Edwardian Architecture and its Origins

Edwardian Architecture and its Origins

Alastair Service

WITH MANY CONTRIBUTORS

The Architectural Press Limited

Acknowledgements

I want to thank many people for help of various kinds with this book, including John Allan, Alexandra Artley, Mark Ricardo Bertram, Sir John Betjeman, Sherban Cantacuzino, Canon Basil Clarke, Mark Girouard, Wendy Glynn, A. S. Gray, Bob Hall, Louisa Hemming, Eva Hunte, Venetia Maas, Jean Isobel Munro, Sir Nikolaus Pevsner, Robert Pite, Mischa Spallone, Rory Spence, Sir John Summerson, Peter Turner, Peter Wentworth-Sheilds, Richard Woollard and Sadie Wykeham. I owe much to the patient help of the Librarian and staff of the Royal Institute of British Architects' library.

I am particularly grateful to John Archer, Alan Crawford, Godfrey Rubens, Andrew Saint and Lynne Walker for advice and generous help with their specialist subjects. Lynne Walker has provided photographs of several buildings by Edward Prior, an architect whose highly original designs will be one of the chief revelations of this book for many readers. Most of all I am indebted to David Walker, whose considerable work and vast knowledge of the extremely important Scottish contribution to architecture of this period have added greatly to the value of the book.

Alastair Service

PHOTOGRAPHIC ACKNOWLEDGEMENTS
Unless stated otherwise below, photographs in this book are the copyright of Alastair Service
Figures refer to pages in which photographs occur: figures in brackets refer to plate numbers

Courtesy of Mewès & Davis: Frontispiece, 426–27, 433–41; Manchester Public Libraries: 14; Walter Kerr 15 (5); The Royal Institute of British Architects, London: 16, 192, 296, 386, 410; John Brandon-Jones: 24, 136 (8), 137 (12), 138; National Monuments Record, London: 43, 47, 50, 51 (13), 52, 87 (18), 135, 198 (7); The Architectural Review: 17–23, 25, 26–37, 45, 46, 48, 51 (12), 81 (3), 83 (6), 90, 93, 94, 97, 125 (4), 127 (11), 128 (15), 156 (7) (8), 160, 187 (5), 188 (7), 205, 208, 209 (21), 255 (5) (6) (7), 260–69, 273, 297, 306 (6), 308 (10), 315 (7), 335, 340, 355 (5), 360 (16), 365 (6), 366, 369, 388 (3) (5) (6), 390 (8), 392, 417–21; Bob Hall/Courtesy of the Ellen Terry Memorial Museum, Tenterden: 70, 72; The Royal Academy, London: 68; Bill Toomey/The Architectural Review: 89 (2), 113; Whyler Photos, Stirling: 108; S. S. Summers: 110, 111, 112; Frances Kelly: 114 (18); Margaret Tomlinson: 124 (2), 144 (4), 146 (8) (9), 147 (10); Greg Edwards: 127 (9), 222 (7), 223, 225, 228 (15), 229; Eric Jarrett: 128 (12); Laurent Sully Jaulmes/The Architectural Review: 129 (16); Godfrey Rubens: 130, 137 (14); The Architect: 133 (4); National Monuments Record of Scotland, Edinburgh: 197 (6), 198 (8), 201, 210, 211, 231, 238; The Architects' Journal: 202; A. L. Hunter/Ian Burke and Colin McWilliam: 203; Colin McWilliam: 204; William Slack: 212 (26); Catalogue of the C. R. Mackintosh Memorial Exhibition, Glasgow 1933: 216; Keith Gibson: 227 (14), 232; Hamlyn Publishing Group, Feltham: 228 (16); Scottish Art Review: 243, 295; Corporation of Glasgow Planning Department: 245; Bob Hall/The Architectural Press Ltd.: 256 (10), 257 (11), 332, 336 (10); Bob Hall/Courtesy of The Art Workers' Guild, London: 280; H. de Burgh Galwey: 284–86; Courtesy of Anthony Symondson: 290; Courtesy of Caröe & Martin: 299; Peter Baistow/The Architectural Review: 311, 322, 323, 324; Colin Westwood: 139 (17); Colin Westwood/The Architectural Review: 314; Eric de Maré: 139 (18) (19), 148, 149, 178, 291, 293 (5); Victoria & Albert Museum, London: 141, 330; John Holtum/The Architectural Review: 143 (3); Lynne Walker: 145 (6), 150, 151; The National Portrait Gallery, London: 152; Peter Wentworth-Sheilds: 162; Richard Woollard: 180; Glasgow Herald: 187 (4); Douglas Scott: 188 (8); Sam Lambert/The Architects' Journal: 190 (11), 246; Studio Seven, Glasgow: 191 (12), 199; David Walker: 196 (4), 200, 207, 212 (25), 212 (27), 224, 240 (6), 241; Peter Joslin, Lancaster: 318; John Whybrow Ltd., Birmingham: 333; John Warren: 339, 342 (5), 346 (13); Country Life: 134 (5), 136 (10) (11), 354, 430 (9), 461–70; Alan Crawford: 355 (4); Mark Ricardo Bertram: 357 (11); John Archer: 360 (15), 374, 376–78, 381–83; Rory Spence: 367 (9), 368; W. J. Smith: 380 (13); C. W. F. Holmes, Abbots Langley: 395; John Maltby, London: 401 (14); Courtesy of the Uganda High Commission: 402 (16); Greater London Council Photographic Library: 406; Letchworth Museum & Art Gallery: 412; Nicholas Taylor: 455; H. de Cronin Hastings/The Architectural Press Ltd.: 473

ISBN: 0 85139 362 4

First published in book form 1975 by
The Architectural Press Ltd

© The Architectural Press Ltd 1975

Printed in Great Britain by BAS Printers Ltd, Wallop, Hampshire

Contents

Introductory Note

Even today, sixty years after the end of the period, it is not yet possible to make convincing value judgements about late Victorian and Edwardian architecture. It probably appeared easier in the 1950s, when everything out of the main stream of development of International Modern architecture seemed irrelevant or just bad. Then most of the buildings of the Arts and Crafts architects seemed quirky and odd, while Edwardian Baroque was simply an enormous bad joke, but opinions change and today we are starting to appreciate the wayward integrity of the first and the visual splendours of the second.

The period as a whole still seems difficult to judge however and although most historians have written on individual architects of the time, a recognised general pattern of development has not yet been established. In preparing this book I have therefore tried to combine the depth that one can find in studies of individual designers with a general framework which places those studies in an historical context. That framework is explained in the outline of the period which begins the book, after which the individual studies are grouped in sections, each with a linking introduction.

These accounts of individual architects and their work were written at various times, one as early as 1897, and many contain invaluable first-hand information about the architects. Owing to this time span, the reader must expect to find much variety in the style and approach of essays in this collection. Where very early essays appear, occasional editorial amendments have been made in the interests of clarity and hindsight. The studies of Lethaby, of Townsend, of Burnet, of Salmon and Gillespie, of Rickards, of Wood and Sellars, of Pite, of the L.C.C. Architect's Department, and of Mewès and Davis have been written especially for the book. Most of the other essays first appeared in *The Architectural Review*: on Philip Webb in 1915, on Norman Shaw in 1941 (subsequently revised), on Nesfield in 1897 and 1898, on Godwin in 1945, on Oscar Wilde and Godwin in 1951, on Robson in 1958, on MacLaren in 1973, on Prior in 1952, on Voysey in 1931, on Mackintosh in 1968, on Sedding in 1897 and 1898, on Belcher and Joass in 1970, on Sir Aston Webb in 1958, on Stokes in 1946, on the Garden City in 1902 and 1905, on Holden in 1960, on Richardson in 1966, on Lutyens in 1951, and Goodhart-Rendel's Roll-Call in 1965. Canon Clarke's piece on Edwardian Ecclesiastical Architecture was originally a lecture given to the Royal Society of Arts in 1973 and we are grateful to the Society for its permission to include it here. It has not been possible to include all the illustrations which appeared with the studies when originally published but I have aimed to include the key buildings in each case.

Alastair Service

The history of late Victorian and Edwardian architecture in Britain is of great complexity, with waves of fashion following each other rapidly and many cross-currents confusing the sequence of developments. But through the surge of new styles and revivals there is one clear story. From the late 1870s onwards there was a consistent effort among progressive architects to develop a new style, for the time and of the time; not a revival of yet another historical style, but a style rooted in national or local traditions adapted to suit the late 19th century. These architects used various words to describe this elusive style – *modern vernacular*, for example – but perhaps the most attractive is the term *free style*. By about 1903 it was clear that, except in domestic architecture, their effort had failed. One of their ace cards, the claim that a style for the day should be recognisably British, was trumped by the success of a modernised version of late-Wren, Hawksmoor, Vanbrugh and Gibbs, a style which we know as Edwardian Baroque. This led the way to a number of large-scale classical styles, and these varieties, which may be seen as celebrating the 1897 Jubilee and the heady days of Edwardian Empire, have collectively been dubbed the Grand Manner. The Grand Manner produced many joyous and magnificent buildings and many ponderously dull ones, but it is only in the 1970s that they have attracted enough attention to justify serious study and to give widespread pleasure.

To return to the early years of the period, the movement towards free design had its roots deep in the Gothic revival. A. W. N. Pugin, the theorist and prophet of the Victorian Gothic style, had ideals of craftsmanship and utilitarianism that find echoes in the words of the progressives until the end of the century, while his flowing decoration can look startlingly as if it dated from 1890 rather than the 1840s. Of the other great Gothic architects and theorists, Butterfield's simple rectories, Street's manner of working, Ruskin's ideas and Burges' late designs all have hints of what was to come. Indeed, when H. H. Richardson, the great American architect who influenced the English progressives so much in the 1880s, visited London, he made a bee-line for Burges' own house in Melbury Road.

All the same, the root figures of the attempt to find an English free style were born in the 1830s. William Morris (1834–96) was a well-off middle-class man who trained as an architect under Street and got a fellow employee in Street's office, Philip Webb (1831–1915), to design and build him a revolutionary non-stylistic house in Kent between 1859–60. Then Morris set up his own firm of furniture designers and makers to revive old standards of design and craftsmanship. Morris did not practise as an architect proper, but he remained the inspiration of much that followed. The firm became Morris and Co. and led to the establishment of the Arts and Crafts Movement. Philip Webb

became the architectural father-figure of the Movement until he retired from practice in 1900.

Next we must look at another main root of the British free style, the Queen Anne Style, a reaction against Victorian Gothic, and in particular at Norman Shaw (1831–1912). Shaw was a genius, if rather a pragmatic one, who took up all fashions and styles and did them more brilliantly than most. He did not invent the so-called Queen Anne Style of the 1870s, but he made it shine. The style itself was usually a combination of early 17th-century English Domestic work with even earlier Dutch features and other motifs added. In fact, it was probably Shaw's former partner W. Eden Nesfield (1835–88) who developed it and it was a Glasgow Scot, J. J. Stevenson, who first brought it to London. It was taken up by E. R. Robson (1835–1917) who formed a loose partnership with Stevenson and went on, as architect from 1871 to 1889 to the London School Board, to build a series of impressively advanced schools in the style. Stevenson came to London in 1870 and his name brings in the important Scottish influence for the first time. His old partner in Glasgow, Campbell Douglas had a thriving practice in altering and adding to country houses, often stern 16th- and 17th-century castles with high bare defensive walls topped by extraordinary oriel turrets and wild skylines. This so-called Scottish Baronial was an architecture that was grand and yet could be called vernacular, though the old Scottish castles had incorporated a number of French features. It was to have much effect on the progressive younger men in Glasgow and features of it were to appear in English work (not always happily) towards the end of the century. An attempt was made to harness the Elizabethan and Jacobean style of Robert Smythson and his contemporaries in the same way in England.

The third main root of the free style lay in a group which was in a way parallel to the Queen Anne architects. This may be described as the Aesthetic Movement, and its chief architect, Edward Godwin (1833–86) was one of the most extraordinary geniuses of English design history. The Movement developed after the disintegration of the Pre-Raphaelites, one of whom, Dante Gabriel Rossetti, was its presiding patron saint of painting.

The Aesthetes aimed at higher standards of taste in literature, poetry, painting and decoration as well as architecture, and a vivid experience of life far from the rustic simplicity that was the ideal of the Arts and Crafts group. Godwin certainly lived up to the Aesthetes' way of life, vivid and varied. As a young man in Bristol he was already decorating his home in a simple but elegant Japanese manner that amazed visitors. He went on to fame as a Gothic architect (he was a close friend of Burges) of town halls and castles, and was a star of hope to younger architects in the 1860s. He was the first architect (Shaw succeeded him) to the first garden suburb at Bedford Park in 1876 and then pro-

1 *Edward Prior. Entrance front, Home Place, near Holt, northern Norfolk (1903–05). An extreme example of Arts and Crafts free architecture, blending local materials and building traditions with original design.*

3

duced a series of startling townhouse designs in Chelsea for the painter Whistler and other Aesthetes, giving up architecture and revolutionising stage design in his last four years. Many artists of the Aesthetic Movement were homosexuals, but Godwin was far from this particular source of scandal. Apart from affairs with many other women, Godwin shocked Victorian society in 1865 by falling in love with the actress Ellen Terry, who had recently married the eminent painter G. F. Watts. Their passionate love affair lasted for twelve years. The same passion can be seen in everything that Godwin said or did. It endeared him to students, but made Morris' disciples suspicious of his principles and so of his innovations.

The fact that his work did influence some of the Arts and Crafts architects in the 1880s may be explained by the fact that a young London Scot, the talented James MacLaren (1843–1890), was a friend of both. In 1886 MacLaren joined the Art Workers' Guild, which became almost a club for the Arts and Crafts architects, and from then until his early death in 1890 his buildings – full of Godwinesque spirit and the American influence of Richardson – were among the most striking produced by the free style progressives.

Such buildings were very much the exception rather than the rule in the late 1880s, and it is time to take a look at the big architectural practices of the time. Alfred Waterhouse was at the peak of his career, dealing with large municipal and commercial buildings in a tough Lancastrian post-Gothic or Romanesque, built of harsh brick and terracotta. Thomas Collcutt and Sir Ernest George were both more sensitive, lacking Waterhouse's talent for the large-scale, but able to produce many admirable buildings in a variety of revived styles. Aston Webb was the architect of numerous public buildings, again in many different styles. He was in successful partnership with Ingress Bell and, though many of Webb's works are ponderous, buildings such as the Birmingham Victoria Law Courts, designed 1887 in a free form of French Renaissance, are admirable of their kind. T. G. Jackson and Basil Champneys, working in a number of styles but preferring a free Elizabethan, both enjoyed considerable practices. In Scotland, the great Alexander Thomson was dead and John Burnet was starting to dominate. And of course there was Norman Shaw, who was almost alone in combining wealthy success with a spirit of progressive adventure. New Scotland Yard, his largest building, was completed at the end of the 1880s.

These were some of the big worldly successful names. In church architecture, the fire had gone out of the Gothic movement, but the style still dominated. Late Victorian Gothic often showed a new finesse, even an elegance, in churches built by Pearson, Bodley, Bentley, Gilbert Scott junior, Brooks and Sedding. And a little later came that strange genius Ninian Comper to bend the Gothic into unexpected forms. Sedding (1838–91), partly through the influence of his

young partner Harry Wilson (c. 1863–1934), was drawn into the Arts and Crafts Movement which is this book's central thread until the end of the century. Of the others mentioned, John Francis Bentley deserves special attention, for in his great Westminster Cathedral built from 1895 onwards he mixed the free manner with the Byzantine and produced a masterpiece of the period.

The weekly architectural magazines of the time largely reflected this picture of British architecture until about 1890, usually illustrating churches and the large buildings almost regardless of their virtues. The biggest exception to this was *The British Architect*, which from its start in the 1870s, sought to encourage progressive ideas. But by 1883 *The Builder* and by 1890 *The Architect*, the most widely read magazines at the time, were following the lead. Soon afterwards others such as *Builders' Journal and Architectural Record* and *Building News* (which published the first plans for Bedford Park in 1876) also started to illustrate Arts and Crafts and other free work fairly frequently.

During the 1890s these were joined by two important new magazines. The first was *The Studio*, devoted to all the visual arts from the viewpoint of the Arts and Crafts Movement. The architecture in its pages was largely domestic and some of its favourite architects were Voysey, Baillie Scott, Townsend, Newton, Mackmurdo and Mackintosh. Perhaps its most important contribution was the number of subscribers it had on the continent of Europe, where it spread the Arts and Crafts influence among artists and architects abroad.

The Architectural Review appeared for the first time in 1896 as the prestige monthly magazine publishing all that was best in British architecture, regardless of style. It was read by architects, but also by many others who wanted to keep themselves informed about what was happening in architecture. The first editor was Harry Wilson, J. D. Sedding's pupil and successor, who was followed by D. S. McColl in 1901, Mervyn Macartney in 1905 and Ernest Newton in 1913.

The last magazine that needs to be mentioned here was a short-lived expression of Arts and Crafts ideals called the *Hobby Horse*. This was in many ways the precursor of *The Studio*, printed on hand-made paper and edited and published for a few years from 1884 by Arthur Mackmurdo (1851–1942). Mackmurdo is a curiously hard man to place, for his most interesting work belongs to the 1870s and '80s. He certainly belongs to the Arts and Crafts Movement and his activities often presaged similar and more lasting efforts by others. In about 1881 Mackmurdo, aged thirty and with little more than a few house designs behind him, gathered together a band of designers and craftsmen (including Selwyn Image the painter, William de Morgan the ceramicist and Heywood Sumner) and formed a group called the Century Guild to produce wallpapers, textiles and metalwork. The Guild was based on the ideas of Morris and Ruskin, but its products were of an originality nearer to 1890 than to 1880.

The word *guild* was again used for a different type of body founded in 1884, the Art Workers' Guild. In effect this was to become a working and social club, with premises in Bloomsbury, where practitioners of all arts and crafts could meet to discuss their common interests informally or at formal evening meetings devoted to particular aspects and craft demonstrations. In a way this guild was a union of Norman Shaw's clever young architect disciples and of the Arts and Crafts ideals, and it was to be of immense importance in the progressive movement of the next twenty years. The idea for the Guild came from a group of five young architects who were working or had worked under Shaw. The most brilliant were William Lethaby (1857–1931) and Edward Prior (1852–1932), but the others, Ernest Newton, Mervyn Macartney and Gerald Horsley, were also to play important parts in British architecture up to the First World War.

The formal aim of the Guild was, after much discussion, expressed by Lethaby as being to reverse "the drifting apart of the arts of Architecture, Painting and Sculpture" and they persuaded one of the few older architects they respected, John Belcher to chair their first meeting. The members of the Guild soon moved on to wider aims to improve architecture, but it is ironical that Belcher clung to these words as his own overall aim to the end of his life. For it was he who was to lead the development that led to the triumph of the Grand Manner and the downfall of the idealistic hopes of the Arts and Crafts architects.

Within a few years the Art Workers' Guild had become the architectural centre of the Arts and Crafts Movement (the Arts and Crafts Exhibition Society, founded in 1888, had a very similar membership). After the middle 1880s one can trace the cross-breeding of ideas and motifs among the group as they tried to develop a 'vernacular' free style. To such an extent is this the case that it is rarely safe to assert that any one of these architects was undoubtedly the originator of any particular feature or type of composition, though it is clear that Philip Webb, Norman Shaw, Edward Godwin and H. H. Richardson were important influences on all of them. Whatever the sources of these ideas, there is no doubt that a series of revolutionary and fascinating buildings were built by architects of the Art Workers' Guild during the 1890s. Apart from Lethaby and Prior, who have already been mentioned, C. F. A. Voysey (1857–1941) and C. Harrison Townsend (1851–1928) were in contrasting ways the most original.

John Brandon-Jones has described another of the breeding-grounds of free ideas in the 1880s, pointing out that Norman Shaw was himself influenced by Philip Webb, and several of his pupils and assistants were in direct contact with Webb through the Society for the Protection of Ancient Buildings: "Lethaby, Gimson and Barnsley, while working for Shaw during the day, were spending their evenings sitting at the feet of Morris and Webb in the Committee Room of the S.P.A.B., and at the suppers at Gatti's which usually followed S.P.A.B. meetings, Webb expounded his views and discussed architectural problems with his juniors . . . not only the men from Shaw's office, but also several members of the newly formed Architect's Department of the London County Council."

Away from London, the free style flourished in various centres, though often without the idealistic discipline of Arts and Crafts theories. In Scotland, the dominant figure was Sir John Burnet (1857–1938), comparable in some ways to Norman Shaw in his ability to handle any style with splendour and originality. During the Edwardian decade he came closer than anyone in Britain to a rational commercial architecture. But the most brilliant of all the Scottish free style architects was Charles Rennie Mackintosh (1868–1928), in close sympathy with the ideas of the Art Workers' Guild men, though not one of them. In February 1893 he quoted from Lethaby's book *Architecture, Mysticism and Myth* (1892) in a lecture in Glasgow "We must clothe modern ideas with modern dress – adorn our designs with living fancy. We shall have designs by living men for living men". And indeed, the best of the buildings he was to design came as close to such ideals as those of any architect of his time. His Glasgow School of Art remains the most marvellously atmospheric masterpiece of the period. Other designers' work, such as that of James Salmon junior (c. 1874–1924) in Glasgow and, in Dundee, of W. G. Lamond remind us that the free design movement in Scotland had more success in terms of buildings built than any region of England.

The chief principles shared by the Arts and Crafts architects and, to some extent, by others who wanted a new free style were these: simplicity, structural honesty, national or regional character with traditional local building materials, and originality blended with tradition in design. Many of them also shared Morris's progressive political ideals.

Thus by 1895 there were architects working all over the country with the common aim of developing a modern free style. They were brilliantly successful in domestic work and, through the medium of Hermann Muthesius, their ideas spread to the rest of Europe. Muthesius was a German architect who was sent to London in 1896 for seven years as an attaché to the German Embassy. His official mission was, astoundingly, to find out what was so impressive about English architectural design that made it the envy of many visitors to Britain. He soon got in touch with Lethaby and others and his reports took the form of a series of books published in Germany, including *Das Englische Haus* in which he illustrated and praised most of the leading Arts and Crafts architects. It was particularly the restraint and honesty of English domestic work that he applauded, compared to the extravagance of

5

Art Nouveau. His books started a school of thought in many parts of Europe which led to the establishment of the Bauhaus ideals many years later.

In contrast to its domestic success, the cause of the free style in Britain for large buildings was a failure, though it had its glorious moments. The last five years of the 19th century saw hopes at their highest. Norman Shaw's free baronial New Scotland Yard (1887–90) was followed by a few other progressive large buildings of varying quality, such as Burnet's Athenaeum Theatre (1891), Townsend's Bishopsgate Institute (designed 1892) and Mackintosh's Glasgow Herald (1893), while Smith and Brewer's Mary Ward Settlement and Gibson and Russell's free Baroque West Ham Technical Institute were both designed in 1895. Then Townsend's Horniman Museum (designed in 1896) Mackintosh's School of Art (1897), Townsend's Whitechapel Art Gallery (revised design 1899), Salmon's Anderston Savings Bank (1899) and Lethaby's Eagle Insurance (1900) closed the century hopefully. At the beginning of 1901 the editor of *The British Architect* wrote, "The dawn of the Twentieth Century is brighter with hope for the art of architecture . . . the present generation may see yet greater architectural progress, and – who knows? – *perhaps* even a new national style!"

The term 'free style' was a loose one, sometimes applied to buildings which attempted to establish a new style for their time, sometimes to anything which used a 'free treatment' of some historical style. Less purist architects than the Arts and Crafts group took up the idea of a free vernacular architecture, with some strange results. The free Elizabethan or Perpendicular had a vogue in the 1890s as a vernacular British but modernised type for larger buildings, especially in the work of T. G. Jackson, H. T. Hare and Basil Champneys. Another variation was the free use of any historical style – with a few fashionable motifs thrown in – as 'modern': thus we see free Renaissance, free Gothic, free Baroque and free Byzantine works of the period and firms like Gibson and Russell worked in all of these. But most important, the Arts and Crafts ideal of a *vernacular* style was transformed by less high-minded designers into that of a *national*-rooted style. After the popularisation of neo-Elizabethan, this led architects to the Baroque of Blenheim and St Paul's Cathedral as being essentially English.

So the hopes for a *new* national style expressed by that editor in early 1901 were not to come true. During the following year, competition after competition for large-scale buildings was won by entries in the neo-Baroque style made popular by John Belcher at Colchester Town Hall in 1897 and by others such as Mountford, Brydon, Young and Hare. Eighteen months later, in June 1902, the same editor was writing in sorrow, "We begin to wonder where we are in the journey of evolution! The phases through which modern architecture has passed, and is passing, must be somewhat bewildering . . . at last the only sheet anchor for the time seems to be a following on of the late Renaissance (i.e. Baroque) again, whence we had made all these diversions."

So headlong was the success of the Baroque that most of the English free style architects had given up the struggle by the end of 1903. Many of the Arts and Crafts men, such as Voysey and Baillie Scott, were only interested in house design anyway – which was as well for them. But of those who had built large free style buildings, some such as Smith and Brewer went over to the Grand Manner for a period, while Townsend, and others who stayed true to their beliefs, built nothing but small commissions of comparatively little interest after 1903. In England, we shall see that only Holden, Stokes and the Mancunian Edgar Wood (with his partner Sellers), continued to develop their free work on any scale during the Edwardian period. In Scotland the position was slightly better and Burnet, Mackintosh, Campbell and Salmon were all to build their finest free work during the reign.

The reasons for the success of the Grand Manner are complicated but not difficult to find. The Imperial Baroque fitted the grandiose mood of most wealthy and successful men of 1900. It could claim to be British, with its roots in the Wren school and was free of the continental tradition of strict classical rules. The competition assessors (with the occasional exception of Norman Shaw) did not select free style entries for the prizes, perhaps knowing their clients' wishes. Finally, the Arts and Crafts progressive architects had simply failed to deliver the goods. After more than a decade of trying, they had failed to develop an accepted modern style suitable for large buildings. Indeed, many of them did not even want to do so, for they were completely out of sympathy with the celebration of Empire and Prosperity.

Even during the peak years of High Victorian Gothic in England, the classical tradition for public and other large buildings had never quite disappeared. Leeds Town Hall of the 1850s was followed by those at Bolton, Portsmouth and elsewhere, while the Greek and Italian manners still dominated in Scotland. The quality of these buildings varied greatly, but all would-be progressive architects, whether they worked in Gothic, Queen Anne or Elizabethan themselves, were united in despising such Victorian classical buildings.

It was against this background that John Belcher (1841–1913) and Arthur Beresford Pite (1861–1934) published their 1888 designs for the Institute of Chartered Accountants building in the City of London in a style which they called free Late Renaissance. The Baroque design caused a stir then and a sensation when the building was opened in 1893, for Belcher and Pite were among the original members of the Art Workers' Guild and were highly respected by the Arts and Crafts men. Yet here was an undeniable gem of a building designed to combine Belcher's current passion for Genoese Baroque with the progressive Arts and Crafts design principles they (and especially Pite) shared with other members of the Guild. And a year later their master Norman Shaw completed his huge neo-Wren country house, Bryanston in Dorset, designed in 1889.

The designs which Belcher and Pite went on to produce during the next nine years, particularly their unsuccessful Baroque entry for the Victoria and Albert Museum competition in 1891, led firstly to a fairly widespread use of what could be called Arts and Crafts Baroque, and then to the fashion for the full-fledged Imperial Baroque. It was Mountford's design for the town hall at Battersea (1893), Gibson and Russell's for Wakefield (1893), Hare's for Stafford (1896) and Brydon's for Bath (1896) that first took up the style suggested by Belcher's museum design. Then Belcher himself won the Colchester Town Hall competition in 1897, followed by Lanchester and Rickards' success with a continental version of the style at Cardiff in the same year: and the Baroque revival was let loose.

It is important to remember that the style could not have found favour with so many young and even idealistic architects if it had not been, firstly, specifically English (the school of Wren) rather than 'foreign' in origin and, secondly, free of the strict scholarly rules which made the classical tradition a laughing stock among the progressives. Any attempt to judge its most splendid buildings by academic standards shows crass misunderstanding of them. Buildings such as Belcher's Colchester Town Hall, Brydon's and Young's government buildings in Whitehall (both designed 1898), Mountford's Old Bailey (designed 1900), Gibson's Walsall Town Hall (started 1901), Hare's Harrogate Town Hall (designed 1902), Belcher's Ashton Memorial (designed 1904), Shaw's Piccadilly Hotel (designed 1905), Brumwell Thomas's Stockport (designed 1905), Woolwich and Belfast town halls (both 1906), Belcher and Joass's Whiteley's department store (designed about 1908) and Edwin Cooper's Marylebone Town Hall (1911) and Port of London Authority (1912) succeed or fail by their siting, their vigour, their masses and accents, and the test of whether their compositions hold together – regardless of the classical rules. On a smaller scale, the Edwardian Baroque added countless enlivening buildings to our street scenery, some of them delicately composed and detailed and others wildly exuberant.

Such was the popularity of the Baroque that many established architects such as Thomas Collcutt (with his Lloyd's Shipping Register Building, built in 1900 in an enchanting Arts and Crafts Baroque) and Sir Ernest George and Yeates (Royal Academy of Music 1910–11) took up the style with their own variations. Perhaps the most successful, in terms of the amount he built, was the formidable Sir Aston Webb (1849–1930). In the quarter-century between the late 1880s and the outbreak of the First World War, the high proportion of really large jobs that were handled by his firm is astonishing. Equally astonishing is the firm's ability to handle any style on even the largest scale with supreme competence, though rarely with inspiration. Aston Webb's first Birmingham University buildings were designed about 1899 in a free Byzantine manner, but in the same year he was designing the huge Naval College at Dartmouth in a free Baroque. Afterwards he started his best known work, that at both ends of the Mall in London which was in part to act as a monument to Queen Victoria. The design was to change many times from 1901 onwards, when Webb won the original competition, but as completed in 1913 it comprised the heavy Baroque Admiralty Arch and the memorial fountain outside the palace, while Buckingham Palace itself was re-fronted in a much less bold Beaux Arts classical design.

For in spite of the dominance of the English-based Baroque, it was not alone. The equivalent period in France saw a grand but scholarly Beaux Arts neo-classical and a flamboyant form of Baroque. According to Goodhart-Rendel, the Paris Exhibition of 1900 astonished visitors just as much by the grand Parisian classical manner as by the *Art Nouveau* work. These continental influences had reached Scotland earlier through the training of J. J. Burnet at the École des Beaux Arts in Paris, but they were brought to England later through the work of Lanchester and Rickards (which shows Austrian Baroque influence as well as French) and of Mewès and Davis.

E. A. Rickards (1872–1920) was a Cockney with a genius for draftsmanship and invention. His partner H. V. Lanchester handled the planning and the engineering of their many large Baroque buildings, but it was Rickards' marvellous inventiveness that won so many competitions from the Cardiff Town Hall and Law Courts in 1897 to the Wesleyan Central Hall, Westminster in 1905.

Rickards' run of successes had ended by 1906, when Mewès and Davis started their most prosperous years and this signifies a definite change of taste and fashion. Arthur J. Davis (1878–1951) represented a far more scholarly, restrained and elegant school of classical architecture than Rickards', and architectural taste was starting to swing away from the flamboyance and ostentatious grandeur of high Edwardian Baroque. Davis was from a wealthy Jewish family in London, who sent him to study at the École des Beaux Arts in Paris. While still a student, he met and impressed Charles Mewès, a French architect who specialised in hotels and had already built the glorious Ritz in Paris. At the age of twenty-two Davis became his London partner and after a few years the young man's urbane charm and sheer talent obtained a series of major London commissions. The Ritz Hotel, with the most pleasurable hotel interior in London, was completed in 1906, the elegant Inveresk House on the corner of the Aldwych (now marred by later upper storeys) in 1907. The Royal Automobile Club (1908–11) in Pall

Mall was followed by a series of company and bank headquarters in the City of London which maintain the highest possible standards of classical design applied to 20th-century buildings.

The other notable figure working in the Beaux Arts tradition was Sir Reginald Blomfield (1856–1942), an aggressive and unpleasant man, but an able neo-classical architect. Apart from their buildings, he and Arthur Davis played a considerable part in establishing the formal architectural education which, for better or worse, was to influence the character of British architecture after 1918.

The purer classical taste of Davis and Blomfield made itself felt in the buildings of architects who had enjoyed the swashbuckling of early Edwardian Baroque. For it was not just a matter of taste. In 1905 a period of depression for the building trade followed the long boom that had started in 1897. Clients were not inclined to be extravagant. Shopkeepers wanted street windows that used every possible foot of frontage, and the new steel frames for city buildings made this possible if the designs were adjusted accordingly.

It was the young Charles Holden (1875–1960) in partnership with the established Percy Adams, and J. J. Joass (1868–1952) in partnership with John Belcher, who produced the most interesting solution. Their stone office buildings between 1905 and 1910 use classical features freely in a vertically emphasised way that expresses the steel frame beneath. There is a new chunkiness and a new surface tension that can only be described as neo-Mannerist, for motifs that have structural functions in classical buildings are here used in a way that makes it clear that they have none. It is a fascinating, though brief, series of designs and it is worth noting in passing that this almost Cubist chunkiness of shapes is part of a widespread taste for such forms at the time, apparent for example in the work of Mackintosh and Edgar Wood.

Structural developments in steel and concrete find expression too in some of the work of older men who had been in the vanguard of progressive work in the 1890s. Mackintosh's Glasgow Art School library of 1907 owes its transcending greatness to other qualities besides structure. But Salmon's Lion Chambers (1906) and Burnet's McGeoch's store (1905), Forsyth's store (1907), Kodak offices (1911) and Wallace Scott factory (1913) show a bold series of moves towards an entirely rational structural architecture.

At the same time Edgar Wood and Henry Sellers were developing along equally far-seeing lines in their work at Stafford and around Manchester, while Leonard Stokes capped a series of idiosyncratically functional telephone exchanges and educational buildings with an office building in Golden Square, London in 1913–14 that combines rationality with Stokes' typical personal flavour. All over London, the L.C.C. Architect's Department was spreading schools, housing, fire stations and other buildings in an unobtrusive but original style that was far ahead of most of Europe until the 1920s. Meanwhile it must be mentioned that some other architects, even those with commercial practices, did hold to the free manner and produced some exciting (and often strange) Edwardian buildings.

The year 1914 saw the outbreak of European war and an end to most building work. Some architects who had been active before the war hardly built anything after it. Others were to go on and make great names for themselves. Sir Edwin Lutyens (1869–1944), a star of the Arts and Crafts Movement in the 1890s and chief architect of Hampstead Garden Suburb in the second five years of the 20th century, took up the Grand Manner and did things with it in New Delhi and later in England that were to make him the most famous English architect of his time. Such an all-round talent for architectural design is a rare phenomenon, whatever we may think of the style of his buildings and his disregard for rationality.

Sir Albert Richardson (1880–1965) went on to uphold the ideals of what came to be called the Stripped Classical of the post-1918 period, well into the post-1945 period. One cannot help admiring his tenacity in the face of fashion, and the severe classicism of his best designs.

Charles Holden, a disciple of Ashbee in the late 1890s, held in some ways to the austere principles of that lonely genius of Chipping Camden. Holden's progressive buildings of the pre-1914 era hardened into a style, neither traditional nor modern, that became a symbol of the enemy to the International Style modernists of the 1930s and even after the Second World War.

These brilliant, obstinate and often hated survivors of the Edwardian era will doubtless attract their own faithful admiring public soon. This book should only be concerned with their activities up to the outbreak of war in 1914, but it is impossible to resist closing the rich Edwardian period without a glance at its succession after the four-year interim of war.

In judging the buildings of the late Victorian and Edwardian period it is important to keep the aims of the architects themselves in mind, rather than assessing their value as forerunners of the International Modern style of the mid 20th century. Thus we can see in the Queen Anne Style of the 1870s an attempt to escape both from the Gothic and from mid-Victorian building-contractors' debased Classical. A succession of stylistic revivals followed, producing a number of fine buildings amidst the confusion, and a slowly growing movement searching for a completely new national free style. This flowered in the 1890s with the buildings of the Arts and Crafts architects that are the most fascinating of the period, though the cross-currents of revivals never died down. The free style architectural experiments continued throughout Edward VII's reign with many notable successes, but the revival of English Baroque in the early years of the century ended the hopes of a new national manner for prestige or public buildings.

This Edwardian Baroque and the subsequent Grand Manner variations produced countless interesting, splendid and even elegant buildings. They have their faults and their nonsenses as well, but we can see now that they are utterly of their own period and as much a part of architectural history as are the contemporary attempts at a rational new style.

Part One: Pioneers of a Free Manner

The great test of Architectural beauty is the fitness of the design to the purpose for which it is intended, and that the style of a building should so correspond with its use that the spectator may at once perceive the purpose for which it was erected." The writer of these words was Augustus Welby Pugin (1812–52) and they appear on the first page of *Contrasts*, his 1836 manifesto for the Gothic style. In the second edition of 1841 Pugin added a preface, in which he wrote, "Revivals of ancient architecture, although erected *in*, are not buildings *of*, the nineteenth century – their merit must be referred back to the period from whence they were copied." These two quotations set the theme for this book's account of attempts by British architects to find a new style that would pass Pugin's test during the following three-quarters of a century. Ultimately they failed, but in the attempt they produced many of the finest buildings that we have.

Some of the domestic buildings of the High Gothic architects, Pugin, Butterfield, Scott, Burges, Street and others, show the first attempts at such a style. In particular, the vicarages sometimes designed with new churches by William Butterfield (1814–1900) and G. E. Street (1824–81) were the ancestors of Arts and Crafts architecture. These brick houses, solid but unpretentious, are stripped of historical features. At the most, pointed windows and a few small details remind us of the Gothic style. William Morris, Philip Webb, J. D. Sedding and Norman Shaw all worked for Street as young men, while Godwin named him as his first inspiration. And those early Victorian vicarages are at the root of the immensely influential Red House that Webb designed for Morris *circa* 1859 and of many other free style buildings until as late as the London County Council work of the early 1900s.

The study of Philip Webb (1831–1915) included here is of historical importance, for its author was one of his many devoted pupils and from it we get a glimpse of what he meant to that younger generation. Webb was a retiring man whose principles rejected publicity. Only one of his designs was published in the architectural magazines during his forty years in private practice. For this reason, his idea of the architect as a designer-craftsman was slow to be taken up by others. Similarly, his aesthetic sense was an austere one and it was not until the 1880s that his manner became influential. When it was taken up during that decade by young idealists, it became one of the dominant themes in free style architecture. But it was left to others to start the reaction: first against the Gothic style and then against stylistic revivals in general.

In passing, we must mention another precursor of the free style. By 1850, two English architects were already widely successful in non-Gothic country house practices for the wealthy. These were Anthony Salvin (1799–1881) and George Devey (1820–86), whose additions to great medieval houses such as Penshurst are often mistaken by guides for original medieval or Tudor work, while their own new country mansions were palatially Tudor or Jacobean in style. In Scotland, William Burn (1789–1870) had been doing similar work as early as the 1820s, so a type of 'vernacular' movement was already well established even though it was known only to the aristocrats and their friends – for these architects rarely published their designs. But there was no sign among such men of a desire to create a *new* style. For that we must turn to Norman Shaw (1831–1912) and to his friend Eden Nesfield (1835–88), a nephew of Anthony Salvin.

These two set up in a loose partnership in 1862. Nesfield had been articled to Salvin, while Shaw (a Scot by birth) had worked for William Burn before joining Street's office. The partnership lasted for six years and it was during this period that the well-connected Nesfield designed Kinmel Park, a big country house in Wales, that is generally accepted as the start of the Queen Anne revival. By 1870, another Scot called J. J. Stevenson (1831–1908) had settled in England and built the Red House in Bayswater, bringing the style to London. Shaw's highly original New Zealand Chambers in the City followed in 1872 and the rest of the decade was marked by so-called Queen Anne domestic buildings, based on the low-key domestic brick manner of the early 17th century in England, with many Dutch features mixed into it.

Nesfield's contribution to this move towards a freer architecture has often been under-rated. Nevertheless, it is Norman Shaw who must be recognised as the dominating genius in England of the period covered by this book. Shaw's sheer brilliance in architectural design was greater than Nesfield's. His early New Zealand Chambers, his own house in Hampstead of 1875 and Swan House on Chelsea Embankment of 1876 added an originality to the Queen Anne manner that lifted it out of period revival. All through the 1880s he remained in the vanguard of the *avant garde* fashions that followed each other in the attempt to find a new national free style. When the influence of vernacular Scottish baronial buildings was felt, Shaw put it to brilliant use in works such as New Scotland Yard. Even after his conversion to the Grand Manner in old age, he outdid most of his rival architects in the daring and anti-scholastic compositions he produced. When his fame was established he became the one regular competition assessor who often premiated the free and bold entries for architectural competitions, while Alfred Waterhouse (who judged most of the big competitions, between 1880 and 1900) was encouraging the Baroque. One may regret Shaw's lack of unshakeable principles and burning idealism for a new free architecture. One may be puzzled that he hardly ever shook off historical detailing. But if one were forced to pick the single greatest architect of the late Victorian period in England, it would be difficult to choose any other.

If Shaw remained a historicist in detail (though not

1 *Philip Webb. House, 19 Lincoln's Inn Fields, London (1868). One of Webb's early influential works, free of stylistic revivalism, but still using historical details.*

in his massing and overall designing), Edward Godwin (1833–86) took the bold steps towards completely original details and town house compositions between 1877 and 1881 that liberated the next generation. Godwin was a romantic genius, flowing with creativity and originality in furniture, decor and stage design as well as in architecture. The early part of his career produced a series of highly praised Gothic town halls and castles. His later career was closely associated with the Aesthetic Movement. Godwin took up the cause of a free architecture with passionate zeal. He disliked the Queen Anne Style as being just another revival and throughout the 1870s wrote articles and travelled around the country lecturing on the need for a new modern style. He inspired the generation of students born in the 1850s and then left that series of extraordinary houses in Tite Street, Chelsea as an example. By 1881 he had almost abandoned architecture for theatre design and by 1886 he was dead. A later chapter in this book considers his influence on James Mac-

Laren (1843–90) and, through him, on the Arts and Crafts architects who disliked most of the Aesthetes so strongly.

It would be wrong to give an impression that all British architecture of the 1870s showed the move away from historicism started by the four architects examined individually here. High Victorian Gothic was almost dead, but one of its finest buildings, the Law Courts in London, was re-designed by Street and built during this decade. And the building of the splendid stern Manchester Town Hall by Alfred Waterhouse (1830–1905) in a hard northerner's version of French Renaissance, was completed only in 1877. These are more typical representatives of most buildings that were going up in England, while the fine neo-Greek of Alexander Thomson (1817–75) continued into this decade in Glasgow. But by 1881 Webb, Nesfield, Shaw and Godwin had opened up new possibilities for the future.

2

3

4

2 *Alfred Waterhouse. Manchester Town Hall, Albert Square, Manchester (1868–77). A magnificent example of an eclectic manner that was used, often without such distinction, by many other architects in the reaction against scholarly Gothic.*

3 *A. W. N. Pugin. Bilton Grange, near Rugby, Warwickshire (1841–46). In spite of the Gothic detailing, there was an underlying rationalism in some of Pugin's secular buildings.*

4 *Anthony Salvin. Scotney Castle, Lamberhurst, Kent (1837–44). Salvin and Devey returned to English traditional forms, though with no intention of escaping from revivalism as such.*

5 *William Butterfield. Choir House, Cumbrae College, Millport, Cumbrae Island, Scotland (1849–51).*

5

An Appreciation of Philip Webb

by George Jack

Philip Webb (1831–1915) worked out with William Morris the principles of architectural truthfulness that were to guide the Arts and Crafts Movement. The honesty and severe aesthetic of his own buildings between 1860 and 1900 remained one of the chief influences on the younger architects of that movement. This account of his work was written in 1915 immediately after Webb's death by one of his most devoted disciples.

The half-century during which Philip Webb lived and worked produced a greater number of changes in building methods and made more adventurous experiments in different styles than any other known to history. Webb was one of the first architects to set these changes in motion, little dreaming then into what a bewildering maze he was helping to lead the architectural designers of the future. For his own part he consistently followed the path which he had first chosen, without faltering, to the end, and without having either to grope his way or change his direction.

That Philip Webb was a great architect in the best sense of the word there can be no manner of doubt. That he spent his life designing beautiful houses for country gentlemen, and left us without once being allowed to prove the power of his genius by the creation of some important public building, only shows that the country gentlemen were much more intelligent than the general public. These houses that he built, beautiful as they are, in no way form the measure of his power; for, quite distinct from his actual performance as an architect, there was in him a most potent quality of silent influence. This influence had always one tendency: it removed 'architecture' from the architect's office to the builder's yard and the craftsman's workshop. It had a very great fascination, more especially for the younger generation of architects. It was so strong that many were under its spell without knowing it, as was proved by their work afterwards. All those who boldly acknowledged his mastership remained his disciples for life, and of these the few who could call him friend came to understand the value of such a master.

I well remember the kind of mental shock which came to me when first I became acquainted with his work; it was like having a flashlight suddenly thrown upon the eyes, blinding at first, but soon lighting up many dark places. No wonder it was startling. The like of such drawings for subtle knowledge of craftwork was not to be seen in any other architect's office in London or elsewhere. Later I came to understand it all better. That wonderful brotherhood of mid-century poets and painters with whom he had been associated in his early years had left a lasting effect upon his mind. The mingled genius and friendship which distinguished that brilliant constellation had warmed his imagination and developed his genius – such a God-given bias is only possible to a good man and in good company.

One remarkable quality which is directly traceable to his early associations, more especially with William Morris, was his keen perception of the proper ways in which all kinds of building materials should be used – it was a kind of instinct with him. His sections for stone mouldings are the stoniest of profiles. They are masculine, because he thought more of the stone than of style. In brickwork, again, he was, I think, the first architect to break through the respectable tradition, common in the early Victorian days, that a uniform colour was the handsome thing to aim at. He always

specified, on the contrary, that the bricks should be 'seconds', as they were more varied in colour and surface than those superior 'firsts' which were more costly and less interesting. That was what he aimed at in brickwork, colour and texture. To which end he always used lime-mortar pointing, never cement, and he got as many 'dark headers' into his walls as he could. He hated pressed bricks and dark pointing. He used to be very proud of his kitchen chimneys, which he often said were the best parts of his houses.

Again, his sections for mouldings on oak are just those suitable for a strong wood, and what he drew by a kind of inspiration was exactly what the carpenter or carver can do best with his tools.

There was no detail about a house in designing which he did not show the greatest interest, from the general plan and scheme to the cupboards and sinks. His chimneypieces were a pleasure for himself to invent, and for others to see – his grates were the outcome of a careful study of the science of smoke and flues – and so it was with everything which he undertook: he put his whole heart into it.

Webb in his early days found house-building on the verge of extreme dullness. The plan of the house then

2 *Philip Webb. The Hare (watercolour drawing for a tapestry).*

was nearly always sacrified in favour of a kind of symmetry which the elevations were supposed to demand. He boldly adopted the opposite extreme, and made his plans the ruling element of his design. In his elevations he sought rather for an effect of variety and balance of parts, and he avoided the handicap of exact symmetry or a particular style.

Webb's own style of design was not one which was ever likely to become popular: it never did so. It had none of the comfortable conventionality so dear to the majority; it offended those of more educated taste who looked for exact conformity to well-known styles. His manner of composition was bold and effective; it abounded in contrast of form and colour. A very inventive imagination was at all times struggling with an austere restraint which feared unmeaning expressions. The result was that his architecture lacked a playful side; there was no relaxation towards innocent architectural nonsense which is often so pleasing as a foil – what little ornament he used was always well placed and effective.

Webb began his practice as an architect in or about the year 1860, and it ended in 1900 – forty years of constant work and invention. His first known work is the house called the 'Red House', near Bexley, in Kent, built for William Morris. It was called the Red House because it was built of red brick, a material then very unusual for such houses. It is in many ways a youthful work, and is planned without his after knowledge of what a modern house should be; yet it is brimful of a kind of joyous experimenting which is of great interest. Webb often said that he never wanted to see it or hear about it again, and that no architect ought to be allowed to build a house until he was forty. The firm of Morris & Company were coming into being just about the time he designed this house, and in conjunction with them Webb did much work in designing decorations of all sorts, wall-papers, panelling, painted decorations, etc., etc. Here it might be noted that Webb was always greatly interested in animals; his drawings of birds and beasts are full of knowledge of their habits and characteristics. He did nearly all the designs for beasts and birds in Morris's wallpapers and textiles – thus they worked together in harmony. He was a most beautiful draughtsman, and his drawings of flowers are marvels of delicacy. His drawings for wood-carving were done so well that they were rather an embarrassment to the carver who had to carry them out.

3 *Philip Webb. The Red House (for William Morris), Upton, Bexleyheath, Kent (1860). One of the foundation stones of the movement away from scholarly revivalism towards a new free architecture.*

A list of Webb's works is appended hereto. It is useless to attempt any description of these houses in this article. Two only I will mention as typical of all, one in the highlands of Scotland, and one in London.

In 1863 he built a remarkable house at Arisaig, a sturdy, strong-looking house – a house of walls and roof, not one of window-frames and cornices, one indeed that does not look ashamed amongst the great hills that surround it. Stern-looking it is, but picturesquely inviting, too. At the time he built this house travelling was no luxury. After a journey by rail to Fort William he had to ride or drive about forty miles to the site, and when he got there few of the men could understand English. He managed, however, to make them understand one thing – that he meant to have his own way; for he set them to work building experimental slabs of walling, in order to settle the kind of facing the house was to have. This was a difficult task, because the walling stone was exceedingly hard, a kind of basaltic formation, and could only be worked to an irregular face. The dressings and lintels were of a similar kind of stone, but of finer texture, and very black. The old traditional way of using this stone had died out in favour of imported stone and fancy surfaces. Webb got his way, however, more or less, as he always did, for he was an obstinate man. He taught the masons their business, much to their disgust at the interfering foreigner.

The other house which I shall mention is the house in Palace Green, Kensington, built for the Hon. George Howard. This house is a good example of Webb's way

4 *Philip Webb. Houses and shops, 91–101 Worship Street, near Liverpool Street Station, London (1862–3).*

5 *Philip Webb. House, 1 Palace Green, Kensington, London (1868). Webb rejected publication of his buildings on principle. But the disciples of his and William Morris's ideas visited the buildings for inspiration.*

6 *Philip Webb. Drawing room, 1 Palace Green, Kensington.*

of combining brick and stone. Whenever he made use of this combination, which was a favourite one with him, he was careful to make it clear that the stone was used for a purpose as well as for appearance – all the stonework is apparently built in with the bricks and looks structural as it is, not a mere facing of stone added to a brick wall for variety. I believe it was originally intended to build this house all of brick, but some difficulty arose with regard to proprietary wishes on this point, and the design was abandoned in favour of the present brick and stone one. The Hon. George Howard (afterwards Earl of Carlisle) was an artist himself, and well understood the value of such men as Webb, Burne-Jones, Morris, and Crane – all of whom were engaged building and beautifying this house. They painted the walls and ceilings of dining and drawing room with beautiful pictures and decorations. Most of the decorative designs – modelled plaster, painted panels, etc. – are Webb's own. The frieze in the dining-room is the work of the other three artists. It is a

noble house, and a worthy monument to the memory of its gifted owner and all the artists he employed.

I shall just add a word or two as to my office recollections of the man and his work, and have done.

The years that I spent in Raymond Buildings with him were made pleasant indeed by his ever kind and gentle manners. The work was interesting, and the man more so. Often he would gossip with us, or laugh over some joke or other in a most unbusinesslike way – for he always appeared as the friend, never as the master. There was no hurry in his office – no maddening telephone or typewriter; such letters as he wrote could never have been done by the aid of machinery or in haste, they were genuine specimens of human intercourse, and he continued to the last to be a letter-writer of the very best kind. His letters are full of thoughts expressed in clear and simple words, enlivened by a wise man's humour, and not less precious because they are beautifully written. His office was a kind of pleasant backwater in this bustling world. Yet withal he some-

7 *Philip Webb. Rounton Grange, Northallerton, Yorkshire (1872–76).*

how managed to build some sixty houses in his time, and for forty years was never without work. There was only one thing in which Webb was autocratic, that was in having his own way in carrying out his designs. If clients questioned them, he used persuasion, and if that failed he recommended them to try another architect. He was equally autocratic in this respect in his office work. There were no 'ghosts' in his office – every separate detail was designed by himself, even to the smallest moulding – he allowed no one else to interfere in these matters.

He had many persuasive methods in dealing with his clients, from reasoning to rude jokes, and always got his way in essentials. One subject or argument was his partiality for large kitchens and offices. If the client, as sometimes happened, suggested cutting them down he would use his best arguments, and offer to cut down the drawing-room instead.

He was a most retiring and self-contained man, especially in later years. He belonged to no society except the 'Antiscrape', as the members called the Society for the Protection of Ancient Buildings. This society he, along with Morris, founded many years ago, and he attended the meetings regularly until he left London. He left London in 1900 to live at Worth, in Sussex. There his friends frequently visited him and had many interesting talks. Once I remember asking him whether he did not think that there might be some

future for the new reinforced-concrete method of building if some appropriate kind of architecture could be invented for it. "Perhaps so," he said; "but, Jack, it's not architecture." I expect he was right. To cast buildings in moulds like pots and kettles may be scientifically the right kind of thing to do, but no one can call it a romantic process. In Philip Webb we may have seen no pioneer of revival, but rather the last great representative of that older manner of building which delighted the world for so many centuries, but which seems, somehow, to be now passing away.

APPROXIMATE LIST AND DATES OF WORKS BY PHILIP WEBB

1860   The 'Red House,' Upton, near Bexley, Kent, for William Morris
1861   Houses and shops, Worship Street, London
1863   'Arisaig House,' Arisaig, N.B.
1864   House in Marlborough Street, Kensington, for Val Prinsep, R.A.
1865   Alterations to 'Washington,' in the County of Durham, for Sir Lothian Bell, Bart.
1867   Dining-room, South Kensington Museum
1868   Offices, 19 Lincoln's Inn Fields
1868   1 Palace Green, Kensington, for The Hon. George Howard
1868   House near Caterham, Surrey, for Sir John Tomes Gen. Pitt Rivers

8 *Philip Webb. 'Joldwynds', Holmbury St Mary, near Dorking, Surrey (1873). Destroyed. Webb's guiding principles involved approaching each design completely freshly and blending the style and materials with local traditions.*

9

10

11

9 *Philip Webb. 'Clouds', East Knoyle, Salisbury, Wiltshire (1881–86). View from south-west. A famous house, whose details were much taken up by younger architects. Now partly destroyed and altered.*

10 *Philip Webb. East front, 'Clouds'.*

11 *Philip Webb. 'Coneyhurst', Ewhurst, Surrey (1886).*

12 *Philip Webb. Staircase, Coneyhurst.*

12

1885   Additions to Tangley Manor, near Guildford; new 'offices'

1886   'Coneyhurst,' Ewhurst, Surrey, for Miss Ewart

1887   25 Young Street, Kensington, for Frederick Bowman

1887   Screen wall to garden of house in Kensington Square

1888   Additions to 1 Holland Park, for A. Ionides

13 *Philip Webb. Office building, Bell Brothers, Zetland Road, Middlesbrough (circa 1890).*

1868   House at Oakleigh Park, Barnet, for Col. Gillum

1868   'Red Barns,' Coatham, Redcar, for Hugh Bell

1868   'West House,' Glebe Place, Chelsea, for G. P. Boyce

1871   Cottage at Hunsden, Hertfordshire

1872   Structural repairs, Hunsden Church

1873   House at Hayes Common, for Lord Sackville Cecil

1873   House in Isle of Wight, for G. F. Watts

1873   'Joldwynds,' Dorking, Surrey, for Sir William Bowman, Bart.

1873   'Nether Hall,' Pakenham

1873   Dining-room, 77 Park Street, Oxford Street, W., for Dr. Dowson

1874   Farm buildings at Pakenham

1875   Church at Brampton, Cumberland, and various works at Naworth Castle, including house for the Estate Agent and The Vicarage at Brampton (1877)

1875   'Rounton Grange,' Northallerton, including farm buildings

1876   The School House at Rounton, for Sir Lothian Bell, Bart.

1876   Additions to 'Red Barns,' including stables

1876   Offices at Port Clarence, Middlesbrough, for Bell Brothers

1876   'Smeaton Manor,' Yorks, for Major Godman

1879   First design for 'Clouds,' East Knoyle, Salisbury, for the Hon. Percy Wyndham, afterwards abandoned for a new design

1880   House at Welwyn, Hertfordshire for H. S. Webb

1881   'Red Barns,' addition of schoolroom wing

1881–
1886   'Clouds,' East Knoyle

1885   Gates to drive, 'Rushmore,' Tisbury, Wilts

1889   'Willinghurst,' Cranleigh, Surrey, for J. C. Ramsden

1890   'Clouds,' rebuilding after fire

1890   Offices at Middlesbrough, for Bell Brothers

1890   Picture Gallery at Hove, Brighton, for Constantine Ionides

1890   Cottage and Gatehouse at Liphook, Surrey, for Mrs. Robb

1890   Gallery for Antiquities, 1 Holland Park

1891   Forthampton Court, Tewkesbury, for J. R. Yorke

1891   Farm-buildings and cottages, Tangley Manor

1891   Addition to house in Kensington, for Val Prinsep, R.A.

1891   Addition to 'Joldwynds.'

1892   Addition to Tangley Manor, library, etc.

1892   'Standen,' East Grinstead, for J. S. Beale

1895   Alterations to old cottage at Much Hadham, Essex, for Miss Morris

1896   'Exning House,' Newmarket, for Captain E. W. Baird

1896   Cottages at Standen, East Grinstead

1896   Chapel at the Rochester Deaconess Institution, Clapham Common

14 *Philip Webb. 'Standen', Saint Hill, near East Grinstead, Sussex (1891–94). At this time the Society for the Protection of Ancient Buildings brought many young architects, especially those of the new London County Council, into touch with Webb and Morris. Webb's influential manner and rather severe aesthetic feeling are finely displayed at Standen, his last major house, which remains almost miraculously preserved.*

1898	'Warrens House,' Lyndhurst, for G. Eyre
1898	Addition to Rounton Grange, new servants' hall
1898	Village Hall, Arisaig
1898	House at Puttenham, Surrey, for Miss Cox
1899	Gardener's Cottage, 'Willinghurst'
1902	Cottages at Kelmscott, Lechlade, Gloucestershire
1905	Completion of Tower to Brampton Church

In addition to the foregoing list there are many works unmentioned, such as early works of decorative design in conjunction with William Morris; designs for furniture, tapestry, metalwork in grates, lamps, etc.; designs for memorial stones and bronzes; designs for chimney-pieces, bookcases, etc.; work in connection with old houses, such as Berkeley Castle, Pusey House, Berkshire, and many others; and also designs for some houses that were never carried out.

William Eden Nesfield

by J. M. Brydon

The special importance of William Eden Nesfield (1835–1888) lies in his development of the so-called Queen Anne Style from the 1860s onwards as a reaction against Victorian Gothic. Nesfield was from a well-connected family and his brief partnership with Norman Shaw in their young days helped Shaw immensely. This study of Nesfield by a friend and successful contemporary architect, J. M. Brydon, was originally published in 1897.

It is somewhat surprising that though nine years have passed away since William Eden Nesfield's death, beyond the briefest obituary notices, no account of his work has, as yet, appeared. This is all the more remarkable because, not only was he a great Artist in himself, but his influence on the contemporary work of his day was second only – if that – to his friend Mr Norman Shaw. Indeed, all during the '60s their names were so linked together, their published sketches from the Continent so similar in character, their work so wonderfully alike in design and intention, the conjunction Nesfield and Shaw so familiar in the artistic world, that it hardly ever occurred to Architects to think of them separately, and yet in spite of a brief partnership in the earlier days of their practice, they never really did a joint work. They shared offices and studies, had the same high aims and aspirations, the same keen artistic instincts; good comrades both, but each devoting himself to his own especial work; advancing along separate yet parallel lines in all that made for the culture and ennobling of the art they mutually loved, and whose highest interests they did so much to promote.

William Eden Nesfield may be said to have come of an artistic stock; his father, Major Nesfield, besides being a well-known member of the old Society of Painters in Water Colours and a constant contributor to its exhibitions, became famous in his day for his facility in designing and laying out ornamental gardens, terraces, and parks. He had the happy gift – inherited also by his distinguished son – of making the mansion house and its surroundings part and parcel of the same design, inter-dependent one upon the other for the harmony of the result he sought for and secured. To Major Nesfield we owe the gardens in Regent's and St James's Parks, the re-modelling of those at Kew, and at many noblemen's seats all over the country. He had a keen eye for architectural effects and may be said to have been the reviver and restorer of the old formal garden, the value of which as an accessory of domestic Architecture is now again admitted to be of the first importance. William Eden, the major's eldest son, was born on the 2nd April 1835, and was educated at Eton. He never forgot the famous school, and to the last was proud of his Alma Mater. Who can say how its associations, historic and otherwise, responded to or called forth the artistic instincts of the boy at the most impressionable time of his life; to its influence also he doubtless owed much of the uprightness and independence of his character, his quick sense of honour, his desire to "keep his shield bright," as he enthusiastically phrased it, declaring that if Eton did not produce great scholars at all events it turned out gentlemen; by birth and education, therefore, he was essentially the latter whatever his claims may have been to the former. How high his ideal was in this respect may be gathered from his facetious remark that old Professor Cockerell was the only gentleman in the profession.

After Eton came the question of his life's vocation; a happy fate decided for Architecture, though his introduction to the mother of all the Arts was somewhat chequered. First of all he went for a few months to Mr J. K. Colling 'to learn to draw'; then afterwards, in 1851, he became an articled pupil with the late Mr Burn. Mr Norman Shaw was also a pupil in the office at this time, though the two met first at Major Nesfield's house at Windsor. Somehow the work in Mr Burn's office proved uncongenial, he could not or would not take kindly to it, the result being that after a couple of years he left and entered the office of his uncle, Mr Antony Salvin, where he remained till the midsummer of 1856, going down to Keele Hall, in Staffordshire – a large house Mr Salvin was then building – for some months, to be under the Clerk of Works. He was then only twenty-one, and it must be remembered at that time the Battle of the Styles was in full progress. Mr Burn may be said to represent the classic, and Mr Salvin the medieval side of the question, and the Gothic revival, then in all its fervour, carried the young student along with it.

Having 'learned to draw' very well, getting through his articles somehow, and seeing a little of practical work on a building in progress, he went off on a foreign tour, and to study in France, Italy, and Greece. He did much travelling, doubtless much observation, and a fair amount of sketching; on his return, finding Mr Shaw at work on his well known book, he was persuaded into following his example, but not having enough material for the purpose, set off again, this time principally to France, to make the sketches and measured drawings, afterwards published. The two volumes became the text books of the Gothic revival, and brought their authors into the most prominent notice, not only as skilled draughtsmen, but as leaders in the movement. These books were marvels of Architectural delineation, and, what is more, could be thoroughly depended upon for accurate information. As Mr Nesfield himself wrote: "My endeavour has been to faithfully represent the subjects as I saw them, avoiding, with few exceptions, such as had been touched by restoration, a process which, as at present conducted in France, frequently tends to destroy the character of the old work." Most of the illustrations in his book were drawn on the stone by himself, and the initial letter on the title page is probably his first published design, the figures on the same page being drawn by his friend, the late Mr Albert Moore.

The period of probationary study being over, Mr Nesfield settled down to work in Bedford Row in 1859, his first important commission being a new wing to Combe Abbey for Lord Craven, the nobleman to whom he dedicated his book of sketches. In 1862, on going into partnership with Mr Shaw, he removed to No. 7 Argyle Street.[1] As already said, the partnership was purely nominal, and lasted but a few years, though they shared offices together till 1876, when, the premises being required for other purposes, Mr Nesfield migrated to No. 19 Margaret Street. His room in Argyle Street was a sight in those days, containing as it did a valuable collection of blue and white Nankin china and Persian plates, Japanese curios, brass sconces and other metal work, nick-nacks of various descriptons, and a well stocked library, in a case designed by himself. It was the studio of an artist, rather than the business room of a professional man; any samples of building materials being conspicuous by their absence. How proud he was of his Persian plates, and how enthusiastic over the flush of the blue in his hawthorn jars, or the drawing of the 'Long Elizas' on his six mark dishes, only those knew who were privileged to hear him discourse thereon; at that time the Japanese craze had not broken out into an epidemic, and, as yet, 'Liberty' as such, existed not, but Nesfield knew all about the movement; he could estimate Japanese Art at its true value, and its place in the grammar of ornament, not hesitating to introduce the characteristic discs and key pattern into his work when occasion served. One loves to think of him amid the congenial surroundings of his room in Argyle Street, working away at the Art in which he delighted, within converse of his friend Shaw, and looked up to with enthusiasm by his fortunate assistants, as the man at his best; a memory that will never fade away. Here the principal works of his life, such as Combe Abbey, Cloverley Hall, and Kinmel Park, were carried out, here o' nights would come his artistic friends – the Painter, the Sculptor, the Poet – and with inspiriting intercourse stimulate each other to higher and nobler efforts. The warm hearted geniality of his nature was infectious; his kindly counsel, and the brilliant example of his conscientious work, both as a designer and a draughtsman, were the highest encouragement to all who came under his influence. Men whose names are now well known in their Profession look back to those days with a feeling of thankfulness akin to gratitude that they were privileged to study under such a consummate master of his craft.

It is no part of the writer's intention to estimate the value of Mr Nesfield's work or classify its standing in the history of 19th-century Architecture in England, but rather to present such characteristic examples as shall serve to show the versatility of his genius, the wide range of his subjects, and the technical knowledge and artistic skill he brought to bear in carrying them out. He was a master of planning and of construction, no detail was too small for his attention; difficulties arose only to be solved, and that too in the simplest and most practical manner. He had a keen eye for the picturesque, and yet never lost sight of the dignity of his work, be it a cottage or a mansion. Nor was there ever any straining after effect for effect's sake; all grew naturally out of the requirements. No one knew better than he the value of mouldings and ornament, drew them better, or used them with more discretion. It was a pleasure to see him drawing out a full-sized detail for some elaborate piece of wood or ironwork; every line instinct with life, and carried out with a thoroughness and vigour which were all his own. He had the true inwardness of decorative art, knowing when to use, and what is often of much greater importance, when to refrain from, ornament. As a result, in his work there is an absence of fussiness and a sense of quietude and dignity which is at once its strength and his reward. For convenience sake, and without attempting any strictly chronological order, it is proposed to consider – firstly, his cottages and lodges; secondly, his mansions; and then his churches, with one or two works which, perhaps, hardly come within either category.

Nothing was more characteristic of Mr Nesfield than his cottages and lodges. He took a pride in these little structures, and was one of the first to show how artistic, and yet so convenient withal, a labourer's cottage or a gate-keeper's lodge could be made. The lodges in Regent's Park, built in 1864, and in Kew Gardens, built in 1866, are landmarks in the history of such buildings. The former, bringing with it a whiff of the breezy weald of Surrey into the heart of London for weary eyes to rest on, was a revelation in red brick, weather tiles, and stamped plaster. It never seems to have been thought of before, yet here it is, no tentative effort either, but a complete little gem. As for the lodge at Kew, with its cut brick pilasters, high-pitched roof, tall, carved chimney, pedimented dormers, plaster cove,

2 *W. Eden Nesfield. Lodge, Regent's Park, London (1864). A strong design, but still in the rustic tile-hung manner Nesfield shared with Norman Shaw (his partner from 1866 for some years).*

and classic detail, it is a bit of fully-fledged 'Queen Anne,' as it was called in those days – thirty years ago, be it remembered – when the Architectural world was still blindly floundering in the throes of the Gothic revival, the predominant note of the hour being Early French – a type on which Mr Nesfield himself was then actually designing his work at Combe Abbey and Cloverley. Yet even at this initial period of his career he was quick to perceive the limitations of this early Gothic work; the Lodges at Regent's Park and Kew were the beginning of the end of the then fashionable craze, the first notes of a change which was presently to bring about such works as Loughton Hall and Kinmel Park. Beginning with the cottage, the movement soon overtook the Manor and the Hall, the leading idea being that all should be thoroughly English, in the letter no less than in the spirit. Anglo-French was tried and found wanting, Anglo-Spanish we were mercifully spared, so the revival under such masters as Nesfield and Shaw settled down to be English first, whatever else it might be in addition. On similar lines were his cottages at Crewe Hall, Hampton in Arden, and Broadlands, and the school at Romsey. His autograph sketch for one of the Broadlands Lodges is published; but even more characteristic than either of

3 *W. Eden Nesfield. Lodge, Kew Gardens (1867). A harbinger of the 'Queen Anne Style', reacting against the Gothic and Victorian Classical alike.*

these, perhaps, is the Gate Lodge at Kinmel Park, a truly delightful bit of English Renaissance. In all these charming little houses there is a freshness of design and an adaptability to their purpose which mark the hand of the true artist. The days of the little Greek temple standing at the entrance to an Englishman's park, and the pointed windows and sham battlements of the Gothic with a 'k' period, are over and gone, and the place thereof shall know them no more.

From the Gate Lodge we naturally find our way to the mansion. As early as 1862 Mr Nesfield was busy with his first important work – a new wing at Combe Abbey for Lord Craven. Fresh from his studies in France, and doubtless swayed by the impulses of the day, it was hardly to be wondered at that Combe Abbey showed a marked Early French feeling throughout. As such it is certainly clever; as such it is just as certain that a few years later it would have assumed an altogether different character. It forms one side of a quadrangle. Two of the other sides – the main body of the house and a wing – are in a somewhat late, not to say debased, type of Elizabethan. The result is a jarring contrast, incongruous to a degree, and quite out of sympathy with its surroundings. For all that, there are, as might be expected, exceedingly clever bits of design – for example, the treatment of the end next the moat, with its boathouse and turreted angles. It is built of stone, with a slated roof, and, given the style, is most carefully worked out in detail, not, perhaps, with the thoroughgoing method of Burges, the apostle of Early French, but with a keen appreciation of its capabilities and – its limits. That he soon became impressed with these limits is apparent in Cloverley Hall, designed in 1864 – when he was only 29 – for Mr Pemberton Heywood, which, though still founded on a French model, is distinctly an English country house.

The plan of Cloverley is remarkable, and may be studied with profit and advantage. The essentially English feature of the Great Hall is introduced with conspicuous success. The house is built on a sloping site, so the treatment of this Hall, its place in and releation to the other portions of the general scheme, with the clever arrangement of the different floor levels, is worthy of all praise. Mark the approach from the Great Hall to the principal staircase, and the skilful treatment of the latter as it rises to the first floor. Few modern mansions can boast such a dignity of entrance, such a clever adaptation of traditional features to modern requirements and the exigencies of the site. Never afterwards, perhaps, did Mr Nesfield plan anything better than Cloverley. It was his first great opportunity, his genius rose to the occasion, he seems to have thrown all his youthful enthusiasm into the task, and worked at it as a labour of love.

The illustrations will serve to give some idea of the general architectural character of Cloverley, the effect of which Mr Eastlake gives very succinctly in his *History of the Gothic Revival.* "Externally the house

4 *W. Eden Nesfield. Entrance front, Cloverley Hall, Shropshire (designed 1864–65, built 1866–70). The author describes this house as being in an 'Early French' manner.*

5 *W. Eden Nesfield. North-West view, Cloverley Hall.*

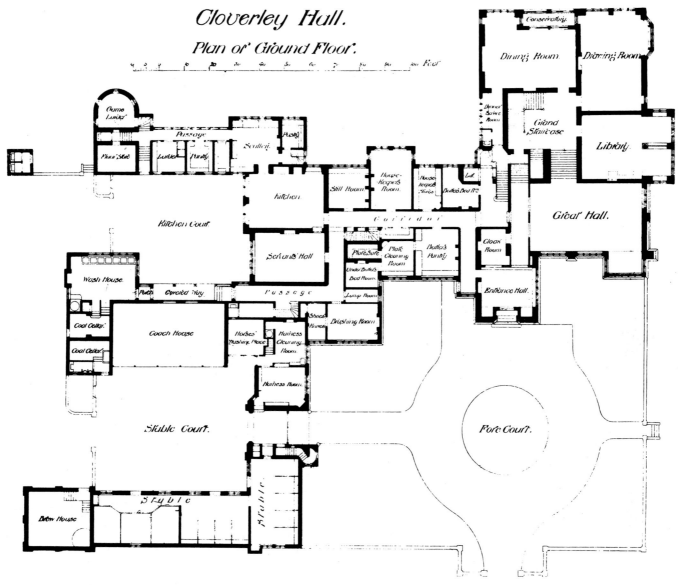

6 *W. Eden Nesfield. Ground Floor Plan, Cloverley Hall.*

possesses, in addition to the general picturesqueness of its composition, many distinctive characteristics of construction and design. The bricks of which the main masses of the walls are built were manufactured expressly for this building on the estate, and are far thinner than usual. They are laid with a thick mortar joint, resembling the style of work in old houses of the time of Henry VIII. The parapets – about 3 feet high – are of wood, covered with lead, which is beaten outwards at intervals in the form of large rose-shaped ornaments, quaintly intersecting each other. Above this parapet on the main (or garden) front rise lofty dormers, bearing in their gables sculptured representations of the seasons, carved by Forsyth from designs by Mr Albert Moore. The effect of these figures, which are about two-thirds of life-size, and are executed in very low relief, is very striking. . . . The whole nature of the Design, refined and skilful as it is, may be described as the reverse of pretentious. Its graces are of a modest,

unobtrusive kind. The work is homely rather than grandiose, and though it bears evidence of widely-directed study, it certainly derives its chief charm from its unmistakably national character.''

Internally the house is remarkable for its thoroughly artistic treatment – its oak panelling, rich plaster ceilings, magnificent stained glass in the bay window of the Hall, and in the staircase, and its sumptuous chimneypieces – that in the Great Hall having carved subject panels from Aesop's fables, executed by Mr Forsyth. The oak screen supporting the music gallery in the Great Hall is also richly carved, and it is noticeable that here as elsewhere in the woodwork the *motif* of the decoration is of a distinctly Japanese character, so cleverly adapted that there is no sense whatever of any impropriety. The touch of the master's hand brings all into a delightful harmony.

About this time also Mr Nesfield was engaged on humbler, but in its way no less remarkable, work in the

7 *W. Eden Nesfield. Entrance front, Kinmel Park, Abergele, Denbigh, Wales (designed 1865 onwards, built 1871–74). Probably the first really large house in the Queen Anne manner, which had many variations, freely based on early 18th-century English buildings influenced by Dutch architecture of that time.*

8 *W. Eden Nesfield. Garden front, Kinmel Park.*

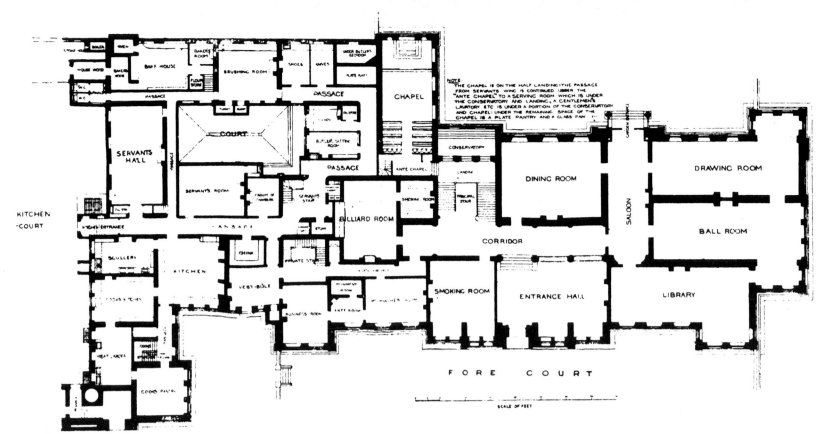

NOTE
THE CHAPEL IS ON THE HALF LANDING. THE PASSAGE FROM SERVANTS WING IS CONTINUED UNDER THE "ANTE CHAPEL" TO A SERVING ROOM WHICH IS UNDER THE CONSERVATORY AND LANDING. A GENTLEMEN'S LAVATORY ETC IS UNDER A PORTION OF THE CONSERVATORY AND CHAPEL. UNDER THE REMAINING SPACE OF THE CHAPEL IS A PLATE PANTRY AND A GLASS PAN...

KITCHEN COURT

FORE COURT

SCALE OF FEET

9 *W. Eden Nesfield. Ground floor plan, Kinmel Park.*

10 *W. Eden Nesfield. The hall, Kinmel Park.*

farm buildings at Shipley Hall, near Derby, and at Croxteth Park, near Liverpool, the features most worthy of note in each case being the dairies, the ceilings of which are enriched with decorative paintings by Mr Albert Moore, who also designed the figures which enrich the fountain in the latter.

The general design of these works may be said to have been influenced by the Gothic revival, but Architecturally they were quite as much a revelation, in their class, as the little lodge in Regent's Park was in its, and the parallel also holds good still further as between the lodges and the mansions, for just as Mr Nesfield designed the Queen Anne Lodge at Kew

immediately after the one in Regent's Park, so Cloverley Hall was still in progress when, in 1866, he began the design for his great English Classic House at Kinmel Park, the two styles running concurrently, as it were, in his mind at this time. Kinmel was not an entirely new house like Cloverley, but extensive additions and alterations to a somewhat unpretending example of 18th-century Classic. The additions, however, proved in the end of such importance that the place is almost a small Hampton Court in its way – indeed Nesfield's enthusiasm for this revived Classic, of which he was a pioneer, ran away with him to such an extent that the first design for Kinmel, when it came to be estimated for, proved too costly, so it had to be reduced and done all over again much to his regret, and to that of everyone who saw and could appreciate so masterly an achievement.

As it stands, however, Kinmel is a splendid house, treated with a broad and dignified grasp of the subject, a sense of proportion, and a skill in detail unrivalled by any of its contemporaries. It is built of red brick, with stone dressings, and grey-green slates for the roof. The chapel is a noteworthy feature in the garden front, and it can be seen at a glance that it is the domestic oratory of a great country house, and does not ape a church-like effect. The same refinement of decorative detail prevails at Kinmel as at Cloverley. The interior is rich in panelling, in plaster work and in chimney-pieces. The hall fireplace is specially noticeable for the splendidly decorative effect gained by the panels of the overmantel, which reaches to the ceiling, being enriched with carved shields with their quarterings emblazoned in their heraldic colours; the result is very striking indeed.

The two great mansions of Cloverley and Kinmel stand out as the typical examples of Mr Nesfield's country houses, so different in style, a contrast in

Design, yet a harmony in Art. Others followed, such as Farnham Royal House, near Slough; Lea Wood (not to be confounded with Leys Wood by Mr Shaw), Loughton Hall, and Westcombe Park, near Greenwich. The types varied, now leaning to the 16th-century Manor House, and again to the so-called Queen Anne, but all characteristically English, and not to be mistaken for anything but what they are – English Country Houses. The multitude of charming features scattered through these Designs is amazing; their variety is seemingly endless. Take, for example, the chimney corner or ingle nook. We have them of all kinds, from the sumptuous to the homely, and yet all are homely. As Mr Eastlake says – "There is, perhaps, no feature in the interior of even an ordinary dwelling house which is capable of more artistic treatment than the fireplace of its most-frequented sitting room, and yet how long it was neglected! . . . How picturesque and interesting an object a fireplace may become when Designed by an Artist's hand."

There is a very striking example of a chimney corner in Mr H. Vallance's house at Farnham Royal. "To draw round such a cosy hearth as this," says Mr Eastlake, "is rarely given to modern gossips." Alas! that this delightful feature has become so much abused in these latter days that it has degenerated into a fireplace in a recess, to be bought in the furniture shops as a 'cosy corner.' *That* is not an ingle nook in the Nesfieldian sense, and never will be. As with his chimney-pieces, so with other features; his staircases – how quaint in plan and design; his bay windows – how restful; his woodwork – how carefully studied for its place and purpose. No detail was too unimportant or to be passed lightly over. All must be worked out to satisfy his fastidious taste. Take his tall chimneys and half-timbered gables: in the former we have every variety, both in plan and Architectural treatment; he loved to picturesquely group them together, enriching them with cut-brick mouldings and carved panels – at that time almost unheard of – and in his half-timber work we have the true spirit as well as the letter of the best English examples. The enormous advance in all that makes for excellence in the planning and design of our modern country houses is the best tribute to the influence men of genius, such as Nesfield and Shaw, have had on its development, and on the ultimate result, till now, at the end of the 19th century, we have a domestic Architecture unsurpassed for its high and artistic qualities by that of any other country in the world. The home is a peculiarly English institution, and certainly no houses, be they stately or be they humble, express the feeling of homeliness more truly than those of England.

The employment of heraldry as a decorative feature is another trait of Mr Nesfield's work, and one he used with rare skill and judgment. We see it in most of his buildings, both externally, in panels, gables, and chimney stacks; and internally, in chimney pieces, ceilings, and windows. One of the earliest examples of the former is in the tall chimney of the lodge at Kew Gardens, where the Royal Arms, carved in red rubber bricks, are quaintly introduced as a panel among the upright moulded ribs of the stack; the effect is a striking as well as novel decorative feature. A particularly rich internal example is the treatment of the chimney-piece and over-mantel in the hall at Kinmel Park, already mentioned. As will be seen from illustrations of this hall, the whole space between the mantel-shelf and the ceiling is covered with a series of carved panels, filled with coats of arms, which are emblazoned in their proper colours – a great family tree in fact, resulting in a splendid piece of decoration, full of interest, no less for its architectural than for its heraldic treatment. Only an artist thoroughly conversant with the subject could venture on such a display as this, and come out of it successfully.

In like manner he shows us what truly appropriate Decoration can be got out of a family crest, or the quartering of a shield, employed as emblems, and used alternately with an initial or monogram as a diaper, as may be seen, in conjunction with the full achievement on the lodge at Kinmel Park, and on the drawing room chimney-piece at Cloverley Hall. When one thinks of the splendid effects obtained by the Medieval and Renaissance builders by the use of heraldry and emblems, it is somewhat surprising Mr Nesfield's lead in these respects has not been more often followed. In the more familiar adornment of hall and staircase windows with heraldic glass, we have many fine examples throughout his work, notably the great windows in the staircase and hall at Cloverley.

Analogous to Kinmel and Cloverley are two urban examples of Mr Nesfield's work, at Saffron Walden, in Essex, where we again have the two distinct types standing side by side. First there is The Bank, built in 1873, and designed quite in his earlier method, if one may use such a term. It reverts to the medieval in style, the semi-public character of the building being emphasised by the great mullioned windows of the banking-room on the ground floor. Unfortunately the front was not carried out as originally designed. It was intended to be finished by a lofty gable, but there seems to have been some fear it would prove too high for the position; it was, therefore, reduced, and one of his favourite leaden parapets, with a dormer behind it, substituted for the gable – a matter for great regret. The banking room, just referred to, is a fine apartment, 32 feet long by 28 feet wide, and 20 feet high, lighted by the large mullioned windows in the front. It was designed with high panelling all round the walls, with a frieze above, a fine fireplace, and a richly panelled ceiling, investing it at once with the dignity befitting its purpose. Next door to the bank is the Rose and Crown Hotel, to which Mr Nesfield built a new Queen Anne front, quite in keeping with the traditions of the old hostelry, quiet and unostentatious in feeling, its red

11 *W. Eden Nesfield. Entrance front, 'Plas Dinam', Llandinam, Montgomery, Wales (1872–75).*

12 *W. Eden Nesfield. Garden front, 'Plas Dinam'.*

brick, stamped plaster, and white painted window-sashes seem to invite a welcome to the hospitality within.

The fine town mansion, No. 26, Grosvenor Square, was almost entirely re-modelled by him for Mr Heywood-Lonsdale in 1878. It is chiefly remarkable again for its fine oak panelling, its rich plaster ceilings, its charming chimney-pieces, and its very cleverly designed conservatory, all bearing the imprint of his skill in clothing with interest and beauty the everyday features of a gentleman's house. A special feature is the smoking room, which has a barrel-vaulted ceiling enriched with very good decorative plaster work, and a quaint fireplace, a cosy, comfortable room, in which to spend a pleasant hour in pleasant chat.

Like many other Architects, Mr Nesfield's designs were not always carried out. His scheme for the alterations and additions to Gregynog Hall in North Wales seems to be one of these, but both the plan and elevation are full of interest, especially the former. It appears the work was subsequently done, but not under his direction, and, of course, to quite another design.

The chapter of Mr Nesfield's church and school work is but a short one. He never seems to have built a large and important church, but rather restorations and rebuilding. Of the latter, St Mary's, Farnham Royal, near Slough, is a typical example. It was begun in 1867, and is carried out mainly on the lines of the old church. The walls are of flint, and have courses of tiles built into them as bonders, in Roman fashion, and showing externally. He was very anxious to preserve the west tower, but its condition was such that it had to go at last, and was rebuilt some years later than the rest of the church. The style is Early Decorated, and the church has a nave and aisles, chancel, and west tower. The mouldings of the piers and arcades, and the tracery of the windows, are drawn with extreme care. The chancel arch is noteworthy for the peculiar outline of its curve, and for the detail of the responds. Over the door from the chancel to the vestry, and at other places, are some of the carved discs Mr Nesfield was so fond of introducing – "pies," as he familiarly called them – sometimes intersecting each other, and again at regular intervals, just as they happened to come in. Farnham Royal Church has an ideal site for a village House of Prayer, and is surrounded with some fine trees.

The restorations of King's Walden Church followed in 1868, and Radwinter Church in 1871. King's Walden Church, near Hitchin, was a restoration pure and simple, though the chancel was nearly rebuilt in the process. The clerestory of the nave was also refaced, the parapets rebuilt, and the windows almost renewed. The walls are faced with flints, and the dressings of the doors, windows, buttresses, etc., are of stone. The south porch, of open timber, with its tile roof, is new. The church is Late Gothic in style; nearly all the internal fittings are new, except the very interesting chancel screen, which was most carefully restored. As will be seen from the plan, the chancel is large for a church of its size – nearly as long as the nave, and not much narrower – and has an interesting chapel on its north side. All the fittings of the chancel, together with the pulpit, reading desk, etc., are most characteristically designed and carefully carried out. The church, as will be seen from the view, has again a fine site. The west tower remains untouched, and is a striking feature in the composition.

Radwinter Church, near Saffron Walden, in Essex, was an enlargement as well as a restoration. The nave was lengthened eastwards by one bay, and the chancel and vestry designed and built by Mr Nesfield; the old chancel arch and the eastern responds of the nave arcade being re-used in the new work. The style is Middle Pointed; the walling is faced with flints, with stone dressings, as in the two previous churches, and the same care is noticeable in the detail of the mouldings and in the window tracery throughout. The roof over the nave is a fine open timber one, and the new portion eastwards is carried out exactly similar to the old work, both over the nave and the aisles. Nothing

could exceed the thoughtfulness, the truly conservative spirit, and the sincere regard for the original work, with which these restorations have been carried out; every bit of the old work that could be saved was carefully preserved and re-used, such as the credence and the sedilia at Radwinter, which are re-fixed in the south wall of the new chancel. The stalls and other fittings there are new, and Mr Nesfield not only designed the organ case, but wrote the specification of the new organ itself. So sure was he of his musical knowledge of his subject that he peremptorily forbade the alteration of any of the stops or pipes without his permission. He also restored Cora Church, near Whitchurch in Shropshire, designing for it a new reredos.

Restoration, as we have had reason to know lately, is a very vexed question, but when it becomes a choice of preserving or losing altogether such charming old churches as the foregoing, it is a matter for thankfulness when they fall into the hands of a conservator like Mr Nesfield. Repairs must be done if the fabric is not to go to ruin; enlargements must sometimes be made if the growing needs of a parish are to be satisfied, and the circumstances will not allow of a new chapel or ease to the Mother Church – and as reasonable men, Architects have to face all these requirements in a reasonable manner – as Artists rather than as engineers, and with a full sense of their responsibilities as well as their opportunities. That the former are as heavy as the latter are sometimes alluring can never be absent from the mind of anyone who approaches his task with that reverence of feeling which must be one of his first qualifications. It is not only a matter of archaeology, or even of construction, but of the knowledge and skill of architectural conservatism, and the experience which comes of them all. An Architect's responsibilities are never light at any time, least of all when a historical monument is entrusted to his care to save from the past for the benefit of the future, and the credit of the present.

The Grammar School at Newport, in Essex, and the Boys' School at Romsey, in Hants, fairly represent Mr Nesfield's contributions to educational purposes. They were built in the pre-School Board days, and are quite in his well-known manner. The Newport School, with its little Quad, its great Schoolroom, Dining Hall, Dormitory, and Head Master's Residence is most picturesque in its grouping, and admirable in plan. The feeling of all being shut in within itself as it were, is eminently suggestive of the seclusion one associates with study, while its quaintness architecturally is still reminiscent of the home. It is astonishing how Nesfield always managed to embody the peculiar qualities of the purposes to which his buildings were devoted, making their outward semblance so easily proclaim their import, that he who runs may read.

It is much to be regretted that we have no public building from the hand of such an artist as Mr Nesfield. Though there is a tradition that he sent in a

13 *W. Eden Nesfield. Bank at Saffron Walden, Essex (1873–74).*

Design in competition for the Manchester Assize Courts, we never hear of him again seeking such an opportunity of distinguishing himself. Perhaps his possession of independent means, which left him free to choose his own path, indirectly contributed to this by depriving him of the necessity of engaging in any such speculative and, to him, probably uncongenial work. Perhaps, also, we owe to the same cause the less extended exercise of his great genius in the more public walks of his profession. Be this as it may, it is remarkable in his case, as in that of others, that a great Artist should have been allowed to pass away without being given the opportunity of enriching his country with any public monument. Surely in England only is such a state of things possible. The State, or other public bodies, seem to think that only in the rush of competition are they likely to secure great buildings, forgetful that it is more than possible the most highly-gifted of our Architects not only never enter the lists at all, but refrain, from the conviction that it is in this method they can do themselves justice, or even that great works of Art are produced.

Again, Mr Nesfield, although he was an Associate of the Royal Institute for a few years in his younger days, never seems to have given his professional brethren, in their corporate capacity, the advantage of his counsel or experience in matters of mutual interest. He never

attended meetings, made speeches, or wrote papers. Indeed it is said, an idea that he was expected to do something of the kind at Conduit Street, led to the resignation of his membership of the Institute. But he was a member of the Foreign Architectural Book Society – familiarly known as the FABS – the social side of which doubtless appealed to his ardent temperament, and met with a ready response. On the burning questions of the day, or what may be called the politics of the profession, it is not difficult to guess the side that Nesfield would have taken, or to imagine the fine scorn with which he would have laughed at registration, and examination, and other shibboleths of latter-day Societies. He had a very strong belief that Architecture was an Art, whatever it might be worth as a profession, that, unless a man was an Artist he was no Architect at all, and had much better become a Builder, with some hope of driving about in his brougham, than struggle on in the endeavour to manufacture buildings at five – or less – per cent – to the detriment of the fair fame of Art and his own probable loss professionally. Yes, it is much to be feared Nesfield would have been a 'Memorialist' of the deepest dye, with a healthy disregard for the pretensions of our friend, the 'Progressive,' or any dictation from him or his like as to what an Architect should or should not be, or any Society that sought to forbid any man from working at his Art as he thought best. The one test with Nesfield was, Could he do it? If so, well and good, he is a Fellow and a Craftsman – if not, well again, and – the less said the better – but it was sure to be forcible, and very much to the point. In private life he was always entertaining, numbering some of the most eminent men in Art and Letters among his friends. In his professional capacity, as one writer said of him, "Among his strongest characteristics were a singular uprightness and a sturdy independence in his bearing towards his clients. He never could be persuaded that he was the servant of an employer, and treated him in something of the same manner as Michael Angelo treated Pope Julius – as a friend and patron and nothing more."

Of his work, as of himself, it may be truly said, one of the chief characteristics is its sturdy independence. He copied no man, followed no school, but struck out a path for himself. A leader rather than a disciple, he showed the way by which, without forgetting old traditions – and especially English traditions – the Architecture of our time can still be made – and is – a living Art, that to be original it is not necessary to forget the teaching and example of the past of any age, that to be picturesque it is not essential to be either restless or even wilfully irregular; that if, in the first place, our houses must be convenient, that is no reason why they should not be beautiful within and without, showered with the quiet dignity, and pervaded by the repose of the home life so dear to our English race. It may be that, as yet, the Art of Nesfield is too close to our own day to enable us to appreciate its true value in

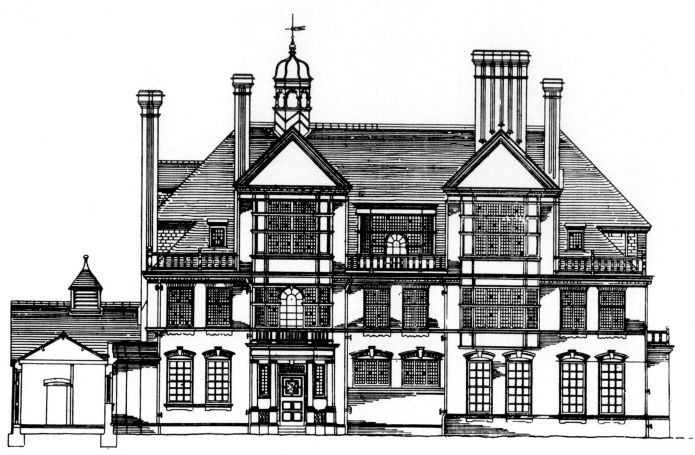

14 *W. Eden Nesfield. Entrance front elevation, Loughton Hall (1878).*

the development going on during his time and since, its place in the revival, not of this style or of that, but of faith in and knowledge of the great and everlasting principle of designing with truth and building with beauty such introspection may, perhaps, become the duty as well as the privilege of the historian of the Architecture of the Victorian Age; but actually we must recognise, and in recognising acknowledge, the inwardness of the true artist in all that he did, in its Design no less than its accomplishment.

Though never losing sight of the fact that Architecture in its very essence is first and foremost a constructive Art, Nesfield never forgot its decorative aspect; the claims of beauty, as such, whether in form or in colour, seem to have been ever present to his mind, and no one was more ready to call to his assistance the painter and the Sculptor, so that labouring together as fellow Craftsmen they might attain to a more glorious result.

Note

[1] It is stated that W. Eden Nesfield, on going into partnership with Mr Shaw in 1862, removed to No. 7 Argyle Street. It should have been stated as No. 30, as, since the year Mr Nesfield removed, the numbering has been re-arranged.

Richard Norman Shaw

by Nikolaus Pevsner

Unlike Philip Webb, Norman Shaw (1831–1912) was no Arts and Crafts idealist. All the same, Shaw's sheer brilliance and originality as a designer in many different styles produced a long succession of the finest buildings of the period and his position as the dominant architectural genius in England in his time is secure. Sir Nikolaus Pevsner's study traces his development and his relationship with other contemporary progressive architects.

Richard Norman Shaw was born at Edinburgh in 1831. His father was an Irish Protestant, "with a Huguenot strain", says E. S. Prior in the *Dictionary of National Biography*. His mother was Scottish. He received his schooling first at Edinburgh, then at Newcastle, and about 1846 entered the office of William Burn to become an architect. Burn (1789–1870) was an extremely competent man, Scottish too, a specialist in country-house work, often additions rather than new buildings, tactful and unostentatious – so much so, in fact, that he never had his designs illustrated in the technical journals. In 1852 Shaw won the Royal Academy Silver Medal, in 1853 the Gold Medal and Travelling Scholarship. The result of his travels to Italy, France, and also such picturesque places as Prague and Lübeck were published in 1858 under the title *Architectural Sketches from the Continent*, a usual thing to do in the mid-Victorian decades, as it established the author as a scholar and an artist and at the same time as a potentially resourceful practitioner. G. E. Street's *Brick and Marble Architecture* and his *Some Account of Gothic Architecture in Spain* are useful to this day. They came out in 1855 and 1865, but Street had travelled in 1850, 1853, 1854, 1861, 1862, 1863. It was Street whose office Norman Shaw joined in the year that the

Architectural Sketches came out. Street, it need hardly be said, was one of the most serious, truthful and conscientious architects of the Gothic Revival. Shaw got the job of chief draughtsman in succession to Philip Webb. Not a year after Webb had left Street, he designed Red House for William Morris, who in his turn, when he had made up his mind to be an architect had also worked under Street. That was in 1856, before Street had moved from Oxford to London. Shaw's earliest published work, a desk-cum-bookcase, illustrated in *The Builder* in 1861 and recently acquired by the Victoria and Albert Museum, is still wholly of the Gothic Revival, Early English, with allusions to shrines, and highly polished colonnettes "closely resembling marble", as *The Builder* writes. At that time, E. S. Prior says in the biographical entry already referred to, Butterfield was his chief admiration, Viollet-le-Duc his classic of Gothic construction.

Then, in 1862 or 1863, he started practice on his own at 30 Argyll Street, off Regent Street, and in partnership with William Eden Nesfield. The partnership lasted until 1868 and must be looked at a little more closely, as Sir Reginald Blomfield's book on Shaw[1] – the only book we have on him – contributes little to clarify it, and as it was in the later '60s that the style

2 *Norman Shaw. Glen Andred House, Groombridge, Sussex (1866–68). Done when Shaw was in partnership with Nesfield.*

1 *Portrait of Norman Shaw.*

emerged which inspired Shaw's mature mastery of the '70s. Webb was born in the same year as Shaw, Nesfield was four years younger. His father had been a military man, a major before he retired, then a painter in water-colours, then the leading formal gardener of the day. The son was a brilliant draughtsman too. He learnt the skill from J. D. Harding. In 1851 Nesfield was articled to Burn and there made friends with Shaw. Shaw on his journey to France in 1854 was accompanied by young Nesfield who had by then moved into the office of Anthony Salvin, a less scrupulous and more inventive architect, who was his uncle. He travelled on the Continent again in 1857 and 1858 (or 1859) and, seeing the success of Shaw's *Sketches*, brought out his as a book in 1862. He called it *Specimens of Medieval Architecture in France and Italy*. Like Shaw he was a convinced medievalist. Together they had measured and drawn not only buildings of the medieval centuries but also of medievalism: Pugin's Houses of Parliament and Pugin's St Augustine, Ramsgate, and in addition they had, while in France, been allowed by the great Viollet-le-Duc to trace some of his drawings.

So, in the years of the partnership both Shaw and Nesfield went on producing Gothic work. Under the joint name of the firm, drawings are signed for the churches of Farnham Royal (1866 etc.) and Kings Walden (1868) and for the English Episcopal Church at Lyons (1868). On the other hand, the beautiful church at Bingley in Yorkshire, of 1864 etc., is Shaw's design, the wing to Coombe Abbey in Warwickshire, of 1862 etc., now demolished, is Nesfield's, though in certain details very similar to Shaw's desk of 1861, and Clover-ley Hall in Shropshire, of 1862 etc., now, alas, also demolished, is by Nesfield, though it was published in *The Builder* as by Nesfield & Shaw. However, the surviving drawings are by Nesfield, and this is con-firmed by C. L. Eastlake's *A History of the Gothic Revival*, which came out in 1873 when the events were still fresh in his and others' memories. Eastlake wrote this of Cloverley Hall:

"To describe a modern building by the general re-mark that its style can be properly referred to no precise period in the history of styles, would, not many years ago, have been equivalent to pronounc-ing its condemnation, and even at the present time there are but few designers who can depart from recognised canons of taste without arriving at a result more original than satisfactory.[2] But in this admirable work Mr Nesfield has succeeded in realizing the true spirit of old-world art, without hampering himself by those nice considerations of date and stereotyped conditions of form which in the last generation, were sometimes valued more highly than the display of inventive power."[3]

3 *Norman Shaw. 'Leys Wood', Groombridge, Sussex (1868–69). Demolished except for a fragment. Nesfield visited the site during construction, but the design was certainly Shaw's.*

Nesfield's inventive power showed itself in other ways as well. Among his earliest work is a lodge in Regent's Park, dated 1864, and representing a pretty, highly picturesque Wealden style, with half-timbering and tile-hanging. Two years later a lodge at Kew Gardens is inspired by the Anglo-Dutch of the mid 17th-century, and more specifically the Dutch House at Kew. The brickwork, the broad pilasters, the hipped roof were a complete innovation, and Nesfield seems almost immediately to have translated this style from the smaller to the larger scale. The exact dating of Kinmel Park, Abergele, is still undecided. The surviving drawings are all of 1871–74, but they are details as demanded only when a building is under construction. J. M. Brydon in *The Architectural Review*, in 1897, says the designs were begun in 1866, but in *The Builder*, in 1888, he calls them begun "twenty years ago". So *circa* 1866–68 is the safest guess. Now Kinmel Park is entirely in what was soon to be called the Queen Anne Style, i.e. a mixture of William and Mary with Louis XIII motifs.[4] Its symmetry, its restraint in decoration, its refined detail are unique at the time and point far forward.

Now as it is precisely this so-called Queen Anne Style that Shaw is remembered for, it may be just as well to ask whether he might not have had a hand in these designs of his younger partner. After all, in 1866 Shaw was at least twenty-five, Nesfield only twenty-

one. But little else than the argument just adduced is in favour of an attribution to Shaw. For one thing the partnership was called Nesfield & Shaw, not Shaw & Nesfield, though that may be due to Nesfield being the wealthy, Shaw the poorer partner. Nesfield had been to Eton. Secondly, Brydon tells us in 1888, when Shaw was very much alive, that the partnership was "purely nominal. They never paid any attention to each other's works and never did a joint work." Thirdly, to account for the seeming conspiracy of silence against Nesfield's historical importance, it must be remembered that Nesfield was a very retiring character, hostile to all publicity, or what he called advertising. So if *The Builder* in its obituary notice after Nesfield's death, writes, "It is an open point whether it is to Mr Nesfield or Mr Norman Shaw that we are most indebted for the great advance which the last twenty years have made in domestic art," we can perhaps now regard that point as closed, and Sir Reginald Blomfield's remark that in the partnership "Nesfield talked about the work and Shaw did it" as unjustified. Another point, however, remains open, that of the sources of Nesfield's tile-hanging and Nesfield's 'Queen Anne'. George Devey (1820–86), it seems, has quite a good claim. Unfortunately Devey was also one of those who refused to have their houses publicised. In *The Building News* for 1886, Percy G. Stone, a pupil – Voysey was another – calls Devey merely "one of the first revivalists of a better state of

4 *Norman Shaw. Cragside, Northumberland (1870–75, extended 1882). Shaw at his most romantic.*

things", but Walter Godfrey, writing in *The Architectural Review*, Volume XXI, in 1907, unfortunately with far too little documentation, insists that the Dutch brick gables at Betteshanger, near Dover, are of 1856. The big bow-window with many mullions and several transoms at St Albans' Court in Kent is dated 1864 ('peractum') and that certainly precedes Nesfield's and by an even longer time Shaw's uses of this motif.

Another unquestionable source for Nesfield as well as Shaw is Philip Webb. Though he was not older than Shaw, he had in William Morris's Red House, at Bexley Heath, already mixed Gothic arches and profiles with Queen Anne windows, and that was in 1859. Finally one more building has recently been mentioned in connection with the introduction of Queen Anne, J. J. Stevenson's Red House, in the Bayswater Road. That, however, dates from 1870 and so does not precede Nesfield even if it precedes Shaw.

For Shaw, at last to return to him, still designed Leys Wood, near Groombridge, in 1868 in a half-timber-gabled, tile-hung, Old English, Sussex style, eminently picturesque and inventive and with a great theatrical virtuosity. There is unlimited promise at Leys Wood, but of the spirit of Webb there is nothing, nor of that of Kinmel Park.[5] Four years later all that has changed, and Shaw's Queen Anne has arrived, and it is a Queen Anne at once very different from Nesfield's, let alone Stevenson's. The key buildings are New Zealand Chambers in Leadenhall Street, designed in 1872 (or, as E. S. Prior says in the *Dictionary of National Biography*, 1871), completed in 1874 and destroyed in the war, and Lowther Lodge in Kensington Gore, now the Royal Geographical Society, which dates from 1873. New Zealand Chambers was a terrace house of no more than three bays, symmetrical except for the charming touch of an oval window pushing the heavily pedimented portal slightly to the left. To the left and right were large office windows, with Georgian glazing bars, but no period motifs at all otherwise, just large windows to let as much light as possible into the dark ground floor. Above, the first- and second-floor windows are vertically connected into oriels, and the motif of the

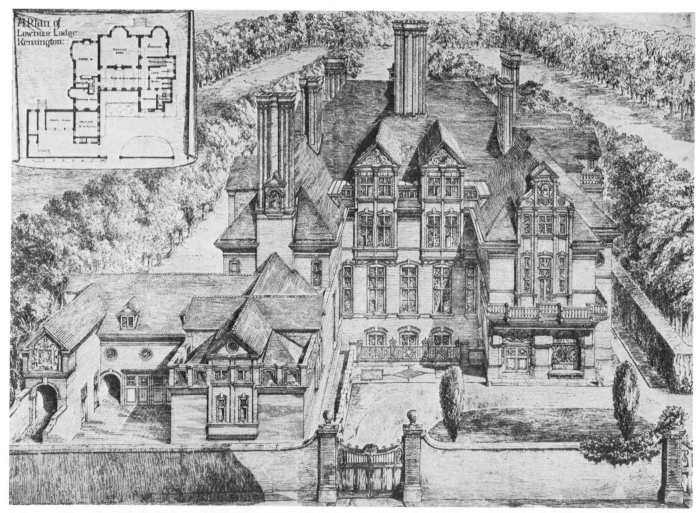

5 *Norman Shaw. Lowther Lodge (now part of Royal Geographical Society), Kensington Gore, London (1873–75). Shaw's Dutch version of the 'Queen Anne Style' introduced by Nesfield, supposedly based on English domestic buildings of the early 18th century.*

6 *Norman Shaw. New Zealand Chambers, Leadenhall Street, City of London (1872–73) destroyed. One of Shaw's earliest buildings in a free style (as distinct from a directly revived one), period motifs being combined with others entirely original, such as the large ground floor windows and asymmetrical doorway.*

bay window such as Devey had done (Adcote, 1877, Flete, 1878, Dawpool, 1882). This attitude distinguishes him from Webb, whose architectural expression is more single-minded and idiosyncratic, besides being more forceful. Shaw said of Webb, so Lethaby tells us:[8] "A very able man indeed, but with a strong liking for the ugly". Webb wrote of Queen Anne, no doubt meaning Shaw, in a letter of 1886, "the dilettante-picturesque of the so-called Queen Anne style", and called it "exceedingly artificial", and William Morris, Webb's friend and client, joined in by writing in an article of 1888 of Shaw's "elegantly fantastic Queen Anne houses at Chelsea", listing them among the examples of a revival of architecture by means of "a quite self-conscious and very laborious eclecticism".[9] Bodley's work at Magdalen College, Oxford, is bracketed with Shaw and also Robson's schools for the newly-created London School Board, work inspired by the Shaw of Lowther Lodge, or perhaps more the Stevenson of Red House, since Stevenson himself worked for the School Board.[10] Shaw's first house in Chelsea was Cheyne House, of 1875–76, followed by Swan House, of 1876–77. Both are in Chelsea Embankment facing the Thames. Both are characterised by the use of exceedingly long, narrow, segment arched windows, and this is indeed a Queen Anne motif. Shaw may have taken it from Church Row, Hampstead, in whose immediate neighbourhood he had just built himself a house. Cheyne House and Swan House have symmetrical façades too,[11] that of Cheyne House very restrained, that of Swan House with the delightfully enterprising motif of three Ipswich oriels squeezed in above a low ground floor and carrying a superstructure which would be too heavy for them, if it were not for the visual lightening by virtue of the equally excessively attenuated little oriels. Here is an originality, a fertility of invention and combination, and an elegance completely new at the time and within our inadequate categories, emphatically post-Victorian. That is Shaw's greatness in the English 19th century. Like Morris in his designs for textiles, like Webb in his buildings, he defeated the grossness of the High Victorian and reintroduced delicacy, sensitivity and a nice sense of composition and proportion.

For composition the finest example is his own house in Ellerdale Road, Hampstead, already referred to, and designed in 1875 – where a big three-storeyed and

9 *Norman Shaw. 'Merrist Wood', Worplesdon, near Guildford, Surrey (1877). A country house that shows many original touches, though the influence of Nesfield's earlier 'Plas Dinam' is evident.*

gabled Ipswich oriel is balanced by a normal canted bay-window, and the fenestration in between is syncopated so as to express the staircase against the rooms. Heights and widths of the windows vary seemingly arbitrarily, but in fact with great subtlety.

Now this was Shaw's stylistic position when the last quarter of the century set in. Adcote in stone, with Elizabethan windows, Merrist Wood, partly half-timbered and partly tile-hung, both date from 1877, and both exhibit in terms of their chosen styles Shaw's unfailing virtuosity in picturesque composition – what E. S. Prior called his "stylistic scenery" – especially in the relations of large, many-transomed windows to tiny openings. It seems easier, when one looks at it, than it really is. Nor did Shaw consider his style, or styles or manner settled. On the contrary, two more changes were to come, the first of them represented by No. 170 Queen's Gate, of 1888, and Bryanston, of 1890. Bryanston, curiously enough, though designed over thirty years after Nesfield's Kinmel Park, comes nearest to it in formal composition and relation of brick-walling to windows. No. 170 Queen's Gate is, except for the pedimented doorway and the central dormer window, unornamented throughout, a three-storeyed block of nine bays, of brick with stone quoins – Wrenish in style and similar, for example, to the tall rows of chambers in the Temple.

From here there runs a direct way to the English domestic neo-Georgian of 1910 and after. And if Shaw in his later years is responsible for this English substitute for modern architecture, he is also responsible for the more reprehensible Baroque Edwardian-Imperial-Palladianism of official architecture. For Shaw in his sixtieth year designed Chesters in Northumberland with grand concave façades, giant detached columns and windows with the rusticated surrounds of alternating sizes that Gibbs was so fond of. Chesters is Sir Reginald Blomfield's favourite of all Shaw's works. No wonder, as it is from there that Blomfield's own style proceeded.

Shaw's most Baroque is also his last work: the Piccadilly Hotel, of 1905, and the unexecuted designs for the Regent Street Quadrant. One cannot help feeling uncomfortable in front of these displays of Shaw's undiminished power. Not only because the responsibility rests with him for breaking Nash's scale of proportions and his skyline, nor only because here the most original of British Victorian architects suddenly recedes into a line with the Belchers and Mountfords, but also because after the delicacy of Shaw's work of the '70s all this seems so massive, so showy, so vulgar. Historically speaking, too, these last works of Shaw are not of anything like the same importance as the earlier ones. Sir Reginald Blomfield, of course, did not share this view of the development. He writes:

"Street ... held with Pugin, not only that Gothic was the only Christian art, but that it was the only possible architecture ... It took Shaw many years to recover

from this unfortunate early start; all his life was spent in working his way from it, to the monumental Classic, the Goal of his ambition, which he never quite reached."

Shaw's position in English architecture is certainly not that, nor is it as simple anyway. His evolution and achievement must be seen in relation to the Victorian age *in toto*. It was the age of historicism in architecture. For the first, the pre-Victorian, generation there was no problem in this. You built Classical or Gothic as your client wished you to, or as the job seemed to require, and you were not too much worried about accuracy of details. Then came a widening of the sources on the one hand – Italian Renaissance, Elizabethan, French Renaissance – and, on the other, the new claims to archaeological exactitude. The former appealed to the more adventurous, the latter to the more responsible architects.

10 *Norman Shaw. Alliance Assurance, corner of Pall Mall and St James's Street, Westminster (1881–82). A brilliant and free composition, historicist only in the detailing. William Lethaby had become Shaw's chief draughtsman in 1879 and, with a group of other Shaw pupils, he founded the progressive Art Workers' Guild in 1884.*

11 *Norman Shaw. 180 Queen's Gate, Kensington, London (1884–85) destroyed 1970. Perhaps the most splendid of all Shaw's free designs and the most tragic loss caused by the spread of Imperial College.*

While Shaw was developing his own style between 1868 and 1875, among the new and spectacular buildings he saw go up were Scott's Gothic St Pancras Station (begun in 1865) and his Italian Government Offices, in Whitehall (1862–75), Street's Gothic Law Courts (1871–82) and Waterhouse's Gothic Manchester Town Hall (1868–77) and Romanesque Natural History Museum (1873–80). He cannot have been in sympathy with any of them, in the first place because up to his fifty-fifth year he was a domestic architect almost entirely and kept away from large-scale official or commercial building.

Yet he was also a historicist, as ultimately Webb and Morris were, too. He added to the then accepted styles two new ones, even if – as we have seen – the original initiative was not his – the Anglo-Dutch style of Kew Palace and Ipswich, and the William and Mary to Queen Anne. The influence of these innovations was great. Shaw's Dutch is the chief source of Ernest George's style of the Cadogan district, and of Harrington and Collingham Gardens, the most popular West End style of the late '80s. Shaw's Queen Anne inspired Mackmurdo, Shaw's country-house felicities Voysey, Baillie Scott, even Mackintosh, and far more of the architects of about 1900 than can here be named. A

12 *Norman Shaw. House for Edwin Long R.A., 42 Netherhall Gardens, Hampstead (1887–88) demolished. The influence of the Arts and Crafts architects on Shaw (Lethaby was his chief draughtsman at the time) is apparent in his free work of the 1880s.*

13 *Norman Shaw. New Scotland Yard (police headquarters), Victoria Embankment, Westminster (1887–90). A fine design, incorporating elements of the Baroque and Scottish Baronial into a strong free manner.*

51

few more examples may be permitted to prove this point. Bedford Park is the first, that earliest of all garden suburbs, begun 1876 – Shaw's drawings for the church are dated 1878, for the inn and store 1880. Look at the inn and store and you would hardly believe that this is separated by nearly thirty years from the Hampstead Garden Suburb. Or go to Swan House and you will recognise at once the source of Voysey's tiny oriels on 14–16 Hans Road. Go to Adcote, and there is the source of Voysey's bay-windows at Wancote and the Broadleys, and Mackintosh's windows on the Glasgow School of Art. And so on.

Shaw was tall, thin and distinguished-looking, so Blomfield tells us, quick of mind, easily amused, suave and persuasive with his clients, and, as Lethaby adds, generous to his clerks. His office, as a school, was with all its variety of personalities no doubt the strongest force in English architecture between 1890 and 1910. There was Lethaby, theorist, prominent member of the Arts and Crafts Movement, a scholarly historian of

medieval architecture and first head of the most progressive of European art schools, the London Central School. Then there was Prior, Slade Professor in Cambridge and author of the best books in English on Gothic art, and T. G. Jackson, the belated medievalist who was engaged on so many Oxford Colleges, and Sir Reginald Blomfield, and Horsley, and Macartney, first editor of *The Architectural Review*, and Ernest Newton, initiator of 20th-century neo-Georgian. Lethaby built little, and what he built is without exception outstanding in quality and character. His first job, Avon Tyrell in the New Forest, was passed on to him by Shaw to whom it had been offered. His aesthetic and moral sympathies were more with Webb and Morris than with Shaw. Prior, on the other hand, was an architect of such *outré* originality that it makes Shaw's own originality appear quite sedate. His play with found materials, reminds one occasionally of Gaudí, his delight in unexpected plan patterns of Lutyens. Jackson took over from the Shaw of the

14 *Norman Shaw. 170 Queen's Gate, Kensington, London (1887–88). The first sign of Shaw's later interest in neo-Wren classicism.*

Jacobean and later 17th-century stone houses; Newton, as we have seen, from 170 Queen's Gate. However differently they developed, they received their initial stimulus from Shaw, and that alone secures him a seat of honour in the Valhalla of the Victorians.

Postscript——X

This paper was originally written as a review of Sir Reginald Blomfield's book in 1940–41. It appeared in *The Architectural Review* LXXXIX 1941. Much had to be done to adjust it to independent publication and bring it up to date in the light of the research of others, especially Mr John Brandon-Jones, and my own maturer knowledge. Mr Brandon-Jones's paper on *The Work of Philip Webb and Norman Shaw* came out in *The Architectural Association Journal* in July–August, 1955. Of 19th-century literature the following was used (apart from Eastlake's *Gothic Revival* – see above): for Nesfield, *The Builder* LIV 1888, pp.225, 244 and 269, *Journal of the Royal Institute of British Architects* 3rd

series II, 1895 (by Phené Spiers), and *The Architectural Review* I 1896–97 (by J. M. Brydon), and II 1897 (by Bulkeley Creswell); on Shaw (apart from Blomfield's book), the *Dictionary of National Biography* (E. S. Prior) and a volume of bound illustrations at the R.I.B.A. called *Illustrations of the Works of R. Norman Shaw*. Drawings by Nesfield are at the R.I.B.A. (U 6) and the Victoria and Albert Museum (DD 7), by Shaw at the R.I.B.A. (V 10–12) and the V. & A. (DD 11).

After this paper had been completed two bits have come to light which ought to be added. Cockerell, so Mr Dodd tells me, refers to Norman Shaw as "quite by far the best pupil I have had" – i.e. at Cockerell's Royal Academy lectures, and Simeon Solomon, the painter, refers to Nesfield in a letter to Swinburne (dated 1869 in the new Yale edition of the letters, Vol. II, pp.32–33) as "one of our best architects, a man of great knowledge, invention and consummate amiability". He is, Solomon adds, "a fat, jolly hearty fellow, genuinely good

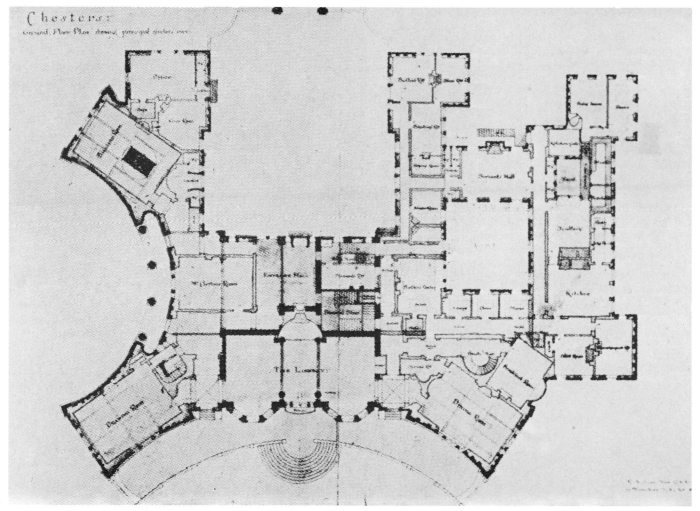

15 *Norman Shaw. Plan of 'Chesters', Shaw's free Baroque house in Northumberland (1889–91). John Belcher's Baroque attracted Shaw, but this plan was to inspire Edward Prior and through him a long series of Arts and Crafts houses in a free style.*

natured, very fond of smoking and, I grieve to say, of women".

Notes

[1] *Richard Norman Shaw,* R.A.*, Architect, 1831–1912,* Batsford, London 1940.

[2] This remark, no doubt, was meant to dispose of the worst mixtures of the Free or Mixed Renaissance and, within the Gothic style, of, say, Thomas Harris.

[3] p.340. Cloverley Hall cost £60,000 and was 450ft. by 440 ft. in size. Nesfield must have been a very well-connected young man.

[4] And, as a matter of fact, just a touch of *japonaiserie* in the lotus-flower friezes which had already appeared at Coombe Abbey and Cloverley Hall – very early cases and memorable as such.

[5] Yet Leys Wood was published in 1868 as by Nesfield & Shaw.

[6] The motif appears also on Devey's Betteshanger, but it is by no means clear whether it belongs to the work of 1856, or to the extensive later works. Nesfield used the Ipswich window in 1878 at Loughton Hall, Essex.

[7] Or Nesfield's equally classical Bodrhyddan, Flintshire, of 1872–73 which is also perfectly symmetrical.

[8] *Philip Webb,* O.U.P., 1935, p.75.

[9] *Collected Works,* XXII, p.329, from *The Fortnightly Review* May 1888.

[10] See H.-R. Hitchcock, *Architecture: Nineteenth and Twentieth Centuries,* Pelican History of Art, 1958, p.212. Also D. Gregory-Jones in *The Architectural Review,* CXXI, 1958.

[11] Though the plan of the whole of Cheyne House is asymmetrical.

16 *Norman Shaw. Detail, Piccadilly Hotel, Piccadilly, London (1905–08). Many have mourned Shaw's ventures in Edwardian Baroque, but here as elsewhere he used the manner freely and with originality.*

Edward Godwin

by *Dudley Harbron*

Webb, Shaw and Nesfield started the movement of English architects into the post-Gothic period in the 1860s. But it was the passionate genius of Edward Godwin (1833–1886) that lit the flames of the campaign by younger architects to find a new modern English architecture, free of historical styles. Godwin's houses in Chelsea, designed between 1877 and 1881, were his chief contribution to the buildings of that movement, but Dudley Harbron's short study shows many other sides to this revolutionary designer.

The editors of Ellen Terry's *Memoirs* express their surprise that none has written a biography of the architect, Edward William Godwin. We can share their regret, for the little that has been told of him is such as to excite the desire to know more: Sir Max Beerbohm calls him a "superb architect," and the late T. P. O'Connor confided – "I knew a lot about him. He was a singularly attractive man to ladies, and had many adventures." Obviously as architect or individual he invites remembrance; and even were not the accomplishments and personality of the man sufficient to warrant the telling of his story, the circle of his familiars should have been enough: Burges, Swinburne, Sandby, Whistler, Wilde, Way, Seddon, Street, Ellen Terry, Rosa Corder and a host of others were his friends – and he the meeting ground of their several arts.

It is true that he is given a place in the *National Dictionary of Biography*; but the account is inadequate. It suggests that had he stayed in Bristol he would have become of more consequence, ignores his work in London, and understates the value of his contributions to the sister arts. Nor were the notices in the press which appeared at his death quite sufficient, for though they pay their respect to his exceptional ability, they are far from complete. His artistic range was too wide. His personality too complex for hasty generalisations.

About the time of his premature death the probable cause of the omission to record his career was that it was no-one's affair; and doubtless any intruding biographer was deterred by anxiety to avoid hurting the feelings of some people then living. Today the psychological interest inherent in his person may lead to reconsideration of Godwin earlier than will the character of his work. The majority of readers are more curious about persons than concerned for the things they created. The time when his works will be generally appreciated is not yet arrived.

The formative years of Edward Godwin were spent in Bristol in which city he was born in 1833. The dashing Elizabethan qualities of some of her earlier citizens infected him. His father was a decorator, and from what we know of the son the occupation of his sire must have contributed through heredity, precept and environment to the growth of the boy's talent and the selection of his objective. Colours, tones, shapes, design were his obsession throughout a period when sensitiveness to such things was almost unknown. When the best designs were adaptations of traditional forms – and the worst traceable to the same fount; when the great architects were connoisseurs – selecting choice bits or choice buildings for their front elevations, and relegating any original talent they had for design to the rear, Godwin by nature creative, was obliged to play the same game as his competitors. It was thus, by and through a union of these two abilities, the selective and the creative, that he was to arrive at the unique position he occupies in the scheme of art in Victorian England.

As a boy at school he is said to have studied Bloxham's works on Gothic architecture, as a youth to have served a pupilage with William Armstrong, a local architect. When barely seventeen he assisted W. C. Border in the production of a serial – *Architectural Antiquities of Bristol*,[1] – only one volume of which appeared, and during and following his training he measured and sketched churches in the neighbourhood. Some of these drawings were published or referred to by him twenty years after they had been made. His training was typical of the time it covered; and he only differed from the rest by the penetrating enthusiasm he had for his work. The Medieval Revival seemed to sensitive souls the recovery of a lost pathway. Seeking for support he discovered the work of G. E. Street. "It was the view of his design for Cuddesdon College, published in the *Illustrated News* of April 23 1858, that first attracted me then a student, to this accomplished architect." From Street he learned the importance of massing and simplicity, rather than the accuracy of detail. It was a similar interest in an illustration which led to the commencement of his lifelong friendship with William Burges. "It was a design by him for a fountain for the city of Gloucester, with a bit of the old city in the background," that led him to call on the author at 15 Buckingham Street. "I introduced myself; he was hospitable, poured wine into a silver goblet of his own design, and placed bread upon the table. With very few words we ate and drank."[2]

Having fortified himself by this apprenticeship, it was not long before Godwin surprised the profession by winning the competition for Northampton Town Hall. Eastlake, the historian, in his comment on the building, says: "The Town Hall at Northampton, begun in 1861, is an excellent example of his early taste. Its plan is at once simple and ingenious. The condition of its site admits of only one façade, but that is treated with becoming dignity. Now, it is impossible to examine this front without feeling that at this period the design was strongly influenced by the then prevalent taste for Italian Gothic and the principles of design which Mr Ruskin had lately advocated. The fenestration of the principal story, the sculptured and star-pierced tympana of the windows below, the character of the balconies, inlaid work, and angle shafts of the Tower – all suggest an Italian origin."[3]

Of course, in a public competition, Godwin, in pursuing this line, was adopting the only road to success, for he, quite unknown, would not yet have been allowed a manner of his own. Indeed, as events will show, he never secured that privileged position.

He was, however, sufficiently confident for the future, to take to himself a wife, a Bristol lady. Their house in Portland Square was decorated and furnished by the bridegroom.[4] Here he was free to exercise his own theories. They differed from those of his friend Burges with whom he frequently argued the subject. Burges was enamoured of strong primary colours,

Godwin of pale or half tones. In his own house the walls were plain washes, the rooms sparsely furnished by pieces chosen for their quality. There were Persian rugs upon the floor and a built-in organ.

It required some courage to make these departures, for not since the Regent had refined taste been exercised. Any tentative return to such simplicity was felt to be immoral; moreover, it was realised as a direct attack upon the foundations of Victorianism – stability.

2 *Edward Godwin. Town Hall, Congleton, Cheshire (designed 1865). The site is narrow and difficult, but this early design already shows Godwin's feeling for strong composition and the play between plain and decorated surfaces. This competition success and that for Northampton Town Hall made the architect famous.*

Everybody knew that the object of man was to increase his comfort. The accumulation of household gods to minister to the insatiable demand for ease and cosiness had rendered any perceptive discrimination superfluous; vacant space was not respectable, it betokened poverty – the merited punishment inflicted by a just God upon idlers. Plenty was the reward of industry. In other parts of the country the same problem was agitating other solutions – in Kent, Morris was making the furniture for the Red House.

Godwin's early married life was brief, his wife died before the year, died to the notes of a Bach Prelude played, at her request, by her husband on the organ. He was left with his sister.

A musician, an artist, and an author, Godwin from his youth had been a frequent visitor to the Theatre Royal; not merely as an idle spectator but as a critic and commentator upon the performances. He had been sufficiently confident to suggest, in a letter in 1858 to Charles Kean, alterations in the way he should produce *Macbeth*. His reviews of the entertainments were published by the local press under the pseudonym *Jottings* (an epithet he used more or less throughout his life); indeed, he must have been an assiduous taker of notes for he was seldom at a loss for the date of any incident years after it had occurred.

Thus early displayed, his concern for the theatre was to grow to be the competing passion in his life. At this date, however, it took the educative form of Shakespeare readings with his friends in the house in Portland Square. There William Burges, James Hine, one of his collaborators on the youthful *Architectural Antiquities of Bristol*, his sister and their circle met to study and discuss the drama. It was thus that, in the spring of 1862, he met the Terry sisters, Kate and Ellen, who were employed in the stock company at the theatre. They were persuaded to join the party of Shakespeare readers.[5]

Ellen was then a girl of fifteen. Her host was twenty-nine. She was a vivacious young lady, sufficiently intelligent to recognise the talent of her entertainer, observant enough to have noted the unusual character of her surroundings, and sufficiently appreciative to allow Godwin to try his hand at the real thing: to permit him to design, make and drape the lovely dress for her part as Titania in *A Midsummer Night's Dream* at Bath. Soon after this happy interlude, Godwin left Bristol for London to pursue his profession. Another Town Hall competition was awarded to him.[6] Of this the invaluable Eastlake continues: "The same architect was employed to erect the Town Hall at Congleton, and a marked difference is at once observable in the character of his work. Venetian angle shafts and Italian tracery have become common property, and Mr Godwin disdains to adopt them. The general outline of the central tower and the open arcade on the street level still indicate a lingering affection for southern art; but a French element predominates in the design, which is simpler and more ascetic in its character. This tendency to shun the minutiae of decorative detail, to aim at effect by sturdy masses of unbroken wall space, and by artistic proportion of parts, is perhaps the main secret of Mr Godwin's artistic power . . ."[7]

But what had in the meantime befallen Miss Terry? On January 20 of the same year she had been married to George Frederick Watts.[8] The bride was now sixteen, Watts an elderly fifty-one. The honeymoon was spent with the Tennysons. This over, the couple returned to Little Holland House. Godwin was a near neighbour.

This nearness was to prove fateful. The juvenile Mrs Watts renewed her association with her congenial tutor of Bristol days. Godwin called upon the Wattses, and they upon him, in an informal friendly way. On one of these casual calls Mrs Watts found the architect ill in bed, and oblivious to the conventions she stayed to attend to his wants. When she returned home she was dismayed to find her husband and parents in conference. They accused her of infidelity and, despite her protestations of innocence, refused to accept them.[9] The upshot was that in June, 1865, a separation was arranged and she returned to the stage.

Godwin, appealed to support her pleas, either could not or would not influence her husband's and parents' decision. Apparently he expected that Watts would follow the breach by divorce of his wife and so enable them to marry. He redoubled his efforts to improve his position in the profession, he submitted no less than *three* designs for the proposed Assize Courts of his native town. The assessor awarded him all three premiums! The reason being that, in addition to the superiority of his suggestions, he was the only competitor who had adhered to the conditions of the competition which stipulated that a strip of land on the site should be left free from building. Notwithstanding the injustice, sufficient pressure was brought to bear upon the promoters to induce them to decide not to build any of these designs, but to hold a second competition.[10] This was held three years later. Godwin sent in one

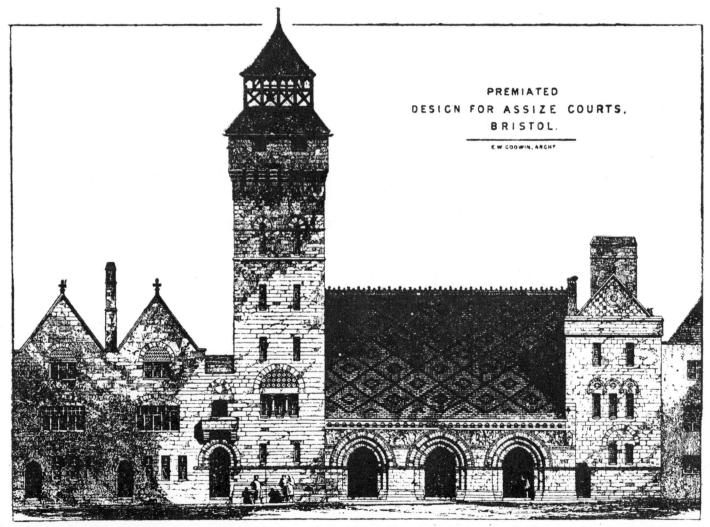

PREMIATED
DESIGN FOR ASSIZE COURTS,
BRISTOL.

E. W. GODWIN, ARCHT

3 *Edward Godwin. Competition design for the Assize Courts, Bristol (1871). The splendid design won the first place, but was never built. Four years later he wrote "The day of architectural revivals may be setting – I for one sincerely hope it is." But he also disliked the Queen Anne style fashionable at the time.*

design for which he was awarded the second premium. It was an ornate effort rather in his early manner because he had been told that an elaborate elevation was wanted. Although better than that which had been awarded the first premium, Godwin's entry in the second competition was not equal to his earlier design, and it was subsequently generally regretted that his first premiated design had not been built.

He joined forces with his friend Burges, six years his senior, in preparing the drawings for the Law Courts competition, staying with Burges's father at Blackheath during the initial discussions. This was followed by the two architects going for a holiday in Ireland together. It was not solely for pleasure. The object of their tour was to visit Cork Cathedral and to glean some insight into local mannerisms, for each of them had buildings in contemplation in the island[11]; Godwin, Dromore Castle, for the Earl of Limerick, and Burges, Finbar Cathedral. On the tour Godwin studied castles as, for the Earl, he had not only to design the building and furniture, but to choose the site.[12]

Watts still proving unrelenting, the architect and the lady he had compromised decided to set up house in a cottage at Gusterwood Common and, when completed, moved to a house designed and built for her at Harpenden.[13] Thus for the second time in her career Miss Terry sacrificed her art for domestic ties. Her mission on this occasion was to keep house, to cook, garden, mend and trace "on £3 a week" for her companion,[14] and to spend the happiest days of her life surrounded by the objects collected or fashioned by her fastidious companion.

In appearance, Godwin was a strikingly handsome man, slenderly built, with brown hair and wide-set eyes. As a speaker he was fluent on the subjects which he had specially studied. They were many and constantly being added to. If fault he had, it was one of temperament in that he was inclined to be dogmatic on matters of opinion and, since he was downright and emphatic and usually in the right, he was feared by less cultivated men. With those like Burges he could dispute and quarrel, argue far into the night, and yet remain

4 *Edward Godwin. First houses (corner design), Bedford Park Garden Suburb, London (1876). Godwin also designed the semidetached houses shown in the background of this sketch. Both were built and survive in The Avenue, but they were unsuccessful and Norman Shaw replaced Godwin for later houses.*

through thick and thin fast friends. Indeed, the wider the knowledge of his opponent, the easier did they find it to agree to differ. At various times, on varied subjects, he crossed swords in public with Fergusson, Butterfield, Sir Edmund Beckett and others. The younger men of his time looked up to him with reason, for he was undoubtedly the most helpful of the senior members of the profession, tireless in giving encouraging advice and assistance to any such who appealed to him and to those who were sent to him by others. There were many of these last, and for all Godwin gave a ready ear and helping hand. To the students of the A.A. he gave an annual prize for design, the solution of some problem set by himself. For years he conducted a Design Club in *The British Architect*, to the running of which he must have given a large amount of time and thought. And seldom, if ever, was his judgment questioned. All these things, plus work for Burges, a pamphlet on St Alban's Abbey, another large house in Ireland, Glenburgh Towers, and the second Bristol Assize competition, filled his days between Harpenden and town. In 1871, he was a member of the Council of the R.I.B.A.[15] In the competitions for the Town Hall, Winchester, and for Leicester Municipal Buildings, he failed, although without question his design for Winchester Town Hall was, as a grouped composition, far superior to that awarded the prize. The contemporary critics said as much. It was revived Gothic in character, as was his Leicester design too, and this seemingly was his last use of any derivative of medieval architecture.

The faith in Gothic for secular buildings was on the wane, Street's New Law Courts were the subject of comment, chiefly condemnatory, in the newspapers and technical journals, the principal objection to the elevation being that that to the Strand was too cut up, so that it resembled a series of buildings and not a building. Godwin, gallantly, and possibly mistakenly, took sides in defence of Street, in particular contesting the criticisms of Fergusson, the writer. He did this by the old controversial device of carrying the war into the enemy's camp.[16]

The tide had turned, and Godwin's fortunes were at a low ebb. The brokers, those unshaven familiars of artists who have something left to appraise, were in possession of the treasures at Harpenden. It was at this crisis that Miss Terry, walking with her children in a country lane, met on a sudden a rider, none other than Charles Reade, the playwright. He was following the hounds. He recognised her and, drawing rein, entered into conversation in the course of which he asked her to return to the stage. Her first reply was "No." But later the call of the stage proved too strong and she changed her answer.[17]

The family returned to London, where in Taviton Street they established themselves. During the interval of Miss Terry's absence on tour, Godwin decorated the house. When the tour of Reade's play, *The Wandering Heir*, ended, Miss Terry returned to London, only to find that her companion's troubles had not abated. The bailiffs were again in possession of his belongings.

Once more fate intervened. This time Mrs Bancroft called unexpectedly to ask Miss Terry to play Portia in *The Merchant of Venice*, the production to be presented and dressed under Edward Godwin's direction. The background of the interview was unusual. The room in which the hostess, dressed in a yellow and brown tabard, received her guest had been stripped of its furnishings. What remained was the matting on the floor, upon which stood a large cast of Venus de Milo.[18] Apparently beauty was not in demand. The engagement was accepted.

As has already been told, Godwin had for more than twenty years thought, written and talked about play production; especially was his criticism directed to errors in scenery and costume. Was the background in scale with the actors? Were the buildings true in character to the time and place they were intended to simulate? Had the shadows been carefully considered? Were the costumes congruous, furnishings in keeping? Did the colour of the whole – background and costumed players – support the mood of the act to the full? These, and the telling grouping of the actors within the scenes, chiefly interested him. He had recently collected these reflections in a series of articles on *The Architecture and Costume of Shakespeare's Plays,* the essence of which was that they should be presented in one or other of three settings: our own day, the writer's day, or the characters' day.

The Bancrofts' confidence was not misplaced. *The Merchant of Venice* was a great success – this particular presentation has been described as "the first in which the modern spirit of stage management asserted itself." It was also the virtual commencement of Ellen Terry's phenomenal career as the greatest English actress of her day. There had at no time been much doubt about her genius. It has never been explained why, soon after this joint success, the architect "went away and shut the door after him."[19]

If a guess may be hazarded, the trouble was due to the refusal of Watts to make possible the marriage of his wife to the architect. Although separated they remained friends, and until her death Dame Terry cherished his memory. Godwin married a second time, and his wife was a vivacious dark-haired young lady, the daughter of Phillips the sculptor. Watts released his wife, who married Charles Kelly. So the legal knots were cut.

Godwin was of a type whose work and society appealed to artists, and for whom they had equal attraction. He designed studios for several of his friends and their friends – Rosa Corder, Frank Miles, Jacomb Hood, Archibald Stuart Wortley, the Princess Louise, Signor Pelligrini, and in their arrangement excelled his only rival (R. N. Shaw) in this special type of apartment.

It was natural, then, that when his companion,

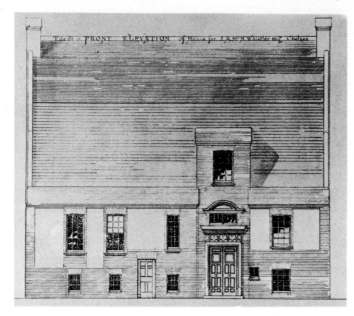

5 *Edward Godwin. First design for James McNeill Whistler, The White House, 35 Tite Street, Chelsea (October 1877). The original bold designs for this and 44 Tite Street were discovered by Mark Girouard in 1972. Godwin had caused controversy years earlier by designing interiors with cool uncluttered spaces, reflecting the current interest in Japan.*

6 *Edward Godwin. Revised design (at the demand of the Metropolitan Board of Works) for The White House (March 1878, completed May 1878). Demolished. In the same year Godwin lectured young architects, "If asked what style your work is, say – 'It is my own.'"*

J. McNeill Whistler, with the intention of accommodating a school, decided to build a house on a site in Tite Street, where some of his studios had been put up, Godwin, who had been associated with the artist in the colour schemes for his picture shows and who had consistently pointed out to the philistines the unique excellences of his friend's work, should be his chosen architect.

The house was built of white brick with a green slate roof, plain in design. In October, 1878, the owner

7 *Edward Godwin. The front door of The White House. Godwin's drawing shows the architect himself being ushered in by his client, the painter James McNeill Whistler. When Godwin died in 1886, Whistler married his widow.*

moved in, and later held a private view, to which his friends and patrons were invited. The works on view in the studios on that occasion were Connie Gilchrist skipping, Three Girls and, in the room below, the Rosa Corder.[20]

In a lecture on Studios which Godwin delivered impromptu to the A.A. (he had mysteriously lost his originally intended address on 'Trimmings' between ten o'clock the previous evening and ten that morning[21]), he told the audience that the Metropolitan Board of Works did not like the design for The White House. "They said it was like a dead house." When asked what was wrong, they said "It is all roof." The design was the subject of a minor sensation. Eventually the architect was obliged to add some unnecessary excrescences to the exterior.

Whistler's term of residence was brief. The costs of the Ruskin case, half of which he had to meet, compelled him to realise money by the sale of the house. It was bought by Harry Quilter, the critic, who altered it; before the sale Whistler had his fling, writing over the door: "Except the Lord build the house, they labour in vain that build it. E. W. Godwin, F.S.A., built this one."

From that time on Godwin grew more and more involved in activities other than architecture: critical journalism, interior decoration, costume design, stage productions.

He continued his applause of Whistler's work, this time the pastels, and drew particular attention to the scheme of decoration, framing and hanging of the exhibits: "As to the few bits of architecture he had drawn, he has given us – with what remains of the marble forms and details, which a knowledge of architecture would have tempted the eye to complete and restore and spoil – that most difficult of effects to render, its gradual decay. Of Venice as it is, in the dethroned, neglected, sad, passing away of it, Whistler tells us with the hand of a master who has sympathised with the noble city's sufferings and loss. This was not what our critics wanted. The Ducal Palace, St Mark's, the Bridge of the Rialto, the Fondaco dei Turchi, San Giorgio, or Sta Maria Della Salute – no matter whether vilely restored or not – are the familiar airs they wanted played again. They have sketches or photographs of them. They or their friends have played them so often that they fancy they know them, and in some cases offends them even to the point of direct misrepresentation. . . ."

To etch the Venus de Milo, to paint the masterpieces of Pheidias, or make pictures of the splendours of architectural genius, would be, to use his own words, "an impertinence. Things that are in themselves mighty and complete works of art should not do service to other arts."[22]

The ridicule of the Aesthetic Movement was now at its height; Gilbert's *Patience* and *The Colonel*, F. C. Burnand's skit, were amusing the public. The last was staged at the Prince of Wales Theatre. It has been con-

8 *Edward Godwin. First design for Frank Miles, 44 Tite Street, Chelsea (June 1878). This brilliant and revolutionary design was rejected by the Metropolitan Board of Works. In it Godwin reached mastery of the balanced asymmetrical composition of a street frontage.*

9 *Edward Godwin. House for Frank Miles, 44 Tite Street, Chelsea (1878–79). As built to a revised design at the insistence of The Metropolitan Board of Works. This house was for Frank Miles the painter, one of the Aesthetic Movement artists for whom Godwin designed much.*

demned as poor stuff by some of the defenders of the movement, notably Walter Hamilton. Godwin, himself a confirmed Aesthete, one of the intended victims, visited the theatre in 1881 and did not find it so effective as satire as he had anticipated.

He told how he had met the leading lady leaving the theatre dressed in a similar dress to that which she had worn in the play. In the play it had been held to be absurd, in the street it passed unnoticed. He says that the rooms and the costumes which the audience were invited to admire, were absurd; and that those they were expected to consider ridiculous, were pleasant. Of one of these last he wrote: "Turning to the other room that is presented to us as wrong, we find it furnished with artistic and simple things: a charming cabinet in walnut, designed by Mr Padgett for the green room; some simple inexpensive black Sussex chairs, like those sold by Messrs. W. Morris & Co.; a black coffee table, after the well-known example originally designed in 1867 by the writer of these notes; a quite simple writing table, matting on the floor, a green and yellow paper on the walls, a sunflower frieze, a Japanese treatment of the ceiling (storks), and a red sun such as we see in Japanese books and on hand screens, make up a scene which, if found wanting in certain details and forced in sunflowers, is certainly an intriguing room, with individuality about it, quiet in tone and, what is most important, harmonious and pleasing."[23]

During the months when *The Colonel* was performed, Godwin, the arbiter of historic costume, dressed *Hamlet* at Sadler's Wells, *Juana* for Wilson Barrett, *Romeo* at the Olympic, and designed the whole of the scenery and dresses for Mrs Scott Siddons' *The Queen and Cardinal* at the Haymarket. His architectural patrons were few but discriminating – Earl Cowper, Lord Ferrers and the Fine Art Society. Godwin was one of the founders of the St Stephen's Fine Art Society; both he and his wife were exhibitors and frequenters of the receptions held by the Society. It was at one of these that he met the youthful Oscar Wilde. When the author later married Miss Lloyd, Godwin was employed to advise on the decoration and furnishing of their house in Tite Street.[24] The top floor study had white walls and woodwork and red painted furniture; downstairs, the walls were buttercup yellow and the woodwork lacquer red. The doors were removed and portières substituted. When this decoration was in progress, Godwin was busy writing a pamphlet, *Dress in relation to health and climate*, for the Health Exhibition. The ideas expressed in the pamphlet enchanted Wilde, who mentioned the work twice in *The Pall Mall Gazette*, and further told the world that "the particular form of dress I wore was very similar to that given in Mr Godwin's handbook from a print of Northcote's, and had a certain elegance and grace about it which was very charming."[25]

Already Godwin had sufficiently impressed Liberty's to induce them to open "artistic and historic costume studios, where any kind of dress, ancient and modern, can be made." The designs were his. There were mannequins (the first time such delectable creatures were thought of) for the dress parade, "All worn by ladies whose stature and general appearance was singularly in harmony with the style of dress."[26]

Apart from architecture, which he had nearly abandoned, the range of his activities was now very wide; producing for Benson at Oxford one week, visiting Copenhagen the next, or writing a series of letters to art students on all manner of themes. They were addressed to art students in general, although their themes mainly concerned architectural students. Into his columns there now nearly always crept his two obsessions: the theatre and his friend Whistler's colour schemes in painting, or on walls: grey, white and flesh colour.

Wilson Barrett was one of his principal admirers and consistent supporters; for him he dressed and environed *Claudian*, and although this was burlesqued in 1884 by Burnand, it was for Barrett that the voyage to Copenhagen in search of inspiration for the costume and scenery of *Hamlet*, at the Princess', was made.

He was growing a little tired of the restless life he had lived. To his readers he counselled: "Be content with a simpler, quieter life than that which is characteristic of the present time."

Perhaps it was this yearning for peaceful life that suggested the idea of performing in the open air. The experiment was made by the Pastoral Players, consisting of Godwin, "Director-General of Entertainment" (so the daily press dubbed him), Lady Archibald Campbell and her friends. The group decided to perform Shakespeare's *As You Like It* and Fletcher's *Faithful Shepherdesse*, in the grounds of Dr M'Geagh's hydropathic at Coombe Wood. It is this series of entertainments which has earned the immortality of Godwin, through the pen of Max Beerbohm.[27]

Three sessions of three days each were proposed; the end of May, the end of June, and the middle of July.[28] Unfortunately the weather over the first two periods was unsuitable, and although they were honoured by the Prince and Princess of Wales and most of society, the venture was voted a failure. Happily, in July the sun smiled and the Prince, who was again present, congratulated all concerned. Thus fortified

10 *Edward Godwin. Pellegrini and Stuart Wortley house, 36 Tite Street, Chelsea (designed June 1878). Demolished.*

11 *Edward Godwin. Design for a house at 42 Tite Street, Chelsea, for Rosa Corder (September 1879). Not built. Godwin did later build the Tower House on this site, which still survives slightly altered. But he did little architecture after 1881, concentrating on the design of stage scenery for the last five years of his revolutionary life.*

they continued the experiment the following year, 1886. This time, with *Fair Rosamond*, in the grounds of Mrs Leo Schuster, known as Cannisaro Woods, there "in a forest glade carpeted with flowers, romantic, secluded, delightful," royalty again graced the day. This year everything conspired to delight: "Delicious too, were the plates of fresh strawberries with clotted cream."[29]

Godwin was now entirely immersed in theatrical ventures. He had a play, *The Fool's Revenge*, at the Opéra Comique, and at Hengler's Circus, Argyll Street, an ambitious production, *Helen in Troas*. Into this last he put all his genius for arrangement, costume, scenery and presentation. The performances were a social success, though some of the press considered the spectacle above the heads of the audience who, they suggested, had assembled because it was fashionable to do so. It is to be divined that the business interests in the theatre were becoming a little alarmed by the revolution he was inaugurating. They need not have worried, for Godwin was already a sick man. Whistler was with him when he died.[30]

They buried him at Northleigh. No stone marks his resting place. Among Dame Terry's papers there was found, when she had died, a manuscript copy of a sonnet in his memory. This read:

"A man of men, born to be genial King,
   By frank election of the artist kind."
and concluded –
"They tell me he had faults – I know of one;
   Dying too soon, he left his best undone."[31]

[1] *Bristol Bibliography*, p.38.

[2] *The British Architect* 29 April 1881, p.213.

[3] C. L. Eastlake, *A History of the Gothic Revival in England*, 1872, p.358.

[4] *Ellen Terry's Memoirs*, 1933, p.37.

[5] *ibid*

[6] *The Builder* July 1864, pp.28–9.

[7] C. L. Eastlake, *op cit* pp.358–9.

[8] *Ellen Terry's Memoirs*, p.43.

[9] Lady Duff Gordon, *Discretions and Indiscretions*, p.34 also *Ellen Terry's Memoirs*, p.46.

[10] *Building News* Vol. 20 1871, p.450.

[11] *The Art Journal* 1886, p.170.

[12] C. L. Eastlake, *op cit* p.423.

[13] *Ellen Terry's Memoirs*, p.74.

[14] *ibid* p.63.

[15] *Building News* Vol. 20, p.213.

[16] *The British Architect* Vol. 21, p.73.

[17] *Ellen Terry's Memoirs*, p.74 or Craig, *Ellen Terry*, p.35.

[18] *Ellen Terry's Memoirs*, p.96.

[19] *ibid* p.96.

[20] T. R. Way, *Memories of Whistler*, p.24.

[21] *The British Architect* 7 March 1879.

[22] *ibid* Vol. 15 1881, pp.98–9.

[23] *ibid* Vol. 16 1881, p.379.

[24] Frank Harris, *Oscar Wilde*, p.64.

[25] *Art and Decoration* p.68.

[26] *The British Architect* Vol. 21 1884, p.226.

[27] *The Works of Max Beerbohm*, p.49.

[28] *The Graphic* 1885, p.488.

[29] *ibid* 1886, p.55.

[30] *Ellen Terry's Memoirs*, p.101.

[31] *ibid* p.97.

N.B. The dating of Godwin's Tite Street designs has now been established precisely by Mark Girouard: see *Country Life* 23 November 1972, pp.1370–4.

Oscar Wilde and his Architect, Edward Godwin

by H. Montgomery Hyde

In 1950 a bundle of letters from Oscar Wilde was discovered among papers left by Edward Godwin. H. Montgomery Hyde traced the story that emerges from this correspondence about Godwin's last architectural work in 1884–85, shortly before his death.

When Oscar Wilde married Constance Lloyd in the summer of 1884, he took the lease of a house in Chelsea – No. 16 (now No. 33) Tite Street – which was to be their future home. While its exterior was that of an ordinary Victorian dwelling, its new tenant planned to convert its interior into something extraordinary and quite unlike the interior of any other Victorian mansion. For this purpose he secured the services of Edward Godwin, who devised and carried out the original and, as some visitors considered, bizarre scheme of interior decoration in addition to designing most of the furniture. In this work he is said to have received some help from James McNeil Whistler. A bundle of Godwin's papers, hitherto unpublished, including a number of letters from both Wilde and his wife, all of which the architect carefully preserved, and which has now come into the present writer's possession, has made it possible to reconstruct this scheme.[1]

No. 16 was a four-storey dwelling with a basement. To the right of the entrance hall was the room facing the street known as the Library where Wilde did most of his work on an antique mahogany writing table which had once belonged to Carlyle. Also on the ground floor, giving on to the back, was the dining room. The whole of the first floor was taken up by a large drawing room, which was divided in two by folding doors, the back drawing room being used by Wilde as a smoke room. There were two bedrooms on the second floor, and another on the third, which was the top. (The Wildes' own bedroom was the second floor front.) At the back of the top floor there was another room originally intended as a workroom for Wilde but he seems to have used it seldom, preferring the Library for such work as he did at home. These were the principal rooms in the house, for which Godwin designed the following scheme of decoration.

"Coloring and Painting Specimens of all the colours will be given by the Architect.

Ground floor.

Dining Room. The whole of the woodwork to be enamel white the walls pt in oils enamel white & grey to the height of 5-6. The rest of the walls & ceilings to be finished in lime-white with a slight addition of black to give the white a greyish tone. At the top of the Dado a band of wood to be fixed of section as per drawing E & painted enamel white to match rest of woodwork.

Library. The walls to the height of 5'-6" to be painted in distemper dark blue. The upper part of the walls cornice and ceiling to be pale gold colour. The woodwork throughout to be golden brown (russet). The wall band to be of thin wood as per drawing F painted golden brown.

Entrance hall: Dado 5' 6" Grey. Wall bank white. Wall over & ceiling yellow. Woodwork white.

Staircase: Walls and ceilings yellow. Dado Grey continuing hall. Woodwork white and wall band to step

with stair at intervals of 4 or 5 steps.

Drawing room front: Woodwork ivory white Walls distempered flesh pink from skirting to cornice. The cornice to be gilded dull flat lemon colour gold and also the ceiling margin to Japanese leather which latter will be provided by Mr Wilde and is to be properly fixed by Contractor. The wall bank to be moulded wood as per sketch pt ivory white.

Drawing room back: Distemper pale green ceiling and cornice walls green darker.

Fireplace & Woodwk painted brown pink.

2nd floor.

Bedroom front: Pink walls woodwork ceiling & 2 feet of top of walls under cornice apple green.

Bedroom back: Dark blue walls 2ft of upper part cornice & ceiling pale blue with greenish tone added.

3rd floor.

Mr Oscar Wilde's room. Greyish-pink-red ceiling & upper part of walls to depth of 4' 0" lower part of walls red russet brown.

3rd floor front: All white woodwork walls and ceilings yellow."

In addition to this specification there were various additions and alterations entrusted to the contractor. Several of Godwin's drawings of parts of the drawing room have survived. One of them shows the elaborate overmantel into which was set a bronze bas-relief by Donaghue, an American sculptor, depicting a scene suggested by Wilde's poem 'Requiescat.'[2] Godwin also prepared sketches showing how several of Whistler's etchings – Venetian studies presented by the artist – and a few drawings by Edward Burne-Jones could best be arranged along the walls so as to form a deep frieze against a background of dull gold. For the dining room furniture Godwin designed a suite in white, and also a sideboard with which he took particular pains. The chairs for this room were modelled in various Grecian styles, while round the walls there was a strip of shelving which served for tea and buffet suppers. "By this arrangement," as one visitor remarked, "the centre of the room was an open space instead of being absorbed by the customary huge table laden with refreshment, and gave an impression of greater size and lightness to the room." Godwin was again responsible for the soft furnishings, and even for such aids to ablutions as were procurable in those days. "I should be very glad," wrote Constance Wilde in one of her letters to the architect, "if a bath of any artistic shape could be found for my room."[3]

While the alterations and decorations were being carried out, the Wildes stayed in the bachelor rooms in Charles Street (now Carlos Street), off Grosvenor Square, where Oscar had lived before his marriage. Like all newly-wed couples, who are waiting to get into the matrimonial home, they were consumed by impatience at the leisurely pace at which English workmen always seem to proceed on these operations. And

2 *Ellen Terry as Camma in 'The Cup', for which Godwin designed the scenery and costumes circa 1880.*

so it happened that one day, soon after the honeymoon was over, Wilde called on the architect at his house in Westminster in the hopes of hurrying on the work. But Godwin was not in. In fact he was busily engaged with Lady Archibald Campbell in directing an open-air performance of *As You Like It* in the grounds of Dr McGeagh's hydropathic establishment at Coombe Wood, near Kingston-on-Thames. Wilde left the following note scribbled in pencil on a sheet of Godwin's notepaper.

"   7 Great College Street,
                    Westminster, S.W.
                         (July 19, 1884)

Dear G.

I suppose you are as busy as you like it (or don't like it)! When can I see you Monday at Tite Street?

I want to press on the laggards – if you like of course after the play will have to do, i.e. Thursday, but Monday wd be best.

                         Ever yrs,
                         OSCAR WILDE.   "

According to Whistler's biographers Godwin had a way of always making his estimates lower than the actual expenses, and then siding entirely with the builders in case of disagreements and misunderstandings. That, they allege, was the way the crash came which obliged Whistler to leave The White House.[4] In the case of 16 Tite Street it cannot be denied that something of this kind happened. The original building contractor was a man named Green, who was already under contract to the landlord to execute certain work, of which the landlord was willing to give the benefit to the incoming tenant. To facilitate this arrangement it appears that Green agreed to allow Wilde to deduct so much from his account. Unfortunately a difference of opinion arose between them as to the exact amount to be credited. Also it appeared that Green skimped some parts of the work besides failing to carry out his instructions in regard to others. The result was that Wilde closed his account and declined to pay it when it was rendered. He then hurried off to the provinces to fulfil a series of lecture engagements, but before leaving he asked Godwin to employ another contractor, which the architect undertook to do.

From Bristol Wilde wrote to enquire whether the new contractor, whose name was Sharpe, had begun work.

"   .   The Royal Hotel,
                         Bristol.
                         (October 14, 1884)

Dear Godwino,

I write to you from your own city to say that Allport[5] estimates work to be done by Green at £72!!! Amazing: now let us for heaven's sake (get a) move on. Is Sharpe in? And can I see you on *Friday* anywhere: it is my first day in town.

I want if possible Sharpe to be in and doing! I am

so overwhelmed with expenses. I will be in town Friday afternoon. Will you send a line to Charles St.
                         Ever yours,
                         O.W.   "

Indeed on the same day as Wilde wrote this letter Godwin approved the new contractor's estimate for the work to be done at £110.

When Wilde got back to town an unwelcome surprise awaited him in the shape of a writ from the old contractor claiming the amount of his account. "What shall I do about Green?" Wilde asked the architect. "He is too horrid." Godwin advised his client to defend the action and apparently he also recommended a firm of city solicitors, Messrs. George and William Webb of 11 Austin Friars, whom Wilde instructed to enter an appearance on his behalf. This meant interviews, affidavits and other tiresome legal documents not to mention costs and a sum of money which the solicitors felt they must pay into court. Of particular importance were the details of the oral agreement which Wilde alleged Green had made with him; on this subject the solicitors were quite explicit. "For greater caution," they wrote to Godwin, "we ought to see Mr Wilde and examine him as he would be examined before a Master, because of course 'understandings' won't do; we have to go upon arrangements."

Meanwhile furniture began to arrive ("the Japanese couch is exquisite"), only to be appropriated by the indefatigable Green. On November 3 Wilde wrote as he was again on the point of leaving London:

"Don't you think a vermilion band in the front room – ground floor – in the recess – to continue the moulding would do for the present – till the bookcase is arranged?

I am in much distress over Green seizing the furniture – you alone can comfort me."

And again, a month later, as he was on the point of returning to town:

"I wish you would choose the colours – the red for the drawing room – as the thing is at a standstill. Is it to be vermilion? Is it not?

The universe pauses for an answer! Don't keep it waiting!"

Later in December Wilde was again away, lecturing this time in Scotland, when the new contractor's bill, amounting in all to £227 17s. 0d., arrived as a further unpleasant surprise.

"   The Balmoral,
                         Edinburgh.
                         (December 17, 1884)

My dear Godwin,

I cannot understand Sharpe's account – enclosed – what is (1) extra painting? What is (2) 12 gas brackets – what is deal shelf overmantel and case in Dining room – etc. Sharpe has been paid first £40 for the overmantel in bedroom and drawingroom, and the sideboard – which by the bye I thought very dear –

then £120 for his contract – but this new £100 takes me by surprise – I thought the £120 was for everything – surely Green fixed the gas stoves? I may be wrong, but would you look over it again?

I hope you have been able to choose the stuffs – I don't think the oriental blue and red hanging is big enough for two curtains on landing at drawing room – would you choose something for that place – and see my wife about them. I do hope to see things nearly ready when I come home – the coverings for settees especially.

I wish you were in Edinboro' with me – it is quite lovely – bits of it.

The house must be a success – do just add the bloom of colour to it in curtains and cushions.

Ever yours,
OSCAR. "

3 *Ellen Terry's dressing table, designed by Godwin.*

Godwin had little difficulty in explaining how "this new £100" was made up. Extra painting throughout the house accounted for £32, four coats of paint with labour to the outside cost a further £21. Then there were such items as "Japan gold paper" for the drawing room, study and the bathroom (£12), "putting Mr Green's mistake right" (£12 17s. 0d.) and the services of a night watchman (£5). Unfortunately for Wilde there was worse to come, since the contractor sent in a further account shortly afterwards. "I am aghast at Sharpe's bill," Wilde expostulated. "His charges are worse than Green's. £3 9s. 0d. for a screen of iron piping! £3 6s. 0d. for hanging lamps!!! £9 for the man who (put up) an array of shelves which is ridiculous. Sharpe told me he had not made much over the furniture in Constance's room. It is clear what he is doing – overclaiming on other things."

With the coming of New Year, 1885, the Wildes were at last able to move in to the house. Although he grumbled about the expenses Oscar was far from ungrateful to the architect. "You have had a great deal of trouble over the house," he told him, "for which I thank you very much, and must insist on your honorarium being not ten but fifteen guineas at (least)." And with the honorarium went in due course a note in Wilde's most graceful style:

" My dear Godwin,

I enclose a cheque and thank you very much for the beautiful designs of the furniture. Each chair is a sonnet in ivory, and the table is a masterpiece in pearl. Will you let me know what I owe you for the plan of the new room? I fear I cannot build it yet – money is as scarce as sunlight, but when I do I will look for your aid. I don't know what you owe Constance – but she will write to you. I was so sorry to miss you. Do come and dine any day this week – and will you come to my wife's box at the 'Hunchback,' Lyceum, on Saturday evening.

Yours ever,
Oscar.   "

It was perhaps ironical that such an enthusiastic exponent of general hygiene as Edward Godwin should now suffer a breakdown of his own health from which he was destined never to recover. For the time being he retired to the country to get some rest before tackling another open-air production at Coombe Wood with Lady Archibald Campbell – Fletcher's *The Faithfull Shepherdesse*, as well as a revival of *As You Like It*. "We are very much annoyed at your being away and not constantly dining with us" Wilde wrote to him. And again –

"
16, Tite Street,
Chelsea.
(April, 1885)

Dear Godwino,

I am glad you are resting – nature is a foolish place to look for inspiration in, but a charming one in which to forget one ever had any. Of course we miss you, but the white furniture reminds us of you daily, and we find that a rose leaf can be laid on the ivory table without scratching it.

We look forward to seeing you robust, and full of vigour. My wife sends her best wishes for your health.

Ever yours,
Oscar Wilde.   "

During this time Wilde completed a long article on 'Shakespeare and Stage Costume' which appeared in the May number of *The Nineteenth Century*.[6] In commenting on the elaborate scenery and costume, which Godwin had designed for W. G. Wills's play *Claudian*,[7] Wilde paid a warm tribute to the architect whom he described as "one of the most artistic spirits of this age in England." Later in the same article he mentioned Lady Archibald Campbell's productions of *As You Like It* at Coombe Wood but does not appear to have emphasised Godwin's contribution strongly enough to please the designer.

" *I was in mourning for my uncle,*
and lo! he speaketh.

Revised version.

Dear Godwino,

I am delighted to know you are somewhere. We thought you were nowhere, and searched for you everywhere, but could not find you anywhere.

Thanks for your praise of my article. The reason I spoke of 'Lady Archie's' production was this. I had spoken before of you in *Claudian* – and was afraid that a second mention would look as if you had put me up to praise you. But every one knows you did it all. The glory is yours entirely.

Do come to town. At Oxford you were mourned with lamentation. The play was charming.[8] See next Saturday's *Dramatic Review* for my account of it. An amazing criticism! with views of archaeology enough to turn Lytton into a pillar of salt.[9]

'My wife has a cold' but in about a month will be over it. I hope it is a boy cold, but will love whatever the Gods send.[10]

How about Coombe this year? I must criticise it somewhere.[11]

Ever yours,
O.W.   "

Meanwhile the proceedings initiated by the contractor Green were dragging their way through the usual interlocutory stages of a legal action. Eventually the plaintiff took out a summons to refer the matter to an arbitrator, which was agreed to, and the reference was fixed for hearing at the Law Courts at the end of May, 1885. Unfortunately when the time came Godwin felt too ill to give evidence, but the solicitors begged him to attend for a few minutes so as to explain this to

4 *Houses in Tite Street, Chelsea. Left to right. Godwin's No. 29 (built 1879–80, now demolished), R. W. Edis's No. 31 (circa 1878), Godwin's 1879 design for No. 33 (not built), Godwin's White House No. 35 built for the painter Whistler (1877–78, now demolished). These designs and their details were highly influential.*

the arbitrator and ask for an adjournment. The result was that the hearing was postponed for a month, and during this period Green's solicitors made overtures for a settlement.

On June 22 Wilde left a note for Godwin at his club which read: "There is a compromise proposed – but it means my paying £125! I cannot do that: but am ill with apprehension. It really rests on your evidence. If you cannot come my case is lost."

When this note was found among Godwin's papers after his death, it was seen to have been endorsed in the architect's handwriting with these words: "Answered that my evidence was his always."

However, on the day before the hearing the parties did finally succeed in coming to terms so that Godwin did not have to go into the witness-box after all. No record has been discovered of the financial details, but the settlement was based on the report of an independent surveyor. And so ended a protracted and irritating dispute. It was Wilde's first experience of the workings of the law. His second experience took place almost exactly ten years later at the Old Bailey. But by this time Edward Godwin was no longer alive, while the contents of the house which he had decorated with such skill had been sold by order of the sheriff, fetching mere knockdown prices.

Sick man as he was when he was working in Wilde's house in Tite Street, the casual notes and sketches which appear on the back of his drawings indicate that he was planning for another great theatrical venture. "One might have thought that to have produced *As You Like It* in an English forest would have satisfied the most ambitious spirit," wrote Wilde; "but Mr Godwin has not contented himself with his sylvan triumphs. From Shakespeare he has passed to Sophocles, and has given us the most perfect exhibition of a Greek dramatic performance that has yet been seen in this country." This was *Helena In Troas*, a lavish production in which Godwin employed the spectacular medium of a circus arena to show off the fine properties of the Greek chorus against a brilliant background combination of scenery and costume.[12] But if Godwin's theatrical genius thus enabled the Philistines to peer into Paradise, it also considerably alarmed the more conservative business interests in the theatre who regarded Godwin's innovations as revolutionary. However, as it turned out. their fears were groundless. Godwin was now suffering from acute inflammation of the bladder. Less than six months later he was dead.

By his own wish no stone marked Edward Godwin's last resting-place. But for many years Lady Archibald Campbell used to tend his grave. She also paid fitting tribute to his memory in the leading article which she wrote, at Wilde's request, for the first number of *The Woman's World* to be published under Wilde's editorship. Her words may serve as a fitting epitaph for "that superb artist," as Sir Max Beerbohm has called him. "No man ever lived with greater singleness of purpose. To create beautiful things for the mere sake of their loveliness, this was his object; not wealth, not position, not fame even. Yet fame surely shall be his, for the muses taught him and the mother of muses had care of him. Poet of architects, and architect of all the arts, he possessed that rare gift, a feeling for the very essence of beauty wherever and whenever it was to be found." For Oscar Wilde he remained, in the perspective of memory, the builder of the 'house beautiful' and the creator of the only home that Wilde was ever able to call his own.

[1] For permission to quote from these letters the writer is indebted to Mrs Vyvyan Holland who owns the copyright.

[2] Written by Wilde, when an undergraduate at Oxford, in memory of his only sister, Isola, to whom he was devoted and who died in childhood.

[3] Anna Comtesse De Brémont, *Oscar Wilde And His Mother* 1911, p.87.

[4] E. R. and J. Pennell, *The Whistler Journal* 1921, p.252.

[5] The surveyor employed when Wilde took the house.

[6] Later republished with some alterations as 'The Truth of Masks' in Wilde's book *Intentions,* 1891.

[7] Produced at the Princess's Theatre, London, in December, 1883, with Wilson Barrett in the title part. The production was applauded among others by Ruskin who wrote "With scene painting like that, this Princess's Theatre might do more for art teaching than all the galleries and professors of Christendom."

[8] Shakespeare's *Henry IV* produced by the University Dramatic Society at the Town Hall, Oxford, on 15 May, 1885.

[9] *The Dramatic Review* 23 May 1885. "Even the dresses had their dramatic value. Their archæological accuracy gave us, immediately on the rise of the curtain, a perfect picture of the time."

[10] Wilde's elder son Cyril was born in Tite Street on 9 June 1885.

[11] For Wilde's criticism of *As You Like It* see *The Dramatic Review* 6 June 1885: "On the whole the Pastoral Players are to be congratulated on the success of their representation, and to the artistic sympathies of Lady Archibald Campbell, and the artistic knowledge of Mr. Godwin, I am indebted for a most delightful afternoon. Few things are so pleasurable as to be able by an hour's drive to exchange Piccadilly for Parnassus."

[12] Among the many female beauties in the large cast was Constance Wilde, who, to please her husband, took the part of one of Helena's handmaidens.

Part Two: From Queen Anne Towards a Free Style 1875-1890

From Queen Anne Towards A Free Style

After the major advances towards a free style by Webb, Shaw and Godwin during the 1870s, the early part of the following decade produced relatively few exciting buildings. But under the surface great things were happening. A new generation of English architects was about to appear, full of the ideas of William Morris and Philip Webb and inspired not only by Godwin's buildings but the aspirations to originality that he had planted. During the 1880s most of them were working in the offices of established architects, particularly that of Norman Shaw, before plunging into independent practice around 1890.

Another group of young men was also establishing itself in London at this time. Glasgow had seen a sudden economic boom during the 1870s, followed by a disastrous banking crash in 1878. The boom produced a rush of young architects at a time when Scotland was turning from Greek classicism and looking at its own impressive ancient castles for a vernacular Scottish style. The bank crash was followed by a depressed period and the drop in building work sent many of these young men south to seek their fortunes in London. We have already mentioned that the Glaswegian J. J. Stevenson was established in London early in the Queen Anne period. His office and that of Sir Gilbert Scott (1811–78) became centres for these progressive young Scotsmen until they established their own practices.

Stevenson was rarely a very interesting designer, but he was important in more than one way. In about 1873 he had established a curious form of partnership with the newly appointed architect to the London School Board, a Durham-born product of Sir Gilbert Scott's office called E. R. Robson (1835–1917). Both partners, but chiefly Robson, went on to adapt the Queen Anne Style to many dozens of high, rationally planned schools all over London. An examination of these schools is a good starting point for what happened during the 1880s, for the Board schools are a Queen Anne precursor of the rationalism of the London County Council architects at the end of the century.

Another influence that became strong early in the 1880s was American architecture, especially that of H. H. Richardson (1838–86) of Boston. What impressed British architects were the long low lines of his houses and railway stations and the rugged naturalistic forms of some features which seemed to link the buildings to the ground on which they stood. James MacLaren (1843–90), one of the young London Scots, combined these features with a type of asymmetrical composition he had learned from Godwin and produced a series of striking buildings between 1886 and 1890 that injected a new spurt of originality into the work of the free style architects.

MacLaren was an early member of the Art Workers' Guild, the most successful of several important organisations founded in the 1880s to develop the Arts and Crafts ideas of Morris and Webb. It was not the earliest.

That privilege probably belongs to the Century Guild, founded in about 1881 by the architect Arthur Mackmurdo (1851–1942) and a group of artist-craftsmen. The far-sighted (but short-lived) venture was typical of

2 *W. Eden Nesfield. Elevation, Lodge, Kew Gardens, Kew, London (1866). One of the first Queen Anne Style designs, initiated by Nesfield and others as a reaction after the Gothic Revival.*

3 *J. J. Stevenson. Red House, Bayswater Road, London (1871). Demolished. The earliest London house in a version of the Queen Anne Style.*

1 *Norman Shaw. 'Hampstead Towers', 6 Ellerdale Road, Hampstead (1875). In this house for his own use, Shaw rejected historical styles and moved towards a new 'free style'.*

81

Mackmurdo, an intriguing figure who was so often ahead of his time in the 1880s but faded into a classicism of much less interest after the 1890s.

The Art Workers' Guild was founded in 1884 by Lethaby, Prior and others. It was followed four years later, by the Arts and Crafts Exhibition Society. These two organisations had many members in common, for the Society existed to arrange exhibitions of the work of the Arts and Crafts designers, most of whom belonged to the Guild, which was a discussion club for architects, artists and craftsmen with its own London premises. The Guild's influence will be discussed more fully in the next part of this book.

The work of J. D. Sedding (1838–91) was done largely in the 1880s and will be dealt with in this book's section on church architecture. But one other architect must be mentioned here, for his most influential work was done in the early years of the Art Workers' Guild. This was Halsey Ricardo (1854–1928), a highly talented and charming pupil of Basil Champneys. He started independent practice as early as 1879 and produced some of the most progressive designs of the late 1880s and early '90s. Perhaps unfortunately, Ricardo had a private income which relieved him of any pressing need to find commissions, and he built few of the outstanding works of which he was capable.

Thus, as far as the free style architects were concerned, the 1880s was a period of formulating ideas and preparation for their great moments in the next decade. But established architects did not escape the influence of the national vernacular theory and the other ideas which their assistants were discussing. Norman Shaw had now stepped up from domestic work to a practice in office and public buildings, and his New Scotland Yard police headquarters and other works show a free mixture of Scottish Baronial and Baroque motifs in a general design that is completely non-historical. Among others, Basil Champneys (1842–1935) and T. G. Jackson (1835–1924) would particularly reward further study.

Of the other large practices in the 1880s, young J. J. Burnet (1857–1938) had now taken over his father's prosperous firm in Glasgow, while in London Thomas Collcutt (1840–1924) and Ernest George (1839–1922) had joined Waterhouse as the big successful names of the time. Then in 1886 the young Aston Webb won the competition for the Victoria Law Courts in Birmingham and launched his firm onto a course that was to make it the biggest in the country. Like the other men mentioned in this paragraph, Aston Webb (1849–1930) was not an architect of any idealism concerning choice of style. Not for any of them the search for a new vernacular British architecture that rejected all historicism. But they must not be under-rated, for they were designers and builders of tremendous confidence and competence, able to work in several different styles with great excellence and, on occasion, to produce a great building.

4

5

4 *Basil Champneys. Harwood Road School, Fulham, London (completed 1875). One of the first of the London board schools in the Queen Anne manner later associated with E. R. Robson.*

5 *Norman Shaw. Lowther Lodge (now part of Royal Geographical Society), Kensington Gore, London (1873). A good example of the Dutch Renaissance variation of the Queen Anne Style.*

6 *Norman Shaw. Tabard Inn and shop, Bedford Park, Acton, Middlesex (circa 1880). Shaw was chief architect of this first garden suburb after 1877, when Edward Godwin resigned or was dismissed after the first year. This public house set a precedent for simple vernacular domestic work for which England later became world-famous.*

7 *Ernest George and Harold Peto. House for W. S. Gilbert, 19 Harrington Gardens, Kensington (1882).*

8 *Edward Godwin. Design for McLean's Art Gallery, at 7 Haymarket, London (1884). Not built, but a striking example of the free taste of the Aesthetic Movement in exterior design. Godwin distrusted the Queen Anne Style as just another revival.*

9 *H. H. Richardson. Lodge at North Easton, Massachussetts (circa 1886). Richardson's strong originality and naturalistic rocky forms at their most extreme.*

6

7

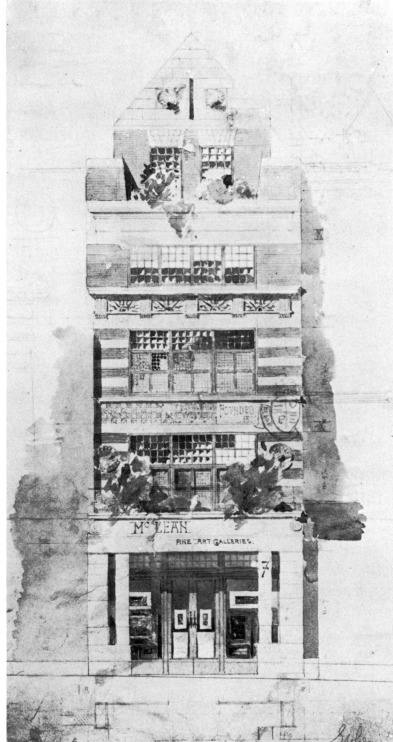

8

9

10

12

10 *Arthur Mackmurdo. 'Brooklyn', Private Road, Enfield, Middlesex* (circa 1887). *A design far ahead of its time in its rational simplicity and freedom of style.*

11 *H. H. Richardson. Crane Memorial Library, Quincy, Massachussetts* (1880). *Richardson's free and vigorous North American Romanesque influenced a number of British architects in the 1880s.*

12 *Halsey Ricardo. Competition design, Aberystwyth College buildings* (1886), *not built. The strong simplicity of the forms are an early example of one type of Arts and Crafts free style.*

13 *John D. Sedding. Vicarage for All Saints' Church, Plymouth, Devon* (1880s).

14 *Halsey Ricardo. Office building, 8 Great George Street, Westminster* (1887) *destroyed. A charming and original design.*

15 *Arthur Mackmurdo. Exhibition pavilion for Cope Brothers, tobacco importers, at the Liverpool International Exhibition of 1886. An extraordinary rationalist design for a temporary structure.*

16 *James MacLaren. 10–12 Palace Court, Bayswater, London (designed 1889, built 1890). MacLaren synthesised many of the features of earlier free style buildings in his brilliant asymmetrical designs.*

17 *H. T. Hare. Oxford Town Hall, St Aldates, Oxford (1892–97). One of the best of many attempts to transform the 'vernacular' English Jacobean style into an accepted modern style for the 1890s.*

18 *Thomas Collcutt. Imperial Institute, off Exhibition Road, South Kensington (1887–93). Demolished, except tower. A fine building, but far from shaking off historical styles.*

19 *Norman Shaw. New Scotland Yard police headquarters, Victorian Embankment, Westminster (1887–90, left hand block added 1904–07). Shaw mixed Scottish Baronial and Baroque features with his own originality in these strong free designs.*

15

16

The London Board Schools
E. R. Robson

by David Gregory-Jones

The London School Board was established in 1870 for the purpose of building dozens of badly-needed new schools all over the capital. These schools, an early adaptation of the Queen Anne Style, remain as landmarks in many parts of London. David Gregory-Jones's essay discusses the social aspirations and aesthetic aims, as well as the financial pressures, that drove the Board's first architect, E. R. Robson (1835–1917), to build so high – and so well.

E. R. Robson, the first architect to the London School Board and the designer of dozens of schools, quite specifically intended them to be landmarks in the urban scenery, dominating their surroundings and expressing the aspirations of their age in the same way as the spires of medieval England had done. Restricted sites may indeed have driven him to build up, but the use of every architectural means at his disposal to intensify the effect of height was quite deliberate: windows were tall and narrow, steeply-pitched slate roofs were furnished with multitudes of lovingly elaborated gables, turrets and soaring fluted chimney stacks, while storey heights were pushed to the 'maximum necessary'. The reasoned deliberation with which Robson emphasised the height of these schools is characteristic of his approach to architecture. In all "good architecture," he said, "there is no vagueness, no indecision, no doing of things by accident, no drifting helplessly from one idea to another. The artist first grasped his building comprehensively as a whole, with a clear definite intention of what he meant to say . . . and he conveyed his meaning and purpose on the face of his work, every moulding and member, window and door architrave, cornice and sculpture being, in his hands, so many opportunities for proclaiming his intention."

E. R. Robson was born in 1835, in Durham, of which his father had been three times mayor. He worked for three years at the bench to gain some practical knowledge of building construction before becoming a pupil, first of a local architect, then of Sir George Gilbert Scott. Scott's office was one of the breeding grounds of that reaction against strict revivalism of which Robson's own work was such a good example. Working there with him were Bodley and Garner, later to be the designers of the London School Board offices on the Embankment near Cannon Street Station, Graham Jackson, whose work at Oxford University and elsewhere has the stylistic freedom if not the vigour of Robson's Board schools, and J. J. Stevenson, designer of the Red House in Bayswater Road – built eight years after its namesake in Bexleyheath and likewise one of the pioneer buildings in the late 19th-century movement that was to place English domestic architecture at the head of the world.

Robson's first important appointment was in his home city where he was for six years architect to the Dean and Chapter of the Cathedral. He restored the central tower, and is reputed to have frustrated Gilbert Scott's ambition to give it a steeple. From here he moved to Liverpool where he was surveyor to the Corporation for seven years. The only work issued under his signature at Liverpool that the author has seen is the Municipal Offices. A contemporary describes the style as "Corinthianesque, treated freely" – and very horrid it looks too. While at Liverpool Robson was forbidden, under the terms of his contract, to undertake private work. He insisted on being freed from this

2 *E. R. Robson. Board School, Rotherhithe, London.*

1 *Portrait of E. R. Robson.*

restriction when he took up his post as Architect to the London School Board, and ran a considerable private practice at the same time as he was pushing through a huge programme of school building.

This is where J. J. Stevenson returns into the picture. Soon after Robson's appointment the two architects entered, for a short period, into partnership. Although Stevenson had no official connection with the School Board, he claimed in his book *House Architecture* that he had been responsible for the design of a few of the earliest Board schools. Robson, however, according to his son, stated that he had been "occupied often in the afternoons rubbing out what John (Stevenson) had done in the mornings." Taking into account both the character of Robson's earlier work at Liverpool and the fact that Stevenson's house in Bayswater Road had been designed in a close forecast of the so-called Queen Anne style developed in the Board schools, it does seem likely that Robson owed a great deal to his partner and that the remark just quoted was made in a rather disgruntled mood.

The London School Board was established in 1870 following the passage of Forster's Education Act. Among the earliest members of the Board was Edwin Chadwick who took his duties sufficiently seriously to write a long report on the construction of schools, in which he suggested a system of hollow interlocking concrete blocks for walls and floors with "iron uprights and ties on the Crystal Palace principle."

After a preliminary period during which buildings were hired for use as schools – we read of warehouses and a rice mill being adapted – the Board embarked on a big programme of school building in 1872. Robson had been appointed Architect to the Board in the previous year, but at first his duties were concentrated on research and site acquisition. It had been hoped that suitable sites could be acquired by advertising for them,

but in fact only one very unsatisfactory site was bought in this way, and the Board was embroiled from the first in the complexities of compulsory purchase orders, arbitration, compensation and the like.

The first thirty schools erected by the Board were all designed in competition. Six different architects were invited to compete in closed competition for each single school, the only reward offered being to the winners who got the job together with their normal 5 per cent fee. Consequently by August 1872, the Board had at its disposal the ideas of 180 architects on the subject of school design. Out of all these schools designed in competition only one gave a foretaste of the future. Its architect was Basil Champneys and it used to stand in Harwood Road near Eel Brook Common in Fulham. It was opened in November, 1873. Its plan was elementary – three superimposed schoolrooms each with a single attached classroom – but its architecture was advanced, and it can claim the distinction of being one of the very earliest schools designed recognisably in the 'L.S.B. style'.

In a talk given in Liverpool in 1888, Champneys gave his opinion as to the principles of limitation which architects might adopt if they were to bring a little order into the chaos of contemporary building. He wished architects to make their work as English as possible, as simple as possible and to abjure unwholesome efforts for originality – "at a premium in the present age of keen competition." These principles had been firmly observed in the Harwood Road school. Its originality was of the unforced kind in which use is made of a traditional language to say new things. It was strongly national in style, being derived from the early period of the Renaissance, which, in England as in all the countries of northern Europe, assumed marked individual characteristics.[1]

The style of Champney's own work at Newnham College, Cambridge, built a good fifteen years later, was forecast in every respect in his Harwood Road school. Thus, at a date when working class tenements were still of the most institutional grimness – the Peabody Trust had been at work since 1861, and it was to be a full quarter of a century before the LCC architects would be bringing some humanity into housing – elementary schools were being built that not only compared with contemporary buildings for the bourgeoisie in their architectural quality – educational standards, space standards, provision of playing fields, etc., were a very different matter – but which led the way in their architectural style. What the London School Board did in the '70s Oxford and Cambridge did in the '90s. This may well demonstrate the importance which ruling circles attached to education – in particular to the need for improved educational standards among the workers in British industry – but it is also a tribute to the determination of the Board, subject as it was to continual sniping on account of supposed extravagance, and to the vision and drive of its architect.

3 *E. R. Robson or J. J. Stevenson. The Cyril Jackson County Primary School, Northey Street, Stepney, London (1874).*

In common with many of the younger architects of the mid-'70s Robson was thinking along the same lines as Champneys. 1873, the year during which the first schools erected by the L.S.B. were opened, also saw the completion of Norman Shaw's New Zealand Chambers: the year was described by *The Architect* as "the first . . . of the Queen Anne revival," which it deplored, particularly as expressed in "several of the schools (of the L.S.B.) which show what the style can descend to when limited to simplicity and severity." It is, of course, partly the "simplicity and severity" of these buildings which appeal to us today. But their qualities are rooted in something more solid than a mere reflex action dictated by the need for economy. Unlike much contemporary work in the 'Queen Anne' manner, in which charm and elegance appear as the most sought-after qualities, these early Board schools have a weight and a seriousness that set one in mind of the work of Philip Webb (or even of Berlage). This weight and seriousness is partly an expression of Robson's own character – he admired as one of the key qualities in architecture "rigidity . . . a particular aesthetic quality opposed to easy softness, incoherence or languid beauty, and having for a result the stamping of the work with a vigorous character" – but also follows from his determination to be clear as to his architectural objectives. The style of his schools was not adopted at the dictates of fashion, but after experiment and careful thought as

to what the objectives of an architect designing a modern elementary school should be. In his book on school architecture, published in 1877 and for long a classic on its subject, Robson recorded this thought. After emphasising that the architect's first job is to understand how his building will be used he then poses the architectural problem as follows.

Schools could not be expensive, and, in London, this meant that they must be built in brick. Nevertheless, they were "henceforth to take rank as public buildings . . . planned and built in a manner befitting their new dignity," and they should have an architectural character that was immediately recognisable as their own. What was to be the content of this new architectural expression? "It is clear that a building in which the teaching of a dogma is strictly forbidden can have no pretence for using with any point or meaning that symbolism which is so interwoven with every feature of church architecture as to be naturally regarded as its very life and soul. *In its aim and object it should strive to express civil rather than ecclesiastical character*. A continuation of the semi-ecclesiastical style which has hitherto been almost exclusively followed in England for National Schools would appear to be inappropriate and *lacking in anything to mark the great change which is coming over the education of the country*." If the Gothic Revival architecture of previous Victorian schools was to be abandoned as inappropriate what was

4 *E. R. Robson. Anglers' Gardens Board School, St Pancras, London (1874). Typical of the U-plan layout evolved by Robson to accommodate the pupil-teacher system. The open arcading marks a ground-floor sheltered play-space.*

to be put in its place? Was it necessary "to abandon all indigenous architecture and to seek something wholly new or 'original'?" (It is interesting that this concept should occur at all to a mid-Victorian architect. Robson may have been thinking of the sort of 'non-period' ornament used by Digby Wyatt at Paddington Station, for instance.) Robson did not think it was necessary to abandon tradition: "History shows that, in all previous cases, new wants have been met by new developments of the prevalent manner of building. Our difficulty lies in the fact that, considered as a vernacular or universally-practised art, architecture has not had a being for many years and there is, consequently, no prevalent architecture of good type from which to develop." The causes of this decline of architecture as a vernacular art lie in the operations of the "speculative builder whose soul is occupied by the scale of rents which he can extract from his scantily-built mansions," in the "ill treatment of the builder's workman" and the consequent "lack of sympathy between him and his employer" that has "too often erased the instincts of good workmanship" and, lastly, in the decadence of "the old spirit of unity" not only in the building industry but among the architects, who, "from having a wholesome rivalry in the same direction" have come to "wage a war of different and conflicting styles." Robson's aim, then, was to look back over history, past the competitive society in which he lived and which

had wrought such havoc on architecture, to the most recent period when there had been a truly vernacular architecture that might make a helpful starting point in the design of modern schools. "The only really simple brick architecture available as a foundation is that of the time of the Jameses, Queen Anne, and the early Georges. The buildings then more nearly approached the spirit of our own time, and are invariably true in point of construction and workmanlike feeling. Varying much in architectural merit they form the nucleus of a good modern style. In looking to the architecture of this period as a basis, a servile copyism need not be attempted, for it may not be impossible to accept its spirit and yet to clothe our rendering with new form and a higher sense of architectural being." "Specimens of good and thoughtful brickwork in sufficient number still remain scattered among the old architecture of the city and its suburbs, to form the basis of a good style suited to modern requirements. Hackney and Putney, Chelsea and Deptford all furnish old examples." The style was not dead: for it was still the preponderant style of London, particularly among the "plainer and less expensive buildings" which were the intimately known settings for countless lives. Thus adherence to its spirit was not an arbitrary act of style-mongering. As well as arising from a careful analysis of the content to be expressed in the architecture of the new Board schools Robson's approach marked a conscious ac-

5 *E. R. Robson. Aldenham Street Board School, London (1874). Another U-plan. In this case the ground-floor was enclosed to contain an infants' school.*

ceptance of the genius loci of London – an act of consolidation in an age of disruption.

After a year's experience of building schools designed in limited competitions the Board decided to call a halt. Not only was it becoming difficult to find "superior architects" who were prepared to compete on this basis, but also continual 5 per cent fees were becoming irksome. It was decided, quite rightly, that now that the initial period of trial and error was coming to an end, the ratepayers would get better value for their money, if Robson himself (who "had given abundant showing of his qualities") were made responsible for the design of all the Board's schools. Robson's salary was raised to the astounding level of £1,000 – the fact that he owned a house in the Paragon at Blackheath brings home the dramatic decline in status of even the most eminent salaried architects since those days – and from then until his retirement in 1889, he was personally responsible for every one of the schools erected by the Board. Late in 1872 he complained to the Board that, with his present staff of eight draughtsmen and juniors (at £80 to £200 a year) it was only possible to complete the drawings for one school a week, but that if this staff were increased by less than one half its cost output would be doubled. After a great deal of argument the board agreed to increase Robson's staff to fifteen – including two tracers, a clerk and "a boy at five shillings a week" – and with this force at his disposal he could, by October 1876, point to an achievement of 134 new schools completed with 40 more on the ground or contracted for. Cost of production worked out at about 1 per cent compared to the 5 per cent which private architects had been paid – and at this time there were no consultants, not even clerks of works to be paid in addition.[2] This saving could be almost exactly balanced against the increased cost – 5 per cent – of a building of some architectural pretensions over the barest piece of mere construction, as was discovered when the Board made a careful study of the economics of architecture in response to complaints by local residents that an unusually plain new school was an eyesore in their neighbourhood. It was decided that, in future, the Board must be prepared to pay for good architecture.

This dramatic reduction in costs of production in the

6 *E. R. Robson. Board School, Goodrich Road, Camberwell, London.*

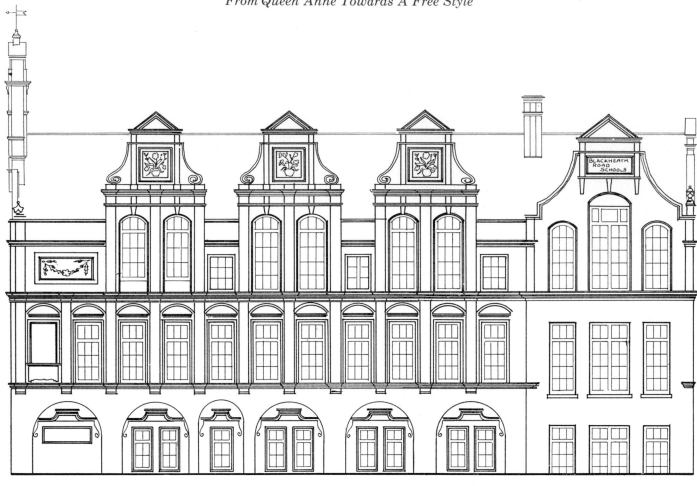

7 *E. R. Robson. Board School, Blackheath Road, London.*

8 *E. R. Robson. Board School, Blackheath Road, London.*

9 *E. R. Robson. Detail, Board School, Blackheath Road, London. The change-over to self-contained classes required drastic alterations and extensions. Here, the added third gable continues the original work so sympathetically as to cause no appreciable break in the facade.*

architect's office could only have been won by treating the Board's work as a programme: plans and detailing were increasingly standardised and there was the minimum chopping and changing of architectural character. By sheer Victorian ruthlessness the L.S.B. achieved a far higher degree of standardisation than most education authorities have achieved since the last war. Although the L.S.B. schools vary from very plain building to the great elaboration according to the openness of their sites, it cannot be said that, in practice, Robson was over-anxious about tailoring each school to suit its locality. The positive result of this is that these buildings, strong in personality, do a very great deal to set a stamp of unified character on the hodge-podge of Victorian London.

Several early Board schools were sited in Deptford – a neighbourhood of tough habits in those days, where it was sometimes necessary to give police protection to building workers on the new school sites. It is not surprising that the voluntary school organisations had not penetrated much into the district! The first school of Robson's designing to be completed was in this area, at Creek Road. It was opened in July 1873. Although it is no longer standing, contemporary descriptions make it clear that it was very similar in planning and appearance to the two schools at Anglers Gardens and Aldenham Street, both opened in August 1874.

These schools were planned at a time when the pupil-teacher system was still being employed; this system was no doubt barbarous, but it could lead to pleasant external architecture. The long school-rooms were planned with windows in the end walls and in the centre of the external long wall, so that as many desks as possible were lit from the side. This meant that there could be large areas of blank wall at the ends of the main façades which gave them breadth and repose. In the '90s most of the early schools, designed for education on the pupil-teacher system, were converted to provide self-contained classrooms, so that the Aldenham Street school now presents a slightly different appearance to that shown in the illustration. The execution of the alterations carried out at this time was admirable.

The grimness of which these early Board schools are so often accused is – at least so far as their exteriors are concerned – the grimness not of the individual buildings, but of 19th-century capitalist London and the conditions which it imposed on the architect. With their constricted sites wrested from the midst of slum housing – one-third of an acre for 1,200 children was by no means exceptional – set in the grimiest parts of London with never a tree in sight, it is remarkable what Robson and his office did achieve. Imagine either of these two schools with plenty of space around them, with decent playgrounds and the greenery of trees and grass to show off the yellows and reds of their brickwork, imagine their sculptured red brick un-pitted by atmospheric pollution and their woodwork white for

more than a few months after redecoration. It is a pleasant picture amply borne out by the rare occasions when an L.S.B. school is placed near an attractive open space, such as the school near Myatts Fields in Camberwell. It is important that the best of these early Board schools should be treated with reasonable respect: the principle to be followed would seem to be that, unless additions in the modern manner can be clearly articulated from the original structure, then the style of the original should be adhered to. Substantial demolition may often be necessary to achieve a clear relation of new and old. One of the greatest services that could be rendered to these buildings would be to open up their forecourts, so often enclosed behind forbidding prison-like fortifications, and to replace at least some of the surrounding asphalt with trees, grass and planting. Exterior woodwork should be maintained a fresh white, and the decorative possibilities of the interior should be revealed by the bold use of colour. In this way the architecture would be given a chance to express its humanity. So far as the interiors are concerned the exceedingly high rooms of these schools are undoubtedly oppressive for small children, but it is difficult to see how adequate lighting could have otherwise been achieved with classes of sixty children and with the limited window widths available in load-bearing brick walls. Edwin Chadwick said that a school should be "an implement fashioned by the best practical sanitary science," and the overpowering importance he attached to 'hygiene' was typical of contemporary educationalists. In the circumstances they may well have been right. Glazed brick and hard, easily cleaned surfaces were favoured at the expense of acoustics and warmth of appearance and in the result humanity was often lacking. Nevertheless, the L.S.B. schools can boast of many splendid interiors (where rescued from the cream, brown and green paint of later generations), in particular the galleried school halls, rising through two or even three storeys, which were nearly always, as befitting their function as focus of the school's life, treated with greater richness than any other room.

The Berger Road School in Hackney possesses a particularly fine school hall, which is now shown to great advantage by its recent redecoration at the hands of the General Division of the LCC Architect's Department, in which a most brilliant use has been made of colour. The school also merits study because it is a typical example of Robson's work at its most mature. The school dates from 1878, by which time classrooms for instruction by separate adult teachers were being provided instead of large schoolrooms for instruction on the pupil-teacher system.

The school is a typical 'three-decker' for 1,200 children, with the infants at ground level, boys above and girls on the top. Each floor consists of six classrooms planned on three sides of a large central space. On the ground floor this space was planned as the infants' covered play area.[3] On the first floor was the school hall, rising through one-and-a-half storeys with a tall arcade on the long side, in which was inserted a gallery which gave access to the girls' classrooms. (This gallery, with its bow-fronted balconies opening on to the hall below, was the only internal connection between the boys' and girls' departments, suggestive of young Romeo and Juliet possibilities!) Above the hall, rising into the pitch of the roof, was the girls' covered play area which was top-lit.[4]

The plan is eminently workable and economical, and it has a straightforward simplicity that the modern architect will find sympathetic.[5]

As with the Champneys school already described the external architectural elaboration of the Berger Road School is concentrated at high level. Unfortunately the Berger Road School has suffered particularly badly from the erosion of its decorative brickwork through atmospheric pollution.

What little decoration – as opposed to architectural embellishment – there is in schools of this period was carefully placed for maximum effectiveness. Although not as highly standardised as the internal detailing – Robson found mechanically reproduced decoration, such as moulded terracotta, lifeless, without the animation of handwork – remarkable consistency exists in the way decoration was used. It always appears set in panels or cartouches and the subjects are similar from job to job. Pre-eminent are the title panels which include the initials of the L.S.B. and perhaps the date. Many years ago Lethaby complained

that the decorative possibilities of lettering and inscriptions on buildings were insufficiently exploited, and the same is abundantly true today. Local authorities and others might take a leaf from the L.S.B.'s book and make it a matter of course to label and date their buildings.

In addition to the title panels the Board schools made use of three other types of cartouche. There were swags and trophies cut in brick or stone, rarely just conventional; there were floral patterns among which a series of designs of flowers in pots, carved in brick or inscribed in stone, were particularly good, because, although nearly always set at the very summit of the buildings, the designs are bold enough to read from ground level while retaining grace and sufficient delicacy. Deep cutting into white stone is probably the secret, so that shadow and the holding of London grime come to the designer's assistance. Robson also made use of a few figural bas-reliefs cut in brickwork – such as the 'Knowledge overpowering Ignorance' designed by McCulloch and repeated in several schools. (It was recut every time from the same model, not cast.) These latter are neither so intrinsically good nor architecturally so effective as the title panels or the floral designs, and the figures in them look absurdly small.

The amount of work turned out by Robson and his office was so vast that it is only possible to look at a tiny fraction of it. Yet what has been shown ought to be sufficient to place Robson's achievement within the

10 *E. R. Robson. Board School, Berger Road, Hackney, London (opened 1878). The school emphasises the qualities of Robson's mature style – tall gabled silhouettes and well-designed relationship of the different storey-heights, while the central hall is clearly defined by the class-room wings that stand, end-on, at either end.*

11 *E. R. Robson. The hall, Berger Road School, Hackney, London (opened 1878). This room, with its bow-fronted balconies set in the arcading of the girls' school access-gallery, gives an excellent idea of Robson's qualities as a three-dimensional designer.*

12 *School plaque, Millbank Board School, London (1901). Typical of the functional-decorative detailing originated by Robson.*

general picture of 19th-century architecture. It would be a mistake to consider him a great stylistic innovator. His search for an architecture that, while rooted in tradition, should not be hag-ridden by the conventions of any one period, was made in common with a fair number of architects working in the '70s, and was not pursued with the singlemindedness of Webb, for instance, to whom the fluctuations of style in Robson's work away from the School Board would have been incomprehensible. Others before him had realized the potentialities of the Carolean vernacular – a style combining Gothic and Renaissance in one body, so to speak – as a basis from which to develop. In 1866, Nesfield had blazed the trail, almost by accident, with a charming gatehouse at Kew Gardens which picked up the style of the adjacent palace; this was followed with a succession of buildings similar in character, including a Grammar School at Newport in Essex that might have been by Robson himself. J. J. Stevenson's Red House dated from 1871, and the likelihood of his influence on Robson has already been suggested. Basil Champneys had been designing in the 'L.S.B.' style at least as early as Robson. Norman Shaw was building Lowther Lodge and New Zealand Chambers just as the first Board schools were going up.

Robson's achievement, on the other hand, lay firstly in his incisive analysis of his objectives, his ready understanding of the challenge which new social

demands had placed before him; secondly, in his prompt understanding that designers such as Champneys and Stevenson had hit upon a stylistic approach that might be developed in answer to this challenge; thirdly, in the superb confidence and virility with which he and his staff carried through the development of this style, giving power and sometimes grandeur where its originators could only achieve charm; and, lastly, in the truly Victorian drive with which he pushed a vast programme of work to completion with architectural standards of the very highest order maintained throughout. Robson's private work, both during and after his days at the School Board, was extensive. The foundation stone of his very enterprising design for the People's Palace in Mile End Road was laid in 1886. It was similar in character to Bentley's Westminster Cathedral but much less earnest. The main hall was approached through a pillared rotunda flanked by two towers so tall and slender that they could reasonably be called minarets, each sporting a gilded cupola. Remembering the importance Robson attached to clarity of intention his admiration for the Greeks is not surprising. Among his recent predecessors he much admired the work of "the late Mr Thomson of Glasgow" – Greek Thomson. Robson himself experimented with the free use of Greek motifs in the Institute of Painters in Water Colours (1881) in Piccadilly. Ruskin admired this building for its freshness and for the purity of its proportions. The large area of blank wall, indicating the top lit exhibition space behind, is unequivocally accepted as the key feature of the façade, while the decoration by portraits of artists shows the same sense of the appropriate which we see in his schools. Robson was an eclectic, but a functional one, in that his shifts of style were an outcome of the varied uses and settings of his buildings rather than of mere whim or fashion. He died in 1917, aged eighty-one.

[1] Robson, while condoning Champney's use of brick because of the adjoining common whose greens showed it off to advantage, was critical of the use of red brickwork in London. He considered that yellow London stock brick, being less pervious, stood up better to the London climate, and consequently built his schools principally in this material with red brick only used – along with stone – in dressings and decorations. Interpretation of what had been a monochrome style in terms of a variety of materials gave Robson's schools their starting point of individuality – though it should be said that Robson more than once urged "the cultivation of an eye for colour" on his fellow architects, so that the structural polychromy of his schools derived from a more positive aim than weather resistance alone. Experience showed that even the limited use of soft red brickwork in moulded ornament was unwise: much of this work in the earlier schools is now eroded beyond recognition by atmospheric pollution. It is possible to explain the less sympathetic character of later L.S.B. schools by the architects' attempts to find materials appropriately hard and unyielding.

[2] The policy of not employing clerks of works was reversed after the board had lost a law-suit in which Robson had been sued for damages following structural failures due to the use of foundation concrete not of the mix specified. It emerged during the hearing that Robson had been kept so busy in the design of new schools that he had often been unable to visit his sites until the jobs were completed. More was brought into the board's affairs by the clerks of works than efficient site supervision. On at least three occasions in 1876 the formal opening of a new school was enlivened by a choral performance conducted by the clerk of works on the job.

[3] As in many other schools this playground has now been adapted as an Assembly Hall.

[4] Between the two classrooms on the long side of the Assembly Hall are inserted staff rooms, two being placed one above the other in each classroom storey height. This favourite planning device, leading to a bay of different function and scale on elevation, was usually treated rather playfully. At Berger Rd., there is a small V-shaped projection. There is a school in Ashmead Way, Lewisham, that rises almost sheer above the railway cutting, where this staff room strip has a semi-circular oriel becoming a circular turret above the roof-line. This must be one of the most inconveniently sited schools in London – suited only to a train-spotters' club – but it does provide a most dramatic picture seen in sharp perspective looking up from a passing train!

[5] An intriguing school was planned in 1873 but never executed for reasons of cost, in which the second floor was carried on cast-iron columns so that the entire first floor comprising school hall, two big school rooms and two classrooms, could be thrown into one space by means of sliding partitions.

James MacLaren and the Godwin Legacy

by Alastair Service

Scotland, and especially Glasgow, produced a sudden plethora of
talented architects in the decades after 1870 and many of them
successfully sought their fortunes by emigrating to London. One
of these London Scots, James MacLaren (1843–1890), developed the
ideas of Godwin and of the American H. H. Richardson and
produced a number of highly original buildings between 1886 and his
early death. These crystallised many progressive ideas of the time
and were to influence free style architecture in Scotland and
England in the 1890s.

When James MacLaren died in October 1890 at the age of forty-seven his obituary in *The British Architect* mourned the early loss of an architect of promise "far above the average in quality". Historians have frequently pointed out[1] the originality of his work and its influence on Charles Rennie Mackintosh in particular, yet the sources of his own inspiration and the general significance of his work have not been fully analysed. MacLaren made a personal contribution to the development of the free style which deserves wider recognition. But the most important point that emerges from a study of his work is that he provided the main link of influence between Edward Godwin's meteoric revolution of town house design in the late 1870s and the work of the generation of progressive architects that became well known after 1890 – Prior, Lethaby, Newton, Stokes, Townsend, Wilson, Mackintosh, Voysey and others.

James Marjoribanks MacLaren was born in Stirling in 1843 and attended the local High School. His father was John MacLaren, J.P., of Middleton, Perthshire. James served his articles in the office of the older James Salmon in Glasgow before moving on to the firm of Campbell Douglas & Stevenson (later Campbell Douglas & Sellars) in the same city. One of the partners, J. J. Stevenson (1831–1908), apparently befriended and influenced MacLaren during these years, but the older man moved to London in 1869. There Stevenson became one of the leaders of the 'Queen Anne' reaction to scholarly historicism, building the Red House at 140 Bayswater Road (1871) and joining a loose partnership with E. R. Robson (1835–1917) in designing the early revolutionary Board Schools. Stevenson was a variable performer, sometimes daring, more often disappointing, but it was probably he who gave MacLaren his first taste of freedom from revived foreign styles. I have discovered only one piece of MacLaren's work before 1877, a previously unpublished pen and ink drawing (signed J. M. MacLaren and dated 1874) of Leckie House, Stirlingshire. But the choice of subject is of great interest, for this old house shows many features that MacLaren later used in his own influential modernised Scottish 'vernacular' buildings. These include the use of white roughcast over stone, stepped gables and the round oriel turret at the inside angle, accentuating a break of levels on either side of it. Little else is known of MacLaren between 1869 and the unknown date when he too came to London. On the

2 *Drawing by J. M. MacLaren (dated 1874) of old Leckie House, Stirlingshire, showing several traditional features later used in his own buildings.*

1 *Doorway of MacLaren's 'Heatherwood', Sussex.*

available evidence[2], it is most likely that he moved south in about 1877 and he may have started work in Stevenson's prosperous office, as did so many other London Scots. Much more important for his own development was the fact that he brought with him an introduction to E. W. Godwin.

In 1877 Edward Godwin (1833–86) was already a guiding star for many progressive young architects and he was about to start the series of startlingly original town house designs which were to open new horizons for the free style of architecture. He had been a highly successful Gothic architect, though his personal eccentricity and the scandal of his long and mutually inspiring love affair with Ellen Terry made it out of the question for him to become an establishment figure. He

3 *Edward Godwin. Design for a house for Mr Slingsby Bethel, 33 Tite Street, Chelsea (1879). Not built.*

openly disliked the Queen Anne school of architects led by Norman Shaw (1831–1912), but agreed with them on the need to reject stylistic revivals and architectural historicism. In 1872 Godwin wrote a troubled article about revived styles in general[3] and in 1875 said "The day of architectural revivals may be setting – I for one sincerely hope it is".[4] His friendship with Whistler and acquaintance with wealthy art patrons made it possible for Godwin to do something about this hope with seven or eight designs for houses in and around Tite Street, Chelsea, between 1878 and 1881. These truly lived up to his words to Manchester architects at about the same time[5] "If asked what style your work is, say 'It is my own'.' When Godwin died in 1886 his obituaries, and indeed comments by some of the more progressive young men years later, made it clear that his influence was very much alive.[6] That influence was chiefly on architects who became well known after 1890 and very little of the work of practising architects in the 1880s reflects Godwin's design principles. The two major exceptions to this were Halsey Ricardo (1854–1928) and James MacLaren, and an examination of their buildings and others has led this author to the conclusion that MacLaren, apart from many original ideas of his own, was the most successful developer and exponent of Godwin's ideas during the second half of that decade.

Before tracing MacLaren's own designs, it is necessary to analyse briefly those principles of free design which Godwin displayed and which his followers took up (often more successfully than in Godwin's own pioneering ventures). In spite of his distrust of the 'Queen Anne' architects, Godwin clearly thought highly of at least one of Norman Shaw's designs. This was Shaw's own house 'Hampstead Towers' at 6 Ellerdale Road, Hampstead (1875), the elevations of which show an extraordinary freedom from both symmetry and historical precedents. It seems likely that it was the street frontage of Shaw's house which gave Godwin the spark to experiment still more freely. The first of his Chelsea designs,[7] twin houses at 5 and 6 Chelsea Embankment, picked up Shaw's idea of a strongly contrasting vertical accent with a free and asymmetrical composition of the rest. Godwin's design is not as successful as Shaw's, being composed of a rather overcrowded collection of his own original – and some Shavian – minor features. But the Chelsea frontage has a greater depth of surface texture and Godwin added a new element in the firm horizontals that bound the design to the vertical accent. In the Tite Street houses that followed – No. 36 for A. Stuart Wortley[8] (demolished), No. 35 for J. A. McN. Whistler[9] (The White House – demolished), and No. 44 for F. Miles[10] and others – Godwin worked out his new principles.

First, he established that it was the balance, not the symmetry, of an elevation that made it satisfying to the eye. By retaining balance of the various features, he was able to compose many varied elements into a harmonious, one might say symphonic, asymmetrical composition. The outstanding examples of this are his surviving house at No. 44 Tite Street, the studio design for Miss Rose Corder[11], and the demolished second Wortley house at No. 29 Tite Street.[12] Second, he demonstrated that the architect should be free to invent completely original and unhistorical detailed components, such as doors and windows, as necessary to fit in with his overall design. Many of these had no historical precedent at all, while others were para-phrases of traditional English features. The White House for Whistler and the surviving 'Tower House' at No. 42 Tite Street[13] demonstrate his invention of such detail.

Finally, he developed a type of asymmetrical design for town elevations of any size that was to have a lasting influence on younger architects, including MacLaren. This consisted of one very strong vertical accent (functionally, this was of course the staircase in many designs) and a series of firm horizontal features, playing with many minor vertical accents. The accents often advance or recede boldly from the overall surface plane of the elevation. Apart from the twin houses on Chelsea Embankment already described, 'Tower House', the Miles house at No. 44 Tite Street (perhaps

his most completely successful design) and the Slingsby Bethell house design (shown in a drawing in *The British Architect* 14 May 1880, but never built) show the various forms which this basic composition can take.

The Chelsea houses were Godwin's most influential buildings for all to come and see, but he planted seeds of an even deeper influence in the series of competitions under the general title 'British Architect Art Club' which he set and judged in the magazine *The British Architect* from 1879 until 1884. These competitions invited and premiated designs for such subjects as 'A Shop Frontage', 'A Village Church' and 'An Artist's Studio' (all 1880) from architectural students under pseudonyms. The entries were commented on by God-win himself and the better ones were reproduced. The results were a series of designs of increasing adventure and originality and pseudonyms such as 'Faust', 'Cichevache', 'Spruce Affectation' and 'Jacopo del Fonte' hide the identities of some noted names of the 1890s. (A few of the real identities were published in 1881 and 1883.) This continuity of Godwin's influence has not been widely appreciated and he has often been treated as an isolated phenomenon rather than as one of the main free style architectural influences, with

4 *James MacLaren. House, Bo'ness Road, near Grangemouth, County of Stirling, Scotland (1877–78). One of MacLaren's first houses.*

Shaw and Philip Webb.

This was the legacy that Godwin left to architecture when he gave it up in about 1881 and devoted himself to stage design for his last five years. And James MacLaren came to London in time to see these Chelsea houses being built. According to his obituary in *The British Architect*, he brought a letter of introduction to E. W. Godwin "whose architectural manners influenced him greatly". Already MacLaren was clearly interested in the cause of each country finding its own 'vernacular' architecture in a modern adaptation. His two stone houses in 1877 in Scotland, Avon Hall and Avondhu House Hotel[14] on the Bo'ness road at Grangemouth, are in a free Jacobean Scottish Baronial style. The larger house already shows the architect's interest in clusters of turrets. Moreover, one of the last jobs of the Campbell Douglas firm before MacLaren left Glasgow (if 1877 is the correct date) was the extension of Mugdock Castle, near Milngavie, north-west of Glasgow, following freely the old Baronial style.[15]

By the beginning of 1878 MacLaren had got the job of designing an artist's house on the Fulham Park Estate, London.[16] It was a strikingly powerful composition, individual if still keeping some Baronial feeling. As a

gesture to the fact that it was in England, not Scotland, it was of brick instead of stone. The high windows and chimneys have obvious links with Norman Shaw. After that, nothing is known of any buildings he actually built until 1886, though some of his competition designs survive and he doubtless 'ghosted' the designs of some established architects. According to *The British Architect* obituary he assisted in the offices of William Young (1843–1900, another London Scot, architect of Glasgow Municipal Buildings 1882–89 and much later of the War Office in Whitehall 1898–1907) and "Mr Howell of the Lunacy Commissioners", as well as Richard Coad (spelt Coads in the obituary) "the late manager of Sir Gilbert Scott". Goodhart-Rendel, a great admirer of MacLaren, tells us[17] that he became the brother-in-law of D. S. McColl, executive editor of *The Architectural Review* from 1901 to 1905, and said that he had the "influence of a Parisian training". Although it is possible to read features of great French chateaux into some of MacLaren's works, it seems likely that Goodhart-Rendel was overstating this influence. *The British Architect's* obituary says that among MacLaren's early work he went to Paris to design some furniture and there studied French style

5 *James MacLaren. Artist's House design, for Fulham Park Estate (1877).*

"but though he admired it much, it never entirely gained on him". It mentioned Godwin's influence on MacLaren and went on to say that "he was at his best in Scotch Baronial": an allegation promptly denied by James's brother Thomas, whose note in the next issue of the magazine pointed out that "Scottish baronial character is not, however, to be seen in these works to any extent, as was stated". It is notable that Thomas did not contradict the alleged influence of Godwin, nor the comment on James's reservations about French architecture in the same obituary.

MacLaren entered the first Glasgow Municipal Buildings competition which was judged in September 1880. Although his design (classical, as the conditions demanded) does not survive, *The British Architect* described it favourably in the 10 September issue, *The Builder* less enthusiastic during the same week. His design for the Liverpool Art School (1881) does survive[18] and gives the architect's address as 21 King William Street, Strand, where he still had an office at the time of his death nearly 10 years later. The Liverpool competition entry is a surprise for it is Neo-Grec – a temple of art which might be viewed as showing French influence, but is more likely to have its roots in the Glasgow work of Alexander Thomson. It is a finely proportioned and well-planned design. The entry for Burnley Municipal Buildings (1884, under the name of MacLaren and Dunn) is a little more adventurous.[19] The comparatively small entrance frontage is orthodox and rather dull Jacobean, perhaps to avoid shocking the assessor. But the rear elevations show a long free design, on a variety of levels, where the influence of Godwin can be seen at work as well as some signs of MacLaren's own originality.

The last of these competition designs of MacLaren's barren years is the most interesting of all. This was a design of 1885 for Fulham Town (or Vestry) Hall,[20] unusually free Jacobean in its use of an order of large Ionic columns combined with an asymmetrical elevation, strong horizontals and a heavy vertical accent with turrets and cupola over the main door. This time it is quite evident that MacLaren was affected by Godwin's pioneering works in Chelsea.

The powerful grouping of turrets above the doorway in this design brings us to two other probable influences on MacLaren from this time on. *The British Architect*, the magazine which drew most attention to both Godwin and MacLaren, was fairly insular in

6 *James MacLaren. Design for Fulham Town Hall competition (1885). The grouping of square and round turrets over the asymmetrical doorway is typical of MacLaren in the mid-1880s.*

7 *James MacLaren. New wing, 'The Park', Ledbury, Gloucestershire (1886). A charming design, showing much of Godwin's influence.*

outlook. But since 1883 it had reproduced a series of illustrations of contemporary American work of the H. H. Richardson (1838–86) school.[21] The editorial comments made it clear that what was considered admirable about these buildings was the powerful adaptation of the Romanesque style to produce a strong 'naturalistic' effect, linking the buildings to the ground they stood on as if they were elemental outcrops from it. Richardson's only work in England, 'Lululand', was started in 1886.[22]

The other influence was that of the Art Workers' Guild, founded in 1884 by a group of Norman Shaw's young pupils who were also strongly affected by the Arts and Crafts principles of Philip Webb. The Guild's declared aim was to halt "the drifting apart of the arts of architecture, painting and sculpture". The founders were W. R. Lethaby, Edward S. Prior, Gerald Horsley, Ernest Newton and Mervyn Macartney, all of them destined to become notable figures in British architecture in the following decades. Most of the progressive architects of the time joined the Guild during its first few years,[23] and MacLaren joined in 1886. We know little about MacLaren's friendships with other young progressives before this, but membership would certainly bring him into frequent contact with them and their ideas, quite apart from the stated aims of the Guild. An examination and comparison of their designs of the late 1880s shows that there was a constant exchange of new features and details between the members. In this way MacLaren, with his concern for local vernacular, appears to have acted as a necessary bridge for Godwin's principles – which were more purely aesthetic and therefore open to suspicion from the Arts and Crafts architects.

This was the year that MacLaren started his successful private practice and *The British Architect* obituary links this with Richard Coad, saying that "from this latter gentleman he received much kindness and several commissions, which encouraged him to set up for himself". The first of these were probably the new wing added to 'The Park', the largest house on the main street of Ledbury, Herefordshire, in 1886.[24] This is a charming work, typical of MacLaren in its care for the local vernacular as well as in the sensitivity of the design. The elevations have striking similarities to Godwin's unexecuted design for Slingsby Bethell's house in Chelsea and there is also the first sign of MacLaren's interest in bands of windows. Apart from the Godwin design, this Ledbury house seems to mark the launching of the angle turret at the junction of two levels or directions – one of the most popular of progressive motifs in the late 1880s and 1890s (e.g. among many instances, Belcher & Pite's Chartered Accountants' design of late 1888, Ernest Newton's Beula Hill house of early 1888 and Leonard Stokes' convent at London Colney a decade later). As we shall see, MacLaren himself used such turrets, usually polygonal in plan, in many of his designs.

MacLaren's first large-scale work was an extensive new wing added to his old school, Stirling High School, in 1887–88.[25] This building's character was partly decided by the need to blend in with the other building of 1854. But there is much more to it than that. The accommodation included art classrooms, science classrooms and an astronomical observatory. MacLaren arranged these sections in a highly expressive and functional way. The art studios are on the outside corner of the 'L' where his range joins the older building and to allow a flood of light the upper windows run straight into rooflights, framed by bold rectangular piers chopped off at their tops, and separated by a strong buttressed chimney.

A hexagonal turret accentuates the break of levels between the studios and long horizontals of the science classrooms, their lines broken by the minor accents of an oriel and three gabled windows (a certain amount of sculpture is worked into the design – perhaps a rather perfunctory bow to Art Workers' Guild ideals). Then there is a slight return angle to the doorway (an old sculpted framework which he incorporated) and the *pièce de résistance* the massive observatory tower. This can be interpreted as Scottish Baronial to some degree, but MacLaren's handling of it shows the influence of contemporary American work. The separate elements of the tower with their rounded corners seem to grow out of and flow into each other as if they are rocky crags rather than part of a man-made building, sympathetic to a work so near to Stirling Castle and its rock. The full description given in *The British Architect* leaves one in no doubt that this naturalistic feeling, together

8 *H. H. Richardson. Remains of 'Lululand', Melbourne Road, Bushey, Hertfordshire (designed 1886, completed 1894). Richardson's Romanesque influenced MacLaren and other Art Workers' Guild members such as Townsend.*

9 *James MacLaren. Observatory Tower and New Wing, Stirling High School, Scotland (1887–88). A powerful mixture of craggy naturalism with Scottish tradition, highly praised in the progressive architectural magazines at the time.*

with MacLaren's emphasis of horizontal lines punctuated by vertical accents (even more evident on the courtyard side of the building[26]), was regarded as a significant contribution to progressive British architecture.

Many motifs from the Stirling tower – such as the battlemented roof line, the horizontal banding and the curious cupola used to emphasise a corner turret – can be found in MacLaren's next building, a studio and house for H. R. Pinker at 22 Avonmore Road, West Kensington (1888–89).[27] This is an example of Mac-Laren's ingenuity in three dimensions, for the porch contains doors to the rooms adjoining the big ground-floor studio, and also to the corner turret stairway up to the apartments above. This fine house is now in a depressingly shabby state.

At some time during the 1880s MacLaren won a competition to build St Michael's Church, Crieff (not executed, according to his brother Thomas in the obituary already mentioned), and (according to the same source) built the Presbyterian Church, Goose Green, Dulwich. This church is something of a mystery. It is a simple, buttressed Gothic building of little interest except for the detail at the west end. Here the foliated doorway, the tracery of the big window, the plaque in the gable and the complex side buttresses show obvious stylistic links with MacLaren and with the intricate foliage of American decoration of the

time.[28] The date and MacLaren's exact part remain elusive.[29]

By the late 1880s MacLaren was living in Hampstead, probably with his brother Thomas who had followed James to London. Both were bachelors. In the same years as he was building the London studio house for H. R. Pinker, James MacLaren also started on the splendid series of buildings he designed and started in the last three years of his life in Scotland and elsewhere. Many of these were commissioned by Sir Donald Currie of Glenlyon, a wealthy man with London and Scottish interests, who could have met MacLaren through Coad or more likely through the Stirling building (of which Currie was benefactor). Mac-Laren's almost frenzied haste in taking on commissions after 1887 may have been increased by a knowledge that his health was failing. He spent some time in Switzerland for this reason, but *The British Architect* obituary says that he had an indomitable capacity for work, "a dangerous endowment without nerves of steel. For a few years past he had suffered somewhat from chest weakness." Like many others at the time, he was almost certainly dying slowly from tuberculosis.

The Town Hall in Aberfeldy, Perthshire (1889), is interesting because it may show some influence of C. F. A. Voysey (1857–1941) in the roof lines.[30]

MacLaren was clearly striving for simplicity and although the strong rounded door arches, banded

10 *James MacLaren. No. 22 Avonmore Road, West Kensington, London (1888–89). A remarkably advanced house, now sadly dilapidated.*

11 *James MacLaren. Doorway, Presbyterian Church, Goose Green, Dulwich, London (mid 1880s). The flowing floral decoration is typical of MacLaren.*

12 *James MacLaren. Town Hall, Aberfeldy, Perthshire, Scotland (1889–90). A new geometrical simplicity is combined with earlier MacLaren features.*

windows and rustic belfry are very much his own, Voysey's simple lines would have appealed to him. By the same token, it seems possible that the banded windows of the courtyard side of Stirling High School may have found a permanent place in Voysey's (and others') vocabulary, though they also have traditional English origins. The continuous interchange of ideas between members of the Art Workers' Guild at this period makes it dangerous to attribute the origin of new features to particular individuals.

The use of white roughcast walls (as in MacLaren's 1874 drawing of old Leckie House) as a valid Scottish vernacular alternative to stone was continued in some of the estate buildings for Sir Donald Currie himself around Glenlyon House, Fortingall, Perthshire, which MacLaren started about the same time.[31] The Thatched Cottages (*circa* 1889) for farm labourers on the estate, use a curious roofing material for Scotland, but show MacLaren's typical power of composition, ingenuity at angles and changes of level (the chimney takes the place of the more formal turret as the vertical accent) and linear feeling in horizontals. The whole corner design reminds one inescapably of Godwin's early

influence on the architect,[32] but MacLaren's own achievement here is remarkable.

The roughcast Tenant Farmer's House (*circa* 1889) at Glenlyon is just as extraordinarily original. As in Aberfeldy Town Hall, the continuity of the roof-line (from the gable set back behind castellation[33] to the long slope over the arched doorway) is reminiscent of Voysey, but it is also indicative of MacLaren's new interest in geometrical forms. Here the castellated upper floor is punched out slightly in a rectangular section that plays with the diagonals and arch of the rest of the elevation. The other doorway around the corner has unfortunately been altered and the boss which supports the upper corner above the chamfered lower storey is covered by a creeper. But these changes do not hide either the interest or the brilliance of Mac-Laren's design.

The third estate building at Glenlyon, the Farm Steading (*circa* 1889), again shows MacLaren's feeling for linear horizontality, anchored by one strong vertical accent and other lesser ones. The main vertical feature here is an octagonal dovecot (or doocot) tower with a pointed roof. The accents are emphasised by the

13 *James MacLaren. Farm Steading Buildings, Glenlyon House, Fortingall, Perthshire* (circa *1889). The long horizontal lines are boldly and asymmetrically punctuated by vertical accents. The traditional Scottish roughcast is used in all this group of buildings.*

14 *James MacLaren. Tenant Farmer's House, Glenlyon House, Fortingall, Perthshire* (circa *1889). One of MacLaren's most powerful geometrical designs, combining a free style with local traditional features according to Arts and Crafts ideas of the time.*

15 *James MacLaren. Cottages, Glenlyon House farm, Fortingall, Perthshire (circa 1889). The large corner chimney plays the same key part in this design that the turret plays in others.*

use of red stone for the tower, the window bands and the horizontal band at ground level, in contrast to the roughcast of the rest. Duncan McAra, like Goodhart-Rendel,[34] found a French chateau effect in the appearance of this building, which one can understand if one compares the doocot with the great towers of Saumur on the Loire. As a whole, the Glenlyon works of MacLaren nevertheless made their most important contribution as simple examples of *avant-garde* free style ideas, intended to be modern designs yet to blend with the traditional or (as the favourite word of the time was) vernacular architecture of their locality.

During 1889 MacLaren was also designing his most complex and perhaps his finest work of all for Sir Donald Currie. This was the pair of houses blended into one composition at Nos. 10 and 12 Palace Court, off the Bayswater Road, London (1889–90).[35] In this building we can see most of the influences on MacLaren synthesised into a masterpiece entirely his own. From Godwin there comes the general type of composition, with a powerful asymmetrical vertical accent,

strong horizontal lines and many subsidiary verticals blending into the whole. Like Norman Shaw's contemporary New Scotland Yard (1888–90),[36] it is of red brick banded with stone, and some windows are also Shavian. The incorporation of much sculpture fitted the ideas of the Art Workers' Guild, while the foliated lines of that sculpture, the rounded arches and the massiveness of the doorways' details show how far MacLaren had developed the American influence. The complexity of the floor levels in the bottom two storeys and the way that the external power of these storeys is carefully balanced by strongly articulated top floors, display the increasing subtlety of MacLaren's designs for town houses. More than anything, it is the sensitive balance and the sheer flow of joyous invention in detail that make the building a pleasure to examine.

By late 1889 MacLaren was an ill man and had been working frantically hard. According to *The British Architect* obituary he had already spent some time in the Engadine in Switzerland for his chest, "and also,

16 *James MacLaren. Nos. 10 and 12 Palace Court, Bayswater, London (1889–90). A complex balanced asymmetrical street frontage, full of boundless invention in detail.*

17 *James MacLaren. Doorway, No. 10 Palace Court, off Bayswater Road, London (1889–90).*

more recently, taking advantage of a commission to build a large hotel at a health resort on Spanish territory, he passed a winter there superintending its erection". This was the Santa Catalina Hotel and its lodges, Las Palmas, Canary Islands, and from these remarks it would seem that it was designed either late 1889 or early 1890, and at least started during the latter year. The design is symmetrical, with an expanded X plan and the main entrance in the centre of one side. It is, essentially, a geometrical white solid. In accordance with MacLaren's principles, the design wears clothes to fit in with the local architecture, but apart from this one sees many typical signs of the architect. The angles of the building are accentuated by strong turrets capped by cupolas, the horizontals are strengthened by a low terrace and a splendid high cedar gallery linking the two turrets. The simple five-storey wings are broken by vertical tiers of carved cedar galleries of three and four bays up to roof level. The stonework around doors and windows shows an odd mixture of MacLaren's inventiveness and local detail. It is a highly individual design for a hotel of its time, though not in the main stream of the architect's best works.

Back in England MacLaren had time to make two more designs before his death, of which one was built. This was a brick and tile-hung house called 'Oaklawn' (now 'Heatherwood'), one of a number of houses set back in their own large gardens near the centre of Crawley Down, Sussex (1890–91).[37] MacLaren's last house is worthy of him in its splendid originality, though the links with the Tenant Farmer's House and the Palace Court building are obvious. The design seems to stem from the great chimney rising immed-

18 *James MacLaren. Santa Catalina Hotel, Las Palmas, Canary Islands (designed 1889–90). The long suspended cedar gallery on the left binds the two cupola turrets at the angles.*

iately beside the front door (which is rugged and irregular as if it were a cave in a cliff-face). From the vertical of the chimney, the volumes of the house spread out with extraordinary complexity of form. There are two main gables – one of them jutting out at the top in a subsidiary triangle – a two-level bow window of MacLaren's favourite form and an arched balcony window on the first floor which penetrates into the mass of the house. No two windows are alike but, in accordance with Godwin's precepts, they fit into an overall balanced composition on each elevation. There is a new feeling of compact, almost compressed, volumes that makes one wonder how MacLaren would have developed if he had lived.

His final known design[38] won the first premium in the competition for a London equivalent of the Eiffel Tower (built for the Paris Exhibition that year) which was sponsored by Sir Edward Watkin. MacLaren's 1200 feet high entry was designed jointly with William Dunn (his partner in the Burnley competition) and an engineer called A. D. Stewart, but the tower was never built. If it had been, MacLaren's name would doubtless be widely known today, though for an odd reason. The designers were content to follow Eiffel's general lines, except that they used an octagonal plan.

A few other buildings remain to be noted. Thomas MacLaren's obituary note mentioned estate work at Garth, in addition to that at Glenlyon. After James's death Dunn formed a partnership with Robert Watson, MacLaren's draftsman, and carried on with the work for Sir Donald Currie. This included the rebuilding of Glenlyon House itself and the Hotel at Fortingall. Both show the influence of MacLaren[39] although Dunn & Watson lack his sheer brilliance in form and detail. *The Building News* obituary also lists alterations at Ripple Court, Kent, for Colonel Sladen among his works, while Goodhart-Rendel's article tantalises us by mentioning other unidentified buildings whose designs MacLaren 'ghosted'.

All through the summer of 1890 MacLaren's health was poor. *The British Architect* obituary said "On his return (from Las Palmas) the benefit hoped for was not

19 *'Heatherwood', Crawley Down, Sussex (1890–91). MacLaren's last house. The power of the free design, with the chimney as its stem, shines through the vernacular Sussex materials.*

20 *James MacLaren, W. Dunn and A. D. Stewart. Winning design, competition for London Eiffel Tower (1890). The ground level buildings were built, but later replaced by Wembley Stadium.*

Wilson and brought about a British adaptation of American naturalistic forms which is often wrongly called *Art Nouveau*. There are signs of a continuing exchange of ideas with other members of the free style generation born a decade later than himself, such as E. S. Prior, Newton, Leonard Stokes and Voysey. Finally, his ideas and Godwin's can be seen at work in the early free works of still younger men such as Robert Lorimer, Smith and Brewer, and even Lutyens.

In one other way, too, the free style architects had reason to regret his early death. Their efforts to establish free design as an acceptable style to clients of large-scale buildings during the 1890s were often hampered by their own temperaments, which tended to be artistically self-indulgent rather than professional. Halsey Ricardo, for example, admitted[42] his own difficult character to clients on more than one occasion, while Lethaby suffered from extreme shyness. MacLaren, on the other hand, showed himself capable of handling rich clients such as Currie and the owners of the Santa Catalina Hotel, and designed and superintended large buildings as competently as small. The obituary expressed this: "Mr MacLaren was an architect who combined good designing power with admirable business aptitude: a combination which is not too usual and which is most pleasing to clients". If this had led to prosperity for MacLaren in the 1890s, it would inevitably have benefited the free style of the Arts and Crafts architects' cause in general.

so complete as could have been wished, but his final illness was, we believe, sudden and unexpected". After this short illness MacLaren died on 20 October 1890 at his house in Hampstead.[40]

Any thorough examination of MacLaren's designs must lead one to the conclusion that he was an architect of great brilliance. His best designs are strong, sensitive and abundantly inventive. His combinations of the various facets of his work – the balanced asymmetrical, the naturalistic, the geometrical and the vernacular – makes his 10 completed buildings perhaps the most impressive group by any of the progressive architects of the late 1880s. But his importance lies just as much in the active link he provides between an even greater designer, Godwin, and the architects of the freest pre-war years of British architectural design in the 1890s. David Walker has already described[41] with admirable clarity the influence he had on Mackintosh. It is impossible to doubt that his Stirling observatory tower and his late foliated detail also influenced Harrison Townsend and Harry

[1] The most important published references for MacLaren are H. S. Goodhart-Rendel's *English Architecture since the Regency*, Constable, London 1953, pp.197–198 and 'Rogue Architects of the Victorian Era' (*Journal of The Royal Institute of British Architects* 1949, p.258), Nikolaus Pevsner's 'Goodhart-Rendel's Roll-Call' *The Architectural Review* Vol. 138, p.259); David Walker's 'Charles Rennie Mackintosh', *The Architectural Review*, November 1968, p.363 and Duncan McAra's good but brief 'James MacLaren – An Architect for Connoisseurs'; *Scottish Art Review*, Vol. XII No 4, 1970, p.28. All contain material of great value. There are obituaries in *The Builder* 1 November 1890; *The British Architect* 7 November 1890 and 14 November 1890; *The Building News* 7 November 1890. Neither James MacLaren nor his architect brother Thomas married. A third brother remained in Scotland and married, having one child (called James after his uncle) who died in 1966. There this branch of the family died out, but after long enquiries I traced the younger James's widow, Mrs Margaret MacLaren, of Drummore, Doune, Perthshire, who gave me what scanty personal details she remembered from her husband and kindly supplied the 1874 drawing reproduced here. This spelling 'MacLaren' is correct for this branch of the family, though it appears in several varieties. No portrait of J. M. MacLaren has been traced.

[2] *The British Architect* obituary 7 November 1890 mentioned that he came south 'following Stevenson', but his first designs were published in 1877 in that magazine (the *avant-garde* leader of the time; it had also promoted Godwin's ideas, and much later published Voysey frequently before he was well-known). These were for two houses in Scotland and they were followed by a house in Fulham, London in 1878. After that MacLaren seems to have built no more in Scotland until 1887. One can imagine that an ambitious man of 33 might well make such a break because he was making no progress in the Campbell Douglas firm. The year of his move south cannot be later than 1877, for *The British Architect* 28 December 1877 gives his address as 102 George Street, Portman Square, London.

3 *Building News* 26 June 1872.

4 *The Architect* 7 August 1875, p.344.

5 Godwin's talk to Manchester Architectural Association, *The British Architect* 29 November 1878.

6 Eg F. S. Granger in *The British Architect* 22 October 1886; Edward l'Anson's R.I.B.A. presidential address 1886 and Beresford Pite in *The Architect* 7 November 1890. Pevsner's *Pioneers of Modern Design*, Pelican, London 1960, pp.62–64 gives a brilliantly concise account of Godwin's originality, but does not trace his continuing influence.

7 Illustrated in *The British Architect* 15 February 1878, though altered in execution. This date (the houses are described as 'approaching completion') points to it being an earlier design than The White House for Whistler at 35 Tite Street (demolished) which was first illustrated 6 December 1878. This is not conclusive evidence, but it fits in with the sequence of Godwin's rapidly developing freedom. In 1878 work had also started on the garden suburb of Bedford Park, where Shaw was the chief architect, and Godwin had designed the first houses (see *Building News* 22 December 1876).

8 First illustrated *The British Architect* 29 November 1878, and No. 29 also for Wortley 4 July 1884. Godwin was closely associated with this magazine, which promoted his views and designs and leapt to his defence when *The American Architect and Building News* attacked his originality (see issue of 22 November 1878).

9 *The British Architect* 6 December 1878.

10 *The British Architect* 6 December 1878.

11 *The British Architect* 3 October 1879. Designed for No. 42 Tite Street, where Tower House was built 1884–85.

12 Built c1880 according to Dudley Harbron, *The Architectural Review* Vol. 98 p.48. Mr Harbron's book *The Conscious Stone*, Latimer House 1949, is valuable as the only biography of Godwin, though it does not analyse his architectural development fully.

13 Designed late 1881, the last of Godwin's Tite Street houses, and completed 1885. One of his last works was the interiors for Oscar Wilde at No. 33 Tite Street in 1884–85, see their correspondence published *The Architectural Review*, Vol. 109, p.175. The detailed dating of these Tite Street houses has been established by Mark Girouard in *Country Life* 23 November 1972.

14 Illustrated *The British Architect* 21 December 1877 and 28 December 1877. I am indebted to Duncan McAra for the present-day names of the houses.

15 Illustrated *The British Architect* 19 January 1883, with the comment that it was built about 1877.

16 Illustrated *The British Architect* 18 January 1878. I have searched the area around Fulham Park Road, but even if the house was built, there is no sign of it there today.

17 *The Architectural Review* Vol. 138, p.263. If Goodhart-Rendel is correct, McColl must have married MacLaren's sister, since MacLaren remained a bachelor.

18 *The British Architect* 11 February 1881.

19 Illustrated *The British Architect* 27 March 1885 and 3 April 1885, though the competition was the previous year (see Halsey Ricardo's highly praised free Jacobean entry *The British Architect* 26 September 1884 and 3 October 1884, with comments p.162).

20 Illustrated *The British Architect* 28 May 1886 under the name T. M. MacLaren. The 'J' of MacLaren's signature looked very like a 'T' and the magazine made the same mistake in the text accompanying his Stirling High School drawing 6 May 1887, though the name was correct on that drawing. His brother Thomas (who joined James in London) always appears as 'Thomas MacLaren' with his drawings

reproduced from 20 May 1885 on, nor is this design like Thomas's known work. There seems to be no doubt that the Fulham design was James's.

21 Richardson's Quincy Library and other buildings 5 January 1883 and 30 March 1883 (the first time wrongly attributed), work by E. M. Wheelwright of Boston, Peabody and Stearns, and McKim, Mead and White in 1885, the Studebaker Building in Chicago by S. S. Beman, a house in Chicago by Andrews & Jacques and a museum in Cincinnati by J. W. McLaughlin in January and February 1886. The series continued for the next few years.

22 Commissioned January 1886, the construction dragged on until 1894. See H. R. Hitchcock *The Architecture of H. H. Richardson*, Hamden, Connecticut 1961. It was not illustrated in magazines in MacLaren's lifetime. A fragment of the house still stands in Melbourne Road, Bushey, Hertfordshire.

23 Apart from the five founders, Sedding, Belcher, Beresford Pite, Voysey and Champneys were among the architect members joining in 1884, Leonard Stokes and MacLaren in 1886, Harrison Townsend and Mackmurdo (and William Morris) in 1888, Bentley, George and Jackson in 1889, Harry Wilson in 1892, Halsey Ricardo in 1893, J. J. Stevenson in 1894, Ashbee and Norman Shaw in 1897. See H. J. L. J. Massé's, *Art-Workers' Guild* Shakespeare Head Press, Oxford 1935.

24 Illustrated *The Builder* 12 June 1886 and *The British Architect* 8 October 1886 as the work of MacLaren and Richard Coad. This wing, running up a side road, survives slightly altered. P.365 (15 October 1886) of the same *British Architect* volume has a delightful essay by MacLaren called 'A Visit to Ledbury', with his sketches of the old village houses in the same issue as 'The Park' drawing. Coad himself would probably merit more research. His rebuilding of Lanhydrock House, Cornwall, from 1881 on after a fire, is good vernacular work. MacLaren may well have been involved.

25 Illustrated *The Architect* 14 October 1887 and *The British Architect* 6 May 1887, with the comment "now being erected". MacLaren's address is here given as No. 3 Duke Street, Adelphi. In the same magazine, 14 November 1890 p.361 Thomas MacLaren implied that his brother won a competition for this commission. Interior detail illustration *The Architect* 17 April 1891.

26 Illustrated in David Walker's 'Mackintosh' article in *The Architectural Review* November 1968, together with telling comments about the influence of the building.

27 Illustrated *The Builder* 19 October 1889, saying it had "lately been finished". For some reason, *The British Architect* illustrated no more of MacLaren's work during his lifetime (but see the issues of 25 September 1891 and 13 November 1891 for posthumous illustrations). MacLaren may have known H. H. Richardson's design for B. H. Warder's house in Washington of 1885, for Mrs M. G. Van Rensselaer's *Henry Hobson Richardson and his Works*, Houghton Miflin, New York 1888 shows a similar approach in an illustration.

28 See the examples of foliated American doorways in *The British Architect* 22 March 1889.

29 The vestry building at the east end is dated 1882, but is clearly of a different building stage. The church officers believe the church itself was built in late 1880s but knew of no documents. MacLaren may have done a minimum cost job, or may have come in only for the trimmings.

30 Dated 1889 by the *Scottish National Buildings Record*. The site was given by Lord Breadalbane in 1887 and the foundation stone laid by Sir Donald Currie on 21 September 1889 (this information was kindly given by Mr Ian Brown, Town Clerk of Aberfeldy, in a 1971 letter). If it was designed that year, Voysey's early published drawings in *The British Architect* 25 January 1911 and 22 February 1889 would have been seen by MacLaren. If it was earlier, the influence may be *vice versa*. One should also point out the similarity to some of the *British Architect Art Club* designs of the first half of the decade. Finally, the similarity to H. H. Richardson's Chestnut Hill Railway Station of 1883 is too great to be coincidental (see Rensselaer *op cit* p.103).

It is often difficult to decide whether any given contemporary group of designers with similarities in their work amounts to a *movement* or not, and this question applies as much to the Arts and Crafts architects as to others. For these men were strongly individualistic. Perhaps the best tests are to establish whether such designers shared important ideas, whether they had regular contact with each other and whether their designs have strong features in common. If these tests are applied, it can be demonstrated that there was indeed an Arts and Crafts architectural movement. It was centred on London and the surrounding counties, but had local adherents in the Midlands and northern England. Its influence had a considerable effect on contemporary Scottish architects, though the Glasgow men went their own way and in turn influenced design in England.

The first point to examine is just how much theory these architects had in common, apart from the general ideas of fine craftsmanship and starting each architectural project completely freshly. One key-note of their architectural theory was simplicity. In 1895, Halsey Ricardo (1854–1928) made the point in an article called 'Architectural Simplicity'. "We are, let us hope, at a measurable distance from the end of this present dissolute style, for dissolute it is. As long as the mouldings and the ornament further and explain the meaning of the design – are organic – all is well . . . Simplicity in architecture means good art in architecture. . . . All this welter of indiscriminate ornament is not practical". So simplicity was an ideal, though it could take a variety of forms in the buildings they built – simplicity of structure, simplicity in almost geometrical forms, a rough rustic simplicity in country buildings, or large areas of plain wall surface that contrasted with the textures of decorated bands and other features.

The next important design theory shared by the Arts and Crafts men was that the structure of any building should be honest and true to its function. It was W. R. Lethaby (1857–1931) who held to this line most tenaciously and, of all the group's theories, it was to be the most influential in later years. Lethaby's years as a teacher were his most important, but the few buildings he himself designed – all done between 1890 and 1902 and all hauntingly idiosyncratic and strange – show a constant eagerness to experiment with new structural techniques. His rational Eagle Insurance building in Birmingham of 1900 and his concrete vaulted church at Brockhampton of 1901–02 were extraordinarily adventurous.

The desire for a national or local vernacular architecture was another important shared idea. In 1899 an editorial in the progressive magazine *The British Architect* commented "The craving after a new and indigenous style of architecture on the part of American architects is perhaps only natural. Even in this country we now and then get a little impatient and a good deal curious to know when and how the long-talked-of new national style is to develop". On a national scale, the country was combed for historic buildings that were essentially British in style, rather than directly imported styles from the continent of Europe. This resulted in many free adaptations of Scottish 16th- and 17th-century castles, English Elizabethan and Jacobean country palaces, Perpendicular churches and Cotswold stone manor houses, without producing anything that satisfied the desire of the progressive architects for a 'new national style'.

On the more localised level, the Arts and Crafts men often did find ways of using regional styles in a modern way. Most of them took care to use the forms and materials that were traditional in the region of each building. At its most extreme, this ideal blended with another: the search for an organic architecture, whose buildings would in various ways seem to grow out of the earth they stood on. The most constant exponent of this, and perhaps the most fascinating of all the English Arts and Crafts architects, was Edward Prior (1852–1932) who tried to obtain all building materials from the immediate area of his buildings, often mixing local stone with local brick in brilliantly original designs that visually linked the building closely to the earth. The organic as a factor in decoration and structure has obvious origins in the work of William Morris and H. H. Richardson but was developed further during the 1890s.

The final shared ideal of the Arts and Crafts architects was that of originality (as one would expect in a movement seeking a new type of architecture), though there was less certainty among them about how far it should go and how it should be balanced with traditional elements. To Philip Webb, and to others who shared his attitudes, this presented few problems, for they felt that the right approach to each individual building would automatically produce an unselfconscious and new result. Thus C. F. A. Voysey (1857–1941), the most boldly and impressively simple designer of these English architects, wrote in 1892 "The myriads of conflicting schools and catechisms fade away into insignificance and we begin to feel the invigorating sensation of being alone with Nature and our own intelligence. . . . Eschew all imitation. . . . Strive to produce an effect of repose and simplicity".

At the other end of the scale from Voysey on the question of originality was Charles Harrison Townsend (1851–1928), who pushed his designs for large buildings further away from traditional forms than any other English Arts and Crafts architects and produced a formula for free design in a talk called 'Originality in Architecture' which he gave to the Architectural Association in 1902. "Remember that in doing your best to make your architecture speak Today rather than the Past, you are not to strive, of set purpose, to be what you or others may call *original*." And Townsend went on to suggest an endearing though simplistic rule-of-thumb of 75 per cent originality and

1 *C. Harrison Townsend. Horniman Museum, London Road, Forest Hill, Lewisham (1896–1901). Townsend built three of the rare large-scale free style buildings in his attempt to escape from historicism.*

25 per cent tradition for architectural design. Until recently little research had been done on this attractive and unpredictable architect.

As we shall see in later sections of this book, the Arts and Crafts Movement established itself in northern England, but not in Scotland. There the Glasgow architects were more successful than their English counterparts in establishing a free national style for large buildings, although (or perhaps because) they lacked many of the high-minded theories of the Arts and Crafts Movement. Only Charles Rennie Mackintosh and a few others combined Scottish hard-headedness with a keen interest in English and Continental ideas.

Of the other centres of provincial Arts and Crafts practice, the north of England was the most active. The most interesting architect in practice there was Edgar Wood (1860–1935), who progressed from rather picturesque works around Manchester in the 1890s to impressively rational designs in the early 1900s in partnership with J. Henry Sellers. Wood did not have the same background training, direct or indirect, by Shaw or Webb that had influenced his southern contemporaries, but he was active in the northern offshoots of the Arts and Crafts Exhibition Society and the Art Workers' Guild. In a 1900 lecture to the Birmingham Architectural Association he described how his attitude to design had now changed, "I find it much more satisfactory to start from the plan entirely, making it thoroughly useful and fit to the extent of almost ignoring the elevation". This rational development certainly gave his work a new impetus that enabled him to survive after the end of the century when so many of his contemporaries became disenchanted.

Another free style architect who continued to develop during the Edwardian period was Leonard Stokes (1858–1925). Never an extreme Arts and Crafts man, he was a widely respected designer of great power who could adapt within reason to changing fashions and still produce startling buildings. His attitude to the question of originality is well stated in an article he wrote in 1895. "Whatever style you work in, do not lose your head. . . . Do not be too slavish, or think yourself bound to do this, simply because it was done before . . . at the same time, do not be too original, or do things simply because they have never been done before".

The Arts and Crafts group contained many strong personalities with their own design characteristics, often conflicting in part. Thus Voysey's houses maintain long continuous horizontals, while Townsend's tend to break such lengths into contrasting sections. All the same, these basic principles (simplicity, honesty of structure, vernacular building materials and character, and originality blended with tradition) were shared by most of the Arts and Crafts men. In addition certain features and details were developed and became widely used by many of them, almost as symbols of the movement. A list of some of these motifs

is almost a description of the whole group of Arts and Crafts buildings – simple surfaces contrasted with textured bands, asymmetry of composition, cupola turrets at corners and junctions of different levels, cupolas or belfries straddling roofs, bands of windows, polygonal bow windows, irregular organic doorways, buttresses and battered walls, roughcast rendering, mixed wall materials, panels of curvilinear carving integrated into the buildings, combinations of battlement with gable, strong horizontals or verticals with equally strong contrasting accents, strong advance and retreat of building lines in small houses, experimental ground plans (skew, linear, X-shaped or L-shaped), layering of surfaces on large wall areas, geometrical forms, and curving rooflines and boundary walls.

Some of these fashionably progressive features were of course spread through the illustration pages of the architectural magazines, but the Arts and Crafts Movement was co-operative in spirit and three organisations played a particularly important part in the development and dissemination of its ideals and ideas. William Morris and Philip Webb dominated the Society for the Protection of Ancient Buildings, although Lethaby became increasingly influential as the founders aged. Many young architects joined the S.P.A.B., as much for general discussion of architectural matters as for its strictly 'anti-scrape' activities.

Even more influential was the Art Workers' Guild, a discussion club founded in 1884 which later built its own premises in London, and the Arts and Crafts Exhibition Society which some of the A.W.G. members founded in 1888 to arrange shows of their designs and products in architecture, painting, sculpture, furniture and all the other crafts.

Again, William Lethaby (who was Norman Shaw's senior draughtsman) was the dominant influence in these organisations. He and some other pupils of Shaw started to have fairly regular gatherings in Ernest Newton's rooms well before 1884, and even founded a group called the St George's Art Society in 1883. The central five of this group were Lethaby, Newton (1856–1922), Edward Prior, Mervyn Macartney (1853–1932) and Gerald Horsley (1862–1917) who became the founders of the A.W.G. The Guild's aims at the time were to reverse the current tendency for architecture, painting and sculpture to drift apart, but by the early 1890s it had become a centre of much wider aims for Arts and Crafts design, holding regular discussion evenings on particular topics of concern to its members and even craft demonstrations. The fact that its members included many painters, sculptors and other designers and craftsmen was of great importance, but we are concerned here chiefly with the architects.

An account of some of the architects who joined the Art Workers' Guild amounts to a roll-call of most of the notable free style men. The five founders were joined in 1884 by Belcher, Sedding, Champneys, Beresford Pite and Voysey. Two years later Stokes and MacLaren joined and were followed in 1888 by Harrison Townsend, Mackmurdo and William Morris. In the following year Bentley, Ernest George and T. G. Jackson spread the character of the membership a little wider and then came W. D. Caröe, Harry Wilson, Detmar Blow, Halsey Ricardo, J. J. Stevenson, C. R. Ashbee, Norman Shaw himself, Roger Fry, Cecil Brewer, George Walton and Edwin Lutyens.

The other most notable architectural names of the free design movement are Baillie Scott, Ernest Gimson, Dunbar Smith, Banister Fletcher, H. Fuller Clark, R. A. Briggs, Weir Schultz, H. B. Creswell, George Sherrin and F. W. Troup – and of course Edgar Wood of Lancashire, W. H. Bidlake of Birmingham, as well as such Scots as J. A. Campbell, James Salmon the younger, J. G. Gillespie and Charles Rennie Mackintosh. Some of these did not join the Guild because their practices were too far from London to make membership useful, but even they were often in touch with the A.W.G. and a Northern Branch was founded in 1896.

The Guild's greatest influence was on the question of the attitude to architecture in the 1890s and on the syllabus of architectural education in the Edwardian period. In 1892 Norman Shaw and T. G. Jackson edited a book, with contributions by several A.W.G. members, entitled *Architecture, a Profession or an Art* as a manifesto against the first Architects Registration Bill then before Parliament. The position taken by these progressive architects was that it was impossible to test a candidate's design or practical building ability by examination. Any attempt to do so would produce a generation of architects who had merely learned the right words by rote, and would cripple the artistic element in design that was so necessary if architecture were to develop healthily.

Gradually the A.W.G. faction lost this struggle against the Royal Institute of British Architects. The Institute introduced voluntary examination and formal schools of architecture started to take the place of the old system of training only by a period of Articles with an established architect. Then in 1904 a Board of Architectural Education was set up by the Institute to establish a syllabus for these schools, and at that point the Art Workers' Guild men changed their tactics.

As so often with this period, we owe much of our knowledge to John Brandon Jones. It appears that several of the Guild members manoeuvred themselves into membership of this education board – Lethaby even joined the Institute with that purpose. And it was Lethaby's draft that formed the backbone of the eventual syllabus. The syllabus laid down a four-year course: two in a school and two in an architect's office. The course was to be governed by the principle that *construction is the basis of architecture* and that, mirror-wise, *architecture is the transformation of structure into aesthetically valuable forms*. A high standard of draftsmanship, a knowledge of historic buildings as

background education, practical knowledge of materials and building would all have to be demonstrated in the candidate's final project. Most important, the aim was the practical but aesthetically pleasing use of materials in abstract forms *without ornament*, and copyism was undesirable.

A syllabus like this was indeed a foundation for a free style, but it was too late. One may regret that the A.W.G. architects had not seen their way to infiltrating the ranks of their opponents in this way a decade earlier than 1904. As it was, the Edwardian revival of interest in classicism caused much of the syllabus to be overlaid by Beaux Arts ideas after a few years, although Lethaby's teaching professorship at the Central School of Arts and Crafts enabled him to ensure that the principle of structure as architecture was embedded deeply in many students. Finally, Lethaby developed yet again a position where he could accept the value of modern industrial techniques if used in the right way and he was active in the foundation in 1915 of the Design and Industries Association that played a central role in the International Modern movement of the 1930s.

To return to the actual buildings of the 1890s, Philip Webb built Standen in Sussex, his last great house, during this decade. The Arts and Crafts men of Lethaby's generation started their own practices around or just before 1890. As one would expect, most of their early commissions were small in scale. MacLaren's Stirling High School of 1887 was a notable early exception, as were one or two free works by established men such as Holy Trinity in Sloane Street and Shaw's New Scotland Yard. But as the 1890s continued, a growing series of public or other sizable buildings in a variety of free styles by A.W.G. members seemed to open the way for a really new architecture. Apart from domestic work, by 1903 Lethaby had built an office building and a church, Prior a variety of educational buildings, Dunbar Smith and Cecil Brewer a large charitable building, Townsend three extraordinary public buildings and two churches, and Voysey a factory. Henry Wilson had put up a notable public library, and Edwin Lutyens's many commissions were increasing in size from the small country houses he had done in the early 1890s. Sadly, what seemed an *hors d'oeuvres* turned out to be the main course in southern England. Edwardian Baroque took over the large commissions, leaving only domestic and a little church work for the Arts and Crafts designers of the Art Workers' Guild.

The free style did survive and develop for large buildings in Scotland, in the London County Council's work, in the work of Leonard Stokes and in a few practices in the north and Midlands of England. But its hope of turning into a new national style for the country as a whole was gone when faced with the harsh facts that architects (who are not all geniuses) like a set of well-worn rules to follow, and prosperous clients like splendour not simplicity.

One final point remains to be made. *L'Art Nouveau* of France and Belgium produced buildings in those countries and some others which are quite unmistakeable. The style, which was partly derived from the tendrils of William Morris's decorative manner, in turn influenced some British artists, designers and decorators. And hints of it appear in designs by Townsend, Wood and others and, most notably, Mackintosh. But the key to *Art Nouveau* is *anti-rationalism*, and in *Art Nouveau* architecture this enters into the structure of the building (as in Gaudi and Guimard). By this criterion, *Art Nouveau* architecture in Britain was almost nonexistent.

2

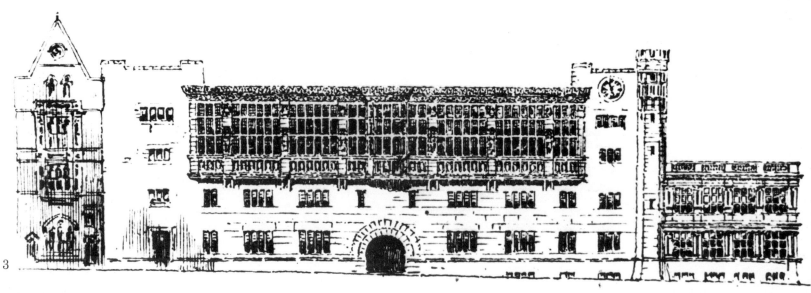

3

2 *Edward Prior. Pier Terrace, West Bay, Bridport, Dorset (designed 1885). An early use of long horizontal lines and original design, combined with Dorset building materials, by one of the leading Art Workers' Guild architects.*

3 *Halsey Ricardo. Competition design, Oxford Town Hall (1892), not built. A brilliant and original design, showing the way the free style might have been developed if the competition assessors had not rejected such entries.*

4 *J. D. Sedding. Courtyard, St Agnes' Industrial Schools, Knowle, Bristol (circa 1888). A striking design combining originality with traditional craftsmanship.*

5 *C. F. A. Voysey. Design for a cottage at Bishops Itchington, Warwickshire (1888). This was Voysey's first published architectural design and already shows the strong horizontals and many of the detailed features that he used all through his career. His emphasis on simplicity and long clean horizontals was to be one of the greatest influences on free architectural design.*

FRONT ELEVATION

BACK·ELEVATION

6

7

8

9

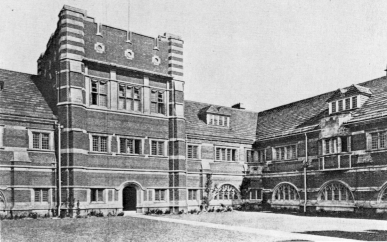

11

6 *Norman Shaw. Design for a church in a hot country at Port Elizabeth (1892). One of Shaw's boldest free designs. A more conventional and less comfortable alternative design by Shaw was chosen and built. Shaw cannot be called an Arts and Crafts designer, but he remained close to many of that loose group who had been his pupils.*

7 *Frank Lloyd Wright. Winslow House, River Forest, Illinois (1893). At this stage, Wright's domestic work was developing in a way that seems to show a knowledge of what Voysey and others were doing in England. Later, Wright corresponded with Ashbee.*

8 *Philip Webb. 'Standen', near Saint Hill, East Grinstead, Sussex (1891–94). Webb's last great house. Younger Arts and Crafts architects were often concerned about the proper balance between originality and tradition in their designs, but Webb's instinct rarely failed him.*

9 *Charles Rennie Mackintosh. School of Art, Renfrew Street, Garnethill, Glasgow (1896–99). Mackintosh cannot be described as a member of the Arts and Crafts group of architects, but he was in touch with them and his free style was influenced by their work.*

10 *Dunbar Smith and Cecil Brewer. The Mary Ward Settlement, Tavistock Place, Bloomsbury, London (1896–97). One of the best free style large buildings of the 1890s. Note the craggy naturalistic doorway (in contrast with the other clean forms) derived from MacLaren and, via him, from H. H. Richardson.*

11 *Leonard Stokes. Central tower, All Saints Convent, Shenley Road, near London Colney, Hertfordshire (1899–1903). Stokes assimilated Arts and Crafts ideals, but kept to his own powerful and individualistic free manner.*

12 *Voysey. Wallpaper Factory, Sanderson's, Chiswick, London (1902). Voysey's only non-domestic building of any size.*

13 *Charles Holden. Belgrave Hospital for Children, Clapham Road, Kennington Oval, London (designed 1900, completed 1903). Holden worked with Ashbee in 1897–98, then took his free style approach into the flourishing hospital practice of Percy Adams, where he soon took over most of the design work.*

14 *Harry Wilson. Design for a fireplace (1890). A good example of the way that the Art Nouveau style influenced the decoration of designs by some English architects, though its anti-rationalism did not get into the structure (as it did on the continent of Europe).*

15 *William Lethaby. Eagle Insurance Buildings, Colmore Row, Birmingham (designed 1899, built 1900). Lethaby was the most influential thinker and writer of the Arts and Crafts architects, but he built only a few houses, a church and this highly original office building.*

16 *Hector Guimard. Coillot shop and house, Lille, France (1898–1900). An example of truly Art Nouveau architecture, with the style expressed in the very structure of the building. Comparable buildings were almost unknown in Britain.*

13

12

14

CERAMIQUE COILLIOT
CARRELAGES ARTISTIQUES   ÉMAILLÉE

William Lethaby's Buildings

by Godfrey Rubens

The 1850s and the following decade saw the birth of a brilliant new
generation of English architects. They grew up under the liberating
influence of Morris, Webb, Shaw and Godwin and most of them
started their own practices around 1890. The most significant to his
own contemporaries and younger men, as talker, writer and
teacher, was William Lethaby (1857–1931). But his own absorbing
buildings are relatively little known. They are described here in a
new study by Godfrey Rubens, current holder of the University of
London Leon Fellowship, who is preparing the first full biography
of Lethaby.

"Then, just as our English free building arrived, or at least 'very very nearly did', there came a timid reaction and the re-emergence of the catalogued 'styles'."[1] As in this country modern architecture was stillborn, so William Lethaby's part in it is almost forgotten. His name we are told now "evokes a diffuse vaguely pleasant, but somewhat fusty image"[2] It was not always so; for many years his urgent message was ignored, he was attacked as the bogeyman of functionalism and dismissed by the pundits of the profession as a crank. His writings are still well known, and books like *Form in Civilization* have been constantly re-published, but his independent buildings, most of which were built in the last decade of Victoria's reign, remain relatively unknown although they are among the freshest and most brilliant of any work in architecture produced at that time.

William Lethaby was born in 1857 in Barnstaple, where his father Richard Lethaby was a carver and gilder. An active Bible Christian and ardent Liberal, he was a man of some standing in the community. Elizabeth, his second wife, brought up William and Emmaline, his only children and the offspring of his first marriage. They seem to have been a close and affectionate family, and William was clearly influenced by his father's opinions and experience. The young Lethaby was educated at the local Grammar school and, as soon as he could, attended evening art classes at the Barnstaple Literary and Scientific Institute, winning the first of many prizes at the age of twelve. His formal education ended shortly afterwards, and his notable independence of mind and willingness to challenge accepted opinion arose, at least in part, from his need to find out things for himself.

At about fourteen, Lethaby was articled to Alexander Lauder, a local architect and here he was fortunate for Lauder was a man of some culture, with an active interest in education. He wrote and illustrated some volumes of verse, ran a brick and tile company, founded the Devon Art Pottery and was a fair draftsman and painter. He worked extensively for local landowners and for the Methodists, for whom he built a number of chapels and schools in London and the West country. A perspective view of one of these London chapels, signed by Lethaby, was published in 1876[3] and although it shows a dull Gothic structure of brick with stone dressings, it is made interesting by Lethaby's lively drawing.

In 1877 *The Building News* started a 'Designing Club', for young architects, the objective of which was to "promote the faculty of design". The subjects were portions or details of buildings and included furniture and the decorative arts. In that year Lethaby, using the pseudonym 'Début', won the £5 prize and Maurice Adams, the editor, who published seventeen of his designs, wrote, "His designs . . . have usually been marked not only by a considerable refinement, as well as feeling but some originality."[4] At the end of the year

Lethaby left Barnstaple and went north to work in Duffield and Leicester. *The Building News* continued to publish his drawings – perspective views of his principals' architectural designs, drawings of old buildings in the neighbourhood and, in 1879, his prize-winning design for the Soane Medallion which was a very striking drawing for a 'House for Four Learned Societies'.

Norman Shaw was, at that time, looking for a new chief clerk, and on the strength of these drawings, he offered Lethaby Ernest Newton's place as Newton was leaving to set up on his own. Lethaby accepted and came to London in 1879. During the ten years he worked for Shaw, Lethaby's views do not seem to have undergone any marked change. In a lecture published in 1883 he said he was "a great admirer of the Renaissance styles" and recommended that "while keeping ourselves open to all new ideas, . . . we should work in our own traditions, . . . but admitting the truth of Bacon . . . when he says, there is no exquisite beauty without some strangeness in its proportion".[5] What this meant in practice was shown in 1882 when he, with Newton and Mervyn Macartney, submitted a competition design for St Anne's Schools, Streatham.

It is an open question exactly what Lethaby contributed to Shaw's style in the years that he was chief clerk and responsible for a busy office where a good deal of freedom was allowed, but on Shaw's own showing it was a good deal. Lethaby may, for example, have been responsible for the designs for 42 Netherhall Gardens, as all the drawings are in his hand.

In 1889 Lethaby left Shaw, and in May, opened an office at 10 Hart Street and in the course of a busy year he worked for many people, including Shaw, J. D. Sedding, Macartney and Emery Walker. The jobs ranged from designing complete buildings to making illustrations for Sedding's unpublished book on Saxon and Norman architecture and he also worked for a number of firms making architectural fittings.

At the Second Arts & Crafts Exhibition Lethaby showed eleven items, including the panel front for E. S. Prior's altarpiece at Bothenhampton, Dorset. For this, Lethaby used techniques he had acquired from his father and produced a boldly asymmetrical design of wild roses, naturalistic but flat, and executed in painted and gilt gesso. Two pieces, made by Marsh Jones & Cribb and exhibited at the Arts and Crafts exhibition the following year, show Lethaby at his most extreme. The rosewood table is about as near as he ever got to an 'Art Nouveau' design and a more conventional cabinet has its walnut veneer laid in such a way as to give the maximum play of light.

Ernest Gimson and Lethaby met for the first time in 1889 and their interest in furniture led to the formation of a co-operative to design and make furniture of which the other members were R. Blomfield, M. Macartney and S. Barnsley. It was called Kenton & Co., after a street they passed through on the way to the 'shop'. In

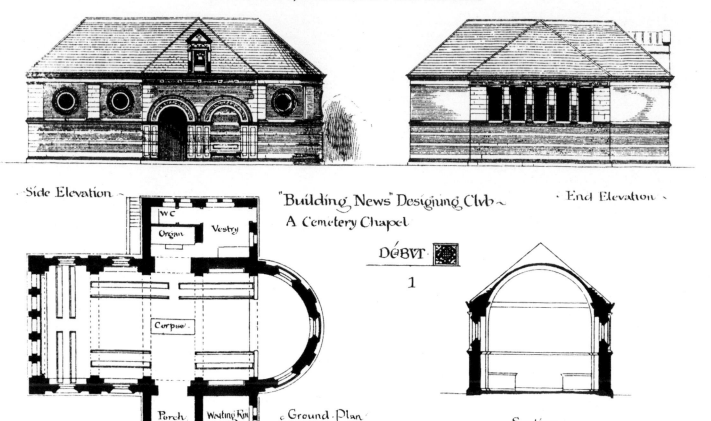

2 *William Lethaby. A Cemetery Chapel. One of Lethaby's drawings for the Building News Designing Club (1877). "In external design, Debut's (Lethaby's pseudonym) idea conveys admirably the expression of a mortuary, there is an almost deathlike serenity of line and feature in the classical style he has chosen, and the calm horizontal repose of lines and roof are thoroughly characteristic, though to some minds the treatment is not sufficiently suggestive of a Christian burial." (Maurice Adams,* Building News, *8 February 1877). At nineteen Lethaby's work was already remarkable for its invention and imagination. In 1879 Norman Shaw employed him as chief draughtsman and assistant until 1889.*

1891 Kenton & Co., held a successful exhibition in the hall of Barnard's Inn, the premises of the Art Workers' Guild, but it was wound up the following year through lack of capital. Though Lethaby was "the dominant personality"[6], it was he who was influenced by Gimson and he later described Gimson's furniture as "one kind of perfect, that is, it was useful and right, pleasantly shaped and finished, good enough but not too good for ordinary use"[7]. The change in his own furniture design was dramatic and marked the beginning of the direct influence on Lethaby of Morris and his friends.

It was through Gimson that he was introduced to the Society for the Protection of Ancient Buildings where he met Philip Webb, who attended all meetings, provided the technical guidance and became his hero. "This Society," Lethaby wrote later, "engaged in an intense study of antiquity became a school of rational builders and modern building".[8] Certainly the influence of the S.P.A.B. on the development of English free architecture has been consistently underestimated.

A year or so before, Lord Manners had asked Shaw to recommend an architect for his new house and Shaw had suggested that Macartney, Newton and Lethaby

send Manners some drawings and photographs. From these, Lethaby was chosen and he started work on Avon Tyrell early in 1891. The house overlooks the Avon Valley towards Christchurch and is designed to take full advantage of this magnificent prospect from the garden front. It is without wings, but there are a number of bays that both catch the morning sun and command the view. The result is a rather long narrow house, unified by the single roof, the composition being closed at one end by a massive chimney breast and at the other by the projection of the drawing room. Lethaby took enormous care with the planning and detailing of the house, as surviving letters and the large number of full-scale drawings show. Although various features can be ascribed either to the influence of Webb or Shaw, the design, which is often very ingenious, is quite unmistakably Lethaby. Like all his subsequent work, it has 'some strangeness in its proportion' and twenty years later when it was described by *Country Life*[9] the author still felt that Avon Tyrell's modernity needed justifying. It is in the interior that Lethaby's transition from eclecticism is notable. The fireplaces, for example, which are simple and rectilinear, are without historical reference. The decorative effects arise from the characteristics of the materials themselves and this is also true of the furniture some of which he designed and which was made by Kenton & Co. The plaster work was carried out in the summer of 1892 by Gimson who lodged for months in a cottage nearby.

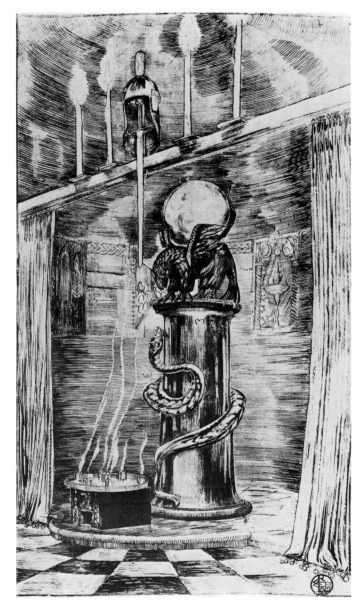

3 *"The altar stood from its curved recess*
In a coiling serpent's life-likeness;
Even such a serpent evermore
Lies deep asleep at the world's dark core
Till the last Voice shake the sea and shore.

From the altar-cloth a book rose spread
And tapers burned at the altar-head;
And there at the altar-midst alone
'Twixt wings of a sculptured beast unknown,
Rose Mary saw the Beryl-stone."

'A Beryl Shrine' by Lethaby was published by The Architect *(20 January 1888); Architectural Illustration Society, No. 137) and was inspired by Part III of D. G. Rossetti's 'Rose Mary'. Four years later, in 1892, he published his first book,* Architecture, Mysticism and Myth, *on architectural symbolism. In 1925 the book was extensively re-written and published as a series of articles by* The Builder.

Lethaby's next commission was for a house at Four Oaks Park, Sutton Coldfield. The Park had been sold to a development company in 1880 and the land divided into building plots. Here Lethaby built The Hurst, which is now destroyed, for Charles Mathews in 1893. It had a tight L-shaped plan and full advantage was taken of the site. The dining room faced east and south and the library westwards across falling ground towards Sutton Park. From the entrance there was a view along the vaulted hall through the dining room to the garden beyond. The fenestration, either sash or casement windows, was a direct expression of the plan, even the venetian window 'expressed' the groin vault of the hall. Exterior decoration was minimal and it was a simplified version of elements used at Avon Tyrell. The decoration of the dining room bay may have been inspired by Newton, who used similar motifs on Redcourt, a house in Haselmere built a year later, but in other respects the houses are dissimilar, Redcourt being of classical symmetry. Lethaby and Newton were soon to go quite different ways, Lethaby saying ". . . the third cornerstone for a modern building is *need* or *utility*. It might be said that as soon as you put pen to paper some distinctive style would come in; but when the drawing has been made, can we not begin again and hunt down every trick of style one at a time. . ."[10]. The Hurst was published by Herman Muthesius in *Das Englische Haus* (1904) and its austere simplicity made an enormous impression. Muthesius wrote that each of Lethaby's houses was a masterpiece, and they certainly influenced his own work.

4 *A part of the third Arts and Crafts Exhibition 1890. Furniture left to right Ford Maddox Brown, Lethaby, Blomfield, Gimson, and Lethaby. Lethaby described the cabinet as "being entirely veneered, the moulding being laid in cross-band. The intention of the design was in laying broad surfaces in varying directions to get a play of light. The table, of the very hardest wood was made as thin and light as possible." Architectural Illustration Society No. 293* The Architect *28 November 1890.*

5 *William Lethaby. Avon Tyrell, near Christchurch, Hampshire, was designed for Lord Manners in 1891, and is now owned by the National Association of Youth Clubs. The builders, Albert Escourt & Son, came from Gloucester, ninety miles away.*

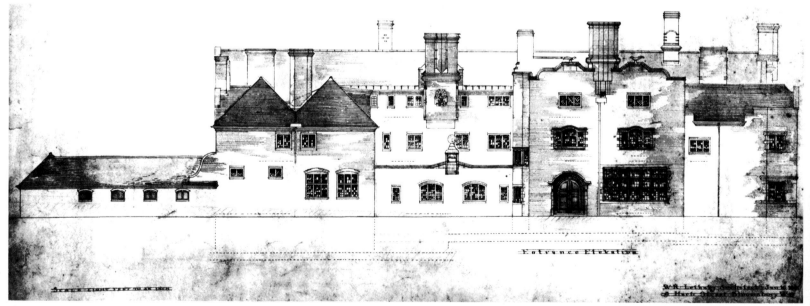

6 *Avon Tyrell. Contract drawing, eighth scale, for entrance elevation.*

Lethaby was appointed as art inspector by the newly formed London Technical Education Board in 1894, and he was much taken up with the improvement and re-organisation of London's art education. His next architectural commission did not follow until 1898 and was for the Eagle Insurance Buildings, Colmore Row, Birmingham, completed in 1900. It was built with the help of a local man, J. L. Ball, who was responsible for the work on the site and later became Director of the Birmingham School of Architecture. Despite its name, it is in fact only one structure. On a narrow irregular site, it is designed to give the largest number of high quality offices, well lit and self-contained. The façade is a restatement of some of the main elements of classicism. It has three rows of superimposed columns, and its symmetry is maintained by increasing the height of the lower doorway. This, incidentally, provides for a step up into the principal office. It is in a most original way related to its surroundings as Colmore Row was then crowded with 19th century classical façades, encrusted with columns. Lethaby was as sensitive to a city site as to a rural one, and he "... most carefully related his building to its neighbours both in adjusting it to its site and taking up local manners in building."[11] There is however almost nothing classical about the actual elements. The columns, for example, are nothing so much as stone versions of the legs of his furniture.

The simple bold façade is virtually in one plane, except where it is broken by the heavy horizontals and the major window springs straight from the ground, while the others are deeply recessed. Access to the building is through the upper entrance, which leads into a high narrow hall, austerely satisfactory. The floor and dado are of marble, the latter white, and the former of black and white rectangles. In the left hand wall there are two blind arches, and above, three intersecting groin vaults. These and the hexagonal glass dome of the director's office all remind one of Soane and it was he that inspired the building next door, now demolished. The stone discs of the parapet acknowledge one of the notable features of the building on the other side.

It was probably the first modern building to have a well-designed inscription as an integral part of the façade. Lethaby was a pioneer in advocating the use of lettering on buildings and was one of the handful of men responsible for the revival of printing and type design. In the same year, he started the first ever lettering class at the L.C.C. Central School of Arts & Crafts, with his protégé, Edward Johnston, in charge.

From 1898 Lethaby also carried out a number of commissions for the Birmingham businessman, Thomas Middlemore. These were Melsetter House and chapel, Rysa Lodge and various small buildings on the Isle of Hoy, Orkney. Shortly afterwards he built High Coxlease, 'a cottage in the Forest', for E. W. Smith, completed in 1901. This is a medium sized house, near

Lyndhurst, in the New Forest. Comparisons between the two illustrate Lethaby's theory of architecture for each building is thought out from 'first principles': the purpose, the site, and local building traditions, materials and techniques. These make two apparently quite different houses but what they have in common is more subtle and arises from their inventiveness and from the quality of the building work. Melsetter, which incorporates an earlier farm house, is large and informal. The main block is to the east and forms two sides of a walled courtyard. From its principal rooms, there are magnificent views across the harbour and the Pentland Firth. In the south-west corner, at a higher level, is the simplest possible chapel with a pointed concrete vault springing directly from high stone walls, which was the inspiration for Brockhampton church. High Coxlease, on the other hand, has a less informal plan and suggests a group of Hampshire cottages. The roofline is broken, and the gables which are not all of the same pitch are differently treated, the composition also being interrupted by tall chimney stacks.

7 *Stanmore Hall, Middlesex. Stanmore Hall was decorated by Morris & Co. for William Knox D'Arcy in 1891. Lethaby designed the fireplaces, the panelling, the staircase and some of the furniture. His massive hall table, here illustrated, was inspired by Philip Webb and probably made by Kenton & Co.*

8

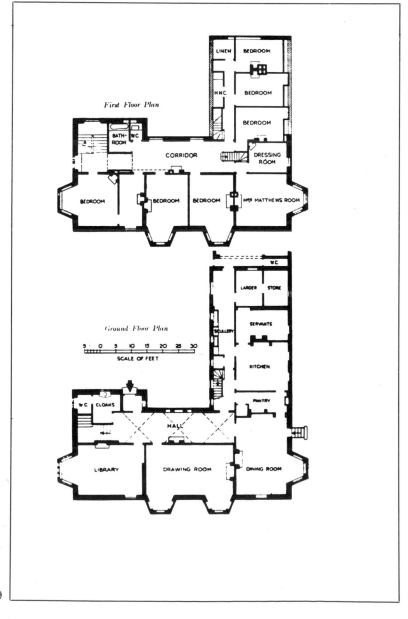

First Floor Plan

LINEN | BEDROOM
H.W.C. | BEDROOM
BATH ROOM | W.C.
CORRIDOR | DRESSING ROOM
BEDROOM | BEDROOM | BEDROOM | MRS MATTHEWS ROOM

Ground Floor Plan

9 0 5 10 15 20 25 30
SCALE OF FEET

W.C.
LARDER | STORE
SCULLERY | SERVANTS
KITCHEN
PANTRY
W.C. | CLOAKS
HALL
LIBRARY | DRAWING ROOM | DINING ROOM

9

10

11

8 *William Lethaby. 'The Hurst,' Hartopp Road, Four Oaks Park, Sutton Coldfield, near Birmingham (1893) for Charles Edward Mathews, was built of thin red Leicester bricks and roofed with hand made tiles from Hartshill. The stables were white-washed. The house has since been destroyed.*

9 *'The Hurst'. Plan.*

10 *'The Hurst.' The Hall, looking toward the dining room.*

11 *'The Hurst.' The drawing room fireplace. The cast iron grate and side panels are two of the many designs that Lethaby made for Longdon & Co., but the fire irons and cinder tray are not his. The plaster work was designed and executed by Ernest Gimson.*

12 *William Lethaby. The Eagle Insurance Buildings, Colmore Row, Birmingham (1900) was built with J. L. Ball, an architect, who practised in Birmingham for about fifty years and died there in 1933.*

13 *Plan, Melsetter House, Orkney (1898). Drawn by John Brandon-Jones.*

14 *William Lethaby. Melsetter House, Hoy, Orkney, Scotland (designed 1898). From the south-east. The house, built of local reddish sandstone, has harled and whitewashed rubble walls, and exposed and dressed trims. Harling, a sort of rough cast, is traditionally Scottish as are the forms of the chimneys and the crow-stepped gables. It is roofed with greenish grey Caithness slates. Now Lethaby was working directly as a practical builder with local craftsmen, putting into practice his revolutionary view of the architect as constructor.*

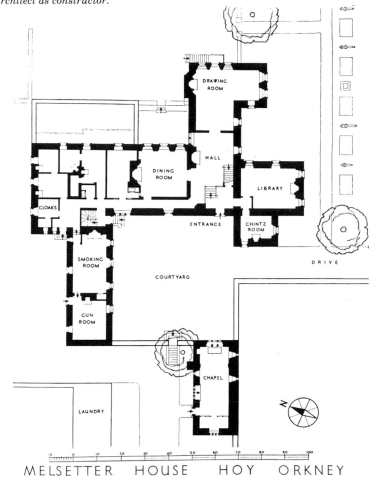

MELSETTER HOUSE HOY ORKNEY   13

15 *William Lethaby. 'High Coxlease,' Lyndhurst, Hampshire, was built as a country retreat for Thomas Eustace Smith, in 1901. It stands in the middle of the New Forest and its walls were originally whitewashed.*

16 *'The Hurst'. The entrance lodge.*

All Saints Church, Brockhampton was commissioned about 1900 by Alice Foster of Brockhampton Court, in commemoration of her parents Eden and Julia Jordan of Boston, U.S.A. and was consecrated in 1902. The general impression of the exterior is of a traditional thatched Herefordshire church. The rough and primitive look comes from the very broad treatment; the walls and buttresses are of local rubble masonry and the irregular quoins and window trims are chisel dressed. Nevertheless the arrises are clear and sharp. It is the interior that seems so entirely new. From the low and massive walls spring single chamfered arches, supporting a mass concrete tunnel vault, "formed on rough boards".[12] The semi-circular relieving arches to the transepts and west windows underline the thickness of the walls and the delicacy of the square-headed window tracery.

Lethaby, because of his increasing distrust for 'paper architecture' used direct labour and employed Randall Wells as Clerk of Works. Thus the architect was involved in the actual building process and the work was a direct expression of structure, of materials, and

17 *William Lethaby. All Saints' Church, Brockhampton, near Ross-on-Wye, Herefordshire, from the south-east (1901–02). The church was commissioned by Alice Foster of Brockhampton Court, as a memorial to her parents, Eden and Julia Jordan.*

18 *All Saints' Church, Brockhampton. The interior looking east, showing the great concrete vaults. E. S. Prior's church at Roker was partly inspired by All Saints', and Randell Wells worked on both. The tapestries, designed by Burne-Jones, were woven by Morris & Co. These designs were made in about 1879 for stained glass in Salisbury cathedral. The furniture, like the lamps, was designed by Lethaby.*

19 *All Saints' Church, Brockhampton. Detail of interior, showing Lethaby's fine font and detailing of stonework.*

20 *Lethaby, Henry Wilson and others. Design for Liverpool Cathedral Competition (1902). Not built. A montage, showing the Cathedral from the north-east.*

of function. Changes could be made during the construction and in fact were. The height of the crossing tower was increased for example and the transept windows were completely redesigned.

"True originality is to be found by those who, standing on the limits of the sphere of the known, reach out naturally to some apprehension and understanding of what is beyond; it is the next step in an orderly development".[13] This seems exactly to describe what Lethaby did at All Saints. There was nothing incongruous in this context of a thatched concrete vault – the thatch

provides excellent insulation.

But, like all original statements, the church indeed poses the question of the next step and this Lethaby attempted in the second Liverpool Cathedral Competition. He invited a number of others, H. Wilson, F. W. Troup, Stirling Lee and Weir Schultz to join with him in making an entry but the design and inspiration was largely Lethaby's though it was sent in under Wilson's name. Lethaby was an enthusiastic advocate of concrete. "If only," he wrote, "we could sweep away our fear that it is an inartistic material and boldly build a

21 *Design for Liverpool Cathedral Competition (1902). Section through the model, from the south-east, showing the concrete vaults designed by Lethaby and his group.*

railway station, a museum, or a cathedral, wide and simple, amply lighted, and call in our painters to finish the walls . . .".[14] A concrete cathedral was, however, too much for the assessors, Shaw and Bodley, and the design was hardly heard of again although the drawings are testimony to what might have been and to the timid reaction that brought English free architecture to an end.

After 1902 Lethaby practised little as he felt that his own training had been entirely inadequate for modern scientific building. "It is absurd, for instance, that the writer should have been allowed to study cathedrals from Kirkwall to Rome and from Quimper to Constantinople; it would be far better to have the equivalent knowledge of steel and concrete construction".[15] Or again, "If I were again learning to be a modern architect I'd exchange taste and design and all that stuff and learn engineering, with plenty of mathematics and hard building experience. Hardness, facts, experiment that should be architecture, not taste."[16] He concentrated mainly on teaching and writing and on attempts to reform both the teaching and practice of design and architecture. Although in these matters he was not entirely unsuccessful, at that time in England few people really understood what he was saying, let alone its implications for the new century.

[1] W. R. Lethaby, 'Modern German Architecture and what we may learn from it'. In *Form and Civilization* O.U.P. 1922 p.100.

[2] R. Macleod, *Style and Society* R.I.B.A. Publications 1971, p.7.

[3] *The Architect* 8 April 1876.

[4] *The Building News* 4 January 1878.

[5] *The Architect* 30 June 1883, p.435. This was the first talk given to the St George's Art Society, which was formed by Norman Shaw's clerks and friends. The following year they helped found the Art Worker's Guild. Lethaby played a leading part in both.

[6] W. R. Lethaby, 'An Impression and a Tribute'. *Journal of The Royal Institute of British Architects* Vol. XXXIX, No. 8, p 6.

[7] W. R. Lethaby, 'Ernest Gimson's London Days' in *Ernest Gimson, his Life and Work* 1924, p.6.

[8] *ibid* p.4.

[9] *Country Life* 11 June 1910, Vol. XXVII, p.846.

[10] H. H. Statham, *Modern Architecture*, Chapman and Hall 1897, p.15.

[11] W. R. Lethaby, *Philip Webb*, O.U.P. 1935, p.129. Though he was writing of Webb, he could equally have been talking about himself.

[12] 'Specifications of Materials for Brockhampton Church': MS in R.I.B.A. Drawings Collection.

[13] W. R. Lethaby, 'The Architecture of Adventure' *Journal of The Royal Institute of British Architects* 3rd Series, Vol. XVII No. 12, p.477.

[14] W. R. Lethaby, *Architecture*, Home University Library 1912, pp.248–9.

[15] *ibid* p.247.

[16] Letter from Lethaby to Sydney Cockerell dated 7 October 1907.

Edward Prior

by Christopher Grillet

The Arts and Crafts Movement was dominated by Lethaby's
ideas, but he was not necessarily its outstanding architect. That
place must probably be allotted either to Edward Prior (1852–1932)
or to Voysey. Prior was at his best an architect of tremendous
originality and power and Christopher Grillet's short study of his
work conveys the character of his genius.

Edward Schroeder Prior is known to some as a scholar, to few as an architect. Yet the relatively few buildings he designed are amongst the most original of their time by anyone in England and possess in addition a remarkable topicality. If ever there was an architect who placed 'the nature of material' foremost it was Prior.

No more can here be done than to discuss eight of his buildings, one in detail, the others more briefly. They date from between 1885 and 1907. Before that time he was a faithful follower of Norman Shaw, after that time a scholar more than an architect. He entered Shaw's office in 1872, after schooling at Harrow and studying at Caius College, Cambridge. At the time Lethaby was chief draughtsman, and Mervyn Macartney, Ernest Newton and Gerald Horsley were also members of the office. Blomfield describes young Prior as an "athletic good-looking" young man, and Shaw wrote to his mother that "once he gets a good start, he won't want much help from anyone."

That estimate was true, less as regards success than style. For after some clearly shavian houses[1] he began quickly to introduce touches of wilfulness quite different from Shaw's own picturesque licence. They seem to appear for the first time in the Harrow School Laundry of 1887 where the coupled segment-headed Shaw windows on the ground floor are crushed by heavy arches around each pair, and there, between the four gabled Shaw oriels big chimneys go up corbelled out of the façade from below eaves level. Similarly odd is the big many-ridged roof of the centrally planned little Billiard Room of 1889 at Harrow. But Prior's zest for originality at all costs went much further. He is said to have built as early as 1885 that long, isolated terrace of houses along the harbour of West Bay, near Bridport, which has the oddest rhythm in its elevation. The houses are four-storeyed, and every storey is a surprise in itself and in relation to the others. The ground floor has no doors – they are at the back – and only small windows eccentrically grouped. The first floor has oriels equally eccentric – a pair always belonging to two different houses. Above the oriels the second floor projects and has an even run of normal windows. The third floor is in the big, heavy gambrel roof, and it is this long roof more than anything that gives the houses its curious massive warehouse quality. At every pair of houses it is stepped up a foot or two, rising as the cliffs in the direction of the sea.

Ten years later Prior exhibited at the Royal Academy his drawings for The Barn, a house at Exmouth and no

2 *Edward Prior. Red House, Byron Hill, Harrow, Middlesex (1883).*

3 *Edward Prior. Henry Martyn Memorial Hall, Market Street, Cambridge (1885–87). Only the unusual restless stonework links this Gothic building with Prior's later work.*

1 *Portrait of Edward Prior.*

4 *Edward Prior. Pier Terrace, West Bay, Bridport, Dorset (1885). An early design of startling originality.*

5 *Edward Prior. Design for Swimming Baths, West Bay, Dorset (circa 1894). Not built.*

this unobtrusively Perpendicular building of flint and ashlar stone dressings, and mixed into his flint pebbles of all kinds and sizes and bigger pieces of rubble; an effect which he must have seen and liked in Cambridgeshire churches. But there is apparently no precedent for that surface effect he introduced at the angle, in the polygonal turret. Here the staircase goes up and he made that visible outside by letting the blocks of the treads pierce the wall so that they appear on the outside. In The Barn again there is a wildly haphazard mixture of stone and pebbles and weatherboarding. The thatch sat on them like a big old straw hat, and the chimneys are round and a little tapering, as if the village craftsmen had made them without any drawings. Prior indeed believed in the village craftsman. In an article in *The Architectural Review* in 1901[2] he recommended that at Liverpool Cathedral the architect should be no more than the supervisor and selector of materials. The design should be left to grow from the efforts of the chief craftsmen of the major trades. In that he expresses – though unusually violently – the principles of the Arts and Crafts Movement – which, since he was one of the founders of the Art Workers' Guild and the Arts and Crafts Exhibition Society, is not surprising.

Prior detested straight lines and right angles, although he firmly believed in symmetry. His columns are cigar-shaped, his gables often canted, the corners of rooms or whole buildings also canted or chamfered off, the arches of vaults stretched into parabolic shapes. His use of thatch represents the same tendency. What was he after? The effect in The Barn is more like Gaudi in Barcelona than one can see anywhere else in England. It makes even the naughtiest Lutyens appear tame. Surely Prior's fundamental belief was in organic

6 *Edward Prior. Superintendent's House, Harrow School Laundry, Alma Road, Harrow, Middlesex (1887).*

doubt Prior's most remarkable house. It is remarkable enough today, though it lost much of its original character when the thatch on its roof was replaced by tiles after a fire. The plan is the first extraordinary thing about it, an X-shape, never, it seems, attempted before in Victorian England. For although Prior's model was no doubt Norman Shaw's Chesters of 1891, the plan here is only a threequarter X, as it were, with the back made into a square *cour d'honneur*. Also Chesters is grand, The Barn is intimate, small in size, low and squat and comfortable in a curiously primeval or native way. That effect is due to Prior's use of materials. Already in his Henry Martyn Hall at Cambridge, in 1884–86, he made up the wall surfaces of

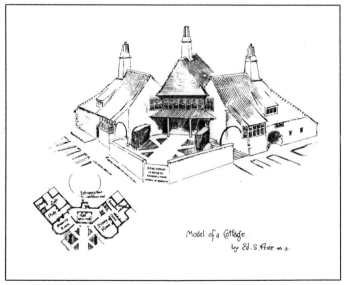

7 *Edward Prior. Design for a country cottage (1895), later developed into The Barn, Exmouth, Devon (1897). This type of highly original plan was taken up by many others, including Voysey, Stokes, Lutyens, Baillie Scott and Muthesius.*

8 *Edward Prior. The Barn. One of the two or three most original and influential houses of the Arts and Crafts Movement in the 1890s both in plan and use of materials.*

9 *Edward Prior. 'The Barn', garden front. The house is superbly sited, overlooking a long garden and the sea. The original thatch was replaced by tiles following a fire shortly after completion.*

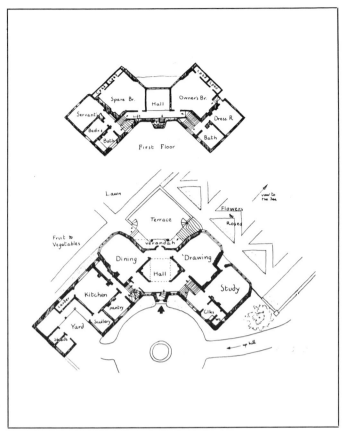

10 *Edward Prior. 'The Barn'. Interior, showing hall and gallery.*

11 *Edward Prior. Plan of 'The Barn'. Prior still worked occasionally with Norman Shaw at the time when Shaw's 'Chesters' was designed (1891) and its X-plan may be the origin of that of 'The Barn'.*

architecture. One hesitates to use this fashionable phrase, but it does apply to Prior – more probably than *au fond* it applies to Frank Lloyd Wright. A building, according to him, should look as if it had grown – grown under the hands of craftsmen sympathetic to their materials, but not concerned with mathematics and the exactness of high finishes.

Home Place at Kelling, near Holt in Norfolk, is an enlarged version of The Barn, on a very similar plan, with all sorts of canted shapes of rooms, and again with a wild and violent mixture of materials outside. It is a little grander perhaps than The Barn, a little less casual and a little more Lutyenesque. It was built in 1904, and the equally remarkable block of cottages nearby with their oddly hollowed-out ground floor façade, was added in 1907.

The same year Prior completed his *chef d'oeuvre*, St. Andrew's Church at Roker, near Sunderland. What he achieved here is (perhaps side by side with Lutyens's St. Jude's at the Hampstead Garden Suburb) the best English church of the early 20th century. There was plenty of money and plenty of space. The church was to seat 700 and to have a tower visible far out to sea. So Prior placed his tower over the chancel end and made his nave one large room without aisles. By placing his buttresses, big heavy buttresses, inside and piercing them, he made it possible to have passage ways

for the congregation to reach their pews from along the walls. Such narrow passages through buttresses were a favourite device of the best Victorian architects, see for instance Pearson's St. Augustine, Kilburn, of 1870–80. But Prior's passages are specially low and narrow and out of the buttresses grow without a break heavy parabolic transverse arches. This form of arch Prior had already used once before, in 1887, at Bothenhampton in Dorset. Towards the nave, the arches rest on pairs of thick short hexagonal piers with a kind of hexagonal block capitals. East of the nave are a pair of transepts and the chancel, considerably narrower than the nave. To link them to the nave diagonal arches are thrown across from the outer walls of the nave to the outer walls of the chancel, thus giving the transepts a canted entrance. Canted also are the inner angles of the nave at the west and the chancel at the east end. The window tracery is Gothic, as is the tower, but in their details they are considered entirely afresh. All curves in the tracery are straightened out, and the chancel is placed so that its roof just appears east of the tower as if it had been tunnelled through. The outline of the tower is splendid with the batter of its windowless angle turrets, and its castellations corbelled out on segmental arches above the bell openings.

Those who deny that in the design of churches inspiration from the Middle Ages can have results

147

12 *Edward Prior. St Andrew's Church, Roker, near Sunderland, County Durham (1904–07). Tower, showing the craggy massing that expresses the nature of the building stone.*

3

15

13 *Edward Prior. St Andrew, Roker (1904–07). West end. One of the most successful of all Arts and Crafts buildings.*

14 *Edward Prior. Interior looking east, St Andrew, Roker (1904–07). The enormous buttresses form ribs for the nave, with dramatic effect, but the passage between walls and the piers from which they rise avoids excessive heaviness. Furnishings by Ernest Gimson.*

15 *Edward Prior. 'Home Place,' Kelling, near Holt, Norfolk (1904). Prior at his wildest, in plan and mixed materials, though perhaps less successfully than in 'The Barn'.*

16 *Edward Prior. Cottage, 'Home Place' (1907).*

1

17 *Edward Prior. 'Greystones', Highcliff-on-Sea, Hampshire (1911–14). The last of Prior's pre-war works shows much of his usual originality of form on this entrance front, though the garden side is much quieter.*

valid in the 20th century, have their answer here, not in Sir Ninian Comper's works.

After Kelling and Roker, Prior did little architecture. He designed a few more houses, two of them excellent (one at Lavant, near Chichester, in 1912, the other Greystones, at Highcliff-on-Sea, in 1914) and a few war memorials, but for the last twenty-five years of his life he was more a writer than an architect. He had always liked to write. He had contributed one of the most trenchant pieces to Norman Shaw's and his group's celebrated attack on professionalism amongst architects, the book of 1892 entitled *Architecture, a Profession or an Art.* He had written an extremely interesting series of papers on gardens in *The Studio* in 1898 pleading for 'artificiality' and 'cobble-stones'. In the same year, he began to write for *The Architectural Review*.[3] and in 1901 joined the newly constituted editorial committee.[4] This consisted of Norman Shaw, John Belcher, F. T. Bagallay, Reginald Blomfield, Gerald C. Horsley, Mervyn Macartney, D. S. MacColl, E. J. May, Walter Millard, Ernest Newton, Halsey

Ricardo, Professor F. H. Simpson, Leonard Stokes, apart from Prior. But the very first editor who had been engaged when this magazine started, Harry Wilson,[5] Sedding's pupil, was also his friend.

In 1900 Prior published his first and best book, the *History of Gothic Art in England*, the most appreciative and sensitive work that exists on its subject. His *Cathedral Builders in England* came out in 1905. Between 1902 and 1904 his *Medieval Figure Sculpture in England* (written with Mr Arthur Gardner) appeared in *The Architectural Review*. In 1912 it came out as a book. In the same year Prior was made Slade Professor at Cambridge. He remained it until he died in 1932.

In an obituary notice in *The Cambridge Gazette* it is said of him that "he was constitutionally incapable of accepting the via media." Blomfield also in his book on Norman Shaw says of Prior that "he enjoyed being in the majority of one." That fits the style of his best buildings, but it remains a puzzle how so headstrong and so gritty an architect can have been so gentle and tender a writer on the nobility and the beauties of the Early English style.

---

[1] High Grove, Harrow, 1881 illustrated in *The Building News* 8 December 1882; Carr Manor, Meanwood, Leeds, 1881 illustrated in *The Architect* 2 May 1890; Manor Lodge, Harrow, 1884 illustrated in *The Architect* 19 July 1889 and mentioned without Prior's name in *The Buildings of England: Middlesex.*

[2] *The Architectural Review* Vol. 10 1901, p.79.

[3] He wrote three short articles: Vol. 4 1898, pp.106–108, 154–158; Vol. 5 1898, pp.132–134 and Vol. 6 1899, pp.42–44.

[4] *The Architectural Review* Vol. 9 1901, p.256.

[5] He did all but the chancel of St Osmund, Parkstone, Bournemouth, in 1913, a church not originally designed but executed with a fantastic exterior by Prior. He also did the sculptured decoration for the proposed Ciborium for Norwich Cathedral (1915) which was never executed. Lynne Walker is now (1974) writing the first full study of Prior and has traced several other interesting buildings by him at Harrow and at West Bay, Dorset.

N.B. Jill Franklin has investigated the development of Prior's house plans in 'Edwardian Butterfly Houses', *The Architectural Review* April 1975, pp. 220–225.

Charles Annesley Voysey

by John Betjeman

Of all the Arts and Crafts architects it is C.F.A. Voysey (1857–1941)
whose aesthetic simplicity can be seen as most strongly expressing
the reaction to Victorian over-decoration and presaging the taste
of the 20th century. In spite of occasional lapses into a coy
prettiness, Voysey maintained high standards of long and strong
horizontals, bold accents and geometrical solids in his architectural
design. Sir John Betjeman's essay of 1931, supported by an
interesting piece of the same year by Voysey himself, is one of
particular value in that it was written when Voysey was still alive
and to his fury, was first being hailed as an originator of the
International Modern Style.

Once it would have been as risky to praise the work of Voysey to, say, Sir Gilbert Scott, as it would be today to praise Le Corbusier to a modern 'traditionalist'. Now, what Ruskin was to Scott probably Voysey is to the 'traditionalist'. Yet it would be a mistake to consider either Ruskin, Voysey or Corbusier as particularly 'dated'; the dates remain with Sir Gilbert Scott and his modern equivalent. The other three are the true pioneers and their messages differ but little. Only in England is Voysey not taken at his true value, for he is dismissed as *Art Nouveau* or even 'arty', and the extravagancies of new architecture at the end of Victoria's reign are considered more of a joke than they really are. Later, when considering the influence of Voysey on European architecture, we can estimate him and his school at their true worth. To understand the architecture and decorations of Voysey it is necessary to know his principles and life, for the man and his work are closely allied. The originality of much that he did is due to the originality of his character, just as the works of Wren and Soane bear the personal imprint of the architect and make them stand shoulder high above the work of contemporaries. It is significant, too, that Voysey should consider A. W. Pugin one of our greatest English architects, for that bold man with his sailor's clothes and outspoken opinions can be compared with Mr Voysey, who has an original and pleasing way of dressing and whose opinions are as brave and outspoken.

Charles Francis Annesley Voysey is the son of the famous Reverend Charles Voysey, who was removed from the Church of England for preaching against the doctrine of hell fire, and founded the Theistic Church. He is descended from the Duke of Wellington, and as has been written of one of his younger brothers: "He perpetuates on his gentle visage the Iron Duke's nose and in his gentle nature the Iron Duke's will." Yet he is probably prouder of the blood of Wesley. What his father preached to thousands in London, Mr Voysey has interpreted in stone and colour. He was articled for five years to J. P. Seddon, one of the more prominent competitors for the New Law Courts, and in 1889 he did his first house. From the first his work was original, yet it would be a mistake to call it revolutionary. As he stated, in a letter he wrote in 1931 to *Country Life,* upon the signing of their buildings by architects, it would be presumption to put the name of one man to a house. Architecture is a growth, and all knowledge of material and construction is the product of generations of experimental architects. Therefore, the house at Bedford Park which he built in 1891, and which must have surprised even the modern Mr Norman Shaw, is the product of necessity, for Voysey allowed his materials to dictate to him. As he himself writes: "... there yet remain certain elements which change, not like certain kinds of stone, which by their nature have dictated certain forms of architecture, as for instance, stone found in large sizes lead to the lintel and column

treatment, while smaller stones called for the arch. These are what we may term enduring qualities. ... The Traditionalist is shocked by what he calls the mixture of styles. Fitness does not appeal to the mind already wedded to definite modes of expression. The fact that the two forms of arch (Tudor and Classical) were seldom, if ever, used together in ancient times, blinds his eyes to the fact that altered conditions of modern life may demand the consideration of requirements non-existent in previous ages. The individualist is always ready to cast off the shackles of a bygone time, and is willing to meet the needs of the present while still holding fast to all enduring qualities." And again, "Certain conventions, dictated by a complete knowledge of material and needs, would naturally lead to the use of many familiar forms. The principles of the lintel and the arch, which are based on material qualities, must for ever remain true principles. But if we cast behind us all preconceived styles, our work will still possess a style, but it will be a living, natural and true expression of modern needs and ideals: not an insincere imitation of other nations and other times." The sincerity of Voysey's architecture refutes all those slurs which might be cast upon it as deliberately unusual. The heavy sloping buttresses by which most of his later houses may be distinguished were the products of necessity for they are there to support a wall only nine inches thick. The bedroom windows high under the eaves of his houses are protected from rain, and by being high "give a feeling of security to the bedroom."

Voysey's architectural principles have remained the same from the time he started. It is not, therefore, necessary to give a detailed history of his career. In 1924 he became Master of the Art Workers' Guild with which he had long been associated. With characteristic sincerity and thoroughness he learnt all the crafts connected not only with the building but also with the decoration of the house. He followed the principles of William Morris. He even carried them further. He must be the only architect who has designed everything, down to the very spoons and forks, for his buildings.

After building nearly two hundred houses with such care, he explained his principles in a book, *Individuality* (Chapman and Hall), which was published in 1915. It is a work of more importance than any detailed biography could be, for it expounds the religion of the architect and the consequent reverence with which he made his buildings.

To him aesthetic and moral values are inseparable, and since he is an individualist, he considers the training of character to be of far greater importance than any knowledge of styles and books. He therefore deplores the foundation of architectural schools and the disappearance of the personal contact between architect and pupil. "Many architects of today say in effect 'Let us have an established mode, a national style

12 *C. F. A. Voysey. Interior, 'The Homestead,' Frinton-on-Sea, Essex (1908).*

Aston Webb was President of the Royal Academy of Arts, for the first time in the existence of that body, an Arts and Crafts Exhibition was held under its auspices in Burlington House.

The period when Norman Shaw was in full practice was certainly more Gothic than Classic, and lasted in Baillie Scott, Lutyens, and the two Barnsleys, Andrew Prentice, Guy Dawber, Mallows and others, with domestic practice. But very soon after Shaw's time the Classicism of the Georgian type became fashionable and corrupted even the Great Lutyens.

Commercial and public buildings were before domestic architecture in manifesting the feeling of the time, as men of known business ability were chosen to do the work because the business man shunned the artistic crank. All artists being regarded as cranky in a thoroughly materialistic age.

It was early in the 20th century that architecture seems to have been completely divorced from Gothic. Temporary dwelling-places taking the place of homes, that is to say, something to go *from* rather than go *to*, were the outcome of the motor-car. And difficulty of finding domestic servants led to the building of flats. Death duties and local councils' powers to interfere with property owners' vested interests, all combined to kill *home* building, and flats, shops and commercial buildings had to be made to pay commercially; their aesthetic qualities being quite unimportant.

Let us, however, sing a *Te Deum* over the fact that in this dark age we had a Bentley, a Giles Scott and a few others producing lovely Gothic work.

When Gothic architecture ceased to be fashionable, away went that lovely quality so often to be seen in the old towns of Holland, where all the houses are different, though sympathetically respecting each other, like gentlemen. Now an angry rivalry, or a deadly dull uniformity, is the dominant feature of our street architecture.

This, indeed, is a commercial age gone game mad.
Facilis est descensus Averni.

Charles Harrison Townsend

by Alastair Service

While Voysey designed in long horizontals, Charles Harrison
Townsend (1851–1928) broke up the exteriors of his early house
designs into contrasting vertical sections. Where Voysey reduced
his buildings to simple geometrical solid forms, Townsend often
sought surging organic shapes that would make the design appear
to grow from the ground. In these and other ways Voysey and
Townsend represent opposite poles within the Arts and Crafts
Movement, with Townsend attempting a modern free style that
strongly asserted its rejection of scholarly historicism.

Townsend's designs during these years (1897 to 1902), in spite of all that it might be possible to say about sources in England and abroad, are without question the most remarkable example of a reckless repudiation of tradition among English architects of the time." Nikolaus Pevsner's remarks in *Pioneers of Modern Design*[1] are typical of many writers on the architect of the most original exteriors of the Arts and Crafts Movement, yet no close study of his work has yet been published and the dates of his many private houses remain elusive. Now, however, the unpublished theses[2] of Peter Wentworth-Sheilds and Richard Allan Woollard have given a sound factual foundation for historians.

At the core of Charles Harrison Townsend's fascination for us today lies the paradox of the surging organic exteriors and the contrasting rational interiors of his famous public buildings. On a first visit to the Bishopsgate Institute, the Whitechapel Art Gallery or the Horniman Museum, the frontages lead one to expect curving lines, dramatic spatial contrasts of solids and voids, and a rich variety of textures inside. Instead one finds a series of simple, almost bare galleries or rooms, well lit and adaptable to changing uses. Indeed the interiors are so flexible and unassertive that they remain impressively functional despite the alterations made in the past seventy years. The explanation of this contrast between outside and inside lies partly in the purpose of the buildings and partly in the nature of the architect himself.

Charles Harrison Townsend was born on 13 May 1851[3] at 27 Price Street, Birkenhead in Cheshire. His father Jackson Townsend was a solicitor with a poorly paid job, who had married Pauline, the daughter of a well-known Polish violinist called Felix Yaniewicz. Their family consisted of six sons and one daughter. They were all musical and artistic but, with little money, their childhood was hard. Townsend was articled to a Liverpool architect named Walter Scott in about 1870, and was able to save enough to make his first trip abroad to Normandy in 1875.[4]

In about 1880 the Townsend family moved to London in the hope of better employment. We do not know Townsend's job at this time, though he may have worked with W. Eden Nesfield[5] and it seems that he was able to afford a trip to Italy in 1881.[6] By 1883 he was working for Thomas Lewis Banks, an architect with a London office at 23 Finsbury Circus, but much practice in the north of England. Townsend went into partnership with Banks in 1884 and published several of the firm's designs, including churches at Turnham Green, Hartlepool and Upton, and a house in West Hartlepool.[7] Only the plan of the school with the Upton Church shows any departure from run-of-the-mill Gothic (or, in the case of the house, a Waterhouse-type Renaissance) and the designs were presumably by Banks.

In 1886 Townsend visited Venice, Ravenna and Verona. Later that year, *The Builder*[8] published its only Banks and Townsend design which is clearly Charles' work. This was a chapel at Lamplugh, Kirkland, Cumberland and already many points of the design, in an Arts and Crafts version of the Perpendicular, with low eaves and a small pointed belfry, are recognisable Townsend, and at a date before Voysey was published.[9] It is worth noting that the same issue of *The Builder* illustrated three American villas by Mead and White and others, using the curved forms that were to be so typical of Townsend's own later work. As we shall see, Townsend's elder brother Horace, a journalist, had met H. H. Richardson in the early 1880s.

One can demonstrate Townsend's interest in the Richardson school of American architecture by a glance at the designs of two houses in Chicago by S. G. Beaumont[10] in *The Builder* in 1887. The comment with these says that they were sent in by Banks and Townsend, in whose office Beaumont had worked before emigrating to Chicago. The powerful rounded style indicates that Beaumont and Townsend must have shared a keen admiration for this type of American work.

By 1888 Townsend had become a fellow of the R.I.B.A. and gone into private practice with an office at 29 Great George Street, Westminster. His first published design under his own name appeared in *The Builder* of 11 February 1888; a simple pair of cottages for Cotleigh in Devon, with much tile-hanging and little chance for displaying his originality of form. In the same year he was elected to the Art Workers' Guild.[11] The Guild brought him into contact with its founders, including Lethaby and Prior, and others such as MacLaren, Beresford Pite and Mackmurdo who had joined since its foundation and shared Townsend's fascination with new forms in architecture. It may also have brought him into touch with William Morris, who joined it in the same year. The Guild was to be the centre of many of his activities and friendships over the following years, for although he was a sociable and amusing man he never married. Aged thirty-seven at this time, he was older than most of the Guild's members, but its records show his obvious popularity.[12]

His practice started slowly. A house called 'Tourelle' in Salcombe, dates from about 1890,[13] described by Richard Allan Woollard as "a strange roughcast building on battered rubble piers". Then in 1892 Townsend rebuilt the west front of All Saints Church,[14] Ennismore Gardens, Knightsbridge, London as a small-scale version of the façade of San Zeno Maggiore in Verona (there is some attractive foliated carving). He was to continue with the replacement of some of the church's internal fittings over the next few years. The tower of the church also seems to be Townsend's work. It is a fine free adaptation of the campanile of the Murano Basilica near Venice, but already shows something of the surface plasticity of his later Horniman Museum. There is no doubt that Townsend had a genuine and lifelong personal passion for the Romanesque.

1 *Charles Harrison Townsend in 1903.*

2 *C. H. Townsend of Banks and Townsend. Chapel, Kirkland, Cumberland (1886). Already, the general proportions of Townsend's two later churches can be seen.*

In the same year of 1892 he obtained another church commission, to build St. Martin's, Blackheath, near Guildford, Surrey.[15] This small village church has great charm and an endearing oddness. Its style could be described loosely as a rustic Romanesque, with a long low line of wall that ties the building to the ground it is on, and a great sweep of tiled roof with a curving belfry. The west front has a massive round-topped door between two great buttresses on the corners. The interior is a pleasing space, with a low tunnel vault and round side arches, much marbling and Arts and Crafts frescoes by a Mrs Lea Merrit. Originally there was a subtle lighting effect over the altar, from a triangular window tucked under the end gable beyond the belfry, which has been foolishly obscured. The church was opened in 1895 and occupies the key visual position in the small valley along which the pretty village is scattered.

This Surrey village of Blackheath is the happiest hunting ground for admirers of Townsend. Originally an undistinguished 19th-century hamlet, its position near Guildford, yet isolated and healthily high on the Surrey downs, led to its being taken in hand by two wealthy men who lived there. These were Sir William

Roberts-Austin, who paid for the church, and Mr Henry Prescott, who paid for the Congregational Chapel and Village Hall. Work continued with the conversion and extension of many cottages, with the object of beautifying the village for middle-class people who valued the rustic scene and the healthy air. Harrison Townsend was the architect for almost all these buildings, working there until as late as 1910. We cannot describe all his work around Blackheath and nearby Chilworth here and the dates of many cottages are unknown.

The Congregational Chapel (*circa* 1893), is a remarkable and charming little white building, its roughcast and buttressed sides owing something to Voysey's house in St. Dunstan's Road, West Kensington (1891) but with a front elevation design that is very original Townsend. It is now to be converted into a cottage. The Village Hall is probably later, built in about 1897.

Two enlarged cottages, 'Rosemary Hill' and 'Blatch-field', are used as illustrations for an article by his brother Horace in *The Studio* of October 1895. They are concerned with comfort, preserving the cottage character and blending with the old buildings. The few unusual points are details such as the battering of the walls in one cottage and, in the other, the bulge in the roof tiles to give just the type of dormer roof-light that Richardson had in his Crane Memorial Library in Quincy of 1880.[16] The garden frontage of 'Blatchfield' is typical of Townsend's way of breaking up his long narrow houses into contrasting sections. The main influence here was probably Philip Webb's 'Standen'.

Mr Woollard's thesis on Townsend puts forward the possibility for various reasons that the Townsend house called 'Dickhurst' near Haslemere, which was built in 1900, may have been designed in the early 1890s. Its long, bent plan is indeed comparable with 'skew' plans by Prior, Stokes and others illustrated in *The British Architect* in March and May 1895 and elsewhere. There was great interest in such elongated plans at the time.

The year 1892 produced the design of the first of Townsend's major buildings and before describing it, an examination of the influences on the architect up to this time is necessary. When Townsend died, his effects included a scrap-book of 'Manuscript notes and newspaper cuttings on Mosaics, collected by C. Harrison Townsend'[17] between the years 1870 (when he was nineteen) and 1912 (almost the end of his career). This lifelong fascination with mosaics – he frequently lectured and wrote about them – certainly influenced his own designs (to the extent that large-scale mosaics appeared in the major ones) and led him on to an interest in Byzantine and Romanesque buildings. It is unlikely to be just a coincidence that his first trips abroad took him to Caen, Verona, Ravenna and Venice.

So we can be reasonably sure that old Romanesque architecture was his personal favourite, though his own progressive ideals were strongly against any form of historicism whatsoever. For this reason we can understand why there is so much evidence of Townsend's interest in American work of the 1880s, for H. H. Richardson, McKim Mead and White, Peabody and Stearns and many others were using strong Romanesque forms in a completely free way[18] that captivated some of the young British free stylers.

Writing in the 1970s, it is difficult to know whether Richardson (1838–86) seemed as pre-eminent among his American peers in the 1880s as he does now, for the British magazines illustrated much other exciting American work. But we do have a full account of his second and last visit to Europe[19] in 1882. Richardson met Phené Spiers, spent an absorbing afternoon with William Morris, and his "aesthete" friends, showed "unbounded enthusiasm" for William de Morgan's ceramic work, was received "cordially" by Burne-Jones and "went through many of the new London houses, but was much impressed with their lack of interest and individuality". Richardson was a huge barrel of a man, overflowing with life and enthusiasm, and his whirlwind visit must have invigorated many young architects of similar ideas that he met during those two weeks. His visit would naturally cause

excitement and we find from *The Magazine of Art* in 1894[20] that Horace Townsend, Charles' brother, had worked for *The New York Herald* in the early 1880s and had gone to the trouble of visiting Richardson in Boston.

So what influence did this splendid American, or his contemporaries, have on young Harrison Townsend? The answer seems to be a great deal in spirit, but very little in the actual elements of Townsend's compositions. A close examination of his work yields surprisingly few details derived from others' buildings. The Richardsonian roof-light already mentioned is one. The foliated friezes inside Louis Sullivan's Auditorium Building, Chicago (1888) and outside his Wainwright Building, St. Louis (1890–91), as well as the figured frieze on Richardson's earlier Brattle Square church tower[21] of 1870 and street fountain in Detroit of 1881, were almost certainly the inspiration for Townsend's rather different use of such decoration. The sweeping surfaces of tiled roof down to low eaves of Richardson's brilliant railway stations and libraries of the early 1880s[22] have echoes in Townsend's churches and houses, and even in the roof of the Bishopsgate Institute, but only echoes. In general Townsend and the Americans share a liking for hints of natural formations, whether of rocks or plants, as a link between a building and the ground on which it stands. But when it comes to the great majority of his details and the way he builds up his compositions from such elements, Townsend is totally fresh in his approach. And most of the elements themselves, especially the great doorways, are very much his own.

As for the possibility of finding traces of his favourite Romanesque buildings in his designs, it is less surprising that (leaving aside All Saints' façade) there is little of significance. This almost puritanical abstention from ancient detail is obviously deliberate, though we have some odd thoughts on the subject in his own words in his lectures and articles.[23]

In 1894 he wrote, "Better too much precedent, that is – Copyism, than too little, that is – Ignorance. . . . What does much of the work of the present day for which the artist claims originality show us? Do we not find in the examples that at once rise up in the minds of all of us that the cardinal idea of the designer has been to differ from the old men by *omitting* what they had done before him? . . . The man of fashion . . . calls the result the 'simplicity of originality'. It is not. It is, instead . . . a negation that is a poor substitute for invention, a cowardice pretending to be courage. . . . We crave no right to start afresh *ab imis*, but on the understructure of our predecessors we strive to rear their buildings higher still, and to see our common edifices capped at last by the soaring spires that sing their soul in stone." Odd words from an architect whose Bishopsgate Institute was going up as he wrote them.

But in 1902 he has altered this theme a fair way. "It is for him (the architect) to throw into the crucible of his

3 *C. Harrison Townsend. St Martin's Church, Blackheath, near Guildford, Surrey (designed circa 1892, opened 1895). Townsend built many houses, as well as the church and the chapel, in this attractive new village.*

4 *C. Harrison Townsend. Interior, St Martin's Church, Blackheath, near Guildford, Surrey (designed 1892, completed 1895). The style might be described as free rustic Romanesque.*

5 *C. Harrison Townsend. Congregational Chapel, Blackheath, near Guildford, Surrey (circa 1893). An unexpected and charming adaptation of Voysey's manner.*

6 *C. Harrison Townsend. Garden Front, 'Blatchfield', Blackheath, near Guildford, Surrey (circa 1894). A typical example of Townsend's long ground-plans with elevations broken into varied sections, the antithesis of Voysey's long horizontal emphasis.*

own nature all his learning and all his knowledge, there to be fused and made one, and out of that melting-pot to draw an ingot that is to be stamped and shaped as his own personality. . . . The attachment of undue importance to formulae and rules causes a positive atrophy of the imaginative and creative faculty. . . . Precedents and traditions must need exist . . . and it would be presumptuous to claim to be in art absolutely free. . . . Yet remember that in doing your best to make your architecture speak Today rather than the Past, you are not to strive, of set purpose, to be what you or others may call 'original'. As Lowell says in one of his letters, 'When a man *aims* at originality, he acknowledges himself unoriginal'." And Townsend continues with a slashing attack on Copyism, leading to the rather pleasing if naive formula that designs might best be 75 per cent original content and 25 per cent traditional.

The other possible sources of Townsend's inspiration were of course his immediate predecessors and contemporaries among free style architects. In 1893 Victor Horta in Brussels and Hector Guimard in Paris were about to launch the decorative movement later called *l'Art Nouveau*.[24] Guimard visited England to look at new buildings in 1894, but we know of no contact between him and the Arts and Crafts architects.

Townsend has often misleadingly been called an *Art Nouveau* architect. In as much as he used patterns of tendrils and leaves and some curvilinear forms, his work certainly has obvious similarities to that of the Continental style. But Townsend was a zealous member of the Arts and Crafts Movement and the Art Workers' Guild, and Pevsner has rightly written[25] "the representatives of the Arts and Crafts loathed *Art Nouveau*. . . . 'The decorative illness known as *l'Art Nouveau*' is what Walter Crane says. Undoubtedly the Arts and Crafts, in fighting for honesty of work and simplicity of form, fought for higher moral values than *Art Nouveau*." Crane was a close friend of Townsend's and worked with him on the Whitechapel Gallery design in 1896. So clearly he did not rate this as *Art Nouveau* architecture, and we have only to compare Townsend's work with say, Guimard's writhing Coilliot shop at Lille (1898–1900) to see why.[26] Guimard's anti-rational style gets into the very structure.

The fact of the matter seems to be that Townsend's relationship with *Art Nouveau* stops at the decorative, while, as we shall see in a moment, he used his own free style of architectural design that kept to Arts and Crafts principles and had roots in Philip Webb's ideas, in Godwin's asymmetrical pioneering work and of course in Richardson's Romanesque. Much the same could be said of the late 1890s work of Mackintosh and Prior, though they show little American influence.

For British stylistic influences on Townsend we might look expectantly to Philip Webb and Norman Shaw's detailing – and find little connection,[27] except on his domestic work. And then there is the influence of the Art Workers' Guild. The Guild formed the

centre of Townsend's life, for he was a gregarious bachelor who loved the atmosphere of a boisterous men's club. He organised the Guild's trips to Europe[28] and some of the periodic banquets and entertainments in London. His chief friends were (according to his family) Crane, Robert Anning Bell, George Frampton, Heywood Sumner, Edward Burne-Jones, William Strang and George Clausen – all artists though none of them architects, but this refers to the latter part of his life. In the late 1880s and early 1890s, his fellow members included James Maclaren (who died at the end of 1890), Halsey Ricardo, Edward Prior, William Lethaby, Charles Annesley Voysey and many others whose published designs show an extraordinary interchange of ideas and motifs. Each kept his individuality as an architect, giving different emphasis to the various parts of the creed they shared. It was probably MacLaren's Stirling High School tower of 1886[29] that confirmed to Townsend that the 'organic' expression of naturalistic forms was a real possibility in Britain. Likewise he held something of Prior's obsession with materials and Ricardo's faith in bright colour on outside walls: Townsend's paper on mosaics in 1901[30] produced an enthusiastic outburst from Walter Crane in the hope that his "glorious vision might one day be realised of London decorated with mural designs and colour." Links with buildings by the other architects mentioned above are too numerous to list here, but it is already abundantly clear that, whatever sparks may have come from outside, the principles of this group (and his own burning and idealistic belief in the importance of originality in architectural detailing with a solid traditional base) were the main sources of Townsend's inspiration.

The first large building Townsend designed illustrates all this clearly. This was the Bishopsgate Institute, in Bishopsgate, City of London, an idea conceived in 1891[31] to provide a library and some cultural activities for the poor. Townsend won a limited competition for the job in 1892 from a field that included T. Chatfield Clarke and four others. The assessor's report by J. Macvicar Anderson makes it clear that the winning design was by far the best from a functional viewpoint, and the foundation stone was laid in May 1893. The Institute was opened on 24 November 1894 by Lord Rosebery, to slightly bemused praise from the building press.[32]

A long, irregular site with a very narrow street frontage is well exploited by the plan and most of the rooms inside are as undecorated and functional as the budget dictated. The Hall on the first floor is of a curious sub-Renaissance character. As for the famous street exterior, the first thing to notice is that the decorative elements (towers, friezes and the rest) do not interfere with the function and that they rise out of a composition that is basically four-square and rock solid. Even the three levels of foliated frieze (one bitten into by the big welcoming entrance arch) are held together by the strong verticals. The winding branches and leaves of the frieze designs have obvious William Morris and American ancestors, but the grouping of the central board room window and the blank arcade below it is typical only of Townsend. And the detail of towers and roof, with the strange horizontal features running across their surfaces, has few if any antecedents.

The major general influence on Townsend was probably Henry Wilson's Ladbroke Grove Free Library of 1891, while the grouping of steeply pitched roof with two turrets can be compared remotely with Richardson's Chamber of Commerce in Cincinatti (designed 1885).[33] Many of the Institute's individual features can be related to those of the Quincy Library (designed 1880)[34], but Townsend had already developed his own style in their detail and in the way they are built up into the overall composition. Mr Woolard has pointed out to me that one other probable source is the Elizabethan

7 *Bishopsgate Institute, Bishopsgate, City of London (designed 1892, built 1893–94). The influence of the North American Romanesque of H. H. Richardson and of Henry Wilson is evident, but Townsend's originality is still considerable.*

mansion of Brereton in Townsend's native Cheshire, illustrated in a 1906 edition of Nash's *Mansions of England in the Olden Times* (1849) with an introduction by Townsend.

Perhaps the key to the individuality of Townsend's compositions may be exactly that feeling for breadth as well as height, flowing and spacious although firmly defined by a general rectangular framework. Examples of it in other fields may be seen in a bookplate[35] for Angus Hooper which he designed in 1894 while the Bishopsgate Institute was being built and in the tremendous fireplace he exhibited at the 1896 Arts and Crafts Exhibition (carving by George Frampton), where it was called "one of the most important objects this year".[36] Lengthy praise for it in *The Studio*'s review of the exhibition is worth partly repeating here. "It is a work that owes little to precedent and yet is infused with the best traditions of the past. Indeed, without eulogising it beyond its legitimate merit, one might claim that it supplies suggestions for a new architectural style."

The author sets up such work against contemporary European design. "Since 1888, when the first Arts and Crafts Exhibition was held at the New Gallery, much has happened. Then, the average man looked upon the new Society as a fresh attempt to revive the so-called 'aesthetic craze', which born in *Punch*, died in *Patience*. Now, eight years after, Paris has an 'Arts and Crafts' – *L'Art Nouveau*; the two great Salons admit examples of the applied arts . . . We see also that English decorative art is less swayed by mere singularity than many Continental movements, whose supporters believe themselves in close sympathy with it. Japan, that has played havoc with Continental design, is scarce felt in the exhibitions of this society. The traditions of the English Gothic revival, purged of their narrowness, still permeate the Exhibition . . . the principles of sound construction and honest work . . ." So, arising out of Townsend's fireplace exhibit, we have here a valuable statement by the organ of the Arts and Crafts Movement of its own relationship to *Art Nouveau* as early as 1896.

The house (also of 1896) for which this fireplace was designed, 'Linden Haus', Dusseldorf in Germany, is a disappointment. Doubtless with the well-intentioned Arts and Crafts notions of fitting a building to local traditions and materials, Townsend's design[37] shows a Teutonic type of mansion with great curling Dutch

8 *Brereton House, Cheshire. An Elizabethan house illustrated in* The Mansions of England in the Olden Time *by Joseph Nash (London 1849). A 1906 edition had an introduction by C. Harrison Townsend.*

9 *Bookplate for Angus Hooper, designed by Townsend 1894. Influenced by* Art Nouveau, *but Arts and Crafts decoration developed a manner of its own, based on a strong rectangular framework.*

10 *C. Harrison Townsend. Fireplace for 'Linden Haus', Dusseldorf (1896). Exhibited at the Arts and Crafts Exhibition that year and widely praised.*

gables and much strapwork.

In the same year's Royal Academy exhibition, Townsend showed an astonishing painting of a design for a picture gallery for Whitechapel in the East End of London, which had been commissioned from him late in the previous year, 1895, by Canon Barnett. Exhibitions of paintings for the East Enders had been arranged annually in a school by Barnett since 1881 and were so successful that a permanent home was now planned. One of the Trustees was Miss P. D. Townsend, a close friend of the Barnetts, and her brother Charles was appointed architect.

This first Whitechapel design of 1896[38], for a broader frontage than was finally available, repeated the symmetry and twin-towered motif seen at Bishopsgate, but put far more emphasis on breadth and massiveness. There is little floral relief tiling here. The walls are battered – sloping up the height of the towers – and the corners rounded, giving an echo of cliff formations. The advance and retreat of the frontage is tremendous, for over the main doorway (an echo of St Martin's church) the upper storeys are pushed right back some 8 feet – then the large but unconvincing pitched roof would have projected 'three or four feet' over the wall to shelter the huge 65 by 17 foot figured mosaic designed by Walter Crane. Apart from the mosaic, the colours were to be yellow stone, marble doorway and bands, and green tiles on the roofs. The towers advance even further than the main doorway and the organic impression is accentuated by the sloping and roughly dressed stone at their bases. In the design of the topmost cupolas, Townsend for once uses a motif that goes

11 *C. Harrison Townsend. First design for Whitechapel Art Gallery (1895). An extraordinary and ambitious composition, later radically revised. The tower design was used in an altered form in the Horniman Museum.*

back to MacLaren's prototypes for the fashion of a decade earlier. These towers are impressive and original, but perhaps the most surprising thing is that within a year Townsend simply lifted one of them, removed the top cupola, raised the ring of the balcony and enlarged its semi-circle into a large clock, made some other small alterations – and there was the tower of the Horniman Museum. The Whitechapel design was to be revised later, so we shall leave it for the moment.

The story of F. J. Horniman MP, is a charming one. A highly successful tea merchant, he collected anthropological items passionately on his travels and so many students visited him that he finally opened his house in Forest Hill, south London to the public in 1890. The collection went on growing and he built an extension in 1893. 90,383 people visited it in 1895. Finally, in desperation, Horniman commissioned Townsend to design a special museum building in January 1896, laid the foundation stone on 16 November that year and paid for the building which he gave to the London County Council (complete with collection) when it was opened on 30 June 1901.[39] The Library and Lecture Hall on the left, seen from the road, were added by Townsend in 1910.

The site was long, narrow and sloping, so Townsend planned it with two halls end to end, one long hall's floor level flowing through to the upper gallery level of the other hall. Both large white spaces are open and flexible, with high light barrel-vaults reflecting the curve of the pediment on the front wall outside. Smaller side galleries give space for exhibits that need such rooms. The clarity of this plan has been obscured by recent ill-advised alterations and Townsend's few touches of foliated decoration on capitals have unbelievably been plastered over.

The plan is a distinguished one, the spaces are open and free and, in spite of the visual contrast between inside and outside already mentioned, the superb exterior makes this one of the few masterpieces of English free style architecture. The tower is the fulcrum of the frontage design, a fascinating piece of flowing solid form that rises from the ground as a square and grows upwards into five circles richly clothed in carved stone foliage. From this tower, the end wall of the exhibition halls form the contrasting horizontal, curved at the top with the lines of the barrel-vault, a blank arcade below that and then the great dominating mosaic by Robert Anning Bell. The visitor's approach is as unobvious as the rest – he is led up steps towards a blank wall, turned right towards a mighty voussoired Romanesque doorway (of Townsend's own patent type, seen in many of his designs) under the tower, turned left into the building, and then back almost to where he started before he finds the first exhibits. It is a masterly spatial sequence.

As far as we know, the museum was completed in 1901 pretty well as Townsend designed it in 1896,

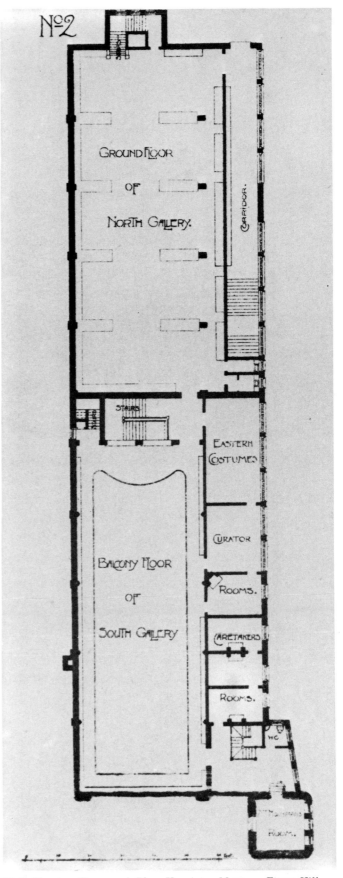

12 C. Harrison Townsend. Plan, Horniman Museum, Forest Hill, London (designed 1896, built 1896–1901). The floor level of the North Gallery flows through into balcony level of the lower South Gallery. Entrance and tower below.

13 *C. Harrison Townsend. Horniman Museum (designed 1896, opened 1901, left-hand block added 1910). The tower starts square in plan, but as it rises turns into four small circles around one large one.*

14 *C. Harrison Townsend. Interior, Horniman Museum (designed 1896, opened 1901) showing high barrel vault, and doorway capital decoration, now vandalised by proprietors.*

except for the absence of the curving-topped wall beside the road shown in earlier drawings. One of the most flowing of all his designs may also have been done that year, for it was complete and reproduced in *The Studio* in 1897.[40] This was a font for All Saints church, Ennismore Gardens, whose exterior he had already rebuilt. The cover of the font, if not quite so organic as Harry Wilson's church work of this period (perhaps the most inspired plate designs of the epoch), flows and ripples with an intriguing fluidity.

The trade mark of the voussoirs or radiating brackets of Townsend's own favourite door-hood design re-appear in one of his best house plans for 'Cliff Towers', above Salcombe Harbour on the Devon coast, designed in 1898.[41] There are touches of Voysey and still hints of Richardson, this time in the curving roofs which remind one of the swooping tiles of the American's marvellous railway stations. But by now Townsend had digested such influences into an individual style of his own. Three of the four walls are battered, sloping inwards on both storeys, again expressing the house's growth from the ground. The lines are long and low, well punctuated by strong accents, and the plan attractive.[42]

Meanwhile, the Trustees of the Whitechapel Art Gallery were having trouble in raising funds for their building and in 1899 they asked Townsend to revise his scheme for a smaller area. This was done promptly and the new design[43] was built and opened on 12 March 1901. Unfortunately, there was no money to carry out Crane's mosaic and the great panel remains blank to this day. The only other omission from the second design was the single cupola above each tower.

The plan makes clever use of yet another long narrow site by providing a full-width, ground-floor hall with a narrower hall above it – thus allowing quite a lot of top-lighting at the sides of the lower level and full top-lighting above. The interiors are determinedly unobtrusive, leaving the exhibits to catch the eye.

The street frontage, however, has the job of drawing attention to the art gallery's presence and it certainly fulfils that function. The 1899 design abandons the symmetry of the earlier 1896 drawings, putting the weight of Townsend's idosyncratic Romanesque doorway on the left. This change is in line with the Horniman frontage (done between the two Whitechapel designs), where the tower acts as the chief accent and the rest grows from that.

Although to some extent we may see the Whitechapel façade as a descendant of Godwin's and MacLaren's asymmetrical house fronts, there is a crucial difference in the composition. These earlier designers built up their compositions by balancing each off-centre accent with one or more carefully calculated accents on the other side, juggling with sizes and textures. Townsend's Whitechapel design, on the other hand, rises from a massive doorway that roots it to the ground (the smaller doorway has little weight). Above and around this, a great blank solid band rises to one of those strips of windows (sometimes arcades) which Townsend by now used in completely his own way. From this level up, the frontage is completely symmetrical, even in the areas of foliated relief tiles. The towers, as designed, have obvious links with MacLaren's Stirling High School, but this disappears without the cupolas.

The Whitechapel Gallery and the Horniman Museum were opened in March and June 1901 respectively. Meanwhile, Townsend's domestic practice continued.

15 *Entrance elevation, 'Cliff Towers', Salcombe, Devon, designed by Townsend 1898, his most ambitious house design. The influences of Richardson, Voysey and others are still apparent, but have been transformed into Townsend's personal style. Apparently not built.*

16 *C. Harrison Townsend. Whitechapel Art Gallery as re-designed by Townsend in 1899, opened 1901. The cupolas and the huge mosaic were never carried out.*

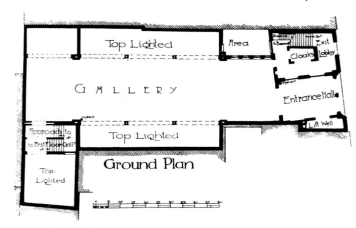

17 C. Harrison Townsend. Ground plan, Whitechapel Art Gallery, Whitechapel, London, as revised in 1899, built and opened in 1901. The smaller upper gallery allowed much top lighting in the ground floor gallery too.

18 C. Harrison Townsend. Whitechapel Art Gallery.

'Dickhurst' is a large house on a hillside near Haslemere, Surrey, built in 1900[44], though I have already mentioned that it may have been designed as early as 1894 or '95. It has a long bending lineal plan and its elevations are made up of contrasting sections of varying cottage materials (half-timbering, then hung tiles, then roughcast) typical of Townsend's earlier work.

In late 1901 or early 1902, Townsend was approached by a Mr Evelyn Heseltine and asked to design a memorial church for his late brother, Arnold Heseltine. Townsend accepted the commission and a group of Arts and Crafts artists joined him; William Reynolds-Stephens did all the inventive interior metal-work and Heywood Sumner the stained glass (mostly lost in 1940, leaving only the original apse windows). This was the church of St Mary the Virgin, Great Warley, southwest of Brentwood in Essex.[45] The foundation stone was laid 3 July 1902 and the church dedicated in 1904, but Reynolds-Stephens worked on at the metal fittings until 1906.

The plan is a straightforward, if slightly irregular, Latin cross; nave, choir and chancel apse with a chapel on one side and vestry on the other. The church is approached through carefully designed gardens. Once again, in Townsend's third church, the outside is simple – we do not know whether it was architect or client who rejected this opportunity for loosing Townsend's imagination on plan and exterior.

As it is, the outside of the small building is pleasing in a simple way, roughcast walls and tiled gable roofs, with a little broach bell-tower and spire. Pevsner has called it 'à la Voysey' and one sees what he means, although the line of windows at the west end, the way the corner buttresses are handled and the rose window are characteristic Townsend.

The detail of the interior has been fully described and photographed in an article by Mr John Malton.[46] Townsend and Reynolds-Stephens worked harmoniously on the decorative scheme for the interior, and the result is one of the culminating church works of the Arts and Crafts Movement, together with the Prior and the Lethaby churches, and comparable with Sedding and Wilson's much earlier Sloane Street masterpiece. Basically, the spaces, walls, ceilings and seating are Townsend's but all other fittings (including font, screens, throne and lights) are Reynolds-Stephens.

The flow of space between areas defined by the twining floral screens creates some mystery as one advances towards the chancel. The architectural style, doubtless intentionally, fits into no historical category. Although the large vaults and arches of nave and chapel are pointed, others are rounded and Townsend's panelling has a round-topped motif. We are nowhere in earlier history, he is saying, we are in 1902. The chancel is the climax of the church, richly decorated and centring on Reynolds-Stephens' altar.

In 1902 and 1903 Townsend must have seemed to himself and to others to be launched on a successful lose all interest in the ideal of a free style for the time and in the originality that Townsend had to offer. He was not alone. Mackmurdo left London in about 1900, Ashbee in 1901. Lethaby ceased practice in 1902 and Prior built little after the middle of the decade. Voysey too made no great advances after the early 1900s, though his practice continued to flourish – as did that of Baillie Scott, who went on experimenting quietly with flowing internal spaces. Mackintosh was still to produce his greatest work in 1906, before his own fading began. But of all the English free style architects, only Leonard Stokes and Lancashire's Edgar Wood, pushed by a young partner called Sellers, were to start on exciting new courses at the start of Edward VII's reign. And Norman Shaw, a jump ahead to the end, joined the Edwardian Baroque movement in his old age and produced some of its best monuments.

In Townsend's case the ebb of fashion left him empty. He rejected the ideas of the Grand Manner and went on building houses, village halls and country schools (besides those already mentioned, twenty other minor works are known, mostly undated) and lecturing on mosaics. He shared a house with his sister and spent much of his time at the St John's Wood Art Club and the Art Workers' Guild – for whom he arranged tours of

Holland, Antwerp, Paris and Ghent between 1906 and 1914. He became a member of the R.I.B.A. Council in 1905, and Chairman of its Literary Committee in 1915. He published a number of articles and, when the Civic Survey was started in 1915, he became Assistant Director. So in general, he busied himself with fringe activities and small commissions. He certainly had no shortage of the latter, uninteresting though most may be. We can date fifteen commissions between 1903 and 1911, while Townsend's *Who's Who in Architecture* entry and other sources give another sixteen undated.[54]

When war broke out in 1914, Townsend was a man of sixty-three, but from 1916 to 1918 he was commissioned as a Lieutenant in the Royal Navy at Avonmouth to supervise the dazzle painting of ships which the painter Norman Wilkinson had invented and persuaded the Admiralty to adopt, with great success.

After the war, Townsend arranged one more Art Workers' Guild trip in 1920, this time to Normandy where his own first foreign journey had taken him. After that, apart from several moves of his own residence (from St John's Wood to Northwood) and two articles in *The Architects' Journal* in 1925 and 1927, there is nothing to note until his death on 26 December 1928 at 30 Murray Road, Northwood. He is buried in

21 *C. Harrison Townsend. 'Cobbins', Blackheath, near Guildford, Surrey (circa 1907, for himself). After 1904 Townsend's only large building was the library added to the Horniman Museum. His many commissions for houses were designed in a quieter local vernacular manner, with only occasional appearances of his earlier originality, as in the long angles of 'Cobbins'.*

Northwood Cemetery with his sister under a grave-stone of his own design.

Townsend was illustrated by Muthesius and was certainly one of the best known British Arts and Crafts architects on the Continent. In Britain, disciples included W. G. Lamond in Dundee[55] and H. Fuller Clark in London, among others, but for a short time only.

The Times obituary in 1928 commented "Townsend's death leaves a gap in the dwindling group of men who, in the 'nineties and later, worked for a revival of interest in architecture and the allied arts on a modern note, respecting tradition but trying to avoid imitation of past styles, a movement which is growing stronger daily as the newer conditions and changes in materials give opportunity."

"He was a man much appreciated by his friends, to whom his wide knowledge and a certain whimsical quippish humour, always accompanied by a touch of old fashioned courtesy, endeared him."

In the R.I.B.A. Journal his obituary appeared aptly beside that of Charles Rennie Mackintosh.

Townsend's reputation stands or falls by his larger buildings, for his domestic work rarely rises higher than the quite interestingly experimental. His linear planning is certainly strange but not as convincing as the experiments by Prior, Baillie Scott and Voysey. Indeed Goodhart-Rendel dismissed Townsend as "of no importance" in his 'Roll-Call'[56] of architects of the period. But then he dismissed Voysey too.

If we were to apply the beliefs of the 1960s and '70s to Townsend's large buildings, the dichotomy between his exteriors and his interiors might well be described as thoroughly bad architecture. But this really will not do, for it is foisting on Townsend principles of external expression of structure which he would have thought nonsense. He would point out that, within reason, the plans and sections of the Whitechapel Gallery (a narrow toplit gallery above a broad one, with a floor of offices between) and of the Horniman Museum (the narrow end of the big double gallery, with the great curve of the rounded vaulting above) were expressed by their street elevations. The interiors moreover, were excellently rational – indeed progressive – *structures*. Further, he would answer that it was the function and spirit of the buildings that he had tried to express on their exteriors, and he could make a very fair case on these grounds. He was also concerned, as were a number of his notable contemporaries, with creating exteriors that used forms and decoration associated with the natural formations of rocky outcrops and trees, but organized into compositions that were clearly man-built and clearly of their own time.

Townsend's exteriors took this ideal of the union of modern organic design with tradition very much further than anyone else in England, and by his very success in applying such principles to three impressive public buildings that were actually built, he is of considerable importance in the history of free design in architecture. As it turned out, his museum and art gallery were to be the final large-scale non-ecclesiastical successes of that movement in London.

[1] Penguin edition 1960, p.165.

[2] P. Wentworth-Sheilds' thesis 1963, a copy of which is in R.I.B.A Library. Richard Allan Woollard thesis, School of Architecture, Cambridge, 1971–72.

[3] General Register Office. The usually given date of 1852 is incorrect. Peter Wentworth-Sheilds has a copy of the birth certificate.

[4] The basic information was given to Peter Wentworth-Sheilds in a personal letter from Miss St Clair Townsend (Townsend's neice) dated 18 January 1963.

[5] Townsend told an R.I.B.A. meeting on 19 March 1906 that he had worked with Nesfield.

[6] Townsend's letter, commenting on an article in a Venice Newspaper, was published in *The Builder*, 16 January 1881.

[7] See *The Builder* 4 August 1883; 12 January 1884; 5 April 1884 and 1 November 1884. One may guess from this that Townsend was an acquaintance of H. H. Statham, who became editor of *The Builder* in 1883 and sought out architects with the new ideas of the time.

[8] *The Builder* 25 December 1886.

[9] Voysey's designs were first published in *The British Architect* 7 December 1888, though it is of course quite possible that Townsend knew him and had seen some of his drawings. The chapel also has a striking resemblance to some of H. H. Richardson's small railway stations designed from 1880 onwards, though I cannot find any publication of these in English magazines before *The British Architect* 23 September 1887. But again, Horace Townsend had met Richardson about 1880 and unpublished drawings may have circulated among young English architects.

[10] *The Builder* 22 January 1887.

[11] See lists and dates of Guild membership in H. L. J. Massé's *Art-Workers' Guild*, Shakespeare Head Press, Oxford 1935.

[12] Lethaby, Newton, Voysey, Pite and most of the other early Guild members were born in the late 1850s or 1860s. Massé's book lists the journeys and festivities organized by Townsend.

[13] Information given in a personal letter in 1972 to Mr Woollard.

[14] The work was not illustrated in the building magazines at the time. See Mr Woollard's thesis.

[15] Illustrated in *The Builder* 30 October 1897. Mr Wentworth-Sheilds now owns the water-colour shown there, which was given to him by Miss St Clair Townsend.

[16] *The British Architect* 30 March 1883.

[17] Now in the Victoria and Albert Museum.

[18] From 1883 onwards *The British Architect* and *The Builder* both illustrated many new American buildings, after largely ignoring them previously. This may have some connection with Richardson's visit to London the previous year.

[19] See M. G. Van Rensselaer, *Henry Hobson Richardson and his Works*, Houghton Mifflin, Boston 1888 and reprinted Dover Publications, New York 1969.

[20] *The Magazine of Art* February 1894.

[21] M. G. Van Rensselaer, *op cit* p.52. It is possible that this feature inspired the appearance of a number of such figured friezes in progressive English architecture (notably Belcher and Pite's Institute of Chartered Accountants, designed 1888), though they are used in a different way.

[22] See M. G. Van Rensselaer, *op cit* pp.83 and 102.

[23] Townsend's articles etc. giving information on his approach to architecture are: 'The Value of Precedent' in *The Studio* Vol. 4 1894, p.88; 'Originality in Architectural Design' read to the Architectural Association with H. T. Hare as chairman in 1902, and causing obvious conservative fury among some of his listeners judging from the discussion afterwards (paper and discussion are printed in *The Builder* Vol. 82, p.133. Further correspondence on the subject in *A.A. Notes* Vol. 17, pp.33–39; 'The Training of the Architect Today' in *The Architect's Journal* 1925, p.431.

[24] See N. Pevsner and J. Richards, *The Anti-Rationalists* The Architectural Press, London 1973 for Sherban Cantacuzino's impressive article on Guimard and the development of *Art Nouveau*.

[25] N. Pevsner, *Pioneers of the Modern Movement*, 1936 edition. The same idea is repeated in slightly different words in the 1960 Penguin edition of *Pioneers of Modern Design*, p.107, the quotation from Walter Crane being from his *William Morris to Whistler*, London 1911, p.232.

[26] See *The Anti-Rationalists* p.22.

[27] But see some of the detail of Webb's 'Clouds' house (1881–86) for possible influence of Richardson or vice-versa.

[28] See Massé, *op cit.*

[29] Illustrated in *The British Architect* 6 May 1887.

[30] *Journal of the Royal Institute of British Architects* Series 3, Vol. 8.

[31] See *The Builder* Vol. 67, p.374.

[32] See *The Builder* as above, and *The Architect* Vol. 54, 1895, p.416.

[33] Wilson's Library design (executed more simply) was illustrated in *The Architect* in June 1890 and elsewhere, Richardson's Chamber of Commerce in M. G. Van Rensselaer *op cit* p.97 (1888).

[34] Illustrated in *The British Architect* as far back as 5 January and 30 March 1883.

[35] *The Studio* Vol. 4, October 1894.

[36] *The Studio* Vol. 9, October 1896.

[37] *The Builder* 11 July 1896.

[38] *Academy Architecture* 1896; *The Studio* 1897.

[39] Three photographs in *The Architect* Vol. 66, 1901, p.40, also illustrated in *The Builder* Vol. 82, 1902, p.138.

[40] *The Studio* Vol. 12, 1897, p.118.

[41] *The Builder* Vol. 75, 1898, pp.230 and 343, *The Studio* Vol. 13, 1898, p.239.

[42] The description in *The Builder* of 10 September 1898 says that the house "is built" but goes on to say that wallpaper "will be used". However, Richard Woollard tells me that efforts to trace it have been fruitless.

[43] Published in *The Building News* 1899, pp.85–92; *The Studio* Vol. 16, 1899, p.196; *The Builders Journal and Architects Record* 1899, p.204.

[44] Mr Woollard's thesis places this design in the early 1890s on stylistic grounds and because the contractor is reported as saying "Mr Townsend should have kept to churches."

[45] See *The Art Journal* 1905, pp.67–78; *The Studio* February 1905, and *The Builders Journal and Architects Record* 1905, p.312.

[46] Originally published in *The Architectural Review* August–September 1959 and reprinted in N. Pevsner and J. Richards, *The Anti-Rationalists* The Architectural Press, London 1973.

[47] *The Builder* 3 October 1903.

[48] A model of the building was exhibited at the Arts and Crafts Exhibition in 1906.

[49] All three were illustrated in Mervyn Macartney's *Recent English Domestic Architecture* London, 1908.

[50] *The Builder* 26 October 1907.

[51] 'The Wakes' is now called 'Peerie Hame', unbelievable as it may seem.

[52] Illustrated in Banister Fletcher's *The English House* London 1910.

[53] *The Builder* 4 June 1910.

[54] Village Cross, West Meon, Hampshire, 1902.
Pulpit, Bristol Cathedral, 1903. Design exhibited at The Royal Academy.
Extension, 'Nut Tree Hall', Plaxtol, Kent, 1905.
Competition design for a school at Richmond, Surrey, 1905.
Arbuthnot Institute Hall, Shamley Green, Surrey, 1906.
House for Sir John Gorst, in The Glade, Letchworth, Hertfordshire, 1906 (illustrated in *The Studio* 14 July 1906 and *The English House* by Banister Fletcher 1910).
'Blatchcombe', Chilworth, Surrey (between 1900 and 1906) (illustrated in *Recent English Domestic Architecture* by Mervyn Macartney, 1908).
'Theobalds', Blackheath, Near Chilworth, Surrey, 1900–1906 (illustrated as above).
'Cobbins' (for self), Blackheath, near Chilworth, Surrey, between 1900 and 1906 (illustrated as above).
Competition design for school at Wimbledon, 1907.
Upper storey, London School of Printing, Elephant and Castle, London 1908. (Now demolished.)
Vicarage, 1907, and probably a number of other cottages at and around Blackheath, Surrey.
Design for a portable garage, Lewisham (*The Builder*, 1908).
Small schools for Penn, Buckinghamshire and for Holmer Green, Buckinghamshire, 1909–10.
'The Wakes' (now 'Peerie Hame'), Guildown, near Guildford, Surrey, *circa* 1910.
Alterations to 'Hallingbury Place', Bishops Stortford, 1910. (Now demolished.)
Village Hall, Panshangar, Hertfordshire, 1910.
Library and Lecture Room, Horniman Museum, Forest Hill, London, 1910–11.
Garden for house in Whitehall Gardens, Westminster, 1910. (Now demolished.)
'Shankhill', near Dublin.
'Llanover Court', Surrey.
'Littleton House', Uxbridge.
'Hall Barn', Robertsbridge.
'Broadlands', Liverpool.
'Cowesfield', Wiltshire.
'Oxford House', Godalming, Surrey.
'Missenden House', Buckinghamshire.
'Ingfield Hall', Settle.
'Highcliffe', Hampshire.
Lodge, Castle Ashby, Northamptonshire.
House for C. E. Masterman, Northwood.
House, 135–141, Hampstead Way, Hampstead Garden Suburb, London. (The R.I.B.A. has a drawing entitled 2 Temple Fortune Lane, Hampstead.)
Restoration at Compton Wynyates.
Memorial, Dehra Doon, India.
Own gravestone, Northwood Churchyard, Middlesex (? 1920s).

[55] See *The Architectural Review* 1958.

[56] 'Goodhart-Rendel's Rollcall', edited by N. Pevsner, *The Architectural Review* 1965, Vol. 138, p.263 and in this volume pp.   – .

Part Four: Scotland at the End of the Century

Nineteenth-century architecture in Scotland is if anything even more complicated than in England, and this account is necessarily over-simplified. The early part of the century in cities was dominated by the Neo-Grec style, of which William Henry Playfair (1790–1857) and Thomas Hamilton (1784–1858) in Edinburgh were the finest practitioners, while Alexander Thomson (1817–1875) in Glasgow took up the style in about 1850 and used it to produce a series of brilliantly original masterpieces in the following quarter-century.

The Gothic Revival was not strong in Scotland, but in the countryside William Burn (1789–1870) had been building big neo-Tudor and neo-Jacobean houses as early as the 1820s. As the 1830s wore on, Burn started to introduce an increasing number of 16th- and 17th-century Scottish-Baronial features into his work, particularly after adding a new wing to the ancient Castle Menzies at the end of the decade. Burn was the favourite architect of the Tory aristocrats and gentry. His equivalent for the Whigs was the same W. H. Playfair who is mentioned above, but by the early 1830s Playfair too was introducing historical Scottish forms into some of his country houses.

Thus it seems to have been from these upper-class practices that the interest in vernacular Scottish forms was brought to the towns. During the 1850s some of the baronial country mansions became almost Wagnerian-Scottish in feeling and scale particularly after William Smith's Balmoral (inspired by Burn) for the Queen in 1852–54 and the work of David Bryce (1803–76), a partner of Burn for a time, at Kinnaird and elsewhere from 1854 onwards. But meanwhile some strange things were happening in the wild designs of James Gowans, Thornton Shiells, F. T. Pilkington and others in Edinburgh, most of whom had been pupils of Burn and Bryce.

More significantly still, the Glaswegian Campbell Douglas (1828–1910) returned from a long spell in England to practice in Glasgow in 1856. Douglas built Gothic churches (Gothic established itself only for ecclesiastical work in Scotland) but also became a fine designer of baronial domestic work and interested in extending and restoring old baronial castles. Many architects who were to become influential worked in his office for various periods, including J. J. Stevenson (another Bryce pupil who became Douglas's partner), Bruce Talbert, William Leiper, James MacLaren, George Washington Browne, William Flockhart and John Brydon. The office was clearly one of the progressive hot-houses in the 1860s and early '70s and, as four of those mentioned above migrated to successful practices in London, had a notable influence on developments in England too. But during the 1870s the firm changed, for James Sellars (1843–88) became Douglas's partner after Stevenson's departure, and Sellars took over the bold neo-Grec mantle of Alexander Thomson in Glasgow for a few years after the latter's death in 1875.

It was in 1881 that George Washington Browne (1853–1939) transferred from Stevenson's and Nesfield's offices to that of R. Rowand Anderson (1834–1921). Anderson was already an interesting architect, ready to experiment with new versions of old Scottish and other forms, though always restrained and scholarly. Browne's arrival in his firm encouraged him to bolder Scottish 16th- and 17th-century style work in the 1880s.

Meanwhile in western Scotland another influence had entered the picture. From the 1870s onwards a series of young Glasgow architects went to Paris for training at the École des Beaux Arts. These included the young John Burnet (son of a prosperous architect), John A. Campbell, R. D. Sandilands, John Keppie and A. N. Paterson. By the end of the decade, Burnet (1857–1938) was back and soon took over much of the running of his father's established practice. For some years (during the slump following the Glasgow bank crash in 1878) this French influence was evident in Burnet's designs, but in 1886 Campbell (1859–1909) joined him as a partner. The two young men started a practice that produced distinguished buildings in many historicist styles, but at the same time began a long slow move towards a free architecture.

This then was the situation in Scotland in the mid 1880s: a splendid series of new Gothic churches was flourishing, neo-Grec and other classical forms were still alive and kicking, with a new Beaux Arts injection of life. Scholarly baronial, with French or Tudor or Jacobean appearing occasionally, dominated the country house practices. The baronial vernacular was increasingly appearing in urban street architecture as well, attracting those who believed in developing a truly Scottish modern style. And a new generation of young architects was working towards a tradition-based but non-revivalist Scottish architecture.

It was not only in buildings that new ideas were appearing, for the Glasgow school produced a number of revolutionary painters during this time. No one interested in the arts in general could be unaware of the strange new shapes coming from the Arts and Crafts designers in England, while before long the influence of the flowing *Art Nouveau* movement on the continent of Europe began to be felt. Finally, the London Scot James MacLaren (1843–90) had built an extraordinary school in Stirling in 1887 and some other Scottish works with overtones of the American school of H. H. Richardson that pre-echoed the new forms that were to appear in the 1890s.

The Glasgow free style – with its own strong and craggy character quite different from the English – emerged early in that decade from the formative influences just mentioned. Burnet and Campbell's Athenaeum Theatre of 1891 and the Glasgow Herald building of 1893, detailed by the young Charles Rennie Mackintosh (1868–1928) for his firm of Honeyman and Keppie, were the trail-blazers, using classical and other historical forms in a way that shattered scholasticism.

1 *Alexander Thomson. St Vincent Street Church, Glasgow (1859). 'Greek' Thomson's influence dominated Glasgow architecture between 1850 and 1875.*

By the end of the century, Mackintosh's great Glasgow School of Art was started, while James Salmon the younger (1873–1924) had built (with his partner J. G. Gillespie) his Mercantile Chambers and started his own individualistic series of buildings. These four architects – Burnet, Campbell, Mackintosh and Salmon – are the most important of a considerable group of men who developed a new Scottish architecture until the end of the Edwardian period. In passing we must also mention interesting free work (some in the '80s and increasingly in the '90s) by John Bridgeford Pirie of Aberdeen, William Gillespie Lamond of Dundee, Charles G. Soutar, the partnership of Patrick Thoms and William Wilkie, the early works of R. S. Lorimer and Mackintosh's friend and collaborator George Walton, who later moved from Glasgow to England to join the mainstream of Arts and Crafts activities.

If the Arts and Crafts existed as a movement in England, it did not do so in Scotland; but its influence can be seen in design and in attitudes. Edinburgh and Aberdeen remained almost completely aloof from these new influences, preferring an eclectic mixture of styles well exemplified by the work of Aberdeen's A. Marshall Mackenzie and Edinburgh's George Washington Browne. Glasgow's J. J. Burnet (later Sir John) was, from several points of view, the leading Scottish architect of his generation. His position in Scotland was in some ways similar to that of Norman Shaw in England: he was immensely successful in worldly terms, he could work wonders in almost any style of design and he remained influential on progressive young architects. In about 1904 Burnet opened a London office and it soon flourished as much as his Glasgow practice. His commercial buildings of the Edwardian period in both countries (and those of his partner John A. Campbell, who practised independently from 1897 onwards) are powerful masterpieces in their own right and milestones in the development of a rational modern architecture.

If Burnet was the Scottish master-architect of his time, Charles Rennie Mackintosh was the soaring genius. All the fashionable influences of the period appear in Mackintosh's work, including the continental *Art Nouveau* in his decoration. But by 1900 he had digested them all and out of the melting pot came a series of highly personal free style buildings of lasting fascination. The chapter on Mackintosh is a *tour de force* of scholarly detective work, tracing the sources of his inspiration and the process by which he turned such influences into the inspired works that have justly become famous.

The other architects of the Scottish free style dealt with here are the younger James Salmon and his partner John Gaff Gillespie (1870–1926). Mackintosh's fame has perhaps obscured the originality of the other highly talented architects working in Scotland at the time, and this study of Salmon and Gillespie should do much to bring two of them recognition. Salmon's

strange 'Hatrack' building and astonishing Lion Chambers in Glasgow are among the most interesting buildings of the Edwardian period.

Indeed Glasgow contributed more large-scale buildings to the harvest of free style architecture than did any other city. By the time that war broke out in 1914 the period of vigour was finished. Burnet had moved to London, and found further success. Campbell was dead. Mackintosh too emigrated to London, but found only failure and obscurity. Salmon and Gillespie stayed in Scotland, though their practice and their original creativity dwindled. But they and their contemporaries left behind a legacy of buildings that makes Glasgow still the treasure house of the free style period.

2

2 *James Gowans. Rockville House (for himself), No. 3 Napier Road, Edinburgh (1858). Demolished. An attempt to create a non-historical style.*

3 *Crathes Castle, Kincardineshire, Scotland (16th century). One of the many Scottish castles whose features were widely taken up after 1880 as a 'vernacular' British architecture.*

4 *John James Burnet and John Archibald Campbell. Interior, The Barony Church, Castle Street, Glasgow (1886). One of the finest of many notable Gothic churches built in Glasgow. The Gothic style was hardly used for secular buildings in Scotland.*

5 *James MacLaren. Courtyard frontage, Stirling High School (1887–88). The American influence of H. H. Richardson is here blended with ideas developing among the Arts and Crafts architects, as well as with MacLaren's own strong individuality.*

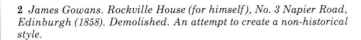

Sir John James Burnet

by David Walker

In some ways the Scottish counterpart of Norman Shaw, Sir John
Burnet (1857–1938) overcame the inhibitions of his Parisian Beaux
Arts training and dominated Scottish architecture by the end of the
19th century. His classical and Gothic buildings have great
splendour, but it is particularly for his powerful free and
increasingly rational buildings of the Edwardian period, both in
Scotland and England, that we value his great work so highly today.

"*How could a man develop from a Beaux Arts training in Paris to the bold and wholly convincing angular neo-Baroque of the narrow front of the Athenaeum Theatre of 1891 and end with the calm and competent classical Edward VII's Galleries of the British Museum on the one hand with the 'Early Modern' Kodak Building in London and the Wallace Scott tailoring factory at Cathcart on the other? Or do all these buildings represent different men in one liberally run office?*"

sir nikolaus pevsner, *1968*

Since Charles Rennie Mackintosh died, his reputation has gradually eclipsed that of Sir John James Burnet. In their lifetime the situation was very different. Mackintosh had a small specialised practice, Burnet a large and varied one which was the mecca of every aspiring Glasgow apprentice. Sir John was all things to all people, a cultured charmer, an excellent classicist, a skilful Goth and a significant modernist without indulging in detail which might outrage the conventional sensibilities of the post-*Art Nouveau* era. He was *apparently* rich, and much honoured in England, Scotland and France in an era which still set great store by that kind of success. Now it is Mackintosh's unique imaginativeness and singleness of purpose which is valued, and the antipathy between the two artists has lived on after them to Burnet's discredit. And paradoxically, Burnet's own success has put him at a disadvantage, for Burnet as modernist has been obscured by his spectacular skill as stylist. But it should never be forgotten that Burnet began designing in the 1870s, Mackintosh in the 1890s. He was of an earlier generation, and that, even more than differences in training, travel, background and range of practice, saw to it that their approach to modern design would be different.

John James Burnet was born on 31 March 1857, youngest son of John Burnet Senior (1814–1901) who had graduated from joinery to one of the largest practices in Glasgow. The elder Burnet was a skilful eclectic architect, but the driving force in the Burnet family was his wife, Elizabeth Hay Bennet, ambitious for both her husband and her sons. John James was sent to the Collegiate School, the Western Academy, and Blair Lodge, and, unlike his parents, grew to only average stature. After a two-year introduction to architecture in his father's office he resolved to train at the École des Beaux Arts, apparently prompted by Phené Spiers whom his father knew through the Architectural Publication Society. His parents did not approve. It was foreign, not to say dangerous, expensive and pointless when there was already a strong architectural tradition in Glasgow. But they were won over, and in the autumn of 1874 Spiers introduced him to Jean-Louis Pascal who became his 'second father'. In Pascal's *atelier* he respected his parents' warnings about Paris to such a

degree that his cheerful moral rectitude earned him the *petit-nom* of 'Joseph' while his fresh Scottish complexion brought that of '*Confiture des Groseilles*'. In 1877 he returned home with the *Diplôme du Gouvernement* in architecture and engineering, and the lifelong friendship of 'Père' Pascal and his pupil Henri-Paul Nénot. In later years Burnet thought he had not been influenced stylistically by Pascal, whose aim was to develop the individuality of the pupil, but Pascal's love of sculptural treatment and of teaching both left their mark as did the École's emphasis on logic.[1] What Theodore Fyfe described as his "child-like" directness of character formed the perfect matrix for the École's teaching. Goodhart-Rendel recalled that he had a "tremendous love of order and system. He never lost hold of the essentials and thought no one in England knew anything about them. He used to say that nothing ought to be done without a decision behind it."[2] Burnet claimed never to start with a preconceived idea, but to allow the design first in plan, then in construction, and finally in elevation to grow out of the requirements of his client. Essentials, decisions and reasons were expounded to clients, staff, family and friends alike, but he wrote little and seldom for publication. Books he used but rarely, though he continued to build up his father's excellent library more for the benefit of the staff than himself; sculptures and good pictures were also added to give a studio, or perhaps we should say *atelier* atmosphere, for he was soon to make his office one of the greatest teaching institutions of its time.

Projects always began with small scale sketches drawn at home. In the office these were drawn up and almost unceasingly experimented upon with tracing paper – rubbing out was not allowed – until a final result was achieved, often studied under a reducing glass and miniaturised again to the smaller scales in which he thought best, methods derived from his father rather than the École. If a scheme failed to satisfy it was laid aside regardless of time spent and a fresh start made. The assistants learned much from working through these experimental design processes, and although, according to custom, he dealt mainly with the leading draughtsmen, occasionally he stopped to give the juniors a few moments' demonstration in draughtsmanship.

Whether John James assisted in any of his father's projects during his student days is unclear. In 1920 he quoted the Glasgow Fine Art Institute as his first building but in 1921 and 1923 the Union Bank head office in Glasgow (now Lanarkshire House) was included in lists of his principal works and it is possible that he had a hand in its lavishly sculptured façade during the 1875 and 1876 vacations, as indeed certain of its details suggest.[3]

It was, however, his competition win for the Fine Art Institute in May 1878 which made his name. Its aim "to combine Greek with modern French Renaissance" and

2 *Sir John Burnet. Fine Art Institute, Sauchiehall Street, Glasgow (1878–79). Neo-Grec with some French Renaissance details. Sculpture by the Mossmans. Demolished.*

the inclusion of a magnificent frieze to be sculptured by the Mossmans was well calculated to appeal in Glasgow where neo-Greek still had a strong hold.[4] The "modern French Renaissance" element was largely confined to the doorpiece, but its three wide distyle in antis bays broke with the even columniation of Alexander Thomson's neo-Greek school, while within, the clever sidelighting of the stairhall recalled the French mastery of *lumière* as much as Thomson's. The neo-Grec proved, however, to be but a fleeting moment, not to be rediscovered for more than twenty years. A tour through France and Italy in 1881 on which he visited intensively but sketched little, confirmed the generally Renaissance preferences inherited from Pascal and his father.

Glasgow's architects took due note of the success of the École's teaching. John Keppie, John A. Campbell and A. N. Paterson followed Burnet to Pascal's in rapid succession, R. D. Sandilands went to Guadet's while in the Glasgow Municipal Buildings competitions of 1880–83 not only Burnet[5] but the well-established architects Leiper, Salmon and Sellars attempted the Beaux Arts manner. It was, however, to be but a brief incident, more impressive on paper than in executed works. It neither won the Municipal Buildings competition nor appealed to private clients. In Burnet's next two quality commissions in Glasgow's central area the French roofs which characterised the Beaux Arts competition designs of the early '80s were absent. The first of these was the Clyde Trust in Robertson Street of 1883 in which he echoed the swaggering scale and spirit of William Young's successful Municipal Buildings design but with a mastery of composition and detail which was pure Beaux Arts.[6] At the Athenaeum Building in St George's Place (1886) however, Burnet was building for clients who, if not actually artists, at least commanded some connoisseurship. Again an academic simplicity was aimed at, but stylistically more forward looking, closer to the forthcoming American Beaux Arts classicism than the old neo-Grec in its highly simplified restatement of the Arch of Constantine theme in three even Ionic bays. It introduced for the first time details characteristic of his mature manner, notably the door architraves of elongated ogival section and the broad banding together of the basement windows.[7]

The other works of John James's early years were mostly completions, alterations and additions. The City Bank failure had brought a slump in building. His largest domestic commission was Deanston House, Doune (1882–83)[8] where he was, however, obliged to retain a remodelled Georgian house in the centre. In style it consisted of Glasgow Italianate and modern French, a mixture not repeated, Norman Shaw type Tudor and Scots baronial taking over from 1886. Within, some of the detailing, particularly the fine drawing room doorcase, has in its Michaelangelesque feeling (doubtless a product of the 1881 tour) strong hints of the characteristic Burnet detailing of twenty years later.

Edinburgh provided the two other large commissions of those years. He won the competition for the Edinburgh International Exhibition of 1886[9] with a triple-domed scheme which recalled on a small scale the 1878 Paris exhibition building. This was a temporary structure, but his Drumsheugh Bath Club Building of 1882 (rebuilt after a fire in 1893) remains to show how perfectly the young Burnet could master anything he put his mind to. Behind the beautifully detailed Islamic arcaded front building lie utilitarian rubble-and-brick masses of picturesque Eastern European character. Within the main pool is even more evocative with its severe plastered walls, open roof, brick arched openings and elegant arcade of cast iron columns.[10]

By 1882 John James had become his father's partner, acknowledging the fact that the design work of the firm had been his for the previous four years. In 1886 he married Jean Watt Marwick, one of the four six-foot tall daughters of Glasgow's town clerk, Sir James Marwick, and a real late Victorian beauty with an enchanting smile. It was an influential match, but although a wonderful hostess Jean Burnet was also hypochondriac, spending much of her time in bed; Burnet could never bring himself to be firm with her. They had no family but John James's elder brother George died early and they undertook the education of his children John and Edith.

On 13 August 1886 Pascal's pupil John Archibald Campbell (1859–1909) became a partner, the firm becoming John Burnet Son & Campbell. Although at

3 *Sir John Burnet. Glasgow Municipal Buildings Competition, first design (1882). The Beaux Arts influence is still strong.*

4 *Sir John Burnet. The Athenaeum, West George Street, Glasgow (1886). A highly simplified adaptation of the Arch of Constantine Theme. Old photo, before sculpture over the roundels was removed. The sculpture is by the Mossmans.*

5 *Sir John Burnet and John Archibald Campbell. Competition design for Clyde Yacht Club, Hunter's Quay (1889). Shaw-Nesfield school but tower and porch show American shingle-style influences.*

first close friends and indistinguishable in architectural style, the two men were quite different in character. Campbell, grandson of William Campbell of Tullichewan, was a tall, reserved, and, it is said, very handsome bachelor who disliked personal publicity, his connections with the old Glasgow mercantile gentry being such that he did not require it. They worked independently, consulting each other but occasionally and collaborating closely only in competition work for which, as in the case of South Kensington, they sometimes sent in separate designs. Neither ever clarified Campbell's contribution to the partnership apart from the Ewing Gilmour Institute at Alexandria, Shawlands Church, and others planned for Elie[11] and Alexandria.

In 1885 the firm designed Newark Church at Port Glasgow which has a tall lancet front and saddleback tower.[12] In the following year they won the Glasgow Barony Church competition (assessed by J. L. Pearson) with a Gerona-type plan (Rowand Anderson had shown Presbyterians how to use it at Govan in 1884) designed in the same manner; very pure Dunblane front and huge battered buttresses, but omitting the tower, the stock Victorian prestige feature, in order to have money enough to build high and detail consistently well. Halls and ancillary apartments (largely 1898–1900) show the same fastidious detailing throughout.[13] In 1888 John A. Campbell built a smaller edition of it without clerestory or Gerona plan at Shawlands, which he appears to have designed in 1885.[14] So although generally credited to Burnet, just whose scheme it was basically is hard to guess. A. R. Scott, who subsequently

practised in London and Edinburgh is known to have assisted with both. Rather more elaborate competition designs were prepared for churches at Paisley (1887) and Largs (1889) but neither was successful. The final expressions of the type were Arbroath Parish Church (1894–96),[15] the rather lower Rutherglen Parish (1900–02)[16] and Glasgow University Chapel (1923–27) which are indisputably Burnet, all fine buildings, but progressively tamer in external composition.

The Low Look was a Burnet rather than a Campbell theme, the churches of this family forming a continuous sequence right down to Kingussie R.C. Church of 1931. His early introduction of low intimate proportions – more generally credited to Voysey who in turn took the theme from some of Devey's smaller scale designs – has not received the attention it deserves. Burnet probably adopted it from American practice, for his earliest and best house in this idiom, Corrienessan, Loch Ard (1886), although of the Shaw half-timber school in its detailing, has an angle veranda and a profile whose origins are unmistakably American shingle style. The larger Nunholme, Dowanhill, Glasgow (destroyed) also of 1886–87, was of the same family but less obviously American in inspiration.[17] In the same year (1887) the late English Gothic Union Building (now John McIntyre Building) at Glasgow University[18] carried the theme into public architecture with a squat topless tower, the idea for which, and perhaps also for an unexecuted tower at Dougarie Lodge, Arran,[19] may have come from Devey's Macharioch in Kintyre which Burnet would know. Other notable early Scottish

6 *Sir John Burnet. Union Building (now John McIntyre Building), Glasgow University (1887). The squat topless tower anticipates Mackintosh a decade later.*

7 *Sir John Burnet. Gardner Memorial Church, Brechin (1896–1900). The most elaborate of Burnet's low-look churches. The ironwork of the cloister gate is tinged with* Art Nouveau.

8 *Sir John Burnet and John Archibald Campbell. 'Garmoyle', Dumbarton (1890). Scots Baronial and Arts-and-Crafts touches in decorative raked-joint treatment of the rubble, with red tiles instead of Scots slate.*

instances of the use of low intimate proportions, just slightly later, are J. M. MacLaren's courtyard façade at Stirling High School (1888) and G. W. Browne's studio house for Martin Hardie near Dean Bridge, Edinburgh (1891). In 1887–89 Burnet introduced it into church architecture at Corrie and Shiskine[20] in Arran, with which churches A. R. Scott's name is also associated. In these the standard elements of the long series of churches of this family are all present – low church with broad eaves, half-timbered porch of excellent wood-work, squat tower with pyramid roof, mixed late Gothic and Romanesque motifs, and fat dome capped pier by the gate. They form a delightful series with interesting compositional variations on the same basic themes. The MacLaren Memorial Church at Stenhouse-muir (1897–1900, 1905–07), the rather more expensive Broomhill Congregational at Glasgow of 1900–08 and the Gardner Memorial Church at Brechin (1896–1900), which omits the half-timber and has interesting borrowings from Mackintosh in the metal work, are the most memorable examples. Burnet's churches, both tall and low, are the only Scottish churches of their

period to match those of the best English Goths. His scholar contemporaries like Anderson and Kinross were estimable figures but none had Burnet's vitality.[21]

The Low Look appeared briefly in Burnet's Renaiss-ance designs, notably at Campbeltown where the Public Library (1899)[22] and Rothmar (1898)[23] are of that family.

In 1888 the Scots Renaissance manner of mid to late 17th-century type, hitherto generally reserved for the country house, overflowed into public architecture, probably under the influence of Rowand Anderson's example. Campbell used it at the Ewing Gilmour Institute at Alexandria from 1888[24] and the wide spacing of Burnet balusters thereafter derives from the old Scots economy of never using two balusters where one would do. Burnet and Campbell built two large mansions in this manner, Garmoyle, Dunbarton (1890)[25] and Baronald, Lanarkshire (1891),[26] before again using it on public buildings at the Pathological Institute at Glasgow Western Infirmary (1894),[27] a design of great simplicity with just a few well-chosen motifs, and Alloa Public Baths (1895–99)[28] which shows Burnet baronial

9 *Sir John Burnet and John Archibald Campbell. Charing Cross Mansions, Glasgow (1890–91). 16th century French Renaissance* with *grande horloge adapted to late Victorian Glasgow. Sculpture by Birnie Rhind. Albany Chambers (on right) was added in 1897.*

at its most unrestrained; ingleneuk gable and cistern tower are bartizaned with rumbustious energy, exploring the possibilities of the style as a modern architectural expression without any thought of emulating the qualities of old work.

In 1891 Burnet and Campbell had in hand two important commissions in central Glasgow. The larger was Charing Cross Mansions, a huge range of well-to-do flats with shops below.[29] The general character was very French with its pavilion towers, Francois Ier dormers and *grande horloge* in the centre of the symmetrical quadrant section, but the bay windows were Glaswegian, and in this growing indifference to academic purity lay the germ of the Burnet and Campbell free style.

Mature Burnet Baroque features appeared in the same year at the Athenaeum Theatre on Buchanan Street. Its façade, as cleanly designed as the Athenaeum itself, was the pioneer vertical composition on Glasgow's narrow houseplots. The arched recess and bay window theme (suggested probably by H. J. Blanc's Edinburgh Café of 1886 and in turn perhaps by Bruce Price) was much copied in Glasgow elevator buildings of the next decade and the mullioned stair tower was itself to become a favourite Burnet feature. Within, the theatre had a simple panelled interior with a Japanese scheme of decoration in blue and – Burnet's favourite colours – yellow and gold. Massive cast iron columns with inverted volute capitals of very original design rose through the single gallery to carry the classrooms above, which had fireproof floors on the Fawcett system.[30]

The *point de depart* of Burnet Baroque, which was in less capable hands to become the common language of Glasgow building at the turn of the century, was no doubt Norman Shaw's Scotland Yard (1887) as indeed the gable aedicule, and other remoter echoes in Burnet and Campbell competition designs (such as the Edinburgh North British Hotel, 1895)[31] testify. Belcher-Pite designs may also have provided helpful suggestions, Pite sharing to the full Burnet's love of Michelangelesque sculpture: Burnet and Campbell's manner of composition is, however, original and peculiarly their own. Around 1893–94 Burnet again visited Italy from which he wrote to Campbell "with the fresh delight of a debutante about her first ball", and a further wider ranging continental tour was made in 1895.

The influence of these tours can be seen in the extended mastery of the Baroque language evinced in the Savings Bank Building in 1895–97.[32] To his father's quiet Glassford Street palazzo he added at the Ingram Street corner a domed single-storey banking hall, the centre of each façade being recessed with extraordinarily rich and inventive aedicules sculptured by Sir George Frampton: the interior was no less elaborate, big in scale with white and black marble columns in thorough-going Edwardian spirit. University Gardens shows the same style on a quiet domestic scale,[33] two

types of bay window in the curved section at Nos. 2–10 (1896) being distributed with a skill which emulates Thomson's mastery of terrace design in the 1870s.

In 1897 Burnet and Campbell's partnership was dissolved by mutual consent, Burnet having no patience with Campbell's drinking. But the latter went on to establish himself as a great architect in his own right. At first at Dundas House (now Britannia Building) in Buchanan Street (1898)[34] which recalled the Athenaeum Theatre opposite, and at the eaves-galleried block on Robertson Street (1901)[35] he still thought on similar lines, but thereafter their styles diverged. The giant cube of the Hope Street – West George Street block (1902),[36] its severe façades crowned by a strong arcaded eaves gallery, is arguably the finest, and certainly the most romantic, of all Glasgow office blocks. In the glazed brick rear elevations of bayed Henry Hope steel casements of his Edinburgh Life

10 *Sir John Burnet and John Archibald Campbell. Athenaeum Theatre, Buchanan Street, Glasgow (1891–93). Mature neo-Baroque detail and the first of Burnet's mullioned towers.*

(1904)[37] and Northern Insurance (1908)[38] buildings in St Vincent Street he achieved a severe early modern somewhat akin to French constructivism of that time, but in fact deriving from Salmon. And in the Portland stone street façade of the latter he adopted soaring lines with sparing modernized Renaissance motifs in a way which verges on expressionism. He died in July 1909, just too soon to establish the national reputation he deserved.

In 1896 Burnet visited America to study laboratory design for the University (where he was unfortunately saddled with Oldrid Scott as consultant)[39] armed no doubt with introductions from Pascal whose excellent English had attracted many American students including McKim, whom Burnet knew well. But it was not so much to McKim as to Chicago (where he may well have called on Sullivan whom he must have known at the École)[40] to which he looked for inspiration in the next few years. The first fruit was probably the American-looking top floor added to his father's Glassford Street Savings Bank (1898–1900) but in two office blocks in central Glasgow, both of 1899, seven-storey and on the dumb-bell plan, American influence is strongly in evidence even although their detailing is of the Athenaeum Theatre Baroque family: Burnet always developed new ideas in his own idiom.[41] At Atlantic Chambers on the Hope Street elevation the

eaves gallery, boldly broken by the central chimney shaft, has the squat proportions and deeply shadowed cornice favoured by the Sullivan school; and at the rear elevation on Cadogan Street close-spaced bay windows are set in pilasters in a very Chicagoan way, again with a low crowning eaves gallery. At the larger Waterloo Chambers the detailing is generally similar, but the doorpiece rises through two floors and above the central facade breaks into a deeply modelled recess framed by slim pylon towers and a deeply shadowed eaves gallery: within the recess, bay windows are banded together by a balcony, and from these rise Greek Ionic columns whose fluted verticals are continued by the triglyphs of the individual doric entablatures right up to the deep cantilever of the eaves gallery: academicism had no relevance to this kind of design and had been rejected in favour of complete freedom of expression. Burnet had, as Goodhart-Rendel observed, "no interest in style as such".

Both these buildings originally had shops in oblong architrave frames. At Skinner's Bakery in Newton Street (1900, destroyed) the frame took its cue from the Waterloo doorpiece and extended up through two storeys, leading on to the design of the first of his department stores, the Professional and Civil Service Supply Association in Edinburgh's George Street, in 1903–04.[42] Twenty years later Goodhart-Rendel noted

11 *Sir John Burnet. Savings Bank, Ingram and Glassford Streets, Glasgow: banking hall (1895–96) and top floor added to his father's 1865 bank (1898–1900) showing increased mastery of neo-Baroque at the former and the influence of McKim on the latter. On right Lanarkshire House with which he assisted his father, 1876–9.*

in some detail that Burnet was "the first to perceive that a façade of superimposed salesrooms should not look like house over shop".[43] Burnet was in fact really restating earlier Glasgow perceptions of this architectural truth, notably Thomson's designs for Howard and Dunlop Streets as early as 1850 and Wylie and Lochhead's building on Buchanan Street of 1855 (destroyed in 1883). The George Street building is developed from the central section of Waterloo Chambers, but the detail is varied with a lavish use of figure sculpture and marble; the pylon towers are dome-capped, the eaves gallery has caryatids, the central opening is developed into a two-storey recessed portico of shop windows flanked by single-storey ones, and at third and fourth floors the windows are vertically linked to express shop over shop rather than office over shop: for these mildly *Art-Nouveau* glazing was at first proposed.

The interior, as originally planned, was a classic example of the formally laid out department store. Curved vestibules led round a big circular cash office from the portico to an oval concourse; a wide easy staircase bowed gracefully outwards from the lift shafts round which it bifurcated as twin geometrical stairs to the upper levels at which, in addition to a complete range of goods and services on the Harrods model, such luxuries as a members' writing room and telephones were provided. The rear elevation, recently altered, was an achievement which matched Campbell at St Vincent Street, slim white piers framing huge windows which reached to the cill levels of the next floor, the ceilings being canted up to them for the greater admission of light.

Forsyth's in Edinburgh's Princes Street (1906–10)[44] was much less stylish in layout but, more modern in plan, has survived the test of time more successfully. It was, for the first time in Scotland, fully steel-framed in the modern sense, providing a plan of total simplicity, six floors of clear floorspace with the columns only one bay out from the walls and a beautifully detailed square stair well near the centre. Externally Burnet made a corner tower of the familiar mullioned pattern the dominant element of his composition, but otherwise he consistently applied to the steel frame a variant of the George Street bay design full of inventive detail: the Ionic columns are subtly banded in to the window architraves, their entablatures are Doric as at Waterloo Chambers but subtly treated with blank triglyphs, and even the minor details are novel improvisations on familiar classic motifs comparable with those of Lutyens. Marble and wrought iron were even more lavishly used than at George Street. Here was Edwardian opulence with real subtlety, imagination and elegance, in Goodhart-Rendel's words, "capricious and learnedly allusive, playing round the stern lines of the structure like a luxurious counterpoint of Bach" – not altogether an extravagant comparison.

Magnificent though Forsyth's is, it was the William McGeoch ironmongery warehouse at 28 West Campbell

Street, Glasgow (1905–10) which was the supreme moment of Burnet's free Baroque.[45] As at George Street the walls were loadbearing with a strong internal framework of steel joists on iron columns, the floors being concrete on the Columbian patent with finned steel bearers. The façades were both an end and a beginning, the finest British expression of the Louis Sullivan idea with great mullioned window grids married to the best of all Glasgow displays of virtuosity in turning the corner – reminiscent, as has been remarked of the prow of a ship – strongly clamped together by vestigial mullioned towers. In total concept it was as modern as anything by Mackintosh himself, the Baroque figures by Phyllis Archibald being but minor incidents in a completely functional design. The recent loss of the building is the most serious the Modern Movement in Britain has yet suffered.

In 1901 the shipbuilder, Elder, commissioned two buildings in Govan. The larger is The Elder Library[46] which has since been deepened in plan. In it, as Goodhart-Rendel noted, Beaux Arts influence is marked, but

12 *Sir John Burnet. Atlantic Chambers, Hope Street, Glasgow (1899). Showing the influence of Burnet's first American tour. The eaves gallery is American-looking, but could derive from 'Greek' Thomson.*

the serpentine portico appears to be of more easterly European origin while the generous proportions of the columns and urns is characteristic of Burnet around 1900. The Elder Hospital is still formal, but on a kindly almshouse scale, low and welcoming, surely one of the happiest hospital buildings ever built: Burnet had clearly benefited from his Belcher and Macartney Later Renaissance folios though no direct prototype will be found there. Their influence is also to be felt in the Clyde Trust extension of 1905–08;[47] the original building determined the bay design but the cupola at the circled corner, framed in a monumental setting of chimneys and Albert Hodge sculpture, recalled Gibbs at the Radcliffe Camera.

This contrast in scales is also evident in Burnet's domestic work. In his sumptuous remodelling of Finlaystone (1900)[48] the monumental scale is apparent both outside and in, the marble columns and eagle-ended handrail of the otherwise moderately sized staircase looking as if they were surplus from the building of Forsyth's. At the remodelling of Carronvale (1901)[49] the scale is more comfortably domestic with some very original variations on Renaissance detail internally. Fairnalie (1904–06),[50] last of Burnet's baronial houses, has the same bold restless energy which

characterises the Victorian baronialist David Bryce at his best, Arts and Crafts simulation of the surface qualities of original castles still being avoided; but later at Duart Castle, restored from ruins in 1911–16,[51] he could command a sympathy with the original which matched that of Lorimer.

In 1904 the Trustees of the British Museum obtained from the R.I.B.A. a list of a dozen candidates for the design of new galleries, these being invited to submit folios of executed work, and on the strength of his three Burnet was appointed. By 1905 a vast scheme had been prepared for extending the museum on all four sides and laying out a very Parisian British Museum Avenue on the north axis. By 1914 the north wing – the Edward VII Galleries – had been built: the rest was never proceeded with. But what was built, even although it never received its full complement of sculptures, was a masterpiece which must have gladdened the hearts of Pascal and Nénot, a giant Beaux Arts Greek Ionic colonnade framing subtly detailed fenestration, set forward slightly from its strong terminal pylons; in true neo-classic fashion the centre is not emphasised, being marked only by a low doorpiece in a powerful but restrained monumental Baroque and a slight central emphasis in the lead cresting. Leonard Eaton has

13 *Sir John Burnet. Civil Service and Professional Supply (later SCWS), George Street, Edinburgh (1903–07). The first of Burnet's departmental stores. The caryatid eaves gallery graced the restaurant. Ground floor now being reinstated, the central part having been remodelled about 1930.*

14 *Sir John Burnet. Civil Service and Professional Supply (later SCWS), rear elevation. Bold early modern, akin to early 20th-century French constructivism.*

15 *Sir John Burnet. R. W. Forsyth's, Prince's Street, Edinburgh (1906–10, left hand bay 1923–25). The George Street bay design adapted to a fully steel framed structure. Sculpture by Birnie Rhind and Reid Dick.*

recently noted a family resemblance to McKim, but doorpiece, window detail and composition are peculiarly his own. Echoes of McKim were perhaps more evident in the up-dated neo-Grec of the interior which reads well with the severe functionalism of Smirke's Greek Revival interiors.[52]

Only the early stages were designed at 239 St Vincent Street, Burnet's Glasgow office. In 1905 a London house and office was established at Montague Place in the sole name of John J. Burnet with Thomas Smith Tait (1882–1954) and David Raeside in charge, the Glasgow office continuing as John Burnet & Son in the care of Norman A. Dick (who died in 1948): all were Scottish and Burnet men of several years' standing. No further commission for a new building came his way in London until 1909[53], however, and then from a Scottish company, the General Accident.[54]

The General Building in Aldwych was the swansong of Burnet Baroque and, although less inventive than Forsyth's was perhaps the supreme work of Burnet as stylist and planner. It adopts the Edinburgh George Street model of a recessed portico through two storeys with integration of the third and fourth floor windows above. Sculpture and fine materials, marble, granite and metal are again most generously applied, but otherwise the treatment is simplified to just a few characteristic motifs subtly disposed in a pyramidical arrangement above the yard-wide architrave frame, the whole being crowned by a big roof with well-placed chimneys over a simple eaves gallery. The detailing is of un-

common excellence, particularly the Cristola marble inner screen of the portico and superb sculpture by Albert Hodge. The interior is simpler but again all is of the very best: it was, according to Tait, "all Burnet's work".[55]

This phase of Burnet's career closed with a now unremembered but astonishing episode. Edinburgh had vacillated on various sites for the Usher Hall since 1896. The Mound was not one of them, but in Playfair's Grecian galleries he saw the same challenge as at the British Museum. He sketched out a scheme which was beautifully worked up by Tait and Dick and sent it in free of charge. This visionary approach was not well received, the Corporation fixed on another site and an open competition, and family and friends were scandalised. Unruffled and unrepentant he exhibited the scheme at the Royal Scottish Academy of 1909.

Burnet's style changed radically in 1910–11. Although his favourite compositional motifs – the broad architrave, the pylon and mullioned tower features, the black bands, and occasionally the eaves gallery were still to be stock features, the Baroque decorative treatment was given up in favour of an uncompromisingly modern severity. The germ of this transition was of course to be seen at McGeoch's, not only in the mullioned grid but in the severe abstract simplicity of much of the detailing. But the final catalysts were undoubtedly two study tours, one continental and taking in Germany and Austria, and the other to America. The first related to the commission for

16 *Sir John Burnet. Elder Library, Govan, Glasgow (1901). Beaux Arts with Edwardian Baroque proportions.*

17 *Sir John Burnet. McGeoch's Warehouse, No. 28 West Campbell Street, Glasgow (1905–06). Demolished 1970. American influence now takes the form of the Louis Sullivan grid in this most imposing of all Burnet's Edwardian buildings.*

Glasgow Sick Children's Hospital, the second to that for the new Kodak building in London, and perhaps also to the Forsyths: William Forsyth was also in America about this time, returning full of American ideas on the organisation of industry, shortly to find expression in the Wallace Scott Tailoring Institute at Cathcart. What Burnet saw on those tours is unfortunately not now known, but the work of Otto Wagner was probably on the first and that of Albert Khan, Dwight Perkins and Richard Schmidt, whose work he would know from *The Architectural Record*, on the second. It is difficult to say more. Burnet never copied. He took in the general concept of what he saw and interpreted it in his own way.

The Kodak Building (1910–11)[56] prototype of countless buildings of the 1920s and 1930s, is, as Leonard Eaton has remarked, basically Sullivanian in its handling of the whole as base shaft and capital. The components of the design were not, however, entirely new; the two-storeyed base is an old Burnet arrangement, the giant piers of the upper floors were perhaps in the first sketch the familiar Glasgow pilastrade since the bases still remained in the final design, the metal spandrels punctuated by ventilators derive from his own experiments in multi-storeyed openings rather than Chicago practice, and the whole might, in its basic concept, be a drastic simplification of the Selfridge building, in the design of which he had been involved in 1908.[57] The plan, too, in its absence of a lightwell was really no more than an extension of the Forsyth's type. Kodak was, technical improvements apart, more remarkable for what was left out of the design rather than what was put in.

In his three main Glasgow commissions of this period the American strain is a good deal more marked and it must be a matter for regret that within recent years the first two have been destroyed and the third 'modernised': Burnet has almost ceased to exist as an early modern master in Glasgow. The Sick Children's Hospital at Yorkhill (1911–16)[58] was the first and least obviously American in inspiration. It consisted of the usual parallel ward blocks fronted by a big administration block and nurses' home. Money was tight: brick-built, the lower areas of the administration block were roughcast to give the tone values of a brick and stone treatment, a small amount of stone trim being reserved for the bay windows (large versions of those at Fairnalie), spandrels, and the familiar broad architrave from which projected a glass-roofed carriage porch on stout columns of mixed Burnet-American inspiration. Urns, centre window and ventilator were Burnet Baroque. The administration block and nurses' home was still a transitional design, but in the ward blocks and ancillary structures functional features such as ventilation towers were expressed with remarkable frankness.

The immense Alhambra Theatre was begun in the same year (1910) but was in its external appearance much more uncompromisingly modern and indeed American, without any Baroque echoes, although the composition was a reworking of old themes, mullioned towers, eaves gallery, broad architrave and black bands in the masonry, here as at the Sick Children's, brickwork. Period features were more in evidence inside, the D-plan foyer being Rococo, the 2,500-seat auditorium an updated Louis Seize, but its construction and arrangement showed familiarity with contemporary American theatre design.[59]

Not much less influential than Kodak, and a stronger design – Leonard Eaton has compared it with Albert Khan at his best – was the Wallace Scott Tailoring Institute, a landmark in its concept as well as its architecture, being planned on American lines as a garden factory with welfare and recreation facilities built in, the Forsyths emphasising the fact with the word *Institute* rather than *factory* or *works*.[60] The original building (1913–16, extended 1919–22) was a simple steel-framed brick mass, in which façades of wide-bayed pilastrades of the Kodak type are powerfully clamped together by slightly recessed pylons: the principle is that of the British Museum colonnade, here applied in the round over three sides of a square, the pylon detail being indeed very similar. The spandrels were of patterned brick instead of metal as in his earlier designs, the only other architectural feature being the familiar distyle recessed portico, here with a glass canopy. Internally, entrance hall and stair were unornamented classical-modern relying solely on good proportions and marble facings. The extensive gardens were laid out on formal lines – almost reminiscent of

18 *Sir John Burnet. 'Fairnalie', Selkirkshire (1904–06). A late example of Burnet Baronial: more vigour than Lorimer and no Arts-and-Crafts detailing.*

19 *Sir John Burnet. Edward VII Galleries, British Museum, London (1904–14). Beaux Arts expertise revived, but with characteristic Burnet Baroque touches.*

20 *Sir John Burnet. Interior, North Library, British Museum, London (1904–14). Destroyed. Since altered.*

New Delhi – with architecturally treated steps, retaining walls, pergolas, urns and even an eastern looking khiosk at the entrance bridge, now almost all swept away.

In a conversation with Sir John Summerson in 1948, Thomas Tait claimed authorship of the Kodak Building and most of the London firm's designs thereafter.[61] Burnet, he recalled, did not like his design, and had another made, but his client Eastman preferred Tait's, the final version being worked out in the office. Burnet, according to his neice Edith, certainly regarded it as his design and used to quote the Second Church of Christ Scientist (1921–26)[62] and Lloyds Bank, Cornhill (1927–29)[63] both in London as the first designs conceived by Tait from the outset, though at those dates, probably still under his own close supervision. In 1910 Burnet was still at the height of his powers, full of new ideas from his travels; the supply of small scale sketches and tracings he handed out for development was hardly likely to have dried up. At the same time it is not hard to believe that the executed scheme, as developed by Tait, did not at first meet with his approval. Even as finalised and executed it is just a little dry and lacks the characteristic Burnet deftness and generosity of spirit in a way the stronger and equally simplified Wallace Scott did not. Nonetheless there can be little

doubt that the concept of the Kodak-Wallace Scott type is his, for by 1911 Burnet was all that the London and Glasgow offices had in common. In that year Norman A. Dick had bought himself a ten year partnership in the Glasgow office and under his supervision Burnet's sketches were developed and sent to Montague Place for amendment, Burnet himself spending only about two days a month at the Glasgow office.

In 1914 Burnet was knighted on the completion of the Edward VII Galleries, secured the Royal Gold Medal for his old master Pascal, and designed the Institute of Chemistry in Russell Square, brick neo-Georgian in deference to the neighbourhood but with some personal touches of late academic Burnet, notably in the omission of the entablatures at the ground floor arcade. But otherwise 1914 brought difficult times. Burnet, scrupulously business-like with clients and contractors, had given little thought to his own finances. The offices were extravagantly run, profitability being subordinated to perfection, and the great study tours had been immensely expensive for everything was done in style abroad as well as at home. [64] By the end of the war some of the Burnets' most-loved possessions had had to be sold.

The London office recovered rather more quickly than the Glasgow one, thanks to Gordon Selfridge who entrusted him with the completion of his Oxford Street

21 *Sir John Burnet. General Buildings, Aldwych, London (1909–11). A late London flowering of his Glasgow style with sculpture by Albert Hodge.*

22 *Sir John Burnet and Thomas S. Tait. Kodak Building, Kingsway (1910–11). Walls reduced to pilasters above second floor level with only vestigial neo-Baroque detail.*

store[65] and the War Graves Commission for which he designed the cemeteries at Gallipolli, Palestine and Suez. Thomas Tait (who assisted much with the latter) and David Raeside were still in the London office, their position being recognised in the change of name to Sir John Burnet and Partners. His neice Edith hoped to work there but Burnet, in spite of having paid for her education, demurred at women in the office. Her husband T. Harold Hughes (1887–1949) also aspired to the London office but Tait demurred. Hughes then joined Dick in the Glasgow office as a partner for the year 1921, but incompatibility with Dick and the financial troubles of that office caused him to leave for teaching. Dick then cleared off the firm's debts, re-purchasing his partnership as Burnet Son and Dick.

Burnet's first large building after the war was the block comprising Vigo (now Empire) and Westmorland Houses in Regent Street, built in 1920–25. Its long three-storey plain-piered façade with columned angle quadrants, framed in vestigial pylons which rise through a beautifully smooth unbroken entablature, again derives from the British Museum, but with an eye on the best contemporary French classical-modern: a visit to Pascal and Nénot had been made in March 1919. The

23 *Sir John Burnet. Alhambra Theatre, Wellington and Waterloo Streets, Glasgow (1910–11). Destroyed 1970. Inspired by contemporary American architecture, but the mullioned towers and big architrave frame are recurring Burnet themes.*

eastern-looking corner domes reflected his travels for the War Graves Commission and can be related to the dome of his chapel at Jerusalem.

The year 1921 brought Adelaide House, an immense office block at London Bridge. Tait was deeply involved in this project and the publication of his sketches for it in *The Architectural Review* of 1925 have given the general impression that the whole concept is Tait's. These may, however, be no more than three-dimensional expressions of Burnet sketch elevations, for by 1921 Burnet rarely drew out anything himself. Stylistically the first sketches with their high colonnades tell us little, but the distyle recessed portico, the Sullivanian grid, the mullioned pylon towers at the river angles, the eaves gallery, the black banding and the generous spirit of the detailing in the final scheme are all classic Burnet themes, having little in common with Tait classical-modern as seen at Carliol House in Newcastle and the Daily Telegraph Building in London. Even if, as Leonard Eaton and others have remarked, the structural expression of the steel frame is less clear than in its predecessors, Adelaide House is now, with the destruction of McGeoch's and the ruination of the Wallace Scott, the finest expression of Burnet early modern.[66]

In Glasgow Burnet was busy at the University. The larger of his two commissions there was the completion

24 *Sir John Burnet. Alhambra Theatre. Destroyed 1970. Interior, reminiscent of contemporary American designs. Circle and balcony were both fully cantilevered.*

of Sir G. G. Scott's main building by constructing a western range with a tall memorial chapel (1923–27)[67] orientated east and west through the middle of it. Burnet designed this building in detail, probably the last occasion on which he did so, working closely with his draughtsman James Napier. Scott's architecture imposed severe constraints, and although his chapel is nobly proportioned the bold massing of his Barony Church is inevitably absent. Within there is more of the Barony spirit, and the use of a flat roof over the presbytery to admit of three small lancets over the chancel arch, answering those of the presbytery itself, is an original and successful touch; rich stallwork, chandeliers, angels at the collar-braced roof and fine trefoiled blind arcading at the presbytery complete a composition remarkable for its spaciousness in a building only 120 feet long.

The Zoology Building (1922–23) was a compromise between Burnet's Edwardian and early modern manners and probably marked the beginning of a conservative trend so far as Burnet's few remaining buildings were concerned.[68] But it is still a remarkable design: lecture theatre, entrance bay and gable of the laboratory block were wrapped together in a channelled mass, the cupola louvre being placed asymmetrically over the theatre whose raked floor is expressed in the stepped windows; the laboratories have a miniature Wallace Scott elevation; and beyond them, at the elementary class, the windows break up into the roof plane. It is perhaps the most lucid expression of the classic Burnet precept of designing from the inside out, expressing the requirements of the client through the plan and into the elevations. The detailed working out of this commission was in the hands of Norman Dick.

In 1923 Burnet, who had procured the award of the Royal Gold Medal for Pascal in 1914, Anderson in 1916 and Nénot in 1917, received it himself, Paul Waterhouse paying a tribute which is still the best interpretation of the Burnet spirit. From then on Burnet became elder statesman rather than architect, leaving most of the designing in the London office to Tait, but in a commission which came to the Glasgow office he made what was really his final statement. The North British and Mercantile (now Commercial Union) Building (1926–29) in St Vincent Street is frankly conservative, a giant subtly tapered Renaissance cube with a huge cornice broken by bold chimneys and an arcaded base which is an extension of the London Institute of Chemistry and Royal Free Hospital Eastman Dental Clinic (1926) theme: the entrance arch is framed by disengaged columns carrying crouching figures in characteristic Burnet-Michelangelesque style. The scheme was developed by Dick and drawn up by Walter J. Knight with nuances in the capital detail which were to be a Dick hallmark; Dick had a difficult time for Burnet had his finger closely upon it, and even after construction was under way made detail changes for which he paid personally. It did not in the end take

25 *Sir John Burnet and Norman Dick. Wallace Scott Tailoring Institute, Cathcart, Glasgow (1913–22). Mutilated. British Museum and Kodak themes combined as a garden factory on American-inspired lines.*

26 *Sir John Burnet and Thomas Smith Tait. Vigo and Westmorland Houses, Regent Street, London (1920–5). French classical-modern, reflecting Burnet's continuing contact with the École.*

27 *Sir John Burnet and Thomas Smith Tait. Adelaide House, London Bridge (1921–25). A modernised version of the McGeoch scheme; the mullioned pylon towers recessed in the angles are an old Burnet favourite.*

shape quite as he conceived it: 1926 was a difficult year economically and 10 feet of the total height was eliminated, but without much detriment to the design. It was still a fitting, if conservative, end to his career.

Great men can, however, sometimes carry on too long. From the time of his knighthood Burnet received the inevitable round of appointments as assessor, member of commission and juror – including the sad affair of the League of Nations competition in 1927 which only harmed his reputation and that of his old friend Nénot who made the compromise design – bringing a decline in creativity which was aggravated by the chronic eczema which compelled him to wear skull-cap and gloves from the very early '20s. His very last major design was the giant Unilever Building at Blackfriars Bridge (with J. Lomax-Simpson);[69] the directors had asked him to do it himself and he was not a little pleased. But by 1930 he had not much left to say. The design with its high colonnade was unbelievably conservative for a pioneer of the Modern Movement, drawing much upon the preliminary designs for Adelaide House and Tait's Lloyd's; Tait did indeed help with the design. Only at the lower levels was something of his old resourcefulness to be seen, and at the colonnade windows he inserted a few touches of Burnet Baroque, the final gesture of a man whose heart was by now in another age.

Thereafter his role in the firm was administrative. The Dudok style of Francis Lorne (who had replaced Raeside as third partner) he approved of but had no active hand in. Francis's sister Helen, who was his secretary, managed his post-war finances well and made retirement in 1935 possible. He moved from Farnham to Colinton, Edinburgh, and there, until shortly before his death on 2 July 1938, he and Lady Burnet were pleased to receive the greater Burnet 'family' of assistants of former days. One recalled that in his retirement "he had no profession and no recreation – nothing of interest for him to turn to, no hobbies of any kind. He passed through life with one all absorbing interest which burned him dry."[70]

The principal sources on Burnet's life and work are the memoirs by A. N. Paterson, T. S. Tait and Theodore Fyfe published in the *Journal of the Royal Institute of British Architects* 2 June and 18 July 1938 (Paterson and Fyfe's being much the best and giving a sympathetic portrait of the man even if at times not entirely accurate as to dates): *The Bailie* 7 April 1886; 6 May 1914; 4 May 1921: *The Builders' Journal* 9 October 1901: *The Architect's Journal* 27 June 1923 (H. S. Goodhart-Rendel): *Journal of the Royal Institute of British Architects* 30 June 1923 (Paul Waterhouse): *Royal Incorporation of Architects in Scotland Quarterly* No. 84 (1951, D. Paterson); No. 85 (1951, W. J. Smith); No. 94 (1953, Robert Rankin thesis and other notes): E. J. Burrows and Co., *Modern Architectural Art* parts I and II: Masters of Architecture Series, Geneva, *The Architectural Work of Sir John Burnet and Partners* (dealing with work from the British Museum onwards only). The most recent writing on Burnet's work is to be found in Gomme and Walker *The Architecture of Glasgow* 1968 and Leonard Eaton *American Architecture Comes of Age* 1972. Information not otherwise referenced has been taken from these sources, but much personal information and help was provided by the late Mrs Edith Burnet Hughes, the late Alfred G. Lochhead, Mr

Colin McWilliam, Mr John Watson, and Dr A. H. Gomme with whom the writer intends to undertake a full monograph.

[1] See Burnet on Pascal *The Architects' Journal* 2 June 1920 with its affectionate account of Spiers's introduction of the young Burnet to Pascal: "the trim untrimness of him struck me then as being so representative of his architecture – with dark long hair and black penetrating eyes in which there shone a light of much kindliness". It is also of interest that visiting Burnet in London, Pascal was "pleased with the *carelessness* in design of the English buildings. The French worked more to rule." See also J. H. Markham on Nénot in *Journal of the Royal Institute of British Architects* 1934.

[2] See 'Goodhart-Rendel's Roll Call' pp. –

[3] *The Architects' Journal* 2 June 1920; 4 May 1921; 27 June 1923; repeated undated by all subsequent writers who listed works. There may be confusion with Burnet's Union Bank at Lerwick (1904–6) as it is sometimes included in the correct chronological order for that building. It was designed from the late summer of 1875: working drawings summer 1876, begun in the autumn. R. S. Rait, *History of the Union Bank.*

[4] *The Bailie* 27 January, 1 May, 22 May 1878; *Building News* 6 February 1880; good illustrations *The Architects' Journal* 27 June 1923.

[5] First scheme *The British Architect* 22 June 1883; second scheme 5 January, 12 January 1883.

[6] *The Architect* 20 January 1888 (showing scheme for campanile, watercolour by Jules Lessore).

[7] *Royal Scottish Academy Catalogues* 1887; photo prior to removal of sculpture at roundel windows *The Builder* 9 July 1898. The original interior work has almost completely disappeared.

[8] Another important Perthshire commission was the remodelling of the interior of William Burn's Auchterarder House with magnificent Renaissance woodwork: externally a conservatory and porte-cochère were added (1886).

[9] With C. C. Lindsay C.E., and A. G. Sydney Mitchell who was responsible for the Old Edinburgh Street part of the project.

[10] *Royal Scottish Academy Catalogues* 1882/5. Elevation of first scheme *The Architects' Journal* 27 June 1923, and photos as rebuilt.

[11] Free Church, Alexandria *Building News* 3 August 1889; Free Church Elie, design with stone dome *The Builder* 20 March 1886; replaced by Sydney Mitchell whose church has now been destroyed. Burnet Son and Campbell also built the Marine Hotel there, 1889, remodelled and enlarged by Burnet in 1900, burnt 1904, rebuilt 1905–8.

[12] *The Architect* 30 October 1885.

[13] *Building News* 29 October 1886; 7 and 14 January 1887.

[14] *Shawlands Old Parish Church Jubilee* 1938. A tower was planned but omitted. Originally to be of red sandstone like the Barony Church.

[15] *The Builder* 12 September 1894; *Academy Architecture* 1895.

[16] *The Builder* 29 September 1900.

[17] Both houses *Royal Scottish Academy Catalogues* 1887; Nunholme *The British Architect* 6 July 1888 with photo of drawing room, very shadowy but evidently of very original design.

[18] *The British Architect* 13 July 1888. The building was deepened in plan on the south side in 1895 and again in 1908–9. The late gothic style is related to their competition scheme for Birmingham Law Courts (with tall tower) *The Builder* 14 August 1886.

[19] *Academy Architecture* 1894. A large boathouse was however built at this time, as was the hotel at Loch Ranza illustrated in the same

issue.

[20] *Building News* 15 July 1887; *The British Architect* 1 March 1889. Also engaged on these were Alexander McGibbon and William Kerr. A. N. Paterson did watercolour perspectives of them. Other buildings on Arran designed about this time include the Congregational Church at Sannox, Hamilton Terrace and a church at Lamlash.

[21] Brechin *The Builder* 23 May 1896; Stenhousemuir *The Architect* 11 April 1902. Two more churches of the same type are Dundas, Grangemouth (*Academy Architecture* 1894i) and St Geraldine's, Lossiemouth (*The Builder* 24 August 1901).

[22] *Academy Architecture* 1899i. Burnet had earlier designed a hospital there *The Builder* 28 November 1896.

[23] *Academy Architecture* 1898i.

[24] *The British Architect* 28 June 1889; *The Architect* 7 February 1902. It is now a masonic lodge.

[25] *Journal of the Royal Institute of British Architects* 12 September 1938, note on p.993.

[26] *The British Architect* 30 January, 6 February 1891.

[27] *Academy Architecture* 1894i; *The Builder* 19 May 1894.

[28] *Academy Architecture* 1897i; *The Architect* 16 May 1902.

[29] *Academy Architecture* 1891. Subsequently extended on Sauchiehall Street by Albany Chambers (1896–99) and on Renfrew Street (Nos. 347–353 with good interiors in style of 17th-century artisan mannerism, *circa* 1896).

[30] *Academy Architecture* 1893; *The Builder* 1 April, 21 October 1893. For Edinburgh Café see *The British Architect* 27 September 1889; and see also Montgomery Schuyler *American Architecture and Other Writings* Fig. 70, p.243. The arch and bay window motif was also used by Anderson, however, at Glasgow Central Hotel, 1884.

[31] *The British Architect* 19 April 1895.

[32] *Building News* 31 January 1896; *The Architect* 10 January 1892. Dean of Guild plans for banking hall and new north facade of old bank August 1894; new top floor of old bank January 1898.

[33] Most have good Burnet interiors: notably No. 4 (*Academy Architecture* 1902i). Burnet Son and Campbell had earlier designed Nos. 11–25 (*circa* 1887, end houses at University Avenue only survive). No. 14 is also Burnet, 1900.

[34] *The Builder* 17 September 1898.

[35] Office Records per late A. D. Hislop: Nos. 63–71 for R. E. Buchanan (*The Builders' Journal* 28 November 1906). Campbell had earlier (1899) designed No. 17 in the same street.

[36] *The Builder* 28 December 1904; *The Builders' Journal* 28 November 1906.

[37] *The Builders' Journal* 28 November 1906.

[38] *Building News* 10 December 1909.

[39] These were the Botanical Building 1899–1902; Engineering Building 1899–1901, extended 1907–08; Anatomical Building, 1901–03, all from sketches by Oldrid Scott whose aim was to match Pearce Lodge, built with stonework from the Old College; and the Surgical Laboratory 1901–03. Various laboratory works at the associated Western Infirmary were also connected with this tour.

[40] Sullivan was in the same year, but attended the Atelier Vaudremer.

[41] Both *Academy Architecture* 1899i; Atlantic *Building News* 2 February 1900; Waterloo *Building News* 5 January 1900, photo

The Architect 23 February 1906. Waterloo was to have been two floors higher which would of itself have given it a more markedly American character but the firemaster demurred.

[42] *Building News* 20 October 1905; 1904 plans in possession of John Watherston & Sons, Edinburgh.

[43] *The Architects' Journal* 27 June 1923.

[44] *The Builders' Journal* 25 December 1907: Burnet had already reconstructed Forsyth's Glasgow store (originally Black's Building, 1858 by Boucher & Cousland) at the corner of Gordon and Renfield Streets, 1896–98, 1900–02 and again 1909; Corinthian column quadrant corner and dome inserted, interesting staircase of semi-octagonal plan.

[45] *The Builders' Journal* 28 November 1906; the National Monuments Record of Scotland has preliminary studies of 1904 showing a Waterloo Chambers type doorpiece and an ogee roofed corner treatment; also a perspective by Alexander McGibbon showing the final scheme but with an earlier version of the corner gable and doorpiece sculpture half the executed size. It is said that Phyllis Archibald misread the scale in carving it, but Burnet was pleased with the result and altered the design to accommodate it.
The construction was an intermediate stage, corresponding to American practice at that time for buildings of less than ten floors. The Edinburgh George Street building had iron columns, steel beams and Fram patent floors, concrete over an arched corrugated iron reinforcement; Skinner's had a similar frame with expanded sheet metal reinforcement. Neither Atlantic nor Waterloo were consistently framed although both, particularly the latter, contain a good deal of steelwork.

[46] *The Architect* 17 March, 7 April 1905.

[47] *The Builders' Journal* 26 August 1908, *The Glasgow Herald* 6 December 1905, 15 September 1908.

[48] *The Architect* 19 August 1904; 30 May 1906.

[49] *The Builders' Journal* 9 October 1901; good photos of interior *Building News* 3 April 1903. An older house of early 19th-century date was incorporated centre front.

[50] Nicoll, *Domestic Architecture in Scotland* plates 5–9.

[51] *Building News* 11 December 1916. Handled by Norman Dick, drawn out by J. McGregor Harvey.

[52] J. M. Crook *The British Museum*; *The Architect* and *The Builders' Journal* 1 April 1914. The magnificent North Library which linked Smirke's quadrangle with Burnet's new wing has unfortunately been destroyed.

[53] An interesting addition, however, was the chancel of King's Weighhouse Church with glass by Anning Bell: see *The Builder* 26 November 1904.

[54] *The Architectural Review* July 1911. The company's head office in Perth (*Academy Architecture* 1899i) also has a marked Burnetian character, their architect George P. K. Young having sent his son Cedric to train at Burnet's in the 1890s.

[55] Eaton, *American Architecture Comes of Age* p.54, note 16.

[56] *The Architectural Review* December 1911, pp.336–341.

[57] Eaton, *op cit* p.49. The architects were D. H. Burnham & Co. whose representative was Albert D. Miller; Francis Swales was responsible for the facade design. Robert Atkinson and Burnet were the British architects consulted.

[58] *Building News* 22 May 1914. Illustration showing Administration block as first designed without wings. Handled by Dick, the drawing out of the Administration block was in the hands of a Mr Bow and that of the Ward blocks in those of J. W. Weddell and J. McGregor Harvey, though many other assistants were employed on it. Considerable

additions were made in the 1920s by Burnet Son and Dick. Burnet was a close friend of Dr Mackintosh of the Western Infirmary who helped with the layout of his hospital projects. Burnet also worked at Cumberland Infirmary, Carlisle 1908–13 and Kilmarnock Infirmary 1912–22, as well as at Glasgow Royal Asylum, Gartnavel, from 1898 onwards.

[59] *Building Industries* 16 March 1910. Handled by Dick, drawn out by W. J. Blain with McGregor Harvey and others. For American theatres whose interiors may have influenced Burnet see for instance those in *Architectural Record* v. 15.

[60] *The Architectural Review* 1922 pp.128–132; Eaton, *op cit* p.46.

[61] Quoted in Eaton, *op cit* p.54 note 16.

[62] In Palace Gardens Terrace. Published in *The Architectural Review* August 1926, pp.66–73 as 'From the design of Thomas S. Tait'. The exterior, particularly the hall which was built first, has Burnetian touches in its early Christian design, but the interior of the church itself is Art Deco.

[63] *The Builder* 20 September 1929; *The Architects' Journal* 30 January 1929.

[64] A good example of Burnet 'doing things in style' was the complimentary luncheon given by Burnet and Forsyth at the Wallace Scott in 1922. The menu cards were etchings by Walcot.

[65] Again with Albert D. Miller, now of Graham Anderson Probst and White. See *The Architects' Journal* 9 December 1925; 15 May 1929.

[66] *The Architectural Review* 1925, pp.61–73; *The Architects' Journal* 7 January 1925.

[67] *The British Builder* March 1923; *The Architect's Journal* 19 October 1927.

[68] *The Architect's Journal* 21 September 1927.

[69] *The Architect's Journal* 21 January, 6 May 1931. The authorship of these post-war London works is a complex subject. Tait's *Journal of the Royal Institute of British Architects* obituarist claimed nothing done in partnership as his alone but emphasised his share in the Kodak building; on the other hand the list of works Tait supplied to the *Journal of the Royal Institute of British Architects* in 1938 (often inaccurate as to date) included only Adelaide House, Selfridge's, the War Memorials and the Ramsgate improvements (*The Architectural Review* August 1923) amongst post-war works for the London office and only work prior to 1923 for the Glasgow one. Paterson, who knew Burnet well, regarded Adelaide House as Burnet's alone – surely an overstatement, even if the design is basically his – and Vigo and Unilever Houses as being done in partnership. Edith Hughes gathered from her uncle that the final concept of Adelaide House was his, but that most of the working out was Tait's. W. H. Godfrey in his *Dictionary of National Biography* account seems to have gone into the matter with particular care, and gives Kodak, Vigo, Adelaide and Unilever Houses as all being done in conjunction with Tait; that seems to get the emphasis right, both in respect of what is put in and what is left out amongst the post-war works as mainly or wholly Tait's work.

[70] *Royal Incorporation of Architects in Scotland Quarterly* No. 94.

Charles Rennie Mackintosh

by David Walker

Charles Rennie Mackintosh (1868–1928) has long been accepted as the transcending genius of British architecture at the turn of the century. Tastes change, but that judgement seems likely to remain. Mackintosh drank deeply of all the progressive influences of his time, including the English Arts and Crafts Movement and the continental European *Art Nouveau*. Then, in a small number of buildings in the decade from 1896 onwards, he fused these influences into a superb architecture that touched great heights. David Walker's study traces Mackintosh's sources and the emergence of his own individuality against the background of his contemporaries' work.

It is over a hundred years since Charles Rennie Mackintosh was born and sixty-five since his last major architectural work was finished. Since, sadly, in 1928 he reminded us of his meteoric ten years as an independent designer in Glasgow by dying, a great deal has been published about him, culminating in Professor Pevsner's book in 1950[1], Professor Howarth's in 1952[2] and Robert Macleod's[3] in 1968. To Howarth we owe a particular debt. He was in the right place at the right time. A little later would have been too late to collect the personal recollections on which every subsequent biographer must depend. But of Mackintosh's precursors and contemporaries, of how he built up his uniquely personal architectural idiom, and why, there is perhaps something left to add.

With a designer so intensely inventive as Mackintosh, quoting firm precedents for his mature work after 1895 is hazardous. Yet no designer can shake off subconscious memory, training and custom altogether. Indeed in his early years he did not try to do so. Howarth tells us that the heroes of his youth were James Sellars and John James Burnet.[4]

The earliest building in which we know Mackintosh was concerned, the Wylie Hill Store in Buchanan Street, Glasgow, was modelled by his first employer John Hutchison (or rather his assistant Andrew Black, Hutchison himself being no designer) on Sellars's Wylie and Lochhead building of 1882–84 across the street. The excellent decorative sculpture suggests Mackintosh's hand; he would then be in the final year of his apprenticeship, and one or two detail drawings he made for it are still remembered.

His interest in Sellars would be further stimulated by his becoming an assistant in Honeyman and Keppie's firm in 1889, for Keppie had assisted Sellars during his tragic gamble with his health in 1888 and had been entrusted both with the design of his tomb and with the finishing of the Anderson Medical College. These twin allegiances show very clearly in Mackintosh's student designs for competitions in 1890. The Thomson Scholarship design is pure Sellars Grecian – down to the lamp standards; the Science and Art Museum is of the same family as J. J. Burnet's Beaux Arts designs of the early 1880s, but the columnar arrangement appears to be related to the designs of Burnet and Sellars for the Glasgow Municipal Buildings competition. Sellars was briefly a Beaux Arts convert, but finding no success with it in competitions promptly gave it up. Keppie may well have had some of these designs about the office, as well as some from his own Beaux Arts days which seem to have profited him little.

So far relatively little attention has been paid to the designs of Honeyman and Keppie's office in 1890–94. They have been generally regarded as 'work of the firm'. It is wrong, however, to look at them as such; for they tell us a great deal about Mackintosh's development. Of that office Honeyman was an Italian Renaissance and neo-classical man, and (given a little money) a very

able Goth, interested no doubt in the Modern Movement but too old to be in touch with it. The office books show that except for the Brechin Cathedral restoration, nearly all the important jobs after 1890 were handled by Keppie or Mackintosh. Alexander MacGibbon, the senior assistant, was a brilliant draughtsman, but suffered chronic indecision in matters of design; and Keppie in his independent work of 1889–90 at 33–9 Greendyke Street, Glasgow, and the Fairfield Shipbuilding Offices at Govan, shows us that he was a rather unimaginative follower of Sellars and J. J. Burnet. This leaves us with Mackintosh, with whom Keppie was, an inscribed watercolour shows, then on terms of exceptional friendship, frequently invited to Keppie's house at Prestwick to work uninterruptedly, particularly on competition designs, leaving Honeyman in charge of the office. Keppie had few ideas of his own; Mackintosh had many. Niceties of employer and employed were sunk, we may be sure, in friendship, the expectation that he would become his brother-in-law and the desire to win.

The oldest of these competition designs (now in the Glasgow University Collection) is for the rebuilding of Glasgow High Street. The competition was won by Burnet & Boston (a different firm from J. J. Burnet's) but the design, entirely in Mackintosh's hand, is of some interest; for it shows appreciative study of Sydney Mitchell's Well Court, Edinburgh (*The British Architect* 23 August 1889), though the prescribed street lines prevented Mackintosh from emulating Mitchell's romantic courtyard grouping.

More interesting is the Glasgow Art Galleries competition, for which Honeyman and Keppie at first competed separately. Honeyman's (*The Builder* 25 June 1892) was a Greek design equal in quality to anything by Sellars and almost approaching Alexander Thomson himself.[5] It is unlikely, though Howarth noted that it is akin to Mackintosh's Thomson Scholarship design in 1890, that Mackintosh did more than draw the friezes and sculpture which appear to be in his hand; Honeyman had already designed the Paisley Museum in this idiom in 1868. Keppie's was also published (*The British Architect* 2 December 1892) and, despite its sculptured frieze below the entablature, apparently copied from Burnet (Glasgow Fine Art Institute 1878), and a big dome rather too obviously borrowed from Rowand Anderson's dome at Adam's Edinburgh University (1887), shows considerable evidence of Mackintosh's hand.

The double-transomed windows are those of the design for a Science and Art Museum of 1890 and so are the French square dome roofs and Sellars-type pedimented doorpiece. The treatment of the main portals seems to be Keppie (cf. Fairfield), the organ case has details like the Glasgow Art Club work of 1893, which was largely designed by Mackintosh. It is already hard to tell where, beyond plan and general outline, Keppie ends and Mackintosh begins.

1 *Portrait of Charles Rennie Mackintosh.*

These designs secured separate places in the final competition for their authors, but they produced one joint design, quite unrelated to their previous schemes. The drawings as published (*The British Architect* 10 June–8 July 1892) are entirely in Mackintosh's hand, and there can be little doubt that beyond the general arrangement the whole design is his. The brilliant penmanship, the unmistakable lettering, the fluent design of ornament and sculpture, the awareness of the contemporary London work of J. D. Sedding, Henry Wilson, and in a few details J. M. MacLaren, are far removed from the work of either of the partners.

Alfred Waterhouse was the assessor. Mackintosh took a good look at what Waterhouse was known to like: the recent transition from Gothic to early Renaissance in Waterhouse's own practice together with the general outline and Romanesque treatment of the Natural History Museum in South Kensington and two competition successes by Aston Webb in which Waterhouse was the assessor. These were the Law Courts at Birmingham and the original design for the Victoria and Albert Museum which had been published in the very week the Glasgow competition was announced (and which also formed the foundation of Edgar Wood and Thomas Taylor's design for the Whitworth Institute at Manchester). Mackintosh managed to encompass all these elements in his design. The combination of strong Romanesque and Late Gothic elements may surprise, but it had the authority of Belcher (whose work Mackintosh acclaimed in his lecture notes of 1893)[6] in a design for Maida Hill, London (*The British Architect* 10 May 1889). Mackintosh put his Italian sketch-books to good use: the interior detail can be directly related to his sketches at Pavia, Verona and elsewhere, while the apse on the east elevation is directly based on his sketch of S. Fedele at Como.[7] His enthusiasm for Michaelangelo shows in the sculpture,

3 *Charles Rennie Mackintosh. Glasgow Herald Building, Mitchell Street, Glasgow, 1893. Preliminary study by Mackintosh, much as executed. Original variations on 17th-century Scots detail and a tower probably deriving from MacLaren's turret at Stirling High School.*

which has curves familiar in his decorative work a little later, while other details are recognisably developed from his competition design of 1891–92 for a chapter house which itself appears to have had its origins in studies of the apse of Como Cathedral.

The origin of the Art Gallery towers is harder to identify. They may be Italian; for some of the sketch books are lost; or they might go back to Sellars's unsuccessful competition design for Renfrew County Buildings at Paisley of 1888. Mackintosh's Soane Medallion design of 1893 for a railway terminus is in some degree related to this design, but save for the lower turret features, which are derived from MacLaren's Stirling High School and which we shall meet again in Mitchell Street, the architectural features are largely inspired by Henry Wilson and to a lesser degreee by Leonard Stokes, whose work also received enthusiastic notice in Mackintosh's lecture notes of 1893. The Art Gallery design has perhaps rather more of the 'living fancy' which Mackintosh sought, and confronted with the present building (Sir John Simpson at his very coarsest) it is impossible not to regret that Honeyman and Keppie did not win. Yet perhaps it was

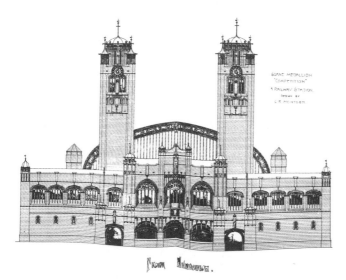

2 *Charles Rennie Mackintosh. Soane Medallion Competition design for a Railway Station. Free Gothic with reminiscences of Harry Wilson and J. M. MacLaren.*

as well; for the pleasure Mackintosh had in working in this eclectic idiom is very evident from the drawings, and the prolonged period of construction might well have retarded his search for a more personal expression.

A little-known Honeyman and Keppie design of this period is that for the Manchester Technical Schools which *The British Architect* published on 4 November 1892, expressing mild surprise that it did not win the competition and suggesting that the assessor might have given his reasons. The unusual combination of early Venetian Renaissance windows at first floor with François Ier detail above strongly recalls Rowand Anderson's similar experiment at Glasgow Central Station, while those at the centre have been re-used from Keppie's Art Gallery design. All these features could be either by Keppie or Mackintosh. The hand of Keppie is recognisable at the portal, features of which go back to his warehouse at Greendyke Street; the unbroken figure frieze above and the centre top floor can be related to other Mackintosh schemes. The big Italianate tower is probably a Mackintosh reminiscence of Italy, though no related sketch survives; the

4 *Charles Rennie Mackintosh. Competition design for Royal Insurance Building, Buchanan Street, Glasgow (1894). Repeats the Glasgow Herald corner treatment with a Belcher-type top; much of the detail is of the same type. The plain parapet heralds the east elevation of the School of Art. Perspective by Alexander McGibbon.*

treatment of the angle strips of the octagonal turret we shall meet again. The whole design seems very much a joint product, but the interesting roof gallery to the internal courts with perky *Art Nouveau* turret features, is plainly Mackintosh.

The year 1893 brings us to the Glasgow Herald Building in Mitchell Street, and here Mackintosh comes much closer to his final style. The memorable feature is the tower, which Professor Howarth believed derived from features in Henry Wilson's design for Victoria (BC) Cathedral of 1893. But this was published late in 1893, by which date Mackintosh had already used the motif in miniature form in his railway terminus design. The real origin was no doubt the angle turret of the High School at Stirling by J. M. MacLaren, in whom Mackintosh apparently took considerable interest.

The expansion of such a turret into a big tower is of course a bold and wholly original stroke, well considered in relation to the constricted nature of Mitchell Street, where a tower of conventional proportions would have been two-thirds hidden. The deep swelling form of the corbelling, with elongated shields at the angles, is unprecedented.[8] The lower floors are a determinedly non-period effort, but the recessed bays were not entirely novel: Ricardo had introduced this feature in his design for a Westminster office (*The British Architect* 18 May 1888), and several others followed.

The top floor is controversial; it is generally believed to be Keppie's, but Mackintosh's sketch-books show clearly that this is not the case. It may be that Keppie did not like the Ionic eaves-gallery proposed in the first sketch, but the second sketch leaves no doubt that the final treatment was Mackintosh's. In any event the swirling *Art Nouveau* forms of the pediments, developed from Scottish 17th-century details, are far beyond anything devised by Keppie unassisted, while the concave-ended balconies (adopted from Burnet and Campbell's Athenaeum Theatre of 1891) and the depressed ogee architraves were to be features of Mackintosh's Martyrs' Scool.

That Mackintosh admired Belcher (or rather, though he evidently did not know it, Belcher's assistant Beresford Pite), may surprise some people. Belcher gets very favourable notice in Mackintosh's lecture notes of 1893. I have noted a possible hint of his influence in the Art Gallery design, and the house designs published in *The Architect* in 1890 must also have impressed. Belcher's use of crowded figured friezes could have influenced Mackintosh, but Colcutt and others also favoured such friezes at the time. A much more obvious borrowing is to be seen in the corner dome of the competition design for the Royal Insurance Building of 1894; for here the aedicules of the subsidiary domes of the Belcher-Pite competition design for the Victoria and Albert Museum have been adopted with only slight modifications. Howarth believed that this was a Keppie design, but in some ways it is the most interesting of all these competition designs. The corner treatment is quite clearly related to the Glasgow Herald, while on the Buchanan Street frontage the wall head without cornice and the slightly advanced bays with curved tops point forward to the east gable of the School of Art.[10] The side elevation is more orthodox (in consideration no doubt for the Wilson and Elliot buildings opposite), but the rustication-linked windows were to reappear in the Martyrs' School of the following year.

I do not suggest that these are entirely Mackintosh's designs. They are the result of that 'happy phase of close collaboration' of which Howarth was told by people then still alive, with Keppie concentrating on the planning and technical, and Mackintosh, we may be sure, on the decorative aspects. There would be suggestions and changes, no doubt, which Mackintosh absorbed into the elevations in his own way. The end of this phase is easily seen in the dull academic design for the Paisley Technical Schools of 1896 in which Mackintosh conspicuously had no hand. From that year, perhaps because of his declining relationship to Jessie Keppie, they seem to have moved apart. The answer to the persistence of the motifs evolved in 1890–94 is that Mackintosh moved on; Keppie left to himself did not. Studies for 'Keppie' detail in Mackintosh's Italian sketch books leave little room for doubt. In the trial and error of joint designing, Keppie may not himself have realised how much Mackintosh had contributed.

Except for the Glasgow School of Art, in which he collaborated with Honeyman on the planning, Mackintosh henceforward became in a large measure autonomous. The Queen Margaret College (now enveloped in additions and poorly recorded) and the Martyrs' School are generally regarded as his. In the College is the first appearance of Mackintosh's characteristic gable set back behind a plain parapet – a feature which goes back to such early Scottish tower-houses as Liberton and had already been re-adopted by MacLaren at Glenlyon. The stepping of the stair windows and the crowning turret might derive from MacLaren's large studio house in Avonmore Road in London, but is more likely to be independently worked, since the turret is a Sellars motif derived from the Tolbooth at Dysart. Most of the other details except for the very original flowing of the roof through an arched opening in the parapet[11] can be paralleled in earlier designs and were to persist in Keppie's work thereafter. The widely spaced Scottish balusters are of a type reintroduced by Sir J. J. Burnet and re-appeared in even more characteristic Burnet form as part of a solid parapet wall curved at the angle (as at Burnet's University Gardens, 1887, the Western Infirmary Pathological Building, of 1894 and so on) in the Martyrs' School.

There are no other special features in this design except for the boldly projecting eaves (Burnet also started using broad eaves about this time), but the section containing this feature is of interest in that the turret feature seems to lead on to the centre bay of the

5 *Charles Rennie Mackintosh. Queen Margaret's College, Hillhead, Glasgow (1894). Now engulfed in B.B.C. extensions. A design of the Scottish school with a severe tower-house like wing on the right, again anticipating the School of Art's east gable. Drawn by Mackintosh.*

School of Art. Apart from the remarkable roof-trusses, the doorway is the most interesting feature with the familiar depressed ogee architrave, here given the characteristic Burnet profile, but flanked by extra-ordinary consoles stretched far beyond anything that Burnet would then have contemplated. The doors themselves show that *Art Nouveau* had invaded the joinery work in no uncertain terms.

So much has been written about the Glasgow School of Art, which was designed between March and October 1896, that it might at first sight seem difficult to add anything new about it. But something more might be said on the difficult question of sources and something about the competition itself. While the design must have stood out startlingly from the others, we should not imagine them all as academic palaces. H. E. Clifford had already designed in the Modern Movement manner[12], Henry Mitchell had followed Mackintosh closely (see his College design in *The British Architect* 23 February 1894) and was building a Modern Movement tenement in Castlebank Street; Salmon and W. J. Anderson had already shown experimental tendencies and were to design Modern Movement work within the next twelve months; and Burnet had used very modern horizontal windows without mullions in the Western Infirmary Pathological Building of 1894 and had visited the United States in that very year. His design may well have had modern characteristics.

The importance of the financial restrictions on the School of Art cannot be overstressed. The challenge was to design a building which would be a worthy image for the School and yet cost much less than an ordinary Board school. It had to be achieved virtually by simple mass and void. Had it not been for the peculiar nature of the competition, it is possible that Mackintosh's style (except in its internal decorative aspects which were already well advanced) would have become established rather later than it did, and that such drastic simplifications would not have been acceptable to the partners.

This radical simplification is evident in the earliest known study for the school, the preliminary sketch illustrated by Howarth, the significance of which has hitherto gone largely unnoticed in print. The centre-and-ends treatment may be conventionally British, but the fenestration is of the kind we think of as American, though the Gage Building, whose fenestration it most nearly resembles, dates from two years later. Such mullioned façades were not entirely unknown in Glasgow: there is a badly mutilated example in St Enoch Square and another in Govan Road, both as yet unattributed, and a warehouse at 50–76 Union Street (of *circa* 1855) where long window bands are divided by widely spaced strips of superimposed orders, but it is hard to believe that this sketch could have been influenced by such unfashionable designs. Although Burnet had been in the United States, in 1896, he did

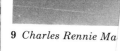

9 *Charles Rennie Ma*

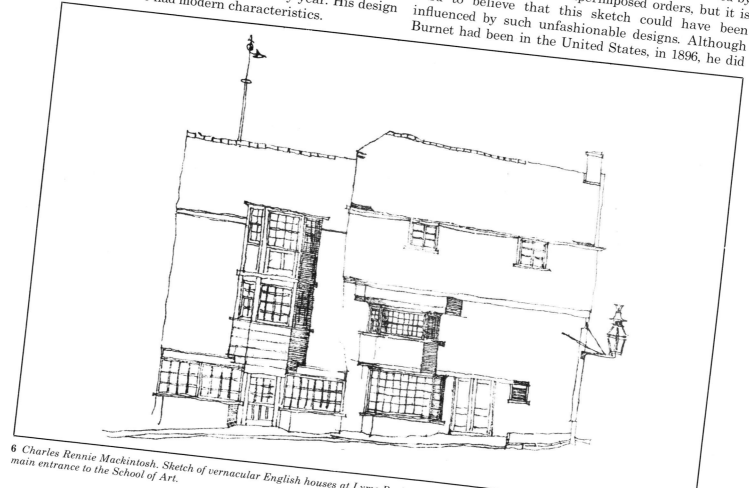

6 *Charles Rennie Mackintosh. Sketch of vernacular English houses at Lyme Regis, Dorset (1895). The bay windows inspired those at the main entrance to the School of Art.*

11 *C...*
Merr...

of the Liverpool design in any event transcends all indebtedness. The Ruchill Church Hall, of 1899, however, is in his own idiom with an elongated version of the School of Art centre window and bowed cills deriving perhaps from the 16th-century Duffus Manse at Elgin. The frontage curves into the stair turret without any break, a treatment earlier adopted by J. J. Burnet in the west gable of the Queen Margaret Union in 1887.

The year 1899 brings us to Windyhill, Kilmacolm, the earlier of his two major houses. And this is perhaps the place to discuss in a little more detail James Marjoribanks MacLaren (1843–90)[19], suggestions of whose influence have been noted from time to time. Rather surprisingly Mackintosh does not mention him in his lecture notes among *The Architect*'s other star performers, although he and his successors came far nearer to the style of Windyhill than any others. It is unlikely that Mackintosh ever met him. But Keppie probably had; for Campbell Douglas's and Sellars's assistants – B. J. Talbert, Troup, J. M. Brydon, Flockhart, G. W. Browne and MacLaren, and J. J. Stevenson, Douglas's ex-partner – were very much a family. MacLaren was actually a pupil of Salmon, but, according to *The British Architect* of 7–14 November 1890, had been with

Douglas for a time before making the predictable transfer to Stevenson in London.[20]

Thereafter he worked with William Young, Howell, and Richard Coad, before setting up on his own. He did not live long enough to do much: the Presbyterian church at Dulwich, additions to Ripple Court in Kent, alterations at Ledbury Park, an hotel at Santa Catalina, Las Palmas, a large studio-house in Avonmore Road in London, the small town hall at Aberfeldy and the extension to Stirling High School, his largest job. Just before he died he collaborated with Stewart, a civil engineer, and William Dunn, and won first premium in the abortive Watkin project for an Eiffel Tower for London. The Curries (who had previously employed Devey) were his best clients: for them he designed the Palace Court houses, the farmhouse and steading and at least two blocks of thatched cottages at Glenlyon, in Perthshire, which were finished by Dunn who had formed a partnership with MacLaren's draughtsman Robert Watson. Dunn and Watson reconstructed Glenlyon House, and built the hotel at Fortingal.

The designs for all these Perthshire commissions were illustrated in *The Architect* in 1891–92, rather early to have an effect on Windyhill unless Mackintosh had filed their plates, but since he explored the country

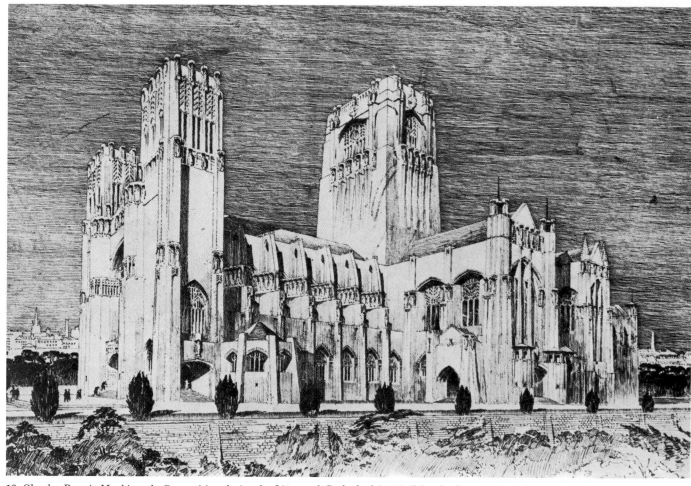

18 *Charles Rennie Mackintosh. Competition design for Liverpool Cathedral (1903). Like the Railway Terminus design of ten years earlier, it owes something to Harry Wilson.*

whenever he could it is very likely that he had seen them. He may even have had friends or relatives in Perthshire; for in 1906 he designed a hitherto unrecorded little house and shop (for P. Macpherson, now Brough and Macpherson) opposite the parish church of Comrie. Fortingal Hotel was unique at its date, as to a lesser degree was Glenlyon House, in its avoidance of the turrets, string courses, moulded openings and sculptured pediments which characterised Scottish baronial up to the turn of the century and beyond; it relied entirely upon a careful appreciation of the proportions of solids and voids and the simple harled finish of true Scots vernacular building. Substitute straight skews for crowstepped ones, take away the solid angles and parapet of the bay, and you have the style of Windyhill almost exactly.

MacLaren's farm house is even more interesting, as we might expect, for he was a far more original designer than Dunn or Watson. This little house has not merely the squareness and robust quality of the Hill House at Helensburgh of 1902 but also a very similar gable treatment and strongly battered chimneys, which had of course been common currency from Voysey's

practice throughout the '90s, and on the east side of the house is another feature which anticipates Mackintosh's inventions, a narrow vertical panel of similar family to that in the 'Town House for an Artist' of 1901.[21]

Yet although I feel sure that Mackintosh found the Glenlyon buildings interesting and suggestive the story is not quite so simple. There is an undated design for a large 'Country Mansion', symmetrical round a courtyard, in simple vernacular style but with tall octagonal bays to the court and other *Art Nouveau* features which have no point of resemblance to the Glenlyon buildings and may well antedate Windyhill. Moreover, a small sketch and the first large finished design for Hill House show that the resemblance to Glenlyon farmhouse was less marked in the early stages. The set-back gable was at first designed quite differently with a small oriel high up, while the round tower in the re-entrant angle was originally corbelled out rather like the Glenlyon House one. The sketch shows that the bow with stone 'shutters' rising directly from the lintel of the window below has no precedent and that it was arrived at by incessant experiment, even

19 *Charles Rennie Mackintosh. Scotland Street School, Glasgow (1904–06). A standard board school plan given original elevational expression. Mackintosh's drawing shows small paned windows, but the School Board demurred.*

20 *Charles Rennie Mackintosh. Glasgow School of Art. Interior of Library from gallery (1907–09).*

although Niven and Wigglesworth had done something similar in swelling the wall area between windows at the Sailors' Rest in West India Dock Road, London, of 1896. The simple 'monolithic' treatment of the main entrance of Hill House, however, so different from the archaeologising effusions common at that point in neo-Scottish houses, seems clearly related to the porch of the Fortingal Hotel, basic though the design is.

Mackintosh's last large house in Scotland, Mosside (now Cloak) at Kilmacolm, shows a more uncompromisingly Scottish approach. As first designed it was a real Scottish castle with severe rubble walls, crowstepped gables and a tall three-storey section which was not built. It had, however, one very original and unexpected feature: the deep internal window splays of the old Scottish tower houses were turned inside out, a good example of Mackintosh's ability to see unusual possibilities in the most conventional things.

From this period two unexecuted designs survive, both very different from Mackintosh's other work after 1895. One is for a house at Kilmacolm (1902), rather in the Franco-Scots style of Leiper and, although attractive, not significant. The other is a very large and ambitious competition design for the National Bank at the corner of St Vincent and Buchanan Streets in Glasgow, of 1898. This design appears to have been suppressed in the past as outside the main stream of Mackintosh's development, and there can be no doubt that he swallowed at least some of his pride to woo the bankers. Very probably he would have drastically re-designed it had he been called upon to execute it and vexed his clients in doing so. Nevertheless the rich *Art Nouveau* Renaissance of this design shows considerable power and resource in the design of ornament, and perhaps even hints at what Mackintosh's style might have become had it not been for the enforced austerity of the

21 *Charles Rennie Mackintosh. Library Wing, Glasgow School of Art (1907–09). The peak of Mackintosh's late work. He worked on the design from 1905 onwards.*

School of Art. It is significant that Mackintosh became friendly with James Salmon Jun., at this time, for the design is related to the Mercantile Chambers, Bothwell Street, Glasgow, designed in 1897. Salmon's design is superior below, but Mackintosh's incomparably finer in the upper parts.

Sir Nikolaus Pevsner (*Pioneers of Modern Design*, Penguin Edition 1970) has remarked upon the increase of Baronial influences after 1897. We see it not merely in Hill House but even more markedly in the Daily Record of 1901, where Scots dormers of a simple Scots 17th-century pattern, with a bold corbelled cornice and wide cantilevered bays below, are allied to a type of frontage then becoming popular in Glasgow for lane elevations, in which large glazed areas are set back between unbroken brick piers. The Daily Record windows have Chicago proportions, but are still sashed.

With the Scotland Street School of 1904 it is possible to be a little more specific in baronial antecedents. The basic plan is standard board-school practice (as may be seen by reference to books of school plans published at the time) and so is the fenestration: the education authorities of the time appear to have jibbed at the proposed small-paned windows. Two features other than the finely designed ornament are novel: the setting back of the mezzanines, perhaps a carry-forward from the functional peripheral vestibule and buttress features of the non-premiated Concert Hall design of 1901, and the stair towers. In plan-type the staircases – parallel flights with a solid wall between – were again standard board-school practice. Mackintosh had used the type himself with a bow end at Windyhill and Hill House in the Scots 17th-18th-century tradition. But at the school he stopped the landing short of the bow so that he could treat it continuously. The suggestion for this mullioned bay through several storeys might be the centre hall-bay of Voysey's Broadleys, which goes back to medieval prototypes via Devey, but Thomas Ross's restoration drawing of the Earl's Palace at Kirkwall seems a more natural and indeed an obvious source.

Mackintosh's last significant Glasgow work – and his greatest – the library wing of the School of Art (1907), shows the final shaking off of all identifiable precedent. The design has a soaring quality far beyond the dreams of the designer of the 17th-century work at Huntly, Aberdeenshire, to which it has sometimes been likened. The library windows have no doubt a distant relationship to Salmon and John A. Campbell's rear elevations of Hope's steel casement bay windows (Mercantile Chambers 1897 and 124 St Vincent Street 1904), the doorpiece might still have a remote connection with Burnet, but the proportions, the strongly Expressionist forms to be misused in the '20s and '30s, the recessed southern bay where a brilliant virtue is made of the necessity of keeping within the building line, are far beyond anything hitherto dreamed of.

Yet while I cannot quote any precedent for this section other than the Daily Record for the eastern part of the south elevation, the executed building shows subtle and significant changes from the original designs of March 1907. In order to emphasise the soaring quality of the library oriels Mackintosh cut the tall parapets of the three northern bays to mere hoods and altered the huge mass of blank masonry above from ashlar to snecked rubble, thus darkening it in tone and making the library stand out, as if it were a tower. At the same time the doorpiece which was originally similar to the eastern one was given a strong and very original Expressionist surround. Subtle changes were also made on the south elevation, chiefly the omission of the conventional masonry top to the uppermost bay. This Expressionist zigzag was to be further developed in the Cloister Room of the Ingram Street Tea Rooms and the Basset-Lowke house at Northampton, but, except for the small Squire and Augustus John studios and Hoppe's cottage, Mackintosh built no more.

However much we may feel for the personal tragedy of his last nineteen years, we may not have missed so very much. From 1914 to 1928 important commissions were few in Glasgow. Neither Salmon nor Gillespie designed anything of significance after 1914, and even Burnet's Glasgow office was much less busy than it had been. And when building picked up again in 1927 James Miller's American Classical was triumphant. Even Burnet in the North British and Mercantile Building followed the American pattern, characteristically excelling at it and contriving to be as original as ever in the details, but nevertheless to declare oneself satisfied with the derivative instead of the original meant that the century of the most individual architectural expression ever experienced by Glasgow ends on a sad note.

---

[1] Nikolaus Pevsner, *Charles R. Mackintosh*, Milan 1950 (in Italian). Translated in Nikolaus Pevsner, *Studies in Art, Architecture and Design*, Vol. II 1968.

[2] Thomas Howarth, *Charles Rennie Mackintosh and The Modern Movement*, Routledge & Kegan Paul, London 1952.

[3] Robert Macleod, *Charles Rennie Mackintosh*, Country Life, London 1968.

[4] For James Sellars see *Scottish Art Review* (old series) December 1888; *Transactions of the Glasgow Philosophical Society* 1888, and *Scottish Art Review* (new series) Vol. XI 1967.

[5] The final published drawings look like Mackintosh's draughtsmanship. The lettering is Roman in deference to the design but the high-pitched diagonal of the 'N' betrays its draughtsman.

[6] Entitled 'Architecture' – a lecture read to the Glasgow Architectural Association.

[7] The window divided by the column of the arcading is of course set back in a gallery at the original.

[8] Bits and pieces of detail reminiscent of this tower also appear in Keppie's Dunloe at Wemyss Bay 1889–90/94. Professor McLaren Young has pointed out to me the remarkable resemblance between the proportions and outline of this tower and a sketch of a late Gothic dome-capped pinnacle for Witchcombe.

[9] No. 8 Great George Street, now destroyed. For illustration see 'Goodhart-Rendel's Roll Call' in *The Architectural Review* Vol. 138, pp.259–264 and this volume pp.   –   . Also Goodhart-Rendel on Pite and Ricardo in *Journal of the Royal Institute of British Architects* Vol. XLIII, p.177.

[10] Edgar Wood had already used this feature though not in a very significant way in the doorpiece of the Manchester and Salford (now William Deacon's) Bank at Middleton in 1892.

[11] I have not been able to find a really likely precedent for this. Something like it occurs at Burnet's University Gardens of 1887, but the part containing it appears to be a slightly later addition. Townsend ran the roof through the balustrade in the Bishopsgate Institute of 1894.

[12] Rather tentatively in a terrace of flats in Terregles Avenue, Glasgow in 1895. His most interesting design is Bell Aird and Coghill's in Cadogan Street, Glasgow 1900–1. Clifford's interior design received considerable coverage in Muthesius' *Das Englische Haus*.

[13] The influence of Voysey does in fact show twice in Mackintosh's work: at the Auchenbothie lodge and in an un-executed design for a golf club house of which only a draughtsman's perspective survives.

[14] Most of these were Goodhart-Rendel favourites – see the 'Roll Call'. *The Architectural Review* ran a rather similar campaign in its early years with long biographical articles which are still not superseded.

[15] Like the Slater design (see below) which, as Howarth noted, Mackintosh would have retained because the issue of *The British Architect* contained a report of his lecture. The issue containing the Voysey studio would be retained, because it also contained the 'Keppie' Art Gallery design. Robert Macleod has shown that Howarth was wrong in thinking that the cornice in the 1896 drawings for the Glasgow School of Art was similar to that in the Voysey design – it is in fact the eaves in dead elevation – but it seems to have been a trick of Mackintosh's to give borrowed motifs a different third dimension. See, for instance, note 7.

[16] Ricardo was a particular favourite of *The British Architect* which complained of the impoverishment of British architecture by the assessors who fought shy of the unorthodox brilliance of his competition designs.

[17] A preparatory drawing of 1907 shows the gable set back behind a parapet and the new storey lightly pencilled in. Mackintosh's studies of Lindisfarne Castle of 1901 show a special interest in severe un-crowned wall planes.

[18] These 'oriels' are very curious. They form one-third of a circle from the inner wall surface and the projection beyond the outer wall surface is quite small. Clifford's are orthodox English canted bays with a straight link, and not curved as here. Though the motif is unusual, the two designs seem unconnected.

[19] MacLaren was a favourite of Goodhart-Rendel. See the 'Roll Call' and 'Rogue Architects of the Victorian Era', *Journal of the Royal Institute of British Architects* Vol. LVI, p.251. Part of his inspiration was undoubtedly H. H. Richardson, see the feathery frieze of Palace Court (adopted by Mackintosh in the final Art Gallery design) and the rear porch at Glenlyon farmhouse.

[20] The 'stepping-stone to London'. On this point see *Journal of the Royal Institute of British Architects* Vol. XV, p.482 and XVII, p.607. For the Salmons see *Scottish Art Review* (new series) Vol. X No. 3. Their circle included Leiper, the painter William McTaggart and the sculptors Albert Hodge and Derwent Wood. James Salmon Jun. ('a social and municipal Bolshevik . . . his views on the Parish Council, School Board and Infirmary Managers cannot be published!') was a friend of Mackintosh and a well-known member of the Chelsea Arts Club. He may have encouraged Mackintosh's move south. Both he and his partner J. Gaff Gillespie's *Art Nouveau* and Modern Movement work deserve better coverage. See pp.   –   in this volume.

[21] MacLaren's brother seems to have continued this idiom at least briefly. See Thomas MacLaren's design for a farmhouse, very similar to Glenlyon, *The British Architect* 25 September 1891 and his Nos. 1–11 George Street, Doune, Perthshire in the same idiom. In 1894, however, he appears to have emigrated to Colorado. His City Hall, Colorado Springs, 1905, is neo-Greek.

Acknowledgement: Andrew MacLaren Young gave generously of his time and knowledge particularly in relation to Mackintosh's sketch books and this article is much indebted to him.

The Partnership of James Salmon and John Gaff Gillespie

by David Walker

The fame of Burnet and, particularly, of Mackintosh has obscured the work of a number of other extremely talented contemporary Scottish architects. This account of the work of the younger James Salmon (1873–1924) and his partner J. G. Gillespie (1870–1926), both impressive Glasgow free style architects, is a welcome attempt to redress this historical injustice.

James Salmon Junior and John Gaff Gillespie are amongst the least-known masters of British *Art Nouveau*. Like Mackintosh, their creative architectural careers had a short run, mainly in the same decade and a half from 1893 to 1909. Even although they adapted themselves to the academic reaction against *Art Nouveau*, they paid the price of having made their names in that idiom. Both died in their fifties, still in business but underemployed. Overshadowed by the supreme genius of Mackintosh, in death history has been no less unkind.

Salmon, born on 13 April 1873, came, like Burnet, of an exceedingly prosperous architectural family. Again like Burnet he was the small son of a tall father (bringing the sobriquet of 'Wee Troot'), an indefatigable traveller, studying architecture in the farthest corners of Europe, and strongly opinionated. But there the resemblance ends, for he never was, nor wanted to become, an establishment figure. Comfortably off from accumulated Salmon wealth he could afford to be a rebel. Gillespie's background more nearly resembled Mackintosh's. Born on 17 April 1870, the son of a small master baker in the Gorbals, he chose architecture as his career and found an apprentice's stool in the office of J. M. Munro, from which, through sheer brilliance as a draughtsman, he graduated to the better-known office of James Salmon and Son. From it, placed equal with Mackintosh, he won the Glasgow Institute of Architects prize in 1889.

His employer, William Forrest Salmon (1843–1911), the 'son' of the firm, was not much of an architect himself, but could number amongst his closest friends the painter William McTaggart and the artist-architect William Leiper, to whom young James was apprenticed; and in Leiper's office at the time was the tragic scholar-architect W. J. Anderson who was, in the later '90s also interested in the possibilities of concrete and a non-period style.

James did not return from Leiper's until about 1893. In the intervening years Gillespie had raised the quality of the Salmon practice, notably at the narrow-frontage Scottish Temperance League building at 106–108 Hope Street, Glasgow in 1893–1905.[1] Its handsomely detailed early Flemish Renaissance front has curvaceous openwork at the gable, hinting at *Art Nouveau* openwork crowns to come, and beautiful sculptured roundels, carved by Ferris, but clearly from models made by one of Salmon and Gillespie's sculptor friends: both personally and through the business they greatly encouraged, among others, the Dutch sculptor Johan Keller (1863–?) at Glasgow School of Art from 1895, Francis Derwent Wood (1871–1926) at Glasgow School of Art 1897–1901, and the Glasgow-born Albert Hodge (1875–1918).

Gillespie became a partner in 1897, but the big commission of that year, Mercantile Chambers on Bothwell Street,[2] then one of the largest office blocks built in Glasgow, was given to young James who

became the firm's third partner in the following year. If it did not have the marvellous simplicity of Mackintosh, the overall pattern of the façade being still late Victorian and in some of its details (e.g. the columnar arrangement at the gables) deriving from Leiper, it was original, inventive, and, thanks to Derwent Wood, superbly detailed. It was however as much of the London school of *Art Nouveau* as of Glasgow's: the softly rounded treatment of the ground-floor arcade has something in common with Townsend, the sinuous pilasters and twisted columns above are of London origin too and have nothing at all in common with Mackintosh and his circle. Here perhaps the influence of

2 *James Salmon. Mercantile Chambers, Bothwell Street, Glasgow (1897). Front elevation. Leiper early Renaissance but with sinuous Art Nouveau detail. Drawing by Salmon.*

1 *Portrait of James Salmon.*

3 *James Salmon. Mercantile Chambers. Rear elevation of wood and metal casement bays.*

Wood and Hodge, the former a cosmopolitan London sculptor, and the latter soon to follow him there, should be stressed for sculpture was an integral part of all early Salmon designs. Salmon himself was in London a good deal, was early a member of the Chelsea Arts Club, and through it knew the latest trends in London just as well as those in Glasgow. More modern in its forms was the Mercantile's rear elevation, close spaced timber and steel canted casement bays with lead spandrels between very slim brick piers, the pioneer design of its kind in Glasgow.

In the same year the firm designed the large Marine Hotel at Troon,[3] a commission which seems to have been Gillespie's rather than Salmon's. The original 1897 section was advanced English Arts-and-Crafts on a symmetrical E plan, but the 1901 section showed a mild kinship with Mackintosh. Some of its details are good enough to linger in the memory, but the composition as a whole had nothing of his intensity. Internally, the influence of Mackintosh was rather more marked, the twinned uprights of the hall chimneypiece being presumably suggested by the twinned beams of the Glasgow School of Art staircase, then building. A much smaller building, but related to the Marine in some of its details was a house Gillespie designed at 12 University Gardens, Glasgow, in 1899–1900.[4] This terminated Burnet's terrace at Nos. 1–10 and in detail

generally deferred to it, the whole composition of Nos. 1–12 being rounded off by a canted bay over the porch with a dormered top. Internally the house is handled with a very distinctive non-period Arts and Crafts simplicity, detailing being concentrated on a little high quality woodcarving, metalwork and stained glass: in the stairwell the canvas-lined walls with green stained strapping, and, in a small square-panelled room at first floor, a simple but wilful stone chimneypiece and open-beamed ceiling all recall Mackintosh at the Glasgow School of Art even although the decorative detailing has a different and personal character.

Concurrently with these Salmon and Gillespie designed two Glasgow branches for the British Linen Bank, both with tenement flats above. The first of these at 162 Gorbals Street, now doomed, is somewhat indecisive in style with very wayward ground-floor arches brought to a horseshoe at the abaci, some good sculpture, and deliberately odd squatly-proportioned fenestration above, partly with quoined surrounds. The second, at Govan Cross (1899)[5] shows a simpler and maturer style. The general composition is pure late Victorian Glasgow with two bold chimneys framing a corner bay, but in the crown of thorns at its truncated roof and in the non-period sculptured details by Wood and Keller at the ground floor, *Art Nouveau* is clearly evident. The Anderston Savings Bank,[6] designed later

4 *John Gaff Gillespie. Marine Hotel, Troon (1897 and 1901). Drawn by Gillespie.*

in the same year, elaborated the same basic design but with a bolder corner oriel and a spectacular doorpiece sculpted by Albert Hodge with mosaic semi-domes and blue Venetian glass. Within a fine chimneypiece of *brèche-claire* marble and specially-designed *Art Nouveau* furniture were provided. If their obituarists' division of their work is to be trusted, these were by Gillespie, but Salmon mentioned the Linen Banks as his in a *Bailie* interview in 1918. Probably both partners had a hand in them as some Leiperish detailing, particularly at Anderston, suggests.

'The Hatrack' (properly St Vincent Chambers) at 142–144 St Vincent Street[7] was Salmon's commission. The site was a narrow Georgian houseplot only 29 feet 6 inches wide but 109 feet deep, and incredibly ten floors on an irregular dumb-bell plan were piled upon it. In order to get as much light into the building as possible, the façade was modelled into two oriel bays flanking central bipartite windows without any solid wall whatsoever, even the red stone mullions being whittled down almost to nothing. Above them the central division rises as the front face of another canted bay almost the whole width of the façade. The lower detail is extraordinary; the central first-floor window has a depressed scrolled crown to its arched head, fanciful cylindrical lantern oriels top the ingeniously stepped doorpieces, the winged corbelling of the main oriels above is marvellously rich, much more in the idiom of his sculptor friends than that of Glasgow *Art Nouveau*; above, in spite of the paucity of stonework, the detail is ingeniously varied, no two floors being identical, the whole terminating in a lively contrast of concave and convex at the balconies and roof which was once topped by an extravagant finial. Within, at the wrought-iron oval on the lift cage Mackintosh's influence begins to be seen even though the main motif is a variant of Salmon's favourite onion, and the curvaceous landing rails seem to show familiarity with more Continental forms of *Art Nouveau*. The transition to a purely Glasgow *Art Nouveau* within the next few years can well be seen at 79 West Regent Street, Glasgow, the façade of which was remodelled in 1903–04.[8] The copper spandrel panels of its bay windows have original beaten relief variations on the coats of arms of Scotland and Glasgow, the latter reminiscent of Mackintosh's wrought-iron versions of the same theme at the School of Art.

Salmon had in fact been friendly with Mackintosh, particularly after the McNairs left for Liverpool in 1898. A degree of Mackintosh influence is indeed to be felt in Salmon and Gillespie's hall of St Andrew's in the East Church, Glasgow still of that extraordinarily busy year, 1899. It has his extreme simplicity of treatment with the interest concentrated on just a few original features, but the scale was too small for the design to be very expansive. Like Mackintosh at Ruchill, Salmon and Gillespie lost the commission for the church itself, which went to James

5 *James Salmon. St Vincent Chambers, No. 144 St Vincent Street, Glasgow (1899). Drawing by Salmon, showing side elevation, probably never executed as adjoining site was redeveloped immediately after it was begun.*

6 *James Salmon. St Vincent Chambers. Detail of lower floors.*

7 *James Salmon. St Vincent Chambers. The upper stories are cantilevered in steel from a double row of iron columns. Affectionately known as 'The Hatrack'.*

Miller in 1904.

Salmon and Gillespie's best interior work for this period, and indeed their richest domestic commission ever, was the embellishment in 1897–99 of 22 Park Circus, Glasgow, internally the work of James Boucher (1872) and already a palazzo worthy of Barry himself.[9] The original chimneypieces failed to please however, and new ones in the *Art Nouveau* idiom, but still with remarkable sympathy for Boucher's work, were installed throughout the principal rooms with probably Derwent Wood – perhaps supplemented by Hodge and Keller – providing the magnificent woodcarving. The figure capitals of that in the dining room, the satinwood examples in the drawing room and its ante-room and the corinthianesque pilasters in the billiard room are amongst the very finest pieces of British *Art Nouveau* and virtually unknown. The glasswork by Stephen Adam is also of very high quality particularly at the front door and at a first-floor overmantel cabinet. Still in that same year, five pages of *L'Art Decoratif* were devoted to their work, and the future must have looked bright indeed.

Tastes changed and they never saw so much business again. As early as 1901 they recognised that they would have to have a foot in the academic camp to survive, and in their Glasgow Technical College competition designs of that year[10] two elevational treatments were submitted, one an elegant simplified treatment of Renaissance forms with arched centrepieces: a central semi-domed recessed porch of the Beresford Pite type, and an asymmetrical wing with a San Lorenzo dome; the other an *Art Nouveau* scheme developed from the designs produced in 1899. These were, judging by the draughtsmanship, by Gillespie and Salmon respectively.

In 1901–03 Salmon and Gillespie were responsible for two small designs for the Glasgow Congregationalists, both in a simplified late gothic manner with *Art Nouveau* references. The first of these, won in competition, was the Lloyd Morris (Hutchesontown) Church[11] in Rutherglen Road (demolished 1972). The squat pend tower showed the influence of the east gable of the School of Art, and perhaps also Burnet's low topless tower at the University Union, in its simplified outline, but the artful detailing, the subtle vestigial crenellation and the dropping of 'AD 1902' in and around the peak of a hood mould is entirely personal: the design was claimed for Gillespie and indeed the close relationship of the pend arch to a chimney piece at 12 University Gardens bears this out. Closely similar in style, but more extended in composition and without a tower, was the unsuccessful competition design for Elgin Place Church mission halls (1903) at the corner of Dobbie's Loan and Ann Street[12]. Still of the same family, but inferior in composition and draughtsmanship is the competition design for Renfrew Parish Halls, also unsuccessful, and also of 1903.[13]

In the competition designs of 1902 for Rutherglen

Public Library[14] and Newton Park School at Ayr[15] (neither was selected) the style of 1899 continued to flourish. The library scheme was still conventional '90s Glasgow in its basic form, a variation on themes from the Anderston and Govan banks with a broader corner octagon reminiscent in proportion of Leiper's Sun building at Glasgow, but the school design which was drawn by Gillespie showed definite stylistic development. The main block wilfully combined reversed symmetrical elements into an asymmetrical square block whose central entrance features extended upwards in a pagoda-like composition developed from a similar theme at the Anderston bank. More novel in their features were the octagonal janitor's house and the gymnasium, in outline simple Arts and Crafts, but with long-keystoned parabolic arches foreshadowing those at the corner turret of Lion Chambers.

Lion Chambers at 170, 172 Hope Street, Glasgow,[16] was Salmon's commission although Gillespie seems also to have had some hand in it. Like St Vincent

8 *John Gaff Gillespie. British Linen Bank, Govan Cross, Glasgow (1899). Drawn by Gillespie. A similar crown of thorns was proposed for St Vincent Chambers but not done.*

9 *John Gaff Gillespie and James Salmon. Anderston Savings Bank, Glasgow (1899). Mainly by Gillespie but with Leiper-Salmon type details inside and out.*

10 *John Gaff Gillespie and James Salmon. Anderston Savings Bank. Detail of doorpiece: sculpture by Albert Hodge.*

11 *James Salmon. Billiard Room ingleneuk, No. 22 Park Circus, Glasgow (1898).*

12 *John Gaff Gillespie and James Salmon. Competition designs for Glasgow Technical College, Glasgow (1901). The large drawing is Gillespie's, developing a free Renaissance manner; the smaller, developing St Vincent Chambers themes, is Salmon's.*

Chambers it was an extreme instance of their skill in designing large buildings for cramped sites, here a mere 33 feet wide by 46. Eight floors of lawyers' chambers were planned upon it, and, as was remarked at the time, had the masonry walls prescribed by the building bye-laws been adopted, the chambers would have been too small for useful occupation. L. G. Mouchel of the Hennebique company was consulted and devised a structure hung on 21 columns, each 13 inches tapering to 8, with membrane walls and floors only 4 inches thick, finished externally in cement with decorative motifs cast in situ. The general outline with its broad corbelled bay was conservative, deriving from J. A. Campbell's Britannia Building on Buchanan Street (1898), but justified on the grounds that it gave relief to elevations whose paper-thin walls were incapable of any but structural modelling with cantilevers, as well as providing a useful bonus in floorspace. In a lecture delivered in 1908[17] Salmon advocated a simple rough-cast treatment inspired by the old Scottish castles for large concrete and steel structures – an echo no doubt of the views of his friend Mackintosh – but no further concrete commission with which to experiment came his way.

It was their last major building in the city. Apart from the large nurses' home at Woodilee Hospital, plainish but with a handsomely-proportioned central pavilion, of 1902–04[18] and a school at Cartsburn, Greenock (1906–08 destroyed in the blitz)[19] it was mainly domestic work, particularly at Kilmacolm, which kept them in business. Forrest Salmon had, about 1898, there built himself a large house, Rowantreehill, probably to his son's designs as the general character is akin to Leiper's half-timber and tile Helensburgh houses, but predictably with some distinctively *fin-de-siecle* touches, such as the gargoyle features and the dormers. It was a good advertisement and several commissions for houses there followed, nearly all developing late Leiper themes in their exteriors but with modern movement detailing within. Mirjanoshta (1905),[20] now the R.C. Bishop's house, is the largest after Rowantreehill, stone-built with mullioned windows and a tiled roof, very simply finished inside. Dilkusha (1907),[21] which was drawn by Gillespie, is a modest Leiperish cottage house with a half-timbered wing, not noticeably modern movement, but in its detailing anticipating features of Salmon's Den o' Gryffe,[22] the most interesting house of the Kilmacolm series. This house has an octagon children's wing linked to the low main house by an angled hall-staircase, whose Leiper-type half-timbering emphasises the separation. The detailing, evidently reflecting the cult of simplicity in his 1908 lecture, was of the simplest kind: by his own account "all constructional woodwork such as joists, safe lintels etc., is exposed, and the walls are finished inside with the second coat of plaster off the float. There are no mouldings, V-joints, beads nor arches." It compares well with houses of similar size and character by

Baillie Scott. Nether Knockbuckle nearby, plain harled with prominent chimneys' also cultivates absolute simplicity of treatment, but Salmon's slightly earlier North Lodge at Edzell (1906) is in a more self-conscious Arts and Crafts version of the Scottish style with uncut boulders extruded from its red rubble walls, good internal woodwork, and canvas-covered walls with wooden strapping. It is impossible to differentiate the individual personalities of Gillespie and Salmon in these houses. The same detailing is common to them all, and can be seen also at Gillespie's very plain Lanfine Cottage Hospital, Broomhill, Kirkintilloch of 1904.[23]

Salmon and Gillespie remained faithful to the Modern Movement throughout the increasing conservatism of Edward's reign. In his 1908 address to the Glasgow Institute Salmon pleaded that "if this new material, reinforced concrete, could induce us to drop all the ridiculous accretion of absurdities which we plaster on to stone, it will indeed have lifted a weight from a world overladen with 'ornaments' and 'decorators'." These were extraordinary words from a man who had made his name with richly sculptured buildings. Yet in the series of competition designs, a good many fortunately published, with which they struggled somewhat unsuccessfully to recover the position they had so briefly held in the late 1890s, they had to follow the academic trend, imbuing it at the same time with *Art*

13 *John Gaff Gillespie. Lloyd Morris Congregational Church, 155–157 Rutherglen Road, Glasgow (1902). Free late Gothic owing something to Mackintosh.*

16 *John Gaff Gillespie. Competition Design for London County Hall (1907). Bold roof forms and some Glasgow reminiscences in a design otherwise sensitive to the current L.C.C. style.*

no building subsequent to a flourishing war-time practice building hutments: Gillespie on 7 May 1926, busy realising at last the basic concept of his 1909 concrete design for *The British Architect* in the exten-extension of the Ca d' Oro Building in Glasgow's Union Street. His partner William Kidd continued it but he too died within a year and the third partner of the firm, Gillespie's most famous pupil, Jack Coia, finished the job.

Biographical information on the Salmons and on Gillespie is scanty. Their obituaries in the *Journal of the Royal Institute of British Architects*; *The Bailie* 23 January 1918 and my brief note in *Scottish Art Review* Vol. X No. 3 provide the best information available. Mr Robert Scott Morton, Mrs Mary Newbery Sturrock, and the late A. G. Lochhead all helped with personal information.

[1] *Academy Achitecture* 1894i; *Glasgow Advertiser and Property Circular* 15 August 1899.

[2] *The Glasgow Advertiser and Property Circular* 6 December 1898; *Academy Architecture* 1901ii.

[3] *The Builder* 11 October 1902, drawing by Gillespie; *The Studio* Vol. 34 (1905) pp.54, 55.

[4] No. 14 has long been assumed to be Gillespie's also, but Mr Francis Worsdall has lately found evidence that it is by J. J. Burnet and of this the interior work gives ample confirmation.

[5] *The Glasgow Advertiser and Property Circular* 22 August 1899. Now the Bank of Scotland.

[6] *Academy Architecture* 1900i; *Building News* 28 September 1900; *The Builder* 21 March 1903.

[7] *Academy Architecture* 1900ii; *The Glasgow Advertiser and Property Circular* 1 August 1899; *The Builders' Journal* 28 November 1906. It was completed by December, 1902. The *Academy Architecture* drawing shows that the roof crown was developed from that of the Govan bank.

[8] *The Builders' Journal* 3 February 1904.

[9] *The Studio* Vol. 18 1900, article by Horace Townsend at pp.34–37 which very annoyingly does not mention any of the craftsmen; *Academy Architecture* 1898i; and *The Studio Year Book of Decorative*

17 *John Gaff Gillespie. British Architect Concrete Design Competition (1909).* Art Nouveau *has gone* Art Deco.

Art 1907 p.109. Salmon and Gillespie also remodelled 14, 15 Woodlands Terrace nearby with very good interior work at No. 14 (see *Academy Architecture* 1904i) but only some choice fragments remain, the house having been partitioned as small offices.

[10] *The British Architect* 11 October 1901. David Barclay's design was selected.

[11] *The Glasgow Advertiser and Property Circular* 13 August 1901.

[12] *The British Architect* 25 December 1903. R. A. Bryden's design was selected.

[13] *The British Architect* 21 August 1903.

[14] *The British Architect* 7 November 1902, 9 January 1903. Sinclair and Ballantine's design was selected.

[15] *The British Architect* 10 October 1902. John Eaglesham's design was selected.

[16] *Building Industries* 16 April 1906; with perspective by Gillespie: *The Builders' Journal* 28 November 1906; Peter Collins, *Concrete: The Vision of a New Architecture*, p.82.

[17] *The Builders' Journal* 25 March 1908, pp.269–273.

[18] *The Builders' Journal* 28 December 1904.

[19] *The Builder* 8 September 1906; *The Builder* 22 August 1908.

[20] *The Studio Year Book of Decorative Art* 1907 pp.74, 75.

[21] *The Builders' Journal* 27 November 1907, house for A. Crosbie Turner. Nether Knockbuckle, also in Kilmacolm, is another house of similar type.

[22] Nicoll, *Domestic Architecture in Scotland*, pp.58–59.

[23] *The Builders' Journal* 29 June 1904.

[24] *The British Architect* 9 October, 23 October 1903. Cullen Lochhead and Brown's design was selected.

[25] *The British Architect* 30 September 1904. Walker and Ramsay's design was selected.

[26] *The British Architect* 26 April, 10 May 1907. A. N. Paterson's design was selected. A good Salmon and Gillespie renaissance design of this period which did see execution was the reconstruction of St Peter's, Brown Street, Glasgow, since destroyed, *The Builders' Journal* 30 September 1908.

[27] *The British Architect* 25 October, 1 November 1907. Ralph Knott's design was selected.

[28] Alexander Koch, *British Competitions* Vol. II 1907–09, pp.194–195. H. E. Clifford's design was selected (by Burnet).

[29] Koch, *op cit* Vol. III 1909–1911, p.185, 3rd Premium. Cullen Lochhead and Brown's design was selected (by George Bell).

[30] *The British Architect* 1 October 1909.

[31] Koch, *op cit* Vol. II, pp.147–152; *The Architects' and Builders' Journal* 31 October 1917. Never finished. J. A. Coia was entrusted with its completion in 1939 but war stopped the work. It has recently been extended to a different design, reslated and denuded of its ventilator cupola.

[32] *The British Architect* 25 June 1909.

[33] *The Architects' and Builders' Journal* 10 April 1912, illustrated. Recently destroyed.

The writer is indebted to John R. Hume for help in respect of Gillespie's designs.

The lingering death of the Gothic Revival in secular British architecture during the 1870s was not followed by any such decline of the style in ecclesiastical work. Indeed the period covered by this book produced a very large number of Gothic churches, and even cathedrals, using the basic pointed style in an unending variety of manners. The only challenges made to its supremacy were a Byzantine Revival in the last two decades of the 19th century and a handful of Arts and Crafts free style churches scattered across the country – and many of the latter were free developments of the Gothic.

The great Goths of the end of the century were William Butterfield (though his best-known works were middle, rather than late, Victorian), J. L. Pearson, William White, James Brooks, G. F. Bodley, J. D. Sedding, J. F. Bentley and George Gilbert Scott the younger. The general characteristic of the period (there were many exceptions, of course) was a new lightening of feeling that approached elegance at times in church interiors. All of the above men had architectural practices predominantly in church work. The study of the work of John Dando Sedding (1838–1891) has been selected for this book not only because of his excellence as a designer, but also because his originality in the use of Gothic made him influential on the young idealists of the Arts and Crafts Movement (indeed, he was the Art Workers' Guild's second Master). The younger Scott, like Sedding, was a sad case of a great talent cut off by early death. But any account of the period must note how Pearson (1817–97) came to eminence late in life with his great Gothic cathedrals at Truro in Cornwall and Brisbane in Australia. Mention must also be made of the flowering of Gothic churches by Leiper, Burnet, Campbell and others in Scotland in the 1870s and '80s.

However distinguished these other Gothic architects, it is to John Francis Bentley (1839–1902) and his works, that contemporaries and historians most frequently return for the finest church work of the time. His Holy Rood church at Watford of 1887 was put forward by H. S. Goodhart-Rendel as "the most lovely church the nineteenth century gave to England". But his next major work brings us not only to a great building but to the fairly widespread Byzantine Revival. This was the Westminster Roman Catholic Cathedral, designed about 1895 with an interior that was never finished to Bentley's plans. Bentley died in 1902, and of the generation of fine English church architects mentioned above, Bodley was the only one to survive him. By 1907 Bodley too was dead – it was as though the end of the century of Queen Victoria's reign had signalled a new wave of church designers.

Those new men were to some extent the Arts and Crafts architects. Sedding's own pupil and successor, Harry Wilson (1863–1934) was one of the great talents of the movement – as church plate designer as well as architect. His work shines out at a level of artistic inspiration that makes most of its neighbours pale. Sadly, he seems to have been no business man, for he let the Sedding practice decay and plunged into architectural journalism for a time before finally retiring to France. Additions to some of Sedding's churches, a library in North Kensington, a splendid but unexecuted church design for Boscombe, some marvellous church plate and the inspired Byzantine furnishing of St Bartholomew in Brighton – this and a little more is all that we have from this brilliant man.

Sedding was not the only Arts and Crafts architect to design churches – examples will be found in the chapters on Lethaby, Prior, Townsend, Pite, Lutyens and Stokes, and there are others (including one by Mackintosh, several by Bidlake in Birmingham and one by Randall Wells). They are among the most impressive achievements of English architecture, but most are small and few are in city centre positions where they would attract the attention they deserve.

The greater part of the good church work of the Edwardian period, often influenced to some degree by the Arts and Crafts manner, was by five men; the aging Basil Champneys (1842–1935), the much younger Temple Moore (1856–1920), W. D. Caröe (1857–1938) Ninian Comper (186 –1960) and Giles Gilbert Scott (1880–1960). Scott rocketed to fame by winning the Liverpool Cathedral competition in 1903. He and Moore preferred to work in a chunky Gothic, using powerful forms and massing. Caroe was less predictable, but again used predominantly strong Gothic forms with generous injections of Arts and Crafts features.

Finally, Ninian Comper started to carve his own refined manner; digesting classical, Gothic, Renaissance and other features and producing highly individualistic works that blended them into a delicate whole.

The last essay in this part sorts out all these strands of Edwardian ecclesiastical architecture and sets them against the ritual and other church reforms of the period that have, as always in church design, so great an effect on the architect's work.

1 *James Brooks. St Andrew's Church, Plaistow, London (1867–70).*

253

2

2 *J. L. Pearson. Truro Cathedral, Cornwall (1880 onwards).*

3 *John Francis Bentley. Church of the Holy Rood, Market Street, Watford, Hertfordshire (1883–90).*

4 *Norman Shaw. St Michael and All Angels, Bedford Park, London (1879–80).*

3

4

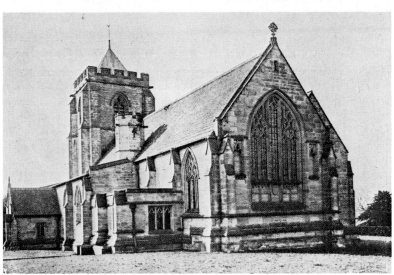

5 *John Francis Bentley. High Altar, Church of the Holy Rood, Watford, Hertfordshire (1883–90).*

6 *Ninian Comper. West end, Chapel of St Margaret, Aberdeen (1891).*

7 *G. F. Bodley. All Saint's Church, Danehill, Sussex (1892).*

8 *Leonard Stokes. Design for a town church (1893). The free manner of the Arts and Crafts architects applied to church design.*

9 *C. Harrison Townsend. St Martin's Church, Blackheath, near Guildford, Surrey (designed circa 1892, opened 1895). One of Townsend's early works, yet showing typically unexpected twists to Arts and Crafts ideas.*

10 *John Francis Bentley. Main doorway, Westminster Cathedral, Victoria Street, Westminster (1895–1903). Bentley's great cathedral was the masterpiece of a widespread revival of Byzantine church architecture.*

11 *John Francis Bentley. Westminster Roman Catholic Cathedral, Victoria Street, Westminster (1895–1903, interior decoration done later not to Bentley's designs). Cardinal Vaughan suggested the early Christian Byzantine style to Bentley.*

8

9

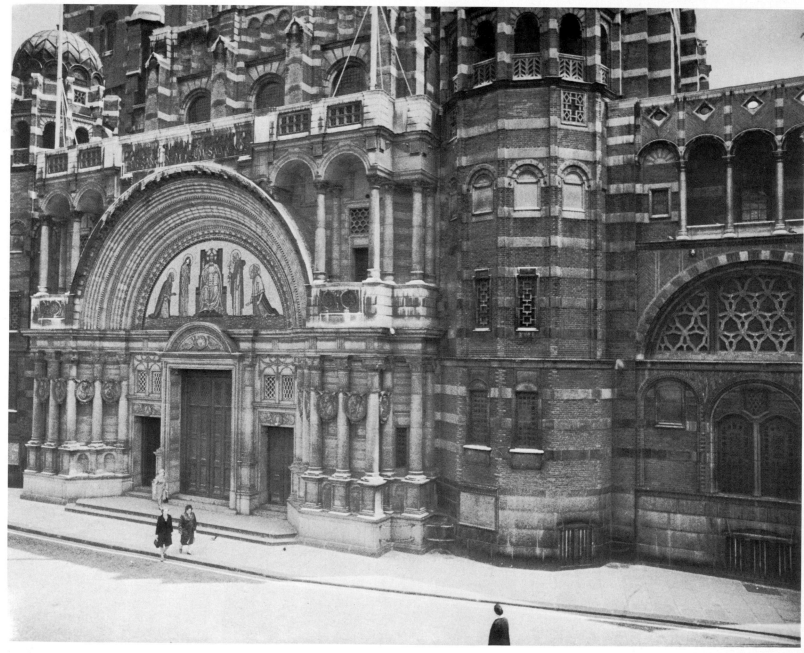

10

The Work of John D. Sedding

by J. P. Cooper, assisted by H. Wilson

The great names in late Victorian church architecture include
Pearson, White, Brooks, Bodley, the younger George Gilbert Scott,
Bentley and Sedding. Of these, John Dando Sedding (1838–1891) has
been chosen here for individual study because his was the most
original and free use of the Gothic style in the 1880s, combined with
a deep interest in Arts and Crafts principles that influenced later
church designs by younger men. The essay was written by one of
Sedding's pupils, J. Paul Cooper, with the assistance of his senior
partner Harry Wilson, six years after the architect's death.

The objects of these papers is to give some account of the early works of John Sedding, to show the connection they had with the time in which he was educated and with his later works, and also to trace their influence on the art of to-day. The artist is, in his generation, often looked upon as a creature too effervescent, too full of whims and fancies, to stand the shock of time; we scarcely recognise him as ever having been of the same stuff as ourselves, because we do not see the links which bind him to the earth. So it was with Sedding. His art was, and is, the despair of the "classifying bookmaker." He did not work in any particular style, but ventured on unknown and, therefore, dangerous seas.

His work divides itself into three parts. First, his early work of the days of the Gothic revival, which is a *resumé* of the past, and an attempt to bring back its romantic character. Secondly, works of additions and repairs done chiefly to country churches, most of which had already suffered at the restorer's hand. Thirdly, his latter day works, when, his connection with Gothic being severed, he struck out in a new direction in the attempt to raise the architecture of the future. Of his country work, lying as it does in out-of-the-way parts of Cornwall and Devon, but little is known. From perspective sketches, however carefully executed, it is impossible to judge them; they were nearly always altered in the process of construction. Some mistake of the builders was taken advantage of, or what had appeared to look well on paper was modified to suit the latter needs. Little as this country work is known, it is probably that by which he will be best remembered. "In old art any good thing is backed by other good things." This cannot be said of our towns nowadays, where one barren street echoes another – one piece of vulgarity caps its fellows. The few good buildings we have left to us stand isolated amid their sordid surroundings, in daily peril of their existence from some pecuniary-minded landlord or his numerous agents. In entering a town church of Sedding's, we nearly always feel that he, too, was glad to get inside and shut out the view. In the country such shudderings are almost unknown – nature and art are in unison. The site is suggestive, and the surrounding buildings themselves give the key for the artist to work in. Proud as Sedding was of his town work, his heart was in the country, and it was in the work done there he felt his fame would eventually rest. "You must write on my gravestone," he said, shortly before his death, 'He made the doors at Holbeton, and was an artist in his way'."

In 1858, at the age of twenty-one, Sedding entered Street's office. The master was then in his thirty-fifth year, with a reputation already established, and work crowding in from every side. With Sedding he had but little in common; their natures were entirely unsympathetic, and Sedding, when the opportunity offered, left him to join his brother at Penzance. Street was one of the sources of the Gothic revival. Traditional art, scotched by Inigo Jones, lingered on in country places till Pugin dealt its death blow. Sir Walter Scott, one of the first to feel the coming storm, gave voice to it in his novels. The classic rule was overthrown all along the line. Renaissance literature was condemned; the Pre-Raphaelite brotherhood was formed with aims, as Street felt, identical with those of the leaders of the Gothic Revival in the field of architecture. Puritanism, later on, received a shock in the 'Oxford Movement', from which it has never recovered. Our village churches, which lay slumbering amidst their hills and meadows, became with our cathedrals, castles, and houses, worthy of note and subjects for restoration. Sedding, in a short account of the 'Revival,' says; "The necessities of the Gothic revival made us 'collectors,' and set us 'species-making.' We had scotched and killed Old English traditional art, and nothing remained but that, like vagabonds without food, we must run to and fro, anywhere and everywhere to beg, borrow, or steal motifs for the purposes of current art. Two men went to France, two to Germany, others strayed to Belgium (Holland was not in fashion then); one dipped into this home style, one into that. So things went on for a time. But 'snaps' were not of much service. This petty nibbling did not go far enough. Individual discrimination was often at fault. Things got mixed. There was not enough system in the classification of styles for the growing acumen of antiquarian circles. Old art must be unravelled – the 'styles' must be deciphered; for it was absurd to attempt a scientific revival of the old periods until we had first reduced them to system, and defined their characteristic details. So the cry went up for more light, and for figured details and classification. Hence Rickman's book. Hence our registered generalisations which reduce the informal elements of old art to formulae." "Archaeology," he goes on to say, "as applied to English architecture, has been conducted upon mischievous lines – the narrow lines of personalities. It was not *all* that is old shall be studied and preserved, but only that which has the approval of passing taste. Out of the hundred and one modern writers upon English architecture, only two men have shown the historic sense or the broad sympathy to appreciate the ripened beauty and concentrated interest of the later Gothic. The rest deal largely in repugnances. The specialist's point of view is not a desirable one: it is defective because it is one-sided. However extensive the acquirements, however gigantic the learning of the specialist, he is an abnormal creature. Like the Cyclops, he has only one eye – in the middle of his forehead." It is interesting to turn from this to the account of that revival, given by one of the revivists themselves. Sir Gilbert Scott, in his autobiography, says: "At first, free choice was allowed in the variety of Gothic which each man should adopt for any of his works. Gradually this was seen to be inconsistent with an organised revival, and it became necessary to unite in the adoption of our one style. The 'Middle Pointed' was soon fixed upon, though some (including myself) held that whatever was valuable in other styles should be translated into it, so as to make it more comprehensive of all which was good. Some among us hated other varieties as much as they did classic, or perhaps even more, and seemed to think the use of Perpendicular, or Norman, or even Early Pointed, as nothing short of heresy." The reign of the 'Middle Pointed' was quickly succeeded by that of the 'First Pointed,' and then foreign features were introduced. The skeleton of art was displayed to the joy of the populace. Members of Parliament wrote and debated on it, and a change of Government involved changes of style. England blazed with enthusiasm. The country squire and the country parson, not to be left behind, became students of archaeology and judges of art. Into this maelstrom of opinion Sedding was thrown. To attempt to stem the flow was impossible, but his individuality was too great to be submerged. Gothic forms he had to use, yet compelled them into modes of individual expression. His work was a continuance of the ancient traditions of design with inevitable modifications. Unable to escape sufficiently from the tyranny of forms, he resorted largely to the use of colour, so much so that he earned a reputation as a colourist before his name as an architect was established. This is all seen in his first work of importance, 'The Downs,' at Hayle. The first set of plans for the house, dated 1867, were executed by his brother Edmund, who died in the following year, about

2 *St Clement's Church, Boscombe, Bournemouth, Hampshire (1873 by Sedding, west end and tower circa 1893 by Henry Wilson).*

the time the work was commenced. These designs were greatly altered in execution. The house, fairly situated on a hill, overlooks the town and harbour of Hayle. The garden holds the house in a quiet embrace, and its levels fall by a series of steps and terraces till the garden melts away into the woods below. The house is linked with the site, wedded to its scenery, blended with nature. The upper terrace, some 300 feet long by 30 feet wide, extends the garden's length, and is broken by beds of clipped holly. On one side it is divided from the lawn by a thick-set hedge, on the other it overlooks the geometrical garden, and bounded on the latter by a clipped hedge of bay, 7 feet thick on the top. A straight avenue of firs, beeches, and elms, leads from the road to a small gravelled courtyard, surrounded by ivied walls. From this courtyard the house is entered by a small porch, the main hall and staircase being cut off from it by a painted screen. The hall is tiled with small red tiles and encaustic tiles ("those abominations," as Sedding called them in after years), let in sparingly to form a pattern. Here they are so carefully used that in the softened light they look delightful. There is a wealth of nooks and corners and unexpected turnings. Every room is interesting, from the dining room, with its panelled ceiling richly moulded, its Gothic fireplace, and small plaster frieze of natural birds and convention-al foliage – all coloured – to the servants' bedrooms, with ceilings coved to give greater height under the roof. On screen and fireplace are small painted panels of birds and flowers, recalling bits of embroidery of later date. The conservatory shows a vigorous attempt to make a feature of what is usually an ugly appendage. The wood cornices throughout the building are capped by diminutive battlement mouldings, to be met with in all his works of early years. Every window frames a view. One is placed in the passage, on purpose, it would seem, to give a glimpse of the out-stretched terrace and the hills beyond, whilst from the front win-dow one sees the laid-out garden falling away to the woods, with the sandy bay and the distant sea. At the same period he built the church, schools, and vicarage at Lower Marple. The church, as the house at Hayle, was erected from designs left by his brother Edmund, who was thought, by all who knew them, to be the more gifted of the two. The site for the church was all that could be desired. Marple lies in a valley on the border of the coal district, a swift stream and a steep hill dividing the town in two. Half way up the hill, ever alive with the creaking drag of descending carts, is a small platform on which the church is built. On the far side are the schools, and higher up the hill is the vicarage. Through a small lych-gate, the path leads from the hill to the church. Dedicated to St Martin, it originally consisted of nave and chancel, vestry and south porch. A lady chapel, however, has lately been added. The building is as simple as possible. Inside, the interest centres in the chancel, which, sombre in tone, is lighted up by a small painted and gilded alabaster

reredos. The chancel windows, rich in colour and strong with life, are an early production of the Morris firm, from designs by Ford Madox-Brown. An oak roodscreen divides the nave from the chancel, origin-ally intended to be painted, for Sedding had no more scruple about painting oak, if the grain was not good, than he had about plastering the inside walls of a stone church. The beauty of stone was one of the discoveries of the 'Revivalists,' who, with innocent enthusiasm, would strip frescoed plaster from the walls to show it.

In 1873 he built the Church and Vicarage of St Clement's, Bournemouth, the best known and the most interesting of these early works. The church stands back from the road, an oasis in a desert of villas. It is dedicated to St Clement, and has a nave, north aisle, north porch, chancel, lady chapel, vestries and a western tower, the latter completed since his death. The nave arcade has pointed arches, with capitals hinted at rather than expressed. Above the arches is a range of stone panels, homes prepared for an army of saints. The chancel and lady chapel are divided from the nave by stone screens. The design of that in front of the chancel is a daring and original combination of intersecting arches, surmounted by a row of angels holding candlesticks, whilst the cusps of the side openings bud out into tiny adoring angels folded up in bract-like wings. Angels, too, strayed from the old Botticelli, stand as pinnacles on the corners of the aisle. The reredos at the back of the high altar is crowded with saints, the panel below them is filled by a figure on horseback, representing Lieutenant Edwin Christie, to whose memory it was erected. The

3 *John Dando Sedding. Lych gate, Ermington Church.*

reredos in the dimly-lighted lady chapel is very interesting, and its design is peculiarly appropriate to a chapel dedicated to the Virgin Mother. Christ crucified on a lily is in the centre, on His right and left are panels typical of the Fall and the Redemption; The Annunciation on one side, The Expulsion from Eden on the other, these, in their turn, bound in by niches containing figures of St Anne and the Virgin crowned. Yet in all this throng of saints and angels, we are never allowed to forget to whom the church is dedicated. The Life of St Clement is figured on the font. His anchor is patterned on the floor throughout the church; large in the nave, and small in the chancel, and on the scutcheons suspended to the lamps. On the pulpit rails we have his anchor and monogram cast in copper; the balustrade is twisted into flowing wreaths of seaweed.

Throughout the Church of St Clement at Boscombe symbols of the Saint abound. In the coloured medallions of the windows, his monogram alternates with roses and with crowns; while on the south-east buttress is a small panel representing his crucifixion. The chancel stalls are of the Gothic of the period, but differentiated from it in the treatment of the carving. On one of the priest's desk ends, St Clement holds his new church, showing the tower already built; on the others are the Annunciation – the Virgin on one side of the choir, the Angel on the other, and on another stall the Virgin and Child. Forming the arms of the boy's bench ends are a lion, a dog, an unmistakable ram with curly wool, and a hart holding a shield, which probably belonged to the arms of the founder, as it occurs again in the vicarage. The spider web glazing, surrounding the monogram in the aisle windows, is most interesting. We see here the germ which developed into that delightful elfin tracery at Ermington. A corridor connects the church with the vicarage. On the right, before entering the house, is a small oratory cut off from the passage by a rood screen, the passage ends in a flight of steps which lead to the hall. To the left is the porch door, in front is the staircase screened in with open-wood work, through which one can see the stairs winding to the upper floor, a delightfully contrived vista full of mysterious suggestion. To the right is the passage leading to the drawing-room, with its stone fireplace and carved spandrels of harts pasturing amid gigantic lilies; above them is a broad frieze of pure Cornish carving. On the garden front are carved stone panels of harts pursued by dogs, let into the brickwork. In front of the house is a sunk garden, with high enclosing walls, from which steps lead up on either side to the front and back entrances. Sheltered from the wind on all sides, it should in summer contain a wealth of flowers. The small red bricks of varied hue, used throughout the house and corridor, give that dignity and richness of texture, which is impossible to obtain with the large and carefully-sorted bricks commonly used.

St Clement's is the most complete of Sedding's churches, but for the decoration, which extends to the second bay of the nave only, it might be called a finished work. What he did here on a small scale, he wished to execute in large at Holy Trinity Church, Chelsea, which he hoped to have seen decorated by some of the leading artists of today, by Gilbert, Burne Jones, and others. These churches, one might say, are similar by contrast. At Bournemouth one is struck by the excellence of the craftsmanship, which he owed to the indefatigable way in which he would search out and train the best workmen. Street, who had not time to attend personally to such matters, said that every architect should himself be able to decorate his buildings with painting and sculpture. It was probably his influence that started Sedding working at the crafts. He would tell how he spent his evenings in his rooms, where he must have had a most amenable landlady, at work with mallet and chisel, on a block of stone he had managed to procure from a neighbouring stone merchant. Whenever there was any painting to be done, he would always mix and try the colours himself. In the apse of a church, at Cardiff, which he decorated, there is a row of white stone figures, on which, for years before his death, he was going to 'try' colours whenever he had a day to spare.

In his architecture and his decoration we continually see the effect Cornish work had on him. It was in Cornwall he first studied building. It was Cornwall that inspired and coloured all his later works. "To my mind," he says, "no place in the world is more vocal with many-voiced music than old Cornwall. It is the nursery-ground of the Saints (almost every 'church town' has its own special local patron Saint), it contains the land of Lyonesse of Arthurian legend; it is the house of the giants; the haunt of fairies, pixies, mermaids, demons, and spectres; the place of dragons. And as for the art of the people, that must not be separated from Nature in Cornwall. They must be allowed to go hand-in-hand now as they ever have gone; they have so long 'sistered' one another's efforts; have kept so close together in tone, texture, spirit and manner, that one cannot consider them apart. The Cornish church is wild, rustic, moorish, singular in type, singular in emotional quality. No Art that has ever graced this world is more strongly local and home-bred than the Cornish. I know of no place in England where Nature in sky, sea and land, can so take hold of and possess the mind as is the case here – no place where Nature can be so obviously moody and masterful – now calm, now full of menace – now bright and caressing – now black with evil omen and gloomy suggestion – now silent and asleep, now furious and lifting up its voice in thunder. What wonder, then, if the Cornishman should be sensitive to the scenery and humours of the place, and that this sensitiveness should foster superstition in his mind and emotionalism in his Art." Much of this description might be applied to Sedding's work. It was to catch and make permanent this feeling of emotion, he chiefly strove in his work. He used the stylism of Gothic, but he used it with a difference. He aimed at making everything vital and full of appeal, to make one form grow out of another, so that each was a natural development of what had gone before. The lines of his tracery and mouldings have a sharpness and vigour one seldom finds elsewhere, they spring out as the branch does from the tree trunk, as leaves from the stem. When he copied old work, it was with the knowledge of the sources from which the old workmen drew their inspiration. He learnt from Nature in lines of flowers and foliage, but the language he expressed himself in was forced upon him by the times in which he lived. He used the stereotyped conventional carving with slight modifications at first, but gradually he learned to dispense with it, till, in such works as that at Holbeton, the crockets, cusps, and finials are turned to thickets of flowering twigs, peopled by birds and beasts of every kind. His work was as vivacious as himself. A friend said, on entering one of his churches, "I feel as if I were looking Sedding in the face." Much of his success in thus expressing himself came because he never sank into organised delegation. When he delegated, he chose carefully the delegate and primed him. Most of his designs for stone and wood-carving he drew on the material, either in the workshop or on the site, and it

was difficult for those who saw him thus at work not to catch some of his spirit. Whenever he found an intelligent workman, he would continually employ him till he gained somewhat of his own mode of looking at things. He would make them study, as he did, from Nature. Of flowers he was passionately fond. He would advise young architects to spend their Sunday afternoons drawing them, and would recommend those who wished to learn embroidery, to take some favourite flower and fill a panel with it, saying that the material would impose its own convention. He himself made innumerable designs for embroidery and filled them as gardens with birds and flowers – designs often based on conventions imposed by the past, but overrun, as a trellis, with roses, honeysuckle, and trailing vine. With his carving it was the same, convention was the trellis over which his fancy flowered. Good as some of it was, it is chiefly effective from rhythmic repetition. It told by masses as a meadow full of daisies, king cups, and cuckoo flowers, a wood thick sewn with bluebells, violets and hyacinths, or a field of poppies. We do not stop to examine each separate flower, but are carried away by the imaginative wealth and 'life rural'. He would never look upon this lavish ornamentation as sculpture, but as 'decorative masonry. *"La sobriété en poésie est pauvreté"* says Victor Hugo. Sedding gave free rein to his fancy. Knowing the value of restraint,

4 *John Dando Sedding. Netley Castle, near Southampton (1889).*

he boldly disregarded it. He had some of the Celtic fire in him, and his work shone with it. This love for flowers is best seen in the homes he made for them; he had not then to depend so much upon his workmen for the effect at which he aimed. Nature at once corrected their impregnated mechanical instincts; he had no enemy to deal with but 'winter and rough weather;' and his gardens show how well he knew how to keep these at bay, how he seemed almost to have divined what the flowers liked and what they needed. A garden was to him "man's recreation ground, children's fairy-land, birds' orchestra, butterflies' banquet," and never was he happier than in creating one of these fairylands, where Art completes Nature, and Nature ransomed from decay, gives in return a fuller and richer life. "The Artist wants neither flattery nor ignorant abuse." William Hunt.

It is only of quite recent years that we have begun to recognize the fact that old buildings are the *deposit* of a nation, and form a most important part in a nation's history, and are not, as seems to have been the general idea in the early part of the century, merely feats in Design and marvels of masonry, to be reconstructed at will by any educated person with sufficient capital. We find that we can no more imitate them than we can reproduce, the language of Chaucer or Shakespeare. Like Nature they are inimitable, and, as Browning says:

". . . Nature is complete. Suppose you reproduce her (which you can't)? There's no advantage! You must beat her, then."

They breathe the spirit of an age with which we have entirely broken, yet we persist in destroying these wonderful creations and giving sham reproductions in place of them – reproductions that might be compared to the mutilated translations of the Classics sold at a penny for the enlightenment of the masses. In these old buildings we read the aspirations, follies, modes of life, and changes of custom of a people. In former times the peculiarities of every county in England were shadowed in each – peculiarities which Sir Gilbert Scott said should not be imitated nowadays because they arose from difficulties as to material, etc., which then existed but since have ceased. Now those peculiarities themselves have vanished. We have so reduced everything to formulæ that we view even with dislike the changes

5 *John Dando Sedding. Flete Lodge, Holbeton, Devon (1889). A bold asymmetrical composition.*

of style an old building exhibits, and quite overlook 'the essential unity.' The Ecclesiologists at one time, we have been told, doubted whether it would not be right to pull down Peterborough Cathedral "if only they could rebuild it equally well in the Middle Pointed style." It was left to another fate – *"Tempus edax, homo edacior,"* or as Victor Hugo puts it, *"Le temps est aveugle, l'homme stupide."*

Sedding, though influenced by the atmosphere in which he was brought up, broke sufficiently free from the Gothic Revival to see that whilst we failed in our new buildings, we doubly failed when in adding to old work we tried to rival it on its own ground. Local characteristics he never ignored; we see them adhered to as much as possible in all his work. The sudden changes from a London office to life in Cornwall must have at once shown him that they were due more to the character of the builders than to difficulties as to materials and site. "The localness of English Art," he said, "is one of its distinguishing marks, a mark that the text-books cannot enforce. How can the textbooks be at once general and local, comprehensive and particular, generic and specific? Study the Art locally, for that is how it grew: its institution was mostly with the horny handed workmen, so far at least as details are concerned; its foster mother was tradition; its cradle was the tradesman's bench. The patron might scheme the building work and direct the work, but he did not invent the details; indeed, you can scarcely say that anything was original in those days, so related was everything to what had gone before, and to what was going on elsewhere. No one supposes that what the books call 'Norman' Architecture was invented by the Norman patron at all: had it been so we should have found a parallel to Durham or Peterborough in Normandy, which you cannot find. Of course it was English earlier than the Early English of the silly books, and quite three hundred years later than the true Early English of Saxon times began. Study the Art where it grew; so much of its historic interest depends on this, for the localness of Art touches the types, features, general aspect, sentiment, of the work of a given district for many centuries." Sedding's knowledge of his Art was "uncorrupted by books." "Love," he says, "furthers knowledge." But love is a flower that will not grow out of book-lore and technical classification. Nor do we find him making Architectural drawings of buildings. It is probable that had the times allowed, he would have done Designs such as those submitted by Baldassari in competition for the completion of the west front of St Petronius, Bologna, where two elevations are sketched in in freehand. His habit of making pencil notes of buildings, with the chief measurements jotted down, not only helped to keep the memory of the place, its lights and shades fresher in the memory, but acted as a stimulus to the imagination in cases of reference. These notes he would often use as a basis for design, but as a basis only. "Of

the relics of old handiwork," he says, "let us learn the secret of their charm, imitate their excellences, and put aside the thought that all good work must necessarily go along the same grooves and conform to the same conditions." We do our work under new conditions, and we mustn't envy the past (envy never advances any one) nor despair of the future just because Art has changed its forms, and no longer radiates from a centre of far-reaching traditions. Let us not blink the fact, the old happy footing of Art is gone – gone as it seems for ever. What of that! The good qualities, the virtues that animated the good old work, are not dead and buried too. Goodness cannot die. Goodness cannot be monopolised. I think there is truth in Quaker Penn's remark that all good people belong to one religion— "Our great society alone on earth. The noble living and the noble dead."

Cornwall, which one might call Sedding's county by adoption, tinctured all his work, and though we find its influence at times less noticeable than at others, it is always present. He says, in his 'Notes on Cornish Churches,' that he had often tried to analyse the sources of peculiar delight one gets from an old Cornish church, but that as often as he tried he had to give it up. "One cannot put that sort of thing into words. There is very little to admire in the rough exterior of the churches of the county, in their unvaried outlines, or their unpretending features and repeated types, and the unsympathetic stranger, coming upon them with his mind stored with finer memories, would think them mean and rude, and deficient in interest. Yet to me they are always full of a peculiar inexpressible charm." This charm which he could not express in words he expressed in his designs. In Cornwall itself, the two old churches of St Eval and St Merryn, one would, perhaps, as an instance of this, first call to mind. Not that much work was done at either of them, but what was done was so in keeping with the local notes that one feels it is Cornwall itself that speaks in them. They are two long low churches of the peculiar country type, situated on a bleak moor overlooking the wild Cornish coast. Their towers stand high over the low roof line, as if to protect them from storms, like crouching beasts with heads raised against the blast. The tower, it is said, of St Eval is still used by sailors as a landmark in preference to the neighbouring lighthouse; the hot lime in the mortar has streaked its grey sides with white. The sailors aver it to be whitewash used for their benefit as a guide on stormy nights, when the tide runs high.

St Eval's tower was rebuilt in 1727 ("We will hope," Sedding said in his report, "as much for the Glory of God as for the safety of their ships"). When called in to examine the building he found that "the gales had at different times stripped the slates off, and the wind sweeping along the roof, torn the timbers apart, bending them from eastward end to end." The interior presented striking contrasts; for, whilst the roof was left open to the weather, the Church had been reseated with new pitch pine seats, in glory of grain and varnish, and some few of the old bench ends adorned with the emblems of the Passion had been fitted to them. The rain poured in on old and new alike. The wall plate, where thoroughly rotten, was renewed, the timbers of the roof patched, and new bosses substituted for the old ones. A facetious workman carved a head of Gladstone on one of these bosses, making the hair and beard die away in foliage in true Cornish fashion. Sedding, only too pleased to find a man who could jest in his work, toned down the caricature, and had it put up with the rest. The roof of the neighbouring church of St Merryn was in a similar condition, and was treated in the same way. Both churches were reseated, the old bench ends of St Eval were re-used, as were parts of bench ends and parts of the old wall plate, which were found under the floor at St Merryn.

In examining the additions and repairs Sedding made to old churches, one invariably finds he has caught the tone and spirit of the building, and that without in anyway binding himself as to 'style'. He worked as the old builders did, not changing the style according to the needs of the day, but catching the spirit of the place, and trying to reproduce that. In his treatment of these old buildings we notice what a strong hold the Gothic Revival had on him to the very last. In early Gothic days, all his work shows his fond-

ness for 'Perpendicular,' and how deeply he had studied it. When there were additions to make to an old building he invariably used it, as if timid of showing more of his own personality than was inevitable in connection with work erected by the masters of old times. At Bovey Tracey and at Callington he added a second north aisle in this style. The church at Bovey Tracey, originally dedicated to St Michael, had been rededicated to St Thomas à Becket, it is supposed in expiation of the part Tracey took in his murder. It is delightfully situated on a hill up which the long village street winds, closing in with houses the view that bursts upon one on reaching the green which bounds the churchyard wall. The church had been restored in 1857, when some old mural decoration was discovered, badly copied, and covered up again with a new coat of plaster. The richly carved and painted roodscreen had been left untouched. Sedding found it in a very rotten condition. The decayed portions were replaced; nearly the whole band of carving running along the top was renewed, and the whole, with the exception of a series of painted figure panels at the bottom, was repainted, the old scheme of colour being carefully followed. I do not think he would have done this when wider knowledge came. A new chancel pavement of Devonshire green and red marble, bordered with black and white, never probably highly polished,

6 *St Germandus (or St Gonand) Church, Roche, Cornwall. A medieval church rebuilt by Sedding in 1890. His careful approach to the restoration of many old churches endeared him to the Arts and Crafts men.*

has had what polish it had worn off, and looks a sea of colour, and exceedingly beautiful. The broad north aisle here and at Callington suggest rather a careful restoration of the old than an entirely new piece of work. Built by the old workmen they would be perfect. That at Callington would seem to have borrowed something from the old market town itself. It is difficult to imagine it having been originally conceived other than it is, so well does it keep touch with the spirit of the place. The chancel was reseated, and a new chancel pavement added, the latter being an unsuccessful attempt to combine marble with encaustic tiles. This is, it would seem, the last time that Sedding used the latter. The choir stalls here and at Madron show the advance he was making in Decorative work, the stereotyped Gothic forms gradually disappearing, cusps and crockets changing into animals, birds, and bunches of foliage.

At Madron the church was reseated throughout, new stone windows were placed instead of the old wooden ones, and north and south porches – unlike any of the past, yet unmistakably Cornish in design –

were added. The only thing to mar the work was the removal of the old slates, which were replaced by new ones laid to a large lap. This, probably done at first to save expense, became a usual practice, and we find the same thing done at Holbeton and Ermington, where the excuse of saving could not be made. In the churchyard at Madron, overlooking Penzance and St Michael's Mount, is the tombstone he erected to the memory of his brother Edmund, a plain slab shaped in the old way, with a cross growing from a heart cut upon it; a little sunk pannel at the end bears the inscription: "This church was repaired in '83."

In '84 the chance he must have long wished for came. He had the opportunity at Holbeton of showing what could be done with an old building when untramelled by want of money. The church stands in the centre of a small village built within an amphitheatre of hills. The village green slopes up to the churchyard, which is entered by a new lychgate and a double flight of steps. The church consists of a nave, north and south aisles, transepts, organ chamber, morning chapel, and a tower at the west end. On the outside the roofs, the long

7 *John Dando Sedding. Chancel, Salcombe Church, Devon (added to older nave in 1890).*

sloping tops to the buttresses, and the south porch – which is richly carved, as if to prepare one for the wealth within – are new. One enters through doors of ironwork and enamel, excellent in design, but in execution bearing rather the mark of the mechanic than that of the craftsman. It is the what they might have been, one feels, inspired the saying: "He made the doors at Holbeton, and was an artist in his way." But the slight disappointment one experiences on the outside is at once obliterated by the interior. The main structure has hardly been touched. Enough of the old woodwork remains to show that the new work has been carried out in harmony with the old. The chancel screen is new, but its continuation across the aisles is old, and untouched save for the most careful patching, some of the pieces of wood let in are not more than an inch square. The tower has been shut off from the nave by a screen with bottle glazing in the upper part, very rich in effect. The north transept has been turned into a vestry, shut off from the rest of the church by another oak screen. The richness of woodwork has been carried round the church by means of panelling the lower part of the walls; the aisle windows above the panelling are also glazed with bottle glazing, spots of colour being given by small medallions and panels of stained glass from designs by Heywood Sumner. The nave and chancel seats are all richly carved, the bench ends in the nave with panels of birds, animals, and foliage, alternating with tracery panels, the beads of the moulding which tie them in being twisted into a pattern of leafwork. Rich as the general effect of this work is in the nave, it is still subordinated to that in the chancel. One might liken the nave to a garden full of flowers on either side, yet the eye is still drawn to the terrace beyond, where the ordered beds all hold the rarer and richer growths. The chancel stalls are more finely carved with panels of lizards, squirrels, frogs and every sort of creeping thing, with birds and flowers innumerable. Beyond the stalls are the altar, reredos and east window, the one strong patch of colour in the church, from which the rest would seem to borrow its brilliancy – the nave windows seem like sparks thrown off from a huge fire, the font at the west end of many coloured marbles, looks a half extinguished brand. The altar panel is of dark red marble divided by strips of white marble from a wide band of lacquered gesso work, depicting the four Evangelists in circular medallions, bound together by a running pattern of roses, lilies and poppies; the whole surrounded by a frame of oak, down the centre of which runs a metal moulding. The reredos frames an old picture of Christ with the crown of thorns; the frame is carved, with figures introduced, all richly coloured and gilded. The floor was relaid with marble. The church was reroofed throughout, the chancel roof being a continuation of that of the nave, but pannelled and embossed with gold bosses at the cross ribs, the panels spotted with stars, while angels support the ribs on either side.

Ermington, a sister church but a few miles off, was treated in much the same way. The church stands at the entrance to the village, as one enters it from Ivy Bridge, above and away from the road. A flight of steps, which jut out on to the road on either side, lead to the churchyard, through a granite lychgate, which in breadth, simplicity, and general design echoes the Jacobean screen within the church. On the outside the stonework has been patched, here and there stackpipe heads added, as at Holbeton. The old richly-carved roof over the crossing of the transepts tells of the wealth of the church in the past, and would seem to have given the key to the work Sedding did here. The seating throughout the church is new, there is a wealth of carving; but the Jacobean screen, with its columns and big frieze, give a broad character to the church other than that at Holbeton – the one tells by its intricacy and mass of details, the other by its very plainness and lack of them. The nave bench-ends nearest the chancel have panels of lilies growing out of pots, and stand like guardians to mark the crossing of the transepts and the entrance to the chancel. The cusps everywhere end in twisted flower and leaf work. The spiderweb glazing in the aisle windows has a magical effect, and gives great breath to the church. The lower stage of the tower has been left open to the nave. Stone steps, bound by a low stone wall, lead from it to the tower, and a wooden staircase, panelled below, rises steeply from the dim floorline to the belfry stage above. The north transept has been turned into a vestry. New parclose screens, chancel seats, and a delightful little communion rail, with balusters and a broad band of carving running along the top have been added. The altar is of red marble, with an oak frame, behind which is a retable, with red and green marble panels, white border, and capping. It is impossible to give an idea of the rich effect of these churches. The arrangement and design everywhere are admirable, the lavish ornamentation is what Sedding would have called "decorative

8 *Chancel screen, St Mary's Church, Stamford, Lincolnshire (restored and refurnished by Sedding in 1890).*

masonry or carpentry." Whilst submitting to the 'jet ascensionnel' of repeated lines and masses, one willingly acknowledges in looking at them that "*La sobriété en poésie est pauvreté.*

To the Artist it is more than a chant, it is an inspiration. It is not the work of the Archaeologist, however talented; it is the work of one in touch with the forces of Nature, of one alive to the tendencies of the age, of one who, learning to see with his own eyes, sees also with the eyes of the generation in which he lives.

The work at Ermington was finished in 1889. In the year following, Sedding repaired and refitted the chancel and Lady chapel at St Mary's Church, Stamford. Here he carried a step further ideas that were probably generated in his work at Holbeton and Ermington. The altar, executed by Stirling Lee, is of alabaster, with bronze panels of the Apostles surrounding a circular medallion of Christ in the centre, bound together by bands of lapis lazuli. The pavement in front of this altar, and likewise that in the Lady chapel, is enriched by squares of cloisonné enamel.

Before the main altar is a panel of lilies bound in with a pattern of vine, before that in the Lady chapel a large fleur de lys, used with black and grey marble, so as to give the fullest effect to the broad masses of gold. The brilliant colour of the east window of the Lady chapel is repeated in more sombre tones in the small north window; they were both of them executed by Christopher Whall. The chancel roof was decorated with panels of foliage, alternating with monograms, whilst immediately above the cornice is a band of warrior angels. The chancel and Lady chapel are cut off from the nave by oak screens, the rood screen being but partially finished. The chancel seat-ends are carved in the likeness of the four Evangelists, with angels above them bearing shields, on which their names are written. Whilst the work here was being finished, Sedding was called in to see to the repairs of the little church at Winsford. Whilst driving here from Dulverton, eight miles off, along a windy valley, he caught a chill, and a few days after died. A quiet out-of-the-world spot it is, hidden away amongst the hills. The churchyard is almost the only piece of flat ground in the neighbourhood, which may account for its having been used as a fives-court in days gone bye. The south aisle windows still bear the hinges on which the shutters hung that used to protect the windows against the balls. Little was done here, but that little was all that was needed. The nave walls, which, seen from the inside, seem to modern eyes to lean dangerously outwards, were found, when the aisle roof was reopened, to have been built so intentionally, for the outside of the wall was almost perpendicular, the inside having been cut back to give the required effect – a fact which lends colour to the supposition that many of our old buildings, which have been pulled down during this century, to be rebuilt or not, have perished from the modern belief that all walls were originally plumb, and

than any leaning must be owing to settlement, and not to intention on the part of the builder. It is this trusting to rule and line rather than to eye and common sense, that has levelled to unutterable dullness the floors of our cathedrals, and probably, but for Street, would have led to the loss of the sea-like pavement of St Mark's, Venice. It was against this tendency Sedding fought all his life. If a pupil wished to enter his office, he would never ask for designs or measured drawings – pencil notes and sketches told him all he wanted to know. Architecture to him was an Art first, and as little of a business as possible. He would do all he could to prevent those who had to make their fortune by it from entering the profession. In the same way that he did all in his power to keep the commercial spirit from entering the ranks, so he did his best to keep it out of his buildings. He was always on the outlook for conscientious workmen, and when found, he trained and kept them to his own work as much as possible. That his work failed in many respects he would have been the last to deny. "The design of the modern architect may be fussy and

9 *John Dando Sedding and Henry Wilson. St Clement's Church, Boscombe, Bournemouth, Hampshire (church 1873 by Sedding, west end and tower* circa *1893 by Wilson).*

lack breadth, and his details be uninteresting – like enough! But who reared the walls and fashioned the wood and stone?... In the old buildings there is characteristic material and intelligent handicraft, in the modern is utter dullness all over ... Here is no corresponding sign of lavish craft in the selection, the ordering, the manipulation of the materials – no obtaining of values from texture, colour, or scale in effortless but unerringly light, instinctive way traceable in the old structure." The output of nervous force in teaching the craftsmen their crafts must have, one feels, been immense, for whatever workman he had to deal with, and he could not always choose his tools, he always managed to get some good out of them, to put some life into his work. He managed to give that touch which words cannot explain. *"La vie ne se vérifie pas, elle se fait sentir, aimée admirer."*

In considering his later works, we shall see how he minimised the inevitable, the at present unsurmountable difficulties inherent in the structure of the building. In all his best work done in the old buildings he dealt with, we see that the structure was only patched by letting in pieces of stone where absolutely necessary, taking care that the new materials were of the same quality, and used in the same manner as the old.

The building which showed the nearest approach to the expression of Sedding's great aim in life was the Church of the Holy Trinity, near Sloane Square, London for which the scheme of decoration, no unimportant part of the main idea, was barely commenced, and is now likely to remain one of those songs composed and never sung, owing no further life than that given by an ephemeral sketch on paper. Just as he began to gain that recognition with all it entailed, for which he had been working all his life, he was taken from us.

The practice which his brother left him had dwindled, bringing him but little fresh work, so that for years much of his time was filled by making designs for wall papers and embroidery, and it was not till he was close upon fifty that he began that work and formed the style by which he is now chiefly known. The years left him were too short to show clearly in execution the ideal at which he was aiming; it is to his writings, as well as to many unfinished buildings, we must turn to find it. The Architect, he recognised, was alone in his work as far as the construction of the building went – any glory to be gained was his, and his alone. No help, he knew by long experience, could come from the workmen who raised the walls and roofed the building. Tradition was dead amongst them; they had been taught to forget the lessons handed down to them by their forefathers, and it was beyond any one man's power to revive it. The masters of the Renaissance had thought for them, drawn their mouldings, and indicated the ornament, and though they had survived the shock and renewed tradition, learning to do feelingly what they could not do lovingly, yet their hold on the new style was slight, and the first shock of the revival killed them. They may

still claim credit for neat and deft work, but any beauty we find in detail, we feel sure, has filtered through them from the mind of the Architect. The Artist had in former times impregnated the workmen with his spirit – the inspiration was strong and the soil fruitful; of the working body, the guilds were the lungs. Sedding had not enough work to be able to continually employ, and so train a band of workmen to his methods, but where feasible he always kept to the same men; nearly all his woodwork in fittings issued from the same workshop in Somersetshire, nearly all his iron work passed through the hands of the same men. But a competitive age was against him, and the A B C of his work was always having to be taught afresh. "Grant that our work lacks the solid merit of the old, and one may fairly attribute some of the blame for this to the miserable utilitarian spirit of the age which clips our wings when we would soar." His hope for Architecture lay in the co-operation amongst artists, and for this he worked all his life. Guilds for artists first; those for workmen would follow in due course.

Mazzini has somewhere said that "All true Art must either sum up and express the life of a closing epoch, or announce, and proclaim the life of the epoch destined to succeed it." Sedding, at different periods of his life, seemed to have aimed at the one and the other. "New and old" was his motto. St. Clement's, Bournemouth, is the work of one saturated with the past. It is not, nor was there the least attempt to make it, archaeologically accurate. It has, however, somewhat of the glamour of the past about it. It appeals to the Medieval spirit that lurks somewhere in most of us. From the year 1887 onward his aim is entirely different. Gothic trappings had in the meantime been abandoned, and a decided step taken towards expressing modern thought in modern language. He aimed at making buildings sing to us, as they had done in former times to our ancestors. With workmen lacking tradition and with the smallest knowledge of their own craft, he could hardly hope to do aught save act as a pioneer, and do his best to make smooth a rugged path. Designs might be good and the result "utter dullness." He saved his work from dullness by treating his workmen as pupils, standing over them and pointing out what effects he wanted them to aim at, often emphasising what he said by handling the mallet and chisel himself. But much was done by simplifying the work, doing away with crockets and finials, carved caps and many mouldings. In themselves they do not add to the expressiveness of the building. In former times they afforded many men the opportunity of displaying their peculiar views and impressions; they were like the various instruments in a great orchestra, but what use in the orchestra when there is virtually but a single instrument through which each must blow in turn. What far-reaching tradition and living handicrafts could no longer give, he hoped to in part supply by the co-operation of the leading Artists of the age. At Marple, as early as 1867, we find him going to Ford

Madox Brown for the cartoons for the stained glass in the windows, and, as opportunity offered, he always sought out the best men he could find to work in his churches. "Are there no dead walls in our cathedrals and parish churches," he cried, "to be made alive by bas-reliefs and paintings? Have you no trumpery 'ecclesiastical Art' reredoses to remove? Will you not prefer a good picture or sculpture to the glaring tiles and marbles, and 'holy beetles' and scribbled monograms that no one understands? . . . In the old days the poor man who 'took a turn' round your unrestored church could at least find a little human interest in the monuments; but these you have banished, and you have left him never a skeleton, nor a weeping cherub, nor a skull and crossbone, nor Maud's 'Angel watching an Urn' – no, not even the lion and the unicorn a-fighting for the crown." "To me," he says elsewhere, "it speaks volumes that the reredos of St Paul's – one of the costliest pieces of sculpture of the century – should go, as a matter of course, to Messrs. Farmer and Brindley, while the successors of Flaxman and Stevens are never thought of!" "Had you," he says in this same lecture to the members of the Liverpool Art Congress, "found the service of Vanity Fair less pleasant and lucrative – had you not so splendidly succeeded in easel painting and 'furniture sculpture' (as Mr Ruskin calls it) as to obscure your ideals – had you not exiled yourselves from the services of religion for this many a long day – there had been another tale to tell. The pity is–

'In this world, who can do a thing will not – And who would do it, cannot, I perceive.'

And why are painting and sculpture so deficient in popular appeal? For these two reasons – they are Arts cultivated exclusively for the rich, and they are not decorative; and on both points they stand condemned by the Art of all lands and all times. It isn't genius; it isn't skill or technique that is wanted to fit them for popularity. It isn't even that the times are against the production of fine decorative designs. It is not that there are not hundreds of new churches to decorate, whose interiors are now just as interesting and soul-inspiring as the inside of a coffin. But it is that the Arts require a new direction. It is that the Artist shall apply his genius to articles of common use, and to the adornment of places that belong to the people." It is not Artists that are needed; they are as numerous now, perhaps, as they ever were, but they are scattered, and their isolation limits their powers of reflection. Were the reredoses, lecterns, altar frontals, crosses, and candlesticks in our churches (which are still the most representative of our public buildings) given to the men most capable of executing them; were our monuments, public and private, put into hands such as those which reared the monument of the Duke of Clarence at Windsor; were the Architects, who allow money to be thrown away on yards and yards of wearying ornament and badly-arranged costly marble fittings, to follow in the

public buildings committed to their charge the example of Mr Waterhouse, when he employed one of the greatest decorative painters of the age to give life to the walls of the Manchester Town Hall – a building destined, probably, to be both the glory and the shame of the century in which it was erected; or were artists employed even to superintend the colour-washing or painting of our public halls and large houses, the house-painter would soon learn his trade; and by like means all that we now attempt to bring about by violent methods would have a natural growth. Schools for 'applied Art' but aggravate the evil. The chatter about them, said Sedding, is not good; "it encourages the fatal notion that Art *is* a thing to be 'applied' – that it is a dispensable commodity, not an integral part of all work of all manufacture whatsoever. If Art were a matter of imitative skill and historical knowledge – a matter of clever designs upon cartridge paper – how happy should we be!"

Sedding's latter churches are admirably suited for great decorative designs on wall and ceiling. All the

10 *John Dando Sedding and Henry Wilson. Detail, Holy Trinity, Sloane Street, Chelsea (1888–90, interior fittings throughout the 1890s). Arts and Crafts features predominate in Sedding's last free Gothic church masterpiece.*

town churches, whether in Falmouth, Cardiff, or London, are what might be termed big preaching churches, the modern type of the Franciscan Church, built for congregations taking an active part in the service. The choir is usually as broad as the nave, with steps up to it, so that the clergy and choristers are above the congregation; another flight of steps leads to the altar and retable, the which, backed by a great broad window filled with stained glass and canopied by the sanctuary roof of gilded stars on a blue ground, would, emphasised by the massive columns and more sombre colouring in the nave, make a blaze of colour and concentrated richness. A low stone wall, with low gates of twisted and enriched ironwork, formed the entrance to the chancel, the stalls of which are low and delicately carved, or have sunk panels of metal work; the pavement is of big slabs of marble, arranged in patterns – the great test of an Architect's ability, Sedding would say. The side chapels are rich in a lesser degree; the pulpit, font, and aisle windows, as brands thrown off from the main altar, carried the colour to die away in the nave.

Each of these buildings was the expression of an idea; the detail but clothed and administered to that idea, and emphasised it, as in Greek statues the gauzy flowing drapery emphasised, but did not hide, the lie of the figure beneath. These ideas were never hastily executed; the production and adaptation might be hasty, but the crystallisation was often the work of years. An instance of this we have in an anecdote concerning the Church of the Holy Redeemer at Clerkenwell. After having decorated the apse of St Mary's, Cardiff, the vicar came one day to Sedding and told him that he had a piece of land on which he was thinking of erecting a barn for him to decorate. "No, don't do that," said Sedding; "I've got a plan in my head for a cheap church, which would be the very thing for you. You give it to me to build, and we'll decorate it afterwards." Time passed, and plans were asked for. Sedding sent a design for a rich Renaissance church, but this was too expensive, and the plans were prepared from which the present church was erected. Later on, when down there on one of his visits of inspection, he said, "I have put up your church of St Dyfrig's at Clerkenwell." This church is in effect the embodiment of those ideas matured. The plans submitted at Cardiff were the outcome, probably, of a suggestion received during a visit to Italy. The church at Clerkenwell was the same idea grown almost beyond recognition, and with the Italian element left out. To the introduction of foreign features into English Architecture he was strongly opposed. "Students," he said, "should be well grounded in a knowledge of English methods of design before they were allowed to travel. We want the tang of the soil in our work, to which no amount of foreign study can help us." "Do you term that perpetual pistareen paste-pot work American Art?" says Walt Whitman of the literature of his country. Sedding was

not a whit less jealous of English Architecture. But had his first design for the church of St Dyfrig's been accepted, the church would never have been built in strict accordance with the plans first submitted. Sedding had learnt to see his buildings in block with their lights and shades before he commenced work; as the work proceeded details not in keeping, or a hindrance to the general conception, or unsuited to the site, were altered or swept away.

To the suggestion received by the site one is inclined to attribute the uninteresting exteriors as compared with the interiors of his town churches. The sites given him were very rarely inspiring. St Dyfrig's, Cardiff, is built in a sordid neighbourhood with the lines running close by the east end, the continual rattle of trains, the dingy streets, row after row of workmen's villas inhabited chiefly by weekly tenants, who can have no time or care to make their abodes cheerful, the canal with muddy banks and iron railings, patches of unkept common, showing that, though the town's bad blood is here pushing towards the country, it has not yet cleansed itself – do much to suffocate the building. It is perfectly plain on the outside, neither attractive nor repellent – not the poorest inhabitant of the district would hesitate about entering it; hardly a passer-by would turn to look at it. The outside appears somewhat warped, but the completion of the nave and the addition of the bell turret would alter that. Inside it is big, airy, and solemn, not lacking in colour, given both by the shadows and by the painting on the roof. The exterior of the church at Clerkenwell was more satisfactory. Its west front, with great shadowy pediment, faces the street coloured by shops and stalls and owning a population of mixed nationality. All Saints', Falmouth, one of his most successful churches outside London, is built on the brow of a hill overlooking the harbour, in one of those rapidly increasing suburbs where squalor and flash gentility struggle for pre-eminence. The front, facing the street which runs down into the town, is a delightful piece of composition, somewhat marred by a turret, which shows the strong influence Street had on him still. Inside it is broad, spacious, and airy. This church would seem to have suggested the Church of the Holy Trinity, Chelsea, or to have come from a cognate idea. Several of Sedding's churches are closely allied; with the large amount of work he had in these years this was inevitable.

In 1890 he added the chancel to the church at Salcombe. In this addition he only showed his appreciation of the former existence of a church by introducing very broad mullions in the chancel window, similar to those used in the aisles, yet this has been sufficient to bring the work into unison. The east end of this church, which is perched on the top of the hill, looks down over the small harbour, and is seen as one approaches the town by boat from Kingsbridge. Then it is that one sees the full effect of the new work. Whether situated on the brow of a hill or on the slope, as at St Paul's, Truro –

another modern church to which he made additions – his buildings always stand well. At the latter church the hill gives a sudden dip by the chancel, of which Sedding took full advantage, making the east end big and broad, so that the church is like an animal with crouching hind quarters, its forefeet firmly planted forwards, broad chested, and thrown back. This church is the connecting link between his early and later work. Its somewhat sombre interior is lit up by a rood screen, painted white and green; beyond it the sanctuary roof is of more sombre colouring, black being largely used in combination with the red and white and gold of the lilies and roses. The lodge built for Mr H. B. Mildmay in 1889 holds good as to what has been said about Sedding's sensitiveness as to site. It is quiet and unobtrusive. As one dips down the lane leading from Ermington to Holbeton, one comes across it as but another feature in the landscape. At Netley Castle about this time he made many alterations, especially to the interior. Enclosing walls seemed to give his fancy play. At the Industrial Schools, Bristol, the school-rooms, dormitories, sitting-rooms, and kitchen, with its big fireplace, the upper and lower passages with windows under the projecting eaves looking out on to the quadrangle, are all delightful, and give an air of fulness and sufficiency, a depth of comfort and homeliness to the building, with that suggestiveness which is the life of Art. The laundry is a conception in itself. No mangles, wash-tubs, or drying clothes are needed to proclaim its use; it never could be taken for anything else but a laundry.

Of the materials used in the structure of his buildings he was very careful. They, he said, contained germs of life in themselves, which by careful use and handling would give breadth and vitality to his work. His materials were to him what his notes are to the musician. His mouldings, for example, were suggested by the material for which they were designed.

By the study of old work he had formed his eye – gained a sense of proportion and fitness in things. Old herbals were his architectural books. With flowers he covered screens and bench-ends. Cusps and crockets he had at first used, but, gradually leaving hold of the past, he learnt to do without them, and natural forms gained ground till they were transformed into knots of foliage, twisted flower patterns, or birds and beasts. The same men were nearly always employed, so that with greater freedom and wealth in design we find corresponding powers of execution. Figures were seldom introduced, for he was not able to afford men capable of executing them, and was unwilling to employ the mechanical carvers who flourish on 'Ecclesiastical Art' and make cemeteries desolate. "He had a fine impatience" to quote Mr Lethaby, "for trade art, ecclesiastical ornament, and the conventions of so-called appropriateness; he wanted the best work of fine thought, and direct appeal from one mind to another; personal vitality and emotion, not forgeries by day labour, farmed out by contract, of past art, for us dead and done. It was the feeling of old work that he felt with penetrating insight, and his originality arose in stimulating himself by a study of old work considered

11 *John Dando Sedding. Altar frontal, Holy Trinity, Sloane Street* (circa *1889*).

not as mere forms, facts, and dates, but as ideas, as humanity, as delight. If he felt this delight in reading their work, might he not delight others in turn – 'by clothing current thought in current shapes'?" It is this leaning on past styles which has been so ruinous to architecture. "They say that modern architecture is a failure, and I partly believe it. What is a failure? It is something that has missed the mark, fallen short, lapsed. It is implied that architecture has lapsed from its ancient ideal; that it has fallen from its high estate as queen of the crafts; that it has lost that amplitude of craft-mastery which distinguished the architect of olden time. Let that pass. Swift remarked that the latter part of a man's life is taken up in curing the follies, prejudices, and false opinions he has contracted in the former. This is somewhat our case. We are conscious of, and are trying to amend, our many failings. And at the head and front of our offending is that naughty pursuit of style-mongering. We have been goaded on from this side and that to revive and copy work of many periods, and the harm that has resulted from this has not been confined to architecture, but has extended to the handicrafts. An accurate history of modern architecture during the last sixty years would be a delightful burlesque on the fallibility of human judgment – delightful for its ill effects upon ourselves, upon the crafts, and upon you. If English crafts are not better, it is mainly owing to the way in which the architect has followed the multitude to do evil. The architect should stand this day before his fellow craftsmen clad in a white sheet, labelled as ringleader of art revolution, prince of electric paper designers, chief culprit in the debauchery of the handicrafts. But to be fair, the disintegration of the arts from which we so much suffer is not his doing. Is your design chaotic? You reap the dragon's teeth that he has sown. Does confusion reign in the workshops? Your fate was linked with his when, in the pride and naughtiness of his heart, he ransacked the centuries and went 'globe trotting' for fresh *art motifs*. Does your work bring you fever and restlessness instead of Art's honest recompense of reward in satisfaction for well-meant toil? It is that we gathered, and gave you to eat, the fell fruit of the tree of the knowledge of good and evil. Do you languish under the coercion of the 'styles'? It is that modern architecture is based upon acquired styles. Are you prone to imitate rather than to invent? The architect, who is pastmaster at this craft, taught you how to forge. Is your art fickle as fashion? It is that the architect has winnowed with every wind, and you have been borne along in such direction as he set the sails."

If Sedding spoke despondingly of the present century architecture, he was far from despairing over that of the future. The past was gone never to be recalled, "but what of that?" He left loose his grasp on it and stepped forward into the unknown, fully convinced that in architecture "the strongest and sweetest songs" might yet remain to be sung. In the rush of civilisation – a word, according to Disraeli, too often mistaken for comfort – the artist has lost his grasp on the world. We see building after building, reared by intelligent hearts, swept away or mauled past recognition, and we gaze horror-struck, as if all the beauty of man's handiwork was to be snatched from us, and we left with a few museums – cemeteries of art – to be viewed with indifference by the populace – places of delight and bitter regrets to those who understand. Green fields are swept away to give place to the mushroom growth of an advanced age; the fairest sites are fouled by the giant hotels raised for the enthusiastic multitudes who come to gaze on them. And yet – as long as there are men and women, flowers and trees, and night which casts a glamour over day's most hideous growths – the artist need never despair, since he need never lack subjects for inspiration.

A man who has learnt to see with his own eyes the beauty of the world cannot, if he takes the trouble to learn to express himself, fail in giving a fresh view. Flaubert's advice to De Maupassant holds good in architecture – "If you have no originality, by all means get some." If each one but did his best to express his own thoughts and visions we should soon have a new style. Architecture is not so divorced from all other arts that the main laws which govern them should not touch her. There was an Elizabethan literature as well as an Elizabethan architecture. There is a Victorian literature; but in architecture the age has been spent in trying to do God's work, and create a national style, which, if we are to have it at all, must be as the growth of a flower. Till architecture ceases to be all but a closed profession to any save capable business men, we are hardly likely to advance much towards an architectural life; till the business faculty become of secondary importance to the architect, we can hardly expect to find places given in our cathedrals, churches, and other public buildings to the painter and sculptor – to promote the cordial relations between whom and the architect Sedding said was the one great desire of his heart, and the purpose of his life.

Some considerations of John Sedding's work. By H. Wilson.

The critic of the art of modern architecture is in a difficult position – first, because there is no architecture; and, second, because what passes for such is not art. I do not mean to say that the men who produce all this work are not artists; they very often are, only the conditions under which we live are absolutely antagonistic to the production of works of building art.

If you took a painter, and, having got from him a sketch for a picture, you were to chain him up in a corner of his studio; were to give him a few decorator's assistants, and then compelled him to produce that picture by their means – the result, if the painter escaped lunacy, might be interesting, but you could not call it a work of art.

12 *John Dando Sedding. Holy Trinity, Sloane Street, drawn by Gerald Horsley. The church contains fine furnishings and decoration by Henry Wilson and other Arts and Crafts designers, done in the 1890s after Sedding's death.*

The modern architect is in much the same position with regard to every craft and art he is supposed to direct – with this difference, that, instead of being chained up opposite one work, there are so many that he sees each less than once or twice a week for an hour or two at a time. In writing, therefore, of the work of any architect, so many allowances have to be made for circumstances of education, of training, of business conditions, that a real criticism becomes almost an impossibility.

In this study of John Sedding I shall, therefore, direct attention more to his intention than to the work itself; more to his aims than to his achievements; explain ideals, not lesser possibilities. In art, as in everything else, the ultimate judgement must be based on the intention and on motive.

I lay stress on this aspect of the work because it is at once the least disputable, and, moreover, of the most value to ourselves. A man's work is the material deposit of his spirit; the only thing about him that cannot be made to lie; at once his best biography and truest epitaph. Where, however, as in the present case, there are so many intermediaries employed in the transmission and execution of the original idea, we cannot base our judgement wholly on the work itself.

After all, the best critic is he who can divine most of the artist's thoughts. It is not alone from the beauty of the achievement of others that we derive most help and inspiration; it is from the stimulus that the work indirectly provides. For this reason the best work is often the least perfected. The greatest, the most suggestive masterpieces, are those which can only be completed in the beholder's chamber of imagery. Just what was wanting in the master the spectator himself supplies; and he, the work, and the master are one.

Thus, in John Sedding's work it is not what it actually is that we most love, but what it makes us think of. It is not what he accomplished that we must admire, but the triumphs he suggested.

Those, too, who knew him best know also that those suggested triumphs, under more favourable conditions, would have been accomplished. But, because the building artist of to-day is bound hand and foot, his spirit swaddled by many bands, his energy curbed by many chains his actual work can never fully represent himself.

Facing all this very keenly, though saying little, Sedding often reminded one of a spirited horse reined in and spurred on at the same time. His energy was almost explosive, and, for want of its true outlet, expended itself in those melancholies known only to the enthusiast – the marvels of mediocrity.

The best work of John Sedding will, I think, never be fully known. It can only be appreciated in its effects. It was not what he did that should command our greatest admiration, but what he made others do. His claim on our regard does not rest, as some may think, on the invention of a new style, nor even upon the more or less successful modification of an old one, nor does it rest wholly or even mainly on the mass of work he left behind, beautiful as much of it is. It rests on his personal influence, on his inspiring enthusiasm, on the intellectual stimulus he provided. Certain natures flash like luminaries across the mental sky, warming us in their passage, lighting us on our way. Their path shines with borrowed radiance long after the source of light has gone. Sedding was one of these. He was a radiant centre of artistic activity; a focus of creative fire; a node of magnetic force. Enthusiasm streamed from him and, like electric waves, vitalised the spiritual atmosphere and raised the mental temperature of those around him. The exponent in his time of personal art, his example taught all to care little for grammarians of art, for the classifier, or the scholarly artist. Yet the classifier is a wholly necessary person, and only ceases to be admirable when he claims to be regarded as a creator. Sedding's art is not scholarly, but his designs are full of himself, and those who knew his nature are the greatest admirers of his work. In him every lineament declared the enthusiast and betrayed his sensitive organisation; showed him vivacious, observant, ardent, intensely affectionate. Such a man is of necessity deeply religious, though his religion may be too great to be compromised within the bounds of any dogma. It is an ever present sense of the mysteriousness of existence, an unbroken communion with the unseen. I feel sure that it was this abiding sense of other-worldliness that gave such force and fulness to Sedding's design. On the dark background of belief in mystery, form and colour glow with new significance. We find this all through the history of art. The greatest, the most moving painters have been the seers. This has nothing to do with morality, nothing with ethics. The minds of men gifted as Sedding was are openings into the unseen. Through their transpiercing vision we see as on a background of lucent darkness, mysteries revealed but not explained, Nature coloured and transformed by the seer's personality, but not distorted.

One feels that the world of artists is divided into two schools, those who see Nature for themselves, and those who see her through the eyes of others. John Sedding was one of the first, and this fact has not a little to do with our admiration of his genius. Yet because of his seriousness he was easily pleased, and, knowing mystery, loved simple things. Flowers and children, trees and skies and common pleasures satisfied him most. His delight in them is everywhere apparent in his design. Brought up on the countryside from early infancy, his growing mind drank in the wildness round him. His earliest impressions were those of country life, and when the days of pupilage were over, and the bondage of London had become oppressive, he returned again to the countryside, made by exile more avid and receptive than ever. His destiny, by a happy chance, took him to Cornwall as partner with his brother Edmund, already settled there. Cornwall was then far more remote, more untravelled than now. In Sedding's day, too, the individuality of the people was more marked. The salient features of their character, its enchanting ruggedness, its unpreparedness, had not been modified by the influence of civic life and thought.

Here Sedding developed and expanded under the teaching of wild Nature in field and sea and sky. The cross-crowned heights, the tumuli, the menhirs, and dolmens of the moors enriched his fancy with those suggestions of remoteness, of weird loveliness, of the engaging quaintness, which sprang to the eyes every-where from his art.

The churches in which his work lay were then, in the main, unrestored, and it is not difficult to imagine the effect on a mind, brought up in the narrow groove of neo-Gothic, of the wealth of fancy, the romantic imagery, the wild exuberance, the naïve expansiveness of mystery-fed imagination contained in those lonely hillside shrines. Tiny churches, built of gigantic granite blocks – rude outside, richly carved within – glowing with colour or made magnificent by the sombre stain of time, spring out of the coombes and pinnacle the moors in the most unlikely places. One thinks of Malory, with his wayside chapels, all overgrown with briars; chapels enclosing fair silver altars, full richly arrayed, whereat stand ministering hermits, with armoured knights kneeling a-row before them. John Sedding felt all this; his spirit was saturated with the legendary aura breathed from out every corner of that fascinating county, and, though his work at this time shows strongly the influence of Street, though it is thin in quality, tentative in character, yet in the glowing colour, in the ever-present evidence of Nature study, in the little oasis of fantastic imagery sprinkled over his designs, we see how deeply his adopted county affected him. Through the thin simulacrum of a style we see the artist eager, impetuous, impatient to realise himself; even thus early we get glimpses of the man as he was, full of a rich vitality: and we see the promises of that fulness of fancy, that wild luxuriance of imagination he later developed. His work at the time was like an old tale retold with a new accent – for, though he was the outcome of the Gothic Revival, he lived a continued protest against it. He felt the tyranny of the arbitrary and ridiculous ideals while striving to be loyal to its principles as practised by his master.

The ideals and example of his elder brother Edmund had also much to do with Sedding's development. Edmund, if report does not err, was by far the more gifted of the two; he had much of the spirit of Rossetti in him but never strong, he went home before he had fully found himself. His ideals and influence survived, and had a new existence in the spirit of his brother John. The first new work the latter undertook was the church of St Martin, at Marple. It had been originally designed by the elder, but was so modified in execution that it became John Sedding's own. Here again, in the comparative hardness of the detail, in the half-timber porch, in the general rectilinearity of the design, we recognise the results of his training. Still, every here and there in the management of the masses, in the arrangement of light and shade, and, above all, in the rich though sombre decoration of the chancel, we see the strong spirit striving to escape from the Gothic armour.

He was too strong to be correct – correctness is the sole privilege of the inane; too untameable to be bound by rule – rules are but crutches for halting intellects. In all this early work one divines him militant against innumerable disabilities, one sees him hampered by the stupidity or ignorance of workmen, by the cupidity of their employers; torn one way by a desire to do the best, and another by the immediate necessity of doing some-thing. Longing for leisure to create, but compelled to design while the workmen were waiting; and, though spurred on by the beauty of outside Nature, found himself driven continually against the dead wall of modern building conditions before the ideas could take proper shape. He was, as indeed we all are, ever at war with circumstance and conditions. That he never faltered in the battle for thirty-seven years says not a little for his courage.

Long after the time when most men give up ideals and take to organisation and the management of business, Sedding went about sketching, measuring and even in the train filling note-books with ideas of design for future working out. His sketches alone would fill many volumes, his written descriptions many more. Yet, when told he should leave sketching to students, replied that he should "never cease to be one."

This receptive attitude of mind kept him ever young. A man only grows old when he ceases to absorb and assimilate. It kept him ever on the alert for new ideas, for new methods.

Throughout a long and busy life Sedding kept untouched the freshness of his nature. Like a child, novelty ever attracted him. His spiritual retina kept its youthful impressionability. Experiments never ceased to fascinate, no failures discouraged him. Though an experimentalist, he was not "at home in all the styles." He dallied with many, as was the fashion of the day, but only one was deeply affected. That one was his own solution of Gothic. It was an attempt to take up the threads of Gothic tradition where they were left in the fifteenth century, and weave into them the weft of modern need and thought. It was a magnificent attempt, but one doomed from the first to failure. The failure was as splendid as the idea. It was an attempt to bridge an impassable chasm by an impossible abstraction.

In Holy Trinity Church, Sloane Street, his most ambitious work this idea is very fully carried out; but, even had the whole conception been realised, the lack of unifying tradition among the executants, the lack of co-ordinated powers of design in the workmen employed would still have prevented the finished work from being a true masterpiece. Nevertheless, it marks a mighty advance on all preceding work, and the mere attempt to combine in one building the best work of all the best artists and craftsmen of our day is one which should endear his memory to all who are striving, as he was, to the founding of a real vital architecture: an architecture which shall be the immediate and harmonious expression of spiritual and social needs.

Probably the best part of Sedding's design, certainly that which is and has been the most widely appreciated, is that in which he was least hindered by the failures of the workers. In embroidery there is only one person between the artist and the finished thing, and feminine intuition often supplied the lack of traditional knowledge. In this branch of art his love of colour showed itself, his wild and wayward fancy had free play, and flowers and trees, birds, beasts, and creeping things emerged from the woven ground in ordered irregularity. Robins with scrolls of greeting to the Virgin, doves and owls, tits, squirrels, dormice, lived in happy-family fashion together on chasubles, altar frontals, copes, stoles, and hangings; at hide and seek behind a tangled maze of flowers. Were all his buildings to crumble to dust tomorrow, and all his other work to decay, John Sedding's name would still live in our memories as a most gifted artist; a designer of incomparable power and initiative.

Still, even here, the very beauty of the work makes one feel what the world loses in having so few who embroider their own designs.

Another branch of Art in which the play of his power of imagery was less impeded was that of metal work. Here his feeling for crisp, curled forms, for brilliant contrasts of light and shade, for cunning juxtapositions of broad, gleaming surfaces with jewel-like patches of richer work, moves one to admiration, even though the work be not personal, but only an imperfect translation of the designer's conceptions. The many drawings for chalices, pattens, ciboria, pastoral staves, mitres, processional crosses, show how strong was his bent towards the art of the metal worker. Indeed, no inconsiderable part of his youth was spent in the workshop of a once celebrated smith, for the purpose of acquiring a deeper insight into the secrets of the craft, in order to avoid the mistakes made by every uninstructed designer.

The wonder is that he had enough vitality to supply all these varied activities. He seemed, in truth, to be able to direct the whole dynamic energy of his nature on the special problem of the moment, withdrawing that energy temporarily from every other avenue of activity, thus accomplishing much in little time.

Yet, after all, one regrets this restless expenditure of energy, though fully conscious that it was the inevitable result of his environment. The natural outlet for the gifts of such a man was the direction of a guild of masons and other craftsmen. He was a medieval master builder, born two centuries too late. But as this outlet was forbidden him, the pent up energy found vents in these varied channels of artistic expression, and the world is the richer by his work.

To sum up: John Sedding was a Romanticist born in an age of Stylists. Between the two there is ever antagonism. The stylist cares for little but the manner, the romanticist everything for the matter. The latter creates, the former re-shapes existing creations. There can be no harmony between the two, yet both are good and both necessary. They represent the two poles of intellectual energy. Sedding came into the world gifted with powers which could never be fully displayed, endowed with ideals impossible of realisation. But, just because he was so full of unused activities, his influence was so dynamic, his personality affected so many. The expression of his aims in his design and his writings is so pervasive, so dominant, that one sees its results even in the works of men who scoff at what they call his eccentricity. Whatever the world may ultimately think about his work, nothing can diminish the value of his achievement. Sedding's place is with Madox Brown, Morris, and Burges, men who have left their mark upon their time, and have earned the grateful admiration of their successors. Time will add lustre to their names.

An appreciation of J. D. Sedding: by C. W. Whall.

The work of John Sedding was the life of John Sedding and his personality. This cannot be said of everybody, perhaps of few. Many men do large works who in their hearts hate them. They would sooner do other things, and do them otherwise. But they assume their life's work like a garment, and the man within it (if you could reach him) is something quite different. So it comes about that, in setting myself to write about the *work*, I found myself, at every sentence, writing about the *man*. His work to me had all the qualities of his character – all the strong qualities of it, also all the weak ones.

Many have known him longer than I, but the few years of our intercourse were busy ones, and full of vivid experiences.

What one chiefly noted in him was his impulsiveness, warmheartedness, brightness. What one chiefly wished for in him was repose.

Repose – not in the sense of indolence and dreaming, but in the sense of serener outlook upon things around him, contemplation, comparison, balance, and judgement.

But of no one perhaps could it be better said that his defects were the defects of his virtues, their exaggeration. Did he seem unrestful, it was the buoyancy of his hopeful, youthful nature and the warmth of his heart that made every goose a swan, and perhaps led him to estimate too light-heartedly and solve too brusquely some of the problems with which he had to deal, and also to change his point of view with a rapidity and energy sometimes too dazzling; especially as, if one may be allowed to remember it, he did, it must be confessed, enjoy giving a dig at the opposite side, and dragging his coat-tail for people to tread on. Yet, as I say, the whole thing being so genuine, so good and sweet-natured, and all meant in such good part, these "defects of his virtues." as I have called them, never gave offence to a breathing being – we loved him all the more.

The reminiscence I shall venture to recount brings me more directly to the question of John Sedding's Art. We went together to see Holy Trinity, Sloane Street. I looked at it in silence, trying to take it in. He cocked his head on one side and said: "Well? Well, is it too naughty? I hope it's not too naughty?" I said, "I don't see your point in mixing the styles. It's using *style* all the same, only you use two styles instead of one. I like your Bournemouth Church better."

I think the same things now, but what I recognise in Sedding's work, apart from the question of dealing with style – where, it seems to me, he hardly saw the question in its real bearings – what I recognise in his work, was a true endeavour to make things what they seemed; a hatred of false motives, and doing things for convention's sake, and a full intention of doing them for their own sake. This led him to the really great point in his position and career, the true help that he gave – I may almost say the impulse and initiative that he gave – to the union of the arts. Many artists, many craftsmen, some living, some dead, have good and grateful cause to remember his enthusiasm in that regard which led him out towards them with such sympathy and generosity.

Byzantium in Brighton

by Nicholas Taylor

Henry Wilson (1863–1934) carried on Sedding's practice after his
death. Wilson was closely involved with the Arts and Crafts
Movement: he was a remarkable architect and one of the great
church plate designers of English history. Unfortunately he was no
business man and he let Sedding's growing practice fade away.
Nicholas Taylor's account of his work at St Bartholomew's Church
in Brighton is a worthy tribute to his last major architectural
achievement, though its description of the building as *Art Nouveau*
is controversial. The architectural part of these designs may
equally well be seen as Wilson's version of the Free Byzantine
manner introduced by Bentley's Westminster Cathedral.

The furnishings designed in 1897–1908 for St Bartholomew's, Brighton, by Henry Wilson, although incomplete, are the grandest example of English *Art Nouveau*. The church of 1872–74 (described in *The Architectural Review* March 1965), with its 135 feet internal height and 58 feet width, was the masterpiece in stock brick of a local High Victorian architect, Edmund Scott. By 1895, however, the church was as cosmopolitan as any rebel Anglican could wish: vast eclectic congregations worshipped at splendid services, augmented from 1896 by a permanent orchestra, and they were conducted to their seats by a Japanese verger, John Kendo Feudiekitchi, who had once worked in the stables of the Mikado. The work of the parish by then included a crêche, lending library, blanket loan society, invalid kitchen and sick relief centre, besides social, musical and sporting societies, and the more exclusively religious groups such as the Confraternity of the Blessed Sacrament and the Ward of St Mary. The second vicar, who arrived in February 1895, was Arthur Reginald Carew Cocks, a flamboyant and capable leader who perfectly matched the confidence and decorative splendour which now overlaid (or enhanced) the simplicity and directness of Fr Wagner's Tractarianism.

Henry Wilson was the ideal designer to realize Cocks's dreams. Born in Liverpool in 1864, he had been trained at Kidderminster Art School and apprenticed to an architect in Maidenhead. He went as assistant, first to the church architect John Oldrid Scott (Sir Gilbert's second son) and then to John Belcher, the free Classicist, in whose office at that time the design for the Chartered Accountants' building was being prepared, perhaps largely by the chief assistant, Beresford Pite. Finally, Wilson became chief assistant to J. D. Sedding, and on Sedding's early death in 1891 he succeeded to the practice. Wilson did much of the detailed design and furnishings of Sedding's great Arts and Crafts churches, including Holy Redeemer, Clerkenwell, Holy Trinity, Sloane Street, and St Peter's, Ealing. Sedding was a master of spatial and liturgical design, and he kept Wilson's fancies within the bounds of constructional possibility. Like Beresford Pite, Wilson on his own had defects equal to his striking merits (their masters, Belcher and Sedding, were incidentally close friends). Immediately after Sedding's death, with the team of pupils kept together (Charles Nicholson, Arthur Grove, Alfred Powell, H. W. Finch, J. Paul Cooper, E. W. Meredith), Wilson did several complete, though abortive, church designs, including the Victoria (British Columbia) Cathedral competition and St Andrew, Boscombe. But by 1895, with only Grove and possibly

2 *Henry Wilson. First design (1890) for Public Library, Ladbroke Grove, London (1891). A design that influenced Mackintosh and Townsend, among others.*

3 *Henry Wilson. Public Library, Ladbroke Grove, North Kensington (1891). This commission was designed while Wilson was still Sedding's chief assistant. The original design was simplified in construction.*

1 *Portrait of Henry Wilson.*

Cooper remaining, he had become an ecclesiastical stage designer, not a real architect. From Sedding, who in 1882–89 had been churchwarden at St Alban's, Holborn, Wilson inherited connections with an increasingly Baroque, almost Firbankian, school of thought among the younger ritualist clergy – Ritual for Ritual's Sake. It is significant that beneath the brilliantly imaginative detail in his Victoria and Boscombe designs, there are completely conventional medievalist plans – not the broad congregational spaces exploited by Sedding.

It was therefore fortunate that at St Bartholomew's, Brighton, Edmund Scott's decisive liturgical space already existed. Wilson's work there was his last on the grand scale; with his unofficial appointment in 1896 as the first editor of *The Architectural Review*, he began to withdraw from architectural practice, and within a few years, working at Hare Court in the Temple (as a tenant of E. S. Prior), at the Royal College of Art (as a lecturer) and at his cottage at Platt in Kent, he became essentially a metalworker and jewellery designer. He was an enthusiast, combining a love of natural flora and fauna à la Ruskin with an excitement for the exotic (he had a Japanese manservant, and his three children were called Guthlae, Orrea and Fiammetta). He had a colossal, sometimes menacing sense of scale, similar to Pite's. He was a close friend of Lethaby and collaborated with him on an extraordinary concrete-vaulted design in the Liverpool Cathedral competition in 1902.[1] President of the Art Workers' Guild in 1927 and of the Arts and Crafts Exhibition Society from 1915, he died at Menton in 1934.

Cocks commissioned Wilson to design a comprehensive scheme of extension and decoration for St Bartholomew's. The strengthening of the existing east wall with tie rods was an admission that it was now semi-permanent. So in his overall scheme, which in its its mature form of *circa* 1905 is shown in a splendid coloured drawing at the R.I.B.A., Wilson treated it as a dramatic backcloth to the ceremonial beneath. What survives can only be explained within this overall plan – the bareness of the baldacchino, for instance, that was intended to be seen against the swirling rhythm of the Baroque *transparente* above. The dominant theme – a self-consciously daring piece of Romanism for an Anglican church – was to be not Christ in Glory, but the Madonna in Glory. Wilson proposed to pierce the east wall behind the baldacchino as an openwork screen, then continue Scott's main structure for three further bays of the full height, and build a new straight-ended east wall, covered with murals, above a Lady Altar. The Madonna, presumably in mosaic, was to be a giant figure about 30 feet high with arms outstreched, in a red and blue robe.[2] Above and below her arms on each side were to be bands of heavenly souls robed in white, and below her figure was to be a continuous frieze of souls terrestrial. The background was to be mainly of blue and gold. The roof was to have, not the

simple tie-beams of the nave, but a rich barrel vault with the gold criss-cross pattern on blue familiar from the 'ceilures' over the high altars of 15th-century churches in the West Country.[3] Extra boldness was to be added by the convex (instead of concave) coving. The three giant arches of the upper screen, inlaid with green marble, were partially infilled on each side by yellow-brown railings, decorated with green and white inlay and in turn enclosing elaborate metal grilles with sculptured heads in relief. Splendid though this projected Queen of Heaven would have been, there is some doubt whether Wilson's figure drawing would have matched in quality his purely abstract conceptions. Spatially the effect would have been magnificent and, incidentally, the semi-permanence of the east wall would have solved the problem of separating from the main body of the church the noise and confusion of years of building work.

What survives is a mighty fragment. The baldacchino, 45 feet high and raised twelve steps above the nave, was erected in 1899–1900 at a cost of over £2,000. It is grandly Byzantine, contrasting a stark outline with the richly abstract streakings of marble (Ruskin's influence). The square columns are reddish-brown, on

4 *Henry Wilson. Design for new west front for St Andrew's Church, Boscombe (1895). A magnificent free design, unfortunately not carried out, but used as the basis for James Miller's Glasgow church of St Andrew-in-the-East (1904).*

green and black bases; the canopy is green, with capitals and thin arches of interlaced vine patterns in white alabaster. The sanctuary paving is of black and grey marble, with a central strip of red marble beneath the present carpet. In front of the altar, on either side, is a giant standard candlestick put up in *circa* 1908, consisting of a Tuscan column of grey-and-white marble on a black base (in the original drawing, red marble on a white base). This supports a curious bronze object, a hybrid between a flaming urn and a pineapple, forming a base for a thick candle. Beyond it can be seen the glittering vault of gold mosaic and mother-of-pearl of the baldacchino itself, with a dove in its centre. Next to each standard candlestick is a short two-bay altar rail not in the original design and added in *circa* 1905. The thick gilt columns, inlaid with red 'boiled sweet' medallions reminiscent of William Burges, reflect the classicism of Beresford Pite (for example, the claws in their plinths). Between the columns is a thickly curvaceous thistle design. Against the side walls of the sanctuary are the simple oak choir stalls, with a round-arched motif at each end.

Above the altar itself, with its paintings of 1874 by S. Bell, is a tall gradine, supporting six superb candlesticks, the rippling brass stems of which are 4 feet 9 inches high. In the centre is a large tabernacle, on the beaten silver doors of which "a draped and crowned figure in the midst symbolizes perpetual youth, ever renewed and sustained by the true Vine to which it clings" (a very Ninetyish subject). This is now hidden normally by curtains. Wilson's central crucifix, seen in its original setting, was unfortunately replaced in 1912 by a crude Oberammergau-style creation by one McCulloch of Kennington. Wilson's crucifix was removed to the Lady Altar in the third bay from the east on the south side, where it is quite out of scale with its surroundings. The silver-gilt crucifix in low relief stands on a tall ebony base; once again, Wilson's figure sculpture is inferior to his virtuoso handling of the background with its angels and vine branches. It is now seen in the incongruous setting of the canopy designed by an orthodox Goth, C. E. Kempe, in 1888 (the hangings in the same style are more recent). Kempe's Lady Altar was replaced in 1902 (it is now in St Alban's, Brighton) by a silver-plated repoussé frontal and gradine designed by Wilson, with a slab of red alabaster on top[4]. The frontal has the Adoration of the Magi in a central roundel, encircled by symbols of the seven planets. On either side, vigorously modelled swastikas (the ancient symbol of the Sun) are embossed in a manner reminiscent of the neo-Celtic book-illustrators of the Glasgow School. Above is a majestic superscription in Roman letters, commemorating a Mrs Louisa Gilpin. It was in that same year, 1902, that Wilson gave Eric Gill his first

5 *Henry Wilson. Overall scheme for furnishing of St Bartholomew's Church, Brighton (largely carried out 1897–1908).*

6 *Henry Wilson. Baldacchino, St Bartholomew's Church, Brighton (1899–1900).*

7 *Henry Wilson. Giant standard candlestick (circa 1908) and baldacchino (1899–1900), St Bartholomew's Church, Brighton.*

8 *Henry Wilson. Crucifix (circa 1900) above Lady Altar (originally above main altar), St Bartholomew's Church, Brighton.*

9 *Henry Wilson. Silver Lady Altar frontal (1902), St Bartholomew's Church, Brighton.*

10 *Henry Wilson. Pulpit, St Bartholomew's Church, Brighton (1906).*

285

letter-cutting job, at Holy Trinity, Sloane Street; it is thus an appropriate coincidence that against the adjoining pillar there is a tablet excellently carved in Gill's style in memory of Fr Smallpiece, curate from 1896 to 1930.

The whole east end is undeniably spoilt by the mosaics, in an over-blown Pre-Raphaelite manner, inserted in 1911, a year after Fr Cocks had resigned and seceded to Rome. His successor, Henry Ross[5], no longer employed Wilson. The mosaic artist was F. Hamilton Jackson[6], who, as one of the art-workers in the Dixon-Paul Cooper circle at Birmingham (and an early contributor to *The Architectural Review*), must have known Wilson and might have been expected to respect his intentions. A relatively minute Christ in Glory was crushed into the space under the baldacchino, where Wilson intended a plainer mosaic with a more youthful figure, and the side walls were filled with overlarge figures of Michael and Raphael (north) and Uriel and Gabriel (south), where there should have been plain green marble panels. After Wilson's dismissal, Fr Ross went ahead with plans for completing the church (it is not clear who was the architect). In the parish magazine for 1912 he recommended "the expenditure of about £2,500, including the building of an apsidal chapel eastward over the vestries, a new High Altar, and the putting of stained glass in the great west window."

Since this would evidently have meant the destruction of Wilson's baldacchino it is fortunate that the 1914 war put a stop to it. Fortunately too, Scott's splendid circular west window was left unglazed, although a sentimental design of 1914 for glass by J. C. Bewsey hangs in the church (Bewsey did the glass in the four lancets below).[7] In 1924, Sir Giles Gilbert Scott (no relation of Edmund) prepared a design for building a new east end, with one and half more bays of the full height plus a polygonal apse. The baldacchino would have remained in the centre and the mosaics would have been replaced by low screens leading to the Lady Chapel in the apse.

At that moment, however, the whole roof had to be reslated at great cost and the remaining funds were exhausted on minor furnishings.[8]

Because the east end has been thrown out of balance by the mosaics, Wilson's most perfect design at St. Bart's is now the pulpit. This is partly because an error of Wilson's own making was remedied. In his drawing shown at the Royal Academy in 1898 (it is now hanging at St. Bartholomew's sanctuary), he proposed ornate stalls and a cancellum wall, with a comparatively small pulpit and a new casing for the Holditch organ of 1874 in the north-east corner. Ambition soon changed this to the scheme shown in the second coloured drawing at the R.I.B.A., in which the pulpit was to be dis-

11 *Henry Wilson. Font (1908), St Bartholomew's Church, Brighton.*

12 *Henry Wilson. Chalice (1898), St Bartholomew's Church, Brighton. Wilson's genius as a designer of plate and enamelwork can scarcely be over-rated.*

placed slightly to the west and a large organ by Walker erected in the recess next to the sanctuary on the north side. No doubt its stout red arches and strongly model-led yellow-brown gallery would have been attractive in themselves – but it is an example of Wilson's fatal con-centration on detail to the exclusion of architectural qualities that he was oblivious of the extent to which the organ would have unbalanced Edmund Scott's noble single-minded space. As can be seen in a con-temporary postcard,[9] the brick core of the gallery was actually built in 1901 and the organ erected on it in an unsightly wooden frame, nick-named 'the cottage'. It was rightly condemned as an eyesore and in 1906 was demolished. The organ was removed instead to a gallery at the west end, where it is divided in two, with a central console. The west gallery, with its thick, primitive columns of wood, is clearly also by Wilson, though virtually undecorated.[10] It was designed for a choir and orchestra of 150 people.

As finally erected in 1906 on the site of the abortive organ gallery, the pulpit is a triumph. Its bulging polygonal gallery, faced with panels of Irish green marble, stands on six piers of red African marble with white alabaster capitals and a plinth of black Tournai marble. The perfect circle of the wooden canopy is suspended in free space from two wall brackets of iron. The gallery has an apsidal dado of alabaster. The one weak link is the crucifix, which dates from 1888 and was salvaged from the previous wooden pulpit. Best of all – the quintessence of Wilsonism – is the scaling down of the spiral staircase to a minute size compared with the flanking columns in front so that there is the con-ceit of a kind of Aladdin's Cave. The Ravennesque capitals are excellently carved with inscriptions (the two end capitals were, by a mischance, transposed, so that they read *Pro Nobis/Orate*). At the west end of the church, in the second bay on the south side, is the baptistery also by Wilson and completed in 1908. It is a curious composition: on a semi-circular plinth of three black marble steps stands the octagonal font of dark green marble, bordered with beaten copper. Measuring 5 feet 7 inches across, it resembles an enormously enlarged casket or snuff-box. The recess behind is lined with light green marble to a height of 12 feet and on a pedestal stands an uninspired statue of St John the Baptist designed by Sir Giles Gilbert Scott and made by W. D. Gough in 1925.

There is one more work of Wilson's in the church; a very pretty chalice presented in 1898 by the Ward of the Confraternity of the Blessed Sacrament. The silver cup and silver-plated base are connected by a richly carved ivory stem of vine tendrils in truly *Art Nouveau* twists and curves. Halfway up the stem is a globular hand-hold, made of green, blue and brown enamel and representing two interlacing dragons. The hexagonal base is also inlaid with green and blue enamel.

It may be questioned whether, apart from the chalice, Wilson's work at St. Bartholomew's justifies the title 'Art Nouveau'. It seems at first sight so formidably chunky. Yet this chunkiness is merely a necessary contrast to the flowing patterns of the marble and the beaten metal. It is the reliance on the curves and twists of natural materials, deriving ultimately from Ruskin, and their contrast with massive rectilinear shapes, that distinguishes English *Art Nouveau* from the work of Horta or Guimard. It was the *unnatural* quality of the French and Belgian work that the English stigmatised as irreverent and pagan – and which turned the English away from the brink of modern architecture. At St Bartholomew's, there is of course an overall impression of the Byzantine.[11] Bentley's Westminster Cathedral (1895–1903) and Lethaby's and Swainson's book on St Sophia (1894) are clear influences. Wilson, however, used the stylistic detail only as the starting point for a dream world of Byzantium – a rich, permanent, setting for worship towering above the mere mortals in the nave[12] – again a strong contrast to the flimsiness of much continental *Art Nouveau*. Wilson's vitality and sense of scale were rejected by the 'good taste' of the next generation. His patron, Fr. Cocks, after his secession to Rome (he became a Monsignor), built another church, St Peter's, Hove (1915), designed by Bentley's pupil and successor, J. A. Marshall. Although decently Byzantine outside, with a slim campanile, its heavily marbled interior has weakly Mannerist detail – the same contrast with the stock brick of St Bart's as there is at Westminster between Marshall's decorations and Bentley's background.

[1] Illustrated and briefly described in John Brandon-Jones's article on Lethaby in the *Journal of the Royal Institute of British Architects* 1957, pp.220–221.

[2] Presumably, if episcopal authority challenged her insertion, the Vicar could reply that she was merely conventional decoration for a Lady Chapel.

[3] A characteristic ornament in the work of Sedding, who practised at Penzance and Bristol for ten years, 1865–75.

[4] Presumably this altar was intended to be transplanted eventually to Wilson's great eastern Lady Chapel.

[5] Vicar of St Alban's, Holborn, 1918–35, he died in 1963 aged 98.

[6] With Barkentin and Krall as executants. They also made the three Bologna-style sanctuary lamps.

[7] In the nave Cock's one conventional choice, W. E. Tower, Kempe's successor, had previously completed four out of sixteen proposed windows on the themes of the Incarnation and the Atonement.

[8] Sir Walter Tapper's design of 1918 for a 'War Shrine', mentioned by Goodhart-Rendel, does not seem to have been carried out either.

[9] I am grateful to Mr W. W. Begley, an expert on Brighton's ecclesiology, for lending me this.

[10] Under the gallery is a conventionally Gothic Children's Chapel of 1929 by Harold Gibbons; on the walls are some good early photographs of the church.

[11] The architectural painter and draughtsman, William Walcot, used the baldacchino and other details of St Bartholomew's in his painting 'Justinian weds Theodora' – the architecture of course, being that of St Sophia. Mr Begley showed me this too.

[12] It was not Wilson's fault that this type of liturgical setting degenerated into the fashion for Baroque furnishings promoted by the Society of St Peter and St Paul after 1911.

Edwardian Ecclesiastical Architecture

by B. F. L. Clarke

Most of the eminent late Victorian Gothic architects died at the end of the 19th century and the field was left to a new generation. Canon Clarke's survey, originally a lecture to the Royal Society of Arts, sums up the developments of the first ten years of the new century.

The 19th-century churchmen aimed at providing a church for almost every community with a population of a few hundred upwards, and by the end of the century this had been done: there were very few villages and hamlets that had not a church of some kind, even if it was only a mission church. So village churches built after 1900 are uncommon: but some of the few that were built are of exceptional quality, and three deserve mention, each of which was a replacement of an older church.

Brockhampton, near Ross, was built in 1901–02 by W. R. Lethaby – member of S.P.A.B., friend of Philip Webb, first Professor of Design at the Royal College of Art, Surveyor to Westminster Abbey, and in 1911 Master of the Art Worker's Guild.

The church is cruciform with a low central lantern tower, roofed with a pointed tunnel vault on transverse arches: concrete is used for the vaulting of the chancel and transepts. The roofs are covered with thatch. Everything is the product of the Arts and Crafts Movement, and suggests honesty and simplicity. There are some distant suggestions of Gothic, but nothing with any precedent.

Kempley, Gloucester, was built in 1903 by Randall Wells, who had been Lethaby's clerk of works at Brockhampton. The materials and labour were local: the iron-work was made by the village blacksmith, and the sculpture over the north doorway was carved by the village carpenter. The furnishings came from the workshop of Ernest Gimson, and the lectern and

candlesticks, of oak and mother of pearl, were by Ernest Barnsley.

Both these churches are good examples of the Arts and Crafts Movement: the interest in craftsmanship, and the cultivation of a rather sophisticated simplicity – the ecclesiastical equivalent of the ingle-nooks, the shutters and the water-butts of the houses of Voysey.

Great Warley, Essex, by C. Harrison Townsend, has the roughcast walls of a Voysey house and a simple timber belfry: the exterior does not prepare one for the treat that the interior provides: a feast of Arts and Crafts and *Art Nouveau*. This is the kind of art that filled *The Studio*, and with which Canon and Mrs Barnett sought to elevate the masses. There is panelling decorated with lilies: the pointed barrel roof has decorated aluminium bands. The apse has marble at the base and silvered ornament above: the bronze screen has an efflorescence of flowers and leaves mingled with angels, red glass fruits and mother-of-pearl flowers, at the top. Another screen is of walnut and pewter: the font is of marble with two bronze angels. All this is by Sir William Reynolds Stephens: the woodwork was designed by Townsend himself.

But country churches are rare, and churches like this are most exceptional: the typical Edwardian church is in the suburbs, which continued to spread round London into Middlesex, Surrey and Essex, and round the cities of the Midlands and the North. Everyone was worried about Church work in the inner districts, but there was no problem about churchgoing

2 *William Lethaby. Brockhampton Church, near Ross-on-Wye, Herefordshire (1901–02).*

in the suburbs: wherever the new houses were built a church – or the first part of one – was erected, and people went to it. Often the west end was not completed, or an aisle was left unbuilt, and the tower rose no higher than the basement: but in the early 1900s no one doubted that it would be only a matter of time before the church was completed according to the architect's design: a half or two-thirds of a church was enough for the moment, and they would built the rest within a few years.

The first part to be built was nearly always the chancel: a few bays of the nave, or a temporary building, would suffice for the congregation for the time being; but the altar must be in its proper setting from the beginning, raised on steps – seven from the nave to the footpace was usual – visible and dignified.

Since the early days of the church building movement the need for ancillary buildings had greatly increased: a much larger vestry was provided for the clergy, and the choir would need a vestry of its own: the organ would require a good-sized chamber – or more usually in the larger church it would be placed in a gallery, with a passage to the vestry underneath. In a very ambitious church there might also be a gallery on the other side of the chancel in case an orchestra were needed. There would be a chapel for weekday services, generally on the side opposite to the organ. Then there would have to be a heating chamber, and

there might be an undercroft under the raised sanctuary for classes and clubs.

There was no doubt that this was the important part of the church, and this would have to be built even if the rest had to wait.

In general the nave would be wide and the aisles comparatively narrow. Many of the bigger and better churches were of the type that Street began at All Saints', Clifton: a wide nave with aisles that were simply narrow passages pierced through the buttresses. Everyone did not favour this: Sir Charles Nicholson said that a church of this plan has to be very lofty and therefore expensive, and he preferred no clerestory, a lower roof, and comparatively wide aisles. It was not necessary, he said, for everyone to see the altar, and some prefer to be in a corner.

Nave and chancel were normally of the same height, perhaps with a bellcote at the junction, but otherwise with an unbroken line of roof.

The traditional place for the font is at the west end of the nave, but at this time there was a fashion for a western baptistery, often combined with a porch on both sides, one of which shows no signs of ever having been used.

All the architects practising at the time were of course Victorians. Some were finishing their careers. J. T. Micklethwaite died in 1906, and only a few of his churches come into the period. St Bartholomew's,

3 *C. Harrison Townsend, metalwork by Sir William Reynolds Stephens. Interior, St Mary the Virgin, Great Warley, Brentwood, Essex (1902–04). Arts and Crafts church architecture at its most attractive.*

was
hard
high
some
– St
the
Luty
nave
cou
Insi
roof
que
requ
a do

I
R.I.
mer
few
unt
Clu
Bo

4 *A. Beresford Pite. Christ Church, Brixton Road, The Oval, London (built 1902–03). An example of the free Byzantine brought in by Bentley's Westminster Cathedral.*

5 *Edward Prior. St Andrew's, Roker, near Sunderland (1904–07). Built in collaboration with Randall Wells.*

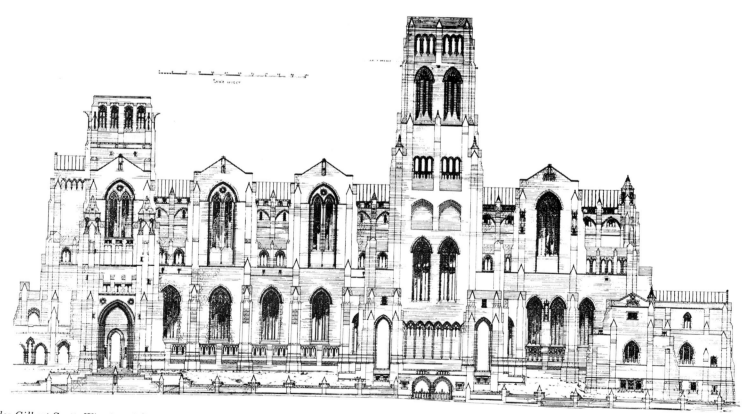

6 *Giles Gilbert Scott. Winning design, Liverpool Cathedral competition (1903). Bodley was assessor of the competition and was appointed to assist the inexperienced young winner. But Bodley died in 1907 and Scott went on with the building, with many revisions of the design.*

7
b

293

8 *Temple Moore. St Wilfrid's, Duchy Road, Harrogate, Yorkshire (1905–14).*

furnishers had served them only too well. Our churches and their services had become pretentious, stuffy and debased: what was needed was a return to the genuine English tradition.

The reform of vestments and of music does not concern us, but we must mention the reform of the altar and sanctuary.

The altar in the average High or Moderate church, from the '70s onward, had been raised on several steps, and had on it, or behind it, a shelf or shelves on which were a brass cross and candlesticks – two, six, or many more: the candles were raised on wooden stocks painted to look like wax. There were also plenty of brass flower vases. Behind the altar there was either a tall reredos, or a tall curtain, with curtains at the sides opened out like wings.

The reformers had no difficulty in showing that an altar like that had no precedent. The medieval altar was low, with a carved or painted reredos below the east window, and with curtains at right angles to the east wall, hung on rods either projecting from the wall or supported by four slender posts. There were two candles at the most, and no other ornaments. The altar stood on a footpace: otherwise it was not raised above the chancel by more than one step.

The propaganda produced a reaction from certain Anglo-Catholics, who spoke disparagingly of the British Museum Use, to which they opposed the living Use of the Western Church – by which they meant modern Roman Catholic ceremonial and vestments, and Baroque altars and altar-pieces such as are to be found in Bavaria and Austria (and, though they did not mention it, in the Lutheran churches of Scandinavia).

Both of these movements reached their climax in the 1920s. Both now seem old-fashioned, but the English Use movement had a very great influence on the design of Anglican churches in the '20s and '30s, and it led to the disuse of many things that were undoubtedly regrettable.

One of its enthusiastic supporters in its early days was J. N. Comper, who had been articled to Bodley and Garner. In 1901 he had the opportunity of designing the church of St Cyprian, Clarence Gate, St Marylebone, which was consecrated in 1903. Comper said that the church "neither seeks nor avoids originality": its aim is "only to fulfil the ideal of the English Parish Church . . . and to do so in the last manner of English architecture."

St Cyprian's is a repro uction of a church on the type of St Peter Mancroft, Norwich, in which a reve-

9 *Ninian Comper. Interior, St Cyprian's Church, Clarence Gate, London (1903).*

10 *Ninian Comper. Interior, St Mary's Church, Wellingborough, Northamptonshire (begun 1906, completed 1930s). Comper's blended style at its best.*

nant from the 15th century would find himself more or less at home, though it would seem very refined and clean, and he would soon discover that the local people did not have guilds which maintained their own chapels and that he must not expect any secular goings-on in the nave. When I last saw it, it struck me that it is not unlike one of the Perpendicular Commissioners' Churches built in the 1820s, minus the tower and vestibules. It is less formal (the aisles differ from one another), and of course there is more expertise in the details: but if the pews and galleries were cleared out of a Commissioners' church, and it was divided up with screens and parcloses, and plenty of space was left empty, it would be much the same as St Cyprian's. All the Victorian movements – Middle-Pointed, Early French, Italian influence, constructional polychrome – have been left behind, and might never have happened at all.

In fact Comper, though he produced one or two other churches something like St Cyprian's, soon went beyond it, and aimed at what he called Unity by Inclusion: classical columns, renaissance details, and pinnacles and tracery from 18th-century Gothic; and he came to believe that the altar should be covered by a full-sized ciborium: the riddel posts of the Middle Ages were the attenuated remains of its columns.

Comper can be seen at his best in the huge church of St Mary, Wellingborough, begun in 1906 but not completed until 1930. Here can be seen in their freshness the Comper features – the dragons beneath the rood, the beardless risen Christ above it, the burnished gold columns . . . and many other things that were repeated so often in later years that they became wearisome. But that was long after the days of King Edward.

The English Use Movement had some effect at the time in the direction of greater simplicity, but its most obvious influence came after the War: it cannot be said that simplicity was much in fashion in the years before 1914. Many old churches and many Victorian churches were adorned with more and more solid fittings: marble or mosaic floors, carved oak stalls and altar rails, alabaster fonts and pulpits, *opus sectile* work in the sanctuary, and larger organs with carved oak cases.

More and more windows were filled with stained glass. The standard was not particularly high. The 19th-century glass firms had passed their prime: Clayton and Bell, and Kempe continued by Tower, were repeating themselves. Heaton, Butler and Bayne filled many windows with intense-looking figures against a cloudy yellow sky. Burlison and Grylls kept up quite a good standard, and there were enterprising glass-painters such as Whall; but most of the glass lacked vigour. Still, it was part of the ensemble, and if I were asked to describe the effect aimed at, I should borrow from Charlotte Yonge and call it a "reverent richness".

Perhaps the best example of all is Sandringham, where King Edward himself worshipped and where he

is commemorated. It would be easy to find fault with it, but the ordinary person admires it greatly. He likes to have something to look at, and he likes the walls and windows to be edifying and interesting, and to express a symbolism that he can understand.

The theory of designing and adorning a church was still what it had been in the days of the Ecclesiologists: that there should be a crescendo to the east with the altar as its climax. The floor should rise step by step. By this time the restorers knew that in a medieval church the old levels should be kept: it was wrong to raise the steps of the sanctuary so high that the sedilia were almost on the level of the floor, and the altar and its reredos filled the lower part of the east window. But there was no reason why it should not be done in a new church in which the chancel was the same height as the nave, and the east window could be placed as high up as the architect wished.

The chancel roof should be more elaborate than that of the nave, and the sanctuary roof more elaborate than that of the chancel. The paving would become richer towards the east. The elaborate tiles of the Victorians were now out of date, but the chancel and the sanctuary were dignified with floors of mosaic or black and white marble squares. Chairs were often used for seating the nave, but carved oak must be in the chancel. Everything suggested to the worshipper as he walked towards the east that he was approaching the most significant part of the church.

The modern fashion is to place a simple altar at the top of the nave, and to leave the chancel and the high altar more or less disused; or even to dismantle the

11 *Edwin Lutyens. St Jude's Church, Hampstead Garden Suburb, London (1910). An impressive example of the free Gothic manner.*

12 W. D. Caröe. St Helen's Church, St Helens, Lancashire (started 1922 but designed earlier).

sanctuary and to put a chair for an absent bishop, and seats for his attendant presbyters who are not there either. This destroys the whole point of the design. No doubt the smaller congregations and the simpler ceremonial of the present time make such churches difficult to use, but it is surely possible to arrange them in a way which will preserve the intentions of the designers. It is certain that things that are little regarded at one time will come to be appreciated again. 18th-century churches came back into fashion years ago, and we regret the attempts made by 19th-century reformers to refashion them into something that suited the taste of the time, but which was only an uneasy compromise. Victorian churches were despised in the '20s, and a good deal later: now they are studied and visited, not least by the younger people. 'Victorian' has now come to include Edwardian: let us hope that the Church of England will not antagonise the coming generation by following blindly the present fashions of destruction and adaptation, but will learn to let well alone.

The Grand Manner

When John Belcher(1841–1913) came back from a holiday in northern Italy in 1888 with his head full of the Genoese Baroque he had seen, and entered the competition for the new Institute of Chartered Accountants building in London, who could have guessed the sequence of architectural events that was being triggered? Both Belcher and his young partner Beresford Pite (1861–1934), were among the original members of the Art Workers' Guild, that centre of Arts and Crafts activities whose original aim in 1884 was to reverse the current drifting apart of the arts of architecture, sculpture and painting. And while Pite moved on to other design developments with the rest of the Arts and Crafts men, Belcher remained fascinated by that original aim. It seemed to him that the Baroque work he had seen in Italy did indeed integrate the arts as fully as possible. Thus the Belcher and Pite entry for the Accountant's competition was basically an Arts and Crafts design, including key motifs such as the sculptured frieze bands and the turret accent at the break of levels, but clad inside and out in luxuriantly Baroque raiment. The design was selected by the assessor Waterhouse to be built and it was only after it was finally completed in 1893 that it had its full effect on contemporary architecture. In the meantime, Norman Shaw's big classical house, 'Chesters' of 1889 and Belcher's own unsuccessful entry for the 1891 Victoria and Albert Museum competition had awoken a new interest in a free use of classical architecture among some progressive architects.

The Gothic Revival had never killed the occasional use of various classical manners for Victorian public buildings, but these had until then been regarded as contemptible remnants of a debased tradition. It was the high artistic quality and freedom from antiquated rules that made the Institute of Chartered Accountants so influential.

By the end of 1892 a number of the younger energetic men, who remained unconvinced by the hopes of a new national free style, were submitting entries to architectural competitions in various classical manners. Entries by Stark and Rowntree, by Gibson and Russell and by E. W. Mountford for the 1892 Glasgow Art Gallery and the 1893 Wakefield Town Hall and Battersea Town Hall competitions show many features reminiscent of Belcher's design for the Victoria and Albert Museum. Then, after the opening of the Chartered Accountants building, a new style which one might call Arts and Crafts Baroque started to appear fairly frequently. Examples include Mackintosh's entry (under the name of Honeyman and Keppie) for the Royal Insurance building in Glasgow in 1895, and one notes that Belcher was one of the architects that the young Scot chose for special praise in his well-known lecture of 1893. By 1899, there were many examples of this Arts and Crafts Baroque appearing in the building magazines, including buildings from the big architectural offices such as Aston Webb's and Thomas Collcutt's.

Nevertheless, the success of a refined and progressive form of Baroque was only one stage towards the development of the Grand Manner. The important steps towards full-blown Edwardian Baroque were taken in 1896 and 1897. The first was perhaps the competition for the Royal Insurance building in Liverpool. Belcher and Pite submitted a truly remarkable and original design, doubtless basically Pite's work, which pre-echoes the more restrained neo-Mannerism of Holden and of Joass a decade later. But the assessor selected another design, by J. Francis Doyle, in a heavily accented High Baroque. In December, John Brydon published his grand classical designs for Bath municipal buildings. The following year, 1897, saw the departure of Pite from Belcher's office and a major success for the older man in a free but far more grandiose English Baroque design for Colchester Town Hall. Three months later, Lanchester and Rickards brought Austrian and French forms of Baroque into the picture by winning the important competition for Cardiff Town Hall and Law Courts. But it was the English Baroque of Wren's Greenwich and Vanbrugh's Blenheim that dominated. It was the year of Queen Victoria's Diamond Jubilee and as if in celebration, England was plunging into Imperial Baroque.

During the next year, acceptance of the Baroque by local government was endorsed by the central government with the commissioning of two London Scots, John Brydon (1840–1901) and William Young (1843–1900), to design respectively the new Government Offices on Parliament Square and the War Office further up Whitehall. These two enormous bureaucratic blocks took a decade or so to build (neither architect lived to see his work here completed) but they brought the English Baroque Revival right to the heart of the Empire. From here it was to spread to the Imperial outposts in India, Africa and Australia.

The most vigorous period of this Baroque Revival was in designs made between that Jubilee year and about 1906 – after that some of the self-assurance went out of Edwardian society and clients for buildings became more careful about the use of space. But in those ten years architects such as Belcher, Mountford, Hare, Brumwell Thomas, James Gibson, Rickards, Cooper, Sir Aston Webb and even Norman Shaw started a host of large buildings, often magnificent in their vigour, that forms a joyous revival of English Baroque.

The attraction of the Grand Manner to many architects and clients was precisely that it was predominantly English in its roots. The style amounted to a free adaptation of the early 18th-century manners of Wren, Hawksmoor, Vanbrugh, Gibbs and Archer to modern building requirements, without any question of scholarly copyism. This fitted well with the fashionable theory of the time that a modern style should have national origins (as was the case with Scottish Baronial

1 *John Belcher and A. Beresford Pite. Institute of Chartered Accountants, Swan Alley, Moorgate, London (1888–93). This adaptation of Baroque style to Arts and Crafts design principles started a series of developments that led to the Edwardian Baroque manner.*

and English Tudor work as well) and that ancient rules of proportion should not be imposed on modern structures. Equally the clients, whether they were politicians or civil servants or businessmen, felt pleasure in the fact that the buildings expressed a sense of patriotic history as well as giving outward evidence of prosperity.

Thus we find Edwardian Baroque making a frequent appearance in office buildings in many parts of the country, as well as in the great town halls. The buildings of C. J. Skipper in Norwich are a particularly fine example of a local practice that specialised in the mode, but is only one of many. In other fields, the theatre took to the style with particular zest and Frank Matcham was especially successful in his Baroque theatrical practice in London and provincial cities. In smaller office buildings too our cities are enlivened by many variations of the style, some superbly done, others wild and extravagant, and others again dull and ponderous.

The only types of building where the Baroque had no success was in church architecture (which one may perhaps regret) and in private housing. In domestic work the early Edwardian period was still dominated by Arts and Crafts ideals, though the 1890s had seen the birth of the quiet neo-Georgian manner sired by Ernest Newton (1856–1922). That was (with a few individual exceptions) the nearest the English house came to the contemporary flamboyance of large buildings.

The following essays on individual architects of the Grand Manner give an account of John Belcher's ever-changing development with his two principal partners, a description of Edwin Rickards (1872–1920) as architect and as man (often through the eyes of his friend Arnold Bennett) and an evocative description of the office of Sir Aston Webb (1849–1930, who had the largest architectural practice of his time) by a man who worked for Webb in the 1890s. More research is needed on other Grand Manner architects, especially on the highly talented E. W. Mountford (1855–1908) and H. T. Hare, (1860–1921), whose buildings are among the best produced during the period.

By the middle of Edward VII's reign a reaction had set in. Several factors were responsible for this, among them the development of economical steel frame buildings which called for a lighter stone skin than the massive Baroque manner provided. Moreover, the establishment of new architectural schools was bringing about a revival of interest in classical purist rules along Beaux Arts lines. Edwardian Baroque did not by any means die out in the first decade of the century – it proved adaptable enough to be used for many years to come. But the most interesting variations of classical architecture during the last eight years before the First World War were very different from the High Baroque of Mountford's Old Bailey and Belcher's Ashton Memorial, as will be seen in the final part of this book.

2

3

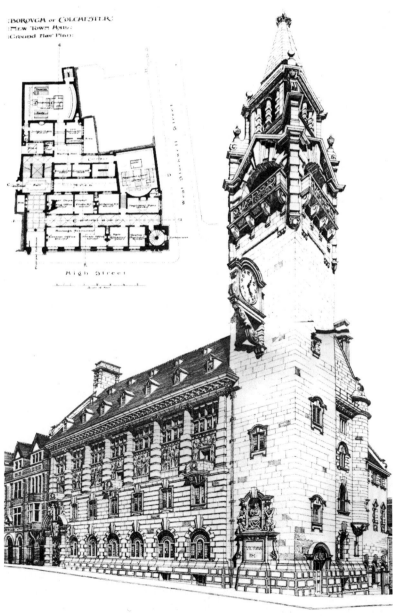

4

1

2 *Sir John Vanbrugh and Nicholas Hawksmoor. Blenheim Palace, Woodstock, near Oxford (1705–25). One of the keys to the appeal of Edwardian Baroque was that its roots were English, in the Baroque of late Wren and his disciples.*

3 *John Belcher. Competition design for Victoria and Albert Museum, Brompton Road, London (1891). Not built, but the design was highly influential on the Baroque Revival that followed.*

4 *John Belcher. Perspective drawing of First Premium design, Colchester Town Hall competition (August 1897). Assessed by Norman Shaw, this competition result was a turning point for the revival of English Baroque.*

5 *H. T. Hare. Perspective drawing of unplaced design, Colchester Town Hall competition (1897). An astonishing and overwhelming design from the architect of the delicate Oxford Town Hall.*

5

6

8

7

6 *Edwin Rickards of Lanchester and Rickards. City Hall, Cardiff (designed 1897). Rickards was the brilliant exception to the rule that the Baroque Revival of 1890–1906 was based on early 18th-century English Baroque.*

7 *William Young. The War Office, Whitehall, Westminster (1898–1907). The Baroque revival was taken up by the government in 1898 for two immense Whitehall buildings.*

8 *Thomas Collcutt. Detail, Lloyd's Shipping Register, Fenchurch Street, London (1900). Collcutt could do any style well. This building is one of the best examples of Arts and Crafts Baroque.*

9 *Edward Mountford. Central Criminal Courts, Old Bailey, London (1900–07). Edwardian Baroque at its most splendid.*

10

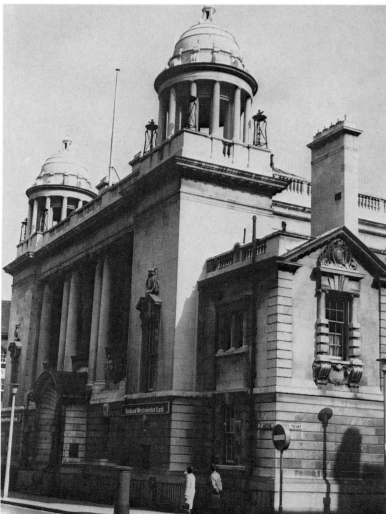

11

12

10 *Sir Alfred Brumwell Thomas. City Hall, Belfast, Northern Ireland (designed 1897). High Edwardian Baroque and generally a success, though the style varies unacceptably in the courtyard and interiors. Thomas's town hall at Stockport, designed two years later, is better integrated.*

11 *S. Perkins and Frank Pick. Westminster Bank, St Martin's, Leicester (1900–02).*

12 *A. M. Jeffers (Province of Alberta architect). Legislative Building, Edmonton, Alberta, Canada (1906–12). The Baroque Grand Manner proved popular in the capitals of the Empire.*

13 *Norman Shaw. Piccadilly Hotel, Piccadilly, London (1905–08). Shaw's Baroque buildings were full of his vigorous originality.*

Belcher and Joass

by Alastair Service

After twenty years of successful commercial practice with an artistic leaning, John Belcher (1841–1913) was introduced to the Arts and Crafts Movement by a new young partner, Beresford Pite, and together they hurtled to fame in 1889 by designing a revolutionary free Baroque building for the Institute of Chartered Accountants. There the success of the Grand Manner started, and Belcher stayed in the forefront of the Baroque Revival with the English Baroque Colchester Town Hall, designed by himself in 1897, and the series of brilliant office buildings which he designed with J. J. Joass (1868–1952) in the Edwardian period.

In the first London volume of *The Buildings of England,* published in 1957, Professor Pevsner wrote of Mappin House, 158 Oxford Street: "A distinguished design . . . Belcher's late style is not yet sufficiently appreciated." Over a decade later the position has changed little, and understanding of this central figure of English architecture at the beginning of this century is so poor that Robert Macleod gives the impression in his recent book on Mackintosh that John Belcher was little more than a front for the designs of Beresford Pite and later of J. J. Joass. In fact, these seem to have been real design partnerships. Belcher and Pite built a small number of buildings, but had widespread influence on the English Baroque Revival of the 1890s, while Belcher and Joass produced many of the most interesting and impressive large buildings of the first decade of this century in England.

The great architectural teacher, Sir Charles Reilly of Liverpool, wrote in his memoirs[1] that for an ambitious young man going into architecture in about 1900 the choice of a major London office lay between those of Norman Shaw, Sir Ernest George, Sir Aston Webb and John Belcher – of which he himself chose Belcher after careful consideration.

Mackintosh praised Belcher's work[2], and so high was his reputation among young men that an advertisement[3] in the press offered architectural instruction in the Gothic, Renaissance, Classic and Belcher styles. To this day writers often refer to him as *Sir* John Belcher – in fact, he was a Royal Academician, Royal Gold Medallist and P.R.I.B.A. but, oddly, was never knighted. This chapter will outline his development and examine more closely the buildings, most of which are in London, designed between 1900 and 1913[4].

John Belcher was born in Southwark on 10 July 1841, the son of an architect of the same name who had a successful practice in City office buildings designed in a classical style similar to Donaldson's (none is known to survive). The younger John Belcher joined his father's office after a private education and periods in Luxembourg and Paris. It seems that he quickly took over most of the design work, for he was a brilliant draughtsman. He was never interested in financial matters and was always to depend on his staff in this respect. He designed one office block in a French classical style before falling under the spell of Burges's famous unexecuted design for the Law Courts and embarking on what he himself later called 'a wild Gothic career'.

Of the many buildings[5] by J. & J. Belcher in the 1860s and 1870s, only one survives. This is the Mappin and Webb building (Mansion House Buildings) on the corner of Poultry and Queen Victoria Street in the City, whose date is *circa* 1870–72. Both in this building and in the Catholic Apostolic Church, Camberwell New Road (1876-77), designed after his father's retirement, the influence of Burges is obviously strong. The church presents a grimly romantic three-sided cloister to the road, but the interior (the upper part of the vault-ing was never completed) has been painted over in pastel shades by its present Greek Orthodox occupants.

In 1865 Belcher had married Florence Parker of Dublin, a Roman Catholic (he was a life-long Irvingite or Catholic Apostolic), and it seems to have been a happy though childless marriage. They shared a particular interest in music – Belcher himself was a fine solo bass singer and performed publicly in many oratorios. He also published in 1872 a small book called *The History of Ecclesiastical Music.* His character seems to have been obsessive but extraordinarily gentle, a mildness that is reflected in his face though by no means always in his work.

In the late 1870s the practice was chiefly concerned with private houses, particularly Stowell Park in Gloucestershire, employing Belcher's own free mixture of Tudor and Gothic styles. In these one sees the influence of Norman Shaw, whom he admired. Belcher also built himself a house, 'Redholm' in Champion Hill, Dulwich (now apparently demolished). This essay will not deal thoroughly with his domestic work, which could do with a separate study[6].

About 1880 he built a large store for Messrs. Rylands in Wood Street in the City. This again has disappeared, but it is worth noting his partner J. W. James's comment[7] that it "had to be framed with iron columns and stanchions and rolled iron joists . . . thus anticipating the later steel framed buildings." Shaw's influence can be seen more strongly in the Cottage Hospital, Hermitage Road, Norwood (1881), with its attractive chimneys, tile-hung gables and informal composition. This building is not recorded elsewhere as Belcher's work, but I was able to trace it from some casual mentions in his obituaries.[8] It has been partly spoiled

3 *J. and J. Belcher. Mappin and Webb building, corner of Poultry and Queen Victoria Street, City of London (1870–72). Belcher took over the design work in his father's office and was influenced by the Gothic manner of Burges at this time.*

by additions and external pipes and flues, but retains some charm. The same style can be seen in the well-known house, now called 'Greenash'[9], which he built for Sir John Thornycroft in Chiswick Mall (1882), though its brickwork has now sadly been painted over.

In 1885 Arthur Beresford Pite became Belcher's partner. Pite was then twenty-four and Belcher forty-four, but they had been friends for some time. Pite had worked in the Belcher office in 1881 until he won the Soane Medallion the following year. He then travelled on the Continent with his brother W. A. Pite, and was joined in Germany by Belcher and J. W. James for part of the time. After returning to England, Pite became a member of the staff of *The Builder*[10] until he rejoined Belcher. The partnership lasted twelve years and had a tremendous effect on Belcher's development. Pite (a close friend of Lethaby) was a vividly original thinker, as is evident from his own later buildings, and between them the two men developed the striking yet intimate Baroque style which made Belcher famous in the 1890s.

At this time Belcher made several further visits to South Germany, Vienna and Italy, and Joass later said[11] that he was "much stimulated by . . . (the) eccentricities of late Italian work at Genoa". Several of the obituaries comment on Belcher's eagerness to take up and develop new ideas and his refusal to talk about his own past buildings. Pite said later [12]: "he never repeated himself, and it is difficult to think of him doing so, for he was always moving freshly from one point to another".

Belcher's reputation among young architects must have stood high, for he was chairman at the very first meeting of the Art Workers' Guild, a society founded by five of Norman Shaw's pupils (led by Lethaby and E. S. Prior) in 1884 to reverse "the drifting apart of the arts of Architecture, Painting and Sculpture". He and Pite (also an original member of the Guild) became excited by this ideal of integrating the arts. It seems likely that they saw Robert Reinhardt's book on Genoese palaces (Berlin, 1886) soon after it was published and that this

4 *John Belcher. Cottage Hospital, Hermitage Road, Norwood (1881). The architect had become an admirer of Norman Shaw at this period and was chairman at the first meeting of the Art Workers' Guild in 1884.*

made Belcher see the possibilities of achieving integration by using the Baroque style.

The first chance that the two men had to put their ideas into effect was their success in the competition for the design of the Institute of Chartered Accountants, off Moorgate in the City of London (1888, built 1890–93). The building, extraordinarily free without losing its discipline and feeling for rhythm, is Belcher's best-known work. It is analysed fairly fully in this writer's study for the I.C.A. on the Institute building, but it is necessary to examine here the vexed question of whose design it was. Pite's contribution was certainly considerable, and one can see the minds of both men at work. A pupil in the office[13] said that Pite's "magnetic personality influenced Mr Belcher very strongly and left its impress on the character of the work turned out", while Mervyn Macartney said[14] that Belcher "expended great and loving labour" on it and 'that every detail was worked out by himself". William Whitfield, architect of the recent restoration and extension, has identified many ideas taken from the Genoese Baroque buildings which fascinated Belcher, while some of the interiors show the influence of Longhena's Venetian work. Pite himself said[15] of his period with Belcher: "viewing his work, as far as possible, from a detached standpoint, his marked originality of proportion, the freedom derived from his earlier Gothic enthusiasm and his underlying love of quaintness led him to experiments in Classical design which might be and are alarming, but I think justify themselves the more they are surrounded by the commonplace". It is fair to conclude that the design was the joint product of their two minds and that neither would have come to it by himself.

In the previous decade there had been some efforts at the Baroque (e.g. Glasgow Town Hall), but Belcher's was a different matter. The building caused a furore among British architects and soon attracted copiers of the style, few of whom had Belcher and Pite's skill in composition. Apart from its grand but intimate scale, it did indeed integrate the arts of architecture, sculpture and painting. The touch of Arts and Crafts individuality which this gave to the building was understandably not preserved in most of the buildings which followed its general Baroque style. Mountford managed it sometimes, and an architect as sensitive as Collcutt could bring it off again with great success in his Lloyd's Shipping Register in Fenchurch Street, several years later (1900); but it was beyond the talents of the majority of architects who took up the fashion. In a paper read to the R.I.B.A. in 1914 Joass mentioned a "member of our profession whose pet topic is the pernicious influence of Belcher and all his works on English architecture". On the other side, Charles Rennie Mackintosh delivered a lecture to the Glasgow Architectural Association in 1893 in which he particularly praised Belcher's work – incidentally, it is possible that Joass heard this lecture[16].

Belcher met Norman Shaw for the first time when Shaw was going over the Chartered Accountants' building. From this time Shaw reciprocated the admiration which Belcher had long had for him and became the younger man's constant advocate for admission to the Royal Academy. They remained friends until Shaw's death in 1912, a year before Belcher's. Baroque features were already increasing in the famous man's work, and there can be little doubt that Belcher and Pite's work helped to nudge Shaw on from his restrained Wren-like classical style (as in the house at 170 Queen's Gate, 1887–88) into his full-fledged, if individualist, Baroque of the 1890s and 1900s. 'Chesters' and 'Bryanston' were designed in the year following the first publication of the design for the Chartered Accountants' building (*The British Architect*, 4 January 1889). Shaw's Baroque was of course quite different from Belcher's. Indeed one could say that there are three categories of English neo-Baroque buildings; the Grand, the Capricious and the Arts and Crafts – though there are many examples which combine any two of these characteristics.

5 *John Belcher and A. Beresford Pite. The prototype of Arts and Crafts Baroque. Institute of Chartered Accountants, Moorgate Place, City of London (designed 1888, completed 1893). The inspiration was Genoese Baroque and its potential for integrating architecture, sculpture and painting.*

6 *John Belcher and A. Beresford Pite. The old Council Chamber, Institute of Chartered Accountants (1888–93). The big murals include a mirror image of the architecture of the room, another indication of Belcher's preoccupation with the integration of the Arts. Before the renovation of the building in 1969, the walls of the apses were painted with flowing foliage.*

The change in style for larger buildings represented by the Institute of Chartered Accountants had less impact on Belcher's domestic work at about the same time. There are two examples of this in London, one before and the other after the building of the Institute. The first is Morden Grange built in about 1887 in Kidbrooke Grove, Blackheath. Its subsequent extraordinary history made it hard to trace, for in the early 1920s it was sliced in two horizontally. The lower half, roofed differently, is now 38 Kidbrooke Grove, while the upper storeys were built as 28 Kidbrooke Grove. Many ground floor interiors survive[17]. The other house was the little studio built for Hamo Thornycroft (the chief sculptor of the Chartered Accountants' building) at 2a Melbury Road, Kensington, in 1892. This has considerable charm and mixes some Baroque motifs

8 *John Belcher. Design for Council Chamber, Colchester Town Hall (interiors designed 1899).*

7 *John Belcher. Colchester Town Hall, Essex (designed 1897, completed 1902). One of the first successes of the High Baroque Revival, significantly referred to by Joass as being 'decidedly English'. This free adaptation of the late Wren and Vanbrugh manner, English rather than foreign in origin, contributed to its popularity at the peak of the British Empire.*

with features of other styles. The upper storey has a flattened oriel window of a type that was to appear, with variations, in many later Belcher buildings. The interior has been altered.

These buildings were followed by a long period during which, rather surprisingly, Belcher and Pite's competition entries were unsuccessful and the office had little work. Belcher seems to have been completely unaffected by financial worries and occupied himself during these slack times by starting work on a book (with Mervyn Macartney) which was to increase his reputation vastly. This was entitled *Later Renaissance Architecture in England*, and the full folio volumes appeared from 1898 on, though they are dated 1901. He was starting to look more seriously at English classical architecture[18] and he spent much time travelling around the country with Macartney[19] collecting examples. The work[20] consists of drawings, brief analyses and photographs of non-ecclesiastical buildings and details from *circa* 1600 to *circa* 1780. Its importance was that it supplied a new textbook for the imminent English Baroque and other classical revivals, as well as having a profound effect on Belcher's own work.

In passing, two competition entries must be mentioned. Both were unsuccessful but they were widely illustrated and praised in the architectural journals and were influential in the establishment of the neo-Baroque style by the late 1890s. The first was for the completion of the Victoria and Albert Museum[21] in

9 *John Belcher. Royal London House, corner of Finsbury Square and City Road, London (1904–05). Edwardian Baroque expressed the growth of British commercial power.*

10 *John Belcher. Elevation of Electra House, Moorgate, City of London (1900–03). Now used as the City of London College. The right-hand section was never built. Freely creative use of the Baroque manner has been lost in exchange for a new pomp.*

Brompton Road in 1891, a competition ultimately won by Sir Aston Webb; and the second was for the Royal Insurance Company's Liverpool offices[22] in 1896. In these designs the Arts and Crafts feeling survives in the detail, but the overall impression is decidely grand.

The following year, Belcher produced one of his most impressive designs and at last won a competition for another major civic building. This was the Colchester Town Hall which was built in 1898–1902. For the first time the high columned bays appeared, taking the eye up two or more storeys to an arch, which were to become a feature of his later work. Frontage, tower and interior are extremely grandiose, but there is freshness and distinction in the design. All the same it must be pointed out that this building, together with some of Mountford's and Shaw's, was the most important step towards the 'Grand Manner' Baroque of the Edwardian era, with all the fine and the overblown things which that style produced. Joass referred[23] to this building as a "decidedly English" design, compared with earlier Continental influences – an interesting comment, presumably made with Vanbrugh in mind. There is much less integrated *external* sculpture in evidence here than in earlier elevations, and the materials, as in the unexecuted museum design, are stone and brick. It seems likely that this design was entirely Belcher's work; for Pite left the office in 1897 and himself entered the Colchester competition[24]. At about the same time Joass became a permanent member of the staff, and though he was not to become a partner until 1905 his influence is felt increasingly in the buildings of the eight years between.

John James Joass was born at Dingwall, on the Cromarty Firth in northern Scotland, in 1868 (the same year as Charles Rennie Mackintosh). His father was an architect at Dingwall and his uncle a clergyman. The family came from Banff, where there are Joass tombstones going back to the 17th century. His father was not prosperous, and J. J., the eldest of three sons, went to the small local school. In his middle teens he entered his father's office, but quickly realized that there was little future there. Borrowing the fare from his grandmother, he went to Glasgow and walked into J. J. Burnet's office, where he started as office-boy. He progressed rapidly, studying part-time at the Glasgow School of Art. About 1890 he was offered and accepted a senior post with an Edinburgh architect. He won the Pugin studentship in 1892 and the Owen Jones studentship in 1895. After winning the former, he travelled in Italy and kept the collection of drawings he made there all his life.

In 1895, at the age of twenty-seven, he also became an A.R.I.B.A. and moved from Glasgow to London. According to Sir Ernest George's obituaries, Joass was in the George and Yeates office at this time. Pite introduced him to Belcher in 1895, and Joass did several drawings for *Later Renaissance Architecture*. It is not known how he met Pite, but he soon became involved

in the Belcher firm and was working full-time there by 1897. Those who knew him then referred to him as a dour and silent young man, a great contrast to Beresford Pite. He kept some of this dourness all his life and was always determined to have his own way, though he later developed an easier manner and could show considerable charm. An obituary by someone in the Belcher offices at the time[25] stated that "he was a brilliant draftsman and a marvellous rapid designer" and that "with his coming the old firm took on a new vitality".

Indeed, Joass arrived at a good time; for the success in the Colchester competition seems to have brought other commissions, and the pace quickened after Belcher and Macartney's book was published. The Cambridge Guildhall[26] and Belcher's entry for the Old Bailey[27] in 1900 were never built, but the Birmingham Post building, 88 Fleet Street, was built in 1900–02. This was the first of a series of cornersite office buildings, and the result is rather curious (it is worth noting that the drawing[28] in *The Builder* was signed by Joass). It is far more restrained than any other stone-faced office building to come from the Belcher office (apparently this was intended to harmonize with St Bride's Church), but the proportions are by no means satisfactory. A corner cupola was not built as designed, and the top of one bay is missing. Altogether one feels that a new expression was being looked for, without success.

This search obviously continued during the design of the next building, Electra House, 84 Moorgate, now the premises of the City of London College. This was designed in 1900 and built in 1901–03, and one can only agree with Professor Pevsner's description, "Belcher at his most intolerable." For the time being he was clearly caught up in the general desire for Imperial grandeur which flooded the country just then. The design was less derived from the English Baroque than Belcher's work in the late 1890s had been. There are traces of the recent Old Bailey competition and a hint of Castle Howard in the main elevation, but the overall feeling is closer to Maderno's façade of St Peter's. On the credit side, the intricate figure-sculpture entwined into the Corinthian capitals is worth examining and the stately bays of the corridors inside are pleasing.

The original published drawings[29] show elevations which would have been more mannered but rather more interesting. Whatever we think of it today, the design was widely illustrated, praised and influential from 1900 on – this is the high 'Belcher style' doubtless meant by the advertisement mentioned at the beginning of this article.

Although I am not dealing with Belcher's country houses here, mention must be made of the elegant and chaste new wing, with its Ionic portico over the main entrance, which he added to Cornbury Park, Oxfordshire, in 1902[30]. It contrasts strongly with his office buildings of the same time, but this was to blend with the existing house.

11 *John Belcher. Ashton Memorial, Williamson Park, Lancaster (designed 1904, built 1907–09). Belcher's last and perhaps finest work in High Edwardian Baroque.*

A general style similar to Electra House is used in the earliest part of Royal London House on the corner of Finsbury Square and City Road (1904–05). It is still not a total success; less heavy, but rather too busy. There is some interesting detailing, and the methods employed to help the vertical emphasis against the strong horizontals are of some ingenuity. The walls are load-bearing. The company has a sketch showing a project to carry the same design along the whole side of the square. The main staircase inside (not the corner door, but the one to its right) is worth looking at. It was modelled on that of a Genoese palace which Belcher had seen, and its lighting and spatial ingenuity are noteworthy. Joass used to tell the story of how Belcher originally obtained this commission. About 1900 there were many doctors in Finsbury Square and it happened that Belcher was ill in a nursing home there. In a neighbouring room was the chairman of the Royal London Mutual Insurance Society, Mr de la Bertouche, and one day Bertouche pointed out of the window across the square. He said "My company is going to build a head office on that corner over there – would you like to design it?" This started a fifty-year job for Belcher's firm.

Belcher's only major building far from London must be examined here, for it was designed in 1904, though not built until 1907–09 (by which time some of the cupola details had become more chunky). This is the Ashton Memorial[31] in Williamson Park, Lancaster, a large composition mounting 220 feet overall to a dome which dominates its surroundings. Lord Ashton gave the park to the city and this was a family memorial built at a cost of over £30,000. There was no other functional purpose (the interior had two high round chambers superimposed), so this is Belcher cut loose, commissioned simply to provide the most splendid monument he could. In these terms it is undoubtedly a success. The superficial resemblance to the Salute and the Invalides is misleading, for a close comparison shows that the proportions of dome to basic edifice resemble Wren's Greenwich domes more closely than any others, while the corner turrets have a family likeness to the west towers of St Paul's Cathedral.

If Belcher and Joass had been looking for a new style for the office building commissions which were now coming in, 1904 marked the time when they seem to have found it. By this time Belcher had been overtaken by many others, and the architectural journals around 1900 are full of competition entries in his Baroque style. He may well have wanted to get away from it when he saw the things that men like Ernest Runtz were doing. But before dealing with Belcher and Joass's next step forward and the buildings of their prime, it would be as well to mention some other aspects of Belcher's life in the early 1900s. It was shortly before 1900 that the young Charles Reilly, Lionel Detmar and W. Curtis Green came into the Belcher office. Reilly describes the office at that time in his memoirs *Scaffolding in the Sky*[32]. "There we were in his outer office on the top floor of 25 (actually 20) Hanover Square at the back bench next the office boy and seeing the great man himself very occasionally in the distance. Between him and his dozen or so draughtsmen was a little office, strategically placed, so that he had to pass through it, and there his head man worked. He was a Scotsman, a Highlander, J. J. Joass, successor in that position to the great Beresford Pite and later on a partner and to carry on his practice after his death. Mr Belcher did not often get by Joass. I wish he had, but I think he was too shy and Joass too strong. If we did not see the great man himself, however, we saw the great Joass every day and very soon with his quick Scottish draftsmanship and his clever use of colour he seemed to us then the greater man of the two. It was he who detailed all the buildings in those days and gave us that curious elongated classical form with pendant blocks and wreaths . . ." In this last sentence Reilly has obviously skipped on to the buildings designed after about 1904.

It is interesting to speculate on the working relationship of Belcher and Joass, using the available information about them. Joass had a granite character, while almost all Belcher's obituaries comment on his very modest, retiring personality; but they go on to say that he always got his way. It must of course be remembered that in 1904 they were aged thirty-six and sixty-three respectively. Joass said in his talk of 1914 about Belcher that "new ideas appealed to him irresistibly" and that he was "never content to reproduce features of a past age". This is perhaps the key to his relationship with his two most important partners. With Belcher's eagerness to try new ideas and to develop new styles, one can understand that the theories brought forward by the two brilliant young men were put into practice as enthusiastically as his own – perhaps more so. But the designs of both Pite and Joass when left to themselves were not as effective on a large scale as when they were worked out in co-operation with Belcher.[33] It was he who seems to have distilled Joass's inspiration (as Pite's before him) into what I believe to be the outstanding office buildings of their time in London (perhaps together with those of Mewès & Davis, working in a refined French style, and of Holden).

In the early 1900s Belcher was also playing an increasingly important part in the affairs of the R.I.B.A. In 1902 he suggested a scheme to Sir Aston Webb which succeeded in bringing other major architectural bodies under the R.I.B.A.'s umbrella, and which resulted in much of the comparative unity of the profession today. In 1904–06 he was President of the R.I.B.A., presided over the seventh International Congress of Architects in 1906 and was awarded the Royal Gold Medal in 1907. His speech on receipt of the medal is typical and almost ridiculously modest.[34] He was assessor for many competitions at home and abroad,[35] and Norman Shaw's continued friendship resulted in his being elected a Royal Academician in

1909. In 1907 he published his third literary work, a small book called *Essentials in Architecture* intended to stimulate public interest in the subject. The book uses many musical analogies and his personal tastes are indicated by the many illustrations of Northern Italian architecture and by the very first illustration in the section on Beauty – Longhena's Chiesa della Salute in Venice. Belcher's words are sometimes contrary to the example of his own buildings, a fault shared with greater architects.

About the middle of the 1900s the firm built a library in 49 Princess Gate and rebuilt 45 Belgrave Square in a conforming fashion. The first of the impressive series of major buildings of these years came when they were asked to build the extension to Winchester House[36] to the corner of Old Broad Street, and London Wall in 1904–05. This is the only important building of Belcher's which has been demolished. The contrast with Royal London House of about the same time was extraordinary. The most immediately striking feature was perhaps the bulging Atlas figures at second floor level which started the strong vertical emphasis of the elevation. The general composition and the integration of much sculpture are a logical development of

12 *John Belcher and John J. Joass. Mappin House, No. 158 Oxford Street, London (1906–08). The new steel frame structure and other factors forced Edwardian Baroque architects to find a vertically emphasised style which developed into a neo-Mannerism.*

13 *John Belcher and John J. Joass. Royal Insurance building, Piccadilly and St James's Street, London (1907–08). Neo-Mannerism at its most extreme, with classical features used anti-rationally as in Michelangelo's architecture.*

Belcher's earlier work. But it was on the upper storeys that the bold chunky detailing by Joass first appeared. The style seems to be an original development of his own. Only Charles Holden's early work at the Law Society is comparable as far as detailing is concerned.

If this new style was not yet fully matured in Winchester House, it certainly was in their next building. This was originally built for Mappin and Webb and called Mappin House, 158–162 Oxford Street (1906–08). It is their most completely successful office building. Both the general design and detailing are individualistic to the point of mannerism, but the proportions are finely suited to the site and the strong vertical succession of elongated Tuscan columns, pillars with a witty reference to the Ionic, coupled Corinthian columns and finally clean round-topped arches, carry the eye directly up five storeys and leave an impression of tension and elegance. The corner is masterfully handled and the area of glass is impressive for such a textured surface.

It is clear the other architects were watching Belcher and Joass's progress, even though this development was not so widely influential as the Chartered Accountants' building. For example, Regency House on the corner of Warwick Street and Brewer Street, Soho designed by Metcalfe and Greig and built in 1910,[37] shows striking similarities to Mappin House, though the tension and vigorous detail are missing.

Belcher is again at his best in the splendid elevation of the bookshop and offices for Mowbray's[38] at 28 Margaret Street, Marylebone (1907–08). This is not a basically original design, but it is here handled superbly. Above the shop, giant columns and a single great arch embrace three storeys, with single bays on either side also vertically accented. In this case the breadth of the arch gives a more expansive feeling, but a peculiarly dynamic effect is achieved by bringing forward the windows in the bay under the arch beyond the line of the columns. Unusually for Belcher and Joass, brick is used together with stone in this frontage.

The other important work built in the same years as Mowbray's is perhaps the most astonishing of all. This is the Royal Insurance building on the corner of St. James's Street and Piccadilly. Here one feels for the first time that Joass must have had the dominating hand, though he made it clear in 1914 in his paper to the R.I.B.A. that it was one of their joint works. This is the Mappin House approach taken to extremes. Again the ground floor columns rise two storeys, though this time they are coupled. But in the three floors above there is an astounding outburst of sculpture and classical motifs used in a way they have never been used before or since. The accents are all vertical and are made up of a riot of recessed and protruding bays; pendant blocks are overlapped by keystones, and the cornice is supported by caryatid cherubs which seem to have climbed out of the blank niches. Above this is a floor with an open gallery, and higher still two storeys of dormers,

though the corner is carried up in stone the full height. The tension is still overwhelmingly present, though one cannot here use the word 'elegant'. It is without doubt the most original and even violent building either man ever produced and, as one might expect, caused tremendous controversy even among Belcher's oldest friends.

Now that this series of striking buildings has been briefly described, it is a suitable time to examine the available clues to the influences which produced them. There is little direct evidence to be gained from Joass's few surviving papers, for he had periodic bouts of throwing papers away; but there is a fair amount of indirect evidence in the available published material. The style of Belcher and Joass in their prime had three main components, which must be considered separately – firstly the tremendous vertical emphasis, secondly the bold, simplified classical detailing and thirdly the anti-logical use of traditional components amounting to a neo-Mannerism.

It was not just the shape of the sites which produced the verticality of these designs, for Royal London House has similar proportions to these later buildings. The most significant factor here was certainly the use of a steel frame, in which respect Winchester House followed only shortly after work had started on Mewès & Davis's Ritz Hotel. It must have seemed obvious to Belcher and Joass that a new style was necessary for a stone skin hung on a steel frame, and the verticality probably reflects their reaction to the new construction method, as well as to the resulting vastly higher American buildings they had certainly seen illustrated.[39] We must also remember that Belcher made a trip to New York and California in 1899, and from what we know of his character he would be fascinated by the new buildings and techniques he saw there. An examination of the English architectural journals from 1900 on gives no other significant clue about this verticality, nor about Joass's sources for his detailing (with one exception mentioned below). It appears likely that the tension and vertical stretch of these designs, especially of Mappin House, seemed to them the best expression of a skin of stone and glass.

Going through the architectural press of this period one is struck by the gradual change in fashion from the numerous busy and rather ponderous Baroque illustrations around 1900 (largely developed from Belcher's own lead of the 1890s) to a preponderance of less fussy, though still Baroque, designs by 1904. Measured drawings of buildings by Vanbrugh, Hawksmoor and Archer appear in *The Builder*, and the detail of one contemporary building stands out like a lighthouse – Holden's Law Society Library, completed early in 1904.[40] Holden had worked from 1897 under Ashbee, whose boldness he interpreted in a classical style (possibly also influenced by Olbrich's *Sezession* of 1898–99) when he joined Adams's office about 1900. In an article of 1931 in *Building* Reilly tells[41] how he mentioned this building to Belcher's staff in 1904 and was greeted with disapproval. But one presumes that this did not come from Joass; for it seems that he rapidly took up Holden's approach, translated it into his own language and used it to fill in the details of all the firm's designs after that time. One sees variations of this Mannerist classical detail on other office buildings throughout England until about 1930.

But there is another element in both this detail and in the Mannerism of the designs that has already been pointed out in a very important paper by Sir John Summerson, and developed by Robert MacLeod in his book on Mackintosh:[42] this is, quite simply, Michelangelo. One sees Michelangelo in much of the sculpture of the time and, in particular, in Beresford Pite's early independent architectural work (e.g. 82 Mortimer Street of 1896 and the entrance to the Marylebone Dispensary[43] of *circa* 1897).[44] Pite remained a friend of both Belcher and Joass after his departure from the firm, and they doubtless discussed Michelangelo's powerful Italian Mannerism, though not under that name. J. Addington Symonds's major *Life of Michael Angelo* of 1893 had been followed by Pite's own three-part article in *The Architectural Review* in 1898, praising his architecture, and a further (poor) book by Lord Ronald Gower in 1903. Even a brief examination of the Biblioteca Laurenziana staircase (illustrated by Pite) and its exterior windows, together with Pope Julius II's tomb and St Peter's apse and dome, is enough to reveal much of the inspiration which must have fired Belcher and, more particularly, Joass. Their buildings are very far from being copies of Michelangelo's works, but some motifs and much of their wilful use of classical forms to achieve a tension and a particular expression clearly reflect his influence.

It will already be clear that Belcher, by himself and when not working under the influence of new ideas (sometimes his own, more often those of his partners), produced work of only minor interest such as Electra and Royal London Houses. But it seems that even in his middle sixties he could jump at new problems and styles and, together with his young partner, could still produce designs that startled his fellow architects.

The final building in whose design Belcher played any significant part seems to have been Whiteley's department store in Queensway, Bayswater. It is not clear when this was designed, but it was built in 1910–12 and the northern end was not completed until much later. The plan is carefully thought out (most of the other office buildings were simple steel frames, very flexible inside their stone skins with deep wells breaking up the interior.

The exterior of the building expresses the four storeys as two stages, with Doric and Corinthian orders respectively. The upper columns are repeated rhythmically, with few breaks, almost the entire length of the frontage on Queensway. But, as is suitable with such a length, the strongest emphasis is horizontal, with a

simplified entablature which runs the entire length of the building, wrapping round the curved ends. This entablature is not even interrupted at the central entrance, though this is expressed by coupled columns. A Mannerist effect is obtained by spacing the lower order at far wider intervals than the upper and then again alternating these lower columns with pillars. This, in visual terms, floats the whole vast frontage. Above the top cornice there is a central tower which looks like Joass's work, while at one end there is a Baroque cupola, more typical of Belcher. Some subtle detail is worth noting. Behind the upper order, the lower windows are brought forward as in Mowbray's, while those above are balconied and arched (the northern end was completed in a somewhat cheaper way). The whole thing is done without heaviness and with considerable restraint and success, although it has been justly criticised for being out of proportion with its surroundings. With Whiteley's the active design partnership of Belcher and Joass comes to an end. Although Belcher did not die until 1913, his health

14 *John Belcher and John J. Joass. Holy Trinity Church, Kingsway, London (1910–12). Joass took over almost all the firm's design work after 1906 and developed a powerful, chunky classical manner at the end of the Edwardian period.*

was poor and he began to be much less active after 1909. Joass said[45] "In his later years illness interfered seriously with his activities . . . an increasing proportion of the responsibility of the work of those years naturally fell into my hands, but I think I may say Mr Belcher was most keenly interested in, and in thorough sympathy with, all that was done". The work referred to included the actual construction of Whiteley's and the design of Holy Trinity Church, Kingsway (1910–12), The Royal Society of Medicine, Henrietta Place, Marylebone (1910–12), offices for the Zoological Society, Outer Circle, Regent's Park (1910–12), a house at 31 Weymouth Street, Marylebone (1912)[46] and the Mappin Terraces at the Zoo (1913). All were nominally the work of Belcher and Joass, though the difference in style is immediately obvious. Joass was interested chiefly in the expression of mass and thrust, and it is clear that he was entirely responsible for these works. (It was only after 1910 that both partners' names were given in the building press when the firm's buildings were mentioned). In these designs the boldness of

Joass's earlier detailing is apparent in the whole composition and only the maintenance of tension prevents the massive forms from becoming ponderous.

The projecting semi-circle of the portico of the church in Kingsway, moving against the strong curve of the concave screen behind, is typical of Joass at this period.[47] It is a highly successful composition of its kind and was meant to be crowned by a huge tower immediately behind the screen, rising in three gigantic stages and crowned by a smaller stage. But there was no money to go beyond the base of the tower and the little belfry which caps the façade today. The building seems to have meant much to Joass, for he used to talk of leaving money in his will for the building of the tower, and the church still owns a large picture showing how it would have been. As late as the 1930s he got his office to prepare half-inch drawings for its construction. Eventually, he was unable to leave this money; for he tied up much of the fortune he made from his practice in annuities for his second wife, who was tragically killed six years before his own death. The

15 *John Belcher and John J. Joass. Whiteley's Department Store, Queensway, Bayswater, London (1910–12). Joass' neo-Mannerism is displayed in the way the visually heavier upper storeys are floated above an apparently weaker ground floor structure.*

16 *John J. Joass. Central section, Royal London House, Finsbury Square, London (1927–30). One of a group of powerful and thrusting major office buildings that Joass designed at this period.*

interior of the church, a fine space, was also never completed. Joass had originally planned to cover it with a huge reinforced concrete dome. When it became clear that this was too expensive, he changed the plans to the present barrel vault. This was built, but never decorated.

The Royal Society of Medicine is again a massive and vigorous work, rusticated on the ground floor, with an imposing doorway and a strong recessed portico above. It is interesting to note the old Belcher and Joass protruding two-storey window around the corner, which expresses the presence of the great library room inside, running along the entire length of the building at that level. This room had sadly been partitioned into two parts, and indeed there are many other alterations inside. Many of these were carried out by Joass himself, notably the top storeys above the stonework, which were added in a zinc material during the last two years of his life. These storeys give the exterior an overbearing appearance which it did not have originally. Of the other important rooms, only the two ground floor rooms and the fine entrance hall survive.

The offices for the Zoo in Regent's Park use much brick as well as stone. This is an unsuccessful experiment, lacking both Joass's vigour and Belcher's refinement. All the same it is worth examining, for it has some points of interest, particularly in the detailing round the door. Only the original small council-room survives inside.

The little-known house in Weymouth Street is far more successful and is an interesting domestic design for this period. It is entirely faced with stone and the frontage makes an intriguing play with volumes. There are three bays, of which the outer ones are brought forward, in one case over the void of a mews entrance, while the porch comes out still further. The interior has doorcases and a few other details typical of Joass.

These buildings and the concrete mountains of the massive Mappin Terraces at the Zoo (Joass's typical rendering of Hagenbeck's experimental zoological terraces at Hamburg) bring to an end the works designed during Belcher's life[48] and with it some of the most striking work done in London at the beginning of the century.

Belcher died on 8 November 1913, after a few days illness at his house in Champion Hill where he had lived most, perhaps all, of his married life. He was buried in Norwood Cemetery. After the paper about him which Joass read to the R.I.B.A. on 14 December 1914, many leading architects paid tribute to him – Pite, George, Aston Webb, Gosse and others.

Had Joass's continuation of the practice not been interrupted, it seems likely that he would have gone on developing his personal style. But towards the end of the war he became involved with the Reginald Blomfield plan for the redevelopment of Regent Street and Piccadilly Circus. Blomfield seems to have imposed his Beaux Arts style on most of the other architects concerned, and though Joass built up a hugely successful practice[49] it was to be many years before the violent aspect of his work emerged again. Dorland House, 14 Lower Regent Street (1924) is typical of his work in the 1920s. Just before 1930 he designed three buildings of great, almost overwhelming power.

These were the amazing central section of Royal London House, the Commonwealth Bank of Australia in the City, and Abbey House, Baker Street. Finally, Finnigan (now Clarendon) House, 17 New Bond Street (1932), shows him, coming to terms with modern trends.

Although Joass had a wide circle of friends, few of them were in the world of architecture. The principal exception to this was Pite, who remained a friend until his death in 1934. As Joass rarely talked of architecture when he was not at work, I have found few clues about admitted influences on his work. I have asked people who knew him, and others who knew Holden, whether they were in touch, but it seems there was little contact. No-one remembers him mentioning Mackintosh, nor did they apparently see each other when Mackintosh moved to London in 1915. Joass did admire Burnet, Lutyens and Arthur Davis, particularly Mewès and Davis's Royal Automobile Club, and he would talk affectionately of Belcher.

Like Belcher, Joass had no children. He was married twice, the second time (to Hilda Sant David) very happily. He lived in a flat in Putney and continued to practise until his death in 1952, though most of the work was small jobs with the exception of further extensions to Royal London House on the corner of City Road and Worship Street in the mid 1930s, and the top storeys of the Royal Society of Medicine in 1950. He had become a wealthy man from his practice, and his interest turned more and more to yacht racing, watercolour painting and his collection of Chinese carvings (many of which are now in the British Museum).

The work of the Belcher firm is of considerable importance in the history of British architecture up to about 1930, though it had little effect abroad. Mackintosh, Voysey and other British architects influenced the architectural developments in Europe which led to the emergence of the 20th-century modern styles. But after the early years of the century the mainstream of European architecture hardly touched Britain for nearly three decades.

[1] Charles H. Reilly, *Scaffolding in the Sky*, Routledge, London 1938.

[2] Lecture to Glasgow Architectural Association, February 1893.

[3] Reference in *Journal of the Royal Institute of British Architects* Vol. XXI, p.50.

[4] I have to thank the owners of many buildings and, in particular, Mr H. Bramhill, F.R.I.B.A. one of the successors to Joass's practice, for much help. Mr J. E. Babbs, the quantity surveyor, and Miss Linda

Sir Aston Webb and his Office

by H. Bulkeley Creswell

The most successful of all Edwardian practices, in worldly terms,
was that of Sir Aston Webb (1849–1930). As with Waterhouse, it was
above all the clarity of his large-scale planning that brought him
success, for the long list of his big buildings includes ponderous
failures as well as some fine achievements. H. Bulkeley Creswell,
himself a notable free style architect and novelist, worked in Aston
Webb's office in the 1890s and wrote his memories of that time in
his old age in 1958.

This article is entirely adventitious. I am writing it because I have been asked: and I have been asked for the reason that if I do not now tell of the architectural scene as it was in the last century, the thing may never be done; for there will soon be nobody left alive who can do it.

Space admits of a peep only. Some knowledge, however, of the peeper must be conveyed and some of the wide-spreading scene. The peeper is the son of a highly-placed Civil Servant; was educated at Bedford and T.C.D., and, after six futile probationary months in the office of a provincial solicitor, was articled in 1890 to Mr Aston Webb, of 19 Queen Anne's Gate, later to become Sir Aston of many distinctions. During the nine years thereafter he enrolled as student at the Institute; was an active member of the Architectural Association and elected to its Council; a Student at Westminster School of Art and the R.A. School of Architecture; travelled in Spain and Portugal, was employed as Clerk of Works and Assistant Architect by H.M. Office of Works, and contributed to a number of weekly and monthly journals and magazines.

The things in the London of 1890 that it best entertains the peeper to recall are those that arrestingly contrast with today. Seventy years is quite a time! When this peeper first opened eyes on the scene, Wren's Temple Bar had but Twelve years before been salvaged to Theobald's Park, and the Newgate Prison of George Dance Junior – where, in the street, the peeper's father might have seen public hangings with the victim's feet dangling a foot above the scaffold floor, while the Chaplain read the burial service to him – still stood for the students of architecture, and their seniors alike to admire very greatly.

The Law Courts of George Edmund Street – then dead nine years, from official badgerings and bankruptcy of contractors, as was said, its echoing vaulted hall still evoking quarry-sap – was raising noisy complaints from judge and counsel for its remoteness from the Courts, and for consequent shuffling crowds in the corridors giving access to them – a lesson well learned by Webb in his competitive planning of the Birmingham Law Courts then building. The Strand of those days, mutilated by Street and freshly uglified by someone's 'special line' in cast-iron dragons, and snaking its delightful course, continuous in width and kinship with Fleet Street, to Ludgate, is the best worthy of peeps since it was the throbbing heart, of the people's essential London. Hedged by a maze of contiguous alleys and courts, the Strand was fronted by numbers of little restaurants whose windows vaunted exquisite feeding; taverns, dives, oyster and wine bars, ham and beef shops; and small shops marketing a lively variety of curious or work-a-day things all standing in rank, shoulder to shoulder, to fill the spaces between its many theatres; with potato ovens, and roast chestnut standings at the kerb-side, and the cat's-meat man and his gruesome haunch of omnibus horse trafficking early. But the mud! And the noise! And the smell! All these blemishes were "ze mark of ze 'horse" – *ecce signum* 'Podsnapery'.

But London had also scenes unforgettable in the rare beauty of them; and here is a peep at one such before we turn to things more near to us. The scene is, again, the Strand; a mild cloudy night in November. The darkness is enchanted by the weak flickering yellow light of dispersed fish-tail gas-jets, and the veiled glow from festive windows. The pavement is alive with plebeian feasters, pit-ites and gallery-ites; the roadway and the cabs and carriages bearing jewelled bosoms and expansive shirt-fronts to stalls and dress circles. These suddenly, with one intent, draw cautiously to the kerbside and foot passengers come to a stand as distant swelling shouts as of terror and alarm, "Hi! Hi! Hi!" demand central roadway for racing fire-engines. Soon, visible in flashing brasswork and vomitings of glowing cinders, they come successively behind the pounding hoofs of horses that, in struggling to gallop against the heavy weight of engine, boiler, and bunkers at their tail which swings pendulum-wise even through thirty degrees, seem to claw desperately at the roadway for foothold. The first thunders dangerously past with coachman leaning back against reins twisted in his separated fists, fire at its funnel and fire in trail from its furnace; and so a second and a third with rush and clamour till all is dimmed to silence in the distance, and the gazers on the pavement and traffic at the kerb-side stir again to life.

Unforgettable moment to a student of architecture. newly savouring London: a London that quite otherwise than now was identified with the aristocracy of the professions, and emphatically with that of architecture. It would be hard indeed to name any architect of those days whose work has preserved memory of him, other than men practising in London; except a certain few celebrating the capitals of Ireland and Scotland. Aston Webb may not have attained highest rank in that aristocracy, but all generalities bearing on his methods and organisation and the ambit of his activities that may be revealed by peeps at them, will be true for the top dogs of those days.

Webb was essentially a happy little man; he gloried in his powers and nothing seemed to bother him or obstruct the fecundity of his ideas. A little man he was, alike in bodily make-up and in his conventional outlook on life and affairs in which, for him, the prominent man was the great man and the only measure of attainment was success. It was beyond thinking that he cared a sniff for the work of Morris, Philip Webb, Nesfield and so forth. His contentment was sumptuous, his demeanour modest to admiration; he was widely esteemed both personally and professionally, and he was truly an artist from his toes to the tips of his fragile lightly boned fingers, characteristically blackened with the soft H.B. lead with which he slapped his designings down on cartridge paper "because it bites so

1 *Portrait of Sir Aston Webb as a young man.*

nicely", hissing through his teeth meanwhile like an ostler curry-combing a horse, in exultation, as it would seem, at his own facility which is demonstrated alike in his Pugin drawings and in his most remarkable gifts as a planner, where every need – and nothing needless – falls into place with a completeness and exactness that seems inevitable and was indubitably the expression of the man's fundamental artistry, and explains his unrivalled success in big competitive layouts.

In 1891, Webb, Hon. Secretary at the Institute, was forty-two, with a narrow head of light-brown hair balding on top, with happy hazel rabbity eyes and an angry nose with a flattening at the bridge of it as though someone had given it a bat, and a complete absence of any mouth, for the whole of it was screened from view by a gingery brown moustache. The cultivation of such things was in those days not unusual, and there were cups sold with perforated projections at the brims to keep the moustache from becoming involved with thick soups that slobbered the chin and dripped

embarrassingly, or bleached by immersions in scalding or corrosive liquids; and there were silver guards to ride on all or any brims, and spoons fitted to like ends. The purpose, in general, of these face-screens undoubtedly was to hide a weak or otherwise detrimental mouth; but Webb's may well have been cultivated at the urge of his natal secretiveness. Further analysis is, however, redundant, for the most excellent portrait of him by Solomon J. Solomon at Portland Place has the rare quality, basic in all great portraiture, of revealing the subject's spiritual make-up. Here Webb confesses to his little tripping, secretive walk with lowered chin and eyes peeping under hat-brim as frankly as to his triumph in his distinctions.

It was said that his predominance in Council at the Institute was won by squatting on the fence till revealed opinion tipped him off on the winning side. This, however, might well have been an unfriendly view of his balanced judgement; and of his clear-sighted persuasiveness well exampled when he returned to the

2 *Sir Aston Webb and E. Ingress Bell. Victoria and Albert Museum, Cromwell Road, South Kensington (designed 1891, built 1899–1909). This free eclectic design is typical of many large public buildings of its time.*

office from submission of the vast, detailed, $\frac{1}{16}$-inch sketch plans and revolutionary layout of Birmingham University, to tell his staff: "They've swallowed the lot." Birmingham Law Courts, Christ's Hospital School the Victoria Memorial, the new frontage to Buckingham Palace, grain silos at Greenwich, mansions, churches, all the output of a smudgy lead pencil on soft paper in the three-windowed front room on the first floor of 19 Queen Anne's Gate!

How was it all accomplished? Webb's staff consisted of: a chief draughtsman aged about twenty-seven at a salary of £3 per week; a tracer and handyman at probably 30s. a week; a secretarial clerk ditto; an office boy, say 7s.; a newly-employed ex-pupil £1, and five live pupils, including this peeper, who, at premiums of £250 for a three-year term, represented an income of £416 6s. 8d., or some £40 more than the total of the salary list. This excellent arrangement – notoriously exampled by Sarah Thorne who ran a theatre at Margate where actors paid Sarah for the opportunity to perform to a public who paid her to see their per-

formance – was fundamental to pupilage throughout the profession.

At times of pressure and of Competition output, one or two seniors came into the office of whom the names of David Niven, Robin Dods and A. S. Scott are memorable; but since Webb owned, or held, the lease of the house; let the two upper floors to quantity surveyors who did much of his work; and housed in the basement the man and wife who serviced the offices; it was an astonishing thing when he confided, with emphasis, that more than half his takings went in expenses. The thing remains beyond understanding, for not many years later, if not then, it was, in general, held that it should cost an architect not more than one pound to gain three. Let it here be noted that it was a high privilege to be accepted as a pupil in the office of one of the outstanding heads of the profession; and that £500 was paid for that privilege. Webb, who was then but newly prominent, no doubt later received top-dog fees.

The organisation of Webb's office relates rather to

3 *Sir Aston Webb and E. Ingress Bell. Christ's Hospital School (1893–1902), near Horsham, Sussex. Until the middle of the Edwardian decade, Webb rejected scholarly revivalism and designed in a free adaptation of a mixture of styles.*

4 *Sir Aston Webb and E. Ingress Bell. Royal United Services Institute, Whitehall, London (1893–95). A quiet version of the free Baroque that was just becoming fashionable. Successful as a neighbour to Inigo Jones's Banqueting House.*

days when Wren could order a forest of oak to be thrown for St Paul's on a half-sheet of notepaper, than to days such as ours. He rode every morning from his home in Ladbroke Grove across Hyde and James' Parks and up Bird Cage Walk on a stout cob with a rigid riding-school seat that promised well for the medicinal benefit he sought by the exercise; and arrived at the office to get out of his breeches by 9.30. Placidity ruled. He read his letters, which were few and brief, and then sat to his drawing-board, where he solidly remained, with few interruptions, other than a short hour's break when he tripped across to his Club in St James's Street for a spot of lunch, till about seven. He had no elevenses; no cup of tea with two digestive biscuits in the saucer was ever taken to him at four o'clock. He rarely went on to his jobs and none of his staff ever did. His clerks of works – often from afar – came to him, reported and received his orders. When a contractor's representative called to protest that the girt of mouldings on a F.S. exceeded specified measure, he took the sheet, rapidly redrew, and nodded the man goodbye with no more ado; and when a bulky report from one of our Colonies – where a prison of adobe was being built from his design – was delivered, he scribbled 'Seen, A.W.' across the corner and it was handed back to the Government office messenger who brought it.

He dictated his letters in the early afternoon when the matters they dealt with had been meditated on at the drawing board. At that time typewriters, and telephones, with motors and electric light, as well as phonograph and bioscope – forerunners of the gram and the movie – were not in being, and telegrams were so great a rarity that the immediate response to the delivery of one was alarm. Letters were written in clerky longhand – if not holograph – on single or double sheets of small social notepaper in a glutinous purple 'copying ink'; and, when dry, blotty and imperfect printings in reverse were obtained from them by pressure on damped flimsy paper, which could be read from the back. These flimsies were strongly bound in a heavy volume and numbered for indexing so that it was possible, after recognising its description in the index, to run any letter to ground by licking the fingers and paging through the book until a point was reached where the wanted leaf could be separated from its neighbours by holding them slackly between the balls of the thumbs and exercising a little patience in blowing upon their edges. Things were, however, by no means so simple when indexing had been postponed for many weeks and it was important that the letter needed should be available within the space of a few hours! Incoming letters were more readily dealt with: they had only to be threaded on laces and thrown into the bottom of a cupboard so that should Webb at any time wish to refer to a letter – as sometimes happened – his secretary had merely to go down on his knees and drag successive lace-loads out into the light until he recog-

nised the bundle he wanted and could beat the dust out of it and settle down to sort it through until the actual letter itself was identified.

We grin: but are we so entitled? In the result all worked smoothly and efficiently without the scrambling complexities that now burden us; and it may be recounted that some twenty years ago Arnold Mitchell, who had recently completed a large block adjoining Berkeley Square in less time than an American architect had taken to put up a comparable building near by, mentioned to an acquaintance that he wrote all his letters with his own hand and that his press-copy book had been in use for fourteen years. When asked how he was able thus to maintain direction of the contractor, he said, "Ask him to lunch!"

In Webb's office all contract drawings were inked in and coloured on hot-pressed Whatman; and after being further dirtied with droppings of tea, and otherwise, by the quantity surveyors, were traced on linen and became the copies due to the contractor. There were no mechanical reproductions then in being. The originals of working drawings were supplied to the contractor after sufficient hurried pencilled records of them on tracing paper had been pasted on lining paper.

5 *Sir Aston Webb and E. Ingress Bell. The Great Hall, University of Birmingham, Edgbaston, Birmingham (1900–09). One of Webb's best buildings, in the then fashionable Byzantine manner that sprang from Bentley's Westminster Cathedral.*

The only Indian ink available was in sticks an inch and a half long embossed in gold with the figure of a dragon to discourage any ideas of lamp black by proclaiming origin in Chinese cuttle fish. This was rubbed to a requisite density on a palette in a half-teaspoon of water to which a little ox-gall was added to ensure viscosity. The ruling pen was loaded by touching it delicately, edge-on, upon the surface of the ink, for capillary completion; and was then ready for service after its nose had been wiped. This nose-wiping called for caution. The adept tracer's efficiency in wiping was brilliant. He turned back the lower part of his waistcoat and all was done in an automatic pass at his belly identical with the instinctive action of a sparrow whetting its bill. The first appearance in an architect's office of a bottle of Indian ink, densely black, flowingly viscous, waterproof and with quill dipper in its cork, was a great event. And yet? – never mind!

Now has come the moment to speak of the soot that incredibly dirtied London even to the begriming of the nostrils, and of the ungloved hands; for flakes of soot drifting continuously down to blacken and greasily deface the laboured drawing was so frequent an annoyance that the plague of it outwearied all cursings. And as for the sea fogs of the estuary chokingly loaded with the smoke of myriad eastern chimneys,

and cheerily accepted as 'London particulars', which once, at mid-summer, created a panic scramble of afternoon shoppers in Tottenham Court Road, by allowing the sun suddenly to pierce it with a flaming redness purporting volcanic origin, they are no longer imaginable.

Before quitting Webb's office to peep at the architectural scene beyond, the mouth that many readers opened in astonishment at the scale of salaries paid by Webb must be closed. Beyond question Webb paid the full market rate for the service he received, for he would have done no less.

At the time spoken of, his pupils came to the office, as did the chief draughtsman, gloved and rigorously dressed in well-tailored morning coat, boiled dress shirt with starched stand-up collar, top-hatted and carrying a closely-rolled silk umbrella; a get-up varied only on social occasions by substitution of a frock coat for a tailed one; but not varied even for crowdings into the galleries of theatres. This peeper 'had diggins' in the two ground-floor rooms of a Cubitt-built house sited in Belgravia at St James, and in Pimlico at Bow Street. He drank beer with a three-course dinner, had full attendance, and, without any sense of deprivation or money shortage, lived for three years on a fixed allowance of one hundred pounds a year, and no more.

6 *Sir Aston Webb and E. Ingress Bell. Great Hall and Chamberlain Tower, University of Birmingham.*

In the years spoken of the aesthetes tailored in pastel plushes and satirised by Gilbert in *Patience* were personified in crowded drawing rooms decorated with crossed Japanese fans and lily-painted door-panels, by a large, soft, cream-coloured man – protagonist of Yellow Book 'decadents' – who was doted on when he extolled the deliciousness of silk underclothing. In these years, also, the intolerances that assailed Browning, Meredith, Wagner, and Rodin, branded every established architect as delinquent for his attachment to Classic, or to Gothic or to the heresy of eclecticism. The animosity thus evoked exceeded any now dividing traditionalists and moderns. The inveteracy of these adhesions and repulsions is exampled by the wide enjoyment at the supposed disgust of Rowand Anderson – a renowned classicist of Edinburgh – on the appeal to him of one of his pupils – "If ye please, Sir, ma mither says I've got tae learn ta go'ick"; and their obstinacy by Charles Annesley Voysey, who, no more than twenty years ago, when a friend, amused at the violence of his prejudices and seeking to flummox him, said: "Well, you can't say you don't admire Church Row, Hampstead!" was answered with: "Ah! but Church Row was designed by *gentlemen*," with emphasis to mark the extreme rarity of such an exception to the rule.

Again in these years the world of architecture was rent by the all-embracing soul-racking question: was Architecture an Art or a Profession? The story is well enough known. T. G. Jackson and Norman Shaw were the protagonists on the side of Art; the Institute represented the Professionals. The intention of the Institute was to introduce Registration – examinations alone qualifying for membership. Anyone who had seen – as he might – a hefty plumber riding his bicycle in the streets of a provincial town inside a coil of service pipe on the first day of one month, and accepted on the second day of the next as a duly brass-plated Architect and Surveyor, on the strength of his appointment as 'Surveyor' (of drains) to a school, could well understand the motive of the Institute's providence of examinations; but providence of the education necessary to pass those examinations was bleakly remote in the eyes of the pupils of the men imposing the examinations who, astonishing to record, in no way concerned themselves with the education of their pupils.

As Webb was the last who would ever seek to avoid his obligations or, for that matter, vary from conduct that was conventionally correct; his official regard for the welfare of his pupils, whose complete loyalty he held, may be taken as the correct one.

His five pupils were all well-connected and at one in public school affinities. They attended daily on the same footing as the salaried staff; each was allotted such tasks as he could tackle by the chief draughtsman and he was free to make himself of use as his abilities allowed, and gain such knowledge of building and design as his curiosity, gumption, or ambition led him to do. Beyond recommending membership of the Architectural Association and, by examination, of the Institute, Webb concerned himself in no way with how his pupils were preparing themselves, or neglecting to prepare themselves, for the career to which they were dedicated, though he entertained them with great kindness at his home. Two of those pupils, charming fellows both, entirely lacked all aptitude, purpose or ambition, and Webb could only have justified their pupilage by feeling that they were as well employed wasting their time in his office as anywhere else. Another became a stained-glass merchant; yet another, distinguished by scholarly taste and outstanding capacity as a draughtsman failed, through a long life, to announce himself in architecture; and the last lived to resent deeply that Webb made use of his pupils' time without regard to whether the time so spent was of use to his pupils.

One lesson his pupils had of Webb was by no means well learned. The hoofmark of the engineer – as it was then regarded by the elect of the Art and/or Profession – was already in evidence; and forgetful of the linked

7 *Sir Aston Webb. Thames Warehouse, Stamford Street, Southwark (1901). A noble and free design for a functional building.*

beams bolstering the Duomo at Florence; and of the dome of St Peter's sustained through generations with successive girdlings; and of the chain of welted iron plates circling the base of London's St Paul's; and of the joggled blocks of Whitbed strung like beads along cast iron girders, in simulation of monolithic lintols, at the British Museum – forgetful of all this, the elect and their disciples deplored lofty frontages carried on the plate glass of shop windows and, regardless of the claims of salesmanship, execrated such examples of engineering skill as, by the use of cantilevers, represented the return angle of a lofty building as entirely unsupported, other than by 'sky hooks' – a term of derision then rife.

Webb, however, appears to have had no attachment to such prejudices of the elect. The offices he built for an insurance company on a corner site in Moorgate are entered diagonally, and have heavy scrolled and foliated brackets of Portland on each side of the doorway supporting the overhanging face above. The design gratifies the viewer's sense of stalwart masonry construction holding the weighty projection it sustains from falling off into the street. Webb, however, had no

such confidence. He employed an engineer to sustain it. The engineer, who was a humble person, came to the drawing office after securing Webb's approval of his devisings, and explained with gusto how his contraption was not, as seemed, graplings from a shipwreck, but a contrivance so combining cantilever and beam as to demand rivetings to meet torsion and shear.

Webb's crowning achievement in this kind is, however, enshrined in the little church he built for the French Protestants in Soho Square. Its frontage of a rarely-seen grey-purple Luton brick, with dressings of red terra-cotta enriched – as are his Birmingham Law Courts – with modellings reminiscent of Blois, exhibits him at his happiest; but its interior reveals him as, constructionally, too far ahead of his time!

This peeper knows that he must be regarded as a mere mortuary attendant on a dead horse which he has spent much of his life in flogging, and which now stinks in the general nose; and that to modern notions it is no discredit to Webb's system of construction that its employment in this little church revolts him. Nave, aisles and apse are of gamboge terra-cotta of ashlar affinity far removed from the traditions of the Holbein

8 *Sir Aston Webb. Royal Naval College, Dartmouth, Devon (1899–1905). The original designs of 1899 were altered and this free rendering of late-Wren Baroque probably dates from about 1901.*

9 *Sir Aston Webb. Admiralty Arch, The Mall, Westminster (1911). Webb was one of the many commercially prosperous architects who turned to the Baroque during its vogue.*

10 *Sir Aston Webb. East frontage, Buckingham Palace (1913) and Victoria Memorial (1901, sculpture by Sir Thomas Brock), London. Webb designed the whole scheme, including* rond-point, *the lay-out of The Mall and Admiralty Arch as early as 1901 but the design was altered greatly over the following twelve years. By the time he re-fronted Buckingham Palace, he had altered his manner to a Beaux Arts classical style, scholarly but not vigorous.*

336

Gateway and Layer Marney; but these concrete-filled boxes of well-puddled and thumbed clay, were requisitioned by the architect only to profess the purpose of their fabrication without performing it; for the terracotta of the piers and arches of the nave merely clothe a framework of steel stanchions and binders.

Webb's constructive prevision, however, as exampled in this church, reaches beyond all conceptions current today; for in an apse, with a periphery of some 25 feet, he has two 7 foot-wide openings with flat arches which, on plan, are accordingly strongly curved. The whole conception, though severely architectural and in spite of its voussoirs being conscientiously joggled, does not, in this peeper's opinion, satisfy the conditions of structural integrity with sufficient emphasis to justify the design; although the engineer who made the enormity possible may think otherwise.

Acceptance by architects of the encroachments of the engineer were general earlier in America than with us. The monumental 'Archives' of John Russell Pope at Washington, for instance, built twenty-five years ago has 20 ton marble cornice-returns anchored to steel roof-members; and the coffered blocks of the barrel vaulting over its side entrances – although with ample abutments – are each suspended by lewis boltings to a raft of steel joists above. Thus are peaceful slumbers ensured to architects – and to their wives!

By comparison, the work-a-day mechanisms of building in those days are no less curious to look back on. This peeper can still recall the moment when he stood in startled admiration on seeing a bucket of mortar being hoiked to a scaffold by a rope passing over a 10-inch pulleywheel, for all loads were at that time humped aloft by men climbing successive ladders from stage to stage of scaffolding which, even on the spires of churches, was uniformly constructed of poles secured by wedges driven into rope bindings. It would seem that masonry must always have been largely slung with lewis bolts; but bricks up to a total of sixteen, and mortar and plasterers' stuff and parge for chimneys – which was always mixed with cow-dung to secure imperviability – were carried uniformly in a thing hardly now ever seen but which will not need describing – namely the hod. The labourers who did this heavy work were hefty men muscularly attuned to it; and as the hod allowed both hands free, so did the ring-pad on the head allow a 2 foot 6 inch square of ledged planks to be carried balanced like the tray of the muffin man whose tea-time bell was welcomed in middle-class residential districts. Upon this square of boards mortar was laddered to the bricklayer, and if at this time anybody may be curious of the origin of the collegiate 'mortar board,' no one in those days was. It was a general rule embodied in a standing clause of specifications, that stone should be worked on the building site, and it was delivered thereon in bulk to that end. This brought into prominence for the transport of worked stone from bench to its bedding, a thing now scarcely known called a 'hand barrow'; a might-be mortar board, supported on bearers with handholds for the two men in service to it.

So the happy work went on in sunshine or in shadow mid clean bracing smells and ringing trowels and manly voices, where the architect still abode in kinship to the tradition of crafts sacred to past ages, and to the attainment of mankind's loftiest aspirations.

Edwin Alfred Rickards

by John Warren

Even when reaction against the Edwardian Baroque was at its
strongest, historians allowed that the period could claim one
extraordinary talent, that of Edwin Rickards (1872–1920). In partnership with the planner and engineer H. V. Lanchester, as Lanchester
and Rickards, he won a series of major competitions for public
buildings between 1897 and 1906 that brought an exuberant touch of
French and Austrian Baroque into the essentially English (Wren
and Vanbrugh) style of the Grand Manner.

By a coincidence of friendship we possess a most remarkable series of insights into the character of Edwin Alfred Rickards – the voluble, volatile, egocentric little Londoner who was the great moving spirit of that outwardly rumbustious and flamboyant style – the Edwardian Baroque. As relentlessly as he caricatured his friend, Arnold Bennett, ("assuredly he did hundreds of caricatures of myself") that famous and immensely popular author wove Rickards into his own writing – into his enormous diary, and into his novels. Witness a letter from Bennett to Rickards,é ..."You will appear in the following two novels . . . and then you will be the hero of the fourth book about London . . ."

This fourth book is *The Roll Call*[2]. Its hero, George Cannon bears to Rickards the architect, exactly the relationship that his own caricatures bore towards the famous author himself – incisive, accurate, perceptive. Every salient characteristic of the subject stands out in this multi-faceted portrait.

The portrayal of Rickards in the novel shows him a highly sensitive man, delighting in artistic creation, and particularly in the esoteric pleasures of his calling; extremely conscious of the world around him, yet self-consciously apart from it, observing it half-quizzically, half sympathetically . . . self-centred and consumed with ambition.

"In the very centre of his mind and occupying nearly the whole of it was the vast thought, the obsession, of his own potential power and its fulfilment. George's egotism was terrific, and as right as any other natural phenomenon. He had to get on . . . he had to be a great architect, and – equally important – he had to be publicly recognised as a great architect . . ." ". . . on matters upon which his instinct had not suggested a course of action, George was ready enough to be taught: indeed his respect for the expert was truly deferential. But when his instinct had begun to operate he would consult nobody and consider nobody."

Passages of pure reportage describe Rickards (George) at work and demonstrate that his designs were not the result of cold calculation, or tentative empiricism. They were the creations of a surge of feeling, of emotion. They were not conceived in an instant, not slowly devised, evolving façade from plan. He worked in bursts of enthusiasm.

". . . the sum of work seemed tremendous; it made the mind dizzy: it made George smile with terrible satisfaction at his own industry . . ."

". . . the perspective drawing did not quite satisfy – and there was still time. The point of view of the perspective drawing was too high up, and the result was a certain marring of the nobility of the lines, and certainly a diminishment of the effect of the tower. . ."

". . . in one second he had decided to finish the original perspective drawing, and in his very finest style. He would complete it sometime during the night . . ."

". . . in a few minutes George was at work, excited,

having forgotten all fatigue . . ."

In all these extracts Rickards is clearly recognisable. Similar verve and intensity characterised his brilliant caricatures, his sketching and water-colour work. In a book produced as a tribute to Rickards,[3] Bennett wrote of his painting:

"He was extremely excitable and while at work would produce in his companions and himself the illusion that nothing on earth matters but water-colour."

There are several records of painting trips shared both in England and abroad. These were no doubt in Bennett's mind when he wrote: "Rickards always had a zest for life . . . such as I have seldom seen equalled and never seen surpassed," and in the same book ". . . he was vastly more bitten by caricature than by any other art except architecture . . . Caricature was second nature to him. He caricatured all the time."

The years of Bennett's success brought him the pleasures of a country house, a yacht and substantial wealth and prestige. Though he had by now married, his friendship with Rickards increased rather than diminished. They shared sailing holidays, and a fluent record of the voyages that Rickards made on Bennett's

2 *Henry V. Lanchester and Edwin Rickards. Detail in entrance hall, Bovril Factory, Old Street, London. Work on the Bovril building started in 1893 and continued with various additions over many years.*

1 *Portrait of Edwin Rickards.*

3 *Lanchester, Stewart and Rickards. City Hall and Law Courts, Cardiff (designed 1897). Success in this competition launched the successful partnership, in which Rickards was the designer with Lanchester the planner and engineer. Stewart's role was less clear (he died in 1904).*

4 *Lanchester, Stewart and Rickards. The Assembly Room, City Hall, Cardiff (designed 1897). Walls, windows and ceiling provide a good example of Rickards' ability to draw from many Baroque sources and produce an inspired and integrated design of his own.*

any good till I met Lanchester."

The qualities which distinguish Rickards' buildings from those of many of his contemporaries, and make them remarkable, are the breadth and vigour of their conception, the fitness of scale and proportion, and his singular version of the Baroque style.

A tremendous facility for perspective drawing – a product of his imaginative powers and his ability with the pencil ensured that every Rickards design was conceived and considered in the solid. Some of the rough sketches, which contributed to the evolution of his schemes still survive and show, for instance, the gradual delineation of the arcs, piers and monumental masses which make up the towers so typical of his buildings. Only when a design had been thoroughly drawn and examined in three dimensions was it reduced to plan and elevation.

Rickards had no mentor. He was essentially self-trained, seizing opportunities for increasing his knowledge as he moved from office to office 'improving himself'. Stylistically he had the deepest admiration for South German Baroque, Salzburg and Vienna were particular sources of pleasure and perhaps of inspiration, though the mainspring of design was so strong in him that he was much less in need of inspiration than of self-control.

The 'cockney' accent which Professor Reilly recalled betrayed, in reality, Rickards' South-London origin. He was born in 1872 and lived his early years in High Street and Disraeli Street, Putney. In *The Roll Call*, Arnold Bennett makes George Cannon's father a bigamist who had fled to America. Whether or not this bore any relation to the facts of Rickards' case, it is difficult to say, as the father never comes into the picture, his family consisting apparently only of his mother and a sister.

About 1884 Rickards' mother moved to the Fulham Road, a winding commercial thoroughfare which straggles from Putney Bridge up to the Brompton Road and Knightsbridge, bordered throughout its length by haphazard commercial development some three or four storeys in height and of varying Victorian and subsequent origin. The Rickards' household was established at number 779 towards the Putney end of Fulham Road. On leaving school, in his early 'teens, Rickards began to work behind the counter of a drapery shop – in all probability the shop which his mother appears to have run at the home address. This seems to have suited the young man very little and, looking for a means of earning his living with some outlet for his growing artistic bent, he hit upon architecture.

At the age of fifteen he joined the office of R. J. Lovell, and before leaving there in his seventeenth year, had begun to attend classes at the Royal Academy. The Professor of Architecture at the Academy at this time was George Aitchison, whom Sir Reginald Blomfield portrays as genial, benevolent and an authority on Roman Architecture, who hated the Gothic as much as

yacht remains in his drawings for The Log of the Velsa.[4]

Rickards personality was extraordinarily vigorous. In stature he was a little smaller than the average. Pale of complexion, and restless, he never sank into the crowd, was never one of it, but remained, wherever he was, the individual. With his emotions always on the surface, and his ready enthusiasm, he could never be the imperturbable man of the world – for this reason the adjective, 'childlike' springs readily to the minds of many who knew him. Dr Lanchester in his notes to the memorial volume gives us a picture of the super-sensitive Rickards, inconsolably hurt by the attribution of an inferior design to his hand, exclaiming, "Can my work be as bad as that?"

"He has a most pungent mind and tongue", wrote Frank Swinnerton.[5] Add to this Dr Lanchester's "always the centre of animated discussion," and the consistent reports of his extraordinarily vivid personality begin to have substance. The vivid imagination which made him so excited and vigorous a talker, and often so destructive a critic, could induce in him tremendous depths of despondency, and made him a formidable opponent in the fierce and explosive arguments to which he could be provoked.

Among the fundamental aspects of Rickard's character is the sheer romanticism which permeated his architecture and coloured his entire view of life. It was so fundamental that those who knew him best have usually failed to mention it directly when describing him.

P. G. Konody, author and art historian, expressed one aspect of it in an article in *The Observer*. He wrote: "More than once have I seen Rickards under the romantic spell woven by his own genius . . . One of these occasions was in the mysterious gloom of dusk under the mighty dome of the then unfinished Central Hall at Westminster; another when he took me by moonlight to see his great group of public buildings at Cardiff. With that curious mingling of supreme egotism and self-abnegating modesty, of hopeless pessimism and romantic exaltation which endeared him to his friends, he spoke of his achievements, of his past career, which began in a draper's shop; of his hopeless prospects; of the romance of his standing there in the moonlight before his own creation which he knew to be something to be proud of; of the difficulties which beset the architect's path, and of professional jealousies and meanness."

Rickards was more at the heart of the resurgence of 'free classic' architecture than any other English architect. He was that unusual thing in the English race – a natural designer in the Baroque. Alfred Stephens, sculptor and painter was another such, and one whom Rickards deeply admired. But the freedom and exuberance of the true Baroque style, the *spumanti* spirit that leads to its peaks of achievement, is unusual among Englishmen – and it is hardly surprising that

the 'free classic' was quickly tamed by an academicism which sapped much of its verve and spirit. Emasculated and academicised it subsided finally into 'Banker's Georgian' in an extraordinary reversal of the natural trends in architectural design.

An understanding of this process is vital to any assessment of Rickard's achievements. At the threshold of his career he plunged into the rising wave of sympathy for the Baroque or free Classical Revival. His instincts were entirely in tune with it, and his youthful abilities carried him up to swim on the crest. The style that ended so sadly in the emasculated pediments of Banker's Georgian really began with the final bold phase of Norman Shaw's career and was carried to its peak by Rickards in the halcyon days of Imperial prosperity and the *Entente Cordiale*.

Writing of Rickard's youthful competition success, Charles Reilly enthused,[6] "It seemed at the time like a new revelation . . . seemed to open the way to a new world . . . every student was full of it." The year was 1897 and the building the civic centre in Cathays Park, Cardiff. Rickards was then in his mid-twenties, self-tutored, hypersensitive, questing and querulous. For some years he had been a close friend of a young journalist who had gravitated from the Potteries to London in pursuit of his career, and who sometimes wished that he himself had 'gone in' for architecture. Later in life, when both had achieved professional eminence, the journalist-turned novelist, Arnold Bennett, wrote "Rickards, the man, influenced my view of life more than any other person I have ever met"; and elsewhere he accorded him, with H. G. Wells, the distinction of being "one of the two most interesting, stimulating and provocative men" he had ever met. More picturesquely, in a speech[7] at a dinner in celebration of Rickard's success in winning the competition for the building now known as Westminster Central Hall, he said: "Rickards is a sea, an ocean and I have always felt myself to be a child wandering by its shore."

Throughout their friendship Bennett's Journals record the impact of Rickard's character, and often it is possible to see the two personalities impinging upon each other.[8] "Rickards dined with me . . . He talked about himself the whole time . . . Of course this exasperating egotism was painful as a disease to witness, but his talk was exceedingly good and original."

"Rickard's conversation remains what it was, the most human and genuinely poetic in texture of any I have ever enjoyed."

"He is now getting hold of me again as a great artist . . ."

". . . did water colours with Rickards."

"Rickards talked incessantly."

". . . Rickards arrived. We had a tremendous deal to say to each other."

". . . Rickards is wonderfully addicted to talking in the early hours of the morning."

Of the friendship, Frank Swinnerton wrote,[9] "They argued the whole time. They never quarrelled. They contrasted each other with complete firmness." The friends shared from their youth the fashionable Francophilia. They made a joint first visit to Paris in 1897 – 'Zola's Paris,' for which Bennett had hungered so long. Rickards was lost in admiration for the Beaux Arts scholarship of the French 'free classic.' Both were irresistably drawn by the romance of the capital: ''as we went home past the Moulin Rouge and met crowds of carriages going towards it each told the other he had no desire to go there and each lied.''

All his great successes were those of the next ten years: thereafter an increasing trend to 'correctness in design', a growing tautness and precision carried the tide of architectural fashion away from his natural tastes and self-tutored schooling. There is something poignant, almost painful, in the vision of so natural an artist curbing himself in his later years to conform to disciplines inherently restrictive to his spirit.

The facet of Rickards' life which complemented his artistry was his professional partnership. Any successful building by Rickards was the success of this partnership with Henry Vaughan Lanchester – a man of utterly different temperament and abilities. The artistry,

5 *Lanchester, Stewart and Rickards. Detail, Deptford Town Hall, New Cross Road, South-East London (designed 1902). The influence of Beresford Pite's interest in Michelangelo is evident, but this is swept up into one of Rickards' most inventive exteriors.*

1 *James S. Gibson. Middlesex Guildhall, Parliament Square, Westminster (1906–13). The Edwardian free style with Gothic clothes to blend with its neighbours.*

The 1890s were the decade of hope for Arts and Crafts and other free style architects that a new non-revivalist national style would emerge and be generally accepted in Britain. By 1903 that hope was drowned in the flood of neo-Baroque large buildings. Lethaby had given up practice by that time, Townsend lost his obsessive originality, Voysey's period of great innovations was past (though his work remained impressive) and Prior too had most, though not all, his striking buildings behind him. As far as large public and commercial buildings were concerned, the progressives had lost the struggle.

But there were survivors from this defeat and we have already seen that the Art Workers' Guild remained influential. Indeed a number of the most impressive free style buildings date from the Edwardian period, particularly in domestic architecture. Within the Arts and Crafts Movement, the most important new talent to arrive at the end of the century was M. H. Baillie Scott (1865–1945). After starting his practice in the Isle of Man, Baillie Scott moved to England and soon made a name for himself by taking up Voysey and Prior's ideas on house design and developing them in his own way. His works are not without an occasional coy touch of the kind to which Voysey was also sometimes liable, but he took the open planning of house interiors boldly beyond anything that had been tried before. Baillie Scott is one of the few Arts and Crafts designers who has so far been the subject of a whole book but, interesting though his work is, one should perhaps not rate him as high as some of his immediate predecessors and contemporaries.

No book has yet appeared on a more powerful designer and more extraordinary man, C. R. Ashbee (1863–1942). Aged only twenty-five, Ashbee had founded an idealistic community called the Guild and School of Handicraft in the East End slums of London in 1888, the same year as the establishment of the Arts and Crafts Exhibition Society. Fourteen years later, at the beginning of the Edwardian period, he moved the entire community of over one hundred people to Chipping Campden in Gloucestershire where it survived for some years. Ashbee himself, an imaginative and dynamic personality, was among the first of the Arts and Crafts Movement to accept the machine as a force in craftsmanship. He exchanged ideas by frequent letters with his progressive American contemporary Frank Lloyd Wright (1869–1959) and before leaving London built some original houses. Chipping Campden is thick with a variety of buildings he designed for his neighbours there, although most of them follow the Tudor and Jacobean Cotswold style to blend with their surroundings.

As far as range of built work was concerned, the slightly older Leonard Stokes (1858–1925) was a more successful (in size of practice) architect than any other member of the Art Workers' Guild of his generation, working in a free manner during the Edwardian years. A Roman Catholic, he built many churches and religious buildings. But he also built many large country houses, office blocks and educational buildings and, as he was married to the daughter of a telephone company manager, he designed and erected an impressive series of big telephone exchange buildings during the early years of the century. Stokes never indulged in extremes of originality, but his designs have great power and rationality. The short study of his work included here will give a good introduction to a most excellent architect, while Sir Albert Richardson's memories of working in the Stokes office (included later in this book) given an intriguing impression of him as a man.

Apart from the London-dominated south of England, the free manner flourished in a number of centres. W. H. Bidlake (*circa* 1860–1938) was only one of several Arts and Crafts architects working in Birmingham, while places such as Knutsford and Queensferry in Cheshire and Bristol too have buildings of interest from this period. But the most progressive work south of Scotland was being done by the Manchester partnership of Edgar Wood (1860–1935) and J. Henry Sellers (1861–1954).

Edgar Wood had been one of the founder members of the northern branch of the Art Workers' Guild in the 1890s. At that time he was very much the artist-architect, working in vernacular styles and dressing ostentatiously in cloak and wide-brimmed hat. But after the end of the century he went into partnership with Sellers and the character of their work gradually changed. Wood's Christian Science Church of 1901 remains one of the more original and attractive products of Arts and Crafts architecture and it was followed by a series of buildings after 1904 in which the partners experimented daringly with flat concrete roofs and almost Cubist forms.

All the same, these practices were isolated developments of the English free style movement of the previous decade. In Scotland the picture was different. Mackintosh's Scotland Street School and Art School Library, Campbell's Northern Insurance building, Salmon's Lion Chambers, Lamond's Dundee schools and Burnet's Forsyth's and McGeoch's stores all date from the years between 1904 and 1908, while there were many other small buildings of interest. And in the last years before the outbreak of war, Burnet took further important steps towards a free rational architecture with his Wallace Scott factory near Glasgow and his Kodak office building in London.

Financial pressures from the property developers helped to ensure that Burnet's was not the only remarkable Edwardian London office building. Commercial firms of architects such as Treadwell and Martin, Gordon and Gunton and Read and Macdonald developed a variety of free style answers to the problems of the time and some of their buildings have much virtue.

More interesting and influential still were the first works of Charles Holden (1875–1960), who joined the established architect Percy Adams after a spell with C. R. Ashbee. Holden designed several large hospitals in a strong and self-assured free style at the beginning of the 20th century, before turning to a vigorously free neo-Mannerist sequence of office buildings. In the Edwardian period Holden came nearer to establishing a successful free style for large buildings than anyone, though his lack of the flexibility to adapt his manner to the expression of new structural systems was to turn him into a reactionary figure after the First World War.

Holden's almost aggressively free early buildings find an echo in the work of Belcher's old partner, Arthur Beresford Pite (1861–1934). Pite was intriguing as an architect, for he spent his first twenty years in private practice seeking, almost with desperation, for new ideas that would provide an architecture for the time. His restless inventiveness fascinated his fellow architects and produced a number of impressive, though strange, buildings.

One sees the influence of Pite and Holden, as well as of Lethaby and Philip Webb, in the many buildings designed by the young men of the London County Council Architect's Department from 1899 until 1920. There is the same rather harsh aesthetic sense and many shared details, though the L.C.C. architects maintained a restraint that Pite, for one, did not. In the immense number of housing schemes, schools, fire stations and other works which the department built during this time the quality inevitably varies. But the overall standard was remarkably high, as were the architects' ideals, and their achievement is one of the high points of free Edwardian architecture.

Finally, no account of idealistic architecture during the Edwardian period could omit some mention of developments in town planning. For it was during this period that the Garden Suburb idea, which started at Bedford Park in the 1870s, was taken up and developed at Hampstead Garden Suburb (with some excellent work by Lutyens). Even more far-reaching was the idea of the Garden City. Ebenezer Howard's dream started to become a reality in 1903 when the first Garden City, planned by Raymond Unwin and Barry Parker, started to rise from the ground at Letchworth, Hertfordshire.

2

2 *Sir Edwin Lutyens. Marsh Court, Stockbridge, Hampshire (1901). Between 1896 and 1903 Lutyens contributed some of the best free designs in England, often with Tudor overtones. Later he turned to the Grand Manner and found fame.*

3 *M. H. Baillie Scott. Design for a house in Switzerland (circa 1903). Baillie Scott's experiments with open planning of house interiors are among the most important developments of the free style in the Edwardian period.*

4 *C. R. Ashbee. Nos. 38 and 39 Cheyne Walk, Chelsea (design 1899, built circa 1901). The irregular gable originally lined up the right-hand roof level with the earlier Ashbee house that stood beside No. 39. Ashbee was the most impressive designer (in many fields) and moving spirit in the latter days of the Arts and Crafts Movement.*

5 *H. Bulkeley Creswell. Willans Factory, Queensferry, Flintshire (1901–03). The chunky battered walls are reminiscent of Frank Lloyd Wright's contemporary Larkin Building.*

6

7

8

9

0

6 *Charles Rennie Mackintosh. The Hill House, Helensburgh, Dunbartonshire, Scotland (1902–04). Baronial features treated in Mackintosh's developing free manner.*

7 *H. Fuller Clark. Boulting and Sons office building, No. 59 Riding House Street, Marylebone, London (1903). One of the most striking examples of Edwardian Free Style applied to street architecture. Fuller Clark was also the architect of the almost Art Nouveau Black Friar public house in Queen Victoria Street, London.*

8 *Gordon & Gunton. Detail, Manor House (flats), Marylebone Road, London (1903). A free style and Arts-and-Crafts decoration used by commercial architects.*

9 *C. F. A. Voysey. Design for proposed house at Woodford, Essex (1905). The year produced a number of designs showing that Voysey's manner had matured without changing its architectural vocabulary.*

10 *M. H. Baillie Scott. Bill House, Selsey-on-Sea, Sussex (1906–07).*

11 *Halsey Ricardo. Fireplace, Woodside (for himself), Graffham, Sussex (circa 1907).*

11

12

12 *James Salmon. Lion Chambers, Hope Street, Glasgow (1906). Every side of this office building explores different possibilities and textures for free design.*

13 *Charles Holden (as chief assistant to H. Percy Adams). Central Reference Library, Bristol (1905–06). Holden's massive inventive energy was highly influential throughout the Edwardian period.*

14 *Frank Lloyd Wright. Unity Temple, Oak Park, Illinois (1906). A new trend towards almost cubist volumes can be seen in the work of architects on both sides of the Atlantic at this period.*

13

4

15

16

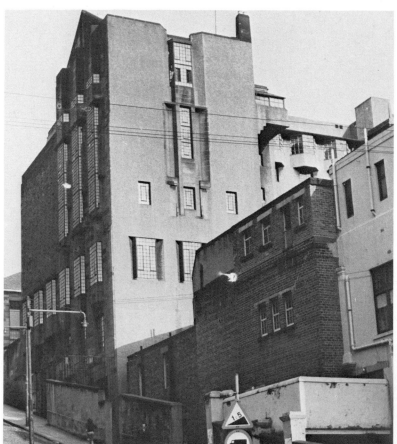

15 *Edgar Wood and J. Henry Sellers. Durnford Street School, Middleton, Manchester (1908–10). Among the earliest large-scale buildings with flat reinforced concrete roofs.*

16 *Sir John Burnet. Kodak Building, Kingsway, London (1910–11). An early attempt in Britain to rationalise office building design. Burnet had designed such elevations for the rear parts of his buildings as early as 1903 in Edinburgh.*

17 *Charles Rennie Mackintosh. Library Wing, Glasgow School of Art, 167 Renfrew Street, Glasgow (designed 1905 on, built 1907–09). This great building again reflects the trend towards solid cubic forms.*

18 *A. Dunbar Smith and W. Cecil Brewer. Heal's Department Store, 196–199 Tottenham Court Road, London (1916, extension by Sir Edward Maufe 1937).*

Leonard Aloysius Stokes

by H. V. Molesworth Roberts

Born only one year after Lethaby and Voysey, Leonard Stokes
(1858–1925) produced much interesting Arts and Crafts work in the
1890s. But his particular interest lies in the fact that he continued to
develop in the Edwardian period when many members of the
movement had finished their most original work. This study by
H. V. Molesworth Roberts summarises the changes in Stokes's
strong and highly personal traditionally-based free style.

By a strange paradox some men of merit, ignored during their lifetime, receive tardy recognition years after their death; others, successful in middle and later life, fade into obscurity shortly after. Leonard Stokes, on the whole, belongs to the second category. Though he carried out few works of major size, he was elected President of the Royal Institute of British Architects in 1910, and awarded the Royal Gold Medal in 1919. More than twenty years before, in 1897, H. H. Statham, in his *Modern Architecture*, had commended and illustrated Stokes's Sefton Park church[1] then built only seven years; and in 1901 Muthesius had mentioned the same church in his *Die Neuere Kirchliche Baukunst in England*, and compared Stokes with Bentley.[2] But there is no reference to him in Platz, *Die Baukunst der neuesten zeit,* 1927, or in Pevsner, *Pioneers of the Modern Movement*, 1936. Was he left out because his work seemed not sufficiently 'advanced', or because it was not sufficiently known?

Whatever the cause of the neglect, it is time now to collect and rejudge his work. When one studies his buildings their most conspicuous quality is seen to be their refreshing balance of verticals and horizontals, which must have seemed strange against the aggressive cornices of classical and the aspiring perpendiculars of Gothic traditions. In a fussier way, T. E. Collcutt, Stokes's one time master, had accomplished a similar effect with his semi-octagonal buttresses and delicate terra-cotta strings.[3] Closer to Stokes than Collcutt is C. Harrison Townsend (1851–1928),[4] although on the whole he relied more on broad surfaces and luscious foliage than on the intersection of lines. In spirit, however, none seems nearer to Stokes than his fellow-Catholic John Francis Bentley (1839–1902), nearly twenty years his senior. Bentley's St John's, Beaumont College, Old Windsor, shows the same dignity and stateliness, the same restrained devotional touch, and above all the same balance of outline as Stokes's All Saints Convent at London Colney, Hertfordshire.

Leonard Aloysius Scott Stokes was born in 1858 at Southport. His father, Scott Nasmyth Stokes (from whom Leonard derived his third prenomen), was an inspector of schools.[5] It was a gifted family. The youngest brother Wilfrid (afterwards Sir Wilfrid) became an engineer; the oldest, Adrian, a painter,[6] survived Leonard by ten years.[7] "During his boyhood (Leonard) had been anything but robust. With maturity, strength and high spirits seem to have come," wrote his fellow pupil Walter J. N. Millard.[8] He came to London in 1871[9] and entered in 1874 the office of S. J. Nicholls (1826–1905), a pupil of Scoles.[10] Nicholls was chiefly an architect of churches, and half a dozen or more of them were illustrated in the architectural magazines of the '70s and '80s. They do not look as if they can have inspired Stokes to any appreciable extent. His unfolding came only, when, after he had left Nicholls and spent a year or two with James Gandy

"the surveyor", he helped George Edmund Street, first as clerk of works and then in the office, on the restoration of Christ Church, Dublin.[11] Later he served under T. E. Collcutt and St Aubyn and then under no less a man than George Frederick Bodley. What better influence, in the late 19th century, could any man employ? Under Bodley and Garner he worked on the Liverpool Cathedral design in the first competition (1885–86). In 1880 he won the Pugin Travelling Studentship with drawings of medieval buildings in Lincolnshire, Yorkshire, and part of Northamptonshire and Nottinghamshire, and the manuscript, his sole attempt at authorship as far as we can discover, is preserved in the Institute's Library; the very complex 14th-century arcading in Ely Lady Chapel was among the subjects, and Millard tells how Stokes doggedly pursued his measuring while a colleague relaxed into perspective.[12]

He visited Germany and Italy in 1881–82 and in the latter year his stay at Florence was cut short by a summons to town on his first commission.

Stokes's work ranged over the years 1883 to 1915 and shows a great deal of development in style. Fortunately an almost complete dated list of executed buildings exists, an appendix to Mr George Drysdale's paper in the *Journal of the Royal Institute of British Architects* (8 January 1927, p. 177). The only disadvantage of this list is that only in a few cases are dates of beginning and completion given. As a rule dates refer to starting only, judging by the later date of published references. The outline of dates and facts in the following account, not otherwise marked, are from this source.

The work falls roughly into three periods: that of very poor imitative 'Gothic' of 1883–86 which may be called 'Late Victorian'; the awakening of a more graceful Gothic – doubtless inspired by his work for Bodley – with windows in the recessed-perpendicular-tracery vogue of the time, purer and more logical ecclesiastical interiors, and original secular works, anticipated in 1888 with Sefton Park and prevailing from *circa* 1890 to *circa* 1913; this tallies with the so-called "early modern" movement, documented by N. Pevsner in *Pioneers of the Modern Movement*, 1936;[13] and thirdly a period of slight decadence (*circa* 1914), due probably to his failing health.

The earliest recorded work, 1883, is a Catholic church, the first of many: the chapel of St Patrick in Portsmouth Road, Woolston, Hampshire.[14] In the following year came Exeter – the chancel of the church of the Sacred Heart in South Street; like many early efforts, this was done in conjunction with a local man, C. E. Ware, an engineer.[15] Started that same year, but not finished till 1913, was his first published work – Maidenhead, St Joseph, in Market Street[16] – poor work of 'Decorated' type. In 1886 having built schools in Westminster Bridge Road, for Pugin's masterpiece, St George's Cathedral, Southwark, Stokes competed unsuccessfully[17] for St James, Spanish Place. The next year saw a school at Southampton and his first town-planning essay, a sketch for improving the north side of Piccadilly Circus.[18]

Then, in 1888, his great religious and secular works began. The Church of St. Clare, at Sefton Park, Liverpool, (presumably begun 1888, finished 1890), in Arundel Avenue, has captured the imagination of architectural illustrators, even to the extent of being selected as a typical work of modern architecture in the pre-last-war *Encyclopaedia Britannica* (11th ed. ii, p. 438). The logical planning of the nave piers, with diagonal-faced roofing-shafts, the cruciform tracery of the east window, and the general loftiness and proportion place it ahead of nearly all other ecclesiastical work of the time. Equally interesting is the "house for Wilfrid Meynell, Esq., in Palace Court," presumably the "47 Palace Court Road" of later record,[19] charmingly broad, simple and balanced, and comparing well with Norman Shaw's contemporary work in the Kensington district.

The next three years saw no work on any design of prime significance; but in 1892 Stokes was busy with the planning of a second church, that for Miles Platting at Manchester, "about to be built" in that year, but never executed.[20] This is a great loss. More traditional than Sefton Park, it yet has that soaring beauty, with its oblique piers and lofty rood beam that is hard to equal.

Of the years 1893 to 1897 only Nazareth House, Bexhill, which received additions not completed until 1909, and the small church of All Souls, Park Road, Peterborough, need here be mentioned. All Souls was built in 1896;[21] Temple Moore's All Saints, further north in the same road, makes a worthy companion. The pulpit, outer rails and south chapel are Stokes's, but the ensemble is unhappily ruined by bad altar fittings. In the same year a beginning was made on the church of the Holy Ghost, Nightingale Square, Balham (near Wandsworth Common Station), still unfinished in 1927, and consecrated, with an ugly temporary west front, in 1934.[22] One town and one country house were built in 1897 – 10 Kensington Palace Gardens, and Shooter's Hill House, Pangbourne, Berkshire;[23] many others followed.

In 1898, at the late age of forty, Stokes married. His wife, Edith N. Gaine,[24] was the daughter of the General Manager of the National Telephone Company. This fact is of considerable importance in the light of his chief activities of a few years later.

The first years of his married life were the high-water mark of his professional career. In 1898 came a suburban house (No. 2 West Drive, Streatham Park, overlooking Tooting Graveney Common). 1899 brought, besides two schools at Oxford (a Board School of traditional type but with the large transomed windows afterwards characteristic of his style,[25] and a Central Boys' School[26] at Gloucester Green), additions to a farm at Worplesdon.[27] Stokes's greatest single achievement was All Saints Convent or Sisterhood at London Colney near St Albans, sometimes called Colney Chapel. The whole layout is excellent and the central entrance tower front noble and fresh;[28] it can "hardly be called stylistic, and yet is rich, balanced and sensitive." [29] The chapel on the tower front was added by Comper.

The years following the beginning of building at

2 *Leonard Stokes. St Clare's Church, Sefton Park, Liverpool (1888–90). Much of Stoke's early work was ecclesiastical; sensitive but not experimental.*

3 *Leonard Stokes. No. 47 Palace Court, Bayswater, London (1889). As original as the other house being built in the same street at the time by MacLaren, who had joined the Art Workers' Guild in the same year as Stokes (1886).*

4 *Leonard Stokes. Design for a new wing, Boxwood Court, Herefordshire (1891). During the following few years Stokes, like other architects of the Art Workers' Guild, experimented with L-shaped and other ground plans for country houses.*

5 *Leonard Stokes. Nazareth House, Bexhill, Sussex (1894). The large arched ground-floor windows remained a favourite Stokes feature throughout his career.*

6 *Leonard Stokes. Courtyard, All Saints' Convent, Shenley Road, London Colney, Herefordshire (1899–1903). Arts and Crafts Gothic as free as Edward Prior's later church at Sunderland.*

7 *Leonard Stokes. Main entrance and tower, All Saints' Convent, London Colney (1899–1903). A strong grid pattern in elevation was another key feature of many Stokes buildings.*

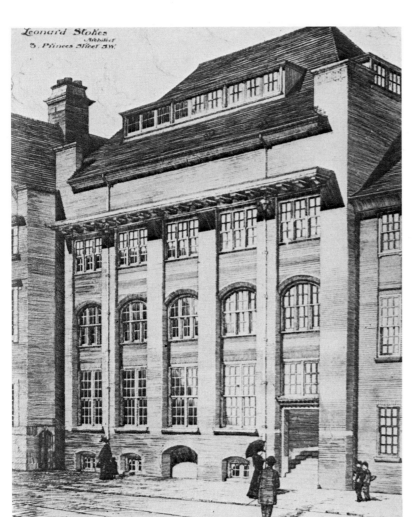

8

9

8 *Leonard Stokes. Telephone Exchange, Ogle Road, Southampton (1900, everything above second floor windows later drastically altered). One of many telephone exchanges by Stokes, experimental designs that always have roots in a historic style.*

9 *Leonard Stokes. Minterne House, Minterne Magna, Dorset (1903–05 for Lord Digby). One of the architect's most powerful compositions.*

10 *Leonard Stokes. Telephone Exchange, Gerrard Street, London (1904). A free and flamboyant design, now destroyed.*

10

London Colney are characterised by the contrast between such conventual and ecclesiastical work as Nazareth House, Southsea, designed ten years earlier[30] and St Philip's Church at Begbroke, near Oxford (1896 according to another source),[31] the latter already possessing the "massiveness of his later work";[32] and a plethora of telephone exchanges. The somewhat surprising move from churches to exchanges is paralleled at a later time by Sir Walter Tapper's transition from churches to gas-holders. These exchanges were built for the pioneering organisation, the National Telephone Company, which subsequently (1911) became nationalised as the Post Office Telephone Service.[33] They are "notable as showing how purely utilitarian buildings can be made architecturally interesting."[34] Stokes was as well qualified as any to achieve this result with distinction and restraint; it is a thousand pities he was not commissioned to design the Company's headquarters on the Victoria Embankment; the actual building has a heavily rusticated front diametrically opposed to the best trend of the time.[35] Nineteen exchanges by Stokes are recorded, and five were built or finished in 1900, including one at Reading[36] and two in Scotland. Of these the specially well sited one at Aberdeen was "still unaltered in 1935". Another big scheme was worked on in Stokes's office in the same year: his Kingsway plan, done for the L.C.C. competition.[37]

1901–03 were predominantly school years. In 1901 two for the Brompton Oratory,[38] and six others; two more followed in 1902, and in 1903 was begun a more ambitious work, the Grammar School at Lincoln, "being built" 1906. A training college, St Mary's, at Fenham, Newcastle-on-Tyne, and additions to another nunnery, Ascot Priory,[40] complete his most educational period.

His best-known telephone building, that at Gerrard Street, south of and parallel with Shaftesbury Avenue (from which it was visible), was begun in 1904; it had a pleasing front, with semi-circular arches to the ground stage, and it is a matter for lasting regret that it had to be rebuilt, for technical reasons, about 1930;[41] it is replaced by a tall and dull Renaissance front of Office of Works type. Paddington went up the same year, with an iron barrel roof, but was partly rebuilt in the '30s.

Stokes's only civic work, the additional King's Road wing (1904–08)[42] to J. M. Brydon's Chelsea Town Hall, is utterly unlike his other work, assimilated to the point of slavishness to the existing buildings (*circa* 1885 onward).[43] To appreciate this contrast the Town Hall wing should be compared with Stokes's largest country house, Minterne House, Cerne Abbas, Dorset, which seems to have been designed in the same year.[44] To 1906 belong five more telephone buildings in different parts of the country, to 1907 (or according to another source 1911) the church at Pickering, Yorkshire – St Joseph, on Potter Hill – a pleasant and sturdy group with low square tower.[45] In the same

year[46] important additions were begun to the school of Downside Abbey. These were opened in 1912[47] and form perhaps Stokes's best-known school work.[48] "With its up-to-date accommodation, the details of this fine plan are worth studying"; Bath stone was used for the exterior, which features to full effect the extensive mullioned and transomed windows so characteristic of Stokes's secular work. This type of design appears again in 1909–10 and 1911 onward in the additions to Emmanuel College, Cambridge, with moulded architraves round the window groups, giving something of a renaissance composition to motifs essentially late medieval in origin. The rock-faced or hammered squared rubble for the plain walls throws up the firm lines of the worked stone features. First Stokes inserted in the south-west corner of the Close a range of lecture-rooms, 1909–10;[49] these were presumably designed in 1908,[50] the date given for an unspecified portion. (In later years, from 1930 onwards, Mr Drysdale converted one lecture hall into a Library, and an existing Library conversely.[51]) The great work here, however, in fact one of Stokes's largest works, was the new North Court, on the far (north-west) side of Emmanuel Street, and facing to the north-east on Drummer Street; the formation here of a central bus station has made Stokes's front one of the most conspicuous college buildings in Cambridge to the public eye, though, strangely, this front does not appear to have been reproduced. Presumably designed 1910 and begun in the earlier year given, 1911,[52] it was "just completed" in 1915,[53] and published in 1913, 1915 and 1916.[54] This quad incorporated a cloister and hostel block.[55]

11 *Leonard Stokes. Downside School, near Bath, Somerset (1907–11). A typical later Stokes design, combining rationalism with powerful originality.*

Meanwhile, in 1908 Stokes was given a place on the Royal Commission on Historical Monuments, England, in its new constitution.[56] He was then Vice-President R.I.B.A., and it is hard to see that he had any other special qualification, as he did little if any restoration work. The Vice-Presidency was followed by a three year tenure of Presidency, 1910–12. Stokes during this time made great efforts for the unification of the profession (i.e. with the Society of Architects, founded in the 1880s) which bore fruit in later years; his work was gratefully referred to by H. T. Hare in 1919.[57] Also during his term of office the pioneer Town Planning Conference was held (in 1910), at which this embryo science was vigorously and internationally discussed.

Of work belonging to the same years the designs for the Admiralty Arch competition[58] and for the completion of St Wilfrid's Hall, belonging to and westward of the Brompton Oratory, [59] just behind the Cardinal Newman memorial, hold first place. The façade of St Wilfrid's Hall had to fulfil the difficult triple function of harmonising with the Victoria and Albert Museum immediately to the west, with the existing renaissance memorial by Bodley and Garner (1896)[60] in front, and with the church itself by Gribble to the east. The end façade is therefore traditional; the cornice and second floor are not yet added.

However, while he was thus busy on designing as well as administrative work of considerable interest, the first signs of his illness must have appeared,[61] a form of paralysis, which ultimately cut short his career. It had already become marked early in the first Great War. This is what Mr Drysdale writes of Stokes about that time: "Making everything into a violent effort, as he did, soon tired him out; much of that which came later looks it."[62]

Meanwhile there had come in 1913–14 the famous office block for A. Gagnière, Nos. 34–5 on the north side of Golden Square, W.1, with the old familiar deeply-moulded arches on the ground stage, a kind of ball-flower hollow carried round the first floor, and a peculiar sunk rustication to the nominal pilasters in the upper part is rather playful and perhaps somewhat worried composition.[63] In 1914 his last building was started, and one of his largest though not his greatest – Georgetown (Catholic) Cathedral in Demerara, British Guiana.[64] This is one of his few works of which scale drawings were published.[65] He "remembered every detail till the end"; it was still unfinished in 1927,[66] and has been continued by Mr Drysdale. Of 1915 only church fittings are recorded, and of 1916 a hospital for cripples, for Alton, Hampshire,[67] apparently never executed.

1919 brought the great day of his life – the bestowal of the coveted Royal Gold Medal. No record of his illness appears in the report,[68] and no explanation of the long period which had elapsed since his last published work, beyond references by H. T. Hare, then President, to an "old friend" whom he had to "greet after a lapse of some years"; but the knowledge of the position must have helped to prompt the award, made "in recognition of the merit of his executed work."[69] Hare spoke of his record as "associated with architectural works of the highest excellence and very strongly marked character" – a just and timely tribute. A selection of drawings and photographs of his work was displayed in connection with the ceremony; but unfortunately there seems no printed record to survive of this exhibition. In the same year, 1919, Stokes was joined in partnership by Mr George Drysdale.

The partnership went on for another six years, until on Christmas Day in 1925 Stokes passed away in his house, No. 3 Mulberry Walk, Chelsea.[70]

It remains to add a few remarks about his treatment of detail. His mouldings, and especially archivolt sections, were the most original of his time; the tablet flower in a wave moulding in the Folkestone design is interesting as a new use of traditional detail, and his junctions of roofing shaft, arch and pier at Peterborough and Balham at once strike the eye on entering. His mouldings "were bold and vigorous .. he had a wish always to design new shapes,"[71] though "he rather overdid it at times; he . . . always drew the contours himself."[72] "He took extraordinary care over the

12 *Leonard Stokes. Office building, Nos. 34–36 Golden Square, Soho, London (1913–14). A rational use of the architect's typical round-arched windows below a firm grid pattern.*

smallest detail" said a Lord Mayor. "His colour sense was not highly developed, nor did carving or sculpture greatly appeal to him"; "the design seemed to be made before it reached the paper stage."[73]

As to his private life and character, he had his office in the early days at 31 Spring Gardens, London S.W.1,[74] but at the time of his death at 17 Buckingham Street, Strand.[75] His clubs were the Arts and Chelsea Arts.[76] He wrote no books and hardly any publication has appeared under his name.[77] He "never seemed to feel the necessity for what we call 'hobbies'"[78] but his part in community affairs is shown by the fact that he was for some years on the Westminster City Council.[79] In later years he tended to be explosive and irritable.[80] He "had a kind heart and more than ingenuous tongue and he hated anything in the way of pose or inefficiency and had no use for fools. . . . He was no respecter of persons and seemed to prefer a good carpenter to an indifferent noble Lord. . . ."[81]

His published portraits reflect these traits: the first, 1890 or earlier,[82] shows him a comparatively young and genial man: another, published in 1919 on the presentation of the Gold Medal but evidently earlier,[83] is front-faced, and shows him firm and serious, possibly a pose; the presidential portrait by Sir William Orpen, *circa* 1910,[84] is also full-faced, a rather scowling figure, standing with clasped hands in a dressing-gown – a circumstance commented on by Hare in 1919.[85]

Whether Stokes, apart from his pupil and partner, Mr Drysdale, and his son, Mr David Stokes, had any followers it is hard to say; the process of simplification and insistence on structural honesty known as the Modern Movement, especially in its international and extreme forms, had made headway independent of his work. Nevertheless, he helped to blaze the general trail and his contribution will prove lasting, beyond vogues and verbiage, beyond our day.

[1] pp.88, 91 illus. p.90.

[2] pp.48, 51. Stokes is, however, not mentioned in Muthesius's *Die Englische Baukunst der Gegenwart* of 1900.

[3] *cf* his well-known Palace Theatre (formerly Hippodrome) in Charing Cross Road, and City Bank on Ludgate Hill (illus. in Statham, *Modern Architecture*, p.256; Muthesius, *Die Englische Baukunst der Gegenwart* title page; *Encyclopaedia Britannica* 11th ed. ii, p.440). Succeeding to his mannerism was R. Huntly Gordon, one of whose pleasant fronts graces Parliament Street (see *Architecture and Building News* 23 June 1944. Leonard Martin stands apart as the apostle of prevailing verticality (see *The Builder* 29 January 1943, p.106), producing at gable level "an effect of joinery" (W.E. Davis).

[4] Pevsner, *Pioneers*, p.154.

[5] *Who was Who*, 1916–28, 1929, p.1003.

[6] *The Builder*, 1926.

[7] He died in 1935, see *Who was Who*.

[8] *Journal of the Royal Institute of British Architecture* 9 January 1926, p.148.

[9] The main facts printed in this article are from *The Times*, reprinted in *The Builder*, 1 January 1926, and *Journal of the Royal Institute of British Architects loc cit.*

[10] M. B. Adams, *Archts. Geo. IV–V*, *Journal of the Royal Institute of British Architects* 1912, p.651.

[11] He is not mentioned in Street's "account of the restoration" in the published report. (Street, E. Seymour & Sir T. Martin, *Cathedral of the Holy Trinity*, 1882).

[12] The 'Soane Silver Medal,' 1882, spoken of in the *Building News* account, 21 March 1890, p.405, seems an error.

[13] *cf.* also *The Builder* 29 January 1943, p.105, etc.

[14] "A school chapel" in one source.

[15] *Building News*, 1890; C. W. Ware according to another source. Not his "earliest work," by another.

[16] *The Builder* 25 October 1884, p.570.

[17] *ibid* 22 May 1886, pl.

[18] *ibid* 26 March 1887, p.484.

[19] *ibid* 11 September 1897, p.203.

[20] *ibid* 15 October 1892, plan p.302, pl. p.303; *Journal of the Royal Institute of British Architects* 1927, p.166; *Academy Architecture*, 1892.

[21] *Academy Architecture* 1895.

[22] *The Architectural Review* Vol I 1897, pp.52–54, pl. p.53; dated 1897 by another source.

[23] *Academy Architecture* 1898, Part 1.

[24] *Who was Who*, 1916–28, p.1003.

[25] *The Builder* 18 May 1901.

[26] *ibid* 25 January 1902; *Academy Architecture* 1901, Part 1.

[27] *The Builder* 18 November 1899, p.466; "Sud" in Drysdale's list, "Soot" in *The Builder* and *Academy Architecture* 1899, Part 2.

[28] *The Builder* 3 February and 15 September 1900. In partnership with G. T. Hine. *cf* also *Academy Architecture* Part 2 1899, Part 1 1900 and *Journal of the Royal Institute of British Architects* 1927, p.170.

[29] *The Builder* 29 January 1943, p.105.

[30] *Building News* obituary.

[31] The "Sefton Park, St Begbroke" of *Who was Who* is a mistake.

[32] Drysdale, p.168.

[33] Information kindly supplied by Mr M. C. Pink, late Deputy Controller.

[34] Hare in *Journal of the Royal Institute of British Architects* 1919.

[35] *The Builder* 25 January 1902.

[36] *The Architectural Review* Vol. XXIII 1908, pp.313–314.

[37] *The Builder* 17 November 1900, pls. pseudonymous and unidentifiable; *Academy Architecture* Part 2, 1901.

[38] Boys', *Journal of the Royal Institute of British Architects* 1927, p.173 (ext.).

[39] *The Builder* 3 February 1906, p.120 and pl.; *Academy Architecture* Part 1, 1905.

[40] *Ibid* Part 1, 1902.

[41] *The Builder* 20 March 1930.

[42] *The Architectural Review* Vol. XXV, 1909, pp.150, etc., views pp.151–152; *The Builder* 13 November 1909; *Academy Architecture* Part 2 1905, Part 1 1909. Not whole building as implied in *Who was Who*. Brydon, who died in 1901, was a close personal friend of Stokes, which doubtless explains why Stokes kept to the earlier style.

[43] *The Builder* 2 May 1885, pp.618 etc.

[44] *Academy Architecture* Part 2 1904, Part 1 1905; *The Architectural Review* Vol. XXV 1909.

[45] Illus., *Journal of the Royal Institute of British Architects* 1927, p.167.

[46] *Drysdale* list, only date; *Academy Architecture* Part 1 1911.

[47] Dom Ethelbert Horne in R.I.B.A., British Architect's Conference, Bath (guide), 1928, pp.97–8.

[48] Illus. *Journal of the Royal Institute of British Architects* 1927, ext. p.163, dormitory int. p.171.

[49] J. Willis Clark, *Concise guide to . . . Cambridge*, 10th ed., 1933, p.92.

[50] Drysdale list.

[51] Willis Clark, and R.I.B.A. Handbook of British Architects' Conference, Cambridge, 1933 (prefixed to Clark), p.16.

[52] *Academy Architecture* Part 1 1910; Drysdale list.

[53] *The Architectural Review* Vol. XXXVIII 1915, p.36.

[54] *The Builder* 19 December 1913, Pl. and plan; *The Architectural Review* ante, pp.36–37 and pl.; *The Builder* 28 July 1916, Pls. and plan.

[55] *The Builder* ditto, p.54, ext.

[56] *Who was Who*; R.C.H.M. *Westminster Abbey*, 1924, pp.x–xi.

[57] *The Architects' Journal* 1919, p.202.

[58] *The Builder* 15 October 1910, p.414.

[59] *The Builder* 2 December 1910, 2nd-floor plan and pl.; *Academy Architecture* 1911.[1]

[60] Muirhead, *Blue Guide to London*.

[61] "14 years before his death," Drysdale, p.168, i.e., 1911.

[62] Letter to the present writer.

[63] Drysdale, p.174.

[64] *The Builder* 13 November 1914, Pl., ext. (design), 7 May 1915, Pl. int. (design). Dedication unfound. *cf.* St George's (Anglican), *Country Life* 10 November 1945.

[65] Plan, secn. and ext., *Journal of the Institute of British Architects* pp.168–169.

[66] Drysdale, p.173.

[67] *The Builder* 5 May 1916, aerial view; *Academy Architecture* 1916.[1]

[68] *Journal of the Royal Institute of British Architects* July 1919, pp.201, etc.

[69] *ibid* March 1919, p.119.

[70] *The Builder* 1 January 1926, p.7, etc; No. of house in *Who was Who*.

[71] Drysdale, p.164.

[72] Ditto – personal information.

[73] Drysdale, pp.166–167.

[74] *The Builder* 25 October 1884, p.570.

[75] R.I.B.A. *Kalendar*, 1924–25.

[76] *Who was Who*.

[77] The *British Architect* in 1893, p.149, *cf.* pp.165–6, printed his unfavourable views on the architectural legitimacy of terracotta; *The Builder*, in 1899, May 6, p.449, a letter of complaint about the architectural limitations of the Royal Academy.

[78] Drysdale, *The Architects' Journal* 1927, p.164.

[79] Drysdale, *ibid* 1927, p.174.

[80] Personal information.

[81] Mr Drysdale, personal information.

[82] *Building News*, 21 March 1890.

[83] *Journal of the Royal Institute of British Architects* July 1919, opp. 201.

[84] Oil painting at R.I.B.A.; photographic print in Library.

[85] *Journal of the Royal Institute of British Architects* 1919, p.203.

Edgar Wood and J. Henry Sellers: A Decade of Partnership and Experiment

by John Archer

Many of the Arts and Crafts architects felt technically unable to cope with the challenge of the steel frames and concrete that were new materials at the beginning of the century. But this was not true of Edgar Wood (1860–1935) who had an established Arts and Crafts practice around Manchester. *Circa* 1904 he took a new partner, J. Henry Sellers (1861–1954) and subsequently they built a succession of flat, concrete-roofed buildings that were among the the most advanced designs of their time in Europe. John Archer, who has done much research on Wood, here gives a fine account of their partnership.

The partnership between Edgar Wood and James Henry Sellers produced a group of buildings so unusual and original that questions of authorship and the respective influence of each partner are inevitable. It appears to have been more a personal than a business relationship which existed between Wood and Sellers, being essentially informal in character, and over the years it changed according to their needs. From its commencement, probably about 1904, each partner was professionally experienced: Wood was then forty-four and Sellers forty-three. Initially the partnership was apparently little more than an arrangement whereby the two men shared office accommodation and discussed their respective projects. Later is assumed the title of a formal partnership, but when in 1908 *The British Architect* incorrectly attributed a design to Wood he responded quickly in a succinct letter:

> "In the sketches you illustrated in your last number . . . you attributed the work to me. It was the work of Mr J. H. Sellers, who works with me on many buildings under the title of Edgar Wood and Sellers."[1]

Few such works have been discovered and it was the partners' more general practice for each to work independently under his own name.

Wood and Sellers appear to have met in 1903–04 and remained friends until Wood's death in 1935. Their period of closest practical collaboration was in the first decade of partnership, and this was extremely fertile for both men, especially up to 1910. Then Wood became financially independent through a substantial legacy and began to devote more time to painting and travel and less to the practice. Between 1910 and the beginning of the First World War in 1914, which virtually ended most private building, independent works by Wood are certainly less common. After the war Wood produced little, and finally retired to Italy about 1922. Sellers continued practising for about another twenty-five years, and even in 1953 the partners' plate remained outside their office at 78 King Street, Manchester.

Both men were native of the north Manchester industrial hinterland. Wood was born in 1860 at Middleton, a cotton-spinning town five miles from Manchester, and Sellers in 1861 at Oldham, the neighbouring town about three miles distant. Physical proximity and a shared environment were about all they had in common, because socially and professionally their early experiences were in marked contrast. Wood came from a well-to-do, middle-class family.

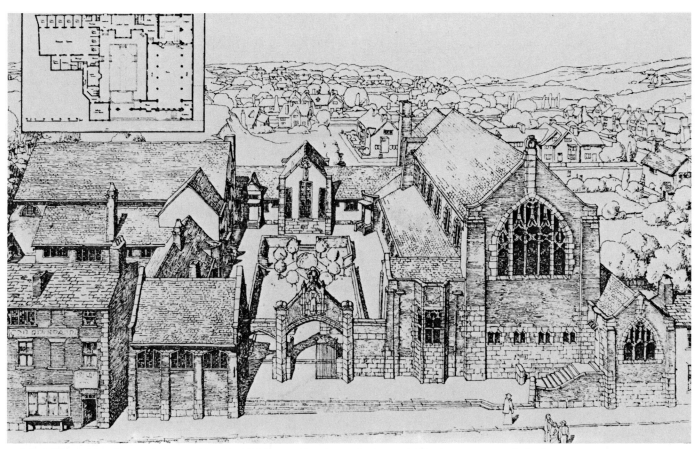

3 *Edgar Wood. Long Street Methodist Church, Middleton, Manchester (1899–1901). Wood was very much the flamboyant artist-architect, especially in his early years, when he was a leading light of the Arts and Crafts Movement in northern England.*

1 *Portrait of Edgar Wood.* **2** *Portrait of J. Henry Sellers.*

successful in business and prominent socially. His boyhood ambition was to be an artist but his father intended that he should enter the family cotton business. Architecture was agreed upon as combining creativity and professional respectability and Wood was articled to James Murgatroyd, of the large Manchester firm of Mills and Murgatroyd, and rapidly discovered that creativity came off second best. He qualified by examination in 1885 and commenced independent practice immediately. Within five years he had gained substantial commissions and opened offices at Middleton and Oldham. By 1893 his main office was in Manchester, and he was executing work in south-east Lancashire and the West Riding generally. He served their textile communities at all levels and was a noted exponent of the Arts and Crafts Movement. His particular *forte* was the revival of the vernacular tradition of his home region, the Pennine foothills, as shown in the house 'Barcroft', Rochdale, of 1894 or in the Long Street Wesleyan Church of 1899–1901, at Middleton, but he paid respect to regional vernacular character wherever he built throughout his career. Wood practised as a craftsmen, drew regularly from nature and followed artistic and architectural precepts drawn from Ruskin and Morris with enthusiasm. An ebullient personality, he enjoyed a Bohemian disregard for orthodoxy, particularly in dress, preferring tweeds, knickerbockers and a cloak to a dark suit and, above all, he utterly despised commercial architectural practice. As an artist-architect his work is highly individual, and his staff consisted of G. A. E. Schwabe, an assistant whom he had trained as a pupil, and an office-boy. By 1904, Wood's reputation was well established and he was recognised amongst the contemporary *avant-garde* by the German critic, Hermann Muthesius (1861–1927), fittingly described by W. R. Lethaby as the "historian . . . of the English free architecture."[2]

Sellers, a year younger than Wood, came from more humble origins, and his introduction to his profession was as office-boy to a local architect, Thomas Boyter of Oldham. After training himself to become a proficient draughtsman Sellers became an itinerant assistant and gained experience in Liverpool, London, Birmingham and York, where he worked for W. J. Penty. He found living in York a memorable experience and often remarked on this, saying "It helped me wonderfully living in an old city like York, full of beautiful old work".[3] Sellers attributed his interest in classical architecture to his years there and he particularly admired Georgian work. This was in the early '90s when the Georgian Revival was gaining momentum.

The ambition which fired Sellers may be gauged from his frequent movements, and from the schemes he successfully submitted for exhibition to the Royal Academy or to periodicals for publication.[4] After a second spell with Penty at York, Sellers became assistant county architect for Cumberland, possibly about 1893 (his memory for dates was uncertain), working and living in Carlisle. The county architect was George Dale Oliver, and he maintained both private and public practices simultaneously. Sellers was employed in both and later described himself in these years as "an architectural ghost". Oliver was responsible for numerous buildings in Cumberland and Northumberland and Sellers 'ghosted' several banks and various school buildings. None of the known designs ranks very high architecturally and no strictly classical example has been discovered. Some are loose and picturesque arrangements of assorted classical motifs, drawn from the repertoires of architects such as E. R. Robson, J. J. Stevenson, Norman Shaw and John Belcher, whereas others are more Tudorish. A bank at Hexham (1896) is a notable illustration of the former type.

At about 1900 Sellers left Carlisle after a disagreement with Oliver and returned to Oldham where he went into partnership with David Jones, who had a substantial but conventional practice in the town. The first record at Oldham of their work is dated 6 May 1901, and is a design for two villas in Abbey Hills Road.[5] The following month they submitted an application to extend Manor House, standing nearby, and in 1903 a further scheme for a house extension in Alexandra Park. Sellers claimed responsibility for these designs which were executed for the proprietors of an expanding firm of ironworkers, Dronsfield Brothers of Oldham.

4 *G. D. Oliver with J. Henry Sellers as assistant. Midland Bank Chambers, Hexham, Northumberland (1896).*

374

5 *Edgar Wood. First Church of Christ Scientist, Victoria Park, Manchester (1903–08). This drawing was published in 1904.*

Sellers arranged for the finished buildings to be professionally photographed by Charles Jackson, of Middleton, who knew Wood well and told him that he had "met an architect who could design a house for a gentleman". Wood met Sellers, visited the houses, one of which had a flat-roofed extension with the roof in reinforced concrete, and this commenced their association. From entries in plan registers it is known that Sellers left Jones and joined Wood between November 1903 and November 1905. No more accurate date for the commencement of their partnership has been obtained.

Wood and Sellers were men of contrasting temperament. Wood, the more volatile, regarded architecture as an art; a means of personal expression and experiment. He had a strong flair for design and a great interest in new forms and developments. Sellers also regarded architecture as an art but was studious and analytical. A great reader, he was deeply interested in architectural history and classicism. In discussions in the early 1950s, he linked his interest in reinforced concrete with historic principles of construction,

Gothic vaulting for example, and he greatly admired W. R. Lethaby as an architectural writer. He disclaimed any suggestion that he had first embarked upon reinforced-concrete construction for abstract theoretical reasons, and recalled that he selected the material because he was building on steeply sloping ground and had been instructed to avoid blocking the view of the house overlooking his site, but there can be no doubt that he and Wood came to appreciate the wider potentialities of the new material, which in 1903 in England was used primarily for utilitarian structure only. Different concrete systems were advertised in the architectural press and the new material was sufficiently publicised for it to have been quite obvious that it was an important new constructional method and one ripe for architectural experiment.

G. A. E. Schwabe, who remained with Wood and Sellers until 1910, described in a letter the effect of the arrival of Sellers on Wood and his practice. He wrote:

"It gave him [Wood] an insight into the beauty of Greek Work, and in planning, the lay out in the grand manner, working for long views and vistas and also an approach to design from a constructional point of view. He started to go in for competitions, such as the London County Hall, National Museum of Wales and similar big work, all under Sellers' guidance. Everything was discussed at length, but Wood stuck to his own jobs. Wood's work began to develop on these new lines with the same old enthusiasm. He never got in a rut but was always hounding some new ideal."[6]

This account was partly confirmed in conversations with Sellers, who said that each partner was responsible for his own work but that he and Wood discussed their work fully. They shared the facilities of the office and, presumably, Schwabe worked for both of them. Sellers was very keen to win a major competition but there is no architectural evidence to suggest that Wood contributed significantly to these, and the character of the designs suggests that Sellers was responsible for them. At the Royal Academy in 1911 the design for the Art Gallery and Museum at Cardiff was exhibited solely under the name of Sellers. Not a single strictly formal building can be traced to Wood throughout this period. What Schwabe did not touch upon is the influence of Wood upon Sellers. Clearly Sellers benefited professionally by an association with an

6 *Edgar Wood. Detail, First Church of Christ Scientist, Manchester. One of the most attractive of the Arts and Crafts church designs, now sadly dilapidated.*

architect with Wood's reputation, but just as Wood's work changed as Schwabe describes, so Sellers' work became lighter, more consistent and controlled. This may have been a consequence of his enthusiasm for Greek art and architecture, then being popularised by scholars such as Percy and Ernest Gardner, but may have developed from Wood's example, vitality and personal flair. Between 1906 and 1914, with the exception of the competition designs, there are close affinities in their most significant independent works. Sellers's design of 1906 for Dronsfield's offices, Oldham, shows a remarkable change from any known earlier work by him. The Collcutt-like exuberant effervescence of his earlier projects has evaporated entirely in this restrained, well-proportioned, symmetrical design. There is no overt suggestion of Greek classicism in its detailing, but in simplicity of outline, orderly disposition of masses, and refinement of detail there is evidence of a fresh inspiration, as though gained from a return to pure classical sources. To resist atmospheric pollution the building is clad in polished grey granite and green-glazed brick, both being virtually self-cleansing. Consequently, the detailing of the building remained permanently legible and effective. The corners of the main blocks are emphasised by inset quadrants, and throughout the detailing is characterised by primary geometrical forms. The large windows at first-floor level and other details are unmistakably reminiscent of Mackintosh's Glasgow School of Art of 1897, both buildings are divided from the street by a carefully designed screen of railings. At Dronsfield's these are a singularly handsome feature of the design and, executed in cast-iron made at Coalbrookdale, add to the sense of quality and richness pervading the design. Of the independent commissions by Sellers this is the most powerful and is the classic of his architectural career.

The principal competition entries by Sellers in this period, for the National Museum of Wales in 1910 and the County Hall, London, in 1912 are less uncompromisingly modern than the design for Dronsfields and conform to the 'Grand Manner' then popular. Both are columnar but reflect the austerity of Neo-classicism rather than the customary lavishness of the Edwardian classical revival.

The last major work by Wood prior to the partnership with Sellers was the First Church of Christ, Scientist, Manchester, commenced in 1903 but not finally completed until 1908. It is probably his best-known building and has been described by Nikolaus Pevsner as "one of the most original buildings of that time in England or indeed anywhere . . ." He added "one can hardly drive originality and wilfulness farther, unless one is called Gaudi."[7] The unconventional forms created severely tax traditional materials and construction, and Wood carried this mode of innovation no further: the First Church has no direct sequel.

It seems probable that Wood quickly grasped the architectural significance of Sellers's application of

7 *J. Henry Sellers (in partnership with Edgar Wood). Dronsfield Bros. office building, Oldham, Lancashire (1906–07). A bold design, pioneering concrete flat roof construction. A key building in the development of a rational architecture in England.*

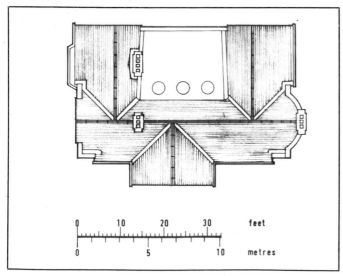

8 *J. Henry Sellers. Detail of Doorway, Dronsfield building, Oldham (1906–07).*

9 *Edgar Wood. No. 121 Park Road, Hale, Cheshire (1906).*

10 *Edgar Wood. Roof plan, No. 121 Park Road, Hale. A combination of concrete flat-roof construction with pitched roofs.*

concrete construction and was attracted by this rather than his classicism. Wood can never be regarded as a classicist. From 1906 axial principles are evident in his planning, but he seldom pursued strict symmetry and only in housing layouts is it a major element in his designs. No sudden changes occur in his work as a result of the partnership. He continued to build traditionally but with more restraint than in the First Church, and classical detail, freely adapted from conventional forms superseded the curvilinear New Art motifs of his earlier years, but classicism remained much subservient to vernacular character which continued to serve as a major expressive theme. Neither did Wood embark upon experimental forms of construction precipitately, but initially he combined concrete flat-roof construction with pitched roofs to simplify construction, as at 121 Park Road, Hale, Cheshire (1906).

In 1907 Wood followed the lead given the previous year by Sellers with the Dronsfield building by designing a house entirely roofed by reinforced concrete. Built at Barley, near Royston, Hertfordshire, for a retired textile manufacturer, 'Dalny Veed' uses flat-roof construction but in a design of markedly different character from Sellers's forerunner. The following year Wood built a very similar house, 'Upmeads', at Stafford for Frederick Bostock of Lotus, the shoe company. As this house received considerable attention in the contemporary architectural press, and has remained almost unaltered, it is the more profitable example to study, but in all major respects the two houses are broadly alike.

'Upmeads' stands on a southern slope facing Cannock Chase. The length of the plot runs approximately north-south and the house is situated at its northern end, with the length of the garden dividing it from the road. The main entrance faces north as do the kitchen and service rooms. The main living-rooms and bedrooms face south overlooking the garden, which is laid out in a series of terraces and neatly rectangular lawns and beds, all defined by walls, hedges or changes in level, and therefore carefully articulated. The entrance drive lies along the eastern edge of the site and is screened by a hedge. The entrance forecourt is formal and its axiality is emphasised by a tall inset panel placed centrally in a wide concave arc in the frontage and rising above the main entrance. In this 'Upmeads' differs from 'Dalny Veed', where the entrance front is similarly organised but with the entrance set in a broad, recessed, flat panel of brickwork. The more elaborate entrance of 'Upmeads' may reflect a growing penchant for formalism, or merely a more affluent client. Both houses are planned about a central, two-storeyed, vaulted hall, overlooked by a balcony at first-floor level. The principal axis extends in both cases through the main entrance and hall, via a series of terraces, to the garden, but the variously shaped rooms, whilst observing both this and a cross-axis, do not rigidly conform to symmetry. In external treatment too the houses are equally free in their interpretation of axial principles, almost as though Wood relished creating asymmetry within a formal framework. This latitude in design, expressed with considerable verve and sophistication, was never attempted by Sellers. A drawing of the entrance front of 'Upmeads' was exhibited at the Royal Academy in 1908 and drew sarcastic fire from *The Builder*,[8] but only because it was thought that the house appeared under-lit. In 1910 'Upmeads' was included in *Small Country Houses of To-day*,[9] edited by Lawrence Weaver. Although likened to architecture in Laputa, it was observed that "Upmeads cannot fail, by its logical qualities, and . . . originality, to rivet the attention of everyone and the admiration of not a few."[10] The article presents Wood's views on the advantages of the flat roof: it permitted an irregular form giving greater freedom in planning; he believed weather proofing would be easier and roof drainage and maintenance facilitated; the roof would provide an additional out-door living-room in summer and its elevation above the garden provided both an overall view of the garden, which, wrote Weaver, "lies open beneath one's eyes like an unrolled map",[11] and a wider prospect over the landscape beyond. These ideas anticipate by twenty years the arguments advanced by the modernist propagandists for flat-roofed construction. Whether they were Wood's, Sellers's, or a result of their joint discussion, which seems most probable, is not known, but Wood made the bolder experiments in domestic design. In addition to the houses mentioned, Wood carried out three smaller schemes along similar lines. One of these is a row of shops at Middleton, designed by February, 1908, and the others are a house at Burnley (1908) and one at 36 Mellalieu Street, Middleton, built in 1910. He also designed two unexecuted housing schemes with flat-roofed construction, one being for Hampstead Garden Suburb.[12] The design for the shops is significant because it marks a further development in Wood's work: the introduction of external tiling in multi-coloured, patterned panels. Wood always had shown an uncommon passion for colour, pattern, and decoration in general. Previously this had always been manifested in interior design but on these shops, built in the centre of Middleton, an extensive panel of tiles, patterned in green and white chevrons, extends above each shopfront to the coping of the parapet of the flat roof. This unusual feature is sometimes mistaken for a period-piece of the 1930s. Wood exhibited a charming rendered drawing of the design at the Royal Academy the same year and in this instance *The Builder*'s critic passed favourable judgement, observing that Wood "is nothing if not original", and that "No one would pass the front of this building without turning to look at it."[13] The origin of the idea is uncertain. The well-known house by Halsey Ricardo, 8 Addison Road, London, illustrating the architectural use of colour, dates from

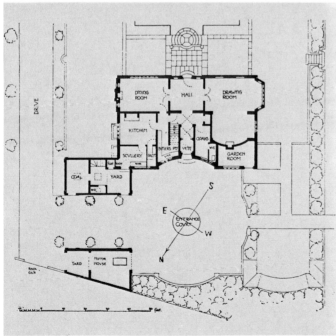

11 *Edgar Wood. Entrance front, 'Upmeads', Newport Road, Stafford (1908). Entirely roofed by flat reinforced concrete, the house is one of an impressive series of progressive designs produced by the two partners.*

12 *Edgar Wood. Plan of 'Upmeads'.*

13 *Edgar Wood. Garden frontage, 'Upmeads'. The lower right-hand window's cill has been lowered since original building.*

14 *Edgar Wood. Design for shops for Middleton, Manchester (1908). The tiled panels are decorated with green and white chevrons. The building survives altered.*

1906 and was exhibited at the Royal Academy in 1907, but there is no similarity between it and Wood's design except in the use of self-cleansing ceramic material. Sellers did not use tiles in this way but designed as an exhibition stand a domed structure for Messrs Pilkington, and the tiled cladding of this corresponds closely to Wood's design on the shops. It was the misattribution of this work which was the occasion of Wood's letter to *The British Architect*[14] referring to its authorship. It is possible that this use of colour was developed by Wood through his travels in Italy, because his sketches abound in notes on decorative finishes in marble and mosaic, but Bentley's great Westminster Cathedral may also have been a potent influence in leading him to experiment with materials providing permanent colour for decorative purposes, as is illustrated by the later additions (1907–08) to the First Church, which include handsome screens of marble and mosaic.

Three major schemes were produced under the joint names of the partners. Two of these, both schools at Middleton designed in 1908, can be attributed principally to Sellers and were exhibited under his name at the Royal Academy in 1908 and 1911 respectively.[15] The remaining one, a garden-suburb type development at Droylsden, near Manchester, was possibly a truly joint enterprise. The schools, in Elm Street and Durnford Street, are substantial and were the first educational buildings commissioned by the incorporated borough. In several respects they are unusually advanced, especially when compared with typical contemporary Board schools. They are planned with an obvious regard for orientation, the minimum number of classrooms have a northern aspect, and natural ventilation. Also, covered play areas, screen walls and planting are included as integral elements in the designs. Both functionally and in the creation of a humane environment the schools appear to reflect liberal and progressive ideas in education, matched by notable modernity in architectural expression. Sellers exploited the flat-roofed construction to serve planning purposes, juxtaposing blocks of different height and extending arms of single-storey construction to separate playgrounds, dividing children by age or sex. Symmetry provided a means of achieving the then customary segregation of the sexes, but also was consistently pursued by Sellers as an architectural aim. The detailing of the blocks is in Sellers' highly personal manner and has the same emphasis upon abstract geometry, e.g. in the stocky towers to each school, as has been observed in his Dronsfield building. Nikolaus Pevsner has described this as "un-period and anti-period",[16] and John Summerson, who cited the schools as examples in his paper "The British Contemporaries of Frank Lloyd Wright", referred to such characteristics as "mannered modernity" when discussing designs of the period by Charles Holden (1875–1960), J. J. Joass (1868–1952), and C. R. Mackintosh (1868–1928).[17] They are prominent in Sellers's work and vary from massive strength, in stressing cubic form, to quirky weakness in inexplicably creating shallow indentations in parapets. Sellers greatly admired Neoclassicists such as Soane and Cockerell, and his zeal for geometric form may be partly attributed to this, in which case modernity and classical revivalism merge in one expression.

The housing estate designed by Wood and Sellers in

15 *Edgar Wood and J. Henry Sellers. Elm Street School, Middleton, Manchester (1908–10). Sellers probably played the principal part in the design of the two schools.*

16 *Edgar Wood and J. Henry Sellers. Durnford Street School, Middleton, Manchester (1908–10). The flat concrete roof construction of both schools is well exploited by the plan.*

1913 adjoins an 18th-century Moravian settlement of considerable distinction, and relates to it successfully. The layout with its informality and skilful adjustment to the site, seems peculiarly typical of Wood, but the immaculately detailed neo-Georgian houses are unquestionably the work of Sellers. Although an attractive scheme, it does not throw more light on the partnership.

The final work designed by Wood before the outbreak of the First World War was a house for his own use at 224 Hale Road, Hale, Cheshire. It is one of his most extreme statements and the architectural concept is carried far beyond normal conventions. A high degree of formalism is combined with plasticity and, as with the First Church, the stretching of means to formal ends even seems to reach the point of Expressionism. Three of the main elevations are concave on plan: a direct expression of the freedom bestowed by concrete construction, but no attempt is made to exploit the structural possibilities of reinforced concrete by means of cantilevers or exceptionally wide spans. The tradition of architecture expressing stability and shelter precluded such effects, and neither Wood nor Sellers ever attempted to display structural gymnastics. Similarly, their interior spaces are designed as sequences of self-contained units, and those at Wood's house are formal in character and are planned with great complexity because the circular motif is repeated in a central hall and elsewhere. Bold arabesques, apparently anticipating the jazz modern, decorate the interior and exterior. Most striking of all is a coloured, tiled panel placed centrally on the front elevation enframing but superimposed above the main entrance, in which the front door is panelled and painted with the same zig-zag patterns. The drive and garden paths echo the

motifs of the diamond and chevron in brick paving and stone flags. Inside the house they are repeated on doors in rich colours and gilt, and their effect is still sumptuous. Much of this decoration, and the laying out of the garden, was carried out by Wood personally during the inactive days forced on the practice by the First World War and Wood retained the interests of an artist-craftsman throughout his life. His enjoyment of the unconventional is recalled by W. C. Young who knew him in 1920. He recalls that it amused Wood, when taking a cab home from his local station, to tell the cabby to take him to "the ugliest house in Hale". Fortunately the house has been well cared for and remains little altered.

In reviewing and interpreting the Wood-Sellers partnership it is evident that Wood gained immensely from it and it adds a major chapter to his career. It was Sellers who introduced reinforced concrete and axial planning and who first gave powerful emphasis to cubic forms. Furthermore, he seems to have grasped these as a direct result of study, reading and architectural acumen. It seems an irony that he was so unsuccessful in innumerable competitions, and it is probable that to some extent he was professionally dependent upon Wood. The evidence of Sellers's influence upon Wood's work is most positive, particularly because so much is known about Wood's earlier career. It is more difficult to assess Wood's influence upon Sellers. Wood's architectural development illustrates continuous movement and experiment. Many of the ideas he adopted were drawn from diverse sources but he showed a marked capacity to develop them to a high degree, having assimilated them within his personal style, and this is clear from his works in the various Arts and Crafts modes which he developed in

17

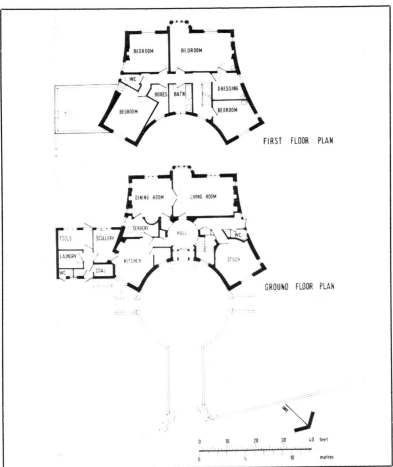

FIRST FLOOR PLAN

GROUND FLOOR PLAN

18

20

17 *Edgar Wood. No. 36 Mellalieu Street, Middleton, Manchester (1910). The flat reinforced concrete roof used for a small town house.*

18 *Edgar Wood. Plan of Royd House, No. 224 Hale Road, Hale, Cheshire (1914–16).*

19 *Edgar Wood. Main Entrance, Royd House. Bold coloured tiling seems to anticipate the Jazz Modern of the 1920s.*

20 *Edgar Wood. Interior, Royd House. Furnished by Wood as his own home, circa 1916–22.*

19

the decade preceding the partnership. He was, perhaps, essentially an interpretative artist, perpetually seeking fresh expression, and not a creator of abstract architectural concepts, but in so successfully developing the ideas he acquired from Sellers it is likely that at least he gave an intense stimulus to Sellers in return. Schwabe referred to Wood's "immense energy and great driving force to everyone he came in contact with" and also mentioned how in the office "everything was discussed at length".[18] There is no record of these discussions but the arguments Wood advanced for the use of the flat roof may be one of their products. It is significant that the ideas which he made explicit in explaining 'Upmeads' are of the kind implicit in the design of the Middleton schools. Although the architectural expression is different, there is discernible in both a common and advanced attitude towards function which is consistent with that also found in Wood's earlier domestic work: Wood was far more than an able stylist. The key to the partnership is not seen as a matter of more stylistic attribution but may well lie in the exchange of ideas and in the quality of architectural thought generated in the discussions shared by Wood and Sellers. This illuminates the works of both men in this period. It is clear that the partnership was a vital force to both its members; after Wood's retirement Sellers turned more towards the neo-Georgian and, with one or two notable exceptions and with these more generally in furniture design, became more conventional.

W. R. Lethaby captures something of the radical spirit abroad in the Edwardian decade in the title he gave to a paper delivered before the R.I.B.A. in 1910, 'The Architecture of Adventure'. The work of the partnership of Wood and Sellers from 1904 to 1914, with its rational, experimental quality and mature but extraordinarily bold expression, is manifestly of this order.

[1] *The British Architect* Vol. 70, 1908, p.185. The sketches, or exhibition stands for the Pilkington Tile & Pottery Co. Ltd. shown at the Franco-British Exhibition, appear on p.159. The stands are described as "one of the most artistic subjects in the exhibition."

[2] *Form in Civilisation* 1922, p.100.

[3] The writer knew Sellers from about 1948.

[4] Before joining Wood, Sellers exhibited at the Academy in 1891, 1892, 1896 and 1897. Examples of his work in journals may be seen in *The British Architect* Vol. 23, 1885, pp.102, 114–115, and Vol. 24, 1885, pp.30–31, 126–127, and 180–181.

[5] Oldham Corporation Plan Register.

[6] Letter to the writer dated 12 April 1950.

[7] *The Buildings of England: South Lancashire* Penguin Books Ltd., London 1969, p.322.

[8] Vol. 94, 1908, p.666.

[9] *Op cit* pp.202–207.

[10] *ibid* p.202.

[11] *ibid* p.205.

[12] See *The Builder* Vol. 98, 1910, p.297.

[13] Vol. 94, 1908, p.629.

[14] See p.1.

[15] Both are indexed under 'Sellers' at the Royal Academy and were published under his name in *Academy Architecture* (Vols. 38 and 39 respectively).

[16] *The Buildings of England: South Lancashire* Penguin Books Ltd., London 1969, p.349.

[17] *Studies in Western Art* Princeton N.J., 1963, Vol. IV, p.84.

[18] Letter to the writer dated 12 April 1950.

Charles Holden's Early Works

by Nikolaus Pevsner

In 1899 H. Percy Adams, an architect well-established in hospital design, employed a young assistant called Charles Holden (1875–1960). Holden was fresh from a year working for C. R. Ashbee and he soon took over most of the design work for the firm (later called Adams, Holden and Pearson). A succession of powerful free style hospitals and other buildings were completed during his first few years, followed by vigorously free neo-Mannerist office buildings in London before 1914. Holden's achievements during these fifteen years were truly remarkable. Later his Underground Railway Stations of the 1930s became famous, though his other designs of that time were often dismissed as reactionary by the *avant-garde*. This account by Sir Nikolaus Pevsner was written shortly after Holden's death.

Charles Holden was eighty-five when he died. For the last twenty-five years of his life he had settled down to a style of architecture – the style of the School of Oriental Studies and the General Electric Company – which shares the absence of period ornament with the current style of the mid-century, but nearly everything else with the neo-Georgians. But in 1930, or, to be precise, in 1930–32, he had made history with his small underground stations on the Piccadilly Line. They were among the first designs in England to be modern in the novel Continental way, and they were at the same time modest, accommodating, not out of sympathy with essential English traditions and sensitively adapted to their surroundings. Moreover, they were part of a house-style more sweeping and successful than any before or after. The conception of the house style was no doubt Frank Pick's, and it is likely that the decision to go so frankly Continental-modern and more exactly north-German-modern was initially Pick's, too, conveyed to Holden or inspiring Holden on a journey which the two men made together to just those parts of the Continent. (See *The Architectural Review* Vol. XCII, 1942, p. 31 etc.).

The great importance of these stations has tended to eclipse Holden's earliest work, though it is equally interesting and historically nearly as significant. Most of the buildings to which this brief essay deliberately confines itself are little known. Some have not been illustrated since they first appeared in the early volumes of *The Architectural Review* and also in other journals.

Volume I of *The Architectural Review* (1896–97) gave a full page to Holden's Soane Medallion design, the design for a Provincial Market Hall – and a remarkable design it was, although the editorial comment in the *Review* was crushing: "lack of knowledge," "waste of space," "motifs without structural ability" were all remorselessly noted, though "considerable latent ability" was recognized. For us that is what matters. Here is indeed an extremely bright student's design, making use, as bright students will, of the most striking motifs most recently put forward by the most go-ahead architects. The nicely asymmetrical composition has no immediate precedent; it was favoured by all the best of the Free-Neo-Tudor addicts. But the frieze of figures in relief was certainly fashionable at that very moment[1] and so was the motif of the flatly spreading-out tree.[2]

The free Neo-Tudor of Holden's, confirmed and no

2 *Charles Holden. Design for a Provincial Market Hall, winner of the Soane Medallion 1896.*

1 *Portrait of Charles Holden as a young man.*

doubt made yet freer by his work in the office of C. R. Ashbee about 1898 and a little later, culminated ten years afterwards in the Bristol Central Library, built in 1906.[3] It is a building whose plan was certainly no longer inexperienced, and it has in addition an extremely pretty façade building up towards the centre with its three oriel windows under arches, the tympana of which have again sculpture in relief. Over and above the sources so far mentioned, one feels distinctly reminded here of Mackintosh's Glasgow School of Art, which had been sufficiently publicised to be not unlikely as a stimulus. The Bristol library was published as by H. P. Adams, for it was in Adams's firm the Holden now worked. He became a partner at just about this time. Before that moment his name did not appear, and even after it no distinction was made between the two men, a failing not unusual among bosses and senior partners.

Thus, in the case of the Midhurst Sanatorium,

3

4

3 *Charles Holden. Entrance to Chapel, Midhurst Sanatorium (1904–05).*

4 *Charles Holden (as chief assistant to H. Percy Adams). Belgrave Hospital for Children, Clapham Road, Kennington Oval, London (designed 1900, completed 1903). Until he became a partner in 1906, all Holden's designs were published under Adams's name.*

5 *Charles Holden. Midhurst Sanatorium, Midhurst, Sussex (1904–05). Holden's aesthetic taste was severe and sometimes harsh, but his free handling of volumes on the largest scale was masterly.*

6 *Charles Holden. Interior, Midhurst Sanatorium (1904–05).*

6

5

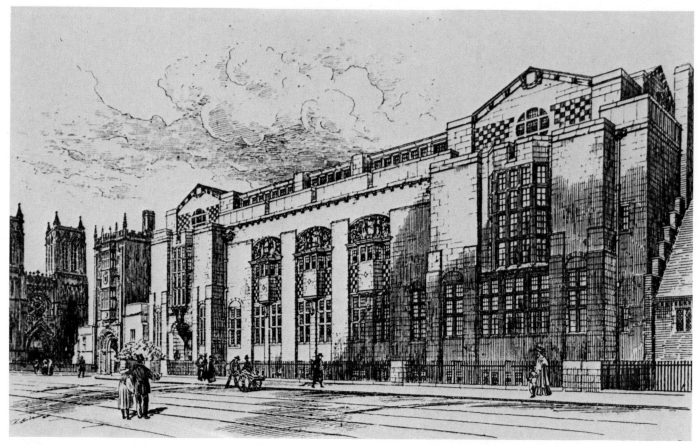

1903–06, not only is the job assigned to Adams, but even the description[4] was provided by him. This Sanatorium certainly is one of the best major buildings in England of the near-modern last phase of Tudor adherence. It can stand a comparison with Voysey's houses of these years and Baillie Scott's Waterlow Court in Hampstead Garden Suburb.

While the sub-division of creative labour here must for the time being be left open, there can be no doubt of Holden's personality in a group of other buildings of the same years, buildings which clearly prepared the ground for his style in the '20s. The first of them is the addition to the Law Society in Carey Street, Chancery Lane.[5] This was designed already in 1902 and is a classical, evenly stone-faced job, with not a touch of Tudor or of the busy and pretty mixture of materials. At first sight it is simply of the Edwardian-Imperial classicism of those years; but there are again very personal touches. The small seated figures below the ground floor arch, it is true, may be inspired by Beresford Pite, but the rest is pure Holden. It is worth memorising the details of the upper side windows and the blank niches above them. This adjustment of classical detail into basic cubic shapes was quite a novelty. The columns without entasis and the heavy attic are clearly in the same spirit.

It was going to be Holden's spirit from now on. Take 127–9 High Holborn[6] of 1904, a monumental composition, with a corner tower and with such details as the spheres at the foot of the tower, the columns without

7 *Charles Holden. Central Reference Library, Bristol (1905–06). One of the most successful free style major buildings, the design was highly influential.*

8 *Charles Holden. Library Block, Law Society, Chancery Lane, London (1903–04). Probably designed as early as 1902, as an addition to an older classical building, Holden here picked up Beresford Pite's neo-Mannerism and combined it with his own strong feeling for piled-up geometrical masses.*

Arthur Beresford Pite

by Alastair Service

Beresford Pite (1861–1934) defies classification. An enthusiastic though lone-wolf member of the Arts and Crafts Movement, he greatly influenced his employer John Belcher during the period when Grand Manner Baroque was launched. His private practice from 1897 onwards produced a stream of experiments in his friend Lethaby's free manner; in free Michelangelesque; in free Grec and most of all in free Byzantine. Pite had no interest in new structural techniques, but aimed to find a modern free style developed from Pugin's precepts.

entasis and also the oddly Mannerist bits round the windows. The fashionable term Mannerism can here be used legitimately; for Holden indeed froze up and invalidated current classical motifs, which is what Mannerist architects did in the Cinquecento. The British Medical Association[7] in the Strand (now Rhodesia House) followed. It was the building in which Holden introduced to a reluctant client and public Jacob Epstein as a monumental sculptor. The later disintegration of his figures has received much publicity. The motifs of the building need not be enumerated. It will be evident to anybody that this and 62 Oxford Street of 1909, are by Holden and no one else. Ultimate confirmation lies in the major job of Holden's early fifties, the stations along the south extension of the Edgware Line designed in 1926, and the Underground headquarters of 1927–29.

10

11

9 *Charles Holden. Rhodesia House (formerly British Medical Association), No. 429 Strand, London (1907). The most impressive of his Edwardian office buildings. Holden became Adams's partner about this time.*

10 *Charles Holden. Norwich House, No. 127 High Holborn, Bloomsbury, London (1904).*

11 *Charles Holden. Evelyn House, No. 62 Oxford Street, London (1908–10).*

In his speech[1] upon receiving the Royal Gold Medal for architecture in 1907, John Belcher listed the principal people who had worked with him. "Then came Mr (now Professor) Beresford Pite, of whose strong personality and versatile genius there is but little need to remind you. I think it was while he was still with me that he won the Soane Medallion with his celebrated design of a medieval West End club. Since then he has surpassed us all in the beauty of his Renaissance designs, and is, too, a distinguished exponent of the pure and refined method of Greek architecture." This quotation, a typical example of Belcher's sly humour, does demonstrate the impossibility of classifying Pite, the least predictable of architects during the Edwardian period. We can view him as a free style man, seeking a valid new English architecture and an active member of the Art Workers' Guild. Or we can see him as the last true successor to the ideals of the Gothic Revival; as a revivalist of Michelangelo's Mannerism; free Byzantine and free neo-Grec; as a witty rogue-architect, determined to be different at all costs; as a brilliant talent that never fulfilled itself; or as an inspiring teacher who encouraged several generations of students to reject dullness. All these views have something to be said for them and he will doubtless continue to fascinate students of the period.

Arthur Beresford Pite was born in London in 1861. The Pite family was and is full of architects. His father, A. R. Pite was a reasonably successful architect in the partnership of Habershon and Pite, while Beresford Pite's brother W. A. Pite later built up a good practice specialising in hospital design.

Beresford Pite was educated at King's College School, then at the National Art Training School (later to become the Royal College of Art). He took a course in drawing from William Richardson, developing a lasting interest in Dürer's techniques, and continued his studies at the Architectural Association and at University College while doing his articles with his father's firm. In 1879 he won the Donaldson Medal and two years later joined John Belcher's staff as a junior assistant. He also attended classes at the Royal Academy schools, where he first met William Lethaby in about 1880 and started a lifelong friendship.

In 1882 Pite won the Soane Medallion with the above-mentioned 'medieval' design for a club[2] and the award enabled him to travel in Europe for a year. He was accompanied by his brother William, who by a happy coincidence was Architectural Association travelling student for the year, and Belcher joined the two young men for a sketching holiday in Germany. In 1883 Pite returned to London and, after a short spell on the staff of *The Builder* magazine, rejoined Belcher as an 'improver'.

His own first building, the infirmary[3] added in Short's Gardens to St Giles' Workhouse in Endell Street at Covent Garden, was designed with his brother William and built in 1884–85. The building still stands, barely distinguishable from the rest of the grim workhouse, though the asymmetrical composition of the low range between Pite's two banded brick towers already shows originality. After that most of his work for fourteen years was done in partnership with Belcher, who was very fond of the clever and articulate younger man. P. M. Johnston, who worked in the office at the time, later wrote[4] that Pite's "magnetic personality influenced Mr Belcher very strongly and left its impress on the character of the work turned out." And indeed one can see many features typical of Pite's later work in a number of the firm's designs of the 1880s and early '90s. Some historians have however fallen into the trap of thinking that all Belcher's interesting works of this period were Pite's designs. In fact, from the stylistic evidence and from what both said later (and they remained friends until Belcher's death in 1913), it appears that most of the designs were worked out together. Only in one or two designs can one say that one or other was clearly dominant (notably the Royal Insurance design for Liverpool mentioned below).

It was doubtless Pite who made Belcher interested in Lethaby and Prior's Art Workers' Guild; as a result Belcher took the chair at the very first meeting in 1884 and, like Pite, was one of the original members – but he wisely refused further office, saying that that was for the other younger members. All the same his interest survived for the rest of his life, and the Guild's original aim to unify the arts of architecture, sculpture and painting has no better realisation than Belcher and Pite's most famous building. That building is the Institute of Chartered Accountants in the City of London, designed in 1888 and opened, with a sensation

2 *John Belcher with A. Beresford Pite as chief assistant. Institute of Chartered Accountants, Great Swan Alley, off Moorgate, City of London (1888–93). The free Genoese Baroque manner was Belcher's, but the design was shared by the two men and details such as the turret at the junction of two levels were fashionable among progressive young architects.*

1 *Portrait of A. Beresford Pite.*

3 *John Belcher and A. Beresford Pite. Design for Royal Insurance Buildings in Liverpool (1896). Norman Shaw assessed the competition, but did not premiate this design. This is probably the earliest design in which Pite's interest in a Michelangelesque neo-Mannerism appears. Several features appear in later Pite designs.*

among architects, in 1893. Belcher felt very strongly that this design was his own child, and we can believe that particularly of the Baroque style, of the integration of sculpture into the architecture of the exterior and of the murals into that of the interior (especially in the old Council Chamber). But it is surely Pite's mind we see in the striking motif of the marvellous band of sculpted frieze, apparently running continuously behind the half-columns and holding the composition together. It is Pite again who probably suggested the contemporary favourite Arts and Crafts feature of the cupola turret marking the break in levels (a James MacLaren speciality) and we see his hand in the fascinating main staircase with its constant changes of character.

Apart from a number of the firm's houses, the other design in which we can detect Pite's influence most strongly is the unsuccessful entry for the Royal Insurance's 1896 competition for its Liverpool offices.[5] The high arches embracing several storeys, the big

semi-circular windows and the high gallery were all to appear in Pite's later work – while there is a new general feeling to the noble design that pre-echoes the neo-Mannerism of Holden and the Belcher and Joass designs of ten years later.

During the same year, Pite accepted three commissions[6] in Marylebone while still working for Belcher. The charming house at 82 Mortimer Street, which is probably his best-known work, shows a similar Michelangelesque Mannerism to the Royal Insurance design. The same style appeared in the St Marylebone General Dispensary at 77 Welbeck Street (demolished 1968) and in the doorway of the otherwise simple brick Church Home at 46–54 Great Titchfield Street. Michelangelo fascinated Pite for the rest of his life. The last of these buildings started Pite on a succession of churches and other buildings connected with the Church. For Pite was, in the words[7] of D. H. S. Cranage, "a devout churchman with pronounced evangelical convictions". This low-churchmanship must have led to some curious

4 *A. Beresford Pite. No. 82 Mortimer Street, Marylebone, London (1896). A charming design done under his own name while he was still working for Belcher.*

5 *A. Beresford Pite. Unplaced design, Colchester Town Hall competition (August 1897). Pite's first design after leaving Belcher, and the most grandiose Baroque work he produced.*

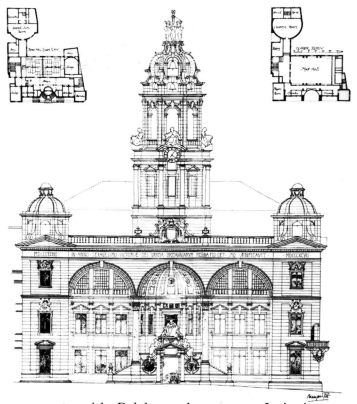

arguments with Belcher, who was an Irvingite or Catholic Apostolic, but there is no reason to think that either this or Pite's outside commissions led to their partnership breaking up in 1897 (as has been suggested to me).

The most likely reason for his parting with Belcher was simply that by 1897 Pite was aged thirty-six, and in that year he was President of the Architectural Association and became a Fellow of the R.I.B.A. It was clearly a good time to start an independent practice. Moreover, he had now married and his wife's brother, a south London clergyman called Mowll, had offered him the job of designing Christ Church and its church hall, to be built on the Brixton Road near Kennington Oval.

In that year Pite entered unsuccessfully the competition for Colchester Town Hall, which Belcher won. But one of the first assistants at his Marylebone office, Theodore Fyfe, wrote[8] that during that period Pite "was making design after design for the Brixton church". The general style was to be Byzantine (which the great John Francis Bentley had made fashionable with his recently started Westminster Cathedral) but the Brixton church hall was built first, in 1897–98, and only shows hints of that manner. It was in fact one of the few really free style buildings Pite did, its entrance front on Mowll Street a powerful and original composition of Arts and Crafts motifs. The church itself may have been designed at any time from 1897 onwards, but was built in 1902–03. The Byzantine frontage, in a now grimy brick dressed with stone, is strikingly restless and in contrast to the fine calm side bays, crossing dome and interior.

Much of Pite's practice was either in south London

or in Marylebone, for he had his home in one district and his office in the other. We have already noted comments about the strength of his personality. He was a tremendous talker, able to carry his listeners away with his eloquence. Theodore Fyfe wrote that "he had a keen if somewhat dry humour" and recalled that "walks with him around London – when he expounded Shaw, Pearson, G. G. Scott, Bodley, Butterfield and Bentley – still remain memorable." Godwin was another architect whom he often picked out for praise in his talks to the Architectural Association.

Another typical Pite house at 32 Old Bond Street and one for church school offices at 126 Great Portland Street[9] followed in 1898, and a more ambitious stone block of flats at 37 Harley Street in 1899. This Harley Street building repays study, for although the Mannerist details are still there, the composition is of an asymmetrical free style type that has roots in Godwin's work of about 1880 – balancing uneven vertical accents. The type of high corner oriel seen here had been

6 *A. Beresford Pite. Detail, Christ Church, Brixton Road, Oval, London (designed 1897 on, built 1902–03). The free Byzantine manner came from Bentley's Westminster Cathedral, but its use by Pite is wholly personal.*

7 *A. Beresford Pite. Church Hall, Christ Church, Mowll Street, off Brixton Road, London (1897–98). A free style, with Pite's favourite type of window.*

favoured by Pite, and indeed by Belcher, since the
Chartered Accountants' building.

In the following year Pite's career took a further turn
which prevented him from developing a full-time
architectural practice. His friend William Lethaby had
been appointed Professor of Design at the recently re-
constituted Royal College of Art and persuaded Pite[10]
to take up the post of Professor of Architecture there –
a job he held until 1923. From then on much of Pite's
time was taken up with teaching, for he also became
Architectural Director of the L.C.C. School of Building
at Brixton from 1905 until 1928. Then in 1912 another
Art Workers' Guild architect friend, the equally
original Edward Prior, was appointed Slade Professor
of Architecture at Cambridge University and Pite
became a teacher and lecturer there with him, retiring
only in 1931.

The commissions that came Pite's way after this
were increasingly connected with church affairs, for
he was, again in D. H. S. Cranage's words, "prominent
in the London Diocesan Conference and latterly in the
National Assembly of the Church of England". This
writer's father and uncle have a curious memory of
Pite during this Edwardian period, for they knew him
at Frinton-on-sea, where he built himself a holiday
house called 'Earlywood' beside the church. As small
boys they naturally spent most of their time on the
beach and clearly remember how the bearded and
cloaked figure of Beresford Pite, accompanied by his
son, would surge onto the beach, gather up all children
in sight and lead them in hymn-singing, kneeling on
the sand.

Pite's next commission was to build a chancel for
Holy Trinity Church, Clapham in 1902 (while the
Brixton Road church was also going up). His tremendous
Byzantine entry for the 1903 Liverpool Cathedral
competition[11] was widely praised but unplaced. In
that year he built only one work, the exotic mosaic
frontage and interiors of Pagani's Restaurant at
42 Great Portland Street, now demolished. Then in
1904 came Ames House, a youth hostel for All Souls',
Marylebone in Great Titchfield Street. This shows a
new departure for Pite, for it is a large building cased
in brick which seems to wrap around the forms that he
introduced to prevent monotony. In the same year he
built an idiosyncratically free office and warehouse
building at 21 Little Portland Street, Marylebone – full
of the intriguing layers and forms that are typical of his
work. There followed a gap in his practice before we

8 *A. Beresford Pite. No. 37 Harley Street, London (1899). A free
asymmetrical composition, with Pite's typical use of sculpture
integrated into the building.*

9 *A. Beresford Pite. Pagani's Restaurant, No. 42 Great Portland
Street, Marylebone (1903). The ground floor front already existed.
Pite added the broad arches and the colourful mosaics above.
Destroyed.*

10 *A. Beresford Pite. Detail, Carnegie Public Library. Pite merged details of Byzantine, neo-Grec and other styles into a manner typical only of himself.*

11 *A. Beresford Pite. Carnegie Public Library, Thornhill Square, Islington, London (1906–08). A variety of geometric volumes are linked to form a relaxed composition.*

12 *A. Beresford Pite. Detail, All Souls School, Foley Street, Marylebone (1906–08). The different layers give some variety to low-cost brickwork.*

come to four of his largest buildings. Of these, the Wesleyan Church in Agincourt Road, Gospel Oak (completed in 1907) has been demolished and only the odd little caretaker's brick cottage beside it survives. The church was almost perfectly preserved example of Methodist lay-out of its time, while the centralised plan and architectural style followed Pite's favourite free use of Byzantine.

The Carnegie Public Library (1906–08) in Thornhill Square, Islington is one of the best of Pite's free designs, full of charm and even wit. But it was his All Souls' School (1906–08) between Foley Street and Ridinghouse Street, Marylebone which added most to his reputation among his contemporaries. Today, thick with grime, it is hard to see the *charm* which commentators mentioned. But it is an interesting low-cost rational structure, relieved by some ingenious uses of layered surfaces. H. S. Goodhart-Rendel described it[12] as being "as new as anything in the so-called new architecture, without any of the fuss or worry of the newer newness".

13 *A. Beresford Pite. London, Edinburgh and Glasgow Assurance Co. Buildings, Euston Square, London (1907 section). The historic sources of the detailing are significant only because of the anti-historic way in which Pite used them in this intriguing design.*

14 *A. Beresford Pite. London, Edinburgh and Glasgow Assurance Co. Buildings, (1907 section on right, 1912 extension on left). The open top-floor gallery of Pite's 1896 insurance building design reappears here in his largest London building.*

The interest in layered surfaces to relieve broad areas of brickwork was shared by many of Pite's students (at the L.C.C. School of Building) and by contemporaries in the L.C.C. Architect's Department. A comparison between their designs and Pite's private practice reveals a shared interest in experimenting with this layering and with new forms of decoration for their occasional stone-faced buildings. The L.C.C.'s Philip Webb and Lethaby type of austere, anti-pretty aesthetic is also present in Pite's brick buildings.

It happened that the Central School of Art (designed by the L.C.C. Architect's Department to Lethaby's specification) was designed and built at about the same time as Pite's only large office building. Again there is a degree of similarity in some of the unusual decorative forms – reminiscent only of Lethaby's Eagle Insurance building of seven years before. Pite's building was the London, Edinburgh and Glasgow Assurance Buildings[13] in Euston Square, London beside the station. The most extraordinary section of this building is the 1907 northerly part in Euston Square, an unprecedented composition at all levels. The larger range on its left, in the wildest form of neo-Grec, was apparently built at the same time. One notices a high open gallery at the top of this range, reminiscent of Pite's 1896 design for the Liverpool Royal Insurance building. In 1912 Pite added a further range to his Euston Square building, running along the Euston Road, but this is much more restrained than the earlier parts.

15 *A. Beresford Pite. Sketch of design for Anglican Cathedral, Kampala, Uganda (designed 1913). The cathedral was completed (slightly altered) in 1918, but the tower was never built. One of the best of all the free style church designs derived from the Gothic.*

16 *A. Beresford Pite. Namirembe Anglican Cathedral, Kampala, Uganda (designed 1913, opened 1918).*

17 *A. Beresford Pite. Entrance, Burlington Arcade, Piccadilly, London (upper storey 1911, entrance arch 1930). Pite's last Michelangelo extravaganza.*

That addition was the only large-scale work Pite did in Britain between 1908 and the outbreak of war. But in the meantime his church interests were starting to bring about some overseas commissions.[14] The most important of these was for Namirembe Anglican Cathedral, Kampala, Uganda. The design was done in 1913 and except for the west towers, which were never built, the cathedral was completed[15] in 1918. It shows Pite at his relaxed best, working in a free and simplified adaptation of the Gothic with a telling use of some of his favourite motifs. The entrance frontage, with his own combination of big arch and buttresses, is a powerful design only spoiled by a weak porch added later. The breadth of the pointed arches over the recessed windows enables Pite to get away with the outrageous change into rounded arches leading up to a dome above the crossing.

This short study will not deal with his few buildings of the post-1918 period[16] except for one final eccentric work. In 1911 Pite had rebuilt the upper storey of the Piccadilly entrance to the Burlington Arcade, providing a three-bay frontage of little distinction. In 1930 he was commissioned to provide a more noticeable entrance for this shopping arcade. His answer was to revive his most flamboyant Baroque manner, with two large head-and-shoulders statues that seem to grow out of their supporting brackets and an arch formed from two enormous scrolls apparently crushing some smaller sculptured figures in the centre. It is a witty and characteristic finale for an enigma among architects.

It is, I believe, useless to seek any logical development in Beresford Pite's buildings. As a young man he believed ardently in the Holy Grail of a new style for his time, freely adapted from tradition but not copyist. That style was never found, but Pite never stopped experimenting. As Theodore Fyfe[17] put it in 1934, "he was a sound constructor, but modern methods in construction or design never interested him very much, perhaps because of his devotion to another cause – the real continuance of an English expression in architecture through the Gothic Revival to Waterhouse. On both counts, his inflexibility tended to isolate him in his later years".

Arthur Beresford Pite died in 1934. A pleasing description of him in old age at R.I.B.A. discussions[18] will close this account aptly; "rising slowly, as often as not on those occasions when the brilliance or perhaps the dullness of the reader of the paper had left others in the audience dumb, he would physically and mentally unbend as he warmed to his subject. Pontifical deliberation would turn to a fluent display of erudition, and by some unexpected turn in argument he would seize on the salient point and clinch the argument – or provoke excited debate by some challenging generalisation."

[1] *Journal of the Royal Institute of British Architects* June 1907. See also the *Journal* of 1901, pp.77 and 96 on Pite. I have to thank several members of the Pite family for their help, especially Beresford Pite's nephew, Robert W. Pite.

[2] Illustrated *The Builder* 1882. See also Pite's design of a spire submitted for Grissell medal, *The British Architect* 1 April 1881.

[3] Illustrated *The Builder* 1888 Vol. 54, p.285, but built 1884–85 according to Pite's F.R.I.B.A. application.

[4] *Journal of the Institute of British Architects* Vol. XXI, p.78.

[5] Illustrated *The Builder* 1896.

[6] Most of Pite's buildings during the earlier part of his private practice were illustrated in the relevant volumes of *The Builder*, whose editor H. H. Statham had taken up that job in 1883, the year when Pite too worked for the magazine.

[7] *Journal of the Royal Institute of British Architects* 1935, p.278.

[8] *ibid* 1935, p.212.

[9] It is not clear from the references whether this was built in 1898 or in 1907.

[10] In *Journal of the Royal Institute of British Architects* 1935, p.212, Fyfe mentions that "Pite's admiration for Lethaby was unbounded."

[11] Illustrated *The Builder* 1903.

[12] *Journal of the Royal Institute of British Architects* 1935, p.152. Goodhart-Rendel's illustrated paper on Pite and Halsey Ricardo is in the *Journal* of 1936, p.117 onwards.

[13] Now used as government offices.

[14] These include Bishop Tucker College, Mukono; the Hospital for the Church Mission to the Jews in Jerusalem; a church for the Mission to the Jews in Warsaw.

[15] A sketch of the original design is in *Journal of the Royal Institute of British Architects* 1936, p.117.

[16] Pite's other works include the roof of St John's Church, Hackney (1929); the top storeys of the Tyler Wing, Homoeopathic Hospital, Queen's Square, Bloomsbury (1929); Pilot Watch House, Dover; chapel at Monckton Combe; Library roof, St John's College, Cambridge; spire of Madingley Church, near Cambridge; parish hall, St Saviour's Church, Champion Hill; two boarding houses at Dulwich College (*circa* 1930).

[17] *Journal of the Royal Institute of Brtish Architects* 1935, p.212.

[18] *ibid* 1935, p.152.

The Architect's Department of the London County Council 1888-1914

by Alastair Service

The teaching and example of Philip Webb reached fruition most strongly in the work of the London County Council Architect's Department, especially after 1899. For most of these young architects were, to greater or lesser degree, Morris-type Socialists and architectural disciples of Webb, Lethaby and to some extent Holden and Pite, who influenced the austere aesthetic of the hundreds of housing blocks, schools, fire stations and other buildings put up by the Department in the pre-1914 period.

The story of the L.C.C. Architect's Department[1] starts shortly after the creation of the London County Council, when the Council was given new powers under the Housing of the Working Classes Act of 1888. The slum problem of London had reached gigantic proportions and a massive re-housing programme was planned. The L.C.C. decided to expand the old Metropolitan Board of Works Architect's Department and received applications for jobs from a stream of young architects attracted by the social idealism of the work. This was a generation born in the 1860s or later and strongly influenced by the political and social ideas of William Morris and Philip Webb. It is Webb's manner above all that one sees in the countless austere but striking, and humanely planned, buildings and housing estates which the department built before the First World War. As a group they form one of the most successful of all the Edwardian fruits of the free style movement – worlds apart from the Grand Manner opulence of the same period.

The large-scale success of the re-housing programme in London really began when the old Metropolitan Board architect Thomas Blashill resigned and W. E. Riley was appointed in his place as L.C.C. architect in 1899. Riley designed none of the L.C.C. buildings, for he was a brilliant building administrator, not an architect at all. He had formerly been in charge of Admiralty building works at dockyards in Britain and overseas, had managed working-class housing schemes before that and had experience of using direct labour. Much of the credit for his department's success is his, for he created the administrative framework in which his brilliant young men such as Owen Fleming, Charles Winmill, R. Minton Taylor, Hiorns and Canning could design and carry out the individual projects. But Fleming had been appointed head of the new Housing Division in 1893, so the establishment of the Department's future success had already started under Blashill.

The first big housing scheme (the first part 1893–95) undertaken was the redevelopment of 'the Jago', a notorious slum east of Shoreditch Parish Church, into the Boundary Road Estate to house 5,380 people. Owen Fleming was in overall charge of the plan, but each group of new buildings was designed by a different architect with certain general guidelines. A new road lay-out provided a large central circular garden, with roads radiating from it. The blocks of flats, mostly five storeys high, show many touches of Philip Webb (and of Norman Shaw) in their brick and terracotta exteriors.

During these early years the Architect's Department was responsible only for housing and other connected services. But after a series of bad fires in 1897 the responsibility to build a large number of fire stations was added and Charles Winmill was given charge of this section. Then in 1908 the architectural work of the London School Board was also given to the L.C.C. architect.

In 1899 work was started on one of the Department's most famous projects, the Millbank Estate behind the Tate Gallery. Hogarth Buildings, the first block, was started that year and the rest of the group, together with many other estates all over London, were built in the next seven years. Those mentioned especially by Mr Gregory-Jones are Bruce Buildings in the Caledonian Road, the Bourne Estate off Clerkenwell Road, the Webber Row Estate in Waterloo Row. Then there were the Totterdown Fields Estate of cottages at Tooting opened in 1903 and other suburban cottage estates at Hammersmith, Norbury and Tottenham. The huge Single Working Men's lodging houses in Drury Lane and off New Cross Road in Deptford are impressive designs, but this is only the tip of the iceberg. Research has not yet been published giving an adequate picture of the Department's full achievement during the Edwardian period.

Some individual buildings must however be mentioned in this brief account. The fire stations designed

2 *L.C.C. Architect's Department, Hogarth House, Erasmus Street, Westminster. The first block in the L.C.C.'s famous Millbank Estate behind the Tate Gallery, started in 1899. The influence of Philip Webb, Lethaby and perhaps Holden is already evident.*

3 *L.C.C. Architect's Department. Detail of housing block in Herrick Street, Millbank Estate, Westminster (1899 onwards).*

4 *L.C.C. Architect's Department. Bruce House (for Single Working Men), Drury Lane, London (1907).*

5 *L.C.C. Architect's Department. St Marylebone Grammar School, Marylebone Road, London (circa 1910).*

6 *Philip Webb. 'Standen', near Saint Hill, East Grinstead, Sussex (1891–94). Many of the L.C.C.'s architects knew Webb through the Society for the Protection of Ancient Buildings.*

7 *Charles Winmill of L.C.C. Architect's Department. Fire Station, Eton Avenue, Hampstead (1914–15).*

by various members of Charles Winmill's division are particularly striking. The Euston Road Fire Station (opened 1902) is an outstanding building, severe but highly original. It is on a level with works by Webb, Mackintosh or Lethaby at their stern best, charged with the feeling of the period. It is not known who was in charge of the design. Winmill himself appears[2] to have designed the Eton Avenue Fire Station in Hampstead (near Primrose Hill) just before the outbreak of the war and it was built 1914–15. If one compares this with Philip Webb's last great house, Standen in Sussex of the 1890s, one sees how deeply his influence was felt by the L.C.C. architects.

Finally we must look at that enigmatic masterpiece, the Central School of Arts and Crafts in Southampton Row, London (1905–08) and here we must turn to the question of William Lethaby's influence. The chief personal contact between the young L.C.C. architects and Webb and Morris was through the Society for the Protection of Ancient Buildings. Several of the L.C.C. architects served on the committee of the Society. According to John Brandon-Jones,[3] they habitually had supper with Webb after its meeting and discussed architecture in general and Socialism. As Webb and Morris aged, their authority was largely vested in Lethaby,

8 *L.C.C. Architect's Department. L.C.C. Fire Station, Euston Road, London (1901–02). One of the most impressive free designs from the Department.*

9 *L.C.C. Architect's Department, A. Halcrow Verstage perhaps in consultation with W. R. Lethaby. Central School of Arts and Crafts, Southampton Row, Holborn (1907). One of the few stone-faced buildings designed by the department.*

whose word became law for the younger members. Certainly his influence can also be seen in some L.C.C. work.

Lethaby was appointed the first Principal of the Central School of Arts and Crafts in 1896 and, even though he had given up architectural practice in 1903, he certainly played an active part in the planning of its new building in 1907. Indeed, Godfrey Rubens has discovered that he prepared the brief to the L.C.C. Architect's Department for the building. We may never discover the exact extent of his involvement in the design, but on stylistic grounds we may guess that either it was considerable or that it was designed with his own works in mind, especially the Eagle Insurance Building of 1900. A. Halcrow Verstage was in charge of the design and Matthew Dawson is said to have helped.[4]

It is a puzzling building, though an impressive one. The planning is clear and the light, taut facing of stone does hint at the structure beneath. There is something of the restlessness in these elevations shown in contemporary buildings by Holden and Joass, seeking external expression for the structure. The strange,

almost Celtic, decoration of the corner shows clear Lethaby influence. One strange feature is a door which appears to have been moved away from the corner and onto the shorter frontage as an afterthought.

Whoever was responsible for the design, the Central School is one of the most fascinating buildings produced by the L.C.C. Department before the war of 1914–18. When war broke out many of the Department's architects were still young and joined the forces. War deaths and the retirement of Riley in 1920 made it a very different department in the 1920s under Topham Forest, with new problems and new solutions, and new architectural manners.

[1] The only published account of this early L.C.C. architectural period is D. Gregory-Jones, 'Some Early Works of the L.C.C. Architects Department' *Architectural Association Journal* 1954 pp.95–105.

[2] *Charles C. Winmill*, by his daughter, Dent, London 1946.

[3] J. Brandon-Jones, 'Philip Webb' in *Victorian Architecture* (ed.) Ferriday, Cape, London 1963.

[4] I have to thank Godfrey Rubens for this information.

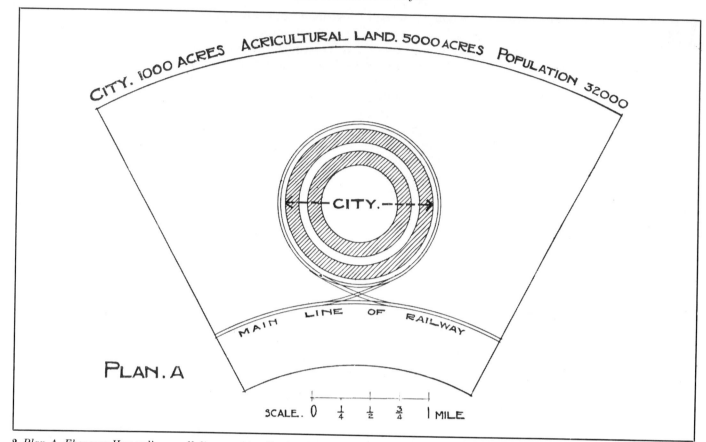

CITY. 1000 ACRES   AGRICULTURAL LAND. 5000 ACRES   POPULATION 32000

CITY.

MAIN   LINE   OF   RAILWAY

PLAN.A

SCALE. 0   ¼   ½   ¾   1 MILE

2 *Plan A. Ebenezer Howard's overall diagram from* Garden Cities of Tomorrow *re-published in 1902.*

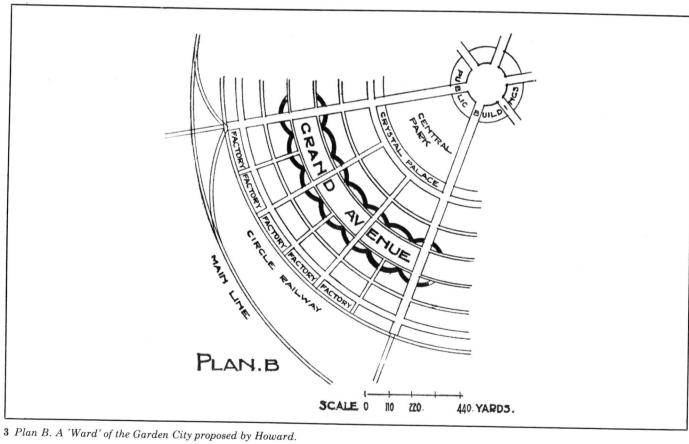

FACTORY   FACTORY   GRAND   AVENUE   CRYSTAL PALACE   CENTRAL PARK   PUBLIC BUILDINGS

FACTORY   FACTORY   FACTORY

MAIN LINE

CIRCLE   RAILWAY

PLAN.B

SCALE 0   110   220.   440. YARDS.

3 *Plan B. A 'Ward' of the Garden City proposed by Howard.*

414

trees, and they may be se
owners, too, without doing
liberty, may be required to
the rusting boilers, brok
many unnecessary pieces o
usual accompaniments of
idea of fitness and tidines:
of the streets and houses. I
under modern condition:
limitations should be fran}
supposed imitation of tl
medieval town, nor on the
make of it a 'model villag
to answer their purpose, si
no unmeaning or redundar
have the beauty proper to
all things the rows of
windowed houses with whi
have made us familiar shou
through some of our nea
anyone with eyes that th
disagreeable in rows and s
the houses themselves are ˌ
these suburbs the old and th
contrast, and the smarting
the glare of the new streets, t
Quiet and ordinary as they ;
reason, a fitness and even (

the furthest removed inhabitant. In this splendid avenue six sites, each of four acres, are occupied by public schools and their surrounding playgrounds and gardens. On the outer ring of the town are factories, warehouses, etc., all fronting on the circle railway, which encompasses the whole town, and which has sidings connecting it with a main line of railway which passes through the estate.

"While the town proper, with its population engaged in various trades, callings, and professions offers the most natural market to the people engaged on the agricultural estate; yet the farmers and others are not by any means limited to the town as their only market, but have the fullest right to dispose of their produce to whomsoever they please. This principle of freedom holds good with regard to manufacturers and others who have established themselves in the town. These manage their affairs in their own way, subject, of course, to the general law of the land, and subject to the provision of sufficient space for workmen and reasonable sanitary conditions. Even in regard to such matters as water, lighting, and telephonic communication – which a municipality, if efficient and honest, is certainly the best and most natural body to supply – no rigid or absolute monopoly is sought; and if any private corporation or any body of individuals proved itself capable of supplying on more advantageous terms, either the whole town or a section of it, this would be allowed. The area of municipal and corporate action is

probably destined to become greatly enlarged; but, if it is to be so, it will be because the people possess faith in such action, and that faith can best be shown by a wide extension of the area of freedom."

Plan C shows the method of expansion when the original city no longer suffices. "How shall it grow? Shall it build on the zone of agricultural land which is around it, and thus for every destroy its right to be called a 'Garden City'? Surely not. Consider for a moment the case of a city in Australia. The city of Adelaide is surrounded by its 'Park Lands'. It grows by leaping over the 'Park Lands' and establishing North Adelaide. And this is the principle which it is intended to follow, but improve upon, in the Garden City. And this principle of growth – this principle of always preserving a belt of country round our cities – would be ever kept in mind till, in the course of time, we should have a cluster of cities, not, of course, arranged in the precise geometrical form of my diagram, but so grouped around a central city that each inhabitant of the whole group, though in one sense living in a town of small size, would enjoy all the advantages of a city, and yet all the fresh delights of the country; field, hedgerow, and woodland – not prim parks and gardens merely – would be within a very few minutes walk."

4 *Plan C. Howard's proposed method of expansion when the original city has reached its limit.*

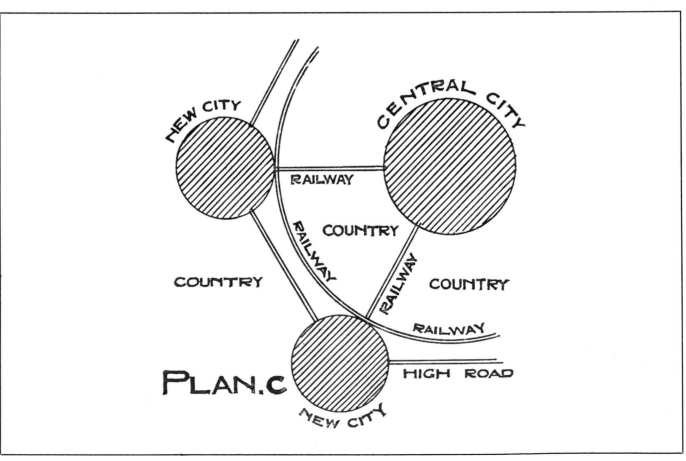

5 *Geoffrey Lucas. Cottages (1905) at*
1903 by Howard and the town plan u

For the benefit of tho
germs of an insidious S
Howard writes: "Comr
principle, for we all be
communistic parks, and
though Communism is
vidualism is no less exce
thought and action are
combination are to be
co-operation are essentia
effort are to be gained; a
most healthy and vigoro
opportunities are afforde
combined effort. Nor is t
socialistic experiment.
property in land and in ;
tion, distribution, and e
such monopoly is claime
work done will be by in
individuals quite other
proposal appeals not or
operators, manufacturer
tions under their control,
under conditions involv
rather securing wider fre

To plan and build a ne
the defects of existing one
first Garden City will ent
author is not perhaps t
scheme is, however, pre
that have been projected,
grasped the conditions of
how to turn natural forc
The experiment being a
melled, and at the same t
precedent, some criticis
architect's point of view

The circular form prope
tion on the hitherto acce
most cities have grown u
but there is an underl;
alignment which is pract
form of a building is re
have shaped the streets (
curved streets would pr
would certainly be diffic
Walking on the inner side
ing that buildings, as they
range of vision, are bein
meet the eye, while the
circling arm perpetually c
the sense of being buried i
motion; the sites, especia
fan shaped and would not

The cities of the Old
rectangular, polygonal, (
are almost invariably fo
angular forms within. T

7 *Houses under construction for the Cheap Cottages Exhibition in 1905 at Letchworth Garden City.*

building will have been put up by the date of the competition. To give a general criticism it may be enough to say that, on the whole, the cottages promise to fulfil their object quite adequately. Here and there, perhaps, the workmanship appeared to have been somewhat slovenly, though in some cases, no doubt, this was due to the work being 'rushed' in order to be up to time. And in some cases, also, the designs were much too stereotyped and of the 'doll's-house' order. Lack of imagination can hardly be excused by the necessity of sternly keeping down the cost price, and when one considers what an excellent opportunity the exhibition will afford, both to builders and architects alike, it is to be regretted both that the designs incline to be rather dull, and that more people have not had the enterprise to seize a golden chance of distinguishing themselves. It is much the same also with the £300 pair cottages. There is far too little originality shown, and in some cases where an attempt has been made to strike a new note the effect has been gained at the expense of the house accommodation, especially of the bedrooms which develop into rooms with hardly anything

straight about them but the floor. If the competition was worth entering for at all it was surely worth a man's best and most careful thought.

The exhibition, however, is not everything. Garden City is now sufficiently advanced to be a fair subject for criticism. A rough outline of the town has already been given, and a few more words of description will be enough, especially as so much has lately appeared in the different newspapers. The plan has been drawn up in harmony with the contour of the country, and can now be executed without the destruction of any existing trees or of such existing features as Letchworth Park and Norton Common. As the official guide book puts it:

"For the Central Square of the town a level plateau has been chosen near the existing station. It is marked on the spot by three isolated oak trees, and lies between the contour lines which mark 290 and 295 feet above sea level. From this plateau the ground slopes gently down on all sides, except towards Letchworth. The roads radiating from this Central Square, which will give ready access to all parts of the town, have been so planned that glimpses of the open country will be obtainable along them from the heart of the town, while they will afford to those approaching from the outskirts good views of the central buildings."

And again, to quote from the same authority:

"Care has been taken to plan the roads so that they will have easy gradients without much departure from the natural ground level, and except where the nature of the contours or other definite reasons have suggested curves, straight roads have been adopted, in many cases for the special purpose of affording views of the parks, commons, country, and main buildings, which may add so much to the charm of the town. Some of the roads shown on the plan may not be considered necessary in actual practice. The width of the roads will probably vary from 40 to 60 feet, with the exception of the Main Avenue, which will vary from 100 feet to 150 feet wide. During the earlier stages of development the roads will not be made the full width, but the Directors will preserve ample space for future widening, and so avoid the necessity of repurchasing land for that purpose.

It is proposed to have considerable variety in the character of the roads, and while the actual roadway will be adapted to the probable volume of traffic, the total width will be increased in many cases by grass margins between the roadway and footway, in which

trees will be planted, or by continuous strips of grass or garden between the roadway and the houses."

It is, of course, obvious that Garden City will not truly begin to be a city until it has got a population of workers. The purely residential buildings are of secondary importance. It is satisfactory, therefore, to be able to say that the gasworks, which are to supply six million cubic feet per annum, are expected to be ready this month, and that the manufacturing district generally is rapidly approaching some degree of completion. But the workers must of course be housed, and, while as yet no large residential houses have sprung up, workmen's houses are being built with astonishing rapidity south of the railway. These houses, either put up by Garden City Company or by private builders, compare very favourably with the competition cottages, and, so far as could be judged from brief conversations with some of the inmates, are giving entire satisfaction. The applications for allotments (no sites on the estate, be it noted, are sold outright) are coming in, it is said, at the rate of about twenty per month, so that the present activity is as nothing to what will shortly be witnessed. A city of some thirty thousand inhabitants is the goal aimed at, and it looks as if this aim were now well on the way towards realisation.

But no description of Garden City, however slight –

8 *Halsey Ricardo. House at Letchworth Garden City (1905).*

and there is the material for many fat books in the subject – would be complete without some reference to Letchworth Hall and church. Dating back to the 15th century, Letchworth Hall is as fine as many a much more famous building. It is one of those low, red-brick, somewhat straggling buildings of which novelists are so fond, with fine chimney stacks, lattice-work windows, quaint doorways, and that wealth of roofs on different altitudes which is one of the greatest charms of old English country houses. It has now passed, after many changes, into the hands of the company, and settled down as a temperance hotel which prides itself upon its old baronial hall and its Jacobean mantelpiece. Even more venerable is the old church only a few yards away, which was built in 1280. Letchworth

Church has only one fault – and that, unhappily, only too common a one – it has been spoiled by some quite unworthy stained glass windows. Outside, and especially in its 'spire', if one may so signify the little wooden structure that bestrides the roof, it is not unlike the church at Perivale, near Ealing, and both churches, curiously enough, look out upon golf links. Inside, the old stone pillars and the simple old wooden pews, and even the floor with its tombs adorned with brass plates picturing and speaking of the departed dead, form a solemn and impressive link between long-bygone ages and a new-born town, the future influence of which upon the whole country may yet prove beyond what has been dreamed of by the most optimistic of modern sociologists.

Part Eight: Variations of the Grand Manner

The years 1905 and 1906 may be regarded as the peak of High Edwardian Baroque. They saw the completion of Lanchester and Rickards' glorious municipal buildings at Cardiff and Deptford, Brumwell Thomas's Belfast Town Hall, Lutyens's Country Life office building, William Young's War Office in Whitehall, Mountford's Old Bailey criminal courts, Gibson's Walsall Town Hall, Belcher's Royal London House in Finsbury Square and many others. They also saw the start of work on almost the last of these ultra-extravagant buildings – for example Brumwell Thomas's Stockport Town Hall and the Methodist Central Hall in Westminster by Lanchester and Rickards. After that the Baroque continued to flourish, but in a restrained form, and the variations of the Grand Manner (which had appeared only occasionally until then) came to the forefront.

The reasons for this change were many. A genuine change of taste is apparent in contemporary comments on the results of architectural competitions, calling for less flamboyant public buildings. The powerful Baroque which had seemed suitable for load-bearing masonry construction no longer appeared valid with the increasing use of steel frames. Developers of office blocks resented the massive stone piers at ground level which blotted out much of the frontage available for profitable letting to shop-keepers. The recently constituted architectural schools were producing young designers with more interest in traditional disciplines than had the old training system of articles with a practising architect. All forms of classical architecture, other than the Baroque, suddenly seemed interesting to many architects.

The chief English representatives of the Parisian form of classicism, backed by the training of the Ecole des Beaux Arts, was a young man called Arthur Davis (1878–1951) who had become in 1900 the London partner of the established Frenchman, Charles Mewès at the age of twenty-two. The firm's early London buildings, such as the Morning Post building and the Ritz Hotel, were a revelation of light elegance to many. The style attracted a number of followers and brought Mewès and Davis a major practice for the next thirty years. Apart from Davis, Sir Reginald Blomfield and Frank Verity became leading exponents of the Beaux Arts manner, while Sir Aston Webb used it for his 1913 refronting of Buckingham Palace.

Other were experimenting with more original uses of classical architecture. One man in particular, Beresford Pite (who remained an unpredictable force among his Arts and Crafts contemporaries), played continuously with free adaptation of all sorts of styles to modern buildings – Byzantine, Baroque, neo-Grec, Gothic and his own non-derivative free manner among them. But it is his experiments with the neo-Mannerist style of Michelangelo that are especially interesting here. Pite's remarkable unexecuted design (under Belcher's name) for the Royal Insurance building in Liverpool of 1896 and his surviving house of the same year at 82 Mortimer Street in Marylebone contain the seeds of the neo-Mannerism which Charles Holden and John Joass (Pite's successor in Belcher's office) were to develop nearly ten years afterwards and architects such as Curtis Green were to take up still later.

That neo-Mannerism produced a handful of the most interesting buildings of the early years of the century, designs that sometimes stretch a skin of stone tautly across the outside of the structural steel frame and sometimes form almost Cubist combinations of shapes. Classical features are often used in a way that is purposely irrelevant to their original functions, and the overall effect is of restless tension. To a limited extent these designs are the equivalent of some buildings of the Secessionist Movement in Vienna – a use of classical architecture that shatters its underlying principles.

Other architects found different ways of adapting the classical appearance, which their clients wanted, to late Edwardian conditions. Some dabbled with the neo-Grec with varying degrees of success, while a few tried a neo-Soane manner. More lasting was a simplified, often astylar, manner which some have called Stripped Classical. One of the most successful practitioners of this mode was Sir Albert Richardson (1880–1965), who employed it, often with distinction, all his long career. He came to be regarded as one of the arch-enemies of the Modern Movement of the 1930s (as did Holden too) and then to inspire something like affection in his old age as an Edwardian survivor.

In spite of these variations on the ancient theme of Vitruvius, the early Edwardian Grand Manner had its truest descendants in the simplified yet still grandiose work of Sir Edwin Cooper (1873–1942) and Sir Edwin Lutyens (1869–1944). Cooper's Marylebone Town Hall of 1911 and Trinity House of 1913 are good examples of buildings which were extravagantly splendid in appearance (and, as far as the reception areas were concerned, in planning) yet on closer inspection consist of relatively severe blocks of offices.

Cooper has much to be said in his favour, but one could not pretend that his was a major architectural talent. Edwin Lutyens, on the other hand, was undoubtedly an architectural genius. Lutyens started as an Arts and Crafts man and his houses of the 1890s in Surrey and elsewhere are among the masterpieces of that movement. Then, as his marriage to the daughter of an aristocrat brought him into contact with the wealthy, his practice in town buildings increased at the start of the new century. Instead of bringing his brilliant free style design to these buildings, he took up the Grand Manner with his own typical individuality. His work at New Delhi in India from 1912 onwards made him famous and for the rest of his life he produced building after building of such brilliance that his tardy clinging to grand classicism has to be forgiven. He is perhaps best regarded as an unexpected late and superb blossom of the Edwardian Grand Manner.

1 *Sir Edwin Cooper. St Marylebone Town Hall, Marylebone Road, London (1911–14). By the end of the first decade of the century there was a widespread reaction of taste against extravagant Edwardian Baroque and a reversion to severer classical forms and even to scholastic rules with Beaux Arts education.*

2 *Halsey Ricardo. Detail, Debenham House, Addison Road, North Kensington (1905–07). The popularity of classical architecture and the quiet neo-Georgian domestic style of Ernest Newton forced even some of the most idealistic Arts and Crafts architects to flirt with things they had rejected. The results were unpredictable; here Ricardo grandly combined shining green glazed bricks with classical stone dressing.*

3 *Charles Mewès and Arthur Davis. Inveresk House, The Aldwych, London (1906–07). The top storey was later disastrously altered. The cool elegance of Arthur Davis's French classical manner contrasts strikingly with the full-blooded Edwardian Baroque of the Gaiety Theatre (by Norman Shaw and Ernest Runtz 1902–03, destroyed circa 1955) on the right.*

4 *Sir Edwin Cooper. Port of London Authority, Trinity Square, Tower of London (1912–22), interior rebuilt 1973. Beneath the Baroque trimmings, many later buildings of the period have solid, almost cubist, forms.*

5 *John Belcher and John J. Joass. Royal Insurance building, Piccadilly and St James's Street, London (1907–08). The anti-rational and anti-scholastic use of classical details by Pite, Holden, Joass and others produced a series of notable neo-Mannerist buildings, often with strong vertical accents.*

6

7

6 *Sir Reginald Blomfield. Piccadilly Circus and Regent Street Quadrant, London (built to Blomfield's design of exterior by various architects. Swan & Edgar by John J. Joass 1917–27. County Fire Insurance offices by Ernest Newton 1924). Blomfield preferred a Beaux Arts manner.*

7 *Charles Holden. Detail, British Medical Association (now Rhodesia House), No. 429 Strand, London (1907). The new steel-frame structure made classical architecture irrelevant. Some architects expressed this by using classical features in an anti-rational way.*

8 *Worthington Simon. Legislative Buildings, Winnipeg, Manitoba, Canada (designed 1913). As grandiose, but less flamboyant than the Baroque government buildings built throughout the Empire a decade earlier.*

9 *Sir Edwin Lutyens. The Viceroy's House, New Delhi, India (1912–31). In Lutyens's best classical buildings the Grand Manner, that had started with Belcher and Shaw's works of about 1890, reached its most original and brilliant conclusion.*

8

9

Arthur Davis of Mewès and Davis

by Alastair Service

The first stage of the Grand Manner period saw the revival of the
late-Wren and Vanbrugh Baroque, usually specifically English in
type, between 1897 and *circa* 1906. But early in the century
variations of the grand classical style started to appear. The famous
Paris Exhibition of 1900 impressed some visitors by its wild *Art
Nouveau* exhibits, others by its elegant classical pavilions in the
Parisian Beaux Arts tradition. The first to introduce this French
style to London was a young English architect, Arthur Davis
(1878–1951), who became the British partner of the established
Parisian architect Charles Mewès, late in the year 1900.

Variations Of The Grand Manner

Most of the celebrated architects of the Edwardian period had practices dominated by either public buildings, of one sort or another, or by private houses and domestic work. In commercial architecture the three famous firms were J. J. Burnet, Belcher and Joass, and Mewès and Davis. All three firms produced designs of strong individuality, but Mewès and Davis were different from the other two in one basic respect. While Burnet and, to some extent, Joass experimented with adaptations of classical design to modern structure and needs, Arthur Davis (the English partner of Mewès) went on trying to use the purest classical forms possible until about 1930. These attempts to clothe steel frames in classical outer garments appear misguided when standards of rationalism are applied to them. But they did produce a lot of the most elegant and visually enriching street architecture of London and other cities, as well as some joyous interiors. Most of Davis's buildings are large – predominantly hotels and clubs around Piccadilly and St James's until 1914, then City banks and company buildings during the 1920s. After that both

his health and his practice collapsed, though the firm still exists.

Arthur Joseph Davis was born in London on 21 May 1878, the son of a successful business man. There were two other sons, Sidney and Leopold, who became a successful pianist. Davis was a Jew, though apparently not a practising one. His childhood was spent in London and from the age of about ten he showed an interest in architecture. Fairly soon afterwards his parents apparently moved to Brussels for business reasons. Davis was of course a full ten years younger than even the second wave of Arts and Crafts architects such as Baillie Scott and Mackintosh and shared none of their ideals. In Brussels in the 1890s he would have had a chance to see the *Art Nouveau* works of Horta, but it was clearly the classicists who made an early and lasting impression on him.

The start of his career is something of a fairy story come true. In 1894 he entered the *atelier* of Godefroy and then passed the entrance examination for the École des Beaux Arts in Paris in fourth place out of all entrants. He followed in Sir John Burnet's shoes by

2 *Charles Mewès and Arthur Davis. The Ritz Hotel, Piccadilly, London (1903–06). The design of the exterior, the earliest large steel-frame building in London, was probably by Mewès, head of the Paris firm.*

3 *Ritz Hotel, London. The Winter Garden. The designs of the interiors were shared by the partners, though Davis the young London partner was only twenty-five in 1903.*

joining Pascal's celebrated *atelier* while at the École. Davis successfully completed the Beaux Arts course in less than four years instead of the normal five, winning three medals on the way.

Practising architects in Paris at that time often got the help of promising Beaux Arts students when preparing designs for competitions and in 1898 Davis was allotted to Charles Mewès (1860–1914) for the competition to design the Grand Palais and the Petit Palais for the famous Paris Exhibition of 1900. Mewès came only fourth, but he was impressed with the young Englishman's talents. When Davis completed his course in 1900, Mewès immediately asked him to become his junior partner to handle the English side of the firm's work. The moment was a good one, for many English visitors had been just as impressed by the Beaux Arts classicism at the 1900 Exhibition as by the *Art Nouveau*. Thus at the age of twenty-two Davis became a partner in an international firm with a large practice specialising in hotels, banks and office buildings. Mewès's other partner, Bischoff, looked after the practice in Germany.

It is obvious that the young man had charm as well as architectural ability. I have to thank Mrs Margaret Lewis, who knew Davis well from about 1910 on, for her help concerning his story.[1] Arthur Davis was rather short, good-looking, something of a dandy and fastidiously neat. A traditional *bon viveur*, he liked conversation, parties and the company of elegant women. He was an expert on good food and wine. He could be devastatingly charming, but his wit was stinging rather than humorous. His closest friend was a stockbroker named Paul Ritcher, but other friends included the painter Sir Gerald Kelly and the architects Stanley Adshead and Sir Edward Maufe. Golf and watercolour painting were his chief recreations.

Davis's first job for Mewès was to supervise the construction in 1901 of the new restaurant and Palm Court of the Carlton Hotel (now replaced by New Zealand House) in the Haymarket, London. The design, probably by Mewès, was an elegant French classical one.

The first of the firm's designs in which Davis played an important part was that of the Ritz Hotel in Piccadilly. Mewès had already done the Ritz in Paris and the London commission was obtained about 1903 (the same year in which the firm largely rebuilt the Adam house of Luton Hoo). It was finished in 1906 and was probably the first large-scale London building to be built entirely with a steel frame. But of course it was a few years too early to expect to find that frame expressed on the exterior. The Norwegian granite façades are, Sir Nikolaus Pevsner writes,[2] "frankly Parisian, with the ground-floor arcading of the rue de Rivoli and pavilion roofs – a clever treatment as evocative as the name of the hotel". The proportions are broad and elegant (an unavoidable adjective in describing Mewès and Davis buildings), but the low relief of the big frontages is so untypical of Davis's later buildings that one feels the hand of Mewès was probably dominant here.

The interior of the Ritz, on the other hand, was largely Davis's design. And it is the finest Edwardian hotel interior I know, with an imaginative use of space and a splendour of decoration that represents the grand architecture of the period at its best. Entering by the Arlington Street door, the wide corridor connecting the main public rooms runs straight ahead through the whole length of the buildings. At this end, Davis kept the feeling cool, though the staircase, curling up gorgeously on the left side of the door towards a round roof-light, hints at the splendours to come. Past the reception desk, the corridor passes the altered Rivoli bar on the right and then the space opens out into the ravishing saloon that occupies the centre of the building. Here space penetrates walls, adding to the lightness of extra height and sweeping plaster-work, for this room is separated only by steps and columns from the corridor. Further on again the sensation of enclosure increases in preparation for the contrast of the dining room. This room is the climax of the hotel, grandly sited with views over Green Park, and itself a glorious design. The space is broad, lined with an opulent Corinthian order and held together by a great ring of hanging garlands suspended overhead – an inspired touch.

The same Edwardian splendour is seen in the 1906 extension and transformation of Polesden Lacey, near Dorking, from an unpretentious classical villa by Thomas Cubitt into a large and – internally – grand mansion. Davis kept to Cubitt's simple stucco two-storey style, but altered all the frontages except the southern and even there he added bays on either end. The style of the rooms was presumably dictated by the client, for there is no cohesion. Davis was clearly unhappy working in the Jacobean of the main hall and the staircase, with poor results. But the cool pilastered library and the contrastingly rich *Louis Quatorze* drawing room are superbly of their time, regardless of the historicism.

Davis's other building that was started in this year, and completed in 1907, was perhaps his finest exterior. This was Inveresk House in London, built as the offices of *The Morning Post* on a sharp corner site at the end of the Aldwych, facing across Waterloo Bridge. The building can still be admired today, but its Parisian gem-like quality was ruined in the 1920s by a new owner who raised its height by adding an extra storey to its Mansard roof. This wrecked the proportions and, worse still, substituted a cruder corner dome for Davis's fine original. As with the Ritz, the steel frame is encased by Norwegian granite. There is no external hint of this structure (such as one finds in contemporary work by Holden and by Joass) but the quality of the façades needs no excuses. The lines are strong and the detail is delicate.

In 1908 Davis carried out a large and harmonious extension to the Cavalry Club at 127 Piccadilly and in the same year started his largest pre-war building, the

4 *Inveresk House, London. Entrance Hall.*

5 *Mewès and Davis. The Morning Post building (Inveresk House), The Aldwych, London (1906–07). The most refined of the partnership's London buildings.*

Royal Automobile Club in Pall Mall (1908–11). Again the flavour is of Paris, but here it is the Paris of the Louvre rather than the rue de Rivoli. The two-storey screen of half-columns holds the great length of the Pall Mall frontage together satisfactorily and the finely detailed portico does its best to provide a central accent without the depth it really needs.

The size of the R.A.C. was the club promoter's responsibility, not the architect's and there were many jokes about it as well as the qualifications for membership. Professor Reilly recalled[3] A. A. Milne writing in 1911 in *Punch* that he might qualify for membership because his aunt owned a motoring veil. It was to be the ultimate in London clubs, with swimming baths and a banqueting hall as well as the usual club facilities.

Faced with the problem of sheer size, Davis seems to have abandoned any possibility of traditional clubland

intimacy and the resulting atmosphere is somewhere between that of a large club and a luxurious hotel. The plan uses an oval reception hall, a fine cool space, as the central ground-floor distribution point with dining room, bars, smoking rooms and other members' rooms disposed around it. There is little of the Ritz's continuity of style in these rooms, but the dining room, the banqueting room and the members' smoking room are strikingly successful in the Grand Manner. Best of all, there are surprises on other floors of the building, for the palatial staircase leads to corridors on the upper storeys where smaller bars and other members' rooms are tucked away. Given Davis's brief, there can be no doubt of his success.

The final pre-war design by the firm was the gigantic Cunard Building on the Pier-head at Liverpool. This strong and dignified palazzo (built 1914–16) is one of the

6 *Charles Mewès and Arthur Davis. Elevation dated 1908, Royal Automobile Club, Pall Mall, London (1908–11). Still very much a Beaux Arts design, but less purely Parisian in feeling. Davis was now taking over all design of the partnership's buildings in England.*

7 *Entrance vestibule, Royal Automobile Club. This oval room shows Davis at his cool best.*

8 *Entrance portico, Royal Automobile Club. The detail shown in the 1908 drawing was altered during building. One of the cherubs in the pediment rides a motorbike.*

glories of the Liverpool waterfront.

By this time Arthur Davis was carrying out all the firm's design work in England. He was endlessly painstaking in design, especially over detail, but left the execution to his junior English partner, a Mr Gage. The firm also employed its own sculptor named Aumonier until the end of the 1920s. There were many smaller jobs in addition to the major buildings mentioned here.

Apart from design work, Davis was well suited to the social and public life necessary for successful architects specialising in commercial work. In about 1910 he met a director of the Westminster Bank at a time when the bank wanted to build offices in European cities. Not surprisingly, the bank welcomed an architect with continental connections and able to speak French fluently. Davis designed the first of these overseas branch banks in 1910 for Brussels, and went on to do others in Antwerp, Nantes and Valencia. Later, he was to do much work for the Westminster Bank in London.

Before closing this outline of Mewès and Davis's Edwardian work, Davis's interest in architectural education must be mentioned. In 1910 Davis was the prime mover behind the opening of a London *atelier* in the Beaux Arts tradition, and was its Patron throughout its brief life. The *atelier* was intended for young newly-qualified architects, to teach them a logical analysis of architectural problems and the classical solutions. Davis believed deeply in these ancient academic principles of architecture and thought them valid regardless of modern structural developments. As late as 1927, Margaret Lewis remembers discussing the matter with him over dinner at the Ritz. She was an art student at the time and full of the ideas of the Bauhaus and Le Corbusier. Davis became quite upset and dismissed the Modern Movement as of no lasting importance. At that time he was involved with the faculty of architecture of the British School at Rome.

In 1914, still aged only thirty-six and newly elected a Fellow of the R.I.B.A., Davis headed a practice that had put up a number of the finest and largest London buildings of the Edwardian period. He and Reginald Blomfield were the leaders of the now fashionable Beaux Arts manner in England. Davis's Westminster Bank connection made the future seem secure. But a troubled period followed. His old Parisian partner Charles Mewès died that year and the outbreak of the First World War put a stop to most building. Davis was commissioned in the army and served behind the lines in France. Then in 1915 he suffered a nervous breakdown, was invalided out of the army and was nursed back to health by Eva Ritcher, the wife of his close friend Paul.

The second boom period of the Mewès and Davis practice started with the commission to build the Westminster Bank in Threadneedle Street, City of London (1922 onwards). This is one of his best works, an elegant variation on the theme of Peruzzi's Palazzo

9 *Mewès and Davis. Westminster Bank, Brussels, Belgium (circa 1910). Davis commented that he designed the low dome in this form to avoid competing with the cathedral opposite. Mewès died in 1914.*

10 *Mewès and Davis. Westminster Bank, No. 51 Threadneedle Street, City of London (designed 1922). After the war most of Davis's large buildings were in the City.*

Massimo alle Colonne, Rome (1532) which Davis felt suitable for a banking palace. This building marked a shift in his practice in more than one way, for most of his large Edwardian buildings were clubs and hotels around Piccadilly, while his major works of the 1920s were in the City.

Of his many buildings[4] during the decade, the following must be picked out. 1923 saw the building of a more modest Westminster Bank at 9 Old Broad Street and the huge but less impressive headquarters for the same bank in Throgmorton Street. His building for the merchant bankers Morgan Grenfell and Company at 23 Great Winchester Street off Old Broad Street (1925) uses a curved recess of the levels above the ground floor to give distinction to a quiet corner. A large development followed in 1928–29, involving a big office block for the Hudson's Bay Company at 52 Bishopsgate – grandly done without a trace of bragging – and a courtyard running through its centre to the Leathersellers' Company building beyond. Then, in 1930, he built another of his most distinguished buildings, the London headquarters of the Cunard line in Leadenhall

11 *Mewès and Davis, executed by the architects Willink and Thicknesse. Cunard Building, Pier Head, Liverpool (1914–16).*
A successful combination of delicate detail with the overall strength of a Florentine palazzo.

Street. A new firmness and feeling for solids and voids can be detected in this work, a worthy fellow to Davis's Cunard Building in Liverpool. All these buildings in the City of London are now sadly threatened by re-development plans. One oddment closes Davis's prosperous 1920s rather endearingly. This is the totally unexpected little Greek Orthodox church of St Sarkis, Iverna Gardens, Kensington (*circa* 1928) which mixes features of many styles in a charming miniature nonsense.

As his practice had grown after 1920, Arthur Davis had flung himself into the almost frenetic social life of prosperous London. His particular set of friends gathered often at the Hyde Park Hotel's restaurant which Davis re-modelled in 1925. There he met his wife Rhona, twenty-three years younger than him, whom he married in 1923. They had one daughter, Anne, in 1925 but it was an unhappy marriage, for she had little education, and Davis was not a patient man. They lived in a house on the corner of Hill Street, Mayfair, which Davis converted attractively from an old public house in 1923.

During the 1930s the international economic depression caused a sharp drop in building work. Mewès and Davis suffered with everyone else, though decor work on the Cunard Company's great liners *Queen Mary*, *Aquitania*, *Franconia* and *Laconia* and some other commissions provided a reasonable income. But Davis

12 *Mewès and Davis. Morgan Grenfell's Bank, No. 23 Great Winchester Street, City of London (1925).*

13 *Mewès and Davis. Hudson's Bay Company building, No. 52 Bishopsgate, City of London (1928–29) and Leatherseller's Hall in courtyard behind.*

14 *St Sarkis Armenian Church, Iverna Gardens, Kensington
(1928). Arthur Davis collected photographs of churches in Armenia
before producing this unexpected design.*

15 *Mewès and Davis. Cunard House, No. 88 Leadenhall Street,
City of London (1930). An impressive design in the 'stripped
classical' manner.*

was depressed by the situation and his condition deteriorated into another nervous breakdown in 1935 following the virtual collapse of his marriage and the death of his friend Paul Ritcher. He was then in a nursing home for some years and, although he was later able to do a little work, Davis never practised fully again. His partners took over the work, but the number of commissions was low without Davis's drive and flair. Rhona Davis died in 1940 and Arthur Davis himself spent most of his time at a new house he bought in Wimbledon until his own death in 1951.

It was a tragic end to a career that had started so brilliantly. Davis's buildings are almost irrelevant to the main stream of development of architecture in Britain, which lay precisely along the lines which he strongly rejected. But he left a series of buildings which are among the finest examples of the ideals he did believe in equally strongly. The Ritz Hotel, Inveresk House, the two Cunard buildings in Liverpool and London, the R.A.C. and the Threadneedle Street Westminster Bank may be chosen as his best works. They add enormously to the visual splendour of the cities in which they stand.

¹ A series of letters to the author from Mrs Lewis in 1973 gave much of the background for this piece. Mr Peter Turner, a partner in the current firm of Mewès and Davis in London, is to be thanked for much help. The other useful source is C. H. Reilly, *Representative*

British Architects of the Present Day, Batsford, London 1931.

² Nikolaus Pevsner, *The Buildings of England: London* Vol. I, Penguin Books Ltd., second edition 1962.

³ Reilly *op cit* p.74.

⁴ The archives of the present-day firm of Mewès and Davis at 78 Wimpole Street contain a list of works by the firm, photographs and newspaper cuttings – but no drawings. The other buildings listed (few are dated) include in the 1920s or earlier: the rebuilding of Luton Hoo (1903); Ritz Hotels in Paris and Madrid; Cunard War Memorial (1921); 42 Upper Brook Street (1921); Mappin and Webb shop at Monte Carlo; 27 Portman Square; interiors for London Library; alterations to Royal Bank of Scotland in Burlington Gardens; National Bank of Scotland in Edinburgh; 42 Hill Street, 11 and 16 Charles Street; 13 Portland Place; Norbury Park near Dorking; Pools Cray Place in Kent, alterations at Luton Hoo; Credit Foncier in Paris; Bramshott Golf Club; R.A.C. Country Club at Woodcote Farm near Epsom; St John the Divine Church at Merton in Surrey; Vicarage at Merton; Spa Hotel at Contrexville; Dormeuil Ltd.; offices 25 Golden Square; 13 Warwick Street; 10 New Burlington Street; Cartier premises at 175 New Bond Street; alterations for Sotheby's at 35 New Bond Street and 5 George Street; Hunt and Roskell at 25 New Bond Street; 1 Burlington Street; Adams and Beeman's factory at Hackney; Garston Match factory at Garston; Morny factory at Perivale. In the 1930s: alterations at Claremont at Esher (1930); interiors for 1 Inverness Terrace; Alliance Assurance Co. in Bartholomew Lane (1932–33); West London Synagogue in Edgware Road (1933); Bagues Lighting Shop at 22 Grosvenor Square (*circa* 1930) and extension of Robert Adam's 20 St James's Square facade to cover No. 21 and remodelling interiors (1936–38). The interiors of the German liners *Amerika*, *Kaiserin Augusta*, *Berengaria* and *Leviathan* and the Esplanade Hotel in Hamburg were done by the Mewès firm, but probably by the German partner Bischoff. More than thirty other private houses are also listed, and Reilly illustrated a model of a strange multi-storey car park which Davis designed in about 1930.

Sir Albert Richardson: A Classic Case of Edwardianism

by Nicholas Taylor

Sir Albert Richardson (1880–1965) was not himself a major architectural figure during the pre-1914 era, but he knew personally many of those who were and worked with several of them. Two years before his death Nicholas Taylor recorded Richardson's recollections of the period, which, though the old man's memory was sometimes questionable, form a fascinating source for historians. Richardson went on to become President of the Royal Academy, a staunch practitioner of late 'stripped classical' in major buildings until late in life and of a life-style that fitted the title of this piece.

The late Sir Albert Richardson was a mythmaker, who embraced the novelty of the mass media with the extrovert eagerness of a Kruschev or a Hastings Banda. His myth, as the obituary notices sedulously repeated, was that he had been 'The Last of the Georgians'. He was no such thing. His love of fast cars and (in his early days) of long-distance bicycling,[1] his crowded accumulation of high quality bric-à-brac, his experienced courting of the world of big business, his outrageous use of the verbal pun, his rotund oratory, his smoking of equally rotund cigars – these were the essence of an Edwardian 'card', a dining club man *par excellence*. Only the outside of his house in the small Bedfordshire town of Ampthill maintained the illusion of symmetrical serenity – particularly as I first saw it, with Henry Holland's simple brick front of 1793 seen across freshly fallen snow. Everywhere within, from the entrance hall crowded with prints to the giant lavatory bowl patterned with roses in blue, happy chaos reigned, with the stubby figure of Richardson as acolyte. I was fortunate in spending two Saturday afternoons with him in 1963 (*aetatis suae* 83) and, at the first of these in particular, his generosity and enthusiasm and remarkable memory were in full spate.

His conversation is unreproducible in print, even though he let me take notes: he was a born actor, and the dramatic pause, the rehearsed spontaneous gesture, the knowing chuckle, and the (sometimes literal) dig in the ribs were an important part of his self-expression. The form of this account is a 'summary with interruptions'; and as such it forms a casebook for historians on the perplexing collapse of the English 'free' style around 1905 and the re-establishment of classicism in Edwardian architecture. It forms a twin testimony to that of H. S. Goodhart-Rendel, reported by Professor Pevsner (*The Architectural Review*, October 1965, also reprinted in this volume).

Richardson, born in 1880, the son of an Islington printer,[2] was articled in London at the age of fifteen to an 'architect and surveyor' named Victor Page. In the evening he went to tutors and to Birkbeck College, where he studied Engineering and Mechanical Construction. At the age of seventeen he became an assistant lecturer there, and a year later went as assistant to Evelyn Hellicar (1862–1929), an admirable Arts and Crafts architect who had been a pupil of T. G. Jackson. It was here that Richardson came in almost at the start of the neo-Georgian movement which had flowed

2 *Ernest Newton. Red Court, Haslemere, Hampshire (1894). Newton did more than anyone else to bring in the quiet neo-Georgian domestic manner at the end of the century.*

1 *Portrait of Sir Albert Richardson in 1955.*

from Norman Shaw's office. While Lethaby had given impetus to the *Art Nouveau* possibilities of Shaw's work, his predecessor as Shaw's chief assistant, Ernest Newton, had exploited in his Red Court at Haslemere (1894), the Early Georgian mode of Shaw's No. 170 Queen's Gate (1887–88).[3] This is turn had been preceded by Philip Webb's Smeaton Manor (1877–79) – Richardson told me that he was "influenced by Webb" and this is no doubt the house he meant. Hellicar was next on the scene after Newton: his Lufton Manor, near Yeovil (1897–98), was started a year earlier than Lutyens's first 'Queen Anne' façade on the east wing of Crooksbury Lodge (1898). Another of Hellicar's houses with Georgian tendencies, on which Richardson worked, was Southill Wood at Bromley (Hellicar's father was vicar of Bromlcy).[4]

How had the neo-Georgian come about? Richardson gave me a medley of answers, some obvious, others unexpected. First, there was Shaw, with his personal taste ("he had seventy-five grandfather clocks" – only a slight exaggeration), his clients ("Kate Greenaway, whom he did a house for, popularised the Regency fashion in her pictures – she sold costumes in Upper Street, Islington"), and his love of Church Row, near his home at Hampstead. Shaw's New Scotland Yard, although not in the Georgian style, was extremely influential in establishing a new kind of domestic monumentality ("an M.P. said it looked like Crosse and Blackwell's jam factory."). Its detail came, not as a pun on 'Scotland' as Hitchcock has suggested, but according to Richardson, "from the Renaissance buildings of Copenhagen". Still more important was the Baroque detail and formal plan of Shaw's Bryanston (1889–94), and Chesters (1891–94). Shaw's clients were

3 *Drawings and book illustrations such as this by Hanslip Fletcher emphasised the quiet street architecture of the Georgian period.*

swayed by the things they read, such as Thackeray's novels, with their pre-Victorian settings, which were paralleled by the author's own remarkable Georgian-style house in Kensington, No. 2 Palace Green (1860–61).[5] Hardy, an ex-architect, who brought to life the vernacular in his novels, had helped to design classical buildings during his time in the offices of Sir Arthur Blomfield (see below) and of Prof. T. Roger Smith, the faithfully orthodox successor to Donaldson and Hayter Lewis at University College. Illustrators such as Hugh Thomson and Hanslip Fletcher depicted the simple Georgian village streets, ("Fletcher lived in Upper Street – it was more like Bond Street in those days."). There was a revival of interest in 18th-century plays and stage design, hitherto considered immoral, and magazines illustrated Chippendale furniture. The aristocracy, who wanted such furniture to match their houses bought it from Waring and Gillow. Above all, architects suddenly 'discovered' the brick precincts of the Inns of Court, in which so many of them had their offices. Pupils and assistants started eagerly to make measured drawings of English classical buildings: Richardson drew, among others, Lindsay House in Lincoln's Inn Fields, Berwick-on-Tweed Town Hall, the Temple gateway, St Paul's Cathedral, old Christ's Hospital, and St Benet Paul's Wharf (the drawings for which are now in the Phené Spiers collection at the Victoria and Albert Museum).

The year before Richardson went to Hellicar at 10 Sergeants Inn, Reginald Blomfield (1856–1942), a young Shaw admirer, who lived in the Temple, published his *History of English Renaissance Architecture*. J. Alfred Gotch had already published his *Growth of Early English Renaissance Architecture*. ("A student asked, 'Have you got Gotch's Growth?' The bookseller answered, 'God help me, I hope not'.") Young architects and pupils of Richardson's age bought these two books eagerly, and also began to read Beaux Arts classics, by such authors as Durand, Charles Blanc, the brothers Goncourt and – the up-to-date masters – Choisy and Guadet. Such studies were encouraged by R. Phené Spiers (1838–1916), the Master of the Royal Academy School, whose Beaux Arts training had been followed by contributions to French publications such as *Croquis d'Architecture* (which Richardson collected), and books on *The Orders of Architecture* and *Architectural Drawing*. Realisation of the internationalism of the classical tradition (as against the nationalism of Gothic) was paralleled by the 'discovery' that the English classical tradition of Chambers and Cockerell had never in fact died. Men born in George III's reign were still alive and practising. Barry's pupil, John Gibson (1819–92) had designed splendid classical banks well into the time of Shaw and Newton; at the western end of Fleet Street his Child's Bank of 1879 was worthily faced by the Bank of England Law Courts branch of 1886–88 by Sir Arthur Blomfield, normally a rather insipid Goth.[6] Richardson was perhaps more aware of this continuity than anyone else: his remarkable book on *Monumental Classical Architecture in Great Britain and Ireland* (1914) contained an appreciation of Victorian richness and plasticity in the classical mode four years earlier than Goodhart-Rendel's celebrated re-evaluation of High Victorian Gothic in three *Architectural Review* articles on 'The Churches of Brighton'. Richardson's own files contained superb early photographs of Cockerell's Ashmolean, and 'Greek' Thomson's Egyptian Halls.

In 1902 Richardson moved to the office of Leonard Stokes (1858–1925), an excellent designer of Arts and Crafts Catholic churches and an admired young ex-president of the Architectural Association. At the moment Richardson arrived, Stokes "was in a mess", trying to convert the old octagonal Architectural Museum on Tufton Street (High Victorian Gothic of 1868–69, by Ewan Christian, and Joseph Clarke) into the new, pre-Bedford Square headquarters of the A.A. itself.[7] Stokes was the natural choice for this job, as his presidency of the A.A. (1889–91)[8] had seen the crucial decisions which ultimately influenced the whole profession away from the individualistic and sporadic upbringing of articled pupilage and towards regular academic teaching in full-time architectural schools.

Why had Richardson gone to become chief assistant to a Gothic architect? The answer lies in Stokes's rational approach to architecture as well as to education. After his training under Street, Bodley and Garner, and T. E. Collcutt (a picturesque Classicist and himself a Street pupil), Stokes became an admirer of J. L. Pearson's Albi- and Gerona-influenced churches. His St Clare, Sefton Park, Liverpool (1888–90), is an Arts and Crafts paraphrase of Pearson. Richardson admired this church and also Pearson's St Augustine,

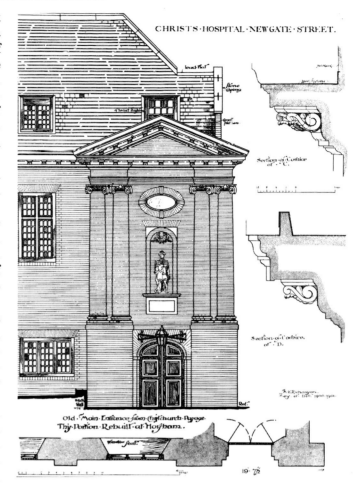

4 *Early drawing by Richardson of old Christ's Hospital, Newgate Street.*

5 *Leonard Stokes. No. 2 West Drive, Streatham, London (1899). A free version of neo-Georgian typical of the architect, for whom Richardson worked in 1902–03.*

Kilburn ("It was very High Church – 'St Disgustin's', the charladies called it") because they displayed a 'classical' handling of Gothic. Pearson's single-minded and systematic build-up of vaulted cells at Kilburn and Red Lion Square (another Richardson favourite) not only reflected the structural theory of Viollet-le-Duc but also – even if coincidentally – shows a similar discipline of elementary composition to that which emanated from the Beaux Arts. Moreover, Stokes himself had turned to a severe stripped classicism for domestic work, after his marriage in 1898 to Miss Gaine, daughter of the general manager of the National Telephone Company, had brought him a rich harvest of telephone exchanges. That at Gerrard Street, Soho (1908, demolished 1936), was perhaps the finest example of his free rationalism. No. 2 West Drive at Streatham, is a fine Early Georgian house by Stokes of 1899. He was a friend of his fellow Roman Catholic, J. M. Brydon, a former Shaw assistant whose Chelsea Town Hall (1885–87) and Bath Guildhall extensions (1891) had shown remarkably early a sympathy with Palladianism (Stokes extended Chelsea in 1904–08 just after Richardson left his office).

Partly because of his rationalism and partly because of his paradoxically impulsive temperament (he was a devout Catholic), Stokes stood a little apart from his admiring contemporaries. Richardson told me of the strict and sometimes alarming atmosphere in the Great Smith Street office. They started at 9 a.m. and had 45 minutes for lunch ("17 for the meal and 28 in the Abbey.") Stokes sat in an end room making sketches and sending them down to be drawn out. His pupils and assistants ('Damned Colonials' and 'Damned Scotsmen' were his two main descriptive labels) frequently felt the whip of his tongue ("One day he was swearing at the top of his voice – and the ceiling of his office fell in. He fell on his knees, prayed and crossed himself, gave cheques to all the assistants – and was worse the next morning."). The assistants used to retreat to the lavatory, where they read *The Daily Mail*[9] until their master shouted for them. Stokes's finest work of those days was All Saints Convent at London Colney, begun in 1899 ("a modernistic version of the Cambridge college gateway with cornices based on the Greek ovulo moulding"). Comper eventually did the chapel there ("Stokes lost the job – he called the Mother Superior a 'Damned Woman' to her face"). Stokes was equally frank about his brother architects: Bodley's churches were "slanting-dicular"[10] and when Voysey left the office after a visit, Stokes said "Did you see his boots? He designed them." Richardson pointed out to me the influence of Stokes on Lutyens, particularly at Grey Walls, Gullane (1901), and also the curious premonition he gave at times of Ostberg's detailing at Stockholm Town Hall. Stokes's disciplined approach to design was best seen in his feeling for scale: so sure was he of the relationship of part to part that "he never put dimensions on his plans." Perhaps it is this precision,

alien to the English picturesque, that has deprived his masterpiece, North Court at Emmanuel College, Cambridge (1910–14), from achieving wide acclaim (Richardson warmly admired it).

At the end of 1903 Richardson moved as chief assistant to the office of Frank T. Verity (1864–1937). Neither Verity nor his father Thomas (1838–91) appears in any of the standard historical works, and several of their major buildings are excluded from Pevsner's London volumes; yet the products of their office are symptomatic of a fundamental change in English architecture that so nearly happened but did not. This revolution – the adoption of the methods and aims, educational in particular, of European, and especially French, classicism – was until recently the very thing that all English modern architects had to disavow in order to keep their self-respect. In the mid-'60s we can now perceive and value the essentially classical genealogies of Schinkel-Behrens-Mies and Garnier-Perret-Le Corbusier. We can see that a significant group of English modern pioneers – Burnet, de Soissons, Robertson, Goldfinger – did their best work[11] directly under the influence of a Parisian training. Moreover, in the world of prefabrication and precasting, such vital things as the correct detailing of a joint require the kind of mental discipline and *expertise* which the Beaux Arts training once gave to the historicist detailing of cornices and drip mouldings. The pioneers, after Stokes, of architectural and town planning education in Britain – Reilly, Adshead, Atkinson – were deeply impressed by the Beaux Arts sense of logic, and all three of them were also notably open to the new architecture when it came. Reyner Banham has briefly drawn attention[12] to the reaction against *Art Nouveau* and the Glasgow School, coupled with the change in attitude of *The Architectural Review* after the appointment as editor in 1905 of another Shaw pupil, Mervyn Macartney. This reaction came much earlier than Banham indicates – long before it reached the publicity of print – and it seems to have sprung from various places more or less simultaneously.

The freedom from Gothic detail that led to the 'free architecture' of Lethaby and Voysey had led simultaneously, and much less satisfactorily, to the development of a relaxed, undisciplined English Baroque manner by architects who had been trained as Goths, but who had large secular practices in the City where clients demanded representational grandeur. It was among the pupils of these men that *expertise* was rediscovered. The pupils despised their masters for their ungrammatical *melange* of detail, but, as Richardson made clear to me, they also admired their masters' courage in using the giant orders once more. Perhaps the key building was John Belcher's Institute of Chartered Accountants (1889–92), which, according to Richardson (and it fits stylistically) was largely designed by Belcher's pupil, Beresford Pite. Jealousy between the two men led to Pite's departure; Pite thenceforth trod a fascinating but unproductive path between Lethabitic Byzantine and revived neo-Grec,[13] with wilful touches intermingled from Michelangelesque Mannerism, Alfred Stevens and English Baroque ("he was very one-sided, very religious – used to preach on Saturdays at Hyde Park").[14] After Pite, Belcher[15] who had originally designed High Victorian Gothic offices with his father, engaged J. J. Joass (from Sir Ernest George's office) as chief assistant); other Belcher pupils included Sir Charles Reilly, S. D. Adshead and Curtis Green. His next important work was Colchester Town Hall ('Belchester') of 1897 and this was followed by Electra House in Moorgate (1902–03), Mappin and Webb in Oxford Street of 1906, ("It's faced with Pentelic marble, though it looks rusty now"), the extraordinary, vertically accented Royal Insurance Building in Piccadilly (1907), Whiteley's store (1908–10), and Holy Trinity, Kingsway (1910–12). T. E. Collcutt, whose claims to monumentality had been established by the Imperial Institute, used a simplified

Baroque for the river block of the Savoy Hotel (1889) and Lloyd's Register of Shipping (1900), the details of which (see *The Architectural Review* June 1963) were much admired ("He was very good, but small in scale; he had been brought up as a joiner and was meticulous in detail"). His Opera House for D'Oyly Carte at Cambridge Circus (1890) was the climax of the 'Reign of Terracotta'. Among his pupils was A. N. Prentice, who published a book with influential drawings of Spanish Renaissance detail. T. G. Jackson, whose success in the Oxford Examination Schools competition in 1876 had been the crucial public victory for the 'pictorial' English Renaissance, was "a fine scholar and writer" but "no good as an architect – no grandeur of effect, too much detail – *Plateresque*". Then there was Aston Webb, yet another ex-Goth and an ambitious competition-winner ("He was the fox, the sneak, worked for himself entirely and against others").[16] Webb's success in winning the Victoria and Albert Museum limited competition in 1891 was followed by his success in the

6 *Frank T. Verity. Flats, No. 12 Hyde Park Place, Bayswater Road, London (1902–03). Richardson became his assistant in 1903.*

similar 1901 competition for the Queen Victoria Memorial in front of Buckingham Palace. This skilfully detailed *rond-point* was a milestone in the introduction of Parisian principles to London; the assistant responsible for it was Ralph Knott, the ill-fated winner of the County Hall competition in 1908, for which Webb was one of the assessors ("A splendid design," remarked Richardson, "until the L.C.C. architect Riley insisted on the curve in the middle, the bite out of the cheesecake.").

Verity's office at 7 Sackville Street, when Richardson arrived at the end of 1903, was among the very small number where authentic Continental classicism had been adopted instead of the bastardised English Baroque of Belcher, Collcutt and Aston Webb. Thomas Verity, Frank's father, had been trained in the days of the Second Empire and was responsible for detailing the Albert Hall under Captain Fowke and Major-General Scott (1867–70). His reputation was chiefly founded on his work in the two building types where Parisian influence remained paramount: restaurants and theatres. The restaurant tradition[17] was rooted in Archer and Green's Café Royal (1865–85); major works were Verity's own competition-winning Criterion (1870–73, since altered) and Archer & Green's Holborn Restaurant (1883–85); Collcutt followed with Frascati's (1893), the Holborn Restaurant extension (1894), Simpson's in the Strand (1903–04) and his interiors of the P & O liners. Theatres were consistently 'continental',[18] in the lavish ungrammatical Baroque of such architects as Phipps and Bertie Crewe, or the Plateresque of Collcutt's two theatres for D'Oyly Carte.[19] In 1884, Thomas Verity had designed the lavishly Parisian Empire Theatre at Leicester Square for Daniel Nicols, the proprietor of the Café Royal; and in 1900–01 Frank was the architect of Lily Langtry's short-lived Imperial Theatre. One of Collcutt's best pupils, experienced in theatre design, joined Frank Verity as an assistant; he was Harold Norton, son of the High Victorian Gothic architect, John Norton.[20] In 1904 Richardson and Norton detailed the richly Baroque rebuilding by Verity (within a plain brick exterior) of the old Regent Theatre in Charlotte Street as the Scala. It was done for a certain Dr Distin Maddick ("we called him Mad Dick"). The influence here was mainly Viennese, but the Verity office had also become fascinated with the Baroque mastery of Garnier's Paris Opéra. Frank Verity was an enthusiastic Francophile,[21] Bohemian in manners, and he visited Paris with Richardson, who collected prints of Rome Prize schemes and other splendidly Imperial fantasies. They made elaborate sketches of Garnier's work, particularly the Opéra's hierarchical staircase, of J.-L. Duc's Palais de Justice[22] and of much work by Hittorff. They watched with approval the neo-classical rebuilding of the Sorbonne by Henri-Paul Nénot. 'Pattern planning' was the new gospel and J.-L. Pascal (1839–1920), the Beaux Arts professor, was the new patron saint, his

elaborate and theoretical 'triple plan' being particularly admired.

Verity's main contacts were with the new moneyed classes, who were then settling in flats in the West End of London.[23] Edward VII himself gave the aristocratic lead in taste which had been so important throughout the 19th century. He was cosmopolitan, secular and Francophile, and his court was consciously that of a great European king.[24] It is not surprising, therefore, that the *nouveau riches* wanted to live in Parisian style. Starting with 12 Hyde Park Place in Bayswater Road (1902–03, just before Richardson arrived), Verity's office developed a smoothly machined Champs-Elysées style of *maisons-de-luxe* which eliminated the traditional and clumsy giant order in favour of big windows, neat stonework and flowing iron balconies. Plans of a well-organised and economical symmetry enclosed interiors of crisp neo-classical detail, in reconstructed stone. Other major examples by Verity are (or were) 25 Berkeley Square (1904, detailed entirely by Richardson), 3–7 Cleveland Row (1905–07),[25] 11a and b Portland Place (1908, demolished), 70–74 Portland Place and 140 Park Lane (1913). The elder Verity, through his theatre work, had been appointed architect to the Lord Chamberlain's Department and it was in succession to him that his son was given the job of redecorating the state rooms of Buckingham Palace itself – a job for which he has never been credited in the books. The work started in 1902 with the ballroom and the Grand Hall; when Richardson joined Verity's office in 1903, he saw inside Buckingham Palace the concluding stages of Edward VII's holocaust of his mother's furniture, piled up over sixty years (Victoria loved her possessions and had never parted with any). The Verity remodelling was basically a return to Nash and Pennethorne, with a few extra French touches: the Thrones for example (Richardson was proud of saying that he had "sat on the Throne") were purchased in Paris by Sir Joseph Duveen, the art collector.[26]

Three architects, two very young, descended on London at that moment: Edwin Rickards (1872–1920), Arthur Davis (1878–1951) and John Burnet (1857–1938). Rickards was a brilliant draughtsman who fell in love with Viennese Baroque and joined in partnership with a Scotsman, Stewart, who died in 1904, and with an able planner, H. V. Lanchester (1863–1953), who was brother of the motor manufacturer. Their victory in the Cardiff Civic Centre competition in 1897 was an important landmark – the assessor was Alfred Waterhouse, the one English Gothic Revivalist who had mastered the planning of public buildings with the skill of the French classicists. The younger men were very much excited by Cardiff and by the same firm's later competition successes, Deptford Town Hall (1901), Godalming Town Hall (1901, not built), Hull Art School (1903), the concrete-framed Central Hall (1905), and the Third Church of Christ Scientist, Curzon Street (1908). Probably as influential as these public

competitors employed him. Hi
was the very French Royal Vict
gate. Richardson and Gill rent
per week an office 7 feet by 6 a
Russell Street, a house formerl
Caldecott, the artist;[38] later the
large room for £1 a week. Th
Reilly, having persuaded the so
(of Port Sunlight) to endow at L
of Civic Design in this country,
brilliant perspectivist's sense
buildings and appointed him
youthful Abercrombie as his as
according to Richardson, "the
that Reilly wanted Adshead to
the Liverpool students' entrie
Reilly was brilliant, unconve
and his influence on architectu
ing. But it was Adshead who
break architecturally – by a cl
holiday in France with Sir
1956), Resident Councillor and

buildings were two shops in Bond Street, Knoedler's and Colnaghi's, which Rickards designed in 1911 in pure Parisian pastiche. Apparently "the slogan was 'Try Lickard's Rococo'."

There was admittedly a certain element of bluff in the superb theatricality of Rickard's work. Arthur Davis by contrast was the real thing: a prize-winning pupil at the Beaux-Arts, selected by the architect of the Hotel Ritz, Charles François Mewès (1858–1914), as the English partner of his international practice.[27] Mewès and Davis together won fourth prize in the

competition for the Grand and Petit Palais, which to the classicists were the finest things at the Paris Exhibition of 1900, now remembered only for its *Art Nouveau* attractions. The Ritz Hotel (1904–06), the Morning Post building in Aldwych (1905–07, now mutilated) and the Royal Automobile Club (1908–11), all steel-framed, established Davis as England's premier classicist at the age of thirty – he was only two years older than Richardson. Davis's clients stank of money – he was able to afford full-scale plaster mock-ups of external details before building commenced. He designed the interiors of several new Cunard liners – *Aquitania, Laconia* and *Franconia*. In 1913 he became the head of the First Atelier (it was also the last), an ambitious attempt to reproduce the École des Beaux-Arts in London, which perished in 1914, but which had a strong influence on the curriculum of the A.A. school under Atkinson and Robertson and of the Bartlett school under Richardson after the War.

Perhaps the most potent of all buildings at this time – singled out by Goodhart-Rendel in his *English Architecture since the Regency* as the ideal of 'Expertise Restored' – was the King Edward VII Galleries added to the British Museum (1905–14), designed by Sir John Burnet. Burnet's background united the Glasgow classical tradition of 'Greek' Thomson, James Sellars and Hippolyte Blanc[28] with a training in the Pascal atelier in Paris, where he was a contemporary of Mewès. A close friend of his was another Pascal pupil, the important American architect C. F. McKim (of McKim, Mead and White). Through Burnet the post-Chicago Exhibition American classical influence came to London[29] – the British Museum building could well be in Washington – and it was confirmed almost immediately by "the big, booming voice" (Pevsner's phrase) of Daniel H. Burnham of Chicago in Selfridge's store.[30] Selfridge's admittedly alarmed students by its vulgarity ("'Don't you be so Selfridge,' we said," muttered Richardson), but in spite of it Robert Atkinson brought the ideas of McKim and Cass Gilbert into A.A. teaching when the became headmaster in 1912. Richardson himself corresponded with Fiske Kimball.

The ill-fated rebuilding of Regent Street became the crucible of all the various experiments in classicism, English, French and American, and Richardson himself played a considerable part, both before and after he left Verity's office. In 1908 he set up in practice in partnership with his fellow assistant, Lovett Gill (1880–1960) who came from Devonshire. It was a complementary arrangement: Gill was in no way an artist-architect but knew the business side well ("he did all the planning in Verity's office and not the artwork at all"). A year earlier, Richardson had been appointed as a lecturer at the Regent Street Polytechnic ("my wages there of £5 a week were a considerable improvement on my chief assistant's pay of £2. 10. 0."). Soon after, he (officially still 'F. T. Verity') got the job of designing the front of the new building for the Poly,

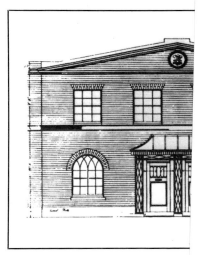

8 *Adshead and Ramsey. Model hous*
Cornwall at Courtenay Square, Ken

9 *Richardson and Gill. Cottages des*
architect's work for the Duchy of Co

7 *Sir Albert Richardson (as assistant to Frank T. Verity). Detail, Polytechnic of Central London, upper Regent Street (designed 1907). A year later, Richardson went into practice in partnership with Lovett Gill.*

which began the transmogrifi
Street. The interior built at th
effort by the then head of the F
school, G. A. Mitchell, and th
executed until 1911, some tim
now hemmed in by amorphou
minor architects. It also needs
it still preserves a monument:
archical organisation of Beau
most other London façades of

Further down Regent Stre
about to be demolished *en ma*
Commissioners. Already ther
matical classicism of Nos. 235
and 184–186 (1899, by Willi:
full-dress English Baroque o
dilly Hotel (1905–08). Normar
for the rest of the Quadrant, w
heavily blocked columns a:
dows,[31] aroused fury among
display space would have l
lighted. It also horrified the
had hitherto valued Shaw for
of his increasing classicism
ignored by the Commission
Shaw on the advice of an ex;
of Shaw himself, Sir Aston
Sir John Taylor of the Of
keepers, led by Swan & Edg
petition, sponsored by *The I*
1912 by Richardson and Gill
Their design was a restrain
("my treatment was a retur
Nash and Pennethorne – w:
IV's son by Mrs Nash – h(
qualities"). It was orname:
detail and, in contrast to Sh
One of the three assessors
tribute was paid to his Bor
son's dashingly Parisian p
had previously asked Rich
him, but Richardson refuse
cularly to a man whose Bar
ally, in 1916, the expert co:
sisted of Webb, Ernest New
Sir Henry Tanner of the
Murray of the Crown Com:
field to design the present c
in 1923–28). For all the m
writing,[34] sketching and le
R.A. from 1907), Blomfic
"contradicted in his own
learnt from the French. In:
spontaneity – the individu
over again."

Meanwhile, Verity, ag
most of the detail, had de
up Regent Street, betwee

he contributed articles and grandiose illustrations of urbanistic reorganisation on the Parisian model to *The Architectural Review* and to *The Architect's Journal*, of which he became Editor in 1919–22. He redesigned the frontage of 59 Tothill Street of Technical Journals Ltd. (the Architectural Press's former name). He wrote books on *London Houses from 1660 to 1820* (1912), *Regional Architecture in the West of England* (1924), both with Gill, and *Monumental Classical Architecture in Great Britain and Ireland* (1914), which was dedicated to the Prince of Wales. It was largely this literary work and his increasing reputation as a provocative lecturer – with a remarkable facility for instant giant sketching on the blackboard – that led to his appointment in 1919 as Professor of Architecture at University College, London, where he remained until 1946.

In 1910 a great classical revival seemed under way. It petered out. "All the time we were hoping for a Great Revolution," said Richardson, "and it never came. It was a period of transition," he added, "producing chaotic results." Sir Charles Reilly's book on *Representative British Architects* (1930) is a record of unrelieved failure – hard though he tried, he could

find virtually nothing of note to add to the career of each architect after 1918. The book on so-called *Modern Architecture* by Charles Marriott, art critic of *The Times*, which came out in 1924, is equally depressing. First, and most obviously, the outbreak of the Great War in 1914 had put a stop to the creation of a grand new Parisian London, of which Richardson and his friends had dreamed and drawn such grand perspectives. After 1918, tastes were simpler and money was scarcer. There was a general failure of nerve amongst the property speculators: the mass of work by Tanner in Regent Street and Treherne & Norman in Kingsway was begun before 1914 and marks the beginning of that general loss of imperial confidence which, for example, transformed Vincent Harris's 1913 Board of Trade design into the sadly emasculated Whitehall Gardens building finished in 1959.[41] The 1909 budget was partly responsible. "It was a time of uncertainty," said Richardson. "The patrons were dying off, and Lutyens worked for the last of them." The Royal Academy plan for London (1944), inspired by Lutyens, was the posthumous fling of the Beaux Arts planners. "Lutyens always had the ambition to rebuild London; he was

10 *Richardson and Gill. New Theatre, Manchester (opened 1912).*

very jealous when Baker got the Bank."

Mention of Lutyens and Baker, however, takes us nearer the heart of the failure. These two architects had come to the top in 1912 – yet (in spite of Lutyens's Heathcote and Hampstead) they were not real classicists. Both were former assistants of Sir Ernest George – George of the pretty Flemish-style houses and watercolours – and their approach to architecture was essentially pictorial. Their antecedents were not Beaux Arts and Parisian, but developed from that bastard 'Wrenaissance' which became the 'competition manner' of the Edwardian period. Its chief exponents were E. W. Mountford (Central Criminal Court) and H. T. Hare (Oxford and Henley Town Halls). Lutyens had turned from his brilliant romantic Surrey houses to the Baroque of Heathcote at Ilkley in 1903. "He was a brilliant elevationist in brick and stone, not a planner," Richardson commented. Baker started with his pretty Cape Dutch houses in South Africa, and made his name with the pictorial Baroque of the Government Buildings, Pretoria, in which porticoes were wrapped nonchalantly round corners, where they would make the prettiest effect. In 1912 Lutyens was appointed to design his greatest work, the Viceroy's House and civic layout of New Delhi. ("He got the job through his marriage to a daughter of Lytton, a former Viceroy.") On the grounds that the job was too large for one man, the Government appointed Baker (on the strength of his Pretoria work) to design the Government Secretariats and Parliament Building. The two men, who hitherto had been close friends, became increasingly incompatible in temperament: Lutyens irreverent, untidy, bawdy and artistic, Baker elegant, hard, dogmatic and practical.[42] Richardson told me how Lutyens learnt of Baker's appointment (which he had earlier recommended). He came into his office one day to find Baker sitting at a desk, leafing through his (Lutyens's) preliminary sketches. As is well known, the partnership turned out badly – Baker's buildings, besides their inferior detailing, were built on a raised platform which cut rudely across Lutyens's central vista and ruined the approach to the superb Viceroy's House. Lutyens said, "That was my Bakerloo." He invited Richardson to help him on the Delhi designs, but once again, "I refused a subordinate role."

"The trouble was," said Richardson, "we were a band of individualists, not a band of brothers."[43] There was tremendous enthusiasm, marked by 'a surfeit of books'. "Every architect had a library . . . and when we hadn't got books, we made our own." Richardson's own crowded sketch books are proofs of the faith of the young men who sketched in Paris – drawing after drawing after drawing of palaces, squares, fountains, finials, giant orders, cornices, entablatures, apses, domes, obelisks, statues, plinths, brackets. Work in the spirit of the 18th-century masters led him to buy in bulk, from the Temple, lawyers' notebooks of the period and to tear out unused leaves; he could then sketch on real

18th-century paper with vivacious little figures echoing his Georgian namesake (some of whose work he possessed). His collection at Ampthill of furniture and pictures was formed for purposes of teaching and study; one of the last of its kind, it is a remarkable survival of the taste of the period. His enthusiasm for all this was infectious – for Piranesian fantasy as much as for rural cottage – but so in 1963 was his sadness. "We were attempting to restore the national heritage and ideal . . . architects are interpreters not originators . . . the people coming on now are not scholars and artists . . . scholarship went out, technology has come in." Yet this is the crucial point – he was quite unable to see that an understanding of technology and structure had formed an essential part of Beaux Arts training. Only Charles Holden and John Burnet of English architects grasped this (significantly, they were left out of the 'top twelve' architects described in Reilly's book). Richardson's bitterness against Holden was intense. After his appointment in 1919 as Professor of Architecture at University College, London, he had unofficially been promised the design of the central buildings of London University in Bloomsbury. Against this there was mounted, perhaps fortunately, a campaign led by the brothers Bone (Muirhead the artist and James the journalist) and other supporters of the Modern Movement, which resulted in Holden's appointment to design the present unsatisfactory building. I have discovered a second and similar reason for Richardson's dislike of Holden (and also a reason for some malicious remarks about Frank Pick);[44] he and Gill had designed (*circa* 1924) the Underground Railway Company headquarters at St James's Park Station. The model shows that it was a conventional essay in the Richardson-Verity Parisian manner, with a rusticated ground floor and six floors of uniform fenestration on a rounded corner.[45] With its flat face to the street and (presumably) grimy inner courtyard, it would have lacked any of the

11 *Richardson and Gill. Model of design for Underground Railway Company headquarters, above St James's Park station, London (1924). Frank Pick later appointed Charles Holden to design the building instead of Richardson.*

qualities that still make Holden's great building of 1927–29 for Frank Pick such a memorably essay in modern civic design. The inadequacy of Richardson's approach was nowhere more evident than in his comments to me about Lethaby (who had nevertheless been a close friend of his).[46] "He was very bitter about imitation and shams. But what was his answer? 'Structure' – a slogan echoed by all the mob of functionalists. Surely the answer is not that, but the *conception*, the *effect*, the *modelling* that make the beauty of a building. Lethaby's books encouraged all these young men who like putting the bowels outside the flesh."

Without a fundamental logic in design, from inner structure to modelled cornice, the neo-classical movement fell apart. Some died (Belcher in 1913, Rickards in 1920), others turned to teaching (of these Richardson was one of the few who kept up a large private practice), others lost their youthful verve (Arthur Davis in particular, after ill-health in the war). Under the later Lutyens and the later Baker, the English picturesque re-asserted itself in the blushing neo-Georgian brickwork which dominated the historicist scene in the '20s (and since). Yet in the last year or two before the Great War, the frame structures of Edwardian classi-cism in London had gone far towards the positions occupied by Behrens in Germany and Perret in France. F. W. Troup's Blackfriars House (1913) for Spicer's, Dunbar Smith and Cecil Brewer's Heal's store (1916); Eustace Frere's General Medical Council, Hallam Street (1915); Sir Richard Allison's Cornwall House, Stamford Street (1912); Sir James West's Ministry of Pensions building at Acton (1914); Sir John Burnet's Kodak building, Kingsway (1911); C. Stanley Peach's W. H. Smith depot, now Reveille, Stamford Street (1915); Walter Cave's Burberry's store, Haymarket (1912); and Charles Holden's British Medical Association, now Rhodesia House, Strand (1907) – none of these are buildings to embarrass the present-day progressive, though none of these architects, not even Holden, maintained similar standards throughout his career. Richardson's Moorgate Hall (1915) shows the same tendency towards stripped detail and purified proportion,[47] spoilt in his case by a failure to persuade shopkeepers to accept flat pilasters which plummeted straight to the pavement (Shaw's old problem).

In the '20s, alas, most of these leaders lost their way somewhere between bypass Tudor and jazz modern. Holden, as all the world knows, did painstakingly

12 *Richardson and Gill. Leith House, Gresham Street, City of London (1925). Richardson valued classical proportions and developed what has been termed a 'stripped classical' manner.*

456

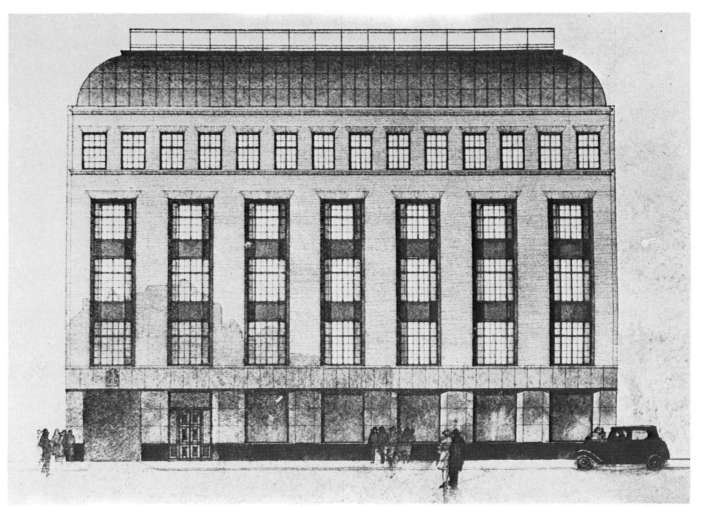

13 *Richardson and Gill. St Margaret's House, Wells Street, off Oxford Street, London (1931). Front and rear elevations remain extremely striking today.*

achieve a modern vernacular; and Tait (Burnet's successor), in spite of a dreadful lapse at the *Daily Telegraph*, eventually reached Ravenscourt Park by way of Adelaide House and Silver End. These two reserved Scotsmen could not fail to appeal to the new puritanism when it came. Professor A. E. Richardson, however, and his successor Sir Albert, came to enjoy an embattled ebullience as the Grand Old Menace, acting out a neo-Classical comedy on the stage of the Bartlett and of Burlington House; and his often deplorable joy in infighting (that extrovert mythmaking with which we started this article) has not surprisingly failed to attract generosity from those he wounded. And yet . . . in two splendid London buildings of the interwar years, Leith House in Gresham Street (1925) and St. Margaret's House in Wells Street (1931)[48] he went quite as far away from historicist detail as most of the more obvious progressives, while keeping a certain scale and depth of splay which are becoming more readily appreciated in the '60s. Once more, at a time when he was otherwise designing developer's hulks in pink brick Georgian, he revived this '20s style in Bracken House (1955–58), the extraordinary Financial Times building close to St Paul's. One has only to compare Bracken House with the deplorable Bank of England offices nearby (the designer of these, Victor Heal, was, oddly enough, one of Bodley's last pupils in 1905–07, and for a time did admirable neo-Gothic with his master's successor, Cecil Hare) to recognise its obstinate warmth and personality. Here indeed we have, *not* neo-Georgian, but (out of time) one of the last of the great 'stripped classic' palaces which formed the transition between historicism and the Modern Movement. The Professor's true position, secure from the myths, can perhaps be found in his contribution to an R.I.B.A. discussion on 'Modernism in Architecture' in 1928.[49]

"We have learned to simplify, to invent, to economise. We have learned to meet new conditions. Planning has shown us the lines on which the art is likely to develop. Concrete has demonstrated new structural possibilities. The copy-book has been relegated to the architectural nursery. But we architects nevertheless still have a just pride in the past, a reasonable view of the present, and a keen desire to invent. In the works of Sullivan, Otto Wagner, Tony Garnier, etc., you will find a vindication of classical principles. These men have advanced the art".

457

I am very grateful for the help I have received from Sir Albert Richardson's family: from his daughter and son-in-law, Mr and Mrs E. A. S. Houfe, and particularly from his grandson, Mr Simon Houfe, who is collecting material for a biography – and yet allowed me access to sketch-books and other unpublished material.

[1] He once cycled up the Great North Road to Edinburgh in three days, timed by W. H. Bidlake, the excellent Birmingham church architect (a pupil of Bodley).

[2] Though his family came originally from Berwick-on-Tweed.

[3] 170 Queens Gate was neo-Georgian because the client wanted it so.

[4] Other Hellicar houses include Cawston Manor, 1896 (given by Pevsner in his *Norfolk* to Sir Ernest George); Luton House, Selling, Kent; Hollands, Yeovil; Lattiford, Wincanton; Peak House, Sidmouth; Buckwell Down, Somerset; Winterborne Whitchurch, Dorset; Raheen, Ireland; and Front House, Bovey Tracey – see Richardson's obituary of him in the *Journal of the Royal Institute of British Architects* 1929.

[5] Yet another, perhaps even more remarkable, example of early neo-Early-Georgian designed by an amateur is Crabbet Park, Worth, Sussex, designed for Wilfred Scawen Blunt (another author) in 1873 by his wife, Lady Anne Noel. See Pevsner's *Sussex*, p.642.

[6] In fact it was to Sir Arthur Blomfield that his nephew, Reginald, was articled in 1881–83 – not to Norman Shaw, as is usually stated.

[7] The site is now occupied by the back parts of 35 Great Smith Street (the National Library for the Blind), designed in 1927 by Sydney Tatchell.

[8] Described in Sir John Summerson's *The Architectural Association*, 1947.

[9] A daring thing to do, only five years after Northcliffe's 1896 revolution.

[10] Richardson himself damned with the nicest praise Bodley's Queens' College Chapel, Cambridge (1890) as "a very ladylike little chapel"—classicism no doubt symbolized virility in contrast to such laciness.

[11] Examples of such 'classical modern' are Kodak House, Kingsway (1910–11) by Burnet; the Shredded Wheat factory, Welwyn (1925) by de Soissons; the British Pavilion at the 1925 Paris Exhibition by Robertson; and the Ministry of Health at the Elephant and Castle (1961–63) by Goldfinger.

[12] *Theory and Design in the First Machine Age*, 1960, pp.44–45, 48.

[13] Pite's best buildings of each type were Christ Church, North Brixton (1898–1902), and the London, Edinburgh and Glasgow Assurance building, Euston Square (1907).

[14] Religious passion may in fact partly have caused Pite's split with Belcher, who was a devoted 'Irvingite' (that is, a member of the ritualistic Catholic Apostolic Church).

[15] Belcher was a close friend of Macartney, the editor of *The Architectural Review*; together they wrote *Later Renaissance Architecture in England*. In his obituary of Belcher (*The Architectural Review* December 1913, pp.127–128), Macartney went out of his way to emphasize that Blecher "expended great and loving labour" on the Chartered Accountants building and that "he told me, more than once, that every detail was designed by himself"—but this smacks of special pleading (why would Macartney say it otherwise?).

[16] "He used to ride on a horse to his office in Queen Anne's Gate," Richardson remembered. It is only fair to Sir Aston Webb to remind readers of Goodhart-Rendel's entirely contrary verdict (*The Architectural Review*, October 1965) that "I never knew anyone who was more popular with his colleagues than he was."

[17] This tradition was analyzed in 'Rococo Grill Room,' *The Architectural Review*, April 1965.

[18] Also concert halls, where (in spite of Sullivan) English music had been virtually excluded in favour of continental masters.

[19] The People's Palace at Mile End (1885–87), by the excellent Board School architect, E. R. Robson, was another brave attempt to be Parisian, as was his Royal Institute of Painters in Water Colours, Piccadilly (1881). Robson incidentally had designed an exceptional, if rather dry, piece of neo-Georgian, Blackheath High School (1879). His horrific extension to Queen Anne's Mansions (1887–89) is another story (*The Architectural Review* April 1966).

[20] Who himself had turned to Renaissance of a sort in the South-Western Hotel at Southampton (1871–72) and the Submarine Telegraph Company's offices, London Wall (1880). Harold Norton, a man of considerable talent, had the misfortune of a severe speech impediment and eventually took his own life.

[21] His French contacts gave him the job of designing the French Hospital, Shaftesbury Avenue (1899).

[22] See Richardson's article on 'The Palais de Justice, Paris, and its remodelling by Joseph Louis Duc,' *The Architectural Review* November 1913, pp.93–94, 102.

[23] See Verity's own article on 'The Designing of Flats-de-Luxe, and the illustrations of his work, in *Flats, Urban Houses and Cottage Homes*, edited by W. Shaw Sparrow, *circa* 1908. See also Richardson's own article on Verity's flats in *The Architectural Review* 1908, pp.286–296.

[24] Symbolized best perhaps by Asquith's kissing hands on his appointment as Prime Minister, not at Buckingham Palace but in the Hôtel du Palais at Biarritz.

[25] At the corner of Cleveland Row and St James's Street Verity's flats adjoin the sober Alliance Assurance (1903) by Norman Shaw and Ernest Newton.

[26] Art collectors were an important influence in favour of Paris. The interiors of Sir Julius Wernher's own house at Luton Hoo, for example, were by Mewès and Davis.

[27] His partner in Germany was A. Bischoff.

[28] Blanc was a genuine Beaux-Arts-trained Frenchman, yet his buildings, oddly enough, are less purely classical than those of several of his native Scots contemporaries.

[29] In 1908–09 *The Architectural Review* ran a series of articles by Francis S. Swales on America.

[30] Burnham was consulting architect to Selfridge. Construction was first supervised by R. Frank Atkinson (1871–1923); when he dropped out, Sir John Burnet took over and built the westward expansion (1919–28) which took up the whole super-block.

[31] Richardson suggested to me that the elderly Shaw turned for much of the detail of this extravaganza to an assistant, Ingleson Goodison, later an expert on furniture.

[32] The full sad story is given in *The Survey of London, Parish of St James, Westminster, Part II: North*, 1963, pp.85–95

[33] The other two were William Flockhart and Alan Munby. For Flockhart, see 'Goodhart-Rendel's Roll-Call,' *The Architectural Review* October 1966 and reprinted in this volume. Rickards' partner Lanchester was at this time briefly editor of *The Builder* (1910–12). The competition results are illustrated in the July 1912 issue, pp.1–2, 12, 35–37 and 46.

[34] The influence of Blomfield's writings was enormous (he had won a First in Greats at Oxford). Besides *English Renaissance Architecture* (already mentioned), his chief books were *The Formal Garden in England* (1893), *The Mistress Art* (1908), *Architectural Drawing and Draughtsmen* (1912) and *A History of French Renaissance Architecture, 1499–1661* (1911–21), Better known nowadays are the pathetically polemical *Modernismus* (1935) and *Richard Norman Shaw, R.A.* (1940).

[35] As with the Polytechnic, the architectural sculptor was A. T. Bradford (see his letter in *The Architectural Review* February 1964). I am indebted to him for lending me illustrations for this article.

[36] Quoted in G. J. Howland's obituary of Richardson in *The Builder* February 1964, pp.273–274. Ramsey had written two volumes on *Small Houses of the Late Georgian Period* (1920–25) which were re-issued in one volume by The Architectural Press in 1972.

[37] Sherrin (1843–1909) was another Gothic man (Ponting's was his) who had turned towards classicism, in his Catholic churches (St Mary Moorfields) as well as in his underground stations (High Street, Kensington).

[38] Caldecott himself, by sheer coincidence, was, as Richardson pointed out to me, an indirect influence on the Georgian Revival, by reason of his drawings which popularized the idea of weekends in the country. Caldecott's house in Hampstead was by Shaw.

[39] Since I wrote this they have received a puff in *Nairn's London*, 1966, p.116.

[40] The latter, of 1910, was originally the Public Schools Club.

[41] A sign of the times was that Frank Verity, with his son-in-law Samuel Beverley, turned from designing theatres to super-cinemas, including the Pavilion, Shepherds Bush (R.I.B.A. London Architecture Bronze Medal, 1923), the Plaza, Regent Street and the Carlton, Haymarket (briefly a theatre).

[42] "Baker was horrid," said Richardson, adding that after the last war he had succeeded in reinstating in the Governor's Room at the Bank a fireplace by Sir Robert Taylor, which Baker had cast into the vaults.

[43] A curious, if minor, aspect of Richardson's own individualism was that, for all his emphasis on professional education and his Polytechnic lectureship, which involved coaching candidates for R.I.B.A. examinations, he himself never took the examination for Associateship. L.R.I.B.A. in 1911, he was elected straight into a Fellowship two year later.

[44] For example a story Richardson had from Churchill's protégé and Minister of Information, Brendan Bracken (the Financial Times patron), that Churchill had dismissed Pick from his wartime job as Director-General of Information with the words, "Will nobody remove this bus conductor from my sight?"

[45] A perspective at Ampthill shows a much richer version, very tall, with a rather vulgar circular tower and cupola on the angle (like an inflated Coal Exchange).

[46] Lethaby's restoration work he had admired, particular at Westminster Abbey, where "he maintained the Percy Dearmer approach, whitewashing the cloisters."

[47] Richardson's historical source for this 'modernism' was almost certainly (though he did not tell me) Sir Charles Barry's remarkable and little-known facade at 16–17 Pall Mall (1833–34), demolished in 1913. It is described and illustrated in *The Survey of London, Parish of St James Westminster, Part I: South,* 1961, p.325.

[48] Built as a wallpaper warehouse for Sanderson's, it was given the R.I.B.A. London Architecture Bronze Medal for 1931.

[49] *Journal of the Royal Institute of British Architects*, June 1928, p.518.

Building With Wit:
The Architecture of Sir Edwin Lutyens

by Nikolaus Pevsner

Sir Edwin Lutyens (1869–1944), the dominating though reactionary genius of British architecture during the first half of the 20th century, bestrides the period covered by this book (and later) like a colossus. From cottages in Surrey after 1890 that blend into their background, he progressed to brilliant free style houses around 1900 and then embraced the Grand Manner, calling it "the High Game". His practice after about 1904 was immense and the standard of his architectural inventiveness remarkably high through the long series of buildings in India, London and other parts of Britain. If anything justifies the long survival of free modernised Baroque in England, it is the work of Lutyens.

I have been unfortunate in my first impressions of the work of Lutyens. When I came to England in 1930, I was full of unquestioning faith in the new style of architecture - my wife's father had just moved into a house built for him with a flat roof and horizontal windows, and I was working on a course of lectures on the Development of Architecture from the 19th into the 20th century, a subject wholly unconsidered then amongst art historians in the German universities. The first two buildings by Lutyens which I saw were Grosvenor House in Park Lane and No. 68 Pall Mall, the one big, red and utilitarian, with unjustifiable bits of classical decoration round a few windows and classical stone-faced hats on the corners, high above the ninth floor, where nobody can see their details; the other tactlessly tall next to St James's Palace and the Marlborough House Chapel, with segment-headed and segment-footed windows suddenly breaking out on the second upper storey, in a rhythm different from all the other storeys, and with silly tricks in the detailing of the pilasters on the ground floor. I remember, these disappearing pilasters irritated me particularly, even more than the fact that an architect should still use pilasters and columns and pediments at all in a building of 1928.

In the meantime, thanks to the intervening years, I

2 *Sir Edwin Lutyens. 'Munstead Wood', Munstead, near Godalming, Surrey (1896) for the great gardener Gertrude Jekyll. Lutyen's first important job after seven years of small commissions which, true to Arts and Crafts principles, blended with existing buildings nearby.*

3 *Sir Edwin Lutyens. Tigbourne Court, Witley, near Godalming, Surrey (1899). During the last years of the century Lutyens designed a number of fairly large country houses in a free style. Some Arts and Crafts influences are apparent, but also great originality and splendour in composition.*

1 *Portrait of Sir Edwin Lutyens.*

do not find them silly any longer, and I know that there is more to Lutyens than belated classical revivalism. What is there to him? Any attempt at an answer is facilitated by the existence of Christopher Hussey's biography of 600 pages and Mr A. S. G. Butler's *Lutyens Memorial* of 3 folio volumes with 338 pages of working designs and 1000 photographs.[1] No English architect except Wren has been recorded on such a scale, and, whatever one's verdict on the aesthetic value of Lutyens's *oeuvre* the bigness of the record is deserved; for his work is big in total volume, his individual buildings are big and his success was big and maintained over a very long period.

So the question arises: why was Lutyens so immensely successful? He was not the type necessarily cast for professional success, as Sir Herbert Baker was, "tall, manly, athletic, outwardly calm" (in Mr Hussey's words), captain at cricket and football at his public school, and in later life outstandingly good on committees. Lutyens was the son of a retired army captain and an Irish girl. His father devoted his time to painting and hunting. His mother was busy trying to bring up

fourteen children on little money. Edwin Landseer Lutyens was the eleventh child. He was born in 1869 (Voysey 1857, Baker 1862, Mackintosh 1868). His education was "irregular and scrappy". At sixteen he went up to the Royal College of Art to study architecture. He did not complete the course, and was articled in 1887 to Ernest George & Peto. Senior assistant at the time was Baker. Lutyens was lazy, disliked sketching, but had a knack of "quickly absorbing all that was best worth learning" (Baker).[2] He left the office after six months and set up in practice on his own. He was twenty years old then.

The credit of having discovered him belongs to Gertrude Jekyll, the formidable garden-maker, "frightening but kind and wise," says Mr Hussey[3] from experience. She commissioned Lutyens to design Munstead Wood, a house for herself. It was built in 1896, not his first building – he had done cottages, lodges and additions to houses before, and in 1896 claimed earnings of about £1,000 a year – but it was his first building of consequence. In 1897, moreover, he married Lady Emily Lytton, daughter of the first

4 *Sir Edwin Lutyens. 'Deanery Gardens', Sonning, Berkshire (1899–1901). Built for Edward Hudson, the owner of* Country Life *magazine. House and garden are an integrated design.*

Viceroy of India. It was the happy end of a romantic love-story, but it also meant connections in a society in which to be a protégé of Gertrude Jekyll was a valuable asset too. And while Baker's success was due to a large extent to his "accommodating architectural conscience and keen sense of practical politics," and of course his sentimentality – Luyens said of Baker that he made architecture "the handmaid of sentiment" (*Life*, p. 285) – Lutyens's line was to be the perennial *enfant terrible*. How much of this was spontaneous, how much methodical will always remain doubtful. Mr Hussey calls him "genial, whimsical, disconcertingly irreverent and facetious . . . habitually schoolboyish and often impish," Miss Sackville West "the most delightful, good-natured, irresponsible, imaginative jester of genius." His jokes never ceased, and ranged from the most atrocious puns to brilliant flashes of genius. He could ask a poor clergyman called Western at a Viceroy's party at Delhi whether he was a relation of the Great Western, but he could also say that the Delhi buildings in their finished form after all the exasperating quarrels with Herbert Baker were his Bakerloo. Herbert Baker on his part found Lutyens's humour, which he had liked when they both worked at Sir Ernest George's, "wearisome in repetition, and less becoming to mature manhood."

But in England the eccentric has as good a chance of social success as the strong, silent, efficient man. Still, it remains remarkable that eccentricity can be a success even in the territory of such material professional accomplishments as architecture. One can understand that in Lutyens's early years, the years of the Arts and Crafts and *Art Nouveau* and the picturesque cottage, eccentricity could pass for originality,

the most desirable quality at the time. But later when Edwardian Palladianism and Classical Re-revival had replaced the Arts and Crafts, and when Lutyens designed in these accepted styles – is one to assume that his clients did not notice his most eccentric details?

The motive, I think, lies deeper. It is connected with the fascination wrought on the British more than any other race by the folly in architecture. Nor need the British be ashamed of that fascination; for to appreciate folly a degree of detachment is needed which is only accessible to old and humane civilisations. Sir Edwin Lutyens was without any doubt the greatest folly builder England has ever seen. Castle Drogo beats Fonthill, the Drum Inn at Cockington beats Blaise Castle, and the Viceroy's house at Delhi beats any other folly in the world. Castle Drogo was to be three times the size it finally assumed, and it is overwhelming as it now stands on the steep edge of Dartmoor. Besides, while Wyatt's and Nash's follies were put up in flimsy materials, for Lutyens only the best and most enduring was good enough. "The Viceroy," he wrote in 1913, "thinks only of what the place will look like in three years time, three hundred is what *I* think of" (p. 282).

How odd it seems to us that such self-confident displays of imperialism could have been made at all. Yet Lutyens himself was not an imperialist, as Baker for instance was. In fact he was not interested in politics at all. He disliked them. "Politics," he wrote, "ought to be included within the Corrupt Practices Act" (p. 269). A committee in his mind was "all sorts and kinds of horrible, ignorant and unsympathetic men" (p. 186), and a democratic government one "that can only work through compromise, leaving its conscience in the hands of accountants" (p. 380).

5 *Sir Edwin Lutyens. Papillon Hall, Leicestershire (1903). Norman Shaw (at Chesters) and Edward Prior (at 'The Barn') had been experimenting with such X-plans and variations a decade earlier. Their influence and Voysey's is evident in Lutyens's work at this time, but so is a strong individuality.*

6 *Sir Edwin Lutyens. 'Little Thakeham', near Pulborough, Sussex (1902). A series of platforms in space, with stairs running up to connect them. The contrast of low and high ceilinged rooms, large and small windows, were devised to give an interior cottage-cum-palace effect that Lutyens aimed at in several houses.*

7 *Sir Edwin Lutyens. Country Life office building, Tavistock Street, Covent Garden, London (1904). His first venture into the Grand Manner.*

Not for him then the commissioning ministry or board of directors. His ideal client was the rich man, preferably self-made or at least not too distant yet in descent from the adventurous stage of self-madeness. And Lutyens was extremely, uniquely fortunate in working at the very last moment in British history when such clients were about. Just as he could complete his work at Delhi five minutes before closing time, so houses of the size of Castle Drogo, Marshcourt, Great Maytham, Nashdom Taplow, Temple Dinsley were only possible in that last Indian Summer of unashamed British prosperity before the First World War. A tendency towards the colossal in size seems to go with the mood of the eve of disaster. So it was at the end of Imperial Rome, so in the years of Louis XVI. But whereas Ledoux's dreams of huge axial compositions for no utilitarian purposes remained on paper, Lutyens's actually rose in solid stone into the air of England and India.

Given the huge scale on which it was permitted to Lutyens to work, and given his universal success, it remains admirable that his work is never, or hardly ever, dead (I except the British Pavilion at Rome of 1910 and the British Embassy at Washington of 1930), as the contemporary campuses and civic centres of the United States so often are. This is no doubt due to two causes which seem at first to exclude each other, Lutyens's *élan vital* and his immense care over details. The many pages of detail drawings in the Lutyens Memorial show clearly how meticulous a worker he was, and how the naughtiness of so many of his motifs is by no means the outcome of faith in accident. Lutyens admired the Norman Shaw of his later period,

that is of Bryanston and Chesters (p. 17) – Shaw had set an example for Lutyens of how an architect of immense picturesque gifts can in later life find a way to Palladio and Wren – but he objected to the manner in which at Chesters all details are "left go lucky beyond a point" (p. 120). Yet Chesters must have impressed him more than any other 19th-century building. Philip Webb he discovered in 1891, and also admired greatly. Voysey is nowhere mentioned in Mr Hussey's *Life*, although his influence on, say, Orchards seems to me beyond doubt – see the bay window with its unmoulded mullions and transomes (a Shaw motif originally) and the batter of the buttresses. Another influence worth considering is that of E. S. Prior on the plan of Papillon Hall with four wings projecting diagonally from a central core. The common source is of course again Chesters, but Lutyens's solution is nearer Prior's than Shaw's. And Prior also possessed a liking for rather crazy primeval details which Lutyens shared.

But Papillon Hall of 1903 has got one feature which neither Voysey nor Prior would have introduced: the circular anteroom and the circular Basin Court with its colonnades. This introduction of motifs which seem to have nothing to do with each other, this playing-up of contrasts sometimes just to amuse, but sometimes also *pour épater le bourgeois*, is in my opinion one of the most characteristic features of Lutyens's style. How he enjoyed such bits as the specially low-silled 'crawling window' in the nursery at Middleton Park, or the one Victorian window left unaltered when he converted Ashwell Bury, or those disappearing pilasters which annoyed me so much at 68 Pall Mall, and which also occur in the Midland Bank in Poultry, and even in the

8 *Sir Edwin Lutyens. Nashdom House, Taplow, Buckinghamshire (1905). A play of words with the style and the name of the house, typical of Lutyens.*

9 *Sir Edwin Lutyens. 'Heathcote', near Ilkley, Yorkshire (1906).
The Grand Manner arrives for Lutyens country houses, in contrast
to his earlier free style designs.*

10 *Sir Edwin Lutyens. Castle Drogo, Drewsteignton, Dartmoor,
near Exeter, Devon (1910–30). A knight's castle par excellence,
originally meant to be three times its size when building finally
stopped.*

British Embassy at Washington, those pilasters which start innocently with Doric bases and then fade away in the close pattern of rustication or brick courses, until much higher up they suddenly reappear and end in correct capitals as if nothing had happened. How he enjoyed adding in completely different styles to houses he had built himself – Crooksbury, the earliest of all his works, was originally in the Caldicott style of picturesque cottages (as Mr Hussey calls it). The addition of 1899 was Lutyens's first effort in a William and Mary, of Shaw derivation. At Folly Farm, on the other hand, the house of 1905 was neo-Georgian, the bold addition of 1912 Tudor with a vast steep roof and hugely battered piers. The entrance side of Homewood at Knebworth of 1901 (not illustrated in the *Memorial*) has a big classical doorway and weatherboarded gables above. Little Thakeham of 1902 is Tudor, but the hall has broad stone doorways towards the staircase with Gibbsian surrounds.

What made Lutyens so fond of this Palladian motif of blocks of alternating sizes for doors and window surrounds? It is due no doubt to the same delight in geometry as the circular room and the circular court at Papillon Hall. The square, the rectangle, the circle occur everywhere in his work. The voluptuousness of the long, swaying curves of the Arts and Crafts and *Art Nouveau* and the single-minded dynamic intensity of the pointed arch of Gothic and Eastern tradition were equally abhorrent to him. When the Viceroy pleaded for pointed arches at Delhi instead of round-headed ones, because these would not be in harmony with the Indian past, Lutyens wrote: "God did not make the Eastern rainbow pointed, to show his wide sympathies" (p. 296). His first conception of the focal monument for graveyards of the First World War in France was "a solid ball of bronze" (p. 373), and wherever one looks in the three volumes of plates of the *Lutyens Memorial*, one is struck by elementary geometrical patterns – the squares of different materials in the Westminster Housing Scheme, the black and white marbles in the paving of entrance and staircase halls, the quadrant front of Gray Walls, the exactly hemispherical domes of Delhi, the Midland Bank in Poultry and the British Pavilion for the 1928 exhibition at Antwerp. This worship of geometry could in some later works lead to most complex and ingeniously thought out ratios of proportions. The memorial arch of Thiepval is as geometrically perfect as any Modulor-designed exercise of Le Corbusier. "In architecture Palladio is the game," wrote Lutyens in 1903 (p. 121).

But where Lutyens's geometry seems to be most successful is where he uses it not for the sake of perfection but for the sake of contrast and surprise. Thiepval and the Poultry façade of the Midland Bank reveal little of the best in Lutyens. For that you have to go to such early houses as Tigbourne Court of 1899. The contrast between the pertly upcurved front wall carrying two absurdly tall chimneys

set diagonally, and the façade itself further back with its low Tuscan loggia and its sheer wall above with windows set wide apart and straight gables on top is irresistible. So is the geometry of the south front of Deanery Garden of 1899, that of the Tank Cloister at Folly Farm of 1912, and also that of the pools and fountains at Delhi, though here and even more, still later, at Liverpool's cathedral the play with geometry gets dangerously near the continental jazz idiom of 1925 – a curiously entirely independent parallelism.

If I look for continental parallels to what is most valuable in Lutyens's work, I find some similarity with Berlage (born 1856) and his Dutch successors, especially de Klerk (born 1884). Here is the same origin in picturesque traditions, the freedom of handling, the faith in elementary cubic forms, the occasional jazziness of detail, and also – and this introduces two more qualities essential to Lutyens's character – the keen interest in a variety of materials and in craftsmanship. But whereas Berlage and de Klerk and then Dudok were led by their *lusus geometricus* to a complete renunciation of period ties, Lutyens's art was petrified by the cold, never wholly relaxing grip of Palladianism.

As for variety of materials, one of Lutyens's earliest buildings, a pair of loggias at Park Hatch, Hascombe, is described as of Bargate stone, Horsham slates, timber in the gables, and pavings of ironstone and of brick. Marshcourt is mainly of chalk, but has an admixture of stone, flint and brick. At 42 Cheyne

11 *Sir Edwin Lutyens. Staircase, Castle Drogo. Tremendous spaces and masses, if theatrical.*

12 *Sir Edwin Lutyens. Stone screen in the garden of the Viceroy's House, New Delhi.*

13 *Sir Edwin Luytens. The Viceroy's House, New Delhi, India (1912–31). The oriental apotheosis of the Baroque Grand Manner.*

Walk, a corridor is wall-papered with varnished sheets of *The Times*. As for craftsmanship, the otherwise not very interesting building at Magdalene College, Cambridge, has the hand-rails of its five staircases designed all completely differently, and with details challenging the skill of any craftsman. At the Midland Bank in Poultry every course of stone had to be 0.273 inch less in height than the one below. The variety of wrought-iron balustrades to staircases is equally remarkable. But Lutyens's liking for delicate and transparent ironwork is characteristic not only of the fun he had with materials and their shaping by craftsmen, but also of the fun he had with space. The library steps at Campion Hall, Oxford, are one of the most endearing examples of this spatial fun. They get you up six steps as any old ladder, but are at the same time spatially and geometrically no less entertaining than a young person's tricks in designs for children's playgrounds are nowadays.

Lutyens's handling of space has not in the past been sufficiently appreciated. The staircase at Little Thakeham is almost as ingenious with quite simple geometrical means as the staircases of the 18th-century which we admire in Germany and Austria. Equally ingenious is the way in which at Ashwell Bury a staircase in a comparatively small well is made to look large. The vaulted corridors at Castle Drogo have a spatial force which one may compare with Piranesi's. No wonder that Lutyens on his first journey to Italy got excited about the staircases of Genoa. "The lavish space given away in staircases makes me sick with envy," he wrote in 1909 (p. 197). If the architects of Genoa had seen the size of Lutyens's staircases at Delhi ten or twenty years later, the envy would have been theirs.

England has never been particularly keen on ingenious or monumental stairs, and Lutyens's are amongst the finest she has produced. The English reluctance to give staircases enough space is connected with the practical, pragmatic, utilitarian side of the national character. But Lutyens had no patience with the utilitarian, and if perfect architecture is defined as a blend of art and use, then Lutyens was certainly not a perfect architect. "Lut was not interested," says Nathaniel Lloyd, "in what held the building up or composed the core, heated or drained it. . . . The office dealt only in surfaces. (p. 493). This is why so often Lutyens's buildings, in spite of all their good solid materials, seem unreal. The best of them are indeed too good to be true. The Drum Inn at Cockington is the cottage straight out of the pantomime, Castle Drogo is a fairy castle, the Viceroy's house a fairy palace, and New Delhi as planned by Lutyens a fairy city. No wonder he could not stick Geddes ("he seems to have talked rot in an insulting way," p. 336). Lutyens was as immune against the social as he was against the structural aspects of architecture. Hence he believed only in axial, symmetrical 'Beaux Arts' planning and never considered the visual variety and intricacy resulting from functional planning, although his architecture looks so much as if he should have been able to appreciate picturesque layouts. But no – in the Royal Academy plans for London which were essentially his, he proceeded to duplicate Burton's screen and Apsley House to get symmetry into the new roundabout at Hyde Park Corner, and to duplicate the Deanery of St Paul's to achieve the same result for the side wings to the left and right of the façade of the cathedral. When Lutyens saw the Acropolis for the first time, he was disappointed. "The Parthenon has no relation to its site," he wrote, "no dramatic sense such as Romans had" (p. 539).

That disgruntled reaction to Athens after Rome is a familiar experience with travellers of untrained visual sense. With a distinguished architect it is curious. But it again helps to explain Lutyens's great popular success. The Lutyens of the Delhi plan, the Viceroy's house, Castle Drogo and the Drum Inn is indeed a laymen's architect. His grandeur, his banality, his jokes – there was everything there to please the common man. "Directly you introspect, you may be sure you are wrong", he could write to Baker (p. 181). Soane would not have written that, nor would Michelangelo.

Yet in his geometrical speculations he was clearly working along lines concealed from the layman, and it is they that betray the inner core of seriousness and intellectual effort in him. That is why Mr Butler in his notes to the folio volumes of the *Memorial* gave so much space to them and analysed them so patiently. Lutyens's supreme faith was in the *divina proporzione*.

14 *Sir Edwin Lutyens. Mobile steps for the library, Campion Hall, Oxford (1934). An endearing example of the fun Lutyens had with space and structure.*

15 *Sir Edwin Lutyens. Midland Bank, Manchester (1929). A splendid piece of geometrical massing, typical of Lutyens's post-war office and bank buildings.*

He did not really care for the Empire, except inasmuch as it was a big client. Nor did he believe with his whole personality in God. "There is that in art which transcends all rules – it is the divine", he wrote to his wife in 1907. "If only the nations would go for beauty with their whole resource and energies . . . the millennium would be ours ! ! . . ." (p. 140).

In such words he seems to be transported far above the conception of architecture as a game to be played with gusto. Yet the two seemingly contradictory aspects of Lutyens's mind are *au fond* one thing. They are both expressive of art for art's sake, or rather architecture for art's sake. Now architecture for art's sake is for good reasons the *bête noire* of the 20th-century architects of all schools. It is therefore quite conceivable that, if once again in the distant future a period may dawn in which the architect can afford to, and will want to, be an artist as elevated above social and structural interests as 'Michel angel divino', Lutyens's wisdom will be recognised as effortlessly as I recognise his folly. In his serious mood he is so completely divorced from all that architects of the last fifty years have striven for, that a balanced judgment of his place in history is perhaps impossible. I am fully aware of that. All I can claim for these pages is that they have emphatically not been written to debunk but to arrive at a judgment at least not consciously biased.

[1] Christopher Hussey and A. S. G. Butler, *Lutyens Memorial*, Country Life, London and Scribner's, New York 1951. (Three folio and one quarto volumes).

[2] Sir Herbert Baker, *Architecture and Personalities*, Country Life, London 1944, p.15.

[3] This and subsequent references to page numbers are from Hussey and Butler, *op cit*.

Conclusion: Goodhart-Rendel's Roll-Call

by Nikolaus Pevsner

The final piece in this book is Sir Nikolaus Pevsner's record of the memories of H. S. Goodhart-Rendel, contemporary Historian Extraordinary of Edwardian architecture. Goodhart-Rendel's comments on the architects of the period may not always agree with our own judgements, but his viewpoints can enrich our understanding of the classicist sympathies of his generation which delayed acceptance of new architectural ideas for so long after the Great War of 1914–18.

H. S. Goodhart-Rendel invented the term 'rogue-architect' and used it both in the neutral sense of the rogue-elephant and in the less neutral one of the rogue pure-and-simple. He was himself a rogue-architect fully in the former sense and more than a little in the latter. For one thing he was never entirely an architect, partly because he could afford leisure and partly because by initial training he was a musician. It is characteristic of him that in his entry in *Who's Who* – an entry of thirty-six lines – he did not refer to a single building of his. He was born in 1887, son of Lord Rendel's daughter. There were large estates in the south of France going with that heritage (he added his grandfather's name to his own), besides the Adam house of 'Hatchlands', near Guildford. He went to Eton and Trinity, Cambridge, taking his B.Mus. under Tovey. Only then did he turn to architecture, working with Sir Charles Nicholson. He went into practice in 1910. He was, apart from a musician and an architect, an enthusiastic and effective Guards officer and a convert to Catholicism. He built a number of churches, perhaps the most interesting one being St Wilfred, Brighton (1932), and restored and remodelled country houses; for example, Tatton Park in Somerset and Farleigh House in Hampshire. Hay's Wharf (1931) is his most familiar work because it is in London; but it is, with its nodding recognition of the normal Modern Movement, an exception in his work. He was as a secular architect inspired by Parisian classicism more than by English trends. Yet another side of his mind and character came out in his passion for Victorian buildings. He was one of the very first to take them

seriously and to study them (see his articles on Brighton's churches in *The Architectural Review*, 1918), and his knowledge of Victorian architects was prodigious. His vast index of Victorian churches and their architects, now at the R.I.B.A. and National Monuments Record, remains his most permanent work of scholarship. The comprehensive book on this subject which he could have written, he never did.

He was the Director of the A.A. School in 1936–38, during the very years of the battle for the new style in architecture. He showed little sympathy for the young and lost the appreciation of many who would otherwise have been his admirers. He was President of the R.I.B.A. in 1937–38, President of the D.I.A. in 1948–50 and Vice-President of the Royal College of Music from 1953 to his death in 1959.

In July 1946, just before Volume 100 of *The Architectural Review* came out, I spent a long evening with Hal Goodhart-Rendel, who was then fifty-nine years old, to ask him about personal memories of *The Architectural Review* in its early years and about the architects who appeared in it or did not appear in it. I had about ten years before brought out my *Pioneers* dealing with the same years; so any information on the situation of the years between 1896 and 1914 was important to me. As the following pages will show, Goodhart-Rendel told me much, but I did not then publish what had been recorded by Miss Horner in shorthand, because it would, twenty years ago, have been of interest only to a small circle. Now this has changed, and I present this arranged version of the interview with full confidence. My own linking explanations are printed in italics.

1 *Cartoon of H. S. Goodhart-Rendel, drawn by H. de Cronin Hastings.*

About the mid-'90s a group of architects who had joined in running the Architectural Publication Society's illustrations in The Architect, demonstrated their dissatisfaction with The Architect by founding the Architectural Illustrations Group, where they published photographic reproductions rather than drawings. Meanwhile in 1895 The Builders' Journal had started, a weekly with the subtitle An Architectural Review. In November 1896 the publishers of The Builders' Journal, the Talbot Newspaper Co., joined forces with the architect-illustrators, and The Architectural Review appeared as a separate monthly.[1]

Goodhart-Rendel saw the Review for this first time when he was at Eton. It was the number (Vol. VII, 1900) with the long article on Butterfield by Halsey Ricardo, who was Goodhart-Rendel's cousin. He took to it, and since then had seen "most numbers" and all since 1903 or 1904. What he originally appreciated most were the long serious articles such as those on Pearson by J. E. Newberry (Vol. I, 1896–97) and on Pugin by Paul Waterhouse (Vol. III, 1897–98).

It stood, he said, for most of what was of interest in current work though it tended to emphasise the grand manner. It kept away from commercial architecture of the Bradshaw Gass type (he went a long way through Hope, and so it soon became Bradshaw Gass & Hope) and it was interested not only in the official but also in the domestic 'artistic' trend. It included the Academicians and kept away from the cranks at the start. It was read as much by educated people of taste as by architects and had elaborate features on Burne-Jones and Sir Edwin Poynter, P.R.A.[2]

The Review, when I first read it, was edited by a board[3] on which Macartney and Reginald Blomfield played first fiddle. Of the two Macartney was infinitely the better man: quiet, scholarly, and as an architect not very inventive, but unselfconscious, and always right. His Queen Anne had a lot of distinction. He did not build much, and is little known nowadays. His design for the Victoria and Albert Museum[4] was much admired. He was the first real editor of the Review. Blomfield stood for the artist-architect. He was really an amateur throughout his life – possessing not much in the way of technique, and very much of academic ambition. But at that time the Academy still meant something – competence and high ideals. Blomfield and Jackson represented academic snobbism. Blomfield's scholarship was all bogus – Latin quotations with false quantities. His early work is quite deplorable. He always abused his uncle Sir Arthur. He did the organ room in our house, 'Hatchlands', the only disfigurement of the place. He was an impatient man, always ready for a fight, to the very end of his days.

But in spite of its classical learning, the Review recognised the Arts and Crafts side as well and was good in picking out the strongest personalities of the Shaw school: E. S. Prior and Lethaby. Prior's houses were something really original, and Lethaby's buildings, the few he did, have all his candid and thoughtful character.

Victorian Gothicists

When the Review started, the great Victorian Gothicists were old or dead. Among them Pearson[5] stands out. His was a wonderfully balanced art: nothing too heavy, nothing too light – scholarly, but never dry. His most talented follower was George Gilbert Scott, Sir Gilbert Scott's son, the only one of the younger generation to achieve that purity. He would deserve to be as well-known as, or better known than, his father.[6] The Review had a special article on him[7] by Walter Millard, himself a hope and a Street pupil. He was one of Phené Spiers's children, much praised by Jock Stevenson. He did very sensitive drawings of old Italian things.

But the most stimulating Gothicist was Street. He was the fountain-head for all those who wanted to get away from imitation. How wilful he could be, you see only in his drawings. His buildings don't show it. The Law Courts are perfect, but nothing to grip your heart. Yet he inspired Shaw, Webb (who is supposed to have done the back of the Law Courts), Sedding and the rest. Sedding[8] was a muddly architect, a soft not a hard, a kind of Browning. He was a sensitive designer of patterns and had wonderful ideas. He liked to use plenty of sculpture and craft, and employ plenty of artists.[9] People fell in love with his buildings.

He was the master of my master, Charles Nicholson. Nicholson was the most remarkable architect who ever lived. He had an extraordinary facility for drawing anything. He designed two cathedrals, Portsmouth and Sheffield, and some forty churches. He did not care much for publicity. The number of things he has done[10] without anyone noticing is simply incredible. His ecclesiastical career kept him rather apart. Also he was violently anti-academic and looked on architecture as an Art. He was in partnership with Major Corlette, but that was an accident, and it took Nicholson thirty years to get rid of him.[11]

But in spite of all Goodhart-Rendel's enthusiasm for his master, he added: My God was Bentley. [12] I admired his grit and cannot to this day see any fault in him.

The Grand Manner

The oldest of the Grand Manner men was Belcher (1841–1913). Belcher was really a bad Gothic architect who also went in for intensely romantic drawings of richly half-timbered houses. Beresford Pite wrote an article on him in the Review.[13] Pite was very tactful, because he did himself most of the earlier classical work of Belcher, such as the Institute of Chartered Accountants with lots of sculpture by academicians. Later, when Joass came in, Belcher's style changed again – to the church in Kingsway, Mappin & Webb's in Oxford Street and Electra House, Moorgate.

2 *Sir Mervyn Macartney. Frithwood House, Northwood, Middlesex*   3 *E. S. Prior. 'The Barn', Exmouth, Devon (1897).*
(1900).

4 *John Belcher. Institute of Chartered Accountants, off Moorgate (1889–93, assistant A. Beresford Pite).*

5 *Frank T. Verity. No. 11a Portland Place (1908).*

6 *Ernest Newton. House at Baughurst, Hampshire (1902).*

Pite (1862–1935) *interested Goodhart-Rendel much.* He was a brilliant draughtsman, [14] and if he had had a little less facility and a few more principles, he would have been a great architect. He was a most inspiring person, always trying experiments that didn't quite come off. His first work was the back of his father's poorhouse in Endell Street. His also is the pretty school behind the Middlesex Hospital (in Foley Street). But he mostly went in for a lot of sculpture. You see that in a house by him in Margaret Street. The sculpture was designed by Slater, but made by Seale. His best thing is the church in Brixton [15], first-class but ugly. He was an enthusiastic member of the World Evangelical Alliance.

Of the other purveyors of monumental and public buildings John Burnet (1857–1938), 'the great Burnet,' was an important influence. He came to the fore in 1886, with the Barony Church in Glasgow, and he also did fine things at Edinburgh, such as Forsyth's store. He was a Frenchified Scotsman, extraordinarily nice, with a tremendous love of order and system. He never lost hold of the essentials and thought no one in England knew anything about them. He used to say that nothing ought to be done without a decision behind it. He had no interest in style as such. His earliest London block of offices is that in Aldwych. [16] He really was a great man, and we were not in the least surprised, when he got the British Museum. The story of Selfridge's is that it was designed by whoever designed for Burnham (of Chicago) and that Burnet added the centrepiece with the hideous enamel clock. Unfortunately he had a weakness for that sort of thing. [17] Our comment was 'gosh' – but what we admired in Selfridge's was the way the storeys were all pulled together between the columns, though Frank Verity had done it earlier and better at the Polytechnic in Regent Street. Burnet can hardly have designed Adelaide House. It must be by Tait, who had first ghosted for Trehearne & Norman in Kingsway.

Aston Webb was at his best while in partnership with Ingress Bell. An example is the Catholic church at Caterham in a 'larky Gothic.' Webb was a marvellous constructor. I never knew anyone who was more popular with his colleagues than he was.

Runtz was the architect employed by the Gaiety Theatre when the L.C.C. got £50,000 to impose Norman Shaw's façades. But, generally speaking, when I was young, Shaw was above everything and no longer in the arena.

Foreign Inspirations
Burnet and Paris have already been mentioned.
Frank Verity (1864–1937) was a sham Frenchman with a little beard and very dapper. As a man he was greatly respected. The flats he designed [18] were a great excitement. They were the first with flat roofs – not a gable, not a turret. Nicholson called them the only sorts of flat. Richardson always said that he ghosted most of Verity's work. My particular group liked Richardson

very much. *No further comment on him followed, and incidentally, no comment on Lutyens as an architect. On Herbert Baker the only comment was:* Such a bad architect, *and on Lorimer:* He did terrible things to old houses, but was a sensitive man.

The Paris exhibition of 1900 made a heavy dent, not only in the *Art Nouveau* way, but also because of the Petit Palais and the Pont Alexandre. That prepared the way for Mewès (1858–1914), whose first London work was the Palm Court of the Carlton Hotel, with his young English partner, Arthur Davis (1878–1951).

Rickards (1872–1920) believed in the Austrian Baroque. He did everything in Lanchester & Rickards. He was a friend of Arnold Bennett, a brilliant draughtsman, and a Bohème type who could only work with exciting amatory experiences. He had an extraordinary talent for all-outness and died young. We admired most his Deptford Town Hall and Hull Art School.

The Studio
The Studio went to the arty people and the art schools. It was sold on the bookstalls, and it also went abroad a lot. The *Review* was much soberer. *The Studio* occupied itself in architecture with the Arts and Crafts and with domestic architects, with Mackintosh and Voysey and very much with Ernest Newton (1856–1922). He had been in Shaw's office and was a simplifier of the Shaw tradition. He paid a great deal of attention to the planning of the moderate-size middle-class house, for doctors particularly. Buller's Wood, Chislehurst, is an unusually big one, inside all Morris. Newton could never get away from the inglenook.

Voysey was not one of Goodhart-Rendel's likes. On Voysey's teacher, the mysterious Devey, he had little to say and probably I asked then too little. He mentioned houses by Devey in Hans Crescent [19] *and old cottages at Penshurst and added without enlarging on it:* He did some amazing major works. Voysey was not a serious architect. Everybody's maiden aunt had a little Voysey house somewhere. They were profoundly uncomfortable to live in. At that time it did not matter much what style a house was in, as long as it looked quaint. Mackmurdo was in the same category. He did a terrible pub in Sloane Street, the sort of thing one's small daughter would design. Much of Mackintosh was rather a fraud, compared with Plumet, Olbrich or Behrens. Also he was influenced by Jessie King. But his drawings with solid blocks and black dots were very impressive. *No more comment.*

Baillie Scott was the most sensitive of that group. His designs may irritate you, but they always hang together. He had an unerring sense of scale.

Draughtsmen
Mackintosh, as we have seen, was one whose technique was praised by Goodhart-Rendel. I asked after the authors of other equally striking illustrations in Academy Architecture.

The best drawings for Niven & Wigglesworth were by Fred Griggs. Fulton was a brilliant draughtsman and never got into building. Curtis Green drew much; but tended to be mannered. Greenslade we all admired as a magnificent draughtsman. He did the Leeds Catholic Cathedral, the National Library of Wales and the Eton Memorial Hall (under the name of Hall). C. E. Mallows was more commercial, but his was the design of the Municipal Buildings at Coventry, submitted as by Brewill & Baily. It is very arty, the sort of thing that looks best in drawings. Gerald Horsley (1862–1917) was another fine draughtsman. He had a scratchy line but a wonderful sense of tone. He was the typical amateur but did much better work than usual among amateurs. By him is the St Paul's Girls' School.

Some Favourites
Among Goodhart-Rendel's favourites when he was young were the following architects, all now forgotten. William Flockhart (*circa* 1850–1913) was an extremely sensitive draughtsman, potentially the best of the lot. His architecture is inventive and original. Examples[20] are Dumbarton House, Palace Court, the Marylebone Presbyterian Church Hall, and a vast Scottish house called 'Rosehaugh'.

James M. MacLaren (1843–90) was a most interesting architect with influence of a Parisian training. *The British Architect* boosted him. He did a studio for Pinker the sculptor and also a house in Palace Court. He was D. S. McColl's brother-in-law.

7 *Halsey Ricardo. Offices in Great George Street, Westminster (1888).*

8 *William Flockhart. 'Rosehaugh', Ross-shire, Scotland (1904).*

Halsey Ricardo (1854–1928), my cousin, was dark, Jewish, spectacularly good-looking, musical and a typical architectural amateur. He was mainly important through his friendship with other people. He had a great theory to make buildings washable. The Debenham House in Addison Road is his most familiar building, but probably most people thought that his best building was that for my great-grandfather, No. 8 Great George Street, which later became the offices of Armstrong Whitworth.[21] It does not exist any longer.

George Sherrin (1843–1909) also was a very good man. He did country houses which were not published and could do without the *Academy* or *The Architectural Review*. There is a block of offices by him above Moorgate underground station and also the Moorfields Catholic Church in Eldon Street nearby.

Miscellaneous Remarks
Ashbee: If you had taken him up, you really were in with the revolutionaries.
Blow & Billerey: The really architectural work is by Billerey who was a very, very good architect[22]. He did the interiors of the Union Club and the Playhouse.
Brewer: Not very rational . . .enormous period charm.

9 *R. A. Briggs. The Old Mill, Aldeburgh, Suffolk (1903).*

10 *E. W. Mountford. Booth's Distillery, Cowcross Street, Clerkenwell (1901).*

Brierley: Studio gossip had it that he did not design his own work, but the churches in Buckingham Palace Road[23] and Kensal Road are his. He practised mainly in Yorkshire.

Briggs: Known as 'bungalow Briggs' ... a slick draughtsman, but in the flesh too frightful.

Bunney: It was he who did all the work of Horace Field and Bunney.

Crawley: Very well known to the rich, but never published anything. Did the interior of Beit's house in Park Lane and *The Lusitania*[24].

Dawber: A pupil of George ... distressing little summer houses.

Dunn & Watson: They were thought highly of. They built pseudo-classical stuff.[25] I used to try to formulate what it was that made them appreciated and then made every effort not to do it.

Eden, F. C.: He was responsible for the second prize in the Eton Memorial Hall competition.[26] He did much stained glass, and Nicholson venerated him.

H. Fuller Clark: Among the people who did wicked things. You find his work near the Middlesex Hospital, such as Boulting's.[27]

Hall, Cooper & Davis: They also were among the naughties – look at their school at Scarborough and their chapel at Slough.

Lutyens: He did a Broadwood piano with a pierced steel music-rack. *This was all Goodhart-Rendel referred to.*

Mountford: He died very young. He did a brewery with one of those sculptured friezes which were a fashion in those years. He is best known for the Old Bailey and Sheffield Town Hall.

Paul Phipps: He was the brother-in-law of Lady Astor, a pupil of Lutyens and a charming man who has either given up architecture, or architecture has given up him.[28]

Prentice: He did half-timbered houses better than anybody else and also the St Martin's Public Library.

Stokes: He was a rugged personality with a great originality of feeling.

Townsend: He was of no importance. By the way, he must have looked carefully at Plumet.

Troup: Arts and Crafts *in excelsis*, an extreme Lethabite.[29].

Fairfax B. Wade: He was a fine gentleman of private means and employed gentlemen to do his architecture. He was a great ghost employer. Leonard Williams, for example, designed Wade's Royal School of Needlework and a house in Sloane Street. Wade also did a filthy Gothic church.[30]

Edgar Wood: Arty and tea-shoppy ... but the flat-roofed house at Stafford is very good.

The Younger Generation

When I was seventeen, I was interested in a kind of Grecian and in Soane. The Grecian was rare then, but there was the Doric competition design for the Chelsea Baths by Tyars & Jago, and also a cinema and house in Waterloo Road by Parnacott or whoever did it really.[31]

11

12

480

11 *Arthur H. Mackmurdo. No. 25 Cadogan Gardens (1899), drawn by W. Curtis Green.*

12 *Fairfax B. Wade. House in Sloane Street, London (1896), drawn by C. H. B. Quennell.*

13 *H. S. Goodhart-Rendel. Proposed No. 27 Berkeley Square (1910). On right, No. 25, by Frank T. Verity (1907).*

Adshead (1868–1946) was the architect most interested in Soane. When he was young he did watercolour perspectives in a loose technique for people like Hare. His most characteristic feature was very attenuated pilasters, rather like Adam or the American Colonial, and of course flutes and reeds. His Ramsgate Public Library I saw with delight. Then there was Reilly. But did he ever design for himself? Adshead did much for him, too.[32] You must not confuse Reilly with R-i-l-e-y: the L.C.C. architect, who certainly did not do his own designing. People were annoyed at the claims he made for himself officially. Clough Williams-Ellis is younger than I, and he came in a bit later. I knew him almost before he became an architect. He married a Strachey, as you know, and his father-in-law, St Loe Strachey, editor of *The Spectator*, instigated a competition for cheap cottages at Letchworth. My step-father was secretary for it. The exhibition of the cottages was an attempt at enlivening the moribund Letchworth experiment. One of the cottages, designed by Williams-Ellis, was financed by his cousin A. H. Clough, son of the poet[33]; another, which cost only £150, was by an amateur, Percy Houfton, who won first prize.

But the man who had the greatest influence over all of us was Charles Holden (we then had to call him Percy Adams; that was his firm). Holden's sketches for County Hall of 1908 went in as Adams & Pearson and were not placed. His Bristol Library excited us a tremendous lot.

It is interesting to note that even an architect so much inspired by the Beaux-Arts and Parisian competence and so much more attracted by the classical than by the line of descent of my Pioneers[33] could appreciate the high originality of Holden'

Goodhart-Rendel's own work appeared first in the Review in 1913; a house (The Pantiles) at Englefield Green and the Eton Club at Hackney Wick, Vol.XXXIII, March, plate VI, and Vol. XXXIV, September, plate V. The former is quiet with a pantile roof and a round-arched side loggia, the latter of brick, with wide eaves and some classical detail. Previously, however, his project for No. 27 Berkeley Square, next to Verity's No.25, had appeared in Academy Architecture 1910 It shows his Parisian sympathies in every detail.

14 *Professor Sir Charles Reilly. Students' Union, Liverpool University (1907), drawn by Professor S. D. Adshead.*

[2] Respectively, in Vol. I, by Henry Wilson, and in Vol. II, by F. Hamilton Jackson, who, with C. E. Mallows, assisted Wilson in the first few issues.

[3] Apparently D. S. McColl was given the executive editorship in place of Wilson in October 1901, soon after Percy Hastings took over the business, and the *Review* was then "edited by a committee of architects," as the title page of each volume put it. This is what Goodhart-Rendel refers to. The committee at first contained ten of the leading figures, including Norman Shaw, but it eventually narrowed to Belcher, Blomfield and Macartney. The first two resigned in a fury early in 1905, when Percy Hastings replaced McColl by Macartney without warning. The secretary to the committee was J. H. Elder-Duncan, who acted as McColl's sub-editor. Ernest Newton took over for a short time after 1913, and then his son William G. Newton, well into the '20s.

[4] In the 1891 limited competition.

[5] To whom, as we have seen, an article was devoted in Vol. I. He died in 1897 aged eighty.

[6] "Temple Moore owed everything to the younger Scott," said Goodhart-Rendel. In fact Temple Moore was Scott's pupil and gradually took over the practice when Scott became deranged.

[7] Vol. V, 1899.

[8] Article by Wilson and Paul Cooper in Vol. III.

[9] Henry Wilson was his principal pupil.

[10] Sir Charles Nicholson (1867–1949) was still alive at the time when Goodhart-Rendel spoke to me.

[11] This was no exaggeration – Nicholson and Corlette were partners from 1897 to 1916.

[12] *Review* articles Vol. XI and XII, 1902.

[13] Vol. IV.

[14] See his article on 'Design in Drawings' in Vol. I, pp.256–64 and

NOTES

[1] The main personalities in the Talbot Newspaper Co. were Charles Rogers the publisher, whose previous business was taken over, his assistant J. W. Worfolk, and two journalists, James Dudley Morgan and Edmund W. Abram. The *Review's* first editor was Sedding's pupil Henry Wilson, though he was never employed on a permanent basis. The firm expanded ambitiously: *Specification* started in 1898 and *The Furnisher* in 1899, the same year that the business had to be wound up. The new firm, Professional and Trades Papers Ltd., had Abram as managing director. It went bankrupt also in the summer of 1900, and Percy Hastings took over, starting Technical Journals Ltd., in April, 1901 (later The Architectural Press). The weekly continued as *The Builders' Journal and Architectural Record*; in 1906 it became *The Builders' Journal and Architectural Engineer*, in 1910 *The Architects' and Builders' Journal,* and finally in 1919 *The Architects' Journal.*

304–11, and his sketches of Prague Cathedral in Vol. VIII, 1900, pp.226–28.

[15] Christ Church; see Vol. XXIII, 1908.

[16] Vol. XXX, 1911.

[17] Goodhart-Rendel did not mention R. Frank Atkinson (1871–1923) the executive architect for the first part. He was certainly more than a draughtsman—see his Waring & Gillow (now Gamages) and his Adelphi Hotel, Liverpool.

[18] Vol. XXIII, 1908.

[19] Did he think of Hans Road and Voysey?

[20] Repsectively, *The Builder* LXI, 1891, *Academy Architecture* XXVIII, 1905, and *Academy Architecture* XXVI, 1904.

[21] *The British Architect*, XXIX, 1888, and *The Builder* LXXV, 1898.

[22] Detmar Jellings Blow (1867–1939) had formerly been a close associate of Lethaby and Gimson, designing in a free style at Happisburgh Manor, Norfolk (1900). Fernand Billery, his partner from *circa* 1905, was a Beaux-Arts-trained Frenchman.

[23] St Philip, demolished in 1958.

[24] The house, No. 26, was by Eustace Balfour and Thackeray Turner (1895–96). Aldford House is now on the site. The *Lusitania* interior was by James Miller, and no mention of Crawley is made in the detailed AR article on it and other liners, by Arthur Davis, Vol. XXXV, 1914.

[25] Curtis Green took over their practice from 1910 onwards.

[26] An interesting case of a pure Gothic pupil of Bodley doing classical for a competition.

[27] This may solve the mystery of a group of very original and attractive houses on the Howard de Walden Estate of which the estate office could not tell me the architect. They are T. J. Boulting & Sons, 59 Riding House Street, dated 1905, and Tower House, Condover Street. Alastair Service points out that Boulting's is certainly by H. Fuller Clark (see *Builders' Journal* 15 April 1903).

[28] Mr Nicholas Taylor tells me that he became Mr Oswald Milne's partner.

[29] His best-known work is the steel-framed Blackfriars House (1913–16), in the City.

[30] *The Architectural Review* XIII, 1903; *The British Architect*, XCVI, 1896; *Academy Architecture* 1894, perhaps for the church.

[31] Perhaps Goodhart-Rendel meant Ambron House, Westminster Bridge Road, by Horace Parnacott (1884–1956), a pupil of Verity. It no longer exists.

[32] Adshead was appointed by Reilly as professor of town planning at Liverpool, and in 1915 he became the first professor of town planning at University College.

[33] Who was officially credited with its design. Clough later designed many cottages himself in Hampshire, as an amateur.

[34] Mr Betjeman in the *Journal of the Royal Institute of British Architects* September 1959, p. 406, confirms that he considered "the architect who was a true artist . . . more worth considering than a heavier handed pioneer."

Postscript: The End of the Edwardian Period

The image we have of the Edwardian age is a dualistic one. On one hand, the benevolent personality of Edward VII himself, the romantically luxuriant clothing of the wealthy, the imperial prosperity of business men, the country house weekends and the pictures of serene summer garden parties leave us with a nostalgic impression of a brief golden age of contentment. But the other side of the period was one of intense social strife.

King Edward died on 6 May 1910 in the middle of the bitter struggle for Asquith's Parliament Act of that year, which at last deprived the House of Lords of its effective veto over Commons' legislation. The rancorous question of home rule for Ireland was reaching a peak. There were social changes too. The women's suffragists turned to violent demonstration in the same year. New ideas and programmes in schools and housing were spreading in local government. In the Trades Union movement, the direct action theories of Syndicalism had increased in popularity after 1908 and a series of widespread strikes led up to the great miners' strike of 1911 and others. That year, 1911, saw a deep rift between Liberals and Tories over Lloyd George's historic National Insurance Act. More ominously, the aggressive Kaiser visited London and in the autumn the Agadir crisis and rumblings of trouble in the Balkans gave warning of the war to come.

In the field of architecture a similar duality can be seen, with the Grand Manner, and classicism in general, representing that largely illusory golden age and the free style expressing some of the new political or social ideas. The war was to kill the movement towards Beaux Arts training and its *ateliers* that had just started, though some such ideas survived in the Schools of Architecture founded early in the century. A generally classical manner, with many variations and simplifications, was to dominate building in Britain for many years.

Indeed, Goodhart-Rendel's view of the pre-1914 period, as expressed in his 'Roll-Call', is distorted by his underlying classicist prejudices. He did not much like the magnificence of high Edwardian Baroque – it was old-fashioned by the time he was twenty years old and perhaps too free of classical discipline for his taste. He himself was one of a generation of architects that admired and followed the attempts of men such as Lutyens, Richardson and even Holden to adapt classical rules and detailing to the new steel and concrete

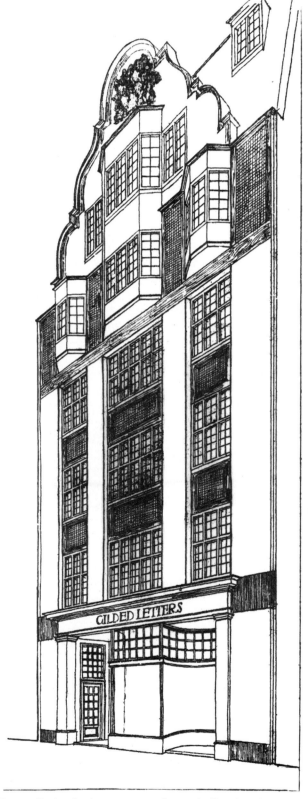

1 *Voysey. Design for ferro-concrete shop and offices (1909).*

frames – a varied group of classicist individualists who designed most of the large buildings in Britain in the 1920s and later. And there is much to admire in the best of such architecture.

All the same, Goodhart-Rendel's airy dismissal of the work of Voysey, Townsend, Lethaby, Mackintosh, Prior and others is illuminating for our understanding of his generation's attitudes. For he is in effect dismissing as unimportant the buildings which are the great original and creative masterpieces of their time. What is more, the problem of inventing an architecture that was true to the new structures and materials available to Edwardian architects seemed almost irrelevant to many of his generation.

This problem was still highly relevant to other architects at the end of the Edwardian decade, particularly those who followed Lethaby's continuing teaching. Lethaby had given up architectural practice, feeling himself ill-equipped to use the new materials. "It is absurd . . . that the writer should have been allowed to study cathedrals . . . it would be better to have the equivalent knowledge of steel and concrete construction," he wrote. Some architects of his school of thought continued in practice. R. Weir Schultz, the designer of the extraordinary Khartoum Cathedral (1909), spoke on the subject of structure and architecture after Lethaby's 1910 paper to the RIBA entitled 'The Architecture of Adventure'. Schultz said "We hear a good deal about the high quality of modern domestic architecture in this country, but after all what does it amount to? Little more, I think, than a parody of the simple traditional types . . . nowadays we have new materials and new constructive methods to deal with. Let us adventure a little way forward with them, discard the worn-out dead forms and evolve fresh ones from the problems they evoke. Recently in London one has watched the growth of two new Post Office buildings (Newgate Street and Wimpole Street) both being constructed with ferro-concrete. One had almost ventured to hope that something interesting and appropriate in the shape of fresh thought would have shown itself on their façades – something evolved out of the lines of the construction within. But no! Outside we now see the same dull dead applied pilasters and arches and cornices, having little relation to what is inside."

Weir Schultz – a Scottish architect of German descent, who changed his name to R. Schultz Weir after the outbreak of war against Germany in 1914 – lived up to his ideals in many of his buildings, though he had little opportunity to do so in large-scale commissions. The same applied to most of the Arts and Crafts architects. The free style was out of fashion even for domestic work. By this time even the great Voysey was reduced to very little work, but he made at least one effort to cope with the new materials and evolve an architecture from them. In 1909 he sent in two designs for a competition for 'Shop and Offices in Ferro-Concrete'; one design chunky and decorated with curious heraldic panels, the other far simpler. The second design certainly lived up to the Weir Schultz's admonition to evolve the façade from "the construction within", for the stripped simplicity of the ground and middle three floors reflects the frame structure, as do the upper bow windows that give depth to the surface. Only at roof level did Voysey feel it necessary to relieve the rectangular forms by a big curling gable. Voysey's offices were not built, but a year later a design was on the drawing board that was to give London its first major building with an exterior true to its frame structure. This was Sir John Burnet's Kodak Building in Kingsway, which put on the front of the building what Burnet and others had earlier used on the rear of buildings in Edinburgh and Glasgow. The magazine *British Architect* commented when the Kodak Building was opened at the end of 1911 that it was built in "a little over a year, with the idea of making a structure suitable in every way for the purpose of a modern office and warehouse, without attempting to copy any style of architecture."

Economy, as well as higher ideals, made the Kodak Building the signpost for the future. That signpost was ignored in the 1920s by some brilliant architects, including Lutyens, and its message adapted to the classical tradition by others such as Richardson. But it foreshadowed the influx of Bauhaus ideas to Britain in the 1930s and the ultimate victory of this approach to architecture after the Second World War.

Principal British Architects of the Late Victorian and Edwardian Period

Adshead, Stanley D. 1868–1946
Anderson, Robert R, (Sir R. Rowand after 1902) 1834–1921
Ashbee, Charles R. 1863–1942

Baker, Herbert (Sir Herbert after 1930) 1862–1946
Belcher, John 1841–1913
Bell, E. Ingress 1926–1914
Bentley, John Francis 1839–1902
Bidlake, W. H. c.1860–1938
Blomfield, Reginald (Sir Reginald after 1919) 1856–1942
Blow, Detmar 1867–1939
Bodley, George F. 1827–1907
Brewer, W. Cecil 1871–1918
Brodrick, Cuthbert 1822–1905
Brooks, James 1825–1901
Browne, George Washington (Sir George afterwards) 1853–1939
Bryce, David 1803–1876
Brydon, John M. 1840–1901
Burnet, John J. (Sir John after 1914) 1857–1938
Butterfield, William 1814–1900

Campbell, John A. 1859–1909
Caröe, William D. 1857–1938
Champneys, Basil 1842–1935
Collcutt, Thomas E. 1840–1924
Comper, J. Ninian (Sir Ninian afterwards) 1864–1960
Cooper, Edwin (Sir Edwin after 1923) 1873–1942
Creswell, H. Bulkeley 1869–1960

Davis, Arthur J. 1878–1951
Dawber, E. Guy (Sir Edward afterwards) 1861–1938
Devey, George 1820–1886
Douglas, Campbell 1828–1910
Drew, Thomas (Sir Thomas afterwards) 1838–1910

Emerson, William (Sir William afterwards) 1843–1924

Fletcher, Banister (Sir Banister afterwards) 1866–1953
Flockhart, William c.1850–1915

Gass, J. Bradshaw 1855–1939
George, Ernest (Sir Ernest after 1911) 1839–1922
Gibson, James G. S. 1861–1951
Gillespie, John G. 1870–1926
Gimson, Ernest 1864–1920
Godwin, Edward W. 1833–1886
Goodhart-Rendel, Harry S. 1887–1959
Gotch, John A. 1852–1942

Hare, Henry T. 1860–1921
Harris, E. Vincent 1879–1971
Holden, Charles H. 1875–1960
Honeyman, John 1831–1914
Horsley, Gerald 1862–1917

Jackson, T. Graham (Sir Thomas after 1913) 1835–1924
Joass, John J. 1868–1952

Keppie, John 1863–1945
Knott, Ralph 1878–1929

Lamond, W. G. 1854–1912
Lanchester, Henry V. 1863–1953
Leiper, William 1839–1916
Lethaby, William R. 1857–1931
Lorimer, Robert (Sir Robert after 1911) 1864–1929
Lutyens, Edwin L. (Sir Edwin after 1930) 1869–1944

Macartney, Mervyn (Sir Mervyn afterwards) 1853–1932
Mackintosh, Charles Rennie 1868–1928
Mackmurdo, Arthur H. 1851–1942
MacLaren, James M. 1843–1890
Mewès, Charles 1860–1914
Moore, Temple L. 1856–1920
Morphew, Reginald 1874–1972
Morris, William (trained, but did not practice as an architect) 1834–1896
Mountford, Edward L. 1855–1908

Nesfield, W. Eden 1835–1888
Newton, Ernest 1856–1922
Nicholson, Charles (Sir Charles afterwards) 1867–1949

Pearson, John L. 1817–1897
Peto, Harold 1828–1897
Pite, A. Beresford 1861–1934
Prior, Edward S. 1852–1932

Reilly, Charles H. (Sir Charles after 1944) 1874–1948
Ricardo, Halsey 1854–1928
Richardson, Albert E. (Sir Albert afterwards) 1880–1965
Rickards, Edwin A. 1872–1920
Riley, W. E. 1852–1937
Robson, Edward R. 1835–1917
Runtz, Ernest 1859–1913

Salmon, James the younger 1873–1924
Salvin, Anthony 1799–1881
Schultz, R. Weir (R. Schultz Weir after 1914) 1861–1951

Scott, George Gilbert the younger 1839–1897
Scott, Giles Gilbert (Sir Giles Gilbert after 1924)
  1880–1960
Scott, M. Hugh Baillie 1865–1945
Scott, John Oldrid 1841–1913
Sedding, John D. 1838–1891
Sellars, James 1843–1888
Sellers, J. Henry 1861–1954
Shaw, R. Norman 1831–1912
Sherrin, George 1843–1909
Simpson, John W. (Sir John afterwards) 1858–1933
Smith, A. Dunbar 1866–1933
Statham, H. H. 1839–1924
Stevenson, John J. 1831–1908
Stokes, Leonard A. 1858–1925

Tapper, Walter J. (Sir Walter afterwards) 1861–1935
Thomas, Alfred Brumwell (Sir Alfred after 1906)
  1868–1948
Thomson, Alexander 'Greek' 1817–1875
Thornely, Arnold (Sir Arnold after 1932) 1870–1953
Townsend, C. Harrison 1851–1928

Unwin, Raymond (Sir Raymond afterwards) 1863–1940

Verity, Frank T. 1864–1937
Voysey, Charles F. Annesley 1857–1941

Wade, Fairfax B. 1851–1919
Walton, George 1867–1933
Waterhouse, Alfred 1830–1905
Webb, Aston (Sir Aston after 1904) 1849–1930
Webb, Philip 1831–1915
Wilson, Henry 1863–1934
Winmill, Charles 1865–1945
Wood, Edgar 1860–1935
Worthington, Thomas 1826–1909

Young, William 1843–1900

Select Bibliography

Books (published)

Archer, J. H. G., *Edgar Wood, a Manchester Art Nouveau Architect,* Manchester 1966.

Aslin, E., *The Aesthetic Movement,* London 1969.

Baker, Sir H., *Architecture and Personalities,* London 1944.

Belcher J. and Macartney M., *Later Renaissance Architecture in England,* London 1898–1901.

Belcher, J., *Essentials in Architecture,* London 1907.

Blomfield, Sir R., *A History of Renaissance Architecture in England 1500–1800,* London 1897.

Blomfield, Sir R., *Memoirs of an Architect,* London 1932.

Blomfield, Sir R., *R. Norman Shaw R. A.,* London 1940.

Brandon-Jones, J.: see Ferriday, P.

Briggs, M. S., *Everyman's Concise Encyclopaedia of Architecture,* London 1959.

Clarke, B. F. L., *Anglican Cathedrals Outside the British Isles,* London 1958.

Ferriday, P. (ed.) *Victorian Architecture* (especially J. Brandon-Jones on Philip Webb and C. F. A. Voysey) London 1963.

Fletcher, Sir H. Banister, *The English House,* London 1910.

Ernest Gimson, His Life and Work, Stratford-on-Avon 1924.

Gomme, A. and Walker, D., *The Architecture of Glasgow,* London 1968.

Goodhart-Rendel, H. S., *English Architecture Since the Regency,* London 1953.

Harbron, D., *The Conscious Stone,* Life of E. W. Godwin, London 1949.

Hill, Oliver, *Scottish Castles (of the 16th and 17th Centuries),* London 1953.

Hitchcock, H. Russell, *Architecture: Nineteenth and Twentieth Centuries,* London 1958.

Hitchcock, H. Russell, *The Architecture of H. H. Richardson,* Hamden, Connecticut, 1961.

Howard, E., *Garden Cities of Tomorrow,* London 1902.

Howarth, T., *Charles Rennie Mackintosh and the Modern Movement,* London 1952.

Hussey, C. and Butler, A. S. G., *Lutyens Memorial Volumes,* London 1951.

Jordan, R. Furneaux, *Victorian Architecture,* London 1966.

Kornwolf, J. D., *M. H. Baillie Scott and the Arts and Crafts Movement,* Baltimore 1972.

Lethaby, W. R., *Architecture, Mysticism and Myth,* London 1892; The Architectural Press: London 1975.

Lethaby, W. R., *Architecture: an Introduction to the History and Theory of the Art of Building,* London 1912.

Lethaby, W. R., *Philip Webb and his work,* Oxford 1935.

Macartney, Sir M., *Recent English Domestic Architecture,* London 1908.

Macleod, R., *Charles Rennie Mackintosh,* London 1968.

Manson, G. C., *Frank Lloyd Wright to 1910, the first Golden Age,* New York 1958.

Massé, H. J. L. J., *The Art-Workers' Guild,* Oxford 1935.

McAra, Duncan, *Sir James Gowans, Romantic Rationalist* Paul Harris Publishing, Edinburgh 1975.

Muthesius, H., *Das Englische Haus,* Berlin 1904–05.

Muthesius, H., *Die Englische Baukunst der Gegenwart,* Berlin 1900.

Nash, J., *The Mansions of England in the Olden Time,* London 1840–49. New edition with Introduction by C. Harrison Townsend, London 1906.

Newton, W. G., *The Work of Ernest Newton R. A.,* London 1923.

Pevsner, Sir N., *Charles Rennie Mackintosh,* Milan 1950.

Pevsner, Sir N., *The Buildings of England,* London 1951 onwards in many volumes.

Pevsner, Sir N., *Pioneers of Modern Design,* London 1960.

Pevsner, Sir N. and Richards, Sir J. (ed.) *The Anti-Rationalists,* London 1973.

Reilly, Sir C., *Scaffolding in the Sky – memoirs,* London 1938.

Rensselaer, M. G. van, *Henry Hobson Richardson and his Works,* New York 1888.

Richards, Sir J.: see Pevsner, Sir N.

Scott, M. H. Baillie, *Houses and Gardens,* London 1906.

Scott-Moncrieff, W., *John Francis Bentley,* London 1924).

Shaw, R. Norman *et al, Architecture, a Profession or an Art,* London 1892.

Statham, H. H., *Modern Architecture,* London 1897.

Winmill, *Charles C. Winmill, by his daughter,* London 1946.

In Preparation

Archer, J. H. G., *A Life of Edgar Wood*

Brandon-Jones, J., *A Life of C. F. A. Voysey*

Crawford, A. and Bury, S., *A Life of C. R. A*

Gray, A. S., *A Biographical Dictionary of E Architecture*

Rubens, G., *The Life and Work of Willian 1857–1931.*

Saint, A., *A Life of Norman Shaw*

Walker, L., *A Life of Edward Prior*

Periodicals

This book draws much on contemporary arc magazines from 1870 onwards, especially *The The Architectural Review* (first published 1 *British Architect, The Builder, Building New Life, Journal of the Royal Institute of British* (first published 1894), and *The Studio* (first 1893), as well as *Academy Architecture* (first 1889).

Many other valuable magazine articles are li footnotes of the individual studies in the book